SAXON® Adaptations for
ALGEBRA 1

Student
Workbook

SAXON®

HOUGHTON MIFFLIN HARCOURT
Supplemental Publishers

www.SaxonPublishers.com
800-531-5015

ISBN 13:   978-1-6027-7483-4
ISBN 10:   1-6027-7483-8

3 4 5 6 7 8   1838   16

4500602510

Table of Contents

SAXON

Introduction

This workbook is designed to supplement and support the instruction and problem sets in *Saxon Algebra 1* and cannot be used independently of the textbook. Included are lesson and investigation worksheets.

Each lesson worksheet contains a brief New Concept section that includes key points and vocabulary from the lesson, selected examples, and page number references to related charts and tables in the textbook. Following the New Concept is formatted workspace for both the Lesson Practice and the Practice problems. The lesson worksheets also provide set-ups and hints to help students complete the problems.

Support for individual problems takes many forms, including:

- identifying a starting point
- restating the problem
- crafting a set-up or partial solution
- citing an *Adaptations Student Reference Guide* page
- referring students to a page in the textbook (with the textbook icon, 📖)
- reminding students to include units in the answer

Investigation worksheets are much like lesson worksheets. They offer support for students through set-ups and hints in problems interspersed with instruction as well as Investigation Practice problems at the end of each Investigation.

Name _____

Class _____

Individual Recording Form   B

Assignment	Date	Assignment	Date	Assignment	Date
1		24		45	
2		25		Test 7	
3		Test 3		46	
4		26		47	
5		27		48	
6		28		49	
7		29		50	
8		30		Test 8	
9		Test 4		Inv. 5	
10		Inv. 3		51	
Inv. 1		31		52	
11		32		53	
12		33		54	
13		34		55	
14		35		Test 9	
15		Test 5		56	
Test 1		36		57	
16		37		58	
17		38		59	
18		39		60	
19		40		Test 10	
20		Test 6		Inv. 6	
Test 2		Inv. 4		61	
Inv. 2		41		62	
21		42		63	
22		43		64	
23		44		65	

Assignment	Date	Assignment	Date	Assignment	Date
Test 11		Test 15		Test 19	
66		86		106	
67		87		107	
68		88		108	
69		89		109	
70		90		110	
Test 12		Test 16		Test 20	
Inv. 7		Inv. 9		Inv. 11	
71		91		111	
72		92		112	
73		93		113	
74		94		114	
75		95		Test 21	
Test 13		Test 17		115	
76		96		116	
77		97		117	
78		98		Test 22	
79		99		118	
80		100		119	
Test 14		Test 18		120	
Inv. 8		Inv. 10		Test 23	
81		101		Inv. 12	
82		102			
83		103			
84		104			
85		105			

Classifying Real Numbers page 2

New Concepts

• This diagram shows subsets of the real numbers.

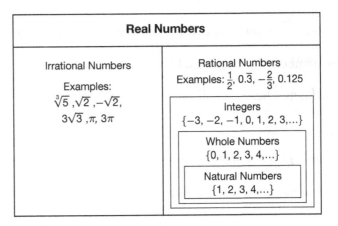

Real Numbers

Irrational Numbers	Rational Numbers
Examples: $\sqrt[3]{5}$, $\sqrt{2}$, $-\sqrt{2}$, $3\sqrt{3}$, π, 3π	Examples: $\frac{1}{2}$, $0.\overline{3}$, $-\frac{2}{3}$, 0.125

Integers
$\{-3, -2, -1, 0, 1, 2, 3,...\}$

Whole Numbers
$\{0, 1, 2, 3, 4,...\}$

Natural Numbers
$\{1, 2, 3, 4,...\}$

Math Language

The **intersection** of sets A and B, **A ∩ B**, is all elements in both A and B.

The **union** of A and B, **A ∪ B**, is all elements that are in either A or B.

Example **Finding Intersections and Unions of Sets**

$A = \{11, 13, 15, 17\}$; $B = \{12, 14, 16, 18\}$

Find $A \cap B$.

There are no elements in both sets, so the intersection is the empty set. This is written $\{\ \}$ or $\varnothing$.

$A \cap B = \{\ \}$, or $A \cap B = \varnothing$

Find $A \cup B$.

The union is all the numbers in A or B.

$A \cup B = \{11, 12, 13, 14, 15, 16, 17, 18\}$

Math Language

A set is **closed** for a given operation if the result of the operation on any two numbers in the set is always a number in the set.

A **counterexample** is an example that proves a statement false.

Example **Identifying a Closed Set Under a Given Operation**

Determine whether the statement is true or false. Give a counterexample for a false statement.

The set of whole numbers is closed under subtraction.

You can subtract two whole numbers and get an answer that is not a whole number.

Counterexample: $4 - 6 = -2$ -2 is not a whole number.

So, the set is not closed under subtraction.

For each number, circle all the subsets of real numbers to which it belongs.

a. -73 natural numbers   whole numbers   integers   rational numbers   irrational numbers

b. $\frac{5}{9}$ natural numbers   whole numbers   integers   rational numbers   irrational numbers

c. 18π natural numbers   whole numbers   integers   rational numbers   irrational numbers

Circle the one set of numbers that best describes each situation. Explain your choice.

d. the number of people on a bus

natural numbers   whole numbers   integers   rational numbers   irrational numbers

_____

e. the area of a circular platform

natural numbers   whole numbers   integers   rational numbers   irrational numbers

_____

f. the value of coins in a purse

natural numbers   whole numbers   integers   rational numbers   irrational numbers

_____

Find $C \cap D$ and $C \cup D$.

g. $C = \{4, 8, 12, 16, 20\}$; $D = \{5, 10, 15, 20\}$

intersection: $C \cap D = \{$_____$\}$

union: $C \cup D = \{$_____$\}$

h. $C = \{6, 12, 18, 24\}$; $D = \{7, 14, 21, 28\}$

intersection: $C \cap D = \{$_____$\}$

union: $C \cup D = \{$_____$\}$

Determine whether each sentence is true or false. Write a counterexample if the statement is false.

i. The set of whole numbers is closed under multiplication.

true   false   counterexample: _____

j. The set of natural numbers is closed under division.

true   false   counterexample: _____

1. Count the decimal places.

   6.15
   × 26.1
   _____

2. Find a common denominator.

   $$\frac{4}{7} + \frac{1}{8} + \frac{1}{2} = \frac{\square}{56} + \frac{\square}{56} + \frac{\square}{56} = \frac{\square}{\square}$$

   = _____

3. $0.9\overline{)954.0}$

4. Find a common denominator. Simplify.

   $$\frac{3}{5} + \frac{1}{8} + \frac{1}{8} = \frac{\square}{40} + \frac{\square}{40} + \frac{\square}{40}$$

   $$= \frac{\square}{40} = \frac{\square}{20}$$

5. $8\overline{)3.000}$

6. Write $0.66\overline{6}$ as a fraction.

   Answer: _____

7. Find a common denominator.

   $$2\frac{1}{2} + 3\frac{1}{5} = 2\frac{\square}{10} + 3\frac{\square}{10} = \text{_____}$$

8.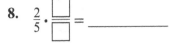

9. Student _____ is correct.

   Student _____ did not _____.

10.

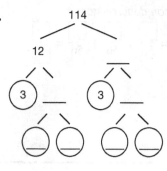

prime factorization: _____

11. *Shift.* ➟

$0.15_{\curvearrowright}$ = _____ ▮

12. *Shift.* ➟

$7.20_{\curvearrowright}$ = _____ ▮

13. natural numbers = {___, ___, ___, ...}

14. Circle the answer.

natural numbers   whole numbers

integers   rational numbers

irrational numbers   real numbers

15. $K = \{0,$ ___, $4,$ ___, ___, ___$\}$

16. Circle the answer.

A   15   **B** $\sqrt{15}$

C   15.15151515   **D** $-\frac{15}{3}$

17. If s is an integer, then $6s^2$ is

a(n) _____ number.

18. Circle the answer: true or false.

If a triangle has both a right angle and an obtuse angle,

then the angle sum is greater than _____ °.

---

19. Use h for the length of the head.

$h = \frac{1}{4} \cdot 19$ in.

$h =$ _____

20. *See page 17 in the* Student Reference Guide.

Circle the answer: true or false.

An acute triangle has _____

acute angles.

---

21. *See page 16 in the* Student Reference Guide.

Circle the answer: true or false.

A trapezoid has only

_____ pair of parallel sides.

22. $7 \cdot \frac{1}{4}$ miles

Circle the answer.

natural numbers   whole numbers

integers   rational numbers

irrational numbers

---

23. *See page 16 in the* Student Reference Guide.

Circle the answer: true or false.

The opposite sides of a parallelogram

are _____.

24. *See page 2 in the* Student Reference Guide.

1248 _____ divisible by 2.

_____

_____

---

25. What kind of number is the hypotenuse?

Circle the answer.

natural number   whole number   integer

rational number   irrational number

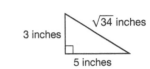

$\sqrt{34}$ inches
3 inches
5 inches

26. a. $A = lw$

_____ [ ]

6 feet

3 feet

b. Circle the answer(s).

natural number   whole number   integer

rational number   irrational number

---

27. $d = r \cdot t$

$d =$ _____ mi/h · _____ hours

$=$ _____ [ ]

28. *See page 2 in the* Student Reference Guide.

207 _____ divisible by 3.

The sum of the digits _____ divisible

by _____ .

---

29. *Find a common denominator.*

$\dfrac{3}{5} \cdot \dfrac{7}{7} = \dfrac{\square}{35}$ $\dfrac{4}{7} \cdot \dfrac{5}{5} = \dfrac{\square}{35}$

$\dfrac{3}{5} \bigcirc \dfrac{4}{7}$

30. Circle the answer.

natural numbers   whole numbers

integers   rational numbers

irrational numbers

Understanding Variables and Expressions page 7

New Concepts

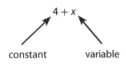
Example Identifying Variables and Constants

Identify the constants and variables.

$71wz + 28y$

The numbers **71** and **28** never change. They are **constants**.

The letters *w*, *y*, and *z* are **variables**. They show unknown numbers.

- $4xy$ shows the product of three **factors**, 4, *x,* and *y.*
- The number 4 in this expression is called the **coefficient.**

coefficient

4xy

factors

Example Identifying Factors and Coefficients in Expressions

Identify the factors and coefficients.

$$\frac{y}{3}$$

$$\frac{y}{3} = \frac{1}{3} \cdot y$$

The factors are $\frac{1}{3}$ and *y*. The coefficient is $\frac{1}{3}$.

cd

$cd = 1 \cdot c \cdot d$ *The coefficient 1 is not written.*

The factors are *c* and *d*. The coefficient is 1.

- Parts of an expression separated by + or − signs are called **terms of an expression.**

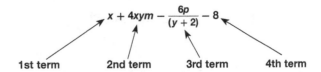

$x + 4xym - \dfrac{6p}{(y+2)} - 8$

1st term   2nd term   3rd term   4th term

Example Identifying Terms

Identify the terms in the expression.

$$6xy + 57w - \frac{24x}{5y}$$

There are three terms: $\mathbf{6xy}$ $\mathbf{57w}$ $\frac{\mathbf{24x}}{\mathbf{5y}}$

Lesson Practice 📖 page 9

Write the constants and variables in each expression.

a. $65qrs + 12x$ constants: _____ , _____   variables: _____ , _____ , _____ , _____

b. $4gh - 71yz$ constants: _____ , _____   variables: _____ , _____ , _____ , _____

Write the factors and coefficients in each expression.
The coefficient 1 is not written.

c. $17def$ factors: _____ , _____ , _____ , _____   coefficient: _____

d. $\frac{uv}{4}$ factors: _____ , _____ , _____   coefficient: _____

e. $-3st$ factors: _____ , _____ , _____   coefficient: _____

f. abc factors: _____ , _____ , _____   coefficient: _____

Write the terms in each expression.
Terms are separated by plus or minus signs.

g. $8v - 17yz + \frac{63b}{4gh}$

_____ _____ _____

h. $\frac{(4 + 2x)}{38q} + 18s - 47jkl$

_____ _____ _____

Bill's Bikes uses this expression to compute rental fees. $6.50 + 3.25h - 0.75b$

i. How many terms are in the expression? _____

j. Write the constants. _____ , _____ , _____

k. Write the variables. _____ , _____

1. Circle the GCF.

factors of 24: _____

factors of 32: 1, 2, 4, 8, 16, 32

GCF: _____

2. Circle the GCF.

factors of 28: _____

factors of 42: _____

GCF: _____

---

3. Circle the LCM.

multiples of 9: 9, 18, 27, 36, 45, ...

multiples of 12: _____ ...

LCM: _____

4. Circle the LCM.

multiples of 3: _____ ,

multiples of 5: _____ ,

multiples of 6: _____

LCM: _____

---

5. $\dfrac{3}{4} \cdot \dfrac{8}{15} =$ _____

6. *Multiply by the reciprocal. Divide out common factors.*

$$\frac{7}{15} \div \frac{21}{25} = \frac{\square}{\square} \cdot \frac{\square}{\square} = \frac{\square}{\square}$$

---

7. *The coefficient 1 is not written.*

coefficients: _____ , _____

variables: _____ , _____ , _____ , _____

8. coefficients: _____ , _____

variables: _____ , _____ , _____

---

9. coefficients: _____, _____

variables: _____, _____

10. *See page 1 in the* Student Reference Guide.

Circle the answer: true or false.

Zero is a _____ number but not

a _____ number.

---

11. *See page 1 in the* Student Reference Guide.

Circle the answer: true or false.

The integers are a _____ of the

real numbers.

12. *See page 1 in the* Student Reference Guide.

Circle the answer: true or false.

There are _____ numbers that are both

rational and _____.

---

13. a. Count the number of times each value appears in the data set.
3, 6, 4, 3, 6, 5, 6, 7, 4, 3, 2, 4, 6

Data item	2	3	4	5	6	7
Frequency	1	3				

b. Complete the line plot.

Frequency of Numbers

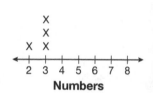

Numbers

---

14. *See page 1 in the* Student Reference Guide.

Circle the answer(s).

whole numbers   rational numbers

integers   irrational numbers

15. *Find a common denominator.*

$$7\frac{3}{8} + 6\frac{1}{3} = 7\frac{\square}{\square} + 6\frac{\square}{\square} = \underline{\hspace{1cm}}$$

Circle the answer.

rational numbers   whole numbers

integers

16.

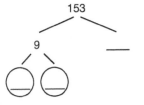

prime factorization: _____

17. Circle the answer: true or false.

The sum of two obtuse angles is greater

than _____°.

---

18. *See page 16 in the* Student Reference Guide.

A line can be classified as a

_____ angle.

19. *See page 2 in the* Student Reference Guide.

2345 _____ divisible by 4.

The last two digits _____

be divided by _____.

---

20. *Shift.* →

$0.00.3 =$ _____

21. whole numbers = {____, ____, ____, ____, ...}

---

22. Circle the answer.

natural numbers   whole numbers

integers   rational numbers

irrational numbers   real numbers

23. *Terms are separated by plus or minus signs.*

Circle the answer.

A $(3x + y)$

B $15gh$

C $\sqrt{8}$

D $\dfrac{gh}{5}$

---

24. π is a constant.

constants: _____, _____

variables: _____, _____

coefficient: _____

---

25. $\$5.75c + \$6.25a$

variables: _____, _____

26. Student _____ is correct.

Student _____ incorrectly listed

two _____.

---

27. a. coefficients: _____, _____

b. variables: _____, _____

28. *See page 16 in the* Student Reference Guide.

Circle the answer.

square	rectangle	trapezoid	rhombus

A	B	C	D

---

29. $\$5 + \$2.25h$

Terms are separated by plus or minus signs.

terms: _____, _____

30. *The natural numbers don't include zero.*

Circle the answer.

irrational numbers   whole numbers

integers   rational numbers

LESSON
3

Simplifying Expressions Using the Product Property of Exponents page 12

New Concepts

• An exponent can be used to show repeated multiplication.

base ⟶ 5^3 ← exponent

Example Simplifying Expressions with Exponents

Simplify each expression.

$(0.3)^4$

The exponent is 4. Use 0.3 as a factor 4 times.

$(0.3)^4 = (0.3)(0.3)(0.3)(0.3) = \mathbf{0.0081}$

$\left(\frac{1}{2}\right)^5$

The exponent is 5. Use $\frac{1}{2}$ as a factor 5 times.

$\left(\frac{1}{2}\right)^5 = \frac{1}{2} \cdot \frac{1}{2} \cdot \frac{1}{2} \cdot \frac{1}{2} \cdot \frac{1}{2} = \mathbf{\frac{1}{32}}$

> **Math Language**
>
> The **base** of a power is the number used as a factor.
>
> The **exponent** tells how many times the base is used as a factor.

• When the bases of two factors are the same, you can add the exponents to find the product.

$5^4 \cdot 5^5 = (5 \cdot 5 \cdot 5 \cdot 5) \cdot (5 \cdot 5 \cdot 5 \cdot 5 \cdot 5)$

$= 5^{4+5} = 5^9$ *Add the exponents: 4 + 5 = 9.*

Product Property of Exponents
If m and n are real numbers and x ≠ 0, then $x^m \cdot x^n = xm^{+n}$.

Example Applying the Product Property of Exponents

Simplify.

$x^5 \cdot x^7 \cdot x^2$

The three factors have the same base, x.

Add the exponents: $5 + 7 + 2 = 14$

$x^5 \cdot x^7 \cdot x^2 = x^{5+7+2} = x^{14}$

Example Applying the Product Property of Exponents

Simplify $m^3 \cdot m^2 \cdot m^4 \cdot n^6 \cdot n^7$.

Add the exponents for the factors with the variable m:
$3 + 2 + 4 = 9$.

Add the exponents for the factors with the variable n:
$6 + 7 = 13$.

$m^3 \cdot m^2 \cdot m^4 \cdot n^6 \cdot n^7 = m^9 \cdot n^{13}$

Lesson Practice page 14

Simplify each expression.

a. 6^4 _____ · _____ · _____ · _____ = _____

b. $(1.4)^2$ _____ · _____ = _____

c. $(2.5)^3$ _____ · _____ · _____ = _____

d. 10^6 *Use 6 zeros in your answer.*   _____

Add the exponents of variables with the same letter.

e. $3 + 5 + 4 =$ _____

  $w^3 \cdot w^5 \cdot w^4 =$ _____

f. y-terms: $6 + 5 =$ _____

  z-terms: $3 + 11 + 2 =$ _____

  $y^6 \cdot y^5 \cdot z^3 \cdot z^{11} \cdot z^2 =$ _____

g. $10^9 \cdot$ _____ = _____

1. Circle the GCF.

factors of 15: _____

factors of 35: 1, 5, 7, 35

GCF: _____

2. Circle the GCF.

factors of 32: _____

factors of 48: _____

GCF: _____

3. Circle the LCM.

multiples of 8: _____, ...

multiples of 12: 12, 24, 36, 48, 60, ...

LCM: _____

4. Circle the LCM.

multiples of 2: _____, ...

multiples of 4: _____, ...

multiples of 7: _____, ...

LCM: _____

5. *Divide out common factors.*

$$\frac{9}{16} \cdot \frac{12}{15} = \frac{\square}{\square}$$

6. *Multiply by the reciprocal.*
Divide out common factors.
Simplify.

$$\frac{6}{15} \div \frac{24}{30} = \frac{\square}{\square} \cdot \frac{\square}{\square} = \frac{\square}{\square}$$

7. coefficients: _____, _____

variables: _____, _____, _____

8. coefficients: _____, _____

variables: _____, _____, _____

9. coefficients: _____, _____

   variables: _____, _____

10. *See page 1 in the* Student Reference Guide.

   Circle the answer: true or false.

   Fractions are real numbers, but they

   are not _____.

11. *See page 1 in the* Student Reference Guide.

   Circle the answer: true or false.

   The set of whole numbers contains

   all the _____ numbers

   and _____.

12. *See page 1 in the* Student Reference Guide.

   Circle the answer: true or false.

   The set of real numbers contains all

   rational and _____ numbers.

13. Compare.

   42.53 ⬭ 42.35

14. *Find a common denominator.*

   $\dfrac{5}{9} \cdot \dfrac{4}{4} = \dfrac{\square}{36}$ $\dfrac{7}{12} \cdot \dfrac{3}{3} = \dfrac{\square}{36}$

   Compare.

   $\dfrac{5}{9}$ ⬭ $\dfrac{7}{12}$

15. *Find a common denominator.*

   $1\dfrac{1}{8} + 7\dfrac{2}{5} = 1\dfrac{\square}{\square} + 7\dfrac{\square}{\square} = $ _____

16. Write the next 5 integers.

   integers = {..., −3, −2, __, __, __, __, ...}

   Circle the measurement that can be described with a negative number.

   temperature   volume

17.

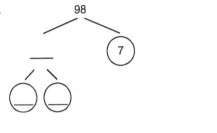

prime factorization: _____

18. Student _____ is correct.

Student _____ multiplied the _____

instead of adding them.

19. *See page 16 in the* Student Reference Guide.

Circle the answer: true or false.

A square has _____ right angles.

A _____ does not always have

_____ right angles.

20. *See page 2 in the* Student Reference Guide.

306 _____ divisible by 6.

The number is divisible by _____ and

_____.

21. a. base: _____

b. exponent: _____

c. ___ · ___ · ___ · ___ · ___ · ___ = ___

22. *Add the exponents.*

$10^3 \cdot 10^6 =$ _____

Circle the answer.

A 10^{18} **B** 10^9

C 10^6 **D** 10^3

23. *Add the exponents.*

____ + ____ = _____

Multiply to evaluate.

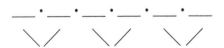

___ · ___ · ___ = _____

24. a. $10^3 =$ ___ · ___ · ___ = _____

b. $10^3 \cdot 10^6 =$ _____

exponential form: _____

Use 9 zeros.

Simplify.

_____

25. *How many decades from 2000 to 2030?*

$25,000 \cdot 3 \cdot 3 \cdot 3 =$ _____ people

$$\begin{array}{r} 25,000 \\ \times \quad 27 \\ \hline \end{array}$$

26. *See page 17 in the* Student Reference Guide.

Circle the answer.

A a triangle with angle measures of 45°, 45 °, and 90°

B a triangle with angle measures of 40°, 110°, and 30°

C a triangle with angle measures of 55°, 45°, and 85°

D a triangle with angle measures of 60°, 60°, and 60°

27. $1 \cdot (2)^8$

$2^8 =$ __ $\cdot$ __ $\cdot$ __ $\cdot$ __ $\cdot$ __ $\cdot$ __ $\cdot$ __ $\cdot$ __ $=$ ____

$1 \cdot 2^8 =$ _____

28. $A = \frac{1}{2} \cdot (hb_1 + hb_2)$

constant(s): _____

29. $V = (3 \text{ feet})^3 =$ _____ cubic feet

30. $P = 2l + 2w$

a. number of terms: _____

b. variables: _____ , _____

Name _____

Using Order of Operations page 17

New Concepts

- To **simplify** an expression means to do all the operations shown.
- If an expression does not have variables, it can usually be simplified to a single number.

Order of Operations
1. Work inside grouping symbols.
2. Simplify powers and roots.
3. Multiply and divide from left to right.
4. Add and subtract from left to right.

- $3 + 2 \cdot 6$ equals $3 + 12$, **not** $5 \cdot 6$.
- To **justify a step** means to give a reason for that step.

> **Example** Simplifying Expressions with Parentheses
>
> **Simplify. Justify each step.**
>
> $(10 \cdot 3) + 7 \cdot (5 + 4)$
>
> $= 30 + 7 \cdot 9$ *Simplify inside the two sets of parentheses.*
>
> $= 30 + 63$ *Multiply 7 times 9.*
>
> $= 93$ *Add.*

> **Example** Simplifying Expressions with Exponents
>
> **Simplify. Justify each step.**
>
> $4^3 + 9 \div 3 - 2 \cdot (3)^2$
>
> $= 64 + 9 \div 3 - 2 \cdot 9$ *Simplify exponents.*
>
> $= 64 - 3 - 18$ *Multiply and divide from left to right.*
>
> $= 49$ *Subtract from left to right.*

Simplify each expression. Complete the steps and the justifications.

a. $45 - (2 + 4) \cdot 5 - 3$

$= 45 - (\underline{\hspace{1cm}}) \cdot 5 - 3$ Add inside the _____.

$= 45 - \underline{\hspace{1cm}} - 3$ _____.

$= \underline{\hspace{1cm}} - 3$ Subtract.

$= \underline{\hspace{1cm}}$ _____.

b. $9 \cdot 2^3 - 9 \div 3$

$= 9 \cdot \underline{\hspace{1cm}} - 9 \div 3$ Simplify the _____.

$= \underline{\hspace{1cm}} - \underline{\hspace{1cm}}$ Multiply. _____.

$= \underline{\hspace{1cm}}$ _____.

c. $\dfrac{15 - 3^2 + 4 \cdot 2}{7}$

$= \dfrac{15 - \square + 4 \cdot 2}{7}$ Simplify the _____.

$= \dfrac{15 - 9 + \square}{7}$ _____.

$= \dfrac{\square}{7}$ Add and subtract from left to right.

$= \underline{\hspace{1cm}}$ _____.

d. Simplify each expression. Then write > (greater than), < (less than), or = to compare.

$\dfrac{1}{4} + 3^2 + 6$ $\bigcirc$ $5 - 2 + 2 \cdot 4 + 3 \div 9$

$= \dfrac{1}{4} + \underline{\hspace{0.7cm}} + 6$ $= 5 - 2 + \underline{\hspace{1cm}} + \underline{\hspace{1cm}}$

$\underline{\hspace{1.5cm}} \bigcirc \underline{\hspace{1.5cm}}$

e. See 📖 page 19.

Simplify.

$V = \dfrac{4}{3}\pi \left(\dfrac{3}{2}\right)^3$

$= \dfrac{4}{3} \cdot \dfrac{3}{2} \cdot \underline{\hspace{1cm}} \cdot \underline{\hspace{1cm}} \cdot \pi$

$= \underline{\hspace{1cm}}$

1. *Find a common denominator.*

$$2\frac{1}{4} + 4\frac{1}{2} = 2\frac{\square}{\square} + 4\frac{\square}{\square} = \underline{\hspace{1cm}}$$

2. *Find a common denominator.*

$$5\frac{2}{5} - 3\frac{1}{4} = 5\frac{\square}{\square} - 3\frac{\square}{\square} = \underline{\hspace{1cm}}$$

3. *Find a common denominator.*

$$1\frac{3}{4} + 4\frac{1}{8} - 2\frac{1}{2} =$$

$$1\frac{\square}{\square} + 4\frac{\square}{\square} - 2\frac{\square}{\square} = \underline{\hspace{1cm}}$$

4. *First convert to improper fractions.*

$$4\frac{1}{3} \div 2\frac{1}{6} = \frac{\square}{3} \div \frac{\square}{6}$$

Multiply by the reciprocal.

$$= \frac{\square}{\square} \cdot \frac{\square}{\square} = \frac{\square}{\square}$$

5.

$$0.3\overline{)3.519}$$

6.   4.16
        $\times$ 2.3
        —————

7. *Terms are separated by plus or minus signs.*

$$14x^2 + 7x + \frac{x}{4}$$

terms: _____

8.   225
                25
        ◯ ◯   ◯ ◯

prime factorization: _____

9. *See page 2 in the* Student Reference Guide.

124,302 _____ divisible by 3.

The sum of the digits is _____.

That _____ divisible by _____.

10. $L = \{-15, \_\_, \_\_, \_\_, \_\_, \_\_, \_\_, \_\_\}$

11. *See page 1 in the* Student Reference Guide.

Circle the answer: true or false.

The _____ numbers are a subset

of the set of _____.

12. *See page 1 in the* Student Reference Guide.

Circle the answer(s).

natural numbers   whole numbers

integers   rational numbers

irrational numbers   real numbers

13.

$6\overline{)1.0000}$

Shift. ⟶

__.___ ___ ___ ___ = _____

14.

$9\overline{)5.0000}$

Shift. ⟶

__.___ ___ ___ ___ = _____

15. *Simplify. Then compare.*
Use the order of operations.

$3 \cdot 4^2 + 4^2$ ◯ $3 \cdot (16 + 16)$

16. *See page 17 in the* Student Reference Guide.

Circle the answer.

  A a triangle with angle measures of 45°, 45°, and 90°

  B a triangle with angle measures of 40°, 120°, and 20°

  C a triangle with angle measures of 55°, 45°, and 80°

  D a triangle with angle measures of 60°, 60°, and 60°

17. Count the number of times each value appears in the data set. Then complete the line plot.

6, 7, 8, 4, 5, 4, 3, 4, 5, 3, 2, 6, 7

Data item	2	3	4	5	6	7	8
Frequency	2	2					

Frequency of Numbers

```
X  X
X  X
+--+--+--+--+--+--+--+--+-->
2  3  4  5  6  7  8  9
```
Numbers

18. *See page 16 in the* Student Reference Guide.

Circle the answer: true or false.

Both squares and rectangles have 4 right angles. Their opposite sides are _____.

19. *Find a common denominator.*

$15\frac{1}{3} - 7\frac{4}{5} = 15\frac{\square}{\square} - 7\frac{\square}{\square} = $ _____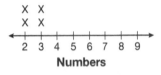

20. Student _____ is correct.

Student _____ has an extra factor

of _____, which results in a product

of _____.

21. *See page 2 in the* Student Reference Guide.

1116 _____ divisible by 9.

The sum of the digits is _____

which _____ divisible by _____.

22. *Terms are separated by plus or minus signs.*

   a. variables: _____, _____, _____

   b. terms: _____, _____, _____

23. increase in wolves: $2300 - 1100 =$ _____

   number of years: $2003 - 1976 =$ _____

   average: _____ $\div$ _____ $\approx$ _____ wolves

---

24. *Use the order of operations.*

   $9 \cdot (\$1.75) + 5 \cdot (\$1.50)$

   Circle the answer.

   A $31.00   **B** $23.25

   C $25.25   **D** $21.75

25. $SA = 2\pi r^2 + 2\pi rh$

   _____

---

26. Ashley: 12 nickels   2 dimes   4 quarters
       Beto: 10 nickels   4 dimes   3 quarters

   a. Ashley: (_____ $\cdot 5¢$) + (_____ $\cdot 10¢$) + (_____ $\cdot 25¢$) = _____ ¢

   b. Beto: (_____ $\cdot 5¢$) + (_____ $\cdot 10¢$) + (_____ $\cdot 25¢$) = _____ ¢

   c. Who has more money? _____

---

27. *Use the order of operations.*

   $8(10 - 3 \cdot 2) =$ _____

28. *See page 15 in the* Student Reference Guide.

   Volume of cube = _____

---

29. $\frac{5}{9}(F - 32) = \frac{5}{9} \cdot$ _____ = _____

30. $28 + 0.07m = 28 + 0.07($_____$)$

       $=$ _____

Name _____

Finding Absolute Value and Adding Real Numbers page 22

New Concepts

Math Language

The **absolute value** of a number is the distance from the number to 0 on a number line.

- Since absolute value is a distance, it is always a positive number. The symbol for absolute value is two vertical bars | |.

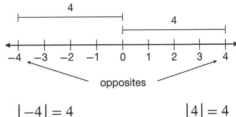

$$|-4| = 4 \qquad\qquad |4| = 4$$

Example Finding the Absolute Value

Simplify $-|11 - 2|$.

$-\|11 - 2\|$	
$= -\|9\|$	Compute inside the absolute value signs.
$= -1 \cdot 9$	Take the absolute value of 9.
$= -9$	Multiply 9 times -1.

Exploration page 23

Use your textbook to complete the exploration.

Example Adding Real Numbers

Find the sum.

$(-19) + (-8)$	Same signs
$19 + 8 = 27$	Add the absolute values.
$(-19) + (-8) = -27$	The sign is $-$ because both addends are negative.

Find the sum.

$(3.2) + (-5.1)$	Different signs
$5.1 - 3.2 = 1.9$	Subtract the absolute values.
$(3.2) + (-5.1) = -1.9$	The sign is $-$ because 5.1 is greater than 3.2.

Simplify.

a. $|-3.4| = $ _____

b. $\left|\frac{6}{7}\right| = $ _____

c. $|14 + (-22)|$

$= |$ _____ $| = $ _____

d. $-|7 + 16|$

$= -|$ _____ $| = $ _____

Find the sum.

e. $(-23.4) + 18.72$

sign of sum: _____

23.40
$\underline{-18.72}$

f. $\left(-\frac{2}{3}\right) + \left(-\frac{1}{6}\right)$

sign of sum: _____

Find a common denominator.

$\frac{2}{3} + \frac{1}{6} = $

_____ $+$ _____ $= $ _____

True or false? Circle your answer. Give a counterexample if the statement is false.

g. The set of rational numbers is closed under addition.

true   false   counterexample: _____

h. The set of positive integers is closed under addition.

true   false   counterexample: _____

i. The temperature at 7:00 p.m. was 34°F. The temperature fell 12°F by midnight. Use addition to find the temperature at midnight.

_____ $+ (-12) = $ _____

1. Find a common denominator.

$$1\frac{1}{6} + 3\frac{1}{3} = 1\frac{\square}{\square} + 3\frac{\square}{\square} = \underline{\hspace{2cm}}$$

Simplify.

$$= \underline{\hspace{3cm}}$$

2. Find a common denominator.

$$2\frac{3}{8} - 1\frac{1}{4} = 2\frac{\square}{\square} - 1\frac{\square}{\square} = \underline{\hspace{2cm}}$$

3. Find a common denominator.

$$3\frac{2}{3} + 1\frac{5}{8} - 1\frac{3}{4}$$

$$3\frac{\square}{\square} + 1\frac{\square}{\square} - 1\frac{\square}{\square} = \underline{\hspace{2cm}}$$

4. First convert to improper fractions.

$$3\frac{1}{3} \div 1\frac{3}{5} = \frac{\square}{3} \div \frac{\square}{5}$$

Multiply by the reciprocal.

$$\frac{\square}{\square} \cdot \frac{\square}{\square} = \underline{\hspace{2cm}}$$

Simplify.

$$= \underline{\hspace{3cm}}$$

5.

$$0.2\overline{)1.506}$$

6.   2.89
     $\times\ 1.2$
     $\overline{\hspace{1.5cm}}$

7. Terms are separated by plus or minus signs.

$$2x^2 + 3x + 7$$

terms: \underline{\hspace{2cm}}

8.

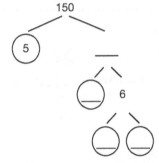

prime factorization: \underline{\hspace{3cm}}

9. *See page 2 in the* Student Reference Guide.

125,000 _____ divisible by 10.

A number is divisible by 10 if the ones

digit is _____ .

10. $L = \{-12, \_\_\_, \_\_\_, \_\_\_, \_\_\_, \_\_\_, \_\_\_\}$

11. Circle the answer: true or false.

Any integer can be written as a fraction

by using the number _____ as a

denominator.

12. Student _____ is correct.

Student _____ was incorrect because

although the number is written as a

fraction, the numerator is an _____

number. So, the ratio is also an

_____ number.

13.

$8\overline{)5.000}$

Shift. ⟶

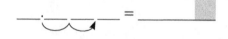

___.___ ___ = _____

14. Order from least to greatest.

1.25 yards   3 feet $1\frac{1}{3}$ yards

↓   ↓   ↓

1.25 yd   _____ yd   _____ yd

_____ , _____ , _____

15. $7\% = \dfrac{\square}{100}$

Convert $\frac{7}{100}$ to a decimal. _____

16. _____ = _____

17. *See page 17 in the* Student Reference Guide.

In an acute triangle, every angle must measure less than 90°.

Circle the answer.

A 45°, 45°, and 90°

B 40°, 110°, and 20°

C 55°, 45°, and 80°

D 30°, 30°, and 120°

18. Round each amount to the nearest 10¢.

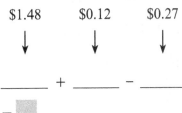

$1.48 $0.12 $0.27

_____ + _____ − _____

= _____

19. $|-5| = 5$

The distance from −5 to _____ is _____.

20. *See page 16 in the* Student Reference Guide.

Circle the answer: true or false.

Both rectangles and parallelograms have

opposite sides that are congruent and

_____.

21. By the order of operations, you find

_____ first.

22. $-3° + 29°$

Subtract the absolute values.

$29 - 3 = $ _____

23. *Subtract the absolute values.*

sign of sum: _____

$8 + \left(-13\frac{1}{2}\right) = $ _____

24. *If you add two numbers in the set, will the answer always be a member of that set?*

Circle the answer.

A integers   B rational numbers

C real numbers   D all of these

---

25. Airplane A: $-43 + 20{,}512 =$ _____

Airplane B: $1924 + 18{,}527 =$ _____

Which plane is farther above sea level?

_____

26. $\$500 + (-$ _____ $) =$ ▨ _____

---

27. a. $3 \cdot \$15.25 + 4 \cdot \$25 =$ ▨ _____

b. $\$145.75 + (0.05 \cdot \$145.75) =$ ▨ _____

28. $(-12.67) + (-31.51) =$ _____ points

sign of sum: _____

$$-12.67$$
$$+\ -31.51$$
$$\overline{}$$

---

29. 1.6^5

Circle the answer.

A $1.6 \times 1.6 \times 1.6 \times 1.6 \times 1.6$

B $1.6 + 1.6 + 1.6 + 1.6 + 1.6$

C $0.6 \times 0.6 \times 0.6 \times 0.6 \times 0.6 + 1$

D $1 \times 1 \times 1 \times 1 \times 1 + 0.6$

30. _____ + _____

Subtract the absolute values.

_____ − _____ = _____ ▨

LESSON

6

Subtracting Real Numbers page 27

New Concepts

Math Language

A positive number and a negative number with the same absolute value are called **opposites**.

-0.5 and 0.5 are opposites.

• The sum of a number and its opposite is 0.

$$-0.5 + 0.5 = 0$$

• To subtract a number, add its opposite.

Example **Subtracting Real Numbers**

Find each difference.

$(-12) - 21$	
$(-12) + (-21)$	To subtract 21, add -21.
$12 + 21 = 33$	Same signs. Add the absolute values.
$(-12) + (-21) = -33$	The sign is $-$ because both addends are negative.
$3.2 - (-5.1)$	
$3.2 + (5.1) = \mathbf{8.3}$	To subtract -5.1, add 5.1.
$\left(-\frac{3}{5}\right) - \left(-\frac{1}{5}\right)$	
$\left(-\frac{3}{5}\right) + \left(\frac{1}{5}\right)$	To subtract $-\frac{1}{5}$, add $\frac{1}{5}$.
$\frac{3}{5} - \frac{1}{5} = \frac{2}{5}$	Different signs. Subtract the absolute values.
$\left(-\frac{3}{5}\right) + \left(\frac{1}{5}\right) = -\frac{2}{5}$	The sign is $-$ because $\frac{3}{5}$ is greater than $\frac{1}{5}$.

Math Language

A set is **closed** for a given operation if the result of the operation on any two numbers in the set is also a number in the set.

• A set of numbers is closed under subtraction if, when two numbers in the set are subtracted, the difference is also a number in the set.

Example **Determining Closure Over Subtraction**

Tell whether the statement is true or false. Explain.

The set of real numbers is closed under subtraction.

The statement is **true** because **the difference of any two real numbers is a real number**.

Find each difference.

a. $14 - (-22)$ *Add the opposite.*

    $14 + (+22) =$ _____

b. $(-7) - 16$ *Add the opposite.*

    $(-7) +$ _____ $=$ _____

c. $(-23.4) - 18.72$

    $(-23.4) + ($ _____ $) =$ _____

d. $\left(-\frac{2}{3}\right) - \left(-\frac{1}{6}\right)$

    $\left(-\frac{2}{3}\right) + \left(+\dfrac{\square}{\square}\right)$

    $\left(-\dfrac{\square}{6}\right) + \left(\dfrac{\square}{\square}\right) =$ _____

Determine whether each statement is true or false. Give a counterexample for false statements.

e. The set of whole numbers is closed under subtraction. _____

    Counterexample: $5 - 12 =$ _____

f. The set of rational numbers is closed under subtraction. _____

_____

g. $(-37,800) - (-13,800)$

    $(-37,800) + ($ _____ $) =$ _____

1. *First convert to improper fractions.*

$$5\frac{1}{3} \div 2\frac{1}{3}$$

$$\frac{\square}{3} \div \frac{\square}{3}$$

Multiply by the reciprocal.

$$\frac{\square}{\square} \times \frac{\square}{\square} = \underline{\qquad}$$

2. *Find a common denominator.*

$$40\frac{1}{8} - 21\frac{1}{4} = \underline{\qquad}$$

3. *Find a common denominator.*

$$5\frac{2}{3} + 2\frac{5}{6} + \left(-2\frac{1}{6}\right) = \underline{\qquad}$$

4. $1\frac{2}{3} \div 1\frac{1}{4} \cdot 1\frac{1}{2}$

First convert to improper fractions.

$$\frac{\square}{3} \div \frac{\square}{4} \cdot \frac{\square}{2}$$

Multiply by the reciprocal.

$$= \frac{\square}{\square} \cdot \frac{\square}{\square} \cdot \frac{3}{2} = \underline{\qquad}$$

5. $0.74 \div 0.2 \cdot 0.3 = \underline{\qquad}$

6. $5.4 \cdot 0.3 \div 0.4 = \underline{\qquad}$

7. $1.24 \cdot 0.2 \div 0.1 = \underline{\qquad}$

8. $112.4 \div 3.2 = \underline{\qquad}$

9.

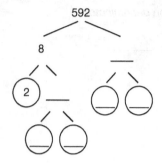

prime factorization: _____

10.

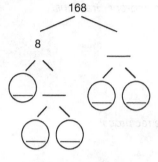

prime factorization: _____

11. 8, 6, 9, 7, 5, 4, 6, 7, 9, 8, 5, 6, 6, 8

Data Item	4	5	6	7	8	9
Frequency	1	2				

Frequency of Numbers

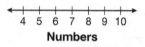

Numbers

12. *See page 2 in the* Student Reference Guide.

2326 _____ divisible by 3.

The sum of the digits is _____ which

_____ divisible by 3.

13. $6\% = \dfrac{\square}{100} = \dfrac{\square}{\square}$

$6\% = 0.$_____

14. $1.25 =$ _____ $\dfrac{\square}{\square} = \dfrac{\square}{\square}$

Compare.

_____ ◯ $\dfrac{5}{3}$

Which is greater? _____

15. $\dfrac{3}{5} = 5\overline{)3}$

$\dfrac{3}{5} =$ _____ %

16. $\dfrac{(3 \cdot 20 + 2 \cdot 20) \cdot 6 - 20}{10^2} = \dfrac{(\square) \cdot (\square)}{\square}$

Circle the answer.

A 2.8   B 58

C −14   D 5.8

17. *Use the order of operations.*

$$\frac{(45 + 39 + 47 + 40 + 33 + 39 + 41)}{(2 \cdot 2)^2 - 12}$$

$$= \frac{\boxed{}}{\boxed{} - 12} = \underline{\hspace{2cm}}$$

18. Which of these differences will be negative?

Add the opposite.

Circle the answer.

A $-4.8 - (-5.2)$ **B** $4.8 - 5.2$

C $4.8 - 3.2$ **D** $6.7 - (-7.8)$

19. *A loss of 15 is −15.*

$25 + (\underline{\hspace{1.5cm}}) = \underline{\hspace{1.5cm}}$-yard line

20. $180 - 105.5 - 38.2 = \underline{\hspace{2cm}}$

21. *16° colder is −16.*

$-5 + (\underline{\hspace{1.5cm}}) = \underline{\hspace{1.5cm}}$

22. *Issuing a check is −$149.99.*

$\underline{\hspace{2cm}} + \$84.50 = \underline{\hspace{2cm}}$

23. *See page 17 in the* Student Reference Guide.

Circle the answer.

A a triangle with angles 45°, 45°, and 90°

B a triangle with angles 60°, 60°, and 60°

C a triangle with angles 55°, 35°, and 90°

D a triangle with angles 30°, 30°, and 120°

24. $-5\frac{1}{3} + 3\frac{1}{4} =$

sign of sum: $\underline{\hspace{1.5cm}}$

$-5\frac{\boxed{}}{\boxed{}} + 3\frac{\boxed{}}{\boxed{}} =$

Can the tour boat leave the dock? $\underline{\hspace{1.5cm}}$

After the rainfall, the lake level is

at $\underline{\hspace{1.5cm}}$ feet, which is $\underline{\hspace{1.5cm}}$ than 2 feet

below normal.

---

25. Simplify.

$|-18.5 + 4.75| \leq |-18.5| + |4.75|$

_____ ≤ _____

26. Student _____ is correct.

Student _____ added _____

instead of _____

---

27. A bit has two values, 0 or 1.
A byte is 8 bits.

a. $8 = 2^{\square}$

b. $32 = 2^{\square}$

c. $8 \times 32 = 2^{\square}$

28. $16c + (-4d) + \frac{8\pi}{15} + 21efg$

a. coefficients: _____, _____, _____

b. The expression has _____ terms.

c. _____

Subtracting a number is the same as

_____ its _____.

---

29. What subset of numbers does the number
$-9.0909090\overline{9}09$ belong to?

See page 1 in the Student Reference Guide.

Circle the answer.

A integers

B irrational numbers

C natural numbers

D rational numbers

30. Depths below sea level are negative
numbers.

Add the opposite.

sign of sum: _____

$-12,925 - (-11,730) =$ _____

LESSON

7

Simplifying and Comparing Expressions with Symbols of Inclusion page 31

New Concepts

• To simplify an expression, begin with the numbers inside the innermost symbol of inclusion and work outward.

Example **Simplifying Expressions with Rational Numbers**

Simplify. Justify each step.

$$\left[5 \cdot (4+2)^2\right] + \frac{4 \cdot 5}{2}$$

$$= \left[5 \cdot (6)^2\right] + \frac{4 \cdot 5}{2} \qquad \textit{Add inside the parentheses.}$$

$$= [5 \cdot 36] + \frac{4 \cdot 5}{2} \qquad \textit{Simplify the exponent.}$$

$$= 180 + \frac{4 \cdot 5}{2} \qquad \textit{Multiply inside the brackets.}$$

$$= 180 + \frac{20}{2} \qquad \textit{Simplify the numerator.}$$

$$= 180 + 10 \qquad \textit{Simplify the fraction.}$$

$$= 190 \qquad \textit{Add.}$$

• To compare two expressions, first simplify each expression. Then compare.

Example **Compare Expressions with Symbols of Inclusion**

Compare the expressions. Use <, >, or =.

$$12 + \left[5(7-5)^3 - 14\right] \bigcirc \left[(9-5)^2 + 7\right] - 3^3$$

$12 + \left[5(7-5)^3 - 14\right]$	$\left[(9-5)^2 + 7\right] - 3^3$
$= 12 + \left[5(2)^3 - 14\right]$	$= \left[(4)^2 + 7\right] - 3^3$
$= 12 + [5 \cdot 8 - 14]$	$= [16 + 7] - 3^3$
$= 12 + [40 - 14]$	$= 23 - 3^3$
$= 12 + 26$	$= 23 - 27$
$= 38$	$= -4$

$$38 \; \large{>} \; -4$$

$$12 + \left[5(7-5)^3 - 14\right] \; \large{>} \; \left[(9-5)^2 + 7\right] - 3^3$$

Simplify each expression.

a. $12 + |5 - 11|$

$= 12 + |\_\_\_\_\_|$

$= 12 + \_\_\_\_\_ = \_\_\_\_\_$

b. $5(8 + 4) \div (15 - 5 - 4)$

$= 5(\_\_\_\_\_) \div (\_\_\_\_\_)$

$= \_\_\_\_\_ \div \_\_\_\_\_ = \_\_\_\_\_$

c. $5 + [6 \cdot (2^3 + 4)]$

$= 5 + [6 \cdot (\_\_\_\_ + 4)]$ *Innermost inclusion symbols first*

$= 5 + [6 \cdot \_\_\_\_]$

$= 5 + \_\_\_\_ = \_\_\_\_$

d. $4(1 + 2)^2 \div 6 + \dfrac{8 \cdot 3}{2}$

$= 4(\_\_\_\_)^2 \div 6 + \dfrac{8 \cdot 3}{2}$ Add inside the _____.

$= 4 \cdot \_\_\_\_ \div 6 + \dfrac{8 \cdot 3}{2}$ Simplify the _____.

$= 4 \cdot 9 \div 6 + \dfrac{\square}{2}$ Simplify the _____.

$= 4 \cdot 9 \div 6 + \_\_\_\_$ Simplify the _____.

$= \_\_\_\_ + 12$ Multiply and _____ from left to right.

$= \_\_\_\_$ Add.

e. Simplify. Then compare.

$(13 + 5) - [5 \cdot 2^2]$ ◯ $[(7 + 11) - 5] - 2^3$

$(13 + 5) - [5 \cdot 2^2]$ $[(7 + 11) - 5] - 2^3$

$= (\_\_\_) - [5 \cdot \_\_\_]$ $= [\_\_\_ - 5] - \_\_\_$

$= \_\_\_ - \_\_\_$ $= \_\_\_ - \_\_\_$

$= \_\_\_$ $= \_\_\_$

$\_\_\_$ ◯ $\_\_\_$

f. $\left(\dfrac{W}{H^2}\right) \cdot 703$

Begin inside the _____ . _____ the height.

Next _____ the weight by the new denominator.

Then _____ the quotient by 703.

1. Use the order of operations.

$(5 + 2)^2 - 50 =$ _____

2. Use the order of operations.

$(3 - 5) + 7^2 =$ _____

3. Find a common denominator.

$3\frac{1}{3} - 1\frac{1}{6} - 5\frac{1}{4}$

$= 3\dfrac{\square}{\square} - 1\dfrac{\square}{\square} - 5\dfrac{\square}{\square} =$ _____

4. First convert to improper fractions.

$2\frac{1}{3} \cdot 3\frac{1}{4} \cdot 1\frac{1}{2} = \dfrac{\square}{\square} \cdot \dfrac{\square}{\square} \cdot \dfrac{\square}{\square} =$ _____

5. Use the order of operations.

$(0.56 + 0.3) \cdot 0.2 =$ _____

6. Use the order of operations.

$3.25 \cdot 0.4 + 0.1 =$ _____

7. $1.2 \div 0.1 \div 0.1$

$0.1\overline{)1.2}$ $0.1\overline{)}$

Answer: _____

8. Count the decimal places.

$20.2 \cdot 0.1 \cdot 0.1 =$ _____

---

9. *See page 1 in the* Student Reference Guide.

All whole numbers are counting numbers.

Circle the answer: true or false.

_____ is a _____ number, but not

a _____ number.

---

10. $\{..., -3, -2, -1, 0, 1, 2, 3, ...\}$

See page 1 in the Student Reference Guide.

Answer: _____

---

11. *See page 17 in the* Student Reference Guide.

An obtuse triangle has two obtuse angles.

Circle the answer: true or false.

A triangle can have only

one _____ angle.

12.

prime factorization: _____

---

13. *A prime number has only itself and 1 as factors.*

prime factorization:_____

---

14. *See page 2 in the* Student Reference Guide.

10,048 _____ divisible by 8.

The number made by the last three digits

_____ divisible by _____.

---

15. $0.345 = \dfrac{345}{1000} = $ _____

$0.345 = $ _____ %

---

16. *Shift.* ⟵

$0.07\% = $ _____

$0.07\% = \dfrac{\square}{10,000} = $ _____

---

17. *Innermost inclusion symbols first*

$$(|-3| \cdot 4) + \left[\left(\frac{1}{2} + \frac{1}{4} \div \frac{1}{3}\right)\right]$$

$$(\underline{\quad} \cdot 4) + \left[\left(\frac{1}{2} + \frac{1}{4} \cdot \frac{\square}{\square}\right)\right]$$

$$(\underline{\quad} \cdot 4) + \left[\left(\frac{1}{2} + \frac{\square}{\square}\right)\right]$$

$$\underline{\quad} + \left[\frac{\square}{4} + \frac{\square}{\square}\right]$$

$$\underline{\quad} + \underline{\quad} = \underline{\quad}$$

18. *Simplify. Then compare.*

$$\frac{1}{3} + \frac{1}{5} \cdot \frac{2}{15} \quad \bigcirc \quad \left(\frac{1}{3} + \frac{1}{5}\right) \cdot \frac{2}{15}$$

$$= \frac{1}{3} + \frac{\square}{75} \qquad = \left(\frac{\square}{15} + \frac{\square}{15}\right) \cdot \frac{2}{15}$$

$$= \frac{\square}{75} + \frac{\square}{75} \qquad = \frac{\square}{15} \cdot \frac{2}{15}$$

$$= \frac{\square}{75} \qquad = \frac{\square}{225}$$

$$\frac{\square}{225} \quad \bigcirc \quad \frac{\square}{225}$$

19. $C = \frac{5}{9}(F - 32)$ $\qquad F = \frac{9}{5}(C + 32)$

The two formulas contain

_____ operations.

20. $C = 2\pi r$

$$P = (2 \cdot \underline{\quad}) + \frac{1}{2}(2\pi \cdot \underline{\quad})$$

$$= \underline{\quad} + \underline{\quad} = \underline{\quad}$$

21. Simplify.

Use the order of operations.

$$\left[(10 - 8)^2 - (-1)\right] + (5 - 3)$$

$$\left[(\underline{\quad})^2 - (-1)\right] + \underline{\quad}$$

$$\underline{\quad} + \underline{\quad} = \underline{\quad}$$

Circle the answer.

A −38 $\qquad$ B 7

C −80 $\qquad$ D 37

22. $S = 2(l \cdot w) + 2(l \cdot h) + 2(w \cdot h)$

Box A: $l = 12$ in., $w = 12$ in., $h = 12$ in.

Box B: $l = 16$ in., $w = 16$ in., $h = 6.75$ in.

a. Box A = ____ + ____ + ____

$$= \underline{\quad}$$

b. Box B = ____ + ____ + ____

$$= \underline{\quad}$$

c. _____ $\bigcirc$ _____

Box _____ uses less materials.

23. 25.6, 12.8, 6.4, 3.2, ...

   a. 25.6 − 12.8 = _____

     12.8 − _____ = _____

     _____ − _____ = _____

   b. If the pattern continues, will the ball

     stop bouncing? _____

     The ball bounces back up

     _____ each time.

24. $P = 2(l + w)$.

   $l = 22.312$ units; $w = 8.42$ units

   $P = 2($ _____ $+$ _____ $)$

   $P =$ _____

25. $|-250| + 78 =$ _____

26. $7 + ($ _____ $) =$ _____ planes

27. Student _____ is correct.

   Student _____ should have _____

   _____.

28. _____ $- ($ _____ $) =$ _____

29. *See page 1 in the* Student Reference Guide.

$$\frac{\sqrt{9ny}}{nx} + a^2 - \frac{n}{4} + \frac{3\pi}{8}$$

Circle the answer.

  A $\dfrac{\sqrt{9ny}}{nx}$ **B** $\dfrac{3\pi}{8}$

  C $\dfrac{n}{4}$ **D** a^2

30. *Use the order of operations.*

$$\frac{180(6-2)°}{6} = \underline{\qquad}$$

Using Unit Analysis to Convert Measures

page 36

New Concepts

- A unit ratio compares two measures that name the same amount.

$$\frac{12 \text{ in}}{1 \text{ ft}} \qquad \frac{1 \text{ m}}{100 \text{ cm}} \qquad \frac{3 \text{ ft}}{1 \text{ yd}}$$

- A unit ratio is always equal to 1.
- A unit ratio multiplied by a measure will always name the same measure.
- Set up the unit ratio so that the units not needed will cancel.

Example **Converting Units of Length**

Math Language

Unit analysis is a process for converting measures into different units.

A cheetah ran at a rate of 105,600 yards per hour. **How fast did the cheetah run in miles per hour?**

$$\frac{105,600 \text{ yd}}{1 \text{ hour}} = \frac{? \text{ mi}}{1 \text{ hour}}$$ *Identify known and missing information.*

$$105,600 \text{ yd} \longrightarrow ? \text{ mi}$$ *Change yards to miles.*

$$1 \text{ mi} = 1,760 \text{ yd}$$ *Equate units.*

$$\frac{1 \text{ mi}}{1760 \text{ yd}}$$ *Write a unit ratio.*

$$\frac{105,600 \text{ yd}}{1 \text{ hr}} \cdot \frac{1 \text{ mi}}{1760 \text{ yd}}$$ *Use a unit ratio.*

$$\frac{\overset{60}{\cancel{105,600} \text{ yd}}}{1\text{h}} \cdot \frac{1 \text{ mi}}{\cancel{1760 \text{ yd}}}$$ *Divide out common factors.*
Cancel units.

$$\frac{60 \text{ mi}}{1 \text{ hr}}$$ *Multiply.*

$$\frac{105,600 \text{ yd}}{1 \text{ hr}} = \frac{60 \text{ mi}}{1 \text{ hr}}$$ *Write the ratio of miles per hour.*

The cheetah ran at a rate of **60 miles per hour.**

Exploration 📖 page 37

Use your textbook to complete the exploration.

a. $\dfrac{35 \text{ mi}}{1 \text{ hr}} = \dfrac{? \text{ ft}}{\boxed{} \text{ hr}}$

Change miles to feet.

5,280 ft = 1 mi

$\dfrac{\boxed{}}{\boxed{}}$ Write a unit ratio.

$\dfrac{35 \text{ mi}}{1 \text{hr}} \cdot \dfrac{\boxed{}}{\boxed{}}$ Cancel units.

$\dfrac{184,800 \text{ ft}}{\boxed{} \text{ hr}} = $ _____ feet per hour.

b. 4.5 yd · 3.25 yd = _____ yd^2 Find the area of the wall in square yards.

_____ ft = 1 yd

$14.625 \text{ yd} \cdot \text{yd} \cdot \dfrac{\boxed{}}{\boxed{}} \cdot \dfrac{\boxed{}}{\boxed{}}$ Yd · yd is the same as yd^2.

$14.625 \cdot$ ___ ft · ___ ft = _____ ft^2

c. 50 cm^3 = _____ mm^3

1 cm = 10 mm

$50 \text{ cm} \cdot \text{cm} \cdot \text{cm} = \dfrac{\boxed{}}{\boxed{}} \cdot \dfrac{\boxed{}}{\boxed{}} \cdot \dfrac{\boxed{}}{\boxed{}}$ Cancel units.

50 · 10 mm · _____ · _____ = _____ mm^3

46,300 mm^3 $\bigcirc$ _____ mm^3

Does Della have enough soil? _____ because _____.

d. 16 pounds = $ _____

1 pound = $2.016

$16 \text{ pounds} \cdot \dfrac{\boxed{}}{\boxed{}}$

16 · _____ = $ _____

1. Use the order of operations.

$$4\frac{1}{3} \div 1\frac{1}{3} + 3\frac{1}{3}$$

First, convert to improper fractions.

$$\frac{13}{3} \div \frac{\square}{\square} + 3\frac{1}{3}$$

Multiply by the reciprocal.

$$\frac{13}{3} \times \frac{\square}{\square} + 3\frac{1}{3}$$

$$= \underline{\hspace{1cm}} + 3\frac{1}{3}$$

$$= \underline{\hspace{1cm}}$$

2. Use the order of operations.

$$2\frac{3}{8} - 1\frac{3}{4} \div 1\frac{1}{2}$$

$$= 2\frac{3}{8} - \frac{\square}{\square} \div \frac{\square}{\square}$$

$$= \underline{\hspace{1cm}}$$

3. Find a common denominator.

$$2\frac{2}{3} + 1\frac{5}{6} - 6\frac{3}{4}$$

$$= 2\frac{\square}{\square} + 1\frac{\square}{\square} - 6\frac{\square}{\square}$$

$$= \underline{\hspace{1cm}}$$

4. First convert to improper fractions.

$$3\frac{1}{3} \div 1\frac{1}{4} \cdot \frac{1}{2}$$

$$= \frac{\square}{\square} \div \frac{\square}{\square} \cdot \frac{\square}{\square}$$

$$= \underline{\hspace{1cm}}$$

5. $0.37 \div 0.2 \cdot 0.1$

$$0.2\overline{)0.37} \qquad \underline{\hspace{1cm}} \cdot 0.1$$

$$= \underline{\hspace{1cm}}$$

6. $1.74 \cdot 0.3 \div 0.2$

Count the decimal places.

$$\begin{array}{r} 1.74 \\ \times \quad 0.3 \\ \hline \end{array}$$

$$0.2\overline{)}$$

Answer: \underline{\hspace{1cm}}

7. $A = \{1, 3, 5\}$

   $B = \{0, 2, 4, 6\}$

   $C = \{1, 2, 3, 4\}$

   True or false?

   a. $A \cup B = \{0, 1, 2, 3, 4, 5, 6\}$ _____

   b. $A \cap B = \{0, 1, 2, 3, 4, 5, 6\}$ _____

   c. $B \cup C = \{2, 4\}$ _____

   d. $A \cap C = \{1, 3\}$ _____

8. *Simplify. Then compare.*

   $$8^2 \div 4 - 6^2 \quad \bigcirc \quad (6 \cdot 7 \cdot 5) \div 6 - 15$$

   _____ $\bigcirc$ _____

9. **Frequency of Numbers**

   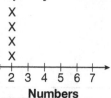

   Numbers

10. *Find a common denominator.*

    $$78\frac{2}{5} - 14\frac{7}{10}$$

    Answer: _____

11.
    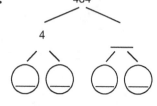

    prime factorization: _____

12. *See page 2 in the* Student Reference Guide.

    22, 993 _____ divisible by 5.

    The _____ digit _____ a 0 or a 5.

13. $125\% = 1\dfrac{\boxed{}}{\boxed{}} = 1\dfrac{\boxed{}}{\boxed{}}$

    $125\% = $ _____._____

14. *Use a unit ratio.*

    $$\frac{105 \text{ km}}{1 \text{ hr}} \cdot \frac{\boxed{}}{\boxed{}} = \text{_____}$$

15. *Use a unit ratio.*

$74 \text{ m} \cdot \text{m} \cdot \dfrac{\square}{\square} \cdot \dfrac{\square}{\square}$

$= \underline{\hspace{2cm}}$

16. *Use a unit ratio.*

$72{,}576 \text{ in.} \cdot \text{in.} \cdot \text{in.} \cdot \dfrac{\square}{\square} \cdot \dfrac{\square}{\square} \cdot \dfrac{\square}{\square}$

$= \underline{\hspace{2cm}}$

---

17. *Add the opposite.*

Which of these differences will be positive? Circle the answer.

A $\ -\dfrac{1}{2} - \dfrac{1}{8}$

B $\ \dfrac{9}{12} - 1$

C $\ \dfrac{5}{7} - \dfrac{3}{10}$

D $\ -\dfrac{14}{15} - \left(\dfrac{4}{15}\right)$

18. Student _____ is correct.

Student _____ incorrectly wrote the

_____ multiplying by _____ to

cancel the units instead of

_____ by _____ .

---

19. *Change cm to inches.*

Answer: _____

20. $1 \text{ knot} = 1.852 \text{ km}$

a. $38 \text{ knots} \cdot \dfrac{\square}{\square} = \underline{\hspace{2cm}}$

b. $\dfrac{\square \text{ km}}{1 \text{ hr}} \cdot \dfrac{1 \text{ mi}}{1.609 \text{ km}} = \underline{\hspace{2cm}}$

---

21. *See page 15 in the* Student Reference Guide.

a. $A = \underline{\hspace{2cm}}$

b. $A = \dfrac{1}{2}\underline{\hspace{0.6cm}} \cdot \underline{\hspace{0.6cm}} \cdot \dfrac{\square}{\square} \cdot \dfrac{\square}{\square} \text{ in}^2$

c. $A = \dfrac{1}{2}(\underline{\hspace{0.5cm}})(\underline{\hspace{0.5cm}}) \cdot \dfrac{\square}{\square} \cdot \dfrac{\square}{\square} \text{ in}^2$

$= \underline{\hspace{1.5cm}} \text{ in}^2$

22. *1 in. is about 2.54 cm.*

Round your answer to the nearest hundredth.

$\dfrac{1 \text{ g}}{\text{cm} \cdot \text{cm} \cdot \text{cm}} \cdot \dfrac{\square}{\square} \cdot \dfrac{\square}{\square} \cdot \dfrac{\square}{\square}$

$= \underline{\hspace{2cm}}$

---

23. *See page 17 in the* Student Reference Guide.

Circle the answer: true or false.

A right triangle contains one _____

angle and two _____.

24. Student _____ is correct.

Student _____ should have simplified

_____ the parentheses first.

25. $s = 8$ in.

$h = 12$ in.

a. $V = \frac{1}{3}s^2h = $ _____

b. I simplified _____ first because

_____

_____

_____

_____

_____

26. _____ + (_____) + (_____) + _____

= _____

27.
$$57\frac{1}{2}$$
$$-\,56\frac{3}{4}$$

$$57\frac{3}{4}$$
$$-\,57\frac{1}{2}$$

Group _____

28. Student _____ is correct.

Student _____ ignored the implied

exponent of _____ on b and c.

29. *Use a unit ratio. 5,280 ft = 1 mi*

$$\frac{32\ \text{mi}}{1\ \text{hr}} \cdot \frac{\square}{\square} = \underline{\qquad}$$

30. $A = s^2$

a. $A = $ _____

b. $A = $ _____

c. $A = $ _____

d. $A = $ _____

Evaluating and Comparing
Algebraic Expressions page 43

New Concepts

- To evaluate an expression, substitute the numbers given for the variables. Then simplify.

Example **Evaluating Algebraic Expressions**

Evaluate the expression $3x - 4x + ax$ when $x = 3$ and $a = 1$.

$3x - 4x + ax$

$= 3 \cdot 3 - 4 \cdot 3 + 1 \cdot 3$ *Substitute.*

$= 9 - 12 + 3 = 0$ *Simplify.*

Example **Evaluating Algebraic Expressions with Exponents**

Evaluate the expression $3(z - y)^2 - 4y^3$ for $y = 2$ and $z = 4$.

$3(z - y)^2 - 4y^3$

$3(4 - 2)^2 - 4(2)^3$ *Substitute.*

$3(2)^2 - 4(2)^3$ *Simplify.*

$3(4) - 4(8)$

$12 - 32$

-20

- To compare two expressions, evaluate each expression and then compare the results.

Example **Comparing Algebraic Expressions**

Compare the expressions $3a^2 + 2b - 4b^3$ and $2a^2b^2$ when $a = 4$ and $b = 3$. Use $<$, $>$, or $=$.

$$3a^2 + 2b - 4b^3 \bigcirc 2a^2b^2$$

$= 3(4)^2 + 2(3) - 4(3)^3$ $= 2(4)^2(3)^2$ *Substitute.*

$= 3(16) + 2(3) - 4(27)$ $= 2(16)(9)$ *Simplify.*

$= 48 + 6 - 108$ $= 288$

$= 54 - 108$

$= -54$

Since $-54 < 288$, $3a^2 + 2b - 4b^3 < 2a^2b^2$ when $a = 4$ and $b = 3$.

Evaluate each expression for the given values.

a. $3x - 4b + 2bx$; $x = 10$, $b = 2$

$3(\underline{\hspace{1cm}}) - 4(\underline{\hspace{1cm}}) + 2(\underline{\hspace{1cm}})(\underline{\hspace{1cm}})$

$= \underline{\hspace{1cm}} - \underline{\hspace{1cm}} + \underline{\hspace{1cm}} = \underline{\hspace{1cm}}$

b. $2ab - 4a^2 + 10$; $a = -1$, $b = 8$

$2(\underline{\hspace{1cm}})(\underline{\hspace{1cm}}) - 4(\underline{\hspace{1cm}})^2 + 10$

$= \underline{\hspace{1cm}} - 4(\underline{\hspace{1cm}}) + 10$

$= \underline{\hspace{1cm}} - \underline{\hspace{1cm}} + 10 = \underline{\hspace{1cm}}$

c. Compare the expressions when $x = 2$ and $y = 5$. Use $<$, $>$, or $=$.

$$\left(6x^2 + y^3\right) - 3x^6 \bigcirc 8x^4 - y^3$$

$= \left(6 \cdot 2^2 + 5^3\right) - 3(2)^6 \qquad\qquad = 8(2)^4 - (5)^3$

$= (6 \cdot \underline{\hspace{1cm}} + \underline{\hspace{1cm}}) - 3(\underline{\hspace{1cm}}) \qquad\quad = 8(\underline{\hspace{1cm}}) - \underline{\hspace{1cm}}$

$= (\underline{\hspace{1cm}} + \underline{\hspace{1cm}}) - \underline{\hspace{1cm}} \qquad\qquad = \underline{\hspace{1cm}} - \underline{\hspace{1cm}}$

$= \underline{\hspace{1cm}} - \underline{\hspace{1cm}} \qquad\qquad\qquad = \underline{\hspace{1cm}}$

$= \underline{\hspace{1cm}}$

$$\underline{\hspace{1cm}} \bigcirc \underline{\hspace{1cm}}$$

$$\left(6x^2 + y^3\right) - 3x^6 \bigcirc 8x^4 - y^3$$

d. $F = \frac{9}{5}C + 32$

$C = -89.4$

$\frac{9}{5}(\underline{\hspace{1cm}}) + \underline{\hspace{1cm}}$

$= 9(\underline{\hspace{1cm}}) \div 5 + \underline{\hspace{1cm}}$

$= \underline{\hspace{1cm}} \div 5 + \underline{\hspace{1cm}}$

$= \underline{\hspace{1cm}} + \underline{\hspace{1cm}} = \underline{\hspace{1cm}}$

The temperature is $\underline{\hspace{1cm}}$° F.

1. *First, convert to improper fractions.*

$$4\tfrac{1}{3} \div 2\tfrac{1}{3}$$

$$\frac{\square}{\square} \div \frac{\square}{\square}$$

$$\frac{\square}{\square} \times \frac{\square}{\square} = \underline{\hspace{1cm}}$$

2. *Find a common denominator.*

$$42\tfrac{3}{8} - 21\tfrac{3}{4} = \underline{\hspace{1cm}}$$

3. *Find a common denominator.*

$$1\tfrac{2}{3} + 2\tfrac{5}{6} = \underline{\hspace{1cm}}$$

4. *First, convert to improper fractions.*

$$2\tfrac{2}{3} \div 1\tfrac{3}{4}$$

$$\frac{\square}{\square} \div \frac{\square}{\square}$$

$$\frac{\square}{\square} \times \frac{\square}{\square} = \underline{\hspace{1cm}}$$

5.

$$0.2\overline{)0.75}$$

6.

$$0.3\overline{)1.74}$$

7. *Count the decimal places.*

$$\begin{array}{r} 1.25 \\ \times\, 0.2 \\ \hline \end{array}$$

8. *Count the decimal places.*

$$\begin{array}{r} 12.2 \\ \times\, 3.2 \\ \hline \end{array}$$

9. *See page 16 in the* Student Reference Guide.

Circle the answer: true or false.

A square has 2 pairs of _____ sides

and its sides are _____ .

10. *Innermost inclusion symbols first*

$4[(6-4)^3 - 5]$

$4[\underline{\quad}^3 - 5]$

$= 4[\underline{\quad} - 5]$

$= 4[\underline{\quad}] = \underline{\quad}$

11. $1.86 \text{ km}^2 = ? \text{ m}^2$

$1 \underline{\quad} = 1{,}000 \text{ m}$

$1.86 \text{ km} \times \underline{\quad} \times \underline{\quad} \times \dfrac{1000 \text{ m}}{1 \text{ km}} \times \square$

$1.86 \times 1000 \text{ m} \times 1000 \text{ m}$

$= \underline{\qquad\qquad}$

12. *Substitute.*

$14c + 28 - 12cd;\ c = 4,\ d = 5$

$14(\underline{\quad}) + 28 - 12(\underline{\quad})(\underline{\quad})$

$= \underline{\quad} + 28 - \underline{\quad} = \underline{\quad}$

13. *See page 16 in the* Student Reference Guide.

A straight angle measures _____ .

14.

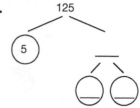

prime factorization: _____

15. *Substitute.*

$\dfrac{t-36}{36} + l;\ t = 72,\ l = 1$

$\dfrac{\square - 36}{36} + \underline{\quad} = \underline{\qquad\qquad}$

16. *Use the order of operations.*

$14 + \dfrac{36}{9} \cdot (2+5)$

$14 + \underline{\qquad} \cdot \underline{\qquad}$

Circle the answer.

A 126   **B** 21

C 42   **D** 140

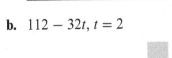

17. Simplify.

$(3 + 12) + (|-4| - 2)^3 + 1$

$(\underline{\hspace{1cm}}) + (\underline{\hspace{1cm}} - 2)^3 + 1$

$= (\underline{\hspace{1cm}}) + (\underline{\hspace{1cm}})^3 + 1$

$= \underline{\hspace{1cm}} + \underline{\hspace{1cm}} + 1 = \underline{\hspace{1cm}}$

18. a. $112 - 32t, t = 1$

_____

b. $112 - 32t, t = 2$

_____

19. *Substitute.*

$\$6.50 + \$1.75h, h = 3$ hours

cost: _____

20. Student _____ is correct.

Student _____ made an error evaluating

the _____ number raised to

a _____ .

21. *Substitute.*

$\frac{s}{n}; s = 30, n = 12$

$\dfrac{\square}{\square} = \underline{\hspace{1cm}}$

22. *Substitute.*

$s + 0.5a; s = 80, a = 53$

$\underline{\hspace{1cm}} + 0.5 (\underline{\hspace{1cm}}) = \underline{\hspace{1cm}}$

23. *See page 2 in the* Student Reference Guide.

224 _____ divisible by 6.

244 is divisible by _____ but not

by _____ .

24. $35.2\% = \dfrac{\square}{1000} = \dfrac{\square}{\square}$

$35.2\% = 0.\underline{\hspace{1cm}}$

25. $A = lw$

The rectangle is 88 cm long and 24 cm wide.

a. $A = (\underline{\quad})(\underline{\quad}) = \underline{\qquad\qquad}$ ▮

b. *Use a unit ratio. 1 cm = 10 mm*

$A = \underline{\qquad} \cdot \dfrac{\square}{\square} \cdot \dfrac{\square}{\square}$

$A = \underline{\qquad}$ ▮

c. $\dfrac{\square \text{ cm}^2}{\square \text{ mm}^2} = \dfrac{\square}{\square}$

26. $V = \pi r^2 h.$

$\pi \approx 3.14, r = 56 \text{ mm}, h = 128 \text{ mm}$

$V = \underline{\qquad}(\underline{\qquad})^2(\underline{\qquad})$

$V = \underline{\qquad}$ ▮

27. $F = P(1 + i)^{n \div 12}$

After adding 1 and i divide

$\underline{\qquad}$ by $\underline{\qquad}$.

28. Find the total for each of the two tournaments, then subtract.

$1 + (-2) + (-3) + 2 = \underline{\qquad}$

$(\underline{\quad}) + (\underline{\quad}) + \underline{\quad} + (\underline{\quad}) = \underline{\quad}$

$\underline{\quad} - \underline{\quad} = \underline{\quad}$

29. Student $\underline{\qquad}$ is correct.

Student $\underline{\qquad}$ did not follow the

$\underline{\qquad\qquad\qquad\qquad}$

and did not work $\underline{\qquad\qquad\qquad}$

$\underline{\qquad\qquad}$ first.

30. *Substitute.*

$35m; m = 15$

words: $\underline{\qquad}$

LESSON

10

Adding and Subtracting Real Numbers page 47

New Concepts

• To subtract a real number, add its opposite.

> **Example** Adding and Subtracting Fractions and Decimals
>
> **Simplify.**
>
> $3.16 + (-1.22) - 4.73 + 5.6$
>
> $= 3.16 + (-1.22) + (-4.73) + 5.6$ *Add the opposite.*
>
> $= 3.16 + 5.6 + (-1.22) + (-4.73)$ *Group terms with like signs.*
>
> $= 8.76 + (-5.95)$ *Add numbers with like signs.*
>
> $= \mathbf{2.81}$ *Add.*

• To compare rational expressions, simplify each expression. Then compare.

> **Example** Comparing Rational Expressions
>
> **Complete the comparison. Use <, >, or =.**
> **Then compare.**
>
> $\frac{3}{8} + \left(-\frac{5}{8}\right) - \frac{1}{8} \bigcirc -2.75 + 6.25 - 3.75$
>
> Simplify each expression.
>
> $= \frac{3}{8} + \left(-\frac{5}{8}\right) + \left(-\frac{1}{8}\right)$ $= -2.75 + 6.25 + (-3.75)$
>
> $= \frac{3}{8} + \left(-\frac{6}{8}\right)$ $= -2.75 + (-3.75) + 6.25$
>
> $= -\frac{3}{8}$ $= -6.50 + 6.25$
>
> $= -0.25$
>
> $-\frac{3}{8} \;\text{\textcircled{<}}\; -0.25$
>
> $\frac{3}{8} + \left(-\frac{5}{8}\right) - \frac{1}{8} \;\text{\textcircled{<}}\; -2.75 + 6.25 - 3.75$

Simplify.

a. $\frac{4}{9} + \frac{2}{9} - \frac{5}{9}$

$\frac{4}{9} + \frac{2}{9} + \left(-\frac{5}{9}\right)$ *Add the opposite.*

_____ $+ \left(-\frac{5}{9}\right) =$ _____   *Add numbers with like signs first.*

b. $16.21 - 21.54 + 12.72$

$16.21 + 12.72 + (-21.54)$ *Group terms with like signs.*

_____ $+ (-21.54) =$ _____

c. Order the numbers from least to greatest: $\frac{3}{4}, -1, 0.85, \frac{5}{8}$.

Write the fractions as decimals.

$\frac{3}{4} = 0.$_____ $\frac{5}{8} = 0.$_____

The numbers in order from least to greatest are: _____, _____, _____, _____.

d. Compare the expressions. Use $<$, $>$, or $=$.

$3.2 + (-2.8) - 5.2 \bigcirc \frac{7}{12} - \frac{5}{12} + \left(-\frac{11}{12}\right)$

$= 3.2 + ($_____$) + ($_____$)$ $= \frac{7}{12} + ($_____$) + \left(-\frac{11}{12}\right)$

$= 3.2 +$ _____ $= \frac{7}{12} +$ _____

$=$ _____ $=$ _____

_____ $\bigcirc$ _____

$3.2 + (-2.8) - 5.2 \bigcirc \frac{7}{12} - \frac{5}{12} + \left(-\frac{11}{12}\right)$

e. Jonah: 32.68 seconds   Gayle: $32.68 + 3.01 =$ _____ seconds

---

1. *Find a common denominator.*

$$\frac{1}{2} + \frac{3}{5} = \underline{\hspace{2cm}}$$

2. *Find a common denominator.*

$$15\frac{1}{3} - 7\frac{4}{5} = \underline{\hspace{2cm}}$$

---

3. *First, convert to improper fractions.*

$$3\frac{2}{3} \cdot 2\frac{1}{4} = \underline{\hspace{2cm}}$$

4. *First, convert to improper fractions. Then multiply by the reciprocal.*

$$3\frac{2}{5} \div 1\frac{2}{3} = \underline{\hspace{2cm}}$$

---

5. *Find a common denominator.*

$$78\frac{3}{5} - 14\frac{7}{10} = \underline{\hspace{2cm}}$$

6. *First, convert to improper fractions.*

$$2\frac{1}{3} \cdot 1\frac{1}{4} = \underline{\hspace{2cm}}$$

---

7. *Count the decimal places.*

$$10.2$$
$$\times 3.15$$

8.

$$2.2\overline{)20.46}$$

---

9. *Count the decimal places.*

$$12.3$$
$$\times\ 2.02$$

10.

$$0.25\overline{)0.80}$$

---

11. Order from greatest to least:

$$\frac{6}{7},\ \frac{3}{5},\ \frac{1}{7},\ -\frac{4}{3}$$

_____, _____, _____, $-\dfrac{4}{3}$

12. *See page 16 in the* Student Reference Guide.

An _____ angle measures less than 90°.

---

13. $8673\ \text{g} = ?\ \text{kg}$

$$1000\ \text{g} = 1\ \text{kg}$$

$$8673\ \text{g} \times \frac{\square}{\square} = \underline{\hspace{2cm}}$$

14. *1 mi is about 1.6 km.*

$$26\ \text{mi} = ?\ \text{km}$$

$$26\ \text{mi} \times \frac{\square}{\square} = \underline{\hspace{2cm}}$$

---

15. $(2 + 5) - (3 \cdot 4) = 2 + 5 - 3 \cdot 4$

Circle the answer: true or false.

The value of each expression is _____.

16. *Group terms with like signs.*

$$1.29 + 3.9 - 4.2 - 9.99 + 6.1$$

Circle the answer.

A −2.9   **B** −1

C 1   **D** 2.9

---

17. Student _____ is correct.

Student B did not complete the operations

within the _____ first.

18. *Find a common denominator.*

$$2\frac{1}{4} - 1\frac{1}{3} = \underline{\hspace{2cm}}$$

19. Draw an X to show the frequency of each
number.

Frequency of Numbers

```
X
X
X
X
←─┼──┼──┼──┼──┼──┼──┼──→
  9  10 11 12 13 14 15
```
Numbers

20. a. distance on map: b

actual block length: _____

b. distance on map: 0.4 ft

actual distance: _____

21. $A = bh$

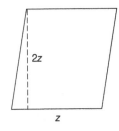

$A = \underline{\hspace{2cm}}$

$A = \underline{\hspace{2cm}}$

22. Student _____ is correct.

Student _____ multiplied by the unit ratio

_____ instead of _____.

23. *1 in. is about 254 mm.*
1 in. is about 2.54 cm.

$$4.5 \text{ mm} \times \frac{\square}{\square} = \underline{\hspace{2cm}}$$

24. *See page 15 in the* Student Reference Guide.

$\text{Area}_{\text{rectangular building}} = 9 \cdot 6$

$\text{Area}_{\text{circular building}} = \pi\left(\frac{4}{2}\right)^2$

$\text{Area}_{\text{plot}} = 16 \cdot 10$

   a. $\text{Area}_{\text{two buildings}} = \underline{\hspace{3cm}}$

   b. $\text{Area}_{\text{not buildings}} = \underline{\hspace{3cm}}$

$$= \underline{\hspace{3cm}} \text{ yd}^2$$

25. Student _____ is correct.

Student _____ the

absolute values of the numbers rather

than _____ them.

26. $500 + (\underline{\hspace{1.5cm}}) + (\underline{\hspace{1.5cm}}) + \underline{\hspace{1.5cm}}$

final balance: _____

27. *See page 1 in the* Student Reference Guide.

Name two subsets of real numbers that
are mutually exclusive.

_____

By definition, the sets of _____

and _____ numbers do

not contain the same numbers.

28. $-8.2 + (\underline{\hspace{1.5cm}}) + \underline{\hspace{1.5cm}}$

total change: _____

29. $4 + (\underline{\hspace{1.5cm}}) + \underline{\hspace{1.5cm}}$

total gain: _____

30. 74 ft ⟶ 73 ft 12 in.
$$\underline{- \ 5 \text{ ft} \ \ 6 \text{ in.}}$$

Name _____

Determining the Probability of an Event page 53

- Probability can be written as a fraction or a decimal from 0 to 1, or as a percent from 0% to 100%

Math Language

The **probability** of an event is the likelihood that the event will occur.

An **outcome** is a possible result of a probability experiment.

An **event** is an outcome in a probability experiment.

Range of Probability

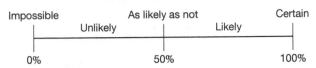

Describe each event as impossible, unlikely, as likely as not, likely, or certain.

1. Jake rolls a number less than 7 on a number cube. _____

   The numbers on a number cube are 1, 2, 3, 4, 5, 6.

2. February will have 30 days. _____

   February usually has 28 days. It has 29 days in a leap year.

3. A tossed coin will land on tails. _____

   There are two possible ways the coin can land, heads or tails.

4. Shayla correctly guesses a number between 1 and 100. _____

   There is 1 right number and 99 wrong numbers.

- Experimental probability $= \dfrac{\text{number of times an event occurs}}{\text{number of trials in the experiment}}$

Exploration 📖 page 53

Use the Exploration in your textbook to complete problems **5** and **6**.

7. A baseball player got 8 hits out of 25 times at bat. What is the probability that he will get a hit his next time at bat? Express the answer as a decimal to the thousandths place.

   $$P(\text{player gets a hit}) = \frac{\text{number of hits}}{\text{number of times at bat}}$$

   $$= \frac{8 \text{ hits}}{25 \text{ at bats}} = 0.\underline{\hspace{1cm}}$$

8. A piston manufacturer finds that 8 out of 250 pistons have defects.

   a. What is the probability a piston will have a defect? Express the probability as a percent.

   $$\frac{8}{250} = 0.\underline{\hspace{1cm}} = \underline{\hspace{1cm}}\%$$

Math Language

Experimental probability is based on trials of an experiment.

b. About how many out of 3000 pistons will likely have defects?

$$3000 \div 250 = \underline{\hspace{1cm}} \cdot 8 = \underline{\hspace{1cm}} \text{ pistons}$$

c. Pistons sell for $35. It costs $25 to make a piston.

How much profit will the manufacturer make on 3000 pistons.

$$\$35(3000 - \underline{\hspace{1cm}}) - \$25(3000) = \$\underline{\hspace{2cm}}$$

Exploration 📖 page 54

Use the Exploration in your textbook to complete problems **9** and **10**.

Investigation Practice 📖 page 55

Describe each event in problems a–d as **impossible, unlikely, as likely as not, likely,** or **certain.**

a. Gavin rolls an even number on a number cube. _____
There are six numbers on a number cube. The even numbers are 2, 4, and 6.

b. In the northern hemisphere, the temperature will get above 90°F in July. _____
The United States is in the northern hemisphere.

c. The first person Sonya meets is left-handed. _____
Most people are right handed.

d. A player with a batting average of .875 gets a hit his next time at bat. _____
An average of .875 is more than half.

e. See 📖 page 55. Express each probability as a fraction and as a percent.
The experiment was performed a total of 25 times.

Probability (landing on A)   _____/_____   _____%

Probability (landing on B)   _____/_____   _____%

Probability (landing on C)   _____/_____   _____%

f. If Jamie spins again, which letter will he most likely spin? _____

The letter _____ was spun most often, so it has the greatest probability of being spun again.

g. A baseball player gets 18 hits in 50 times at bat. What is the probability that he will get a hit his next time at bat? Express your answer as a decimal number in thousandths place.

_____

h. See 📖 page 55.

New Concepts

Properties of Real Numbers	
Multiplication Property of −1	
Change the sign.	Example: $9 \cdot -1 = -1 \cdot 9 = -9$
Multiplication Property of Zero	
Anything times 0 is 0.	Example: $9 \cdot 0 = 0$
Inverse Property of Multiplication	
A number times its reciprocal is 1.	Example: $3 \cdot \frac{1}{3} = \frac{1}{3} \cdot 3 = 1$

Math Language

The multiplicative inverse of a number is called its **reciprocal**. The reciprocal of 4 is $\frac{1}{4}$.

Multiplying and Dividing Signed Numbers	
Same signs: product or quotient is positive.	$(+)(+) = (+) \qquad (-)(-) = (+)$ $(+) \div (+) = (+) \quad (-) \div (-) = (+)$
Opposite signs: product or quotient is negative.	$(+)(-) = (-) \qquad (-)(+) = (-)$ $(+) \div (-) = (-) \quad (-) \div (+) = (-)$

Example **Multiplying Rational Numbers**

Simplify.

$4(-8) = \mathbf{-32}$	*Opposite signs: product is negative.*
$(-6)(-0.7) = \mathbf{4.2}$	*Same signs: product is positive.*

Example **Raising a Number to a Power**

Simplify.

$(-3)^4 = (-3)(-3)(-3)(-3) = \mathbf{81}$	*Use repeated multiplication.*
$-3^4 = -1 \cdot 3^4 = -1 \cdot [(-3)(-3)(-3)(-3)] = -1 \cdot 81 = \mathbf{-81}$	

Example **Dividing Real Numbers**

Simplify.

$-16 \div (-2) = \mathbf{8}$	*Same signs: quotient is positive.*
$(2.8) \div (-7) = \mathbf{-0.4}$	*Opposite signs: quotient is negative.*

Simplify each expression. Justify your answer.

a. $9(-0.8) =$ _____

The product of two numbers with *different* signs is _____.

b. $-12(-2.5) =$ _____

The product of two numbers with the *same* signs is _____.

Simplify each expression.

c. $(-4)^3 = ($___$) \cdot ($___$) \cdot ($___$) =$ _____

d. $(-8)^4 = ($___$) \cdot ($___$) \cdot ($___$) \cdot ($___$) =$ _____

e. $-5^4 = - ($___$) \cdot ($___$) \cdot ($___$) \cdot ($___$) =$ _____

Simplify each expression. Justify your answer.

f. $-105 \div (-7) =$ _____

_____sign(s): quotient is_____.

g. $63.9 \div (-3) =$ _____

_____sign(s): quotient is_____.

Evaluate each expression.

h. $-\dfrac{4}{5} \div -\dfrac{9}{10} = -\dfrac{4}{5} \cdot \dfrac{\square}{\square} = \dfrac{\square}{\square}$

i. $\dfrac{3}{8} \div -\dfrac{3}{4} = \dfrac{\square}{\square} \cdot \dfrac{\square}{\square} = \dfrac{\square}{\square}$

j. See page 59.

Homer, Alaska temperature: _____ °F

Bethel, Alaska temperature: $2 \cdot$ _____ °F = _____ °F

1. Circle the answer: true or false.

   $7 \times (\underline{\hspace{1.5cm}}) = (\underline{\hspace{0.8cm}}) \times \frac{1}{7} = 1$

2. Simplify.

   $-(-4)^2 = -(\underline{\hspace{1.5cm}}) \times (\underline{\hspace{1.5cm}})$

   $= (\underline{\hspace{1.5cm}})$

3. Student ___ is correct. Student ___ did

   not find a _____ _____.

4. Simplify.

   $\dfrac{2 \cdot 14 + 3 \cdot 7}{71 - 15}$

   $= \dfrac{\square + \square}{\square} = \dfrac{\square}{\square}$

5. Complete the line plot.

   Frequency of Numbers

   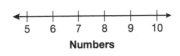

   Numbers

6. *See page 16 in the* Student Reference Guide.

   A(n) _____ angle measures more
   than 90° and less than 180°.

7. $3(x + 4) + y$ when $x = 8$ and $y = 7$

   Substitute.

   $3[(\underline{\hspace{0.6cm}}) + 4] + (\underline{\hspace{0.6cm}}) = 3(\underline{\hspace{0.6cm}}) + (\underline{\hspace{0.6cm}})$

   $= (\underline{\hspace{0.6cm}}) + (\underline{\hspace{0.6cm}})$

   $= \underline{\hspace{2cm}}$

8. $3x^2 + 2(x - 1)^3$ for $x = 6$

   Substitute.

   $3(\underline{\hspace{0.5cm}})^2 + 2[(\underline{\hspace{0.5cm}}) - 1]^3 = 3(\underline{\hspace{0.5cm}}) + 2(\underline{\hspace{0.5cm}})^3$

   $= (\underline{\hspace{0.5cm}}) + 2(\underline{\hspace{0.5cm}})$

   $= (\underline{\hspace{0.5cm}}) + (\underline{\hspace{0.5cm}})$

   $= \underline{\hspace{2cm}}$

9. Which rate is fastest?

Divide.

Circle the answer.

A $\dfrac{660 \text{ ft}}{15 \text{ s}}$

B $\dfrac{645 \text{ ft}}{11 \text{ s}}$

C $\dfrac{616 \text{ ft}}{12 \text{ s}}$

D $\dfrac{1100 \text{ ft}}{30 \text{ s}}$

10. Simplify. Justify each step.

$$5 + \tfrac{9}{3}[4(\tfrac{1}{2} + 4)]$$

$$= 5 + \tfrac{9}{3}\left[4\left(\dfrac{\square}{2}\right)\right] \quad \text{symbols of} \underline{\hspace{2cm}}$$

$$= 5 + \tfrac{9}{3}(\underline{\hspace{1cm}}) \qquad \underline{\hspace{3cm}}$$

$$= 5 + (\underline{\hspace{1cm}}) \qquad \underline{\hspace{3cm}}$$

$$= \underline{\hspace{1.5cm}} \qquad \underline{\hspace{3cm}}$$

11. Temperature at 12 noon: 20°C
Rate of temperature change: −2°C/h

Hours from 12 noon to 11 p.m.: _____ h
Temperature drop between noon and
11 p.m.:

$$\left(-2\,\tfrac{\text{C}}{\text{h}}\right) \times \underline{\hspace{1cm}} \text{h} = \underline{\hspace{1cm}} °\text{C at 11 p.m.}$$

Circle the answer.

A 22°C

B −2°C

C −30°C

D −22°C

12. $a = \dfrac{v^2}{r}$ $r = 200$ cm; $v = 35$ cm/s

Substitute.

$$a = \dfrac{v^2}{r} = \dfrac{\square^2}{\square} = \dfrac{\square}{\square}$$

$$= \underline{\hspace{1cm}} \text{ cm/s}^2$$

13. 560 pints of strawberries
$0.16 loss per pint

number of pints × loss per pint = total loss

$$\underline{\hspace{2cm}} \times \$\underline{\hspace{1.5cm}} = \$\underline{\hspace{1.5cm}}$$

14. Depth of first dive:
rate: $-400\,\dfrac{\text{m}}{\text{min}}$; time: 10 min

rate × time = depth

$$\underline{\hspace{2cm}}\dfrac{\text{m}}{\text{min}} \times \underline{\hspace{0.5cm}} \text{min} = \underline{\hspace{1.5cm}}\text{m}$$

Depth of second dive:
rate: $-400\,\dfrac{\text{m}}{\text{min}}$; time: 4 min

$$\underline{\hspace{2cm}}\dfrac{\text{m}}{\text{min}} \times \underline{\hspace{0.5cm}} \text{min} = \underline{\hspace{1.5cm}}\text{m}$$

15. $-1.06 + 2.01 + 4.13 =$

$$[(\underline{\hspace{1.5cm}}) + (\underline{\hspace{1.5cm}})] + (\underline{\hspace{1.5cm}})$$

$$= (\underline{\hspace{1.5cm}}) + (\underline{\hspace{1.5cm}})$$

$$= \underline{\hspace{2.5cm}}$$

16. a. Use fractions. Round to the nearest
quarter of a meter.

$$\underline{\hspace{1cm}} \text{ m} - \underline{\hspace{1cm}} \text{ m} = \underline{\hspace{1cm}} \text{ m}$$

b. $\dfrac{\square}{100} - \dfrac{\square}{100} = \dfrac{\square}{100} = \dfrac{\square}{\square\text{m}}$

17. Student ___ is correct. Student ___ should

have _____ 4 and 17 first.

18. height: $2.6f + 65$ cm

Substitute.

2.6 ____ $+ 65$

$=$ _____

19. Student ___ is correct. Student ___

subtracted _____ instead of _____.

20. a. _____

b. _____.

c. fraction won: $\dfrac{\square}{\square}$

_____

21. *Opposite signs: product is negative.*

$5(-2)$

$=$ _____

22. *Same signs: product is positive.*

$(-3)(-5)$

$=$ _____

23. Simplify.

$-|-15 + 5|$

$= -|-(\underline{})|$

$= -|\underline{}|$

$=$ _____

24. Simplify.

$(-3)(-6)(-2)(5)$

$= [(\underline{})(\underline{})] \cdot [(\underline{})(\underline{})]$

$= \underline{} \cdot \underline{}$

$=$ _____

25. Simplify.

(3)(5)

= _____

---

26. $P = 2(l + w)$

_____ the sides of a rectangle are

_____ integers.

The _____ of a rectangle

cannot be a _____

number.

27.

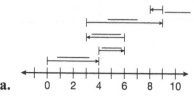

a.

b. ____ + ____ + ____ + ____ + ____

c. _____

---

28. Jan has: 2 yd = 2 × ____ in. = ____ in.

Jan needs: ____ in.

Jan has   Jan needs

(___) in. ◯   (___) in.

Does Jan have enough ribbon? _____

2 yd is _____ in.

---

29. temperature at 7 a.m. ____°F

temperature at 5 p.m. ____°F

temperature change from 7 a.m. to 5 p.m.

5 p.m.   7 a.m.   change

____°F ◯ ____°F = ____°F

---

30. $20 + 0.10m$

Substitute.

$20 + 0.10($____$)$

= ____ + ____

= ▒▒▒▒

Using the Properties of Real Numbers to Simplify Expressions page 63

New Concepts

Math Language

0 is the **additive identity.**

1 is the **multiplicative identity.**

- Use the properties of real numbers to simplify expressions and write equivalent expressions.

Properties of Addition and Multiplication
Identity Property of Addition
Adding 0. $\qquad$ Example: $5 + 0 = 5$
Identity Property of Multiplication
Multiplying by 1. $\qquad$ Example: $5 \cdot 1 = 5$
Commutative Property of Addition or Multiplication
Order is changed. $\qquad$ Example: $5 + 2 = 2 + 5$ $5 \cdot 2 = 2 \cdot 5$
Associative Property of Addition or Multiplication
Groups are changed. $\qquad$ Example: $(1 + 2) + 3 = 1 + (2 + 3)$ $(1 \cdot 2) \cdot 3 = 1 \cdot (2 \cdot 3)$

Example Identifying Properties

Name the properties illustrated.

$1 \cdot 8 = 8$ **Identity Property of Multiplication**

$13 + 5 = 5 + 13$ **Commutative Property of Addition**

$(3 \cdot 4) \cdot 7 = 3 \cdot (4 \cdot 7)$ **Associative Property of Multiplication**

$(12 + 9) + 5 = (9 + 12) + 5$ **Commutative Property of Addition**

Example Using Properties to Justify Statements

Tell whether each statement is true or false. Justify your answer using the properties.

$gh = hg$ **True; Commutative Property of Multiplication,** for example, $3 \cdot 4 = 4 \cdot 3$

$b + 1 = b$ **False; Identity Property of Addition,** for example, $3 + 1 \neq 3$

$d + (e + f) = (d + e) + f$ **True; Associative Property of Addition,** for example, $5 + (7 + 9) = (5 + 7) + 9$

Example **Justifying Steps to Simplify an Expression**

Simplify. Justify each step.

$$16 + 3x + 4$$

$16 + 3x + 4 \ = 3x + 16 + 4$	*Commutative Property of Addition*
$(3x + 16) + 4 = 3x + (16 + 4)$	*Associative Property of Addition*
$3x + (16 + 4) = 3x + \mathbf{20}$	*Add.*

Lesson Practice 📖 page 66

Identify each property shown.

a. $5 + (9 + 8) = (5 + 9) + 8$ _____

b. $0 + 10 = 10$ _____

c. $15 \cdot 3 = 3 \cdot 15$ _____

d. $17 \cdot 1 = 17$ _____

Circle "True" or "False". Justify your answer with properties.

e. $(ab)c = a(bc)$ True   False   _____

f. $m - z = z - m$ True   False   _____

g. $w + 0 = w$ True   False   _____

Simplify. Use a property to justify each step.

h. $18 + 7x + 4 = 7x + 18 + 4$ _____

   $7x + 18 + 4 = 7x + (18 + 4)$ _____

   $\qquad = 7x + \underline{\quad}$ _____

i. $\frac{1}{3}d \cdot 3 = d \cdot (\frac{1}{3} \cdot 3)$ _____

   $d \cdot (\frac{1}{3} \cdot 3) = d \cdot \underline{\quad}$ _____

   $d \cdot 1 = \underline{\quad}$ _____

j. Fill in the blanks. Use a property to justify the first step.

   $\$1.45 + \$3.35 + \$2.65 = \$1.45 + (\underline{\quad} + \underline{\quad})$ _____

   $\$1.45 + (\underline{\quad} + \underline{\quad}) = \$1.45 + \underline{\quad}$

   $\$1.45 + \underline{\quad} = \$\underline{\quad}$

1. $100 \cdot 1 = 100$

_____ Property of

_____

2. *Opposite signs: quotient is negative.*

$-18 \div 3 =$ _____

3. *Work within the absolute value bars.*

$|12 - 30| = |$_____$| =$ _____

4. *Same signs: product is positive.*

Multiply the first two terms and the last two terms.

$(-3)(-2)(-1)(-8) = ($__$)($__$) =$ _____

5. Circle the answer: true or false.

The Associative Property only applies

when the operations are all _____

or _____.

6. Multiply the numerator and denominator by the same number.

$\frac{2}{3} = \dfrac{\square}{\square}$

7. *Complementary angles form a corner.*
Circle the answer: true or false.

The sum of the measures of
complementary angles is 90°.

8. operation: _____

additive identity: _____

Circle the answer.

  A $a \cdot 0 = 0$ **B** $a + 0 = a$

  C $a \cdot \frac{1}{a} = 1$ **D** $a + 1 = 1 + a$

9. *Find a common denominator.*

$$\frac{11}{15} + \frac{1}{30} + \frac{3}{60}$$

$$= \frac{\square}{\square} + \frac{\square}{\square} + \frac{\square}{\square}$$

$$= \underline{\hspace{2cm}}$$

10. Student ____ is correct.

The quotient of a _____ number and

a _____ number is negative.

11. *Simplify.*

Use a property to justify each step.

$$5 + x + 15$$

$$5 + x + 15 = x + 5 + 15 \qquad \underline{\hspace{2.5cm}}$$

$$x + 5 + 15 = x + (5 + 15) \qquad \underline{\hspace{2.5cm}}$$

$$x + (5 + 15) = x + 20 \qquad \text{Add.}$$

12. *Substitute.*

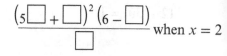

Circle the answer.

A 288

B 200

C 400

D 28

13. $(4x^3y^2)^2$ when $x = 2$ and $y = 1$

Substitute.

$$[4(\underline{\quad})^3(\underline{\quad})^2]^2 = [4(\underline{\quad})(\underline{\quad})]^2$$

$$= (4 \cdot \underline{\quad})^2$$

$$= \underline{\quad}^2$$

$$= \underline{\quad}$$

14. *1 lb = 16 oz*

Use a unit ratio.

$$\frac{588 \text{ oz}}{1} \cdot \frac{\square}{\square} = \underline{\hspace{2cm}}$$

15. The _____ Property of

_____ says that the order

of factors does not change the

_____ .

16. $P = 2(10 + 6) \overset{?}{=} 2(6 + 10)$

_____ the _____ Property of

_____ states that the order of the

terms does not affect the _____ .

17. Using the _____ Property of

Addition, both are _____ .

18. $A = lw$

width: _____

length: _____

_____ $\cdot 2.3 =$ _____

---

19. Find the sum.

Tyra's scores:

28, five times _____

−41, three times _____

−16, two times _____

total score:

$5(\underline{}) + \underline{}(-41) + 2(\underline{}) =$

$(\underline{}) + (\underline{}) + (\underline{}) = \underline{}$

20. *Change the fractions to decimals. Then compare.*

Circle the answer.

A $-0.24, 0.23, \frac{1}{4}, \frac{1}{3}$

B $\frac{1}{4}, \frac{1}{3}, 0.23, -0.24$

C $-0.24, 0.23, \frac{1}{3}, \frac{1}{4}$

D $\frac{1}{3}, \frac{1}{4}, 0.23, -0.24$

---

21. *1 yd = 36 in.*

Use a unit ratio.

$\dfrac{124 \text{ in.}}{1} \cdot \dfrac{\square}{\square} =$ _____

22. Student ____ is correct. Student ____ did not

follow the _____ of _____ .

---

23. $4(8 - 9 \div 3)^2$

1st step: Divide ____ by ____ .

2nd step: _____ ____ from 8.

3rd step: Square ____ .

4th step: _____ (____) by 4.

5th step: The answer is ____ .

24. Find the k's. ____ , ____$^{\square}$, and ____

Find the x's.

____$^{\square}$, ____ , ____$^{\square}$, and ____$^{\square}$

Find the y's. ____

Add the exponents

_____

25. Student ____ is correct. Student ____

did not treat the _____ and the

_____ as _____ in the

expression "5x".

26. beginning balance: $_____

deposit(s): $_____ and $_____, or $_____

beginning balance + deposits = new balance

$_____ + $_____ = $_____

withdrawal(s): $_____

new balance − withdrawals = final balance

$_____ − $_____ = $_____

27. *Draw a diagram.*

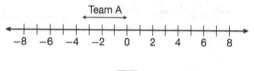
Team A

Answer: _____

28. *Distance = rate × time*

distance 1: ____ × 2.5 = _____ mi

distance 2: (___) × (___) = _____ mi

between ____ and _____

29. $2^2 + 24 - (3 - 12)$

$= 2^2 + 24 - ($___$)$ _____

$= $___$ + 24 - ($___$)$ _____

$= $___$ - ($___$)$ _____

$= $___

30.   number   opposite

↓   ↓

____   +   _____ = 0

Name _____

Calculating and Comparing Square Roots page 69

New Concepts

• A square number can only end with the digits: 0, 1, 4, 5, 6, or 9. Not all numbers that end with these digits are squares.

Math Language

A **perfect square** is the product of an integer and itself.

The **square root** of a number x is the number whose square is x.

A **radicand** is the number under a radical sign.

Example Finding Square Roots of Perfect Squares

a. Is 50 a perfect square? No.
   Explain. No integer multiplied by itself equals 50.

b. Is 64 a perfect square? Yes.
   Explain. $8 \cdot 8 = 64$

Example Estimating Square Roots

Estimate $\sqrt{50}$ to the nearest integer. Explain your reasoning.

Step 1: What is the closest perfect square that is less than 50? 49

Step 2: What is the closest perfect square that is greater than 50? 64

Step 3: Is $\sqrt{50}$ closer to the square root of 49 or 64? 49

Step 4: $\sqrt{50} \approx 7$

• When comparing expressions that contain radicals, simplify first.

Example Comparing Expressions Involving Square Roots

Compare using $>$, $<$, or $=$.

$$\sqrt{4} + \sqrt{36} \; \bigcirc \; \sqrt{9} + \sqrt{25}$$

$\sqrt{4} + \sqrt{36} \; \bigcirc \; \sqrt{9} + \sqrt{25}$	
$2 + 6 \; \bigcirc \; 3 + 5$	*Simplify the expressions.*
$8 = 8$	*Add.*

Is the radicand a perfect square? Explain.

a. $\sqrt{225}$

$= \sqrt{(\underline{\quad})(\underline{\quad})}$ _____, the product of a number multiplied by

$= \underline{\quad\quad}$ itself is a _____ _____.

b. $\sqrt{350}$

$= \sqrt{(\underline{\quad})(\underline{\quad})}$ _____, there is _____ number multiplied by

$= \underline{\quad\quad}$ itself that equals _____.

c. Estimate $\sqrt{37}$ to the nearest integer. Explain your reasoning.

closest perfect square less than 37: _____

closest perfect square greater than 37: _____

$\sqrt{37}$ is closer to _____ than to _____

$\sqrt{37} \approx$ _____

d. Complete and compare using >, <, or =.

$\sqrt{16} + \sqrt{441} \;\bigcirc\; \sqrt{81} + \sqrt{361}$

$\sqrt{16} = \underline{\quad\quad}$

$\sqrt{441} = \underline{\quad\quad}$

$\sqrt{81} = \underline{\quad\quad}$

$\sqrt{361} = \underline{\quad\quad}$

$\underline{\quad} + \underline{\quad} \;\bigcirc\; \underline{\quad} + \underline{\quad}$

$\underline{\quad} \;\bigcirc\; \underline{\quad}$

e. Area of square sandbox: 169 square feet

$A = s^2$

$169 =$ length of side $\times$ length of side

$\sqrt{169} = \sqrt{(\text{length of side} \cdot \text{length of side})}$

$\underline{\quad\quad\quad} = $ length of side

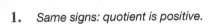
1. *Same signs: quotient is positive.*

$-16 \div -2 = $ _____

2. $\dfrac{4 + 7 - 6}{2 + 7 - 3}$

$\dfrac{\boxed{} - 6}{\boxed{} - 3} = \dfrac{\boxed{}}{\boxed{}}$

3. *Collect terms with the same sign.*

$-2 + 11 - 4 + 3 - 8$

= _____ − _____

= _____

4. $(-2)(-3) + 11(2) - 3 - 6$

___ $+ 11(2) - 3 - 6 = $ ___ $+$ ___ $- 3 - 6$

___ $-$ ___ $= $ ___

5. $3p - 4g - 2x$ when $p = 2$, $g = -3$, and $x = 4$

Substitute.

$3(\underline{}) - 4(\underline{}) - 2(\underline{})$

$= \underline{} \bigcirc \underline{} \bigcirc \underline{} = \underline{}$

6. $3xy - 2yz$ when $x = 3$, $y = 4$, and $z = 3$

Substitute.

$3(\underline{})(\underline{}) - 2(\underline{})(\underline{}) =$

$3(\underline{}) - 2(\underline{})$

$= \underline{}(\underline{}) = \underline{}$

7. Label $\sqrt{40}$ on the number line.

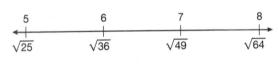

$\sqrt{40}$ is between _____ and _____.

8. $\sqrt{200} = \sqrt{(20)(\underline{})}$

$\sqrt{289} = \sqrt{(\underline{})(\underline{})}$

$\sqrt{410} = \sqrt{(\underline{})(10)}$

$\sqrt{150} = \sqrt{(\underline{})(10)}$

Circle the answer.

A 200   **B** 289   **C** 410   **D** 150

9. $b = \sqrt{4}$

_____ • _____ $= 4$

$\sqrt{\underline{} \cdot \underline{}} = \sqrt{4}$

$b = $ _____

10. *Find a common denominator.*

$\dfrac{1}{3} = \dfrac{\boxed{}}{12}$

Shade.

11. *Use a unit ratio.*

1 yd = _____ ft

$$\frac{25 \text{ ft}}{1 \text{ hr}} \cdot \frac{\square}{\square} = \frac{\square \text{ yd}}{\text{hr}}$$

12. Circle the answer: true or false.

odd numbers: 1, 3, 5, 7, 9, 11, 13 ...

counterexample: _____

---

13. $A = s^2$

A of square 1 = _____

A of square 2 = $\dfrac{\square}{2}$

= _____

s^2 of square 2 = _____

s of square 2 = _____

Circle the answer.

A 14 meters

B ≈ 20 meters

C 196 meters

D 96 meters

---

14. *See page 3 in the* Student Reference Guide.

_____ because of the _____ Property of _____.

---

15. True or false?

a. $4^2 + 15 \cdot 20 \overset{?}{=} 316$

_____ $+ 15 \cdot 20 \overset{?}{=} 316$

_____ $+$ _____ $\overset{?}{=} 316$

_____

b. $(4 + 5)^2 \overset{?}{=} 4 + 5^2$

$(\underline{\quad})^2 \overset{?}{=} 4 +$ _____ ^{2}

_____ $\overset{?}{=} 4 +$ _____

_____ $\overset{?}{=}$ _____

_____

---

16. a. *Find a common denominator.*

$8\dfrac{1}{4}$　$8\dfrac{3}{16}$　$8\dfrac{5}{8}$　$8\dfrac{1}{16}$

↓　　↓　　↓　　↓

$8\dfrac{\square}{\square}$　$8\dfrac{\square}{\square}$　$8\dfrac{\square}{\square}$　$8\dfrac{\square}{\square}$

b. Order from least to greatest.

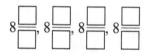

$8\dfrac{\square}{\square}, 8\dfrac{\square}{\square}, 8\dfrac{\square}{\square}, 8\dfrac{\square}{\square}$

---

17. Order from least to greatest.

1.11, 1.5, 1.09, 1.05

Five tenths is how many hundredths?

1.5 = 1.5___

_____ , _____ , _____ , _____

18. *Simplify.*

$(20k^3 \cdot 5v^5)9k^2$

$= (\underline{\quad}k^3 \cdot v^5)9k^2$

$= \underline{\quad\quad}k^{\square}v^{\square}$

Compare.

$900k^3v^5 \bigcirc \underline{\quad\quad}k^{\square}v^{\square}$

19. $A = s^2$

$1{,}690{,}000 = s^2$

$\sqrt{1{,}690{,}000} = \sqrt{s^2}$

$\underline{\quad\quad} = s$

20. $t = \dfrac{\sqrt{d}}{4}$

Substitute.

$t = \dfrac{\sqrt{\square}}{4}$

$t = \dfrac{\square}{4} = \underline{\quad\quad}$

21. $f = 120 \cdot \sqrt{p}$

Substitute.

$f = 120 \cdot \sqrt{\underline{\quad\quad}}$

$f = 120 \cdot \underline{\quad} = \underline{\quad\quad}$

22. *Use a unit ratio.*

1 ft = 12 in.

$210 \text{ in.} \cdot \dfrac{1 \text{ ft}}{12 \text{ in.}} = \underline{\quad} \text{ ft}$

Since the diameter can be expressed as a

ratio, it _____ a rational number.

23. *Area of a circle* $= \pi r^2$

$A = 3.14 \times (\underline{\quad})^2 = 3.14 \times \underline{\quad} = \underline{\quad}$

Area of a square $= s^2$

$A = (\underline{\quad})^2 = \underline{\quad}$

A of shaded part = A of circle − A of square

$A = \underline{\quad} - \underline{\quad} = \underline{\quad}$

24. Round deposit to the nearest dollar: $_____

Round withdrawal to the nearest dollar:

$_____

deposit − withdrawal = change in balance

$_____ − $_____ = $_____

25. Simplify.

$52 + (1 + 3)^2 \cdot (16 - 14)^3 - 20$

$= 52 + (\underline{\quad})^2 \cdot (\underline{\quad})^3 - 20$

_____

$= 52 + \underline{\quad} \cdot \underline{\quad} - 20$ _____

$= 52 + \underline{\quad} - 20$ _____

$= \underline{\quad} - 20$ _____

$= \underline{\quad}$ _____

26. Student ___ is correct. Student ___

incorrectly used the _____ Property

when adding _____ .

27. $30 + 7x - 12$

$30 + (-12) + 7x = $ _____

$[30 + (-12)] + 7x = $ _____

$18 + 7x = $ _____

28. *See page 3 in the* Student Reference Guide.

Simplify.

Circle the answer.

A $(-6)^2$ _____

B $(-6) \div (-6)$ _____

C $-\frac{3}{4}(6) \div (-4)$ _____

D $-1 \cdot (-6)^2$ _____

29. *Use a unit ratio.*

1 drachma $= \$0.004$

1,295,800 dollars $\cdot \dfrac{\square}{\square} = $ _____ drachmae

30. a. numbers on a standard number cube:

1, 2, 3, 4, 5, 6

So, 10 is _____ .

b. 900 numbers to guess from

So, _____ .

c. Heads and tails are _____ .

So, _____ .

LESSON
14

Determining the Theoretical Probability
of an Event page 74

New Concepts

- **Theoretical probability** is the ratio of favorable outcomes to all outcomes.

$$P = \frac{\text{favorable outcomes}}{\text{all outcomes}}$$

- In theoretical probability, all outcomes must be equally likely.

┌─ **Exploration** 📖 page 74
│ Use your textbook to complete this exploration.

Math Language

A **sample space** is the set of all possible outcomes of an event.

An event with only one outcome is a **simple event**.

The **complement** of an event is the set of all outcomes of an experiment that are not in a given event.

┌─ **Example** Identifying Sample Spaces

A number cube labeled 1–6 is rolled. List the outcomes of each event.

a number less than or equal to three

all outcomes	outcomes less than or equal to three
{1, 2, 3, 4, 5, 6}	**{1, 2, 3}**

- The sum of the probability of favorable outcomes of an event and the probability of "unfavorable" outcomes of an event equals one.

$$P(\text{outcome}) + P(\text{complement of an outcome}) = 1$$

┌─ **Example** Calculating Theoretical Probability

Sample space: 4 green marbles, 3 blue marbles, 3 red marbles

What is the probability of randomly choosing a red marble?	**What is the probability of randomly not choosing a green marble?**
$P(\text{red})$	$P(\underline{\text{not}}\ \text{green})$
favorable outcomes: 3 red marbles	green marble outcome: 4 marbles
total outcomes: 10 marbles	<u>not</u> green outcomes: 3 + 3 or 6 marbles
$P(\text{red}) = \dfrac{3\ \text{red}}{10\ \text{total}}$	$P(\underline{\text{not}}\ \text{green}) = \dfrac{\underline{\text{not}}\ \text{green}}{10\ \text{total}}$
$= \dfrac{1}{3}$	$= \dfrac{6}{10} = \dfrac{3}{5}$
$= 0.3$ or 30%	$= 0.6$ or 60%

A number cube labeled 1–6 is rolled. List the outcomes for each event.

sample space for a number cube: {1, 2, 3, 4, 5, 6}

a. a number ≤ 4 _____

b. an even number _____

c. a number > 2 _____

There are 4 green, 3 blue, and 3 red marbles in a jar.

d. Probability of randomly choosing a blue marble?

$$\frac{\text{number of blue}}{\text{total number in bag}} = \frac{\square}{\square} = \underline{\quad}$$

e. Probability of randomly not choosing a red marble?

$$\frac{\text{number of not red}}{\text{number in bag}} = \frac{\square}{10} = \underline{\quad}$$

$$1 - P(\text{red}) = \underline{\quad}$$

f. What is the probability of drawing a ball with a number less than 6?

sample space: {1, 2, 3, 5, 5, 6, 7, 7} number of outcomes: _____

numbers < 6: {1, 2, 3, 5, 5} number of outcomes < 6: _____

$$P(\text{number} < 6) = \frac{\text{number of outcomes} < 6}{\text{number of outcomes}} = \frac{\square}{\square}$$

Do you have a greater chance of drawing a 7 or a 6?

number of outcomes of 6: _____   number of outcomes of 7: _____

$$P(6) = \frac{\text{number of outcomes of 6}}{\text{number of outcomes}} = \frac{\square}{\square}$$

$$P(7) = \frac{\text{number of outcomes of 7}}{\text{number of outcomes}} = \frac{\square}{\square}$$

$$P(6) \bigcirc P(7)$$

g. total outcomes: 52   total favorable outcome, kings: 4

$$P(\text{king}) = \frac{\text{number of kings}}{\text{number of outcomes}} = \frac{\square}{\square} = \underline{\quad}$$

1. *The probability of any outcome stays the same for each roll.*

sample space for each roll: $\{1, 2, 3, 4, 5, 6\}$

$$P(\text{number} > 4) = \frac{\text{outcome} > 4}{\text{total outcomes}}$$

$$= \frac{\square}{6}$$

$$= \frac{\square}{\square}$$

2. *The probability of green is the same for each draw.*

sample space: 5 green and 9 purple marbles

$$P(\text{green}) = \frac{\text{outcome of green}}{\text{total outcomes}}$$

$$= \frac{\square}{14}$$

3. *Use a unit ratio.*

$$\square \text{ in.} \cdot \frac{\square}{\square}$$

$$= \underline{\qquad}$$

4. *Use a unit ratio.*

$$\frac{2.54 \text{ cm}}{1 \text{ in.}} \cdot \frac{\square \text{ in.}}{1 \text{ ft}} \cdot 25 \text{ ft}$$

$$= \underline{\qquad}$$

5. *Use the order of operations.*

$$3 - 2 \cdot 4 + 3 \cdot 2$$

$$= \underline{\qquad}$$

6. *Same signs: product is positive.*
Opposite signs: product is negative.

$$-3(-2)(-3) - 2$$

$$= (\underline{\qquad})(-3) - 2$$

$$= \underline{\qquad} - 2$$

$$= \underline{\qquad}$$

7. *Use the order of operations.*

$$5(9 + 2) - 4(5 + 1)$$

$$= \underline{\qquad}$$

8. *Use the order of operations.*

$$3(6 + 2) + 3(5 - 2)$$

$$= \underline{\qquad}$$

---

9. $\sqrt{31 + z}$ when $z = 5$

Substitute.

$\sqrt{31 + (\underline{})} = \sqrt{(\underline{})} = \underline{}$

10. *Find a common denominator.*

$\frac{4}{5} = \frac{24}{\square}$ ◯ $\frac{5}{6} = \frac{25}{\square}$

11.
$$A = x^2$$
$$49 = x^2$$
$$\underline{} = x$$

12. *See page 3 in the* Student Reference Guide.

Which equation demonstrates the Associative Property of Addition?
Circle the answer.

A $(a + b) + c = a + (b + c)$

B $ab + c = ba + c$

C $a(b + c) = ab + ac$

D $a + (b + c) = a + (c + b)$

---

13. *Same signs: product is positive.*
Opposite signs: product is negative.

Either x or y is \underline{} and the

other is \underline{}.

Either x or y is \underline{}.

Both x and y are \underline{} or

both x and y \underline{}.

14. *See page 3 in the* Student Reference Guide.

\underline{} Property of \underline{}

---

15. set of all outcomes: {\underline{}}

set of favorable outcomes: {\underline{}}

Circle the answer.

A $\frac{1}{2}$ \qquad **B** $\frac{1}{3}$

C $\frac{1}{4}$ \qquad **D** $\frac{2}{3}$

16. sample space: {A, B, B, I, I, L, O, P, R, T, Y}

number of Bs: \underline{}

$P(\text{letter B}) = \dfrac{\square}{\square} = \underline{}$

---

17. $P(\text{blue}) = \dfrac{\text{number of blue marbles}}{\text{total number of marbles}}$

$$= \dfrac{\square}{\square} = \underline{\quad}$$

Circle the answer.

A $\dfrac{1}{16}$ B $\dfrac{4}{15}$

C $\dfrac{1}{4}$ D $\dfrac{4}{32}$

18. Student ____ is correct. Student ____ did not

find one number which equals ____ when

_____ by itself.

---

19. $s = \sqrt{\dfrac{d}{0.04}}$

$d = 4^2$ feet

$s = \sqrt{\dfrac{\square}{0.04}} = \dfrac{\square}{\square} = \underline{\quad\quad}$

20. centripetal force $= \dfrac{mv^2}{r}$

$$F = \dfrac{(\square)(\square)^2}{\square} = \dfrac{(\square)(\square)}{\square}$$

$$= \underline{\quad\quad}$$

---

21. *Use a unit ratio.*

$\dfrac{\square}{\square} \cdot 2.35 \text{ lbs}$

$= \underline{\quad\quad}$

22. _____, since π is a(n) _____

number, the program will

_____.

---

23. *See page 1 in the* Student Reference Guide.

86 m below sea level is a _____

number.

24. $C = \dfrac{5}{9}(F - 32)$

   a. How many terms? _____

   b. Name the constant(s). _____

---

25. *Collect terms with the same signs.*

$-7 + 3 - 2 - 5 + (-6)$

$-$ _____ $-$ _____ $-$ _____ $-$ _____ $+$ _____

$=$ _____

26. Student ____ is correct. Student ____ did

not put _____ around _____.

Without parentheses, _____ is the first

operation.

27. *Use a positive number for those entering, and a negative number for those leaving.*

(_____) $+$ (_____) $=$ _____

28. $22 - (-11) - 11 - (-22)$

Simplify.

$= 22 \bigcirc 11 \ominus 11 \bigcirc 22$

$=$ _____

29. If the operations are not completed in the

_____ _____, the

answer will be _____.

30.

$A = s^2$

$144 = s^2$

$\sqrt{} = s$

_____ $= s$

$P = 4s$

$P = 4 \cdot$ _____

$P =$ _____

Name _____

Using the Distributive Property to Simplify Expressions page 80

New Concepts

- The Distributive Property can be used to simplify expressions.

$$5(2 + 1) = 5 \cdot 2 + 5 \cdot 1 = 15 \qquad 5(2 - 1) = 5 \cdot 2 - 5 \cdot 1 = 5$$

The Distributive Property	
$x(y + z)$	Example: $5(2 + 1) = 5 \cdot 2 + 5 \cdot 1 = 15$
$x(y - z)$	Example: $5(2 - 1) = 5 \cdot 2 + 5 \cdot -1 = 5$

Example Distributing a Positive Integer

Simplify.
$6(4 + 8)$

$6(4 + 8)$

$= 6(4) + 6(8)$ *Distribute the 6.*

$= 24 + 48$ *Multiply.*

$= 72$ *Add.*

$4(5 - 3)$

$4(5 - 3)$

$= 4(5) + 4(-3)$ *Distribute the 4.*

$= 20 - 12$ *Multiply.*

$= 8$ *Subtract.*

- Use the Multiplication Property of -1 to simplify an expression like $-(5 + 2)$. Rewrite as $-1(5 + 2)$ and then distribute the -1.

Example Distributing a Negative Integer

Simplify.

$-(9 + 4)$ $-9(-6 - 3)$

$-(9 + 4)$ $-9(-6 - 3)$

$= (-1)(9) + (-1)(4)$ *Distribute.* $= (-9)(-6) + (-9)(-3)$

$= -9 - 4$ *Multiply.* $= 54 + 27$

$= -13$ *Simplify.* $= 81$

• The Distributive Property applies not only to numeric expressions but also to algebraic expressions.

Example **Simplifying Algebraic Expressions**

Simplify.

$-4(x + 7)$ $(5 - x)6$

$-4(x + 7)$ $(5 - x)6$

$= (-4)(x) + (-4)(7)$ *Distribute.* $= 6(5) + 6(-x)$

$= -4x - 28$ *Multiply.* $= 30 - 6x$

Example **Simplifying Algebraic Expressions with Exponents**

Simplify.

$mn(mx + ny + 2p)$

$mn(mx + ny + 2p)$

$= m^2nx + mn^2y + 2mnp$

Lesson Practice 📖 page 82

Simplify.

a. $8(2 + 7) = 8(\underline{\quad}) + 8(\underline{\quad}) = \underline{\quad}$ **b.** $4(6 - 2) = (\underline{\quad})(6) + (\underline{\quad})(\underline{\quad}) = \underline{\quad}$

c. $-(9 + 3) = (-1)(\underline{\quad}) + (\underline{\quad})(3)$ **d.** $-14(4 - 2) = (-14)(\underline{\quad}) + (\underline{\quad})(-2)$

$= \underline{\quad}$ $= \underline{\quad}$

e. $-10(m + 4) = (-10)(\underline{\quad}) + (-10)(\underline{\quad})$ **f.** $(7 - y)8 = 8(\underline{\quad}) + 8(\underline{\quad})$

$= \underline{\quad\quad}$ $= \underline{\quad\quad}$

g. $4xy^3(x^4y - 5x)$ **h.** $-2x^2m^2(m^2 - 4m)$

$= (\underline{\quad\quad})x^4y + (\underline{\quad\quad})(\underline{\quad})$ $= (-2x^2m^2)(\underline{\quad}) + (\underline{\quad\quad})(-4m)$

$= \underline{\quad\quad} - \underline{\quad\quad}$ $= \underline{\quad\quad} + \underline{\quad\quad}$

i. adults: 4   children: 8   price per ticket: $15 for adults or children
total cost = $15 × (number of adults + number of children)

$= \$15 × (\underline{\quad\quad} + \underline{\quad\quad})$

$= \$\underline{\quad\quad}$

1. $-7(-8 + 3) = (\underline{})(-8) + (\underline{})(3)$

$= \underline{} - \underline{}$

$= \underline{}$

2. $5(-3 - 6) = 5(-3) + 5(\underline{})$

$= \underline{} - \underline{}$

$= \underline{}$

3. $10,000 = (\underline{} \cdot \underline{})$ *Same number times itself*

$\sqrt{10,000} = \underline{}$

4. $25 = \underline{} \cdot \underline{}$ *Same number times itself*

$c = \sqrt{25} = \underline{}$

5. Let $b =$ number of broken eggs

$\dfrac{2}{25} = \dfrac{b}{800}$

$2 \cdot \underline{} = \underline{} \cdot b$

$\underline{} = \underline{}$

$\underline{} = b$

6. outcomes: $\{0, 1, 2, 3, 4, 5, 6, 7, 8, 9\}$

odd outcomes: $\{1, \underline{}, \underline{}, 7, \underline{}\}$

odd and greater than 5: $\{\underline{}, \underline{}\}$

number of outcomes: $\underline{}$

number of odd and greater than 5: $\underline{}$

$\dfrac{\text{number of odd outcomes} > 5}{\text{number of outcomes}} = \dfrac{\square}{\square} = \underline{}$

7. outcomes: $\{1, 1, 2, 3, 4, 4, 4, 5, 6, 6\}$

numbers less than 7: $\{\underline{}\}$

$\dfrac{\text{number of outcomes} < 7}{\text{number of outcomes}} = \dfrac{\square}{\square} = \underline{}$

All outcomes < 7 so the outcome is

$\underline{}$ and has a probability of $\underline{}$.

8. Simplify the expression $-5(x + 6)$.
Use the Distributive Property.

Circle the answer.

A $-5 + x - 11$ **B** $-5x + 1$

C $-5x + 30$ **D** $-5x - 30$

9. $18 - x = y$ if $x = -4$

Substitute.

$18 - (\underline{\hspace{1cm}}) = y$

$\underline{\hspace{1cm}} = y$

10. *Use a number line.*

3 feet *below* normal: -3

5 feet *above* normal: $\underline{\hspace{1cm}}$

change: $\underline{\hspace{1cm}}$

11. Student $\underline{\hspace{0.7cm}}$ is correct. Student $\underline{\hspace{1.5cm}}$

$\underline{\hspace{4cm}}$ the numbers instead

of $\underline{\hspace{3.5cm}}$ them.

12. Multiply each number in parentheses

by $\underline{\hspace{0.7cm}}$. Add the $\underline{\hspace{2.5cm}}$.

$(-8)(\underline{\hspace{0.7cm}}) + (\underline{\hspace{0.7cm}})(-15) = \underline{\hspace{0.7cm}} + \underline{\hspace{0.7cm}}$

$= \underline{\hspace{0.7cm}}$

13. number of lots: $6(\underline{\hspace{0.7cm}} + 7)$

$= (6)(\underline{\hspace{0.7cm}}) + (\underline{\hspace{0.7cm}})(7)$

$= \underline{\hspace{0.7cm}} + \underline{\hspace{0.7cm}}$

$= \underline{\hspace{0.7cm}}$ lots

14. Circle the answer: true or false.

See page 3 in the Student Reference Guide.

Any number plus $\underline{\hspace{0.7cm}}$ is the number itself.

$\underline{\hspace{2.5cm}}$ Property of $\underline{\hspace{2.5cm}}$

15. *1 yard = 3 feet*

$3.4 \text{ yd}^3 \cdot \dfrac{(3 \text{ ft})^3}{(1 \text{ yd})^3}$

$= \underline{\hspace{1.5cm}}$

16. How many cards per child? $\dfrac{\Box}{\Box}$

value of each child's collection:

$\$14 \cdot \dfrac{\Box}{\Box} = \underline{\hspace{2cm}}$

17. number of boys: b; number of girls: $b + 7$

cost per girl: $\$6$

$\$\underline{\hspace{0.7cm}}$ per girl $\times$ number of girls

$(\$\underline{\hspace{0.7cm}})(\underline{\hspace{0.7cm}} + \underline{\hspace{0.7cm}}) = \underline{\hspace{0.7cm}} + \underline{\hspace{0.7cm}}$

18. number of outcomes: $\underline{\hspace{0.7cm}}$

number of 5 or 6 outcomes: $\underline{\hspace{0.7cm}}$

$P(5 \text{ or } 6) = \dfrac{\Box}{\Box} = \underline{\hspace{0.7cm}}$

19. Student ___ is correct. Student ___

incorrectly applied the _____

in the first step.

20. *See page 3 in the* Student Reference Guide.

_____ Property of _____

21. Method 1:   Justify.

$7x \cdot 8 = (x \cdot 7) \cdot 8$ _____

$\quad = x \cdot (7 \cdot 8)$ _____

$\quad = x \cdot 56$ _____

$\quad = 56x$ _____

Method 2:

$7x \cdot 8 = 8 \cdot 7x$ _____

$\quad = (8 \cdot 7)x$ _____

$\quad = 56x$ _____

22. Rickie's age = Raymond's age + $3\frac{3}{4}$ yr

Raymond's age = Ryan's age − $2\frac{1}{2}$ yr

Ryan's age = $14\frac{1}{4}$ yr

Raymond's age: Ryan's age − $2\frac{1}{2}$

$= \underline{\quad} - 2\frac{1}{2}$

$= \underline{\quad}$

Rickie's age: Raymond's age + $3\frac{3}{4}$

$= \underline{\quad} + 3\frac{3}{4}$

$= \underline{\quad}$

23. $16f^2g^3 - 4f^8 + 12$

Substitute 3 for f and 5 for g.

$16(\underline{\quad})^2(\underline{\quad})^3 - 4(\underline{\quad})^8 + 12$

Evaluate _____ left to right.

$16(\underline{\quad})(\underline{\quad}) - 4(\underline{\quad}) + 12$

_____ left to right.

$\underline{\quad} - \underline{\quad} + 12$

_____ and _____ left to right.

$(\underline{\quad}) - (\underline{\quad}) + 12 = \underline{\quad}$

24. Model $x - 8$ when $x = -6$.

$= \underline{\quad} - 8$

$= \underline{\quad}$

25. star Sirius magnitude: -1.5

moon's magnitude: -12.5

difference in magnitude:

____ $-$ ____ $=$ ____

difference in brightness: $2.512^{\square}$

26. Student ____ is correct. Student ____

combined the two ____ ____

before taking the ____

____.

27. $x - |x - 2| = y$ when $x = -3$

$y =$ ____

28. Is $3 + \frac{2}{3} + |-5|$ positive or negative?

____, because each term is

____. The ____ ____

of -5 is ____.

29.

a. $P(\text{red}) = \dfrac{\square}{\square} =$ ____ $=$ ____ %

b. $P(\text{green}) = \dfrac{\square}{\square} =$ ____ $=$ ____ %

c. $P(\underline{\text{not}} \text{ green}) = 1 - P(\text{green}) =$

$1 -$ ____ $=$ ____ $=$ ____ %

30. $A = x^2$

____ $= x^2$

$\sqrt{} = \sqrt{x^2}$

____ $= x$

$P = 4x$

$P = 4(\underline{})$

$=$ ____

LESSON
16

Simplifying and Evaluating Variable Expressions page 86

New Concepts

- To evaluate an expression that contains variables:
  1. Substitute the given numeric value for each variable.
  2. Find the value of the expression.

- Use parentheses when substituting a number for a variable, so that the negative signs and the subtraction signs are not confused.

> **Math Language**
>
> To **evaluate** means to substitute, then simplify.

Example Evaluating Expressions with Variables

Evaluate $(-x + a) - (x - a)$ for $a = -2$ and $x = 7$.

$$(-x + \quad a) - (x - \quad a)$$
$$\downarrow \quad \downarrow \quad \downarrow \quad \downarrow$$

$\quad = [-7 + (-2)] - [7 - (-2)]$ *Substitute.*

$\quad = (-9) - [7 - (-2)]$ *Add inside the 1ˢᵗ set of brackets.*

$\quad = (-9) - (7 + 2)$ *Take the opposite of −2.*

$\quad = (-9) - (9)$ *Add inside the 2ⁿᵈ set of parentheses.*

$\quad = -18$ *Subtract.*

Example Evaluating Expressions with Exponents

If $a = 3$ and $b = -1$, what is the value of $2\left(\dfrac{a}{5 - b}\right)^2$?

$2\left(\dfrac{a}{5 - b}\right)^2$

$= 2\left(\dfrac{3}{(5 - (-1))}\right)^2$ *Substitute.*

$= 2\left(\dfrac{3}{(5 + 1)}\right)^2$ *Take the opposite of −1.*

$= 2\left(\dfrac{3}{6}\right)^2$ *Perform operations inside the parentheses.*

$= 2\left(\dfrac{1}{2}\right)^2$ *Write the fraction in simplest form.*

$= 2\left(\dfrac{1}{4}\right)$ *Evaluate the exponent.*

$= \dfrac{1}{2}$ *Multiply.*

Evaluate each expression for the given values of the variables.

a. $ax[-a(a - x)]$ for $a = 2$ and $x = -1$

$2 = (-1)[-2(2 - (-1))]$

$2 = (-1)[-2(\underline{\quad})]$

$2 = (-1)[\underline{\quad}] = 2(\underline{\quad}) = \underline{\quad}$

b. $-b[-b(b - c) - (c - b)]$ for $b = -2$ and $c = 0$

$= -(\underline{\quad})[-(\underline{\quad})((\underline{\quad}) - \underline{\quad}) - (0 - (\underline{\quad}$

$= 2[2(\underline{\quad}) - \underline{\quad}]$

$= 2[\underline{\quad} - \underline{\quad}] = 2(\underline{\quad}) = \underline{\quad}$

c. $(5y)(2z)4xy$ for $x = 3$, $y = -1$, and $z = \frac{1}{2}$

$= (5(\underline{\quad}))(2 \cdot \underline{\quad})4(\underline{\quad})(\underline{\quad})$

$= (\underline{\quad})(\underline{\quad})4(\underline{\quad}) = \underline{\quad}$

d. $\frac{4rs}{6st}$ for $r = -1$, $s = -3$, and $t = -2$

$= \frac{4(\boxed{} \cdot \boxed{})}{6(\boxed{} \cdot \boxed{})}$

$= \frac{4(\boxed{})}{6(\boxed{})} = \frac{\boxed{}}{\boxed{}} = \underline{\quad}$

Simplify each expression. Then evaluate for $a = 2$ and $b = -1$. Justify each step.

e. $-b(a - 3) + a$

$= -ba \bigcirc 3b + a$ *Distribute.*

$= -(\underline{\quad})(\underline{\quad}) + 3(\underline{\quad}) + (\underline{\quad})$ *Substitute.*

$= \underline{\quad}$ *Simplify.*

f. $-a(-b - a) - b$

$= \underline{\quad} \bigcirc \underline{\quad}^2 - b$ _____

$= (\underline{\quad})(\underline{\quad}) \bigcirc (\underline{\quad})^2 - (\underline{\quad})$ _____

$= \underline{\quad} + \underline{\quad}^2 \bigcirc \underline{\quad}$ _____

$= \underline{\quad}$ *Simplify.*

Evaluate each expression for the given values of the variable.

g. $\frac{-b(a - 4) + b}{b}$ for $a = -2$ and $b = 25$

$= \frac{-\boxed{}(\boxed{} - 4) + \boxed{}}{25}$ *Substitute.*

$= \frac{\boxed{}(\boxed{}) + \boxed{}}{25}$ *Subtract.*

$= \frac{\boxed{} + \boxed{}}{25} = \underline{\quad}$ *Simplify.*

h. $\frac{x^2 - x|y|}{x^3}$ for $x = -4$ and $y = -2$

$= \frac{\boxed{}^2 - (-4)|\boxed{}|}{\boxed{}^3}$

$= \frac{\boxed{} \bigcirc 4(\boxed{})}{\boxed{}}$

$= \frac{\boxed{} \bigcirc \boxed{}}{\boxed{}} = \frac{\boxed{}}{\boxed{}} = \frac{\boxed{}}{\boxed{}}$

i. $P_y = 1.04(P_{y-1})$ so $P_8 = 1.04(P_7)$ *Use P_6 to find P_7 and then P_7 to find P_8.*

$P_7 = 1.04(1600)$ *Substitute value of P_6 for P_{7-1}.* $P_8 = 1.04(\underline{\quad})$ *Substitute P_7 for P_{8-1}.*

$P_7 = \underline{\quad}$ *Multiply.* $P_8 = \underline{\quad}$ *Multiply.*

1. Simplify.

$2 + 5 - 3 + 7 - (-3) + 5$

$=$ _____

2. Simplify.

$3(7) + 5 - 3 + 7 - 9 \div 2$

$=$ _____

3. Use braces to represent a set.

$K =$ _____

4. Counterexample?

_____ because the product of any

two _____ is _____

within the set of _____ _____ .

5. Counterexample?

_____ because _____ is an integer, but

it is ____ a _____ number.

6. See page 3 in the Student Reference Guide.

$-4y(d + cx)$

$= -4$_____ ◯ _____

7. $(a + bc)2x$

$= (a)(\_\_\_) + (\_\_\_)(\_\_\_)$

$= \_\_\_\_\_ + \_\_\_\_\_$

8. Substitute.

$pa[-a(-a)]$ when $p = 2$ and $a = -1$

$= (2)(-1)[-(\_\_)(-(\_\_))]$

$= (2)(-1)[\_\_\_ \cdot \_\_\_]$

$= (\_\_\_)(\_\_\_)$

$= \_\_\_$

9. $x(x - y)$ when $x = \frac{1}{5}$ and $y = \frac{6}{5}$

$= \frac{1}{5}(\underline{} - \underline{})$

$= \frac{1}{5}(\underline{})$

$= \underline{}$

10. $\left[\frac{(x - 3)}{y}\right]^2$ when $x = -5$ and $y = 2$

$= \left[\frac{(\boxed{} - 3)}{\boxed{}}\right]^2$

$= \left[\frac{\boxed{}}{\boxed{}}\right]^2 = \underline{}$

11. $4(b + 1)^2 - 6(c - b)^4$ when $b = 2$ and $c = 7$

$= 4(\underline{} + 1)^2 - 6(\underline{} - \underline{})^4$

$= 4(\underline{})^2 - 6(\underline{})^4$

$= 4(\underline{}) - 6(\underline{})$

$= \underline{} - \underline{}$

$= \underline{}$

12. $P = 4(\underline{})$

$P = \underline{}$

Because a square has _____ equal sides,

multiplying _____ by _____ can be used

to find the _____.

13. $2 + (1 + 7) = (2 + 1) + 7$

_____ Property of _____

14. *Substitute and solve.*

$v = 195 - 0.5(\underline{})$

$v = 195 - (\underline{})$

$v = \underline{}$

Answer: _____

15. ✎ *Substitute and solve.*

a. $V_{\text{cone}} = \frac{1}{3}\pi \underline{}^2 \underline{} = \underline{}$

b. $V_{\text{cylinder}} = \pi \underline{}^2 \underline{} = \underline{}$

c. $V_{\text{cone}} - V_{\text{cylinder}} = \underline{} - \underline{}$

$= \underline{}$

16. $P_i = \underline{}$ atmosphere; $V_i = \underline{}$ L;

$V_f = \underline{}$ L

Substitute and solve for P_f.

$P_f = \dfrac{(\boxed{})(\boxed{})}{\boxed{}}$

$P_f = \dfrac{(\boxed{})}{\boxed{}}$

$P_f = \underline{}$

17. $V_f = \$$ _____ $i =$ _____ % $t =$ _____ yr

Substitute and solve for V_p.

$$V_p = \frac{V_f}{(1 + i)^t}$$

$$V_p = \frac{\square}{(\square)^{\square}}$$

$$= \underline{\quad\quad}$$

18. Circle the answer.

A $y = x^3 + 5$

B $y = \frac{x^2 + 5}{x}$

C $y = |x^3 + 5|$

D $y = \frac{x^3 + 5}{x}$

19. *Substitute and solve.*

a. $A = 50(\underline{\quad})^2 = \underline{\quad\quad}$

b. $A = \underline{\quad}(\underline{\quad})^2 = \underline{\quad\quad}$

c. $A = \underline{\quad}(\underline{\quad})^2 = \underline{\quad\quad}$

20. a. total miles = _____ $\cdot b +$ _____ $\cdot r$

b. total money = _____ (_____ $b +$ _____ r)

= _____ $b +$ _____ r

21. *Circle the numbers* ≥ 5.

1, 1, 2, 3, 4, 4, 4, 5, 6, 6

Student ____ is correct. Student ____ used

only the numbers _____ ____ 5.

22. *Estimate roots of nonperfect squares.*

Compare the sums.

$$\sqrt{36} + \sqrt{40} \;\bigcirc\; \sqrt{25} + \sqrt{80}$$

_____ + _____ $\bigcirc$ _____ + _____

_____ $\bigcirc$ _____

23. title: $A = (18 \text{ in.})^2 =$ _____ in^2

Convert square inches to square feet.

$$\underline{\quad} \text{ in}^2 \cdot \frac{(1 \text{ ft})^2}{(12 \text{ in.})^2} = \underline{\quad} \text{ft}^2$$

$$81 \text{ ft}^2 \div \underline{\quad} = \underline{\quad}$$

24. *Depth is expressed as a negative number.*

2.6 (_____) ≈ _____ ft

25. The sign of the sum is _____

because the number with the _____

absolute value is _____ .

26. Europe uses the _____ system.

The U.S. uses the _____ system.

27. Justify each step.

$10(8 - 6)^3 + 4\big(\,|-5 + (-2)| + 2\big)$

$= 10(8 - 6)^3 + 4(\underline{\quad} + 2)$ _____

$= 10(\underline{\quad})^3 + 4(\underline{\quad})$ _____

$= 10(\underline{\quad}) + 4(\underline{\quad})$ _____

$= \underline{\quad} + \underline{\quad} = \underline{\quad}$ _____

28. Student ____ is correct. Student ____ added the _____ _____

instead of _____ to find the change.

29. volume of playhouse = volume of cube + volume of prism

volume of playhouse $= (10 \cdot 5.8 \cdot 8) + \left[\frac{1}{2}(10 \cdot 5.8)\right] \cdot 4$

$= \underline{\qquad\qquad} + \underline{\qquad\qquad}$

$= \underline{\qquad\quad}$

30. **a.** $\dfrac{\textit{defective balls}}{\textit{total balls}} = \dfrac{\square}{\square} = \dfrac{\square}{\square}$

b. $\dfrac{\square}{\square} \cdot \underline{\qquad}$ balls $= \underline{\qquad}$ balls

LESSON
17

Translating Between Words and Algebraic Expressions page 93

New Concepts

Translating Words and Phrases into Algebraic Expressions		
Words	**Phrases**	**Expressions**
Addition sum, total, more than, added, increased, plus	4 added to a number 7 increased by a number	$x + 4$ $7 + x$
Subtraction less, minus, decreased by, difference, less than	difference of 5 and a number 8 less than a number	$5 - x$ $x - 8$
Multiplication product, times, multiplied	product of a number and 12 a number times 3	$12(x)$ $3x$
Division quotient, divided by, divided into	quotient of a number and 6 10 divided by a number	$x \div 6$ $\frac{10}{x}$

Math Language

Numeric expressions contain only numbers and operations.

Algebraic expressions contain at least one variable.

Math Language

"Less than" phrases are written in the reverse order of the given form:

"two less than x" translates as $x - 2$.

Example Translating Words into Algebraic Expressions

Write an algebraic expression for the phrase "8 less than the quotient of m and 15."

"8 less than" means 8 is subtracted from another quantity.

"The quotient of m and 15" means m, which is mentioned first, is divided by 15.

$\frac{m}{15} - 8$

Example Translating Algebraic Expressions into Words

Use words to write this algebraic expression two different ways.
$5 \cdot n$

For multiplication, use the word "times" or the phrase "multiplied by."

5 times n   or   **5 multiplied by n**

Any operation can be described by its result. For multiplication, the result is the "product."

the product of 5 and n

Write each phrase as an algebraic expression.

a. the product of x and 8

A *product* is the result of _____.

____ ◯ ____ = ____

b. 18 minus y

____ ◯ ____

c. 7 more than 5 times x

More indicates the operation _____.

Times indicates the operation _____.

____ ◯ ____

d. Raquel is 2 years older than Monica, who is x years old. Write an expression for Raquel's age.

Older means _____ old than and should be shown by a _____ sign.

____ ◯ ____

Use words to write each algebraic expression in two different ways.

e. $\frac{10}{s}$

10 _____ by s

the _____ of 10 and s

f. $5 - r$

r _____ _____ 5

the difference of ____ and ____

g. $3m + 7$

7 ____ than ____ times ____

the ____ of 3 ____ m and ____

h. $\frac{3}{4}x + 9$

three-fourths ____ plus ____

the ____ of ____ - ____ of ____ and ____

i. $\frac{x - 3}{2}$

the _____ of ____ less ____

and ____

the _____ of ____ and ____

divided by ____

j. Jon has d dollars in a savings account and withdraws x dollars every week. Write an algebraic expression to represent the money he has left after 15 weeks.

The term *withdrawal* indicates the operation _____.

Total amount withdrawn:

____ – ____x

1. Distribute.

$(4 + 2y)x$

$= (\underline{\quad})(\underline{\quad}) + (\underline{\quad})(\underline{\quad})$

$= \underline{\quad} \bigcirc \underline{\quad}$

2. Distribute.

$-2(x - 4y)$

$= (\underline{\quad})(\underline{\quad}) + (\underline{\quad})(\underline{\quad})$

$= \underline{\quad} \bigcirc \underline{\quad}$

3. A term is a part of an _____

that is _____ to or _____

from the other parts.

4. *See page 1 in the* Student Reference Guide.

True or false?

a. $A \cap C = \{-3, -2, -1\}$ _____

b. $A \cap B = \{-3, -2, -1, 1, 2, 3\}$ _____

c. $B \cup C = \{-3, -2, -1, 1, 2, 3\}$ _____

d. $A \cup B = \{-3, -2, -1\}$ _____

5. *Times* means the operation is _____.

A *sum* is the result of _____.

The unspecific phrase *a number* means a

_____ appears.

To show the *opposite,* use a _____ sign.

$\underline{\quad} (\underline{\qquad} + \underline{\qquad})$

6. The word *of* means the operation is

_____.

The word *is* means _____.

$\underline{\quad} (\underline{\quad}) = \underline{\quad}$

7. Add.

$4.7 + (-9.2) - 1.9$

$= \underline{\qquad}$

8. Compare.

$\sqrt{36} + \sqrt{121} \quad \bigcirc \quad \sqrt{100} + \sqrt{49}$

$\underline{\quad} + \underline{\quad} \bigcirc \underline{\quad} + \underline{\quad}$

$\underline{\quad} \bigcirc \underline{\quad}$

9. Label $\sqrt{15}$ on the number line.

between _____ and _____

10. *Substitute.*

_____, the _____ Property of

_____ states that $k \cdot$ _____ $= k$.

11. $(a + 4)^3 + 5x^2$ when $a = -3$, and $x = -1$

$(\underline{\quad} + 4)^3 + 5(\underline{\quad})^2$

$= (\underline{\quad})^3 + 5(\underline{\quad})$

$= \underline{\quad} + \underline{\quad}$

$= \underline{\quad}$

12. *Substitute.*

$yx^2m^3 = -4$, when $x = -1$, $y = 2$, and $m = -2$

Circle the answer: true or false.

$(\underline{\quad})(\underline{\quad})^2(\underline{\quad})^3 = -4$

$(\underline{\quad})(\underline{\quad})(\underline{\quad}) = -4$

_____ ◯ -4

13. The word _____ indicates

multiplication.

The word _____ indicates the result

of addition.

Three _____ the _____ of

a _____ and _____.

14. The word *times* indicates _____.

A *sum* is the result of _____.

Circle the answer.

A $4 + 9g$ **B** $4(9 + g)$

C $4 \cdot 9g$ **D** $(4 + 9)g$

15. *Younger* means _____ old than and

should be shown by a _____ sign.

Because Paul's age is not specified,

represent it as a _____.

_____p ◯ _____

16. The unknown amount of money Miles

started with can be shown as a _____.

Since Miles spent $7, _____ $7 from

the amount of money he started with.

Doubled means _____ by _____.

___(___ ◯ ___)

17. a. _____ = number of apples; _____ = number of bananas

    b. The word *total* indicates a _____.   _____ ◯ _____

    c. _____ the number of each fruit by its _____.

      (____)(____) ◯ (____)(____)

---

18. Student _____ is correct. Student _____ should have found that (___)^2 = ___.

19. $A_{rectangle} = l \cdot w$

$$A_{rectangle} = \underline{\quad} \cdot \underline{\quad}$$

$$A = \underline{\quad\quad}$$

$A_{circle} = \pi r^2$

$$A_{circle} = \underline{\quad} (\underline{\quad})^2$$

$$A = \underline{\quad\quad}$$

$$A_{\frac{1}{2}\,circle} = \underline{\quad\quad}$$

$$A_{rectangle} + A_{\frac{1}{2}\,circle} = \text{Total Area}$$

$$\underline{\quad\quad} = \text{Total Area}$$

20.

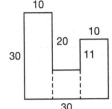

$A_{left} = \underline{\quad} \cdot \underline{\quad} = \underline{\quad}\ ft^2$

$A_{center} = (30 - \underline{\quad} - \underline{\quad}) \cdot (30 - \underline{\quad}) = \underline{\quad}\ ft^2$

$A_{right} = \underline{\quad}\, (\underline{\quad} + \underline{\quad}) = \underline{\quad}\ ft^2$

$A_{total} = \underline{\quad} + \underline{\quad} + \underline{\quad} = \underline{\quad}\ ft^2$

1 gallon covers 305 square feet. How many gallons are needed? _____

---

21. Student _____ is correct. Student _____

___ the _____ of the like _____

instead of _____.

22. $P(\text{tenth grader}) = \dfrac{\square}{\square}$

_____ ÷ _____ = _____

Shift ⟶

_____ = _____ %

---

23. Student _____ is correct. Student _____

did not move the _____ sign with the

_____ when the _____

Property was used.

24. *Multiply by the reciprocal.*

$$-\frac{2}{3} \div \left(-\frac{8}{9}\right)$$

= _____

25. _____, the variables _____ and _____

_____ have _____ different values, so the

expression _____ _____ have to represent

just one value.

26. *Use a unit ratio.*

1 kg = 2.2 lbs

$$\frac{85 \text{ lbs}}{1} \cdot \frac{\Box}{\Box} = \text{\_\_\_\_\_ kg}$$

27. $P = ad^2v^3\frac{\pi}{4}e$

Isolate.

_____ the fraction.

Raise base numbers to their _____

and _____.

28. A deposit is recorded as a _____

amount, and a withdrawal as a _____

amount.

(_____) + (_____) = $_____

29. *See page 2 in the* Student Reference Guide.

_____ _____ from _____.

30. 40(___ + ___)

= _____

New Concepts

- Two or more terms that have the same variable or variables raised to the same power are called **like terms.**

Math Language

Like terms are terms that have the same variables raised to the same power: $4a^2b$ and $-6a^2b$ are like terms.

- Like terms can be combined.

$$\overset{\frown}{3x^3} + 4z^3 + 2x - \overset{\frown}{5x^3}$$

Underline, circle, or box like terms to make it easier to combine them.

- $3x^3$ and $-5x^3$ have the same variable *and* power. They are like terms.
- $4z^3$ does not have the same variable as any other term. $2x$ does not have the same power as any other terms. They are **unlike terms.**

Example Combining Like Terms Without Exponents

Simplify $6xy - 3a + 4yx$.

$\overset{\frown}{6xy} - 3a + \overset{\frown}{4yx}$	Identify any like terms. The order of the variables is not important.
$= (6xy + 4yx) - 3a$	Group the like terms together.
$= (6xy + 4xy) - 3a$	Rearrange the factors, if necessary.
$= 10xy - 3a$	Add the like terms.

Example Combining Like Terms With Exponents

Simplify $3k^2 - 2k^2 + 4k^2 + 2kx^4 + kx^4$.

$\overset{\frown}{3k^2} - \overset{\frown}{2k^2} + \overset{\frown}{4k^2} + \boxed{2kx^4} + \boxed{kx^4}$	Identify like terms.
$= (3k^2 + 4k^2 - 2k^2) + (kx^4 + 2kx^4)$	Group the like terms together.
$= 5k^2 + 3kx^4$	Add the like terms.

- Some expressions cannot be simplified.

$$3xy + 2x^2y - 6ab + 4ab^5 + 9ax$$

This expression has no like terms. It is already in simplified form.

Simplify each expression.

a. $-2xy - 3x + 4 - 4xy - 2x$

$(-2xy - \underline{\quad}) + (- 3x - \underline{\quad}) + \underline{\quad}$

$= \underline{\quad}xy \bigcirc \underline{\quad}x + 4$

b. $7m - (-8m) + 9m$

$7m \bigcirc 8m + 9m = \underline{\quad} m$

c. $3yac - 2ac + 6acy$

Rearrange factors.

$(3\underline{\quad} \bigcirc \underline{\quad}) \bigcirc \underline{\quad}$

$= \underline{\quad} - \underline{\quad}$

d. $x^4y + 3x^4y + 2x^4y$

The coefficient of x^4y is $\underline{\quad}$.

$= \underline{\quad}x^4y + \underline{\quad} + \underline{\quad} = \underline{\quad}$

e. $x^2y - 3yx + 2yx^2 - 2xy + yx$

Rearrange factors.

$(x^2y \bigcirc \underline{\quad}) + (\underline{\quad} \bigcirc \underline{\quad} + xy)$

$= \underline{\quad}x^2y \bigcirc \underline{\quad}xy$

f. $m^3n + m^3n - x^2y^7 + x^2y^7$

$(\underline{\quad} \bigcirc \underline{\quad}) + (\underline{\quad} \bigcirc \underline{\quad})$

$= \underline{\quad}$

g. A triangular-shaped display case has the dimensions shown in the diagram. Write a simplified algebraic expression for the perimeter of the case. Then evaluate the expression for $x = 2$ feet.

$P = \text{side a} + \text{side b} + \text{side c}$

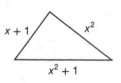

$P = x^2 + 1 + (\underline{\qquad}) + (\underline{\qquad})$

$P = (x^2 + \underline{\quad}) + (\underline{\quad}) + (\underline{\quad} + \underline{\quad})$ *Group like terms.*

$P = \underline{\quad}x^2 \bigcirc \underline{\quad} \bigcirc \underline{\quad}$ *Add like terms.*

$P = 2(\underline{\quad})^2 + (\underline{\quad}) + 2$ *Substitute 2 for x.*

$P = 2(\underline{\quad}) + \underline{\quad} + 2$ *Evaluate the exponent.*

$P = \underline{\quad} + \underline{\quad} + 2 = \underline{\quad}$ ft   *Multiply and add.*

1. *A sum* is the result of _____ .

The phrase *5 times a number* can be

written as _____ .

_____ ◯ (_____)

2. $m + 4 + 3m - 6 - 2m + mc - 4mc$

Rearrange factors.

$(m + \underline{\ } - \underline{\ }) + (\underline{\ } - \underline{\ }) + (cm - \underline{\ })$

$= \underline{\ \ \ } \bigcirc \underline{\ \ \ } \bigcirc \underline{\ \ \ }$

3. $xy - 3xy^2 + 5y^2x - 4xy$

Rearrange factors.

$= (-3xy^2 + \underline{\quad}) + (xy \underline{\quad})$

$= \underline{\quad} \bigcirc \underline{\quad}$

4. Simplify.

$$2x^2 + 3x$$

Like terms have the same variables and powers.

Circle the answer.

A $5x^2$ **B** $5x^3$

C $6x^3$ **D** cannot be
         simplified

5. a. Pages Read Per Night Per Class

  class 1: _____x + _____y

  class 2: _____x + _____y

b. Total Pages Read Per Night

   class 1   +   class 2

  (_____) + (_____)

$= \underline{\quad} x + \underline{\quad} y$

6. John's conclusion: Any addition problem involving a negative number must have a negative answer.

Counterexample:

_____ + _____ = + _____

Is John correct? _____ Explain.

Many addition problems with _____

numbers have _____ answers.

7. original = final − (time)(change)

original = −40 − (_____)(_____)

original = −40 ◯ _____ = _____ in.

8. *1 in. = 2.54 cm*

Use a unit ratio 3 times for volume.

$48 \text{ in}^2 \cdot \dfrac{\square}{\square} \cdot \dfrac{\square}{\square} \cdot \dfrac{\square}{\square} = \underline{\quad} \text{ cm}^3$

Round to nearest cm³.

$5274 \text{ cm}^3 - \underline{\qquad} \text{ cm}^3 = \underline{\qquad} \text{ cm}^3$

9. $\dfrac{-16 + 4}{2\left(\sqrt{13 - 4}\right)}$

$= \dfrac{\boxed{}}{2\left(\sqrt{\boxed{}}\right)}$

$= \dfrac{\boxed{}}{2\left(\boxed{}\right)}$

$= \dfrac{\boxed{}}{\boxed{}} = \underline{}$

10. $-7 - (2^4 \div 8)$

$= -7 - (\underline{} \div 8)$

$= -7 - (\underline{})$

$= -7 \;\bigcirc\; \underline{} = \underline{}$

11. Combine like terms and rearrange factors.

$6bac - 7ac + 8acb$

$= (\underline{} + \underline{}) - \underline{}$

$= \underline{} - \underline{}$

12. Combine like terms.

$2x^3y + 4x^3y + 9x^3y = \underline{}$

13. $\left|-15 + \sqrt{81}\right|^2$

$= \left|-15 + \underline{}\right|^2$

$= \left|\underline{}\right|^2$

$= \underline{}^2 = \underline{}$

14. $\dfrac{\sqrt{6 - 2}}{2 \cdot |-7 + 3|}$

$= \dfrac{\sqrt{\boxed{}}}{2 \cdot \left|\boxed{}\right|}$

$= \dfrac{\boxed{}}{2 \cdot \boxed{}}$

$= \dfrac{\boxed{}}{\boxed{}} = \underline{}$

15. Analise started with 0 bows.

Susan's bows per minute = $\underline{}x$

Analise's bows per minute: $(\underline{})\underline{}x$

a. Susan's bows after x min.: $\underline{}x + \underline{}$

Analise's bows after x min.: $\underline{}x$

b. Total after 11 min.

$= \underline{}x + \underline{} + \underline{}x$

$= \underline{}x + \underline{}$

16. a. Jean's age $= j$

Hank's age $= \underline{}j$

Marshall's age $= \underline{}j + \underline{}$

b. Substitute 12 for j.

Hank $= \underline{}$

Jean $= \underline{}$

c. Substitute 14 for Hank's age and solve for j.

Jean $= \underline{}$

17. $8x + x(2x + 5)$

$8x + x(\underline{\quad}) + x(\underline{\quad})$ $\underline{\qquad}$
Property

$8x + \underline{\quad\quad} + \underline{\quad\quad}$ *Simplify.*

$\underline{\quad\quad} + 8x + \underline{\quad\quad}$ $\underline{\qquad}$
Property
of $\underline{\qquad}$

$\underline{\quad\quad} + \underline{\quad\quad}$ $\underline{\qquad\qquad}$.

18. Evaluate $\dfrac{8ak}{4k(2a - 2c + 8)}$ when $a = \frac{1}{2}$, $c = 3$, and $k = -2$.

$$\frac{8\square\square}{4\square\left(2\square - 2\square + 8\right)}$$

$$\frac{\square}{\square\left(\square - \square + 8\right)}$$

$$\frac{\square}{\square\left(\square\right)}$$

$$\frac{\square}{\square} = \frac{\square}{\square}$$

19. $pm^2 - z^3 = 27$; $p = -5$, $m = 0$, $z = -3$

$(\underline{\quad})(\underline{\quad})^2 - (\underline{\quad})^3 \overset{?}{=} 27$

$(\underline{\quad})\underline{\quad} - (\underline{\quad}) \overset{?}{=} 27$

$\underline{\quad} \bigcirc \underline{\quad} \overset{?}{=} 27$

$\underline{\quad} \bigcirc \underline{\quad}$

The statement is $\underline{\qquad}$.

20. $x^2 y - |4x|^2 z$ when $x = -2$, $y = \frac{1}{2}$, $z = -1$

$(\underline{\quad})^2(\underline{\quad}) - |4(\underline{\quad})|^2(\underline{\quad})$

Student $\underline{\quad}$ is correct. Student $\underline{\quad}$

substituted the $\underline{\qquad}$ values for

$\underline{\quad}$ and $\underline{\quad}$.

21. Finding a common denominator shows

that the first fraction is $\underline{\qquad\qquad}$

than the second fraction.

A greater $\underline{\qquad\qquad}$ number minus a

lesser $\underline{\qquad\qquad}$ number results in

a $\underline{\qquad\qquad}$ number.

22. a. Tamatha $= x$ minutes

grandmother $= \underline{\qquad}$ minutes

b. Tamatha $= \underline{\quad} x$ peaches

grandmother $= \underline{\quad} (\underline{\quad})$ peaches

together $= \underline{\quad} x + \underline{\quad}(\underline{\quad})$

$= \underline{\quad} + \underline{\quad} \bigcirc \underline{\quad}$

$= \underline{\quad} \bigcirc \underline{\quad}$

23. *sum of the squares of the legs:*

___ ◯ ___

square of the hypotenuse: _____

___ ◯ ___ = ___

24. a. $P =$ ___ ◯ ___

b. doubled width = ___ w

tripled length = ___ l

= ___ + ___

25. *Use the Distributive Property.*

Simplify $7(10 - y)$.

Circle the answer.

A $70 - y$ **B** $70 - 7y$

C $70 - 7 + y$ **D** $70\,y - 7y$

26. $-m(mn^2 - m^2n)$

$(-m)(\underline{\quad}) + (\underline{\quad})(\underline{\quad})$

___ + ___

Using the _____ Property,

each term is _____

by _____.

27. Of the _____ numbers from 1 to 5, _____ are odd.

$P(\text{odd}) = \dfrac{\square}{\square}$

28. $A = s^2$

$A = 140 + 4 =$ _____

$s^2 =$ _____

$s =$ _____

29. *Counterexample?*

$24 \div$ _____ $= 6$

___ $\div 24 =$ ___

6 ◯ ___

30. Student _____ is correct. Student _____

squared the _____ of the terms, but should

have _____ each term.

LESSON 19

Solving One-Step Equations by Adding or Subtracting page 103

New Concepts

Math Language

A **solution of an equation with one variable** is a value of the variable that makes the equation true.

- To decide if a number is a **solution of an equation,** substitute it for the variable.

Example **Identifying Solutions**

State whether the value is a solution of the equation.

$$x + 6 = 9$$
$$(3) + 6 \stackrel{?}{=} 9 \qquad \text{Substitute}$$
$$9 = 9$$
$$x = 3 \text{ is a solution.}$$

$$x - 6 = 9$$
$$(3) - 6 \stackrel{?}{=} 9$$
$$-3 \neq 9$$
$$x = 3 \text{ is not a solution.}$$

Exploration 📖 page 104

Use your textbook to complete the exploration.

- **Addition Property of Equality:** If you add the same number to both sides of an equation, the equation stays balanced.

Example **Solving Equations by Adding**

Solve $x - 3 = 12$.

$$\begin{array}{rcl} x - 3 &=& 12 \\ +3 &=& +\ 3 \end{array} \quad \text{Add 3 to both sides.}$$
$$x \quad = \quad 15$$

Check.

$$15 - 3 = 12 \qquad \text{Substitute.}$$
$$12 = 12 \qquad \text{It checks.}$$

Math Language

Addition and subtraction are **inverse operations.** Addition and subtraction "undo" each other.

- **Subtraction Property of Equality:** If you subtract the same number from both sides of an equation, the equation stays balanced.

Example **Solving Equations by Subtracting**

Solve $k + 7 = 13$.

$$\begin{array}{rcl} k + 7 &=& 13 \\ -7 &=& -\ 7 \end{array} \quad \text{Subtract 7 from both sides.}$$
$$k \quad = \quad 6$$

State whether the value of each variable is a solution of the equation.

a. $h - 14 = 2$ for $h = 12$

_____ $- 14 \overset{?}{=} 2$

$h = 12$ _____ a solution because $12 - 14 = -2$.

b. $-11 = j - 4$ for $j = -7$

$-11 \overset{?}{=}$ _____ $- 4$

-7 _____ a solution because $-11 = -7 - 4$.

Solve. Then check.

c. $x - 5 = 17$ 　　　　　　　　　*Substitute to check.*

$x - 5 + 5 = 17 +$ _____ 　　　_____ $- 5 = 17$

$x =$ _____ 　　　　　　　_____ $= 17$

d. $-30 = m - 12$ 　　　　　*Substitute to check.*

$-30 +$ _____ $= m - 12 +$ _____ 　$-30 =$ _____ $- 12$

_____ $= m$ 　　　　　　$-30 =$ _____

Solve.

e. $p + 3 = 37$

$p + 3 -$ _____ $= 37 -$ _____

$p =$ _____

f. $-14 = y + 8$

$-14 -$ _____ $= y +$ _____ $-$ _____

_____ $= y$

g. Subtract like fractions.

$d + 4\frac{1}{2} = 3\frac{1}{6}$

$d + 4\frac{1}{2} -$ _____ $= 3\frac{1}{6} - 4\frac{3}{6}$

$d =$ _____

h. $f =$ first score

$f +$ ____ $= 87$

$f +$ _____ $-$ _____ $= 87 -$ _____

$f =$ _____

1. Write the variables in order.

$-3mx^2y -$ _____ $+$ _____ $+$ _____

$=$ _____ ◯ _____

2.
$$x + 5 = 7$$

$x + 5 -$ _____ $= 7 -$ _____

$x =$ _____

3. $x + 5 = -8$

$x =$ _____

4. $x - 6 = 4$

$x =$ _____

5. Seven times the sum of a number and -5

_____ (_____ $+ ($ _____ $))$

6.
$$-3(-x - 4) =$$ _____ $x +$ _____

7. $xm^2xm^3x^3m =$
Add exponents.

$x: 1 + 1 + 3 =$ _____

$m: 2 + 3 + 1 =$ _____

$=$ _____

8. $3 + 8 = 8 + 3$

_____ Property of _____

9. True or False: $-5^4 = (-5)^4$

_____

Explain.

_____

_____

_____

10. lost 8

gained 5

_____ ◯ _____ = _____

---

11. Student _____ is correct.

Student _____ should have _____ $\frac{1}{3}$ from both sides of the equation.

---

12. _____ $- x =$ _____

$\frac{4}{5} = \frac{}{15}$ $\frac{1}{3} = \frac{}{15}$

Circle the answer.

A $\frac{1}{5}$ **B** $\frac{3}{2}$ **C** $\frac{7}{15}$ **D** $\frac{17}{15}$

---

13. $T_{Celsius} + 273.15 = T_{kelvin}$

$T_{Celsius} + 273.15 =$ _____

$T_{Celsius} =$ _____

14. _____ $- x =$ _____

↑   ↑

needed   sold Friday

$x =$ _____

---

15. $x - 2.5 = 7.0$

_____ 2.5 to both sides of the equation.

16. Which equation relates a and b?

Substitute.

Circle the answer.

A $a - b = 5$ **B** $a - b = -5$

C $-5 - b = a$ **D** $a - 5 = b$

---

17. Student _____ is correct.

Student _____ added

_____ terms.

18. _____ + _____ + _____

= _____

19. *Distance = rate × time*

  a. Julio ran _____ *t.*

      Jorge ran _____ *t.*

      Sam ran _____ *t.*

  b. The family ran

      _____ *t.*

  c. The family ran

      _____ miles.

20. Student _____ is correct.

Student _____ wrote an expression using a _____ rather than the product.

21. $|1.5^2 + (-2)^3|$

  $= |\_\_\_\_\_ + \_\_\_\_\_|$

  $= |\_\_\_\_\_|$

  $= \_\_\_\_\_$

22. *Look for the pattern.*

Level	1	2	3	*l*
Number of cans	1	4	9	

Circle the answer.

  A $3l$ **B** $4l$

  C l^2 **D** l^3

23. a. $-x \cdot -x \cdot -x = -x^3$

  The resulting value is _____.

  b. $|-x|$

  The resulting value is _____.

24.

a. P (exactly 1250 feet) $= \dfrac{\text{number of 1250 foot buildings}}{\text{total number of buildings}} = \dfrac{\square}{\square}$

b. P (exactly 1046 feet) $= \dfrac{\text{number of 1046 foot buildings}}{\text{total number of buildings}} = \dfrac{\square}{\square}$

c. P (built between 1960 and 1980) $= \dfrac{\text{number of buildings built 1960 to 1980}}{\text{total number of buildings}} = \dfrac{\square}{\square}$

---

25. A perfect square is a number that is

the _____ of an _____ .

26. $P(1 + i)^2$ $P = \$500$ $i = 3\%$

Convert percent to decimal.

value: _____

---

27. Simplify $\left(\frac{\pi}{4}\right)b^2 s$ using the order of operations.

See page 2 in the Student Reference Guide.

_____

_____

_____

---

28. _____ is the additive inverse of 12.

The sum of a number and its additive inverse is _____ .

---

29. Adults (a): \$14 each. Children (c): \$8 each. Everyone $(a + c)$: \$5 each

$(\_\_\_ a + \_\_\_ c) + 5(\_\_\_ + \_\_\_) = \_\_\_ a + \_\_\_ c$

---

30. *Simplify.*

P (ace) $= \dfrac{\text{number of aces}}{\text{number of cards in deck}} = \dfrac{\square}{\square} = \dfrac{\square}{\square}$

P (another ace) $= \dfrac{\text{number of aces left in deck}}{\text{number of cards left in deck}} = \dfrac{\square}{\square} = \dfrac{\square}{\square}$

New Concepts

- Every point on the coordinate plane is located by an ordered pair of numbers called a coordinate.
- No two points have the same coordinate.

Math Language

A **coordinate plane** is made of two perpendicular number lines.

The **x-axis** is the horizontal line.

The **y-axis** is the vertical line.

The number lines divide the plane into four **quadrants**.

| Example | Graphing Ordered Pairs on a Coordinate Plane |

Graph the ordered pair $(-3, 0)$ on the coordinate plane. Label the point.

Start at the origin $(0, 0)$.

The x-coordinate is -3. The negative sign moves the coordinate 3 units to the left of the origin.

The y-coordinate is 0. Since it is at 0, the point does not move up or down from the x-axis.

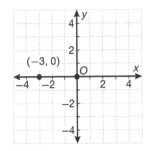

Math Language

The **x-coordinate** is the first number in an ordered pair. It tells the distance to move right or left from the origin.

The **y-coordinate** is the second number in the ordered pair. It tells the distance to move up or down from the horizontal axis.

- When there is a relationship between two variable quantities, one variable is independent and the other is the dependent variable.

Variables
Independent variable: The variable whose value can be chosen. It is also called the input variable. It is usually the x-coordinate.
Dependent variable: The variable whose value is determined by the input value of another variable. It is also called the output value. It is usually the y-coordinate.

| Example | Identifying Independent and Dependent Variables |

For each pair of variables, identify the independent variable and the dependent variable.

number of traffic violations, cost of auto insurance

Since the cost of auto insurance goes up when you have more traffic violations, *the cost depends on the number of violations.*

independent variable: number of traffic violations
dependent variable: cost

Graph each ordered pair on a coordinate plane. Label each point.

a. (0, 5)

b. (−1, −6)

c. (−2, 0)

d. (−3, 4)

e. (5, −1)

f. (2, −4)

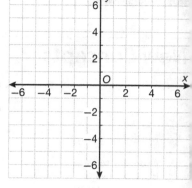

For each pair of variables, identify the independent variable and the dependent variable.

g. the amount paid, the number of toys purchased

amount paid _____; number of toys purchased _____

h. the number of hours worked, the number of yards mowed

number of hours worked _____; number of yards mowed _____

i. Complete the table for the equation $y = 2x - 1$.

$y = 2x - 1$

$y = 2(-3) - 1 = $ _____

$y = 2(-2) - 1 = $ _____

$y = 2(-1) - 1 = $ _____

x	−3	−2	−1
y			

j. Substitute 25, 50, 75, and 100 in the equation $y = 3x - 75$. Identify the x- and y-coordinates. Graph each ordered pair on a coordinate plane and label each point.

$y = 3x - 75$

$y = 3(25) - 75 = $ _____   (25, ___)

$y = 3(\underline{\ \ }) - 75 = $ _____   (___, ___)

$y = 3(\underline{\ \ }) - 75 = $ _____   (___, ___)

$y = 3(\underline{\ \ }) - 75 = $ _____   (___, ___)

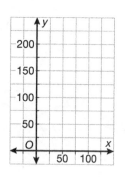

1. $(+3) + (-14)$

= _____

2. $4xyz - 3yz + zxy$

= _____

3. $3xyz - 3xyz + zxy$

= _____

4. $x - 4 = 10$

$x - 4 + \underline{\hspace{0.5in}} = 10 + \underline{\hspace{0.5in}}$

$x = \underline{\hspace{0.5in}}$

5. $x + \dfrac{1}{5} = -\dfrac{1}{10}$

$x + \dfrac{1}{5} - \underline{\hspace{0.5in}} = -\dfrac{1}{10} - \underline{\hspace{0.5in}}$

$x = \underline{\hspace{0.5in}}$

6. Graph $(3. -4)$.

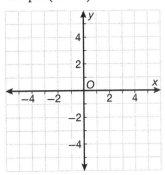

7. Graph $(0, 5)$

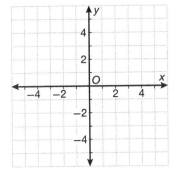

8. Point Z is ___ units _____ (of) the origin.

Point Z is ___ units _____ the x-axis.

Circle the answer.

A $(3, 0)$ **B** $(0, 3)$

C $(-3, 0)$ **D** $(0, -3)$

9.

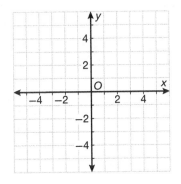

c	r
1	
2	
3	
4	

10.

x	y
15	
20	
30	
50	

11. Student _____ is correct.

Student _____ should have first performed

the operation of _____

on _____ and _____ rather than the

operation of _____ on _____

and _____.

12. a.

x	5	10	20	50
y				

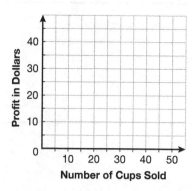

b. Substitute $x =$ _____ into the equation to find the profit if 30 cups were sold.

13. $$P = x + \underline{\quad} + \underline{\quad}$$

$$\underline{\quad\quad} = x + \underline{\quad\quad}$$

$$\underline{\quad\quad} = x$$

14. $\frac{1}{4} \cdot 1860 =$ _____

_____ $- 310 =$ _____ steps

15. Student _____ is correct.

Student _____ made an error by adding

the _____ of x.

16. Mathematicians use symbols rather than

words because _____

_____

_____.

17. Which equation demonstrates the Associative Property of Addition? Circle the answer.

A $6 - 3c = 3c - 6$

B $c^3 - 6 = c^3 + 6$

C $(6 - c)^3 = (c - 6)^3$

D $(6 - c^3) - 4 = 6 + (c^3 - 4)$

18. a. $a^2 =$ _____

b. $-a^2 =$ _____

c. $-a^3 =$ _____

d. $(-a)^3 =$ _____

e. $\left|(-a)^2\right| =$ _____

19. $\dfrac{\text{students with Type A blood}}{\text{all students}}$

$= \dfrac{\square}{\square}$

_____ ÷ _____ = _____

20. $\sqrt{441} + \sqrt{1089}$

= _____ + _____

= _____

21. Associative Property:
$(a \cdot b) \cdot c = a \cdot (b \cdot c)$.
Simplify the equation.

$(3 \cdot 2) \cdot 4$_____ = _____ · (_____ · _____)

_____ · _____ = _____ · _____

_____ = _____

22. _____ + _____ + _____ + _____ + _____ = _____

_____ ÷ 5 = _____

23. $79\dfrac{5}{7} -$ _____ = _____ points

24. A gram is equal to 100 milligrams.

0.3 g · _____ = _____ mg

25. a. A hexagon has _____ sides.

Substitute _____ for n and simplify.

$\dfrac{n^2 - 3n}{2}$

$\dfrac{\square^2 - 3\square}{2}$

$\dfrac{\square^2 - 3\square}{2}$

$\dfrac{\square - \square}{2} = \dfrac{\square}{2} =$ _____

b. Draw the diagonals from each vertex to every other vertex.

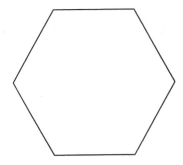

26. Separate the words into parts.

fourteen ⟶ 14

minus ⟶ −

3 squared ⟶ $3^{\square}$

the sum of three plus six. ⟶ 3 ◯ 6

$14 - \dfrac{\square}{\square + \square}$

Simplify.

$14 - \dfrac{\square}{\square + \square}$

$14 - \dfrac{\square}{\square + \square}$

$14 - \dfrac{\square}{\square}$

$14 -$ _____ = _____

---

27. True or false? Explain.

a. _____ ; _____

_____

b. _____ ; _____

_____

28. $b^2 - 4ac$

coefficient(s): _____ , _____

variable(s): _____ , _____ , _____

term(s): _____

number of term(s): _____

---

29. a. Use p to represent the number of pencils and e the number of erasers.

_____

b. _____ · _____ + _____ · _____

= _____ + _____

30. $d = 5t$ Solve for d.

t	0	1	2	4
d				

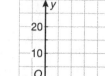

The graph is _____.

Graphing a Relationship page 117

- A graph is a visual representation of how data change and relate to each other.

- A graph can show the numeric relationship between data like time and distance.

This graph shows the different speeds at which a horse runs.

1. Use the graph to complete the table. Describe the horse's speed in each of the five intervals as
increasing,
no change,
or decreasing.

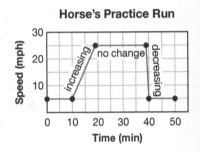

Interval	Description
0 to 10 minutes	_____
10 to 18 minutes	_____
18 to 38 minutes	_____
38 to 40 minutes	_____
40 to 50 minutes	_____

When drawing a graph,
- choose appropriate intervals for the units on each axis
- space intervals equally
- only use values that make sense, such as whole numbers of people

Customers pay $3 per pound for pecans. They can buy the pecans in fractions of a pound.

2. When drawing a graph of this situation, would you use negative values for the number of pounds of pecans? Why or why not?

_____

3. What is a reasonable maximum number

of pounds to include on your graph? _____

4. How much does 1 pound of pecans cost? _____

How much does 4.5 pounds of pecans cost? _____ = 4.5 • $_____

Math Language

A **continuous graph** is a graph without gaps, jumps, or asymptotes.

A **discrete graph** is made up of separate, disconnected points determined by a set of data.

5. Draw a graph to show the cost of pecans.

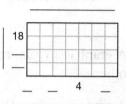

Since you can buy any positive amount of pecans, this graph is a **continuous graph** that is shown by a solid line.

If you could only buy pecans by the whole pound, the graph would show individual unconnected points. This would be a **discrete graph**.

A sheet of photos in a photo booth costs \$5. Customers can buy only full sheets of photos. The booth can print up to 10 sheets per customer.

6. What will the graph look like?

Circle the answer.   line   separate points

7. least number of sheets you can buy: _____

greatest number of sheets you can buy: _____

8. ✎ Draw a graph of this situation.

9. Use the Windy Hill Hike graph to describe Maura's hike. Use the phrases:

increasing   no change   decreasing

Maura walks along a trail with _____ in her elevation.

Then she walks up a hill and her elevation is _____.

Then she walks along the top of the hill with _____ in her elevation.

Finally she walks down the hill to the base with her elevation

_____.

• A graph represents the relationship between two quantities.

In problem **9**, the quantities are _____ and _____.

10. Another quantity that could be related to the hiker's time is the

hiker's _____ from the starting point.

11. Use the graph of the plane's altitude.

plane's altitude at beginning: _____

plane's altitude at end: _____

Since the plane begins and ends its journey at ground level, its altitude

is _____ miles at the _____ and _____ of the trip.

12. Use the phrases:

decreasing   no change   increasing

At the beginning of the flight, the plane's altitude was _____.

At the end of the flight, the plane's altitude was _____.

13. Use the phrases:

decrease   no change   increase

For the middle part of the trip there was (a/an) _____ in altitude.

Investigation Practice 📖 page 119

Graph each situation. Tell whether the graph is continuous or discrete. Then describe the graph as increasing, no change, and/or decreasing.

a. One box of greeting cards sells for $5. The income from selling the cards depends on the number of boxes sold.

Circle the answer.   continuous   discrete

Describe the change. Circle the answer.

increasing   no change   decreasing

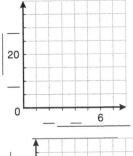

b. A scuba diver dives to a depth of 100 ft, then stays at that depth for a while. Then he dives to a depth of 250 ft and stays there for the rest of the dive. (Assume the diver descends about 100 ft per 5 minutes.)

Circle the answer.   continuous   discrete

Describe the changes.

increasing, _____, _____, no change

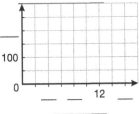

c. A driver slows down and stops at an intersection. She looks both ways, and then continues on.

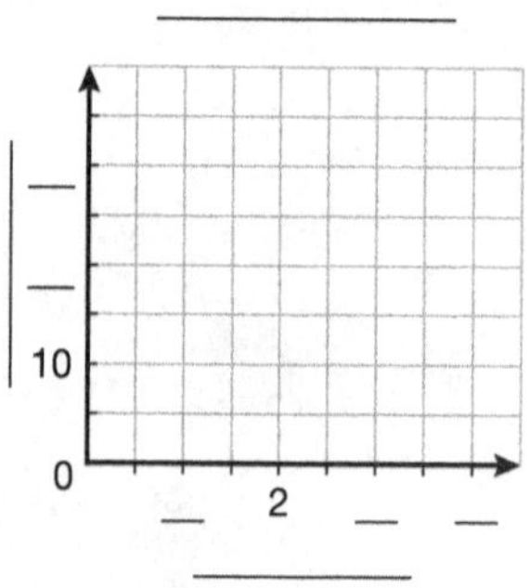

Circle the answer.   continuous   discrete

Describe the changes.

_____, _____, _____

d. The temperature of an ice cube increases until it starts to melt. As it melts, the temperature of the ice cube stays the same.

Describe the change. Then circle the one that matches the situation.

A _____, _____   B _____, _____   C _____, _____

e. ✎ *Draw a sketch.*

A rocket is launched into orbit and, in time, returns to Earth. The graph relates time to the rocket's distance from Earth.

The rocket goes _____, stays up a while, and comes _____.

The graph is shaped like_____.

f. ✎ *Draw a sketch.*

The ink in a printer is used until the ink cartridge is empty. The graph relates time used to the amount of ink in the cartridge.

Circle the answer.   continuous   discrete

The ink in the cartridge _____ until it is empty.

The graph is a _____ that _____ from _____ to _____.

g. An employee of a delivery service earns $3 for every package she delivers. The graph shows the employee's total earnings based on the number of packages delivered.

Circle the answer.   continuous   discrete

The employee's total earnings will _____ with each delivery.

The graph is a series of _____ that fall on a _____ that

_____ from _____ to _____.

LESSON

21

Solving One-Step Equations by Multiplying or Dividing page 120

New Concepts

- To solve an equation, isolate the variable by using inverse operations.

Exploration 📖 page 121

Use your textbook to complete this Exploration.

Math Language

For a real number $a \neq 0$, the **reciprocal** of a is $\frac{1}{a}$. The product of a number and its reciprocal is 1.

Example **Solving Equations by Multiplying**

Solve the equation. $\qquad -11 = \frac{1}{4}w$

Multiplying by the reciprocal of $\frac{1}{4}$ is the same as dividing by $\frac{1}{4}$.

$$-11 = \frac{1}{4}w$$

$$\frac{4}{1} \cdot -11 = \frac{4}{1} \cdot \frac{1}{4}w \qquad \textit{Multiplication Property of Equality}$$

$$-44 = w \qquad \textit{Simplify.}$$

Check: Substitute -44 for w in the original equation.

$$-11 = \frac{1}{4}w \qquad \textit{Original equation}$$

$$-11 \stackrel{?}{=} \frac{1}{4} \cdot -44 \qquad \textit{Substitute.}$$

$$-11 = -11 \checkmark \qquad \textit{Multiply.}$$

Example **Solving Equations by Dividing**

Solve the equation. $\qquad -12 = 3n$

$$-12 = 3n$$

$$-\frac{12}{3} = \frac{3n}{3} \qquad \textit{Division Property of Equality}$$

$$-4 = n \qquad \textit{Simplify.}$$

Check: Substitute -4 for n in the original equation.

$$-12 = 3n \qquad \textit{Original equation}$$

$$-12 \stackrel{?}{=} 3 \cdot (-4) \qquad \textit{Substitute.}$$

$$-12 = -12 \checkmark \qquad \textit{Simplify.}$$

Solve each equation. Then check the solution.

a. $\dfrac{k}{9} = 3$

$9 \cdot \dfrac{k}{9} = \underline{\hspace{1cm}} \cdot 3$

$k = \underline{\hspace{1cm}}$

Check: Substitute 27 for k.

$\dfrac{\boxed{}}{9} = 3$

$\underline{\hspace{1cm}} = 3$

b. $-20 = \dfrac{1}{5}m$

$\underline{\hspace{1cm}} \bigcirc (-20) = \dfrac{1}{5}m \bigcirc \underline{\hspace{1cm}}$

$\underline{\hspace{1cm}} = m$

Check: Substitute $\underline{\hspace{1cm}}$ for m.

$-20 = \dfrac{1}{5} \cdot \underline{\hspace{1cm}}$

$-20 = \underline{\hspace{1cm}}$

c. $8y = 24$

$\dfrac{8y}{8} = \dfrac{24}{\boxed{}}$

$y = \underline{\hspace{1cm}}$

Check: Substitute $\underline{\hspace{1cm}}$ for y.

$8 \cdot \underline{\hspace{1cm}} = 24$

$\underline{\hspace{1cm}} = 24$

d. $-15 = 3x$

$\dfrac{-15}{\boxed{}} = \dfrac{3x}{\boxed{}}$

$\underline{\hspace{1cm}} = x$

Check: Substitute $\underline{\hspace{1cm}}$ for x.

$-15 = 3 \cdot \underline{\hspace{1cm}}$

$-15 = \underline{\hspace{1cm}}$

e. $\dfrac{3}{4y} = 11$

$\dfrac{3}{4}y \cdot \dfrac{4}{3} = 11 \cdot \underline{\hspace{1cm}}$

$y = \dfrac{\boxed{}}{3}$

Check: Substitute $\underline{\hspace{1cm}}$ for y.

$\dfrac{3}{4} \cdot \dfrac{\boxed{}}{\boxed{}} = 11$

$\underline{\hspace{1cm}} = 11$

f. $8 = \dfrac{-5}{12n}$

$\dfrac{\boxed{}}{\boxed{}} \cdot 8 = \dfrac{\boxed{}}{\boxed{}} \cdot \dfrac{-5}{12n}$

$\dfrac{\boxed{}}{5} = n$

Check: Substitute $\underline{\hspace{1cm}}$ for n.

$8 = \dfrac{-5}{12} \cdot \dfrac{\boxed{}}{\boxed{}}$

$8 = \underline{\hspace{1cm}}$

g. Use the formula: $A = lw$.

$140 = 16 \cdot w$

$\dfrac{140}{\boxed{}} = \dfrac{16w}{\boxed{}}$

$w = \underline{\hspace{1cm}}$ ft

Check: Substitute $\underline{\hspace{1cm}}$ for w.

$140 = 6 \cdot \underline{\hspace{1cm}}$

$140 = \underline{\hspace{1cm}}$

1. *Rise of the ladder divided by 4 = the distance of the base from the building*

 $= $ _____

The ladder rises _____ .

2. The *term* in an algebraic expression is the part to be _____ or subtracted.

3. The equation $\frac{2}{3}x = 8$ shows multiplication. The inverse of multiplication is _____ .

To solve $\frac{2}{3}x = 8$, divide both sides by ____ , or multiply by the _____ of $\frac{2}{3}$.

4.
$$\Delta v = v_f - v_i$$
$$2 \text{ mi/s} = v_f - 5 \text{ mi/s}$$
$$2 = v_f - 5$$

_____ $= v_f$

5. Graph $(-2, 6)$.

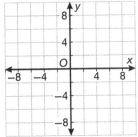

6. **a.** Draw a sketch. Let w = width. Label the width and length.

b. $A = lw$

$A = $ _____ • _____

$A = $ _____

7. Use $y = 2x + 7$ to complete the table.

x	-5	1	4
y	3		

8. *Use inverse operations.*

$$\frac{x}{3} = 5$$

$$\frac{x}{3} \cdot \text{_____} = 5 \cdot \text{_____}$$

$$x = \text{_____}$$

9. *Use inverse operations.*
Circle the answer.

  A Multiply both sides by $\frac{1}{9}$.

  B Multiply both sides by -9.

  C Divide both sides by -52.

  D Divide both sides by 52.

10. Let n = total number of cones sold

money made each day = _____ • n

profit = money made − daily cost

200 = _____ − _____

n = _____ cones

11. The terms _____ and _____ have the same variables and powers as $3z^2y$.

The term _____ has the same variables and powers as $2yz$.

The term _____ cannot be combined with any other term.

12. w = weight of an object on Earth
$2.364w$ = weight of an object on Jupiter

_____

13. Use $A = 8w$ to complete the table. Graph the ordered pairs on the grid.

w	A
2	16
4	
6	
8	

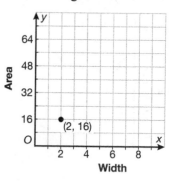

14. $-4 - 3 + 2 - 4 - 3 - 8$
Combine like terms.

$2 + ($ _____ $)$

$= 2 -$ _____

$=$ _____

15. *Combine like terms.*
Circle the answer.

  A $9 - 3p$ **B** $3p - 9$

  C $13p + 5$ **D** $13p - 9$

16. Method 1:
Multiply each number in the parentheses

by _____. Then add.

Method 2:
First add ____ and _____. Then multiply

by _____.

📝 Verify the solution using each
method.

17. Ⓐ B C D Ⓔ F G H Ⓘ J K L M
N Ⓞ P Q R S T Ⓤ V W X Y Z

Number of letters? _____ vowels? _____

$P(\text{vowel}) = \dfrac{\square}{\square}$

18.
$$A = s^2$$
$$100 = s^2$$
$$\underline{\phantom{\hspace{3cm}}} = s$$

The area of a square equals the side length

times itself. So, the side length is the

square root of the _____.

19. *See page 3 in the* Student Reference Guide.

_____ because the _____ Property

of _____ allows the order of the

addends to be switched without changing

their sum.

20. a. Use $y = 1200 - 150x$ to complete the table. Graph the ordered pairs on the grid.

x	y
1	1050
4	
6	
8	

b. It takes her _____ minutes to walk from _____ to _____.

21. _____, dividing by $-\frac{3}{4}$ is the same as

multiplying by its reciprocal _____.

22. a. $4^3 = 4 \cdot 4 \cdot 4 = $ _____

$\left(\frac{1}{4}\right)^3 = \frac{1}{4} \cdot \frac{1}{4} \cdot \frac{1}{4} = $ _____

b. $4 \cdot 4 \cdot 4 \cdot \frac{1}{4} \cdot \frac{1}{4} \cdot \frac{1}{4} = $ _____

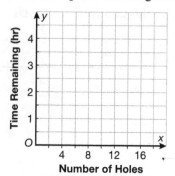

23. *See page 1 in the* Student Reference Guide.

_____, the _____ of two integers

is always a _____ number.

24. _____ units are related by a factor of 10.

The student may be converting square

_____ to square millimeters.

25. Use $y = 4.5 - 0.25x$ to complete the table. Graph the ordered pairs on the grid.

x	y
4	3.5
8	
12	
16	

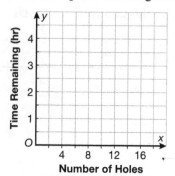

26. *Work within the absolute value bars.*

$-|15 - 5| = -|_____|$

$= _____$

27. Let s = number of strawberries
Let k = number of kiwis

a. first fruit stand: _____ + _____

second fruit stand: _____ + _____

b. Add the two expressions from part **a.**

_____

28. Put time on the horizontal axis and height on the vertical axis.

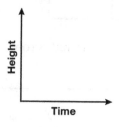

Tomato Plant Growth

29. 0.21 of what number is 7.98?
0.21 times x is 7.98

_____ = _____

30. Student _____ is correct.

Student _____ should have added _____ to

both sides of the equation to isolate x.

LESSON 22

Analyzing and Comparing Statistical Graphs page 127

New Concepts

- Graphs are used to present numerical data. Some frequently used graphs are bar graphs, line graphs, circle graphs, and stem-and-leaf plots.

Exploration 📖 page 127

Use your textbook to complete the exploration.

- A stem-and-leaf plot uses some digits as "stems" and others as "leaves." The "stems" have a greater place value than the "leaves".

Example **Interpreting Stem-and-Leaf Plots**

Find the age that occurs most often.

This stem-and-leaf plot separates numbers into tens and ones digits. The stems represent tens and the leaves represent ones. The first three ages on this plot are 10, 10, and 17.

Look for the leaf that occurs most often. It is 1 in the fourth row. So, the age **41 years** occurs most often.

Age of Hiking Club Members

Stem	Leaf
1	0 0 7
2	4 6
3	2 3 4
4	1 1 1 3
5	3 6 6 9

Key: 1|0 means 10

- A **circle graph** uses sections of a circle to compare parts of the circle to the whole circle. The whole circle represents the entire set of data.

Example **Application: Yearly Sales**

If the yearly sales are $20 million, find the sales for the first quarter.

A year can be divided into four quarters, with three months in each quarter. The circle graph compares the sales for the four quarters.

To find the dollar amount for the 1st quarter, multiply 12% times the yearly total of $20 million.

12% of 20 million

$= 0.12 \cdot 20$ million

$= \$2.4$ **million or 2,400,000**

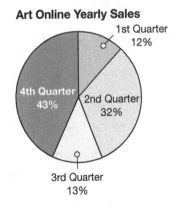

Art Online Yearly Sales

1st Quarter 12%
2nd Quarter 32%
3rd Quarter 13%
4th Quarter 43%

a.

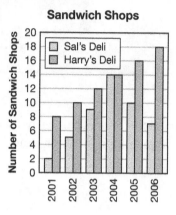

Sandwich Shops

What year shows the greatest difference between the number of shops Sal and Harry owned? _____

b.

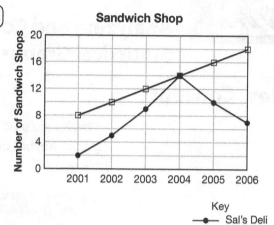

Sandwich Shop

Key
— ● — Sal's Deli
— □ — Harry's Deli

Sal owned 2 shops in 2001. In 2002 he had 5 shops. He opened 3 shops in 2002. What was the greatest number of shops he opened in one year? _____

c. Cross out each number in the list as it is entered into the stem-and-leaf plot.

Height in Inches
56, 52, 68, 49, 49, 40, 72, 71, 43, 54

Complete the stem-and-leaf plot.

What height occurs most often? _____

Height of Jackson Grandchildren (in inches)

Stem	Leaf
4	0
5	
6	
7	

Key: 4|0 = _____

d.

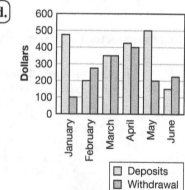

Deposits
Withdrawal

Which month shows the greatest difference between deposits and withdrawals?

_____

e. **Art Online Yearly Sales**

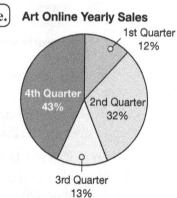

1st Quarter 12%
2nd Quarter 32%
3rd Quarter 13%
4th Quarter 43%

12% of the total sales is $3,000,000.

Let x = total sales

1. A stem-and-leaf plot shows change over time.

Circle the answer: true   false

If false, explain what stem-and-leaf plots do show.

_____

2. *Use the order of operations.*

x	-1	0	1
y	-6		

---

3. $2p(xy - 3k) = 2p(xy) - 2p(-3k)$

$$= \underline{\hspace{3cm}}$$

4. $y - 3 = 2$

$$\underline{+\,3} = \underline{+\,\hspace{1cm}}$$

$$y = \underline{\hspace{1cm}}$$

---

5. *Remember that $\frac{1}{4} = \frac{2}{8}$.*

$$x - \frac{1}{4} = \frac{7}{8}$$

$$\underline{+\frac{1}{4}} = \underline{+\,\hspace{1cm}}$$

$$x = \underline{\hspace{1cm}}$$

6. *First convert to improper fractions. Then multiply by the reciprocal.*

$$4x = 2\frac{2}{3}$$

$$4x \cdot \underline{\hspace{1.5cm}} = \underline{\hspace{1.5cm}} \cdot \underline{\hspace{1.5cm}}$$

$$x = \underline{\hspace{1cm}}$$

---

7. *Use inverse operations.*

$$7x = 49$$

$$x = \underline{\hspace{1.5cm}}$$

8. Consider the following types of graphs:

circle graph   stem-and-leaf plot
line graphs   bar graphs

(A) _____ show(s) changes in data over time.

---

9. *A set of numbers is closed under a given operation if the outcome of the operation results in another number in the set.*

a. true   false   counterexample: _____

b. true   false   counterexample: $\sqrt{3} \div \sqrt{3}$ is a _____ number.

c. true   false   counterexample: _____

10. Complete the graph.

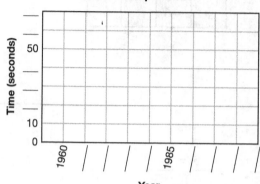

**Fastest Lap Times
in the Indianapolis 500**

Conclusion: The lap times have become

_____ since _____.

11. Graph $(-4, -1)$.

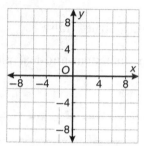

12. Student _____ is correct.

Student _____ graphed (____,____) instead of graphing $(-4, 3)$.

13. 12 eggs + x eggs to buy = 25 eggs in all

Circle the answer.

A $12 - x = 25$ **B** $12 + x = 25$

C $25 + x = 12$ **D** $x - 12 = 25$

14. Write *positive, negative,* or *zero.*

a. If $y > 14$, then x is _____.

b. If $y = 14$, then x is _____.

c. If $y < 14$, then x is _____.

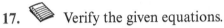

15. *The graph compares the ages of two different groups of people.*

Circle the answer.

A circle graph   **B** stem-and-leaf plot

C double-line graph   **D** double-bar graph

16. Let d = distance driven

_____ ◯ _____

17. Verify the given equations.

a. $x\left(\dfrac{y}{y-x}\right)^2 = -\dfrac{4}{9}$; $x = -4$ and $y = 2$

b. $\left|(x-y)^3\right| = 27$; $x = -1$ and $y = 2$

18. A sample space is _____

_____ .

19.   **Threatened and Endangered Animals**

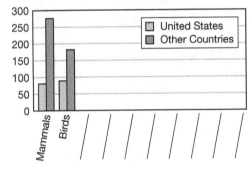

Conclusion: _____

_____

_____

_____ .

20. $9 - 5 = 4$ and $5 - 9 = -4$

$12 - 6 = 6$ and $6 - 12 = -6$

$7 - 3 = 4$ and $3 - 7 = -4$

The Commutative Property _____

apply to the operation of _____ .

21. *See page 15 in the* Student Reference Guide.

$\dfrac{1}{2}($____ + ____$)$____ = _____

= _____

22. *Combine like terms.*

$4 + (-7 - 3 - 3 - 2)$

$= 4 -$ _____

$=$ _____

23. 16 is $\frac{4}{9}$ of the circumference C.

_____ = _____ • _____

$C =$ _____ ▢

24. a. new area $= lw =$ _____ • _____

b. _____ $+ ($ _____ • _____ $)$

c. _____ ▢

25. See 📖 page 133.

_____

_____

26. Add the terms with the variables ab^2.

$3ab^2 +$ _____ $=$ _____

Add the terms with the variables ab.

$-2ab -$ _____ $=$ _____

Answer: _____

27. $1187\overline{)380.000}$

Answer: _____

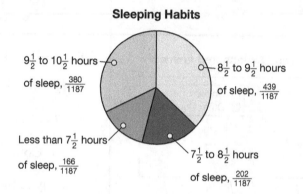

Sleeping Habits

$9\frac{1}{2}$ to $10\frac{1}{2}$ hours of sleep, $\frac{380}{1187}$

$8\frac{1}{2}$ to $9\frac{1}{2}$ hours of sleep, $\frac{439}{1187}$

Less than $7\frac{1}{2}$ hours of sleep, $\frac{166}{1187}$

$7\frac{1}{2}$ to $8\frac{1}{2}$ hours of sleep, $\frac{202}{1187}$

28. *Use the properties for exponents.*

$(x^2 \cdot x^3 \cdot x) \cdot (y \cdot y \cdot y \cdot y)$

$=$ _____ • _____

$=$ _____

29. a. Let $p =$ sale price per book.

_____ $p = \$31.92$ $p =$ ▢ _____

b. Let $c =$ original cost per book.

$\frac{4}{5}c =$ _____ $c =$ ▢ _____

30. *Add the number of cards drawn. Use that as the denominator of each probability fraction.*

a. $P(\text{heart}) = \dfrac{8}{\Box} = \dfrac{\Box}{\Box}$

b. $P(\text{not club}) = \dfrac{\Box}{\Box} = \dfrac{\Box}{\Box}$

Outcome	Frequency
Hearts	8
Diamonds	8
Clubs	6
Spades	4

New Concepts

To solve two step equations:

1. Isolate the term with the variable.

2. Isolate the variable.

Example **Solving Two-Step Equations with Positive Coefficients**

Solve the equation.

$4x + 5 = 17$

Step 1: Isolate the term with the variable.

$$(4x) + 5 = 17$$
$$\underline{-5 = -5} \qquad \text{\textit{Subtract 5 from both sides.}}$$
$$4x = 12 \qquad \text{\textit{Simplify.}}$$

Step 2: Isolate the variable.

$$4(x) = 12$$
$$\frac{4x}{4} = \frac{12}{4} \qquad \text{\textit{Divide both sides by 4.}}$$
$$x = 3$$

Example **Solving Two-Step Equations with Negative Coefficients**

Solve the equation.

$8 = -5m + 6$

Step 1: Isolate the term with the variable.

$$8 - 6 = (-5m) + 6$$
$$\underline{+6 = +6} \qquad \text{\textit{Add 6 to both sides.}}$$
$$2 = -5m$$

Step 2: Isolate the variable.

$$2 = -5(m)$$
$$\frac{2}{-5} = \frac{-5m}{-5} \qquad \text{\textit{Divide both sides by -5.}}$$
$$-\frac{2}{5} = m$$

Check: Substitute $-\frac{2}{5}$ for m in the original equation.

$8 = -5m + 6$	*Original equation*
$8 \stackrel{?}{=} -5 \cdot \left(-\frac{2}{5}\right) + 6$	*Substitute.*
$8 \stackrel{?}{=} \left(-\frac{5}{1}\right) \cdot \left(-\frac{2}{5}\right) + 6$	
$8 \stackrel{?}{=} 2 + 6$	
$8 = 8 \checkmark$	*Both sides equal 8.*

Lesson Practice page 137

a. Which step would you use first to evaluate $9y + 6$ for $y = 2$?

$(9 \cdot \underline{\quad}) + 6.$ *Use the order of operations.*

First _____.

b. Which step would you use first to solve $9y + 6 = 24$?

_____ 6. To isolate the term with the variable, use _____ operations.

Solve.

c. $8w - 4 = 28$

$$8w - 4 = 28 \qquad \textit{Add 4 to both sides.}$$
$$\underline{+ 4 = + 4}$$
$$8w = \underline{\quad}$$
$$\frac{8w}{8} = \frac{32}{8} \qquad \textit{Divide both sides by 8.}$$
$$w = \underline{\quad}$$

d. $-10 = -2x + 12$

$$-10 = -2x + 12 \qquad \textit{Subtract 12 from both sides.}$$
$$\underline{-12 = \qquad -12}$$
$$\underline{\quad} = -2x$$
$$\frac{-22}{-2} = -\frac{2x}{\square} \qquad \textit{Divide both sides by -2.}$$
$$x = \underline{\quad}$$

e. $\frac{1}{8}m + \frac{3}{4} = \frac{7}{12}$

$$\frac{1}{8}m + \frac{3}{4} = \frac{7}{12} \qquad \textit{Subtract } \frac{3}{4} \textit{ from both sides.}$$
$$\underline{-\frac{3}{4} = -\frac{3}{4}}$$
$$\frac{1}{8}m = \frac{7}{12} - \frac{\square}{12} \qquad \textit{Find a common denominator.}$$
$$\frac{1}{8}m = \frac{\square}{12}$$
$$\frac{1}{8}m \cdot 8 = \frac{\square}{12} \cdot 8 \qquad \textit{Multiply both sides by 8.}$$
$$m = -\frac{16}{12} = \frac{\square}{\square} \qquad \textit{Simplify.}$$

f. amount of savings = cost of bulbs.

$$7m + 25 = 125$$
$$7m + 25 = 125 \qquad \textit{Subtract 25 from both sides.}$$
$$\underline{- 25 = - 25}$$
$$7m = \underline{\quad} \qquad \textit{Divide both sides by 7.}$$
$$m = \underline{\quad}$$

Round to the nearest month. _____

1. *Substitute.*

$$= (3.5 - \underline{\quad}) - (\underline{\quad} - \underline{\quad})$$

$$= \underline{\quad} - \underline{\quad} = \underline{\quad}$$

2. To graph $(-2, 4)$, start at the origin.

Go _____ units left and

then _____ units up.

---

3. $3x + 5 = 32$

$3x = \underline{\quad}$

$x = \underline{\quad}$

Circle the answer.

  A 24   **B** 9   **C** 81   **D** $12\frac{1}{3}$

4. Student _____ is correct.

Student _____ should have divided

both sides of the equation by _____.

---

5. starting altitude $+ (6 \cdot 350 \, m)$

$= \underline{\quad} + 2100$

$= \underline{\quad}$

6. *Substitute.*
Use inverse operations.

$3 \cdot (\underline{\quad}) - 8 = \underline{\quad}$, so $x \neq 9$.

Solve.

$3x - 8 = 22$

$\underline{+ 8 = + 8}$

$3x = \underline{\quad}$

$x = \underline{\quad}$

---

7. $\frac{3}{5} \cdot 5 = \underline{\quad}$

This is a counterexample because the product _____ is an _____.

---

8.   **a.** most popular: _____

  b. 15% of $300 = 0.15 \cdot 300 = \underline{\quad}$

  c. $30\% - 20\% = \underline{\quad}$ 10% of $300 = \underline{\quad}$

---

9. Circle the best answer.

bar graph   circle graph

double bar graph   stem-and-leaf plot

_____ graphs can compare

_____

_____.

10. Use the data in the table to complete this vertical bar graph.

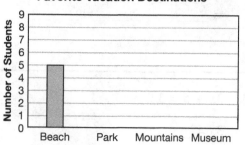

11. $C = 2\pi r$

Use inverse operations.

$$\frac{8}{9}\pi = 2r\pi$$

$$\frac{8}{9} = 2r$$

$$\frac{8}{9} \cdot \frac{1}{2} = r$$

$$\boxed{} = r$$

12. Use the point $(0, -1)$ from the graph. Find the equation where $y = 0$ when $x = 0$.

Circle the answer.

A $y = 2x + 1$ **B** $y = 2x + 3$

C $y = -2x$ **D** $y = -2x - 1$

13. a. Jenny: $(25 \cdot x) + (10 \cdot \underline{})$

Sam: $(50 \cdot h) + (\underline{} \cdot \underline{})$

b. $50h + 25x + \underline{} + \underline{}$

14. Substitute 2 for x.

$3x + 12 = 3(\underline{}) + 12 = \underline{}$

$12 + 3x = 12 + 3(\underline{}) = \underline{}$

15.

$24 + \dfrac{16}{4} - (4 + 3^2) \cdot 2$ ◯ $24 + \left(\dfrac{16}{4} - 4\right) + 3^2 \cdot 2$

$= 24 + \dfrac{16}{4} - (\underline{}) \cdot 2$ $= 24 + (\underline{}) + 3^2 \cdot 2$

$= 24 + \dfrac{16}{4} - \underline{}$ $= 24 + \underline{} + (\underline{}) \cdot 2$

$= 28 + \underline{} - \underline{}$ $= 24 + \underline{} + \underline{}$

$= \underline{}$ $= \underline{}$

$\underline{}$ ◯ $\underline{}$

16. *Use inverse operations.*

$$y - \frac{1}{2} = -2\frac{1}{2}$$

$$y - \frac{1}{2} = -2\frac{1}{2}$$

$$+\frac{1}{2} = + \underline{\quad}$$

$$y = \underline{\quad}$$

17. *Use inverse operations.*

$$2x + 3 = 11$$

$$-\underline{\quad} = -\underline{\quad}$$

$$2x = \underline{\quad}$$

$$x = \underline{\quad}$$

18. *Use inverse operations.*

$$3x - 4 = 10$$

$$3x = \underline{\quad}$$

$$x = \underline{\quad}$$

19. *Use inverse operations.*

$$2.2x + 2 = 8.6$$

$$2.2x = \underline{\quad}$$

$$x = \underline{\quad}$$

20. Divide to three decimal places.

$$1789\overline{)801.000}$$

Round to the nearest hundredth. _____

21.
  a. $P(\text{George}) = \dfrac{\square}{43}$

  b. $P(\text{William or John}) = \dfrac{8}{\square}$

  c. $\dfrac{[43 - (6 + 4 + 4 + 3)]}{43} = \dfrac{\square}{43}$

22. $A = s^2$
  Substitute.

$$361 = s^2$$

$$\underline{\quad} = s$$

23. cold temperature $= 6 \cdot$ highest temperature

$$= 6 \cdot \underline{\quad}$$

$$= \underline{\quad}$$

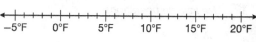

24.

-5°F   0°F   5°F   10°F   15°F   20°F

high temperature on Monday: _____

25. *Combine like terms.*

balance: _____

26. *Use the order of operations.*

$4 \div 2 + 6^2 - 22$

= _____

27. Use the _____ Rule for

Exponents by _____ the

exponents of like _____ .

28. *Use a unit ratio.*

$\dfrac{332 \text{ m}}{1\text{s}} \cdot \dfrac{100 \text{ cm}}{1\text{m}} =$ _____ cm/s

29. *gain − loss*

Circle the answer.

A $247,275 million

B $24,926 million

C $1.2 million

D −$24,577 million

30. Circle each answer.

a. First shoe pulled from the box is a left shoe.

impossible   unlikely   as likely as not   likely   certain

b. Rolls a number less than 7 on a number cube.

impossible   unlikely   as likely as not   likely   certain

c. November will have 31 days.

impossible   unlikely   as likely as not   likely   certain

Solving Decimal Equations page 140

New Concepts

- To write decimals as integers, multiply by a power of 10.

    To move the decimal 1 place to the right, multiply by 10^1.

    To move the decimal 2 places to the right, multiply by 10^2.

    To move the decimal 3 places to the right, multiply by 10^3.

Example Solving by Multiplying by a Power of 10

Solve the equation.

$$8 + 0.5x = 10.5$$

$$(10)8 + (10)0.5x = (10)10.5 \qquad \text{Multiply every term by } 10^1.$$

$$80 + 5x = 105 \qquad \text{Move the decimal 1 place to the right.}$$

$$\underline{-80 = -80} \qquad \text{Use inverse operations.}$$

$$5x = 25$$

$$\frac{5x}{5} = \frac{25}{5} \qquad \text{Use inverse operations.}$$

$$\boldsymbol{x = 5}$$

> **Math Language**
>
> A **coefficient** is a factor in front of the variable. In 0.5x, the coefficient is 0.5.

- Decimal equations can be solved without multiplying by a power of 10.

Example Solving Two-Step Decimal Equations

Solve the equation.

$$0.2m + 0.8 = 1.8$$

$$\underline{-0.8 = -0.8} \qquad \text{Use inverse operations.}$$

$$0.2m = 1$$

$$\frac{0.2m}{0.2} = \frac{1}{0.2} \qquad \text{Use inverse operations.}$$

$$m = 1 \div 0.2 \qquad \text{Simplify.}$$

$$\boldsymbol{m = 5}$$

Solve each equation.
Use inverse operations.

a. $0.25 + 0.18y = 0.97$

$25 + \underline{\hspace{0.6cm}}y = \underline{\hspace{0.8cm}}$ *Multiply both sides by 10^2.*
$-25 \qquad\quad = -25$ *Subtract 25 from both sides.*

$\underline{\hspace{0.8cm}}y = \underline{\hspace{0.6cm}}$

$\dfrac{\square y}{\square} = \dfrac{\square}{\square}$ *Divide both sides by 18.*

$y = \underline{\hspace{0.6cm}}$

b. $\quad 0.05 = 0.5 - 0.15q$

$\underline{\hspace{1cm}} = \underline{\hspace{1cm}} - 15q$

$\underline{\hspace{1cm}} = -15q$

$\dfrac{\square}{\square} = \dfrac{-15q}{-15}$

$q = \underline{\hspace{0.8cm}}$

c. $-0.5n + 1.4 = 8.9$

$\underline{\hspace{1cm}} = \underline{\hspace{1cm}}$

$-0.5n = \underline{\hspace{0.6cm}}$

$\dfrac{-0.5n}{-0.5} = \dfrac{\square}{-0.5}$

$n = \underline{\hspace{0.8cm}}$

d. 0.6 of 24 is what number?
"Of" means multiply.

$0.6 \cdot 24 = n$

$\underline{\hspace{1cm}} = n$

e. $x + 2x = 52.8$

$\underline{\hspace{1cm}} = 52.8$

$x = \underline{\hspace{1cm}}$ so $2x = \underline{\hspace{1cm}}$

Practice 📖 page 142

1. *Multiply by the reciprocal.*

$\dfrac{4}{5}x \cdot \underline{\hspace{1.5cm}} = -24$

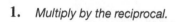

$x = \underline{\hspace{1.5cm}}$

Circle the answer.

A -30 **B** $-\dfrac{96}{5}$ **C** $\dfrac{96}{5}$ **D** 30

2.   **a.** Add first.

$3(2x + 5x) = 3 \cdot \underline{\hspace{1.5cm}} = \underline{\hspace{1.5cm}}$

b. Use the Distributive Property.

$3(2x + 5x) = (3 \cdot \underline{\hspace{1cm}}) + (3 \cdot \underline{\hspace{1cm}})$

$= 6x + \underline{\hspace{1.5cm}}$

$= \underline{\hspace{1cm}}$

---

3. *Multiply by 10^3.*

$(1000)0.45x - (1000)0.002 = (1000)8.098$

$\underline{\hspace{1.5cm}} - \underline{\hspace{1.5cm}} = \underline{\hspace{1.5cm}}$

$x = \underline{\hspace{1cm}}$

4. If you multiply both sides of the equation by the same $\underline{\hspace{2.5cm}}$, you create an equivalent $\underline{\hspace{2.5cm}}$.

The new equation will have the $\underline{\hspace{1.5cm}}$ solution as the original equation.

5. Let s = number of shares of stock

$(\$6.57 \cdot s) + \$25 = \$846.25$

$6.57s = \underline{\hspace{2cm}}$

$\dfrac{6.57s}{6.57} = \dfrac{\square}{6.57}$

$s = \underline{\hspace{1.5cm}}$

6. *"Of" means multiply.*

0.8 is 0.32 of what number?

↓ ↓ ↓ ↓ ↓

$0.8 = 0.32 \cdot n$

Circle the answer.

A 2.5 **B** 0.25 **C** 0.4 **D** 0.4

7. Method I
$0.45x + 0.9 = 1.008$

$\underline{\hspace{0.7cm}}x + \underline{\hspace{0.7cm}} = 1008$

$450x = \underline{\hspace{1.5cm}}$

$x = \underline{\hspace{1.5cm}}$

Method II
$0.45x + 0.9 = 1.008$

$0.45x = \underline{\hspace{1.5cm}}$

$x = \underline{\hspace{1.5cm}}$

8. *Terms are separated by plus or minus signs.*

variable: $\underline{\hspace{1cm}}$

coefficient: $\underline{\hspace{1cm}}$

number of terms: $\underline{\hspace{1cm}}$

9. Method I: $0.25x + \dfrac{1}{2} = 0.075$

$0.25x + \underline{\hspace{1.5cm}} = 0.075$

$x = \underline{\hspace{1cm}}$

Method II: $0.25x + \dfrac{1}{2} = 0.075$

$\underline{\hspace{1cm}}x + \dfrac{1}{2} = \dfrac{3}{40}$

$x = \underline{\hspace{1cm}}$

10. Student _____ is correct.

Student _____ found the total number of students with 0 or 1 sibling and used it as the _____.

11. $C = \pi d$

$C = 3.14 \cdot$ _____

$C =$ _____

12. apples: _____% of $12

_____ $\cdot 12 =$ _____

peanut butter: _____% of $12

_____ $\cdot 12 =$ _____

juice: _____% of $12

_____ $\cdot 12 =$ _____

strawberries: _____% of $12

_____ $\cdot 12 =$ _____

13. Graph (2, 1).

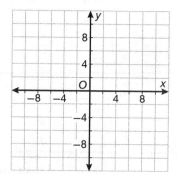

14. total number of outcomes: _____

a. even numbers: 10, 12, 54, 76, x $P(\text{even}) =$ _____

b. odd numbers: _____, _____, _____, x $P(\text{odd}) =$ _____

c. less than 20: _____, _____ $P(\text{less than 20}) =$ _____

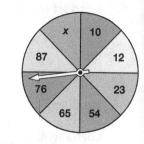

15. Let x = number of counselors who walked
Let y = number of campers who walked

Number of miles walked = _____ x + _____ y

$0.50($ _____ $x +$ _____ $y)$

Use the Distributive Property.

_____ $x +$ _____ y

16. *Use the Product Property of Exponents.*

$(11w^4 \cdot 3z^9)(2w^7z^2)$

$= (11 \cdot$ _____ $) \cdot (w^4 \cdot w^7) \cdot (z^9 \cdot z^2)$

$=$ _____ $\cdot$ _____ $\cdot z^{11}$

_____ because the _____ side of the

equation is equal to the _____ side.

---

17. $100\% - (12\% + 18\% + 20\%) =$

$$100 - \underline{\hspace{1cm}} = \underline{\hspace{1cm}}$$

P (not winning a prize) = _____

18. Total number of people shown on the graph:

_____ + _____ + _____ + _____ = _____

a. $P(\$40 \text{ or more}) = \dfrac{\square}{100} = \dfrac{\square}{25}$

b. $P(\$30 \text{ or less}) = \dfrac{\square + \square}{100} = \dfrac{\square}{25}$

---

19. $P = 2(l + w)$ is equivalent to $P = 2(w + l)$

because the _____ Property

of _____ says you can

switch two addends without changing

the _____ .

20. $\left[\left(-\dfrac{3}{8}\right) \cdot \left(-\dfrac{8}{3}\right)\right] =$ _____

Any number divided by _____
equals itself.

$\dfrac{4}{7} \div \left[\left(-\dfrac{3}{8}\right) \cdot \left(-\dfrac{8}{3}\right)\right] = \dfrac{4}{7} \div$ _____ $=$ _____

---

21. $\dfrac{2}{5} \div \left(-\dfrac{7}{2}\right) \cdot \left(-\dfrac{5}{2}\right)$

$= \dfrac{2}{5} \cdot \left(\dfrac{\square}{\square}\right) \cdot \left(-\dfrac{5}{2}\right)$

$= \dfrac{2}{5}\left(-\dfrac{5}{2}\right)\left(\dfrac{\square}{\square}\right)$

$= \left(-\underline{\hspace{0.6cm}}\right)\left(\dfrac{\square}{\square}\right) = \dfrac{\square}{\square}$

22. The exponents cannot be added to simplify

$k^2 \cdot m \cdot b^4 \cdot c^3$ because no two of the

_____ are the same.

---

23. *See page 3 in the* Student Reference Guide.

$6(ab + ef) =$ _____ $+$ _____

_____ Property

24. Use 21.12122122212222 ...

a. The pattern _____ a repeating pattern.

b. This decimal number does not _____

or _____ .

Circle the kind of number.

rational   irrational

25. *Use a unit ratio.*

$630 \text{ cm}^3 \cdot \left(\dfrac{1 \text{ in.}}{2.54 \text{ cm}}\right)^3$

$= 630$ _____ $^3 (2.54 \cdot 2.54 \cdot 2.54)$

$= \dfrac{630}{(2.54 \cdot 2.54 \cdot 2.54)}$

$=$ _____

26. Complete the chart to find the pattern.

Time (a.m.)	6	7	8	9	10	
°C	30		38	6	46	50

temperature at 9 a.m. = _____

time when temperature is 50°C = _____

27. $-|10 - 7| = -|$ _____ $|$

$= -1 \cdot$ _____ $=$ _____

28. a. 20% of 1,154,358,778

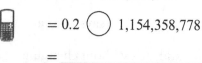

$= 0.2 \bigcirc 1{,}154{,}358{,}778$

$=$ _____

b. $35\% - 20\% =$ _____

15% of 1,154,358,778

$= 0.15 \bigcirc 1{,}154{,}358{,}778$

$=$ _____

29. *Draw a sketch.*

$\sqrt{784} =$ _____ yd

_____ $\div 7 =$ _____ spaces between the trees

$1 +$ _____ $=$ _____ trees

30. a. $\dfrac{495}{500} = \dfrac{\boxed{}}{100}$

b. $\dfrac{99}{100} \cdot 20{,}000 =$ _____

LESSON
25

Differentiating Between Relations and Functions page 146

New Concepts

Math Language

A **relation** is a set of ordered pairs where each number in the domain is matched to one or more numbers in the range.

The **domain** is the set of possible values for the independent variable (**input values**) of a set of ordered pairs.

The **range** is a set of values for the dependent variable (**output values**) of a set of ordered pairs.

Example Determining the Domain and Range of a Relation

Write the domain and range of the relation.
$\{(2, 6), (2, 10), (8, 6), (5, 1), (4, 6), (3, 9)\}$

Use set brackets { } when you write the domain and the range.

Domain: **{2, 3, 4, 5, 8}**

Range: **{1, 6, 9, 10}**

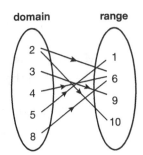

• A **function** pairs each value in the domain with exactly one value in the range.

Example Identifying a Set of Ordered Pairs as a Function

Determine whether $\{(3, 3), (10, 1), (0, 3), (8, 9), (4, 4), (10, 2)\}$ represents a function.

Each domain value must map with exactly one range value.

The diagram shows that the domain value of 10 maps to the range values 1 and 2.

The relation **is not a function**. Each domain value does not have exactly one range value.

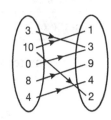

Math Language

Vertical line test: A graph on the coordinate plane represents a function if any vertical line intersects the graph in exactly one point.

• The vertical-line test is used to determine if a graph represents a function.

Example Identifying a Graph as a Function

Determine whether the ordered pairs represent a function.

Any vertical line that is drawn intersects only one point at time. **The graph represents a function.**

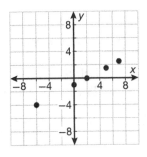

a. relation: {(1, 2); (2, 1); (4, 6); (8, 5); (7, 7); (3, 10)}

Domain: x-values   *Range: y-values*

values in the domain: {_____, _____, _____, _____, _____, _____}

values in the range: {_____, _____, _____, _____, _____, _____}

b. relation: {(11, 12); (12, 1); (5, 5); (14, 10); (13, 7)}

Match the elements of the domain with the elements in the range.

Is each number in the domain matched with exactly one element in the range? _____

If yes, then this is a _____.

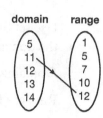

domain   range

c. Graph the equation $y = 3x - 1$. Make a table of values.

Domain (x)	−4	−1	0	2	3	9
Range (y)						

No matter what value is substituted for the input value x, the equation outputs exactly

_____ value for *y*.

The equation $y = 3x - 1$ _____ represent a function.

d. Graph the ordered pairs in this table.

x	−1	0	1	−2	0
y	3	0	3	6	6

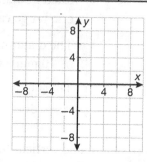

Use the _____ line test.

This _____ a function.

e. *In function notation y = f(x).*

Let c = the number of copies printed. Then $f(c)$ = the total cost.

$f(c) = \boxed{} \cdot c$

f. Let d = the number of days the author writes. Then $f(d)$ = the number of pages left to write.

_____d = the total pages written

$f(d) = 400 - \underline{}$

1. *Use inverse operations.*

$$0.3 + 0.05y = 0.65$$

$$0.05y = \underline{\hspace{1.5cm}}$$

$$\frac{0.05y}{\square} = \frac{\square}{\square}$$

$$y = \underline{\hspace{1cm}}$$

2. *Substitute.*

a. $103 + (\underline{\hspace{1cm}}) = 99$

$$\underline{\hspace{1cm}} = 99$$

b. $\frac{1}{2} - (\underline{\hspace{1cm}}) = \frac{3}{4}$

$$\frac{2}{4} + \underline{\hspace{1cm}} = \frac{3}{4}$$

$$\underline{\hspace{1cm}} = \frac{3}{4}$$

3. Use $y = x + 2$ to complete the table.

Domain y	-2	0	2	4	5
Range x		2			7

$y = x + 2$ _____ represent a function.

4. *In function notation $y = f(x)$.*

Let $m = $ number of miles
So $f(m) = $ amount of time to walk m miles

$$f(m) = \underline{\hspace{1cm}} m$$

5. *Add the opposite.*

$$3.16 + (-1.01) + (-0.11)$$

$$= 3.16 + (\underline{\hspace{1.5cm}})$$

$$= \underline{\hspace{2cm}}$$

6. *The x-values in a function do not repeat.*

Circle the answer.

A $\{(1, 1); (2, 2); (3, 3); (4, 4)\}$
B $\{(1, 0); (2, 1); (1, 3); (2, 4)\}$
C $\{(1, 1); (1, 2); (1, 3); (1, 4)\}$
D $\{(10, 1); (10, 2); (12, 3); (12, 4)\}$

7. *In function notation $y = f(x)$.*

$$f(\underline{\hspace{0.5cm}}) = s + s + s + s$$

$$f(\underline{\hspace{0.5cm}}) = \underline{\hspace{1.5cm}}$$

8. _____, because like a _____,

a function is a _____ of ordered _____.

9. Circle the answer.

function

relation

The circle _____
pass the vertical
line test.

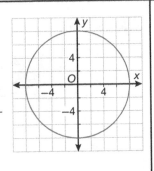

10. $C = \pi d$

$$C = 3.14 \cdot \underline{\hspace{2cm}}$$

$$C = \underline{\hspace{2cm}}$$

11. 1 AU = 93 million miles

$$\frac{5{,}200{,}00 \text{ mi}}{1 \text{ AU}} \cdot \text{_____ AU}$$

_____ million miles or

_____ miles

12. 1 postcard costs _____ cents.

_____ bus holds 40 people.

____ person contributed _____ dollars.

13. *Use inverse operations.*

Let d = number of DVDs rented.

_____ $\cdot\, d +$ _____ = 55.79

$d =$ _____

14. Student _____ is correct.

Student _____ should have _____

from both sides instead of _____ 4.

15. *Look for choices that can be eliminated.*

Circle the answer.

A Michaela is the best player on the team.

B Michaela usually scores more points than Jessie.

C Neither player will score more than 18 points in the next game.

D Jessie does not play as much as Michaela.

16. A _____ graph helps _____ the amounts of water and juice sold each month.

A _____ graph can show how the amounts sold of each beverage _____ from month to month.

Stem-and-leaf plots _____ the data from least to greatest.

17. A _____ compares parts to a whole.

18. *Substitute.*

$(3 \cdot \text{\_\_\_\_\_}) - 2(\text{\_\_\_\_\_} - 1)^2 + 2$

$= (3 \cdot \text{\_\_\_\_\_}) - 2(\text{\_\_\_\_\_})^2 + 2$

$= \text{\_\_\_\_\_} - \text{\_\_\_\_\_} + 2$

$= \text{_____}$

19. Use the equation $y = 2.5x$.

Complete the table. Label each axis using "Batches" or "Cups". Then plot the points.

Batches (x)	Cups (y)
1	2.5
2	
3	
4	

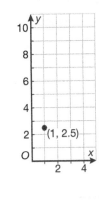

_____

20. Subtraction is not _____, so $x - 3$ does not have the same value as $3 - x$.

The correct way to write "three less than x" is _____.

21. This table shows the pattern up through the sixth generation.

initial	first	second	third	fourth	fifth	sixth
$45 \cdot 2^0$	$45 \cdot 2^1$	$45 \cdot 2^2$	$45 \cdot 2^3$	$45 \cdot 2^4$	$45 \cdot 2^5$	$45 \cdot 2^6$
$45 \cdot 1$	$45 \cdot 2$	$45 \cdot$ _____	$45 \cdot$ _____	$45 \cdot$ _____	$45 \cdot$ _____	$45 \cdot$ _____
_____	_____	_____	_____	_____	_____	_____

The difference between the fourth and sixth is _____.

22. 4890 feet to the nearest hundred:

_____ feet

Square the answer.

(_____) · (_____)

= _____

23. _____, because the Associative Property

is used with the operations of _____

or _____.

24. *Change the mixed numbers to improper fractions.*
Then use inverse operations.

$$1\frac{1}{2}y = 6\frac{3}{4}$$

$$y = \underline{\hspace{2cm}}$$

25. *Use inverse operations.*

$$\frac{1}{8}m - \frac{1}{4} = \frac{3}{4}$$

$$+\frac{1}{4} = + \underline{\hspace{2cm}}$$

$$\frac{1}{8}m = \underline{\hspace{2cm}}$$

$$m = \underline{\hspace{2cm}}$$

26. a. Substitute 2 for x.

$$\frac{(5-x)^3 + 12}{(4x)} = \frac{41-x}{x^3}$$

$$\frac{(5-2)^3 + 12}{4(2)} = \frac{41-2}{2^3}$$

$$\underline{\hspace{1.5cm}} = \underline{\hspace{1.5cm}}$$

Circle: true   false

b. Substitute 3 for x.

$$\frac{(5-x)^3 + 12}{(4x)} = \frac{41-x}{x^3}$$

$$\frac{(5-3)^3 + 12}{4(3)} = \frac{41-3}{3^3}$$

$$\underline{\hspace{1.5cm}} = \underline{\hspace{1.5cm}}$$

Circle: true   false

27.

$$\left|\longleftarrow \text{312.78 mi} \longrightarrow\right|$$

A   B   C

191.9 mi

distance A to B = $\underline{\hspace{1.5cm}} - \underline{\hspace{1.5cm}}$

$$= \underline{\hspace{1.5cm}}$$

28. *Use the properties of exponents.*

$$2^3 \cdot 2^6 = \underline{\hspace{2cm}}$$

Answer: $\underline{\hspace{1.5cm}}$ bits

29. The area of a rectangle is found using the

formula: $\underline{\hspace{3cm}}$

$$(4x - y) \cdot xy = \underline{\hspace{1.5cm}} - \underline{\hspace{1.5cm}}$$

30. *Work within the absolute value bars.*

$$|-2 - 3| - 4 + (-8)$$

$$= \underline{\hspace{1.5cm}} - 4 \bigcirc 8$$

$$= \underline{\hspace{1.5cm}}$$

Name _____

Solving Multi-Step Equations page 153

New Concepts

- To simplify a complex equation, combine like terms first.
- To solve a complex equation use inverse operations and the properties of equality.

Math Language

Like terms have the same variable(s) raised to the same power.

In this example $5x$ and $-3x$ are like terms. 8 and 2 are like terms.

Justify means to give a reason for the step.

Example **Combining Like Terms**

Solve $5x + 8 - 3x + 2 = 20$. Justify each step.

$5x + 8 - 3x + 2 = 20$	
$5x - 3x + 8 + 2 = 20$	*Group like terms.*
$2x + 10 = 20$	*Combine like terms.*
$\underline{-10 = -10}$	*Subtraction Property of Equality*
$2x = 10$	*Simplify.*
$\dfrac{2x}{2} = \dfrac{10}{2}$	*Division Property of Equality*
$x = 5$	*Simplify.*

- Use the Distributive Property to eliminate symbols of inclusion such as parentheses and brackets.
- A negative sign in front of an expression means to multiply it by -1.

Example **Simplifying before Solving**

Solve $5x - (x - 3) - 1 = 18$. Justify each step.

$5x - (x - 3) - 1 = 18$	
$5x - x + 3 - 1 = 18$	*Distributive Property*
$4x + 2 = 18$	*Combine like terms.*
$\underline{-2 = -2}$	*Subtraction Property of Equality*
$4x = 16$	*Simplify.*
$\dfrac{1}{4} \cdot 4x = 16 \cdot \dfrac{1}{4}$	*Multiplication Property of Equality*
$x = 4$	*Simplify.*

Solve. Justify each step. Check the solution.

a.
$$3x + 2 - x + 7 = 16$$

$$3x - \underline{} + 2 + \underline{} = 16 \qquad \text{Arrange} \underline{} \underline{}.$$

$$\underline{}x + \underline{} = 16 \qquad \underline{} \text{ like terms.}$$

$$\underline{} - \underline{} = - \underline{} \qquad \underline{} \text{ Property of Equality}$$

$$2x = \underline{} \qquad \text{Simplify.}$$

$$\frac{1}{2} \cdot 2x = \underline{} \cdot \frac{1}{2} \qquad \underline{} \text{ Property of Equality}$$

$$x = \underline{} \qquad \text{Simplify.}$$

Check: Substitute ___ for x.

$$3x + 2 - x + 7 = 16$$

$$3(\underline{}) + 2 - \underline{} + 7 \overset{?}{=} 16$$

$$\underline{} = 16$$

b.
$$6(x - 1) = 36$$

$$6x - \underline{} = 36 \qquad \text{Distributive Property}$$

$$6x - 6 = 36 \qquad \underline{} \text{Property of Equality}$$

$$+ \underline{} = + \underline{}$$

$$6x = \underline{} \qquad \text{Simplify.}$$

$$\frac{6x}{6} = \frac{\square}{6} \qquad \underline{} \text{ Property of Equality}$$

$$x = \underline{} \qquad \underline{}.$$

Check: Substitute ___ for x.

$$6(x - 1) = 36$$

$$6(\underline{} - 1) \overset{?}{=} 36$$

$$6(\underline{}) \overset{?}{=} 36$$

$$\underline{} = 36$$

c.
$$5x - 3(x - 4) = 22$$

$$5x - 3x + \underline{} = 22 \qquad \underline{} \text{ Property}$$

$$\underline{}x + \underline{} = 22 \qquad \text{Combine} \underline{} \underline{}.$$

$$2x + 12 = 22 \qquad \text{Subtraction Property of Equality}$$

$$\underline{} - \underline{} = - \underline{}$$

$$2x = \underline{} \qquad \underline{}.$$

$$\frac{2x}{\square} = \frac{\square}{\square} \qquad \underline{} \text{ Property of Equality}$$

$$x = \underline{} \qquad \underline{}.$$

Check: Substitute ___ for x.

$$5x - 3(x - 4) = 22$$

$$5(5) - 3(5 - 4) \overset{?}{=} 22$$

$$5(5) - 3(1) \overset{?}{=} 22$$

$$\underline{} - \underline{} \overset{?}{=} 22$$

$$\underline{} = 22$$

d. $90 + x + x = 180$

$$x = \underline{}^{\circ}$$

The measures of the angles are $\underline{}^{\circ}$, $\underline{}^{\circ}$, $\underline{}^{\circ}$.

1. $\frac{3}{4} + \frac{1}{2}x + 2 = 0$ *Add like terms.*

$\frac{1}{2}x +$ _____ $= 0$

_____ $=$ _____

$\frac{1}{2}x =$ _____

_____ $\cdot x =$ _____ $\cdot$ _____

$x =$ _____

2. *The value of the dependent variable depends on the value of the independent variable.*

Circle the answer.

A independent: value of 1 quarter; dependent: number of quarters

B independent: value of 1 quarter; dependent: value of quarters

C independent: value of quarters; dependent: number of quarters

D independent: number of quarters; dependent: value of quarters

3. *Look for expressions that have two or more terms with the same variable.*

Simplify.

Circle the answer.

A $6(5x + 1)$ B $2x(3 + 8)$

C $7x + 5$ D $9x - 6y + 4$

4. a. A circle graph is used to show

_____ of a _____.

b. A _____ graph is the best way to display the data showing change over time.

5. Let $s =$ the number of songs

$2($_____$) - 16 =$ _____s

_____ $=$ _____s

_____ $= s$

6. Methods for solving $12(x + 7) = 96$:

Method I: Use the _____

Property first, then use _____ operations.

Method II: _____ by _____ first,

then use _____ operations.

7. $-5(3x - 7) + 11 = 1$

$-15x +$ _____ $+ 11 = 1$ _____ Property

$-15x +$ _____ $= 1$ Combine _____ _____.

_____ $= -$_____   _____ Property of Equality

$-15x =$ _____   Simplify.

$\frac{x}{\square} = \frac{\square}{\square}$ _____ Property of Equality

$x =$ _____   Simplify.

8. *Use the vertical line test.*

The graph

_____

a function.

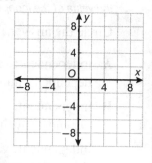

9. *Use the vertical line test.*

The relation

_____

a function.

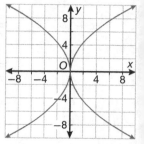

10.
$$0.4m + 2.05 = 10.45$$

$$100(0.4m) + \underline{\quad}(2.05) = \underline{\quad}(10.45)$$

$$40m + \underline{\qquad} = \underline{\qquad}$$

$$\underline{\qquad} = \underline{\qquad}$$

$$40m = \underline{\qquad}$$

$$m = \underline{\qquad}$$

11. Student _____ is correct.

Student _____ did not multiply each

_____ by the correct _____

of ten.

12.
$$7x - 12 = 44$$

$$7(\underline{\quad}) - 12 \overset{?}{=} 44$$

$$\underline{\qquad} - 12 \overset{?}{=} 44$$

$$\underline{\qquad} \overset{?}{=} 44$$

Is $x = 8$ is a solution for

$7x - 12 = 44$? _____

If not, explain. _____

13. Let $h =$ the number of hot dogs in a package

a. _____ $h +$ _____ $=$ _____

b. _____ $h +$ _____ $=$ _____

$$h = \underline{\quad}$$

Evaluate the answer.

$$\underline{\quad}(\underline{\quad}) + \underline{\quad} = \underline{\quad}$$

There are _____ hot dogs in each package.

14. _____ $h =$ _____

$$h = \underline{\qquad} \text{ hops}$$

15. Substitute $x =$ _____ into $y = 2x + 9$ to see if the result is true.

$$y = (2)\underline{\quad} + 9$$

$$y = \underline{\quad} + 9$$

$$y = \underline{\quad}$$

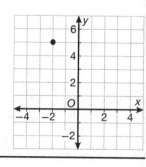

16. $(3p^2qd^3) + (2qdp \cdot -5d^2p)$

$= (3p^2qd^3) + (-\underline{\hspace{2cm}})$

Combining the terms _____ possible

because there are _____ terms.

17. $P(\text{rain on Monday}) = \underline{\hspace{1cm}}$

$P(\underline{\hspace{3cm}}) = \underline{\hspace{1cm}}a$

18. $r = 2$ micrometers $\pi = 3.14$

$V = \frac{4}{3}\pi r^3$

$V = \frac{4}{3}(\underline{\hspace{1cm}})(\underline{\hspace{1cm}})^3$

$V = \frac{4}{3}(\underline{\hspace{1cm}})(\underline{\hspace{1cm}})$

$V = \underline{\hspace{1.5cm}}$

The volume of the cell is about

_____ micrometers³.

19. $P(\text{waiter})$

$= \underline{\hspace{2cm}}$

20. $\sqrt{324} - \sqrt{144} \bigcirc \sqrt{400} - \sqrt{289}$

$\underline{\hspace{1cm}} - \underline{\hspace{1cm}} \bigcirc \underline{\hspace{1cm}} - \underline{\hspace{1cm}}$

$\underline{\hspace{1cm}} \bigcirc \underline{\hspace{1cm}}$

21. $\frac{6}{2}[5(3 + 4)]$

$= \frac{6}{2}[5(\underline{\hspace{1cm}})]$

$= \frac{6}{2}(\underline{\hspace{1cm}})$

$= \underline{\hspace{1.5cm}}$

22. Model $-8 - (-4) - (-6)$.

Simplify.

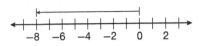

$-8 - (-4) - (-6) = \underline{\hspace{2cm}}$

23. $2 \cdot (3 + 4)^2 + 15$

$= 2 \cdot$ _____ $+ 15$

$=$ _____

24. $\dfrac{1}{4} - \dfrac{1}{3}$

$= \dfrac{\square}{\square} - \dfrac{\square}{\square}$

$= \dfrac{\square}{\square}$

25. $\dfrac{1}{6} \cdot \dfrac{\square}{\square} \cdot \dfrac{\square}{\square} \cdot \dfrac{\square}{\square} \cdot \dfrac{\square}{\square}$

$= \dfrac{\square^{\square}}{\square}$

26. a. $P\left(1 + \dfrac{r}{4}\right)^{4t}$ has _____ term(s).

b. $P\left(1 + \dfrac{r}{4}\right)^{4t}$ has _____ variable(s).

c. In $P\left(1 + \dfrac{r}{4}\right)^{4t}$, the coefficient of t is

_____.

27. $\dfrac{1}{3}Bh$

coefficient(s): _____

variable(s): _____

number of terms: _____

28. *1 acre = 4840 square yards*

a. 6,574,481 × 4840 = _____ yd²

b. *1 mile = 1760 yards*

_____ yd² $\times \dfrac{1 \text{mi}}{1760 \text{ yd}} \times \dfrac{1 \text{ mi}}{1760 \text{ yd}}$

$\dfrac{\square}{3,097,600} =$ _____ mi²

29. The volume measured using formulas

$V = lwh$ and $V = wlh$ is the _____.

The _____ Property of

_____ states that the

terms can be multiplied in a different

_____ and the product stays

the _____.

30.

Color	Tally	Frequency
Blue		
Red		
Yellow		
Green		

The frequency of the spinner landing on

blue is _____

Identifying Misleading Representations
of Data page 159

New Concepts

Example **Identifying Misleading Line Graphs**

The line graph shows the number of members of a health club each month since it opened. **Explain why the graph may be misleading.**

The graph's scale does not start at zero. The graph is misleading because the membership appears to have increased more than it actually did.

When there is a large gap in data values the **broken axis symbol** is used in a scale.

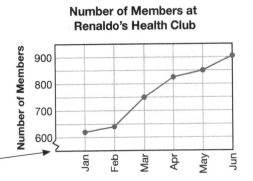

Number of Members at Renaldo's Health Club

Example **Identifying Misleading Bar Graphs**

A radio station conducted a survey of music preferences of listeners. The bar graph shows the results. **Explain why the graph may be misleading.**

The large increments of the vertical scale (0–500) make the data values appear to be closer than they actually are.

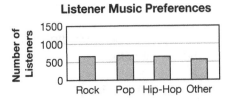

Listener Music Preferences

Example **Identifying Misleading Circle Graphs**

The circle graph shows the number of some types of sandwiches a deli sells in one day. **Explain why the graph may be misleading.**

The title does not specify that these were the only sandwiches the deli sold. The circle graph may not represent all categories. The deli may also serve other types of sandwiches, making the graph misleading.

A circle graph shows parts of a whole. If all of the parts are not shown, the graph will be misleading.

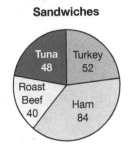

Sandwiches

Explain why each graph may be misleading.

a. The graph shows the number of miles a car traveled each year.

The vertical scale does not begin at _____,

so the change in the number of _____ driven is more noticeable.

The title does not specify whether the _____

or the _____ traveled the miles shown.

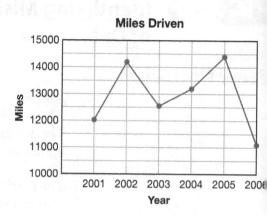

Miles Driven

b. The graph shows the baking temperatures of various foods.

The large increments make the _____ appear

to be _____ than they actually are.

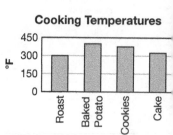

Cooking Temperatures

c. The circle graph shows the number of some kinds of dogs sold by a pet store.

The graph's title does not specify that these were the only

_____ sold in the pet shop. The graph may not

represent all _____ sold.

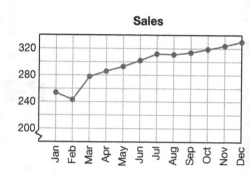

Types of Dogs Sold

A sales person created this graph to display the number of products he sold each month.

d. Explain why the graph may be misleading.

The vertical axis has a broken _____, so the

number of products sold appears _____

_____.

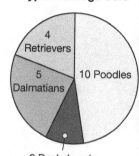

Sales

e. Why might the salesperson have created this graph? The salesperson may have wanted it to appear that

sales _____ from the beginning to the end of the year.

f. Make a graph of the sales data that is not misleading.

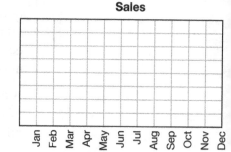

Sales

1. $(-2 + 3) \div (4 - 5 + 3)$

   $=$ _____ $\div$ _____

   $=$ _____

2. $0.5x - 0.2 = 0.15$

   Multiply by 10^2.

   _____ $\cdot 0.5x -$ _____ $\cdot 0.2 =$ _____ $\cdot 0.15$

   _____ $x -$ _____ $=$ _____

   _____ $x =$ _____

   $x =$ _____

3. *Combine like terms.*

   $\frac{1}{4} + \frac{2}{5}x + 1 = 2\frac{1}{4}$

   _____ $+ \frac{2}{5}x = 2\frac{1}{4}$

   $\frac{2}{5}x =$ _____

   $x =$ _____

4. *Use inverse operations.*

   $-0.4n + 0.305 = 0.295$

   Circle the answer.

   A 0.025

   B −0.025

   C 0.0004

   D −0.7375

5. Draw two parallel lines perpendicular to the y-axis.

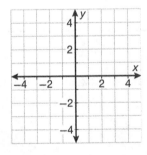

   The graph _____ a function.

6. $3 \cdot (9 \cdot 5) = (3 \cdot 9) \cdot 5$

   _____Property of

   _____

7. $y = f(x)$

   Let $s =$ speed

   Let $d($____$) =$ stopping distance

   $d($____$) =$ _____^{2}

8. Only _____ animals are shown on the graph.

   The title does not specify that the animals listed are only _____ of the _____ species in the petting zoo.

9. *Evaluate.*

$$5x + 8 - 3x + 4 = 20$$

$$5(\underline{}) + 8 - 3(\underline{}) + 4 = 20$$

$$\underline{} + 8 - \underline{} + 4 = 20$$

$$\underline{} = 20$$

4 _____ a solution to the equation.

10. The result of Brand A is _____.

The result of Brand B is _____.

The result of Brand C is _____.

The result of Brand D is _____.

Twice as many people preferred Brand A

over Brand D is a _____ statement.

11. Since all of the numbers are in _____,

the student could use a scale of 0 to _____

and state on the graph that the numbers

are given in _____.

12. Machine _____ appears to produce about

_____ times more parts than Machine

_____ each day.

Machine _____ appears to be less

efficient.

13. Large intervals on a scale can make changes in data appear less than they actually are.

Circle the answer: true or false?

14. Let h = number of hours spent kayaking

(# of persons)(___ per hr)(h) + (# of persons)(___ per life jacket) + parking = cost

The friends spent _____ hours kayaking.

15.

$$S = (4 \cdot \tfrac{1}{2}bh) + b^2$$

$$\underline{} = (4 \cdot \tfrac{1}{2}\underline{}h) + \underline{}^2$$

$$\underline{} = \underline{}h + \underline{}$$

$$\underline{} = h$$

$$h = \underline{}$$

16. To solve $0.35 + 0.22x = 1.67$, the first step

is to use inverse _____.

Begin by _____ 0.35 from both

_____ of the equation.

17. Plot the missing data.

Minutes of first ten calls

___	___
0	2, ___, 9
___	___, ___, ___, ___
___	2, ___
___	___

Key: 1|0 means 10

_____ appears most in the leaves column.

18. *Solve one of the equations.*

$$-\frac{3}{4}x = 12$$

$$\underline{}\left(-\frac{3}{4}x\right) = \underline{}(12)$$

$$x = \underline{}$$

$$\frac{5}{32}x = -2\frac{1}{2}$$

$$\frac{5}{32}x = -\frac{\square}{\square}$$

$$\underline{}\left(\frac{5}{32}x\right) = \underline{}\left(-\frac{\square}{\square}\right)$$

$$x = \underline{}$$

19. Graph the ordered pair $(-1, 0)$.

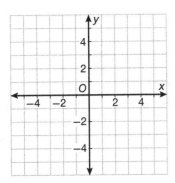

20. $r = $ _____ − _____

$r = $ _____

21. 1 rupee = 0.025 dollars

37 dollars · $\dfrac{\square}{\square}$

37 American dollars = _____ Indian rupees

22. data set: $\{8, 9, 11, 12, 15\}$; mean: 11

absolute deviation for 12:

$$|12 - \underline{}| = |\underline{}| = \underline{}$$

absolute deviation for 11:

$$|11 - \underline{}| = |\underline{}| = \underline{}$$

absolute deviation for 9:

$$|9 - \underline{}| = |-2| = \underline{}$$

absolute deviation for 8:

$$|8 - \underline{}| = |\underline{}| = \underline{}$$

23. Let x = number of calendars
Let y = number of candles
$3 profit made on each item sold

Answer: _____

24. $P(\text{heads}) = \dfrac{\text{\# favorable outcomes}}{\text{total \# of outcomes}}$

$P(\text{heads}) = \dfrac{\Box}{\Box}$

For each toss of the coin, the probability of heads remains the _____.

---

25. *Use the order of operations.*

$11 \cdot 3 + 7$

= _____

26. Let $d =$ _____   Let $q =$ _____

a. _____ · _____ + _____ · _____

b. *Evaluate.*

_____ + _____ = _____

The value of change in the machine with 21 quarters and 13 dimes is

_____ .

---

27. $\dfrac{1}{3} + \dfrac{1}{5} \cdot \dfrac{2}{15}$ ◯ $\left(\dfrac{1}{3} + \dfrac{1}{5}\right) \cdot \dfrac{2}{15}$

$\dfrac{1}{3} +$ _____ ◯ _____ $\cdot \dfrac{2}{15}$

_____ ◯ _____

28. The number of stairs the man runs up

_____ the number of stairs the man runs

_____ gives the man's position at the

end of his run.

---

29. *See page 2 in the* Student Reference Guide.

$10 \cdot 4^2 + 72 \div 2^3$

= $10 \cdot$ _____ + $72 \div$ _____

= _____ + _____

= _____

_____ the _____ .

_____ and _____ from left to right.

_____ .

---

30. *A financial report often uses decimals and fractions.*

The numbers in a financial report are _____ numbers because _____

numbers cannot be shown as _____ or _____ .

Solving Equations with Variables on Both Sides page 164

New Concepts

Exploration 📖 page 164

Use your textbook to complete the exploration.

Example **Simplifying Before Solving**

Solve $5(2x + 4) - 2x = 6 + 2(3x + 12)$. Justify each step.

$$5(2x + 4) - 2x = 6 + 2(3x + 12)$$

$10x + 20 - 2x = 6 + 6x + 24$	*Distributive Property*
$(10x - 2x) + 20 = 6x + (6 + 24)$	*Commutative Property*
$8x + 20 = 6x + 30$	*Combine like terms.*
$\underline{\quad -6x \qquad = -6x}$	*Subtraction Property of Equality*
$2x + 20 = 30$	*Simplify.*
$\underline{\quad -20 = -20}$	*Subtraction Property of Equality*
$2x = 10$	*Simplify.*
$\dfrac{2x}{2} = \dfrac{10}{2}$	*Division Property of Equality*
$x = 5$	*Simplify.*

Lesson Practice 📖 page 167

Solve each equation. Justify each step. Check the solution.

a. $6x = 3x + 27$

$\underline{\quad -3x = -\rule{1cm}{0.4pt}}$ _____ Property of Equality

$3x = \rule{1.5cm}{0.4pt}$ Simplify.

$\dfrac{3x}{\square} = \dfrac{\square}{\square}$ _____ Property of Equality

$x = \rule{1cm}{0.4pt}$ _____.

Check:

$6x = 3x + 27, x = \rule{1cm}{0.4pt}$

$6(\rule{1cm}{0.4pt}) \stackrel{?}{=} 3(\rule{1cm}{0.4pt}) + 27$

$\rule{1.5cm}{0.4pt} \stackrel{?}{=} \rule{1.5cm}{0.4pt} + 27$

$\rule{1.5cm}{0.4pt} = \rule{1.5cm}{0.4pt}$

b. $2 + 3(3x - 6) = 5(x - 3) + 15$ Check: 📓

$2 + 9x - 18 = \underline{\quad} x - \underline{\quad} + 15$ Distributive Property

$9x - \underline{\quad} = 5x$ Combine like terms.

$\underline{\quad -5x = -5x\quad}$ _____ Property of Equality.

$\underline{\quad} x - \underline{\quad} = \underline{\quad}$ Simplify.

$+ \underline{\quad} = + \underline{\quad}$ _____ Property of Equality.

$\underline{\quad} x = \underline{\quad}$ _____.

$\dfrac{\Box x}{\Box} = \dfrac{\Box}{\Box}$ _____ Property of Equality.

$x = \underline{\quad}$ _____.

Solve each equation. Justify each step. If the equation is an identity, write identity. If the equation has no solution, write no solution.

c. $2(x + 3) = 3(2x + 2) - 4x$

$2x + \underline{\quad} = 6x + \underline{\quad} - 4x$ _____ Property

$2x + \underline{\quad} = \underline{\quad} x + \underline{\quad}$ Combine _____ _____.

$\bigcirc \underline{\quad} x = \bigcirc \underline{\quad} x$ _____ Property of Equality

$\underline{\quad} = \underline{\quad}$ Simplify.

Since $\underline{\quad} = \underline{\quad}$ is always true, the equation is an _____.

d. $3(x + 4) = 2(x + 5) + x$

$3x + \underline{\quad} = 2x + \underline{\quad} + x$ _____ Property

$3x + \underline{\quad} = \underline{\quad} x + \underline{\quad}$ Combine _____ _____.

$\bigcirc \underline{\quad} x = \bigcirc \underline{\quad} x$ _____ Property of Equality

$\underline{\quad} = \underline{\quad}$ Simplify.

Since $\underline{\quad} = \underline{\quad}$ is _____ true, the equation _____ solution.

e. Let x = number of days   Members pay: $\$\underline{\quad} + \$5\underline{\quad}$ Nonmembers pay: $\$10\underline{\quad}$

$\underline{\qquad\quad} = \underline{\qquad\quad}$

$\underline{\quad} = x$

The total cost is the same for both members and nonmembers after _____ days.

1. *Multiply by the reciprocal.*

$$\underline{\hspace{1.5cm}} \cdot \frac{3}{4}y = 4\frac{7}{8} \cdot \underline{\hspace{1.5cm}}$$

$$y = \underline{\hspace{1cm}}$$

2. $3p - 4 - 6 = 2(p - 5)$

$$3p - 4 - 6 = \underline{\hspace{1cm}} - \underline{\hspace{1cm}}$$

$$3p - \underline{\hspace{1cm}} = \underline{\hspace{1cm}} - \underline{\hspace{1cm}}$$

$$p = \underline{\hspace{1cm}}$$

3. Let n = the number of nickels

Let n = the number of dimes

The amount in each pocket is the same.

$$\underline{\hspace{2.5cm}} = \underline{\hspace{2.5cm}}$$

$\underline{\hspace{1.5cm}}$ dimes

$\underline{\hspace{1.5cm}}$ nickels

4. Student $\underline{\hspace{1cm}}$ is correct.

Student $\underline{\hspace{1cm}}$ incorrectly distributed

$$\underline{\hspace{6cm}}$$

$$\underline{\hspace{6cm}}$$

5. Let p = the number of $\underline{\hspace{3cm}}$

$$\underline{\hspace{1cm}} + \underline{\hspace{1cm}} p = \underline{\hspace{1cm}} + \underline{\hspace{1cm}} p$$

$$p = \underline{\hspace{1.5cm}}$$

6. $(x + 15)\frac{1}{3} = 2x - 1$

Use the distributive property.

$$\frac{1}{3}x + \underline{\hspace{1.5cm}} = 2x - 1$$

Circle the answer.

A $\frac{18}{5}$ **B** $\frac{5}{18}$

C $\frac{18}{7}$ **D** $\frac{7}{18}$

7. Student $\underline{\hspace{1cm}}$ is correct.

Student $\underline{\hspace{1cm}}$ did not $\underline{\hspace{2.5cm}}$

$$\underline{\hspace{6cm}}$$

8. For yx and zx to be equal, zx must be

$\underline{\hspace{3cm}}$. Since z is negative, x must

be $\underline{\hspace{3cm}}$.

9. *Use the appearance of the graph.*

    a. The length of the bar for sheet 4 is

        about _____ times the length of the bar

        for sheet 3.

    b. $\dfrac{\square}{\square}$ = about _____

10. A broken scale makes the changes in the

    data appear _____ (greater/

    lesser), so the statement is _____.

---

11. a. Use the data in the table to complete this graph.

    b. Compare the lengths of the bars for Dunston
        and Reefville.

        On average, a house in Dunston would cost

        _____ times more than a house in Reefville.

    c. The clients may conclude that the prices of homes

        in Reefville are much _____ than the prices of
        homes in other cities.

Average Home Prices

Price (in thousands): $400, $360, $320, $280, $240, $200, 0

Woodside, Reefville, Boynton, Dunston, York

---

12. a. *Find the greatest and least x-values.*

    Domain: {_____ $\leq x \leq$ _____}

    Find the greatest and least y-values.

    Range: {_____ $\leq y \leq$ _____}

    b. The relation _____ a function.

        Each value is paired with exactly

        one value.

---

13. *Find the coordinates of each point.*

    Circle the answer.

    A $\{(1, 4.5), (2, 6), (3, 10), (4, 14.5)\}$

    B $\{(1, 5), (2, 6), (3, 10), (4, 15)\}$

    C $\{(4.5, 1), (6, 2), (10, 3), (14.5, 4)\}$

    D $\{(5, 1), (6, 2), (10, 3), (15, 4)\}$

14. *"Of" means multiply.*

    0.28 of what number is 18.2?

    _____ = _____

    $x =$ _____

---

15. a. Let $C =$ _____ Let $m =$ _____

$C = \$0.05$_____ + _____

b. *Convert hours to minutes.*

$1\frac{1}{2}$ hours: 2 hours:

$C = \$0.05($_____$) +$ _____ $C = \$0.05($_____$) +$ _____

It will cost between $\$$_____ and $\$$_____ to do the research.

---

16. A line graph can analyze change over time.

The statement is _____.

If the statement is false, explain why.

_____

17. See 📖 page 169.

Answer: (_____ , _____)

---

18. Let $x =$ _____

_____ + _____

$=$ _____

19. a. Let $m =$ _____

George: _____$m +$ _____

Frank: _____$m +$ _____

b. *Combine like terms.*

_____

---

20. Let $g =$ the old grade.

_____

21. $F = \dfrac{m_1 m_2}{d^2}$

$F = \dfrac{\square\,\square}{\square^2}$

$F =$ _____

---

22. Method I: *Use the Distributive Property.*

$8(10 - 4) =$ ____ $\bigcirc$ ____ $=$ _____

Method II: *Use order of operations.*

$8(10 - 4) = 8($____$) =$ _____

23. $\sqrt{49} + 4^2$

$=$ _____ $+$ _____

$=$ _____

---

24. Circle the answer: true or false?
Justify your answer.

_____; _____ Property of

_____

25. $n = -3$ $p = 1$

$3(\underline{\quad})^2 \cdot (\underline{\quad})^5 + 4(\underline{\quad} - 8)^2$

$= 3(\underline{\quad}) \cdot (\underline{\quad}) + 4(\underline{\quad})$

$= (\underline{\quad}) \cdot (\underline{\quad}) + (\underline{\quad})$

$= \underline{\quad}$

26. *A counterexample proves a statement is not true.*

Example: $\sqrt{3} - \sqrt{3} = \underline{\quad}$

An irrational number subtracted from

itself equals _____. _____ is not an

irrational number.

27. *Combine like terms.*

$(7x + 1) + (3x + 3) + 1 + (4x + 2) + x + (2x + 6)$

$= \underline{\quad} + \underline{\quad}$

28. The probability for each toss of the coin is _____.

a. _____ numbers

b. The probability of an event certain to occur is _____. The probability of an event that
is impossible is _____.

_____, _____ and _____ can be a probability.

29. *1 mile = 5,280 feet*

The student will _____ because

the the conversion is from a _____

unit, miles, to a _____ unit, feet.

30. A graph that shows change over

_____ could be represented by a

continuous graph.

For example: _____

_____

LESSON 29

Solving Literal Equations page 171

New Concepts

- To solve for one variable in a literal equation, isolate it on one side.
- The solution will be written in terms of the other variable(s).

Example **Solving for Variables on Both Sides**

Solve for p: $4p + 2a - 5 = 6a + p$. Justify each step.

$$4p + 2a - 5 = 6a + p$$

$$\underline{-p = -p}$$ *Eliminate the p on the right side.*

$$3p + 2a - 5 = 6a$$ *Combine like terms.*

$$\underline{-2a + 5 = -2a + 5}$$ *Eliminate the 2a − 5 from the left side.*

$$3p = 4a + 5$$ *Combine like terms.*

$$\frac{3p}{3} = \frac{4a}{3} + \frac{5}{3}$$ *Divide both sides by 3.*

$$p = \frac{4a}{3} + \frac{5}{3}$$ *Simplify.*

- You can solve for any variable in a formula.

Example **Solving a Formula for a Variable**

The formula $C = \frac{5}{9}(F - 32)$ expresses Celsius temperature in terms of Fahrenheit temperature. **Find the Fahrenheit temperature when the Celsius temperature is 20°.**

Step 1: Solve for F. $C = \frac{5}{9}(F - 32)$

$$\frac{9}{5} \cdot C = \frac{9}{5} \cdot \frac{5}{9}(F - 32)$$ *Multiplication Property of Equality*

$$\frac{9}{5}C = F - 32$$ *Simplify.*

$$\underline{+32 = +32}$$ *Addition Property of Equality*

$$\frac{9}{5}C + 32 = F$$ *Simplify.*

The formula $\frac{9}{5}C + 32 = F$ expresses Fahrenheit temperature in terms of Celsius temperature.

Step 2: Substitute 20 for C.

$$\frac{9}{5}(20) + 32 = F$$

$$36 + 32 = F$$

$$68° = F$$

---

a. Solve for n. $3m + 2n = 8$

Isolate n.

$$3m + 2n = 8$$

$$-\underline{}m = -\underline{}m$$

$$2n = 8 - \underline{}$$

$$\frac{2n}{\square} = \frac{8}{\square} - \frac{3m}{\square}$$

$$n = \underline{} - 3m\square$$

b. Solve for x. $3x + 2y = 8 + x$

$$3x + 2y = 8 + x$$

$$\underline{} - \quad x = - \quad \underline{} x$$

$$\underline{}x + 2y = 8$$

$$2x + 2y - \underline{}y = 8 - \underline{}y$$

$$2x = 8 - \underline{}y$$

$$\frac{2x}{\square} = \frac{8}{\square} - \frac{2y}{\square}$$

$$x = \underline{} - \underline{}$$

c. $F = \frac{9}{5}C + 32$. Find the Celsius temperature when the Fahrenheit temperature is 86°.

Solve for C.

$$F = \frac{9}{5}C + 32$$

$$F - \underline{} = \frac{9}{5}C + 32 - \underline{}$$

$$F - 32 = \underline{}$$

$$\underline{}(F - \underline{}) = \left(\frac{5}{9}\right)\frac{9}{5}C$$

$$\frac{5}{9}(F - \underline{}) = C$$

Substitute 86 for F.

$$C = \frac{5}{9}(F - 32)$$

$$C = \frac{5}{9}(\underline{} - 32)$$

$$C = \frac{5}{9}(\underline{})$$

$$C = \underline{}°$$

d. $V = lwh$. $V = 6\text{ ft}^3$, $l = 24$ in., $w = 12$ in. Find h.

First convert volume to in.^{3}

$$V = 6\text{ ft}^3 = 6 \cdot \underline{} \cdot \underline{} \cdot \underline{} = \underline{}\text{ in.}^3$$

Solve for h.

$$V = lwh \quad \longrightarrow \quad \frac{V}{\square \cdot \square} = h$$

Substitute.

$$h = \frac{\square}{\square \cdot \square}$$

$$h = \frac{\square}{\square} = \underline{}\text{ in.}$$

e. $F = \frac{m}{g}$. $F = 28$ miles per gallon, $m = 350$ miles. Find g.

Solve for g.

$$F = \frac{m}{g}$$

$$g = \frac{\square}{\square}$$

Substitute.

$$g = \frac{\square}{\square} = \underline{}\text{ gal}$$

1. *Use inverse operations.*

$$3x + 2y = 5 - y$$

$$\underline{\quad} = \underline{\quad}$$

$$3x = 5 \bigcirc \underline{\quad} y$$

$$3x - \underline{\quad} = \underline{\quad} y + 5 - \underline{\quad}$$

$$\frac{3x}{\square} - \frac{\square}{\square} = \frac{\underline{\quad} y}{\square}$$

$$\underline{\quad} x + \frac{\square}{\square} = y$$

2. $-2y + 6y - x - 4 = 0$

$$\underline{\quad} - x - 4 = 0$$

$$+ \underline{\quad} + \underline{\quad} = + \underline{\quad} + \underline{\quad}$$

$$4y = \underline{\quad} x + \underline{\quad}$$

$$\frac{4y}{\square} = \frac{\square x}{\square} + \frac{\square}{\square}$$

$$y = \frac{\square x}{\square} + \underline{\quad}$$

3. Without the $35 coupon, the total cost of the order is

$$\underline{\quad} \bigcirc \underline{\quad} = \$\underline{\quad}.$$

$$\text{average cost} = \frac{\square}{\square} = \boxed{} \underline{\quad}$$

4. *See page 15 in the* Student Reference Guide. Circle the answer.

A $A = s^2$ **B** $A \cdot l = w$

C $A = lw$ **D** $A = \frac{1}{2}ab$

5. The domain is the set of _____-values:

$$\{\underline{\hspace{5cm}}\}.$$

The range is the set of _____-values:

$$\{\underline{\hspace{5cm}}\}.$$

6. Which operation is first when solving $12x + 6(2x - 1) + 7 = 37$?

Circle the answer.

A Divide both sides of the equation by 12.

B Multiply $(2x - 1)$ by 6.

C Add 1 to both sides of the equation.

D Subtract 37 from both sides of the equation.

7. _____ or subtract so that terms with

an _____ variable are on one side of the

equation.

Simplify by combining _____ terms.

Multiply or _____ so the coefficient of

the _____ is _____.

8. On average Lee scored a total of

$$(\underline{\quad} t + \underline{\quad} s) \text{ points per game.}$$

Therefore, the total points he scored in all 22 games could be expressed as:

$$\underline{\quad} (\underline{\quad} t + \underline{\quad} s)$$

9. $x + x + 90 = 3y + y + 90$

$x + x = $ _____

_____$x = $ _____y

$x = $ _____y

Triangle ____ will contain the smallest angle.

10. Student _____ is correct.

By using _____ increments,

Student _____ makes the differences

appear _____.

11. If y is negative, y^3 must be _____.

Given that y^3 is _____, in

order for xy^3 to be positive, x must be

_____.

12. When analyzing a circle graph, check to see

that all categories of the _____

set are represented.

13. $3^2 = $ _____ $4^2 = $ _____

$5^2 = $ _____ $6^2 = $ _____

$\sqrt{26} \approx $ _____

14. $\frac{1}{2}($____$)(x + $____$) = 5($____$x - $____$)$

____$x + $____ $= $ ____$x - $____

____$x = $ ____

$x = $ ____

 Substitute to find areas.

Each has an area of _____ .

15. a. If Raquel pays $10 per class, c classes a month at $10 each would cost her _____ .

b. If Viola pays $15 a month for membership plus $5 per class, her monthly cost would be

_____ .

c. Solve for c.

$c = $ ____

16. *Substitute.*

$6(\underline{\hspace{1cm}}) + 8 = 74$

$\underline{\hspace{1cm}} + 8 = 74$

$x = 11$ _____ a solution.

17. A _____ is the best

graph for _____ the data.

18. *Evaluate i = 12f.*

f	i
3	
5	
8	
10	

 Graph the points on a
coordinate grid.

19. _____ because repeating decimals are

_____ numbers because

they can be expressed as _____.

The repeating number multiplied by a

variable could be _____. For

example:

_____

20. If the temperature varies by 148°F, the

_____ between the highest and

lowest temperature is 148°F.

lowest temperature: _____

21. Let $s =$ _____

$\underline{\hspace{1cm}} + \underline{\hspace{1cm}} s$

22. *Combine like terms. Order of variables within a
term does not matter.*

$x^2 - 3yx + 2yx^2 - 2xy + yx$

$= x^2 + 2yx^2 - \underline{\hspace{1cm}} xy$

23.

$-3y + \dfrac{1}{2} = \dfrac{5}{7}$

$\dfrac{-\underline{\hspace{0.5cm}}}{\underline{\hspace{1cm}}} = \dfrac{-\underline{\hspace{0.5cm}}}{\underline{\hspace{1cm}}}$

$-3y = \dfrac{\Box}{14} - \dfrac{\Box}{14}$

$-3y = \dfrac{\Box}{14}$

$\dfrac{\Box}{\Box} \cdot -3y = \dfrac{\Box}{14} \cdot \dfrac{\Box}{\Box}$

$y = \underline{\hspace{1cm}}$

24. $k + 4 - 5(k + 2) = 3k - 2$

$k + 4 - \underline{\quad} - \underline{\quad} = 3k - 2$

$- \underline{\quad} - \underline{\quad} = 3k - 2$

$+ 4k + \underline{\quad} = + \underline{\quad} + 2$

$\underline{\quad} = \underline{\quad} k$

$\dfrac{\square}{\square} = k$

25. If z plus 2 is an odd integer, then z must be an _____ integer.

26. *The farther a number is to the left of zero, the less its value.*

Answer: _____

27. $(3 + 5) - 2^3$

$= \underline{\quad} - 2^3$ Simplify inside _____.

$= \underline{\quad} - \underline{\quad}$ _____.

$= \underline{\quad}$ _____.

28. *Evaluate.*

$x = 2$

$-x - (-2) = y$

$y = \underline{\quad}$

29. $303{,}000{,}000 \times (1.015)^t$

_____ $\times$ _____ $=$ _____

30.

a. $\text{P(own a truck)} = \dfrac{\boxed{}\,\text{families own trucks}}{\boxed{}\,\text{families on the block}} = \dfrac{\square}{\square}$

b. $\underline{\quad} \times \dfrac{\square}{\square} = \underline{\quad}$ families

Graphing Functions page 179

New Concepts

- To graph an equation, use a table of ordered pairs. Substitute negative and positive numbers and zero for the x-values.
- Use the vertical line test to determine if the graph represents a function.

Math Language

A **linear equation** is an equation whose graph is a line.

A **linear function** is a function whose graph is a line. It can be written in the form $f(x) = mx + b$, where m and b are real numbers.

Example   Using Tables to Graph Functions

Use a table of values to graph the equation $y = x$. Decide whether the graph represents a function and whether it is linear or nonlinear.

Substitute values into the equation for x and identify the corresponding y-values.

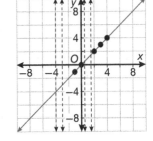

x	-1	0	2	3	4
y	-1	0	2	3	4

To draw the graph, plot the coordinate pairs and connect the points.

No vertical line will intersect the graph at more than one point, so the graph represents a function. The graph is a line, so **it is a linear function.**

Example   Identifying the Domain and Range

Use the graph to identify the domain and range of the function.

The x-values include all of the negative and positive real numbers plus zero. **The domain is all real numbers.**

The graph includes no y-values less than -2. One y-value is -2. All other y-values are greater than -2.

The range is $y \geq -2$.

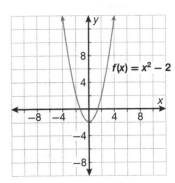

$f(x) = x^2 - 2$

a. Graph $y = 2x + 5$. Determine whether the graph shows a function and whether it is linear.

x	-2	-1	0	1	2
y					

✎ Graph.

No _____ line intercepts the graph in more than one point, so it _____ a function. The graph is a _____, so the function is a _____ function.

b. Graph $y = x^2 + 1$. Determine whether the graph shows a function and whether it is linear.

x	-2	-1	0	1	2
y					

✎ Graph.

No _____ vertical line intercepts the graph in more than one point, so it _____ a function. The graph _____ a line, so the function is _____.

c. Match the equation $y = -2x^2$ to the correct graph.

x	-2	-1	0	1	2
y					

Graph _____ includes these ordered pairs.

Use the coordinates in the tables to match the graph with each table.

d. The ordered pairs in the table for $y = \frac{1}{3}x + 1$ match Graph _____.

e. The ordered pairs in the table for $y = 3x + 1$ match Graph _____.

Identify the domain and range of the function shown in each graph.

f. The x-values begin at _____ and continue to the right of that value, so the domain is

x ◯ _____.

The y-values begin at _____ and continue above that value, so the range is y ◯ _____.

g. The x-values extend continuously to the _____ and _____, so the domain is all _____ numbers.

The y-values begin at _____ and continue _____ that value, so the range is y ◯ _____.

h. Make a graph from the table. Extend the line beyond $x = 4$. Use the graph to find how many emails were sent from 8 classes. Write the rule in function notation and use it to check your answer.

✎ Graph.

The line includes (8, _____), so _____ emails were sent from 8 classes.

The rule for the graph is $f(x) =$ _____x since _____(___) = 240 and the point (8, _____) is on the line.

1. $x + \frac{1}{2} = 2\frac{1}{5}$

$$-\frac{\square}{\square} = -\frac{\square}{\square}$$

$$x = 2\frac{1}{5} - \frac{\square}{\square}$$

$$x = \frac{\square}{10} - \frac{\square}{10}$$

$$x = \frac{\square}{10} = \underline{\qquad}$$

2. Multiply each term by _____.

$$(\underline{\quad})0.4x - (\underline{\quad})0.3 = (\underline{\quad})(-0.14)$$

$$\underline{\quad}x - \underline{\quad} = -\underline{\quad}$$

$$+\underline{\quad} = +\underline{\quad}$$

$$\underline{\quad}x = \underline{\quad}$$

$$x = \frac{\square}{\square}$$

$$x = \underline{\quad}.\underline{\quad}$$

3. Combine like terms.

$$\frac{1}{3} + \frac{5}{12}x - 2 = 6\frac{2}{3}$$

$$\frac{5}{12}x \bigcirc \underline{\qquad} = 6\frac{2}{3}$$

$$x = \underline{\quad}$$

4. Combine like terms.

$$\frac{2}{3} - \frac{4}{9}x + 1 = 2\frac{7}{9}$$

$$x = \underline{\qquad}$$

5. $x - \underline{\quad}x \bigcirc \underline{\quad} + 7 = 6 - x \bigcirc 4$

$$\underline{\quad}x \bigcirc \underline{\quad} = \underline{\quad} - x$$

$$\underline{\quad} = \underline{\quad}x$$

$$\frac{\square}{\square} = x$$

 Substitute to check.

6. Use the vertical line test.

_____ because a _____ line

crosses the circle at more than _____ point.

7. Complete the table using the graph.

c	0	50	100	150	200
s					

These ordered pairs match Graph _____.

8. Complete the table using the graph.

x	−2	0	2	4	6
y					

Answer: _____

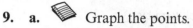

9. **a.** Graph the points.

b. *Use the vertical line test.*

_____ because a _____ line crosses

the graph _____ point at a time.

c. Because the graph does not represent a

_____ function, a prediction for
what the y-value will be when $t = 3$
cannot be made.

10. Use the table to make a graph.

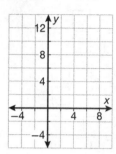

The graph _____ linear because

_____.

11. Student _____ is correct.

Student _____

_____.

12. $A_{rectangle} = $ _____ (_____ $x - $ _____)

$A_{unshaded} = $ _____ x

Subtract to solve.

Area of the shaded part: _____

13.
$$\frac{x}{2} + \frac{y}{3} = 2$$

$$\underline{\quad}\left(\frac{1}{2} - x + \frac{1}{3} - y\right) = \underline{\quad}(2)$$

$$\underline{\quad}\, x + \underline{\quad}\, y = \underline{\quad}$$

$$\underline{\quad} \qquad\qquad \underline{\quad}$$

$$2y = -\underline{\quad}\, x + \underline{\quad}$$

$$\frac{2y}{\Box} = \frac{\Box\, x}{\Box} + \frac{\Box}{\Box}$$

$$y = \underline{\quad}\, x + \underline{\quad}$$

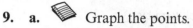 Evaluate for $x = 3$.

$$y = \underline{\quad}$$

14. $I = Prt$

$r = \underline{\quad}$

15. *Use the order of operations.*

Answer: _____

16. Student _____ is correct. Student _____

_____

_____.

17. 1 cm = 50 km

_____ $x =$ _____

$x =$ _____

18. Circle the answer.

  A Using a broken scale on the horizontal axis

  B Using a broken scale on the vertical axis

  C Using larger intervals

  D Using smaller intervals

19. On graphs with large intervals, changes in data appear _____ than they actually are.

20. A circle graph is best for displaying data to show _____ of a whole. The title implies that fruit punch and orange juice are the _____ drinks sold. A _____ graph would be more appropriate to compare the data.

21.

Woodmont Temperatures (°F)

Stem	Leaves
5	
6	
7	2
8	

Key: 7|2 means 72

22. $h = 2 + 0.5m$

m	h
4	
6	
10	
20	

 Graph.

23. From 0 to 9, there are _____ possible keys from which to choose.

The chance of choosing 5 is _____ out of a total of _____ possible choices.

$\dfrac{\square}{\square} =$ _____ = _____

24. *Multiply by the reciprocal.*

$18x \div 6$

$= 18 \cdot \dfrac{1}{6} \cdot x$

_____
Property of Multiplication

$= \left(18 \cdot \dfrac{1}{6}\right)x$

_____
Property of Multiplication

$=$ _____ x

_____.

25. *See page 2 in the* Student Reference Guide.

$$5.2 - 1.6 + 4.08 + 8$$

$$= \underline{\hspace{1cm}} + 4.08 + 8 \quad \text{Subtract} \underline{\hspace{1.5cm}}$$
from left to right.

$$= \underline{\hspace{1cm}} + 8 \qquad \underline{\hspace{1cm}} \text{ in order from}$$
left to right.

$$= \underline{\hspace{1cm}} \qquad\qquad \underline{\hspace{1.5cm}}.$$

26. To convert cm^2 to m^2, the unit ratio was

applied _____ times.

To convert cm^3 to m^3, the unit ratio would

be applied _____ times.

To convert a unit u^n, apply the unit

ratio _____ times.

27. *See page 2 in the* Student Reference Guide.

$$3 + \left(\frac{5 - 2}{4} + 2^2 \right)$$

28. $15 \cdot \$2 + (23 - 15) \cdot \frac{1}{4} \cdot \$2$

$$= 15 \cdot \$2 + (\underline{\hspace{0.8cm}}) \cdot \frac{1}{4} \cdot \$2$$

$$= \underline{\hspace{0.8cm}} + (\underline{\hspace{0.8cm}}) \cdot \underline{\hspace{0.8cm}}$$

$$= \underline{\hspace{0.8cm}} + \underline{\hspace{0.8cm}}$$

$$= \underline{\hspace{1cm}}$$

29. As the exponent grows larger, _____

becomes smaller because when a number

_____ than 1 is multiplied by itself the

product _____.

30. The graph shows a line with a _____

slope. The y-values decrease as the x-values

_____.

Situation that the graph might model:

_____

_____

Name _____

Analyzing the Effects of Bias in Sampling, Surveys, and Bar Graphs page 187

Math Language

A **population** is a group that someone is gathering data about.

A **sample** is a part of a population.

A sample is **random** if every member of the population has an equal chance of being chosen.

A **biased sample** does not represent the entire population.

- Researchers often use data from part of a population to draw conclusions about the entire population.
- Refer to the Sampling Method chart on 📖 page 187 for five sampling methods that describe part of a population.
- A good survey chooses a representative sample.

Give reasons why the sample may be biased.

1. To decide whether to add a new cheese sauce to the menu, a chef asks the first four customers who order the new cheese sauce if they like it.

   Customers who order cheese sauce probably like _____.

2. To find out what subject teachers preferred when they were in high school, a group of science teachers is asked what their favorite subject was in high school.

   Most science teachers' favorite subject is _____.

3. To find out what library services people use most, a librarian sends questionnaires to families with children.

   Families without _____ are not surveyed.

4. Give an example of an unbiased sample.

   _____ survey visitors leaving the zoo.

5. Describe a systematic sampling method.

   Survey every _____ visitor leaving the zoo.

6. Would it be biased to only survey families with children? Explain.

   _____; People visiting with children might only visit the zoo

   because _____.

- A good survey uses unbiased questions.

Create one biased and one unbiased question for each survey.

*A **biased question** attempts to exclude unwanted responses and lead participants to respond in a certain way.*

7. A restaurant owner polls ten patrons on whether they enjoyed the chef's special.

   _____ question: Didn't you like the special tonight?

   _____ question: How was the special?

8. A music store questions five customers about their listening habits.

Biased: _____

_____

Unbiased: _____

_____

Exploration 📖 page 189

Use your textbook to complete the exploration.

Investigation Practice 📖 page 189

Managers of an apartment complex want to know what visitors to the complex think of the complex and the complex employees. They survey every fifth person who signs a lease.

a. What is the population? *What group do the managers want to know about?*

_____

b. Identify the sample. *What group was surveyed?*

_____

c. Which sampling method was used? *Review sampling methods on* 📖 *page 187.* Circle the answer.

A random   **B** systematic   **C** stratified   **D** voluntary

d. What is a possible bias for this survey?

People who _____ the complex but do not _____ will not be included.

e. The areas of four oceans are shown on the chart in your textbook. Create a graph that is misleading on the left. Then redraw your graph so it is not misleading on the right.

Large increments will make the data values appear to be closer to each other than they really are.

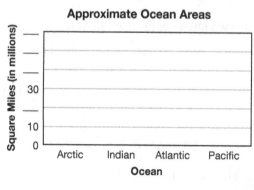

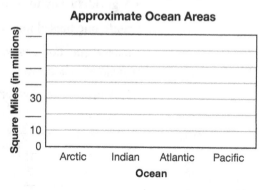

New Concepts

Example **Converting Rates**

A bus driver drives 30 miles per hour. What is the rate of the bus in miles per minute?

$$\frac{30 \text{ mi}}{1 \text{ hr}} \cdot \frac{1 \text{ hr}}{60 \text{ min}} \qquad \textit{Multiply by a conversion factor.}$$

$$\frac{^1 30 \text{ miles}}{1 \text{ hour}} \cdot \frac{1 \text{ hour}}{_2 60 \text{ minutes}} \qquad \textit{Cancel and simplify the units of measure.}$$

The driver drives 1 mile per 2 minutes or $\frac{1}{2}$ **mile per minute.**

Example **Solving Proportions Using Cross Products**

Solve each proportion.

$$\frac{(x-1)}{12} = \frac{1}{6}$$

$$6(x-1) = (1)(12) \qquad \textit{Write the cross products.}$$

$$6x - 6 = 12 \qquad \textit{Distribute and multiply.}$$

$$6x - 6 + 6 = 12 + 6 \qquad \textit{Addition Property of Equality}$$

$$6x = 18 \qquad \textit{Simplify.}$$

$$\frac{6x}{6} = \frac{18}{6} \qquad \textit{Division Property of Equality}$$

$$x = 3 \qquad \textit{Simplify.}$$

Example **Solving Multi-Step Proportions**

How many boys and how many girls are in the class?

The ratio of boys to girls in a class is 3:2. The class has 25 students in all.

There are 3 boys to each group of 5 students.

$$\frac{3}{5} = \frac{\text{number of boys}}{\text{total in class}} \qquad \textit{Write a ratio for boys.}$$

$$\frac{3}{5} = \frac{b}{25} \qquad \textit{Write the proportion.}$$

$$3 \cdot 25 = 5 \cdot b \qquad \textit{Write the cross products.}$$

$$75 = 5b \qquad \textit{Multiply.}$$

$$15 = b \qquad \textit{Divide both sides by 5.}$$

There are **15 boys** in the class. So, there are $25 - 15$ or **10 girls** in the class.

a. Which is the better buy: 8 boxes for $4.96 or 5 boxes for $3.25?

$\dfrac{\$\square}{8 \text{ boxes}} = \$\_\_\_\_\_$; $\dfrac{\square}{5 \text{ boxes}} = \$\_\_\_\_$ Compare: $\$\_\_\_\_$ per box $\bigcirc$ $\$\_\_\_\_$ per box

____ boxes for $ _____ is a better buy.

b. A chemist raised the temperature of a liquid 45° F in 1 minute. What is the amount in degrees

Fahrenheit per second? $\dfrac{45 \text{ degrees}}{1 \text{ min}} \cdot \dfrac{\square \text{ min}}{\square \text{ s}} = \dfrac{\square ° \text{ F}}{\square \text{ per second}}$

c. Jamie typed 20 pages in 2 hours. How many pages did she type in 1 minute?

$\dfrac{20 \text{ pages}}{\square \text{ hr}} \cdot \dfrac{\square}{\square} = \dfrac{\square}{\square}$ page(s) per minute

Solve each proportion.

d. $\dfrac{c}{7} = \dfrac{3}{21}$:

____ $\cdot c =$ ___ $\cdot$ ___

____ $c =$ ____

$c =$ ____

e. $\dfrac{5}{(n+2)} = \dfrac{10}{16}$

$5 \cdot$ ___ $=$ ___ $\cdot ($ _____ $)$

___ $=$ __ $n +$ ____

___ $=$ __ n

___ $= n$

f. The ratio of blue chips to red chips is 5:7. The bag has 60 chips in all. How many blue chips

and how many red chips are in the bag? $\dfrac{5}{12} = \dfrac{b}{6}$ _____ $=$ ___b ____ $= b$

There are ____ blue chips and ____ red chips.

g. A map shows a 5.5-inch distance between Orange City and Newtown, and a 3.75-inch distance from Newtown to Westville. The map's scale is 1 inch:100 miles. What is the actual distance from

Orange City via Newtown to Westville?   Orange City to Newtown: 5.5 $\cdot$ ____ $=$ ____ miles

Newtown to Westville: ____ $\cdot$ ____ $=$ ____ miles   Total: ____ $+$ ____ $=$ ____ miles

h. If Jeff walks 4 miles in 48 minutes, how far can he walk in 72 minutes?

$\dfrac{4}{\square} = \dfrac{x}{\square}$ ___ $\cdot x =$ ___ $\cdot$ ___   ___$x =$ ____ $x =$ ____

He can walk _____ miles in 72 minutes.

1. $7 - 4 - 5 + 12 - 2 - |-2| =$ _____

2. $-6 \cdot 3 + \left| -3(-4 + 2^3) \right| =$ _____

3. $-0.05n + 1.8 = 1.74$

$n =$ _____

4. $-y - 8 + 6y = -9 + 5y + 2$

$y =$ _____

5. $2x - 4.5 = \frac{1}{2}(x + 3)$

Multiply both sides by 2. Then solve for x.

Circle the answer.

A 9   B 2.4

C 2   D 4

6. Solve for y.
$4 + 2x + 2y - 3 = 5$

$2y = 5 -$ ____ $-$ ____ $+$ ____

$2y =$ ___ $-$ ___x

$y =$ ___ $-$ ___

7. *See page 3 in the* Student Reference Guide.

$4k(2c - a + 3m)$

$=$ _____ $-$ _____ $+$ _____

8. $3x^2 + 2y$ when $x = -2$ and $y = 5$

$3(\_\_\_)^2 + 2(\_\_\_)$

$= 3(\_\_\_) +$ ____

$=$ ____ $+$ ____

$=$ ____

9. $2(a^2 - b)^2 + 3a^3b$ when $a = -3$ and $b = 2$

$2(\underline{\quad} - \underline{\quad})^2 + 3(\underline{\quad})^3(\underline{\quad})$

$= 2 (\underline{\quad})^2 + 3(\underline{\quad})(\underline{\quad})$

$= \underline{\quad} + \underline{\quad} = \underline{\quad}$

10. 10 boxes for $42.50

$\dfrac{\$\square}{\square}$ boxes

$= \underline{\quad}$ per box

---

11. *Write and solve a proportion.*

$\dfrac{4}{\square} = \dfrac{n}{\square}$

$\underline{\quad} \cdot n = \underline{\quad} \cdot 10.5$

$\underline{\quad}\, n = \underline{\quad}$

$n = \underline{\quad}$

12. *Write and solve a proportion.*

$\dfrac{3}{13} = \dfrac{\square}{\square}$

$\underline{\quad} \cdot x = 13 \cdot \underline{\quad}$

$\underline{\quad}\, x = \underline{\quad}$

$x = \underline{\quad}$ foxes

---

13. $170 + 40 = \underline{\quad}$

$s = 1.05\sqrt{\underline{\quad}}$

$s \approx 1.05 \cdot \underline{\quad}$

$s \approx \underline{\quad}$

falling speed $\approx \underline{\quad}$ ft/sec

14. Complete the table.

x	−3	−1	0	1	3
y	11	3	2		

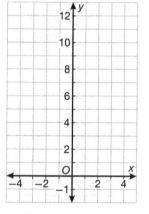

---

15. $\dfrac{\$2800}{\square} = \dfrac{c}{\square}$

$\underline{\quad}\, c = \underline{\quad} \cdot \underline{\quad}$

$\underline{\quad}\, c = \underline{\quad}$

$c = \underline{\quad}$

16. $\dfrac{\text{experimental}}{\text{probability}} = \dfrac{\text{number of times an event occurs}}{\text{number of trials}}$

A or D occurred $\underline{\quad}$ times.

Number of trials $\underline{\quad}$

The experimental probability that the next

spin lands on A or D, is $\underline{\quad}$ out of $\underline{\quad}$.

---

17. a.

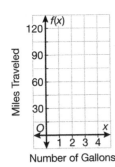

Miles Traveled

Number of Gallons

b. $f(x) =$ _____ x

c. (_____)$x =$ _____ • _____

_____ = _____

18. a. Sally: gardening __ hr; babysitting __ hr

_____ • $d +$ _____ • $g =$ _____ $d +$ _____ g

Sally's brother: gardening ___ hr;

housework ___ hr

_____ • $d +$ _____ • $g =$ _____ $d +$ _____ g

b. (__$d +$ __g) + (__$d +$ __g) =

__$d +$ __g

c. $5 •$ _____ $+ 4 •$ _____ $= $_____

19. $\frac{x}{2} + x + 90 =$ _____

$\frac{x}{2} + x =$ _____

Multiply by 2.

$\frac{x}{2}($__$) + ($__$)x = ($__$)($__$)$

(__$)x =$ _____

$x =$ _____ and $\frac{x}{2} =$ _____

three angles: _____°, _____°, _____°

20. $\{(12, 2); (11, 10); (18, 0); (19, 1); (13, 4)\}$

Domain: {_____, _____, _____, _____, _____}

Range: {_____, _____, _____, _____, _____}

21. $f(x) = x^2 - 1$

x	-2	-1	0	1	2
y					

Domain: _____ numbers

Range: __ ◯ – _____

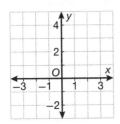

22. $\frac{3}{2}x + 5 = 2x - \frac{1}{2}x + 5$

$\frac{3}{2}x + 5 =$ _____ $x + 5$

$\dfrac{\_}{\_} = \dfrac{\_}{\_}$

$\frac{3}{2}x =$ _____ x

_____ = _____

In the equation $x =$ _____,

x _____ value.

23. Let $m =$ value of an appliance

   a. salary if one appliance is sold:

$$65 + \left(\frac{\square}{\square}\underline{\quad} - \underline{\quad} \right)$$

   b. salary if n appliances are sold:

$$\underline{\quad} + (\underline{\quad})\left(\frac{\square}{\square}\underline{\quad} - \underline{\quad} \right)$$

   c. $\underline{\hspace{2cm}}$ m by $\underline{\quad}$.

---

24. $4(x^2 - 4) + 3z^3(4z^7)$ is equivalent to $\underline{\quad}$

Circle the answer.

A $4x^2 - 16 + 3z^{10}$

B $4x^2 - 16 + 12z^{10}$

C $4x^2 - 16 + 12z^{21}$

D $4x - 16 + 12z^{10}$

---

25. Student $\underline{\quad}$ is correct.

   Student $\underline{\quad}$ did not $\underline{\hspace{2cm}}$ both

   sides by $\underline{\quad}$.

26.

$$A = \underline{\hspace{1.5cm}} \left(1 + \frac{\square}{1} \right)^{\square}$$

$$A = \underline{\hspace{1cm}} \times (\underline{\hspace{1.5cm}})^{\square}$$

$$A = \underline{\hspace{1.5cm}} \times \underline{\hspace{1cm}}$$

$$A = \underline{\hspace{1.5cm}}$$

After 10 years, the account will have

 $\underline{\hspace{3cm}}$.

---

27. *Cross multiply.*

$$(\underline{\quad})100 = \underline{\quad} x$$

$$\underline{\quad} = \underline{\quad} x$$

$$\underline{\quad} = x$$

Divide by $\underline{\quad}$ to get $\underline{\hspace{1.5cm}}$.

---

28. Let $m = \frac{2}{3}$

$$\frac{1}{3}(\underline{\quad}) + \frac{5}{6} \stackrel{?}{=} \frac{11}{18}$$

$$\underline{\quad} + \frac{5}{6} \stackrel{?}{=} \frac{11}{18}$$

$$\frac{\square}{\square} \bigcirc \frac{11}{18}$$

If false, solve for m. $\frac{1}{3}m + \frac{5}{6} = \frac{11}{18}$

$$m = \underline{\quad}$$

 Check the solution.

---

29. $20 \cdot \$9 + 10 \cdot \$13$ Given.

   $\$\underline{\quad} + \$\underline{\quad}$ $\underline{\hspace{3cm}}$

   $\$\underline{\hspace{2cm}}$ $\underline{\hspace{3cm}}$

---

30. $\underline{\quad} s = 916$

   $s = \underline{\hspace{2cm}}$

Simplifying and Evaluating Expressions with Integer and Zero Exponents page 197

New Concepts

- See "Negative and Zero Exponent Properties" on 📖 page 197 and "Quotient Property of Exponents" on 📖 page 199.

- Exponents in algebraic expressions can be positive, negative, or zero.

- Simplified expressions contain only positive exponents. Simplified expressions do <u>not</u> contains negative or zero exponents.

Example **Simplifying Expressions with Negative Exponents**

Simplify. x^{-3} *Write with only positive exponents.*

$x^{-3} = x^{0-3} = \dfrac{x^0}{x^3} = \dfrac{1}{x \cdot x \cdot x}$ *Quotient Rule for Exponents*

                          Zero Exponent Property

              $= \dfrac{1}{x^3}$ *Negative Exponent Property*

Simplify. $\dfrac{y^{-4}}{x^2}$

$= \left(\dfrac{y^{-4}}{1}\right) \cdot \left(\dfrac{1}{x^2}\right)$

$= \left(\dfrac{1}{y^4}\right) \cdot \left(\dfrac{1}{x^2}\right)$ *Negative Exponent Property*

$= \dfrac{1}{x^2 y^4}$ *Multiplication*

Example **Evaluating Expressions with Negative and Zero Exponents**

Evaluate if $a = -2$ and $b = -3$.

$a^2 b^0$

$= a^2(1)$ *Zero Exponent Property*

$= a^2$ *Identity Property, Multiplication*

$(-2)^2$ *Substitution*

$= 4$

When the values are substituted first, the answer is the same.

$(-2)^2(-3)^0 = 4 \cdot 1 = 4$

Simplify each expression.

a. $x^{-5} = \dfrac{1}{\square}$ by the _____ Exponent Property.

b. $\dfrac{p^{-8}}{q^4} = \dfrac{1}{\square}$ by the _____ Exponent Property.

c. $\dfrac{1}{d^{-8}} = \underline{\quad}^{\square}$ by the _____ Exponent Property.

Evaluate each expression for $a = 4$, $b = 6$, and $c = 3$.

d. $a^0bc^2 = (\underline{\quad})bc^2 \longrightarrow (\underline{\quad})(\underline{\quad})^2 = (\underline{\quad})(\underline{\quad}) = \underline{\quad}$

e. $4a^{-2} = \dfrac{4}{\square} \longrightarrow \dfrac{4}{\square} = \dfrac{4}{\square} = \dfrac{1}{\square}$

Simplify each expression.

f. $\dfrac{x^{10}}{x^4} = x^{\square - \square} = x^{\square}$

g. $\dfrac{x^9}{x^{-2}} = x^{9 - \square} = x^{\square + \square} = x^{\square}$

h. $\dfrac{xy^{-3}z^5}{y^2x^2z} = x^{1-2} \cdot y^{-3-\square} \cdot z^{5-\square} = x^{-1} \cdot y^{\square} \cdot z^{\square}$ Quotient Rule of Exponents

$\qquad\qquad = \dfrac{z^{\square}}{x^{\square}y^{\square}}$ _____ Exponent Property

i. How much more intense is the sound of a jet taking off than running a vacuum cleaner?

$10^1 : 10^{-5}$ The ratio is jet : _____

$= \dfrac{10^{\square}}{10^{\square}}$ *Write as a ratio.*

$= 10^{\square - \square}$ *Quotient Rule of Exponents*

$= 10^{\square}$ *Exponential form*

$= \underline{\qquad\qquad}$ *Standard form*

1. $\dfrac{y^0 y^6}{y^5}$

$= (\underline{\quad})\left(\dfrac{y^{\square}}{y^{\square}}\right)$

$= y^{\square - \square}$

$= y^{\square} = \underline{\quad}$

2. $\dfrac{m^3 p^2 q^{10}}{m^{-2} p^4 q^{-6}}$

$= \left(\dfrac{m^{\square}}{m^{\square}}\right)\left(\dfrac{p^{\square}}{p^{\square}}\right)\left(\dfrac{q^{\square}}{q^{\square}}\right)$

$= m^{\square + \square} p^{\square - \square} q^{\square + \square}$

$= m^{\square} q^{\square} p^{\square} = \underline{\quad\quad}$

---

3. $\quad 9x - 2 = 2x + 12$

$9x - \underline{\quad\quad} = 12 + \underline{\quad}$

$\underline{\quad\quad} = \underline{\quad\quad}$

$x = \underline{\quad}$

4. $\quad 3y - y + 2y - 5 = 7 - 2y + 5$

$\underline{\quad} y - 5 = \underline{\quad\quad} - 2y$

$\underline{\quad} y = \underline{\quad\quad}$

$y = \dfrac{\square}{\square}$

---

5. $\quad 2y + 3 = 3(y + 7)$

$2y + 3 = \underline{\quad} y + \underline{\quad\quad}$

$\underline{\quad} y = \underline{\quad\quad}$

$y = \underline{\quad\quad}$

6. $\quad 5(r - 1) = 2(r - 4) - 6$

$\underline{\quad} r - \underline{\quad\quad} = \underline{\quad} r - \underline{\quad\quad} - 6$

$\underline{\quad} r - \underline{\quad} = \underline{\quad\quad} - \underline{\quad\quad}$

$\underline{\quad} r = \underline{\quad\quad}$

$r = \dfrac{\square}{\square}$

$r = \underline{\quad}$

---

7. $A_c = \pi r^2 \qquad A_s = s^2$
area of circle:area of square

$\pi(\underline{\quad} x)^2 : (4x)^2$

$= \dfrac{\square\, x^{\square}\, \pi}{\square\, x^{\square}}$

$= \dfrac{\pi}{\square}$

8. $\quad \underline{\quad} n + 17 = \underline{\quad\quad}$

$\underline{\quad} n = \underline{\quad\quad}$

$n = \dfrac{\square}{\square}$

$n = \underline{\quad\quad}$

---

9. Student ____ is correct.

Student ____ did not find the _____

products of the proportion.

10. The title of the graph does not specify that

the data only apply to _____

_____. Someone may

conclude that 75% of people suffer from

_____ and _____ allergies.

---

11. By combining like terms, the equation,

$3n + 9 - 2n = 6 - 2n + 12$ is _____

_____.

Combining _____ contributes to the

process of _____ the variable.

12. *Substitute.*

$-28 = -4n + 8$

$-28 = -4(\_\_) + 8$

$-28 = \_\_\_\_ + 8$

$-28 = \_\_\_\_\_$

$n = 9$ is a solution.

True or false? _____

---

13. The relation (is/is not) a function.

For the input ____, there are ____

outputs, ____ and ____. For the relation

to be a function, each _____ would

have only _____ output.

14. *Set up a proportion.*

$\dfrac{\square}{\square} = \dfrac{p}{1}$ pencils
carton(s)

$\_\_\_\_ \cdot p = \_\_\_\_ \cdot 1$

$p = \dfrac{\square}{\square}$

$p = \_\_\_\_\_$

There are _____ dozen pencils in 1 carton.

---

15. *Use conversion factors.*

$\dfrac{\square\,\text{s}}{1\,\text{min}} \cdot \dfrac{\square\,\text{min}}{1\,\text{hr}} \cdot \dfrac{\square\,\text{hr}}{1\,\text{day}}$

$= \dfrac{\square\,\text{s}}{1\,\text{day}}$

There are _____ seconds in 1 day.

16. The bar graph will show the exact _____

of roller coasters in _____.

The circle graph will show the _____

number of roller coasters in each country

to the _____ number of roller

coasters.

---

17. *Set up a proportion.*

$$\frac{\square}{\square} = \frac{p}{1} \quad \begin{array}{l} \text{pencils} \\ \text{carton(s)} \end{array}$$

$$\underline{\quad} p = \underline{\quad} \cdot \underline{\quad}$$

$$p = \frac{\square}{\square}$$

$$p = \underline{\quad}$$

There are ____ dozen pencils in 10 cartons.

---

18. *Use conversion factors.*

1 meter = 100 centimeters

1 kilometer = 1000 meters

$$\frac{1\text{ km}}{1} \cdot \frac{\square\text{ m}}{\square\text{ km}} \cdot \frac{\square}{\square} = \frac{\square}{1}\text{ cm}$$

There are _____
centimeters in 1 kilometer.

---

19. *Set up a proportion.*

$$\frac{2.5}{m} = \frac{\square}{\square} \quad \begin{array}{l} \text{inches} \\ \text{miles} \end{array}$$

$$\underline{\quad} m = \underline{\quad} \cdot \underline{\quad}$$

$$m = \underline{\quad}$$

The two towns are _____ miles apart.

---

20. Complete table for $y = |x| + 10$.

x	−3	−2	−1	0	1	2
y						

✎ Use the table to graph the equation.

The graph _____ (is/is not) a function.

---

21. Which expression is simplified?

Circle the answer.

A $\dfrac{6xy^2}{z^0}$ **B** $\dfrac{6x^3y^{-2}}{z}$

C $\dfrac{6x^3y^2}{z}$ **D** $\dfrac{6x^3y^2z}{z}$

---

22. mass of proton : mass of an electron

$$10^{\square} : 10^{\square}$$

$$= \frac{10^{\square}}{10^{\square}}$$

$$= 10^{\square - \square}$$

$$= 10^{\square} \qquad \textit{Exponential form}$$

$$= \underline{\quad\quad} \qquad \textit{Standard form}$$

The proton mass is _____ times
greater than the electron mass.

---

23. a. second side: $x + \underline{\quad}$

   b. $x + (x + \underline{\quad}) = 28$

$$\underline{\quad} x = \underline{\quad}$$

$$x = \underline{\quad}$$

$$x + 4 = \underline{\quad}$$

---

24. $72 - 15 = \underline{\quad}$

$$\underline{\quad} + \underline{\quad} = 85$$

In the second step, the liquid was warmed

$$\underline{\quad}\,° \text{ F.}$$

---

25. Molly is 8.

Megan is 6 years older than Molly.

_____ + _____ = _____

Megan is _____ years old.

26. Let x = number of gallons of gas

a. $ total without tax

= ($ per gal with tax − $tax) · x

= ($ _____ − $ _____) · x

= $ _____

b. Solve for x.

(_____) · x = 73.25

$x = \dfrac{73.25}{\square}$

$x =$ _____

27. Distribute.

$(5p - 2c)4xy$

= $(4xy)(\underline{}) - (\underline{})(2c)$

= $(\underline{}) - (\underline{})$

28. Cross multiply.

$\dfrac{7}{x} = \dfrac{1}{0.5}$

_____ · $x =$ _____ · _____

_____ $x =$ _____

$x =$ _____

29. Cross multiply.

$\dfrac{1}{x} = \dfrac{-3}{(x + 2)}$

$(\underline{})x = (\underline{})(x + \underline{})$

_____ $x = x +$ _____

_____ $x = -$ _____

$x =$ _____

30. a. Complete table for $y = 25x$.

x	1	2	3	4	5
y					

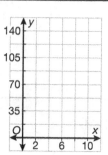

b. The points lie _____ line.

c. $80 = 25x$

_____ = x

Name _____

Finding the Probability of Independent and Dependent Events page 204

New Concepts

> ### Example Calculating the Probability of Dependent Events
>
> Two squares and three circles are in a bag. **Find the probability of drawing a circle, keeping it, and drawing another circle.**
>
> $$P(1^{st} \text{ circle}) = \frac{\text{circle outcomes}}{\text{circle and square outcomes}} = \frac{3}{5}$$
>
> $$P(2^{nd} \text{ circle}) = \frac{\text{circle outcomes}}{\text{circle and square outcomes}} = \frac{2}{4}$$
>
> $$P(1^{st} \text{ and } 2^{nd} \text{ circles}) = P(1^{st} \text{ circle}) \cdot P(2^{nd} \text{ circle}) = \frac{3}{5} \cdot \frac{2}{4} = \frac{3}{10}$$

> ### Example Solving Multi-Step Problems Involving Probability
>
> Isaac has 6 blue and 4 white shirts in his closet. He also has 2 pairs of navy pants and 3 pairs of khaki pants.
>
> **What is the probability Isaac will choose khaki pants and a white shirt?**
>
> $$P(\text{khaki pants}) = \frac{\text{khaki pants}}{\text{all pants}} = \frac{3}{5}$$
>
> $$P(\text{white shirt}) = \frac{\text{white shirts}}{\text{all shirts}} = \frac{4}{10} = \frac{2}{5}$$
>
> $$P(\text{khaki pants, white shirt}) = P(\text{khaki pant}) \cdot P(\text{white shirt}) = \frac{2}{5} \cdot \frac{3}{5}$$
>
> $$= \frac{6}{25}$$

Lesson Practice 📖 page 208

Identify each set of events as independent or dependent.

a. A card is chosen from a deck of cards, replaced, and a second card is chosen. _____

b. A marble is drawn from a bag, kept, and a second marble is drawn. _____

c. A coin is flipped, and a number cube is rolled. _____

d. A spinner is spun and the result is recorded. Then the spinner is spun a second time. _____

e. ✎ A coin is flipped and a 6-sided number cube is tossed. Make a tree diagram showing all possible outcomes. The probability of landing on tails and on an even number is

$P(\text{T, even}) =$ _____.

A bag contains 4 red blocks and 3 blue blocks.

f. Find the probability of drawing a red block, keeping it, and drawing another red block.

1st event: $P(1^{st}$ red draw$) = \dfrac{\text{red outcomes}}{\text{all outcomes}} = \dfrac{\square}{\square}$

2nd event: $P(2^{nd}$ red draw$) = $ red outcomes $- \dfrac{\text{one red block}}{\text{all outcomes}} - $ one block $= \dfrac{\square}{\square} = \dfrac{\square}{\square}$

$P(1^{st}$ red draw and 2nd red draw$) = P(1^{st}$ red draw$) \cdot P(2^{nd}$ red draw$) = \dfrac{\square}{\square} \cdot \dfrac{\square}{\square} = \dfrac{\square}{\square}$

g. Find the probability of drawing a blue block, keeping it, and then drawing a red block.

1st event: $P(1^{st}$ blue draw$) = \dfrac{\text{blue outcomes}}{\text{all outcomes}} = \dfrac{\square}{\square}$

2nd event: $P(2^{nd}$ red draw$) = \dfrac{\text{red block outcomes}}{\text{all outcomes}} - $ one block $= \dfrac{\square}{\square} = \dfrac{\square}{\square}$

$P(1^{st}$ blue draw and 2nd red draw$) = P(1^{st}$ blue draw$) \cdot P(2^{nd}$ red draw$) = \dfrac{\square}{\square} \cdot \dfrac{\square}{\square} = \dfrac{\square}{\square}$

Use the spinner to answer the questions.

h. What are the odds of spinning black? black outcomes to non-black outcomes ___ : ___

simplify to ___ : ___

i. What are the odds against spinning gray? non-gray outcomes to gray outcomes ___ : ___

There are 5 inside activities and 8 outside activities.

j. What is the probability of choosing pottery and horseback riding on the first day?

$P(\text{inside activity}) = \dfrac{\square}{\square}$ $P(\text{outside activity}) = \dfrac{\square}{\square}$

$P(\text{inside activity and outside activity}) = P(\text{inside}) \cdot P(\text{outside}) = \dfrac{\square}{\square} \cdot \dfrac{\square}{\square} = \dfrac{\square}{\square}$

k. Inside activities can be repeated, but outside activities cannot be repeated.

What is the probability of choosing pottery and swimming on the second day?

$P(\text{inside activity}) = \dfrac{\text{one inside activity}}{\text{all inside activities}} = \dfrac{\square}{\square}$

$P(\text{different outside activity}) = \dfrac{\text{one outside activity}}{\text{all outside activities}} - $ one $= \dfrac{\square}{\square}$

$P(\text{inside activity and different outside activity})$

$= P(\text{inside activity}) \cdot P(\text{different outside activity}) = \dfrac{\square}{\square} \cdot \dfrac{\square}{\square} = \dfrac{\square}{\square}$

1.

$$-5v = 6v + 5 - v$$

$$-5v = \underline{\quad} + 5$$

$$-5v - \underline{\quad} = \underline{\quad} - \underline{\quad} + 5$$

$$\underline{\quad} v = 5$$

$$\frac{\boxed{}v}{\boxed{}} = \frac{5}{\boxed{}}$$

$$v = \underline{\quad}$$

2.

$$-3(b + 9) = -6$$

$$\underline{\quad} b - \underline{\quad} = -6$$

$$\underline{\quad} b - \underline{\quad} + \underline{\quad} = -6 + \underline{\quad}$$

$$\underline{\quad} b = \underline{\quad}$$

$$\frac{\boxed{}b}{\boxed{}} = \frac{\boxed{}}{\boxed{}}$$

$$b = \underline{\quad}$$

3.

$$-22 = -p - 12$$

$$p = \underline{\quad} - 12$$

$$p = \underline{\quad}$$

4.

$$-\frac{2}{5} = -\frac{1}{3}m + \frac{3}{5}$$

$$\frac{1}{3}m = \frac{3}{5} + \underline{\quad}$$

$$\frac{1}{3}m = \underline{\quad}$$

$$m = \underline{\quad}$$

5.

$$\frac{2}{x} = \frac{30}{-6}$$

$$\underline{\quad} x = (2)(\underline{\quad})$$

$$x = \underline{\quad}$$

6.

$$\frac{(x - 4)}{6} = \frac{(x + 2)}{12}$$

$$\underline{\quad}(x + \underline{\quad}) = \underline{\quad}(x - \underline{\quad})$$

$$\underline{\quad} x + \underline{\quad} = \underline{\quad} x - \underline{\quad}$$

$$\underline{\quad} x = \underline{\quad}$$

$$x = \underline{\quad}$$

7.

$$\frac{y^6 x^5}{y^5 x^7}$$

$$= \left(\frac{y^6}{y^5}\right)\left(\frac{x^5}{x^7}\right)$$

$$= \left(y^{\boxed{} - \boxed{}}\right)\left(x^{\boxed{} - \boxed{}}\right)$$

$$= \left(y^{\boxed{}}\right)\left(x^{\boxed{}}\right)$$

$$= \frac{y^{\boxed{}}}{x^{\boxed{}}}$$

8.

$$\frac{w^{-5} z^{-3}}{w^{-3} z^2}$$

$$= \left(\frac{w^{-5}}{w^{-3}}\right)\left(\frac{z^{-3}}{z^2}\right)$$

$$= \left(w^{\boxed{}}\right)\left(z^{\boxed{}}\right)$$

$$= \left(\frac{1}{w^{\boxed{}}}\right)\left(\frac{1}{z^{\boxed{}}}\right)$$

$$= \frac{1}{w^{\boxed{}} z^{\boxed{}}}$$

9. $\dfrac{4x^2z^0}{2x^3z}$

$= \left(\dfrac{4}{2}\right)\left(\dfrac{x^2}{x^3}\right)\left(\dfrac{z^0}{z}\right)$

$= \left(\dfrac{\square}{\square}\right)\left(x^{\square - \square}\right)\left(z^{\square - \square}\right)$

$= (\underline{\quad})\left(x^{\square}\right)\left(z^{\square}\right)$

$= \dfrac{(\square)}{x^{\square}z^{\square}} = \dfrac{(\square)}{(\square)}$

10. Draw a picture to represent the contents of the bag before (10 little marbles and 4 big marbles) and after a draw of a big marble that is not replaced.

11. Probability is the ratio of _____ outcomes to _____ outcomes.

Odds is the ratio of _____ outcomes to _____ outcomes.

12. Circle the answer: true or false?

Two rolls of a number cube are independent events.

13. The set of whole numbers _____ closed under subtraction because $3 - 7 = -4$ and -4 is not a _____ number.

14. $P(\text{blue \underline{and} white}) = P(\text{blue}) \cdot P(\text{white})$

$= \left(\dfrac{\square}{\square}\right)\left(\dfrac{\square}{\square}\right) = \dfrac{\square}{\square}$

Circle the answer.

A $\dfrac{3}{50}$ **B** $\dfrac{1}{15}$ **C** $\dfrac{3}{28}$ **D** $\dfrac{1}{2}$

15. 3 × price drop last week = price drop this week

$3 \times \dfrac{-\square}{4} = \dfrac{-\square}{4} = -\underline{\quad}$ points

16. $P(3) = \dfrac{\square}{\square}$

$P(\text{3 and 3 on two rolls}) = \dfrac{\square}{\square} \cdot \dfrac{\square}{\square}$

$= \dfrac{\square}{\square}$

17. A student who wants to make it appear that test grades have not dropped dramatically could _____ on the graph to persuade people to _____.

18. $x^3 \cdot x^{-3}$

$= x^3 \cdot \left(\dfrac{1}{x^{\square}}\right)$

$= 1 \cdot \left(\dfrac{x^3}{x^{\square}}\right) = 1 \cdot \underline{\quad}$

x^3 and x^{-3} are _____.

19. $1 \text{ s} = 10^{\square}$ nanoseconds

$1 \text{ s} = 10^{\square}$ microseconds

ratio: $\dfrac{\text{slower}}{\text{faster}}$

$\dfrac{10^{\square} \text{ microseconds}}{10^{\square} \text{ nanoseconds}}$

$= \dfrac{10^{\square} \times 10^{\square} \text{ microseconds}}{1 \text{ nanosecond}}$

$= \dfrac{10^{\square + \square} \text{ microseconds}}{1 \text{ nanosecond}}$

$= \dfrac{10^{\square} \text{ microseconds}}{1 \text{ nanosecond}}$

1 nanosecond is _____ times faster than a microsecond.

20. $1 \text{ gal} = $ _____ quarts

$\dfrac{30 \text{ quarts}}{\text{mi}} \times \dfrac{\square \text{ gal}}{\square \text{ quarts}}$

$= \dfrac{\square \text{ gal}}{\text{mi}}$

21. Student _____ is correct.

Student _____ multiplied _____ by _____

instead of _____ _____ by _____ .

22. m = number of miles driven

total cost to rent a van: $\$19.85 + $ _____ m

total cost to rent a truck: $\$24.95 + $ _____ m

van cost = truck cost

$\$19.85 + $ _____ $m = \$24.95 + $ _____ m

_____ $m - $ _____ $m = $ _____ $- $ _____

_____ $m = $ _____

$m = $ _____ mi

23. If a set of ordered pairs is not a relation,

the set _____ be a function because

all functions are also _____ .

24. To find the solution of $0.09n + 0.2 = 2.9$:

First, _____ each term by _____ .

Then, _____ from both sides.

Finally, _____ both sides by _____ to get

the answer $n = $ _____ .

25. $B = 377lw$

$12,252.5 = 377 \cdot l \cdot$ ____

$\dfrac{12,252.5}{\square . \square} = l$

_____ $= l$

$A = lw$

$A =$ ____ $\cdot$ ____ $=$ _____ m²

26. a. Complete table, then graph the solution

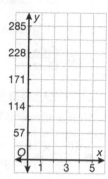

x	y
2	
3	
4	
5	

b. $y = 30x + 125;\ y = 300$

_____ $= 30x + 125$

$x = \dfrac{\square}{\square} =$ ____

He will have thrown the ball more than

300 times after _____ games.

27. qualifying speed $= \dfrac{\text{distance}}{\text{time}} = \dfrac{\square}{\square}$

$=$ ____

The qualifying speed should be _____ Jill's speed in order for her to qualify for the Boston marathon.

qualifying speed $=$ ____ $\bigcirc$ ____ $=$ Jill's speed

Jill _____ qualify for the marathon.

28. a. $\dfrac{\text{short side of small rectangle}}{\text{short side of large rectangle}}$

$= \dfrac{\square}{\square}$ or $\dfrac{\square}{\square}$

b. $\dfrac{\text{long side of small rectangle}}{\text{long side of large rectangle}} = \dfrac{\text{short side of small rectangle}}{\text{short side of large rectangle}}$

$\dfrac{\square}{x} = \dfrac{\square}{\square}$

____ $x = ($____$)($____$)$

$x =$ ____

29. $A = s^2$

_____ $=$ ____ sq ft $= s^2$

_____ $= s$

30. Circle the answer: true or false?

Whole numbers include negative numbers.

LESSON
34

Recognizing and Extending Arithmetic Sequences page 211

New Concepts

Example Recognizing Arithmetic Sequences

Determine if the sequence is an arithmetic sequence. If yes, find the common difference and the next two terms.

7, 12, 17, 22, …

Differences between consecutive terms:

$12 - 7 = 5$ $\qquad$ $17 - 12 = 5$ $\qquad$ $22 - 17 = 5$

The sequence is **arithmetic** with a common difference of **5.**
The next two terms are $22 + 5 = \mathbf{27}$ and $27 + 5 = \mathbf{32.}$

3, 6, 12, 24, …

Since $6 - 3 = 3$ and $12 - 6 = 6$ there is **no common difference,** the sequence is **not arithmetic.**

• See "Arithmetic Sequence Formula" on 📖 page 212.

Example Using a Recursive Formula

Use a recursive formula to find the first four terms of an arithmetic sequence where $a_1 = -2$ and the common difference $d = 7$.

$a_n = a_{n-1} + d$	*Recursive formula*
$a_2 = a_{2-1} + 7$	*Substitute $n = 2$ and $d = 7$ to find a_2.*
$a_2 = a_1 + 7$	*Write a_{2-1} as a_1.*
$a_2 = -2 + 7 = 5$	*Substitute $a_1 = -2$.*

$a_3 = a_{3-1} + 7 \longrightarrow a_3 = a_2 + 7 \longrightarrow 5 + 7 = 12$
$a_4 = a_{4-1} + 7 \longrightarrow a_4 = a_3 + 7 \longrightarrow 12 + 7 = 19$

The first four terms of the sequence are -2, 5, 12, and 19.

• See "Finding the nth Term of an Arithmetic Sequence" on 📖 page 213.

Example Finding the nth Term in Arithmetic Sequences

Use the rule $a_n = 6 + (n - 1)2$ to find the 4th and 11th terms of the sequence.

4th term, $n = 4$:
$a_4 = 6 + (4 - 1)2$ $\qquad$ *Substitute*
$\quad = 6 + (3)2$
$\quad = 6 + 6$
$\quad = \mathbf{12}$

11th term, $n = 11$:
$a_{11} = 6 + (11 - 1)2$
$\quad = 6 + (10)2$
$\quad = 6 + 20$
$\quad = \mathbf{26}$

Determine if each sequence is an arithmetic sequence. If yes, find the common difference and the next two terms.

a. 7, 6, 5, 4, …

common difference: _____   The sequence _____ arithmetic.

$a_5 =$ ____ $+ ($ ____ $- 1)$ ____ $=$ ____ $+ ($ ____ $)$ ____ $=$ ____ $-$ ____ $=$ ____

$a_6 =$ ____ $+ ($ ____ $- 1)$ ____ $=$ ____ $-$ ____ $=$ ____

b. 10, 12, 15, 19, …

common difference: _____   The sequence _____ arithmetic.

$a_5 =$ ____ ; $a_6 =$ ____

c. Find the first 4 terms of an arithmetic sequence. $a_1 = -3, d = 4$

$a_n = a_{n-1} + d$

$a_2 = a_{2-1} + 4 = a_1 + 4 =$ ____ $+ 4 =$ ____

$a_3 = a_{3-1} + 4 = a_2 + 4 =$ ____ $+ 4 =$ ____

$a_4 = a_{4-1} + 4 =$ ____ $+ 4 =$ ____ $+ 4 =$ ____

d. Use $a^n = 14 + (n - 1)(-3)$ to find the 4th and 11th terms.

4th term: $a_4 = 14 + ($ ____ $- 1)(-3) = 14 +$ ____ $=$ ____

11th term: $a^{11} = 14 + ($ ____ $- 1)(-3) = 14 +$ ____ $=$ ____

e. Find the 10th term. 1, 10, 19, 28, …

$a_{10} =$ ____ $+ ($ ____ $- 1)$ ____ $=$ ____ $+$ ____ $=$ ____

f. Find the 11th term. $\frac{2}{3}, 1, 1\frac{1}{3}, 1\frac{2}{3}, …$

$a_{11} = \dfrac{\square}{\square} + ($ ____ $- 1)\dfrac{\square}{\square} = \dfrac{\square}{\square} + \dfrac{\square}{\square} = \dfrac{\square}{\square} =$ ____

g. Write a rule to model the situation.

$a_n =$ ____ $+ ($ ____ $-$ ____ $)$ ____

h. Use the rule to find the number of flowers for 15 tables.

$a_{15} =$ ____ $+ ($ ____ $- 1)$ ____ $=$ ____ $+ ($ ____ $)$ ____ $=$ ____ $+$ ____ $=$ ____ flowers

1. $\dfrac{2}{10} = \dfrac{x}{-20}$

Cross multiply.

_____ · $x =$ _____ · _____

$x = \dfrac{\square}{\square}$

$x =$ _____

2. $\dfrac{32}{4} = \dfrac{x+4}{3}$

$(x + 4)(\underline{\quad}) = (\underline{\quad})(\underline{\quad})$

_____ $x +$ _____ $=$ _____

$x = \dfrac{\square}{\square}$

$x =$ _____

3. $a_n = a_1 + (n-1)d$

number of seats in the first row: $a_1 =$ _____

number of rows: $n =$ _____

difference in the number of seats

in the previous row: $d =$ _____

$a_{15} =$ _____ $+ (\underline{\quad} - 1)$_____

$=$ _____ $+$ _____ $=$ _____ seats

4. Complete the table for $y = 2x^2 - 5$.

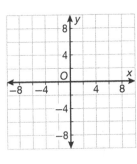 $y = 2(-2)^2 - 5 = 3$

x	y
-2	3
-1	
0	
1	
2	

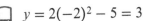

5. Solve for z. $\qquad y = \dfrac{x+z}{3}$

_____ $-$ _____ $= \dfrac{z}{3}$ *Isolate the z-term.*

_____ · $(\underline{\quad} - \underline{\quad}) = z$ *Isolate z.*

6. $4x + 2 = 5(x + 10)$

$4x + 2 = 5\underline{\quad} + 50$ *Distribute.*

_____ $x =$ _____ *Collect like terms.*

$x =$ _____

7. $2\left(n + \dfrac{1}{3}\right) = \dfrac{3}{2}n + 1 + \dfrac{1}{2}n - \dfrac{1}{3}$

_____ $n + \dfrac{\square}{3} = \dfrac{3}{2}n + 1 + \dfrac{1}{2}n - \dfrac{1}{3}$

_____ $n + \dfrac{\square}{3} = \dfrac{\square}{2}n + \dfrac{\square}{3}$

$2n + \dfrac{2}{3} = \underline{\quad}n + \dfrac{2}{3}$

_____ $=$ _____ Since this is always true, the

solution is all _____ numbers.

8. A bead is drawn from a bag and *not replaced*. Then second bead is drawn. This is a(n) _____ event.

9. *Check for a common difference.*

The sequence $0.3, -0.5, -1.3, -2.1, \ldots$

_____ an arithmetic sequence.

If so, the sequence has a common

difference of _____ .

10. The sequence 2, 4, 8, 12, ... is not

arithmetic because the first _____ terms

have a difference of _____ , while the

other terms have a difference of ____ .

11. In the rule for the *n*th term,
$a_n = a_1 + (n-1)d,$

d represents the _____ .

Circle the answer.

A the number of terms

B the first term

C the nth term

D the common difference

12. The sequence 7, 14, 21, 28, ...

_____ an arithmetic sequence.

first term: $a_1 =$ ____

common difference: $d =$ ____

$a_n = a_1 + (n-1)d$

$a_5 = a_4 + (5-1)$ ____ = ____ + ____ = ____

$a_6 = a_5 + ($ ____ $-1)\, 7 =$ ____ + ____ = ____

13. *Independent events*

yes on Q1 $\dfrac{\square}{\square}$

yes on Q2 $\dfrac{\square}{\square}$

$P(\text{yes on 1 and yes on 2})$

$= P(\text{yes on 1}) \cdot P(\text{yes on 2})$

$= \dfrac{\square}{\square} \cdot \dfrac{\square}{\square} = \dfrac{\square}{\square}$

$= \dfrac{\square}{\square}$

14. *Independent events*

$P\,(2 \text{ and } 3) = P(2) \cdot P(3)$

$P(2) = \dfrac{\text{outcome of } \square}{\text{all outcomes}} = \dfrac{\square}{\square}$

$P(3) = \dfrac{\text{outcome of } \square}{\text{all outcomes}} = \dfrac{\square}{\square}$

$P\,(2 \text{ and } 3) = \dfrac{\square}{\square} \cdot \dfrac{\square}{\square}$

$= \dfrac{\square}{\square}$

15. a. 1st rectangle: $a_1 = $ ____

2nd rectangle: $a_2 = $ ____

$d = $ ____ $-$ ____ $= $ ____

$a_n = a_1 + (n-1)d$

$a_n = $ ____ $+ ($ ___ $- 1)\, 6$

b. Find the perimeter for 12 rectangles.

$a_{12} = $ ____ $+ (12 - 1)$ ____

$= $ ____ $+$ ____

$= $ _____ units

---

16. a. *Independent events*

$P(\text{pants}) = \dfrac{\text{pants}}{\text{pants \& skirts}} = \dfrac{\square}{\square}$ $\qquad P(\text{shirt}) = \dfrac{10}{10} = 1 \qquad P(\text{tie}) = \dfrac{\text{ties}}{\text{ties \& vests}} = \dfrac{\square}{\square}$

$P(\text{pant, shirt, \& tie}) = P(\text{pants}) \cdot P(\text{shirt}) \cdot P(\text{tie}) = \dfrac{\square}{\square} \cdot \underline{\quad} \cdot \dfrac{\square}{\square} = \dfrac{\square}{\square}$

b. $P(\text{pants}) = \dfrac{\text{pants}}{\text{pants \& skirts}} = \dfrac{\square}{7} \qquad P(\text{shirt}) = \dfrac{9}{9} = 1 \qquad P(\text{tie}) = \dfrac{\square}{\square}$

$P(\text{new pant, new shirt, \& tie}) = P(\text{pant}) \cdot P(\text{shirt}) \cdot P(\text{tie}) = \dfrac{\square}{\square} \cdot \underline{\quad} \cdot \dfrac{\square}{\square} = \dfrac{\square}{\square}$

---

17. *Substitute.*

$d = 6 \cdot \dfrac{1}{c^{-2}}$ if $c = 2$

$d = 6 \cdot c^{\square}$

$d = 6 \cdot 2^{\square} = 6 \cdot$ ____ $= $ ____

18. $10^{-3} = \dfrac{1}{10^{\square}}$

$10^{-1} = \dfrac{1}{10^{\square}}$

$\dfrac{\square}{10\text{ m}}$ to $\dfrac{\square}{\square\text{ m}}$

---

19. *Set up a proportion.*

How many minutes are in 3 hours? ____

$\dfrac{36}{\square} = \dfrac{c}{\square} \quad \begin{matrix}\text{cookies}\\ \text{minutes}\end{matrix}$

____ $c = 36 \cdot$ ____

____ $c = $ _____

$c = \dfrac{\square}{\square} = $ ____

Circle the answer.

A 45 cookies

B 81 cookies

C 64 cookies

D 144 cookies

20. The equation $y = x^2 + 2$ _____

represent a function because for every value

of ____ there is only _____ value(s) of y.

A vertical line drawn through the graph

of the equation strikes the graph

_____.

---

21. *Set up a proportion.*

$\dfrac{15}{a} = \dfrac{\square}{20}$ model height (in.)
  actual height (ft)

___$a = 20($___$)$

$a = $ _____ ft

22. $\dfrac{2}{b} = \dfrac{1}{a}$ *Solve for a.*

____$a = $ ____b *Cross multiply.*

____$a = b$

$a = \dfrac{b}{\square}$

---

23. The tuition increments are _____, making the _____ in tuition costs seem _____ than they actually are.

24. The equation $x + 5 = x - 5$ has no solution because the resulting equation ____ − _____ is a _____ statement.

---

25. $16x + 4(2x - 6) = 60$

$16x + $ ____ $x - $ ____ $= 60$ *Distribute.*

____$x = 60 + $ ____

$x = \dfrac{\square}{\square}$

$x = $ _____

26. Any irrational number divided by an irrational number will be an irrational number is a (true / false) statement. For example, $\sqrt{5} \div \sqrt{5} = $ _____. Any number divided by itself, even an irrational number, equals _____.

---

27. \$____$x - 250x + \$400 = $ _____

_____$x = $ _____

$x = \dfrac{\square}{\square} \approx $ ____

28. *Set up a proportion.*

$\dfrac{8}{\square} = \dfrac{\square}{h}$ distance (miles)
  time (hours)

___$h = ($___$)($___$)$

$h = \dfrac{\square}{\square} = $ _____ hours

---

29. \$45(____$) + m($____$) = \$395.50$

____$m = 395.50 - $ ____

$m = \dfrac{\square}{\square}$

$m = $ _____ miles

30. Student _____ is correct.

Student _____ confused the_____

_____ and _____ variables.

New Concepts

- The **solution of a linear equation in two variables** is an ordered pair.

  $(2, -4)$ is a solution for $4x - y = 12$.

- The **x-intercept** is the x-coordinate of a point where the graph of an equation intercepts the x-axis.

  The x-intercept of $4x - y = 12$ is 3, the x-coordinate of $(3, 0)$.

- The **y-intercept** is the y-coordinate of a point where the graph of an equation intercepts the y-axis.

  The y-intercept of $4x - y = 12$ is -12, the y-coordinate $(0, -12)$.

Example Finding x- and y-Intercepts

Find the x- and y-intercepts for $3x + 4y = 24$.

Substitute $y = 0$ to find the x-intercept. Substitute $x = 0$ to find the y-intercept.

You can also let the y-term equal zero by covering it up with a pencil, then solve for x. Then let the x-term equal zero by covering it up with a pencil and solve for y.

Find the x-intercept.　　　Find the y-intercept.

$3x + 4y = 24$　　　$3x + 4y = 24$
$3x + 4(0) = 24$　　$3(0) + 4y = 24$
$3x = 24$　　　　$4y = 24$
$\dfrac{3x}{3} = \dfrac{24}{3}$　　　　$\dfrac{4y}{4} = \dfrac{24}{4}$
$x = 8$　　　　　$y = 6$

x	y
8	0
0	6

Example Locating x and y-Intercepts on a Graph

Find the x- and y-intercepts.

First, determine the interval used on each axis. Every tick mark on the x- and y-axis of this graph represents 2 units.

The x-intercept is **−4** because the line crosses the x-axis at $(-4, 0)$.

The y-intercept is **7** because the line crosses the y-axis at $(0, 7)$.

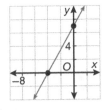

a. *Substitute y = 0 to find the x-intercept.*   *Substitute x = 0 to find the y-intercept.*

$$-6x + 9y = 36$$ $$-6x + 9y = 36$$

$$-6x + 9(\underline{\quad}) = 36$$ $$-6(\underline{\quad}) + 9y = 36$$

$$-6x = \underline{\quad}$$ $$9y = \underline{\quad}$$

$$x = \underline{\quad}$$ $$y = \underline{\quad}$$

The *x*-intercept is _____.   The *y*-intercept is _____.

b. Graph the line.   *Substitute y = 0 to find the x-intercept and x = 0 to find the y-intercept.*

x-intercept: $4x + 7(\underline{\quad}) = 28$

$$4x = \underline{\quad}$$

$$x = \underline{\quad}$$

point: $(\underline{\quad}, \underline{\ 0\ })$

y-intercept: $4(\underline{\quad}) + 7y = 28$

$$7y = \underline{\quad}$$

$$y = \underline{\quad}$$

point: $(\underline{\ 0\ }, \underline{\quad})$

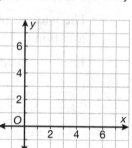

c. Every tick mark on the *x*- and *y*-axis of this graph represents 1 unit.

The line crosses the *x*-axis at ($\underline{\quad}$, $\underline{\quad}$).   The *x*-intercept is _____.

The line crosses the *y*-axis at ($\underline{\quad}$, $\underline{\quad}$).   The *y*-intercept is _____.

d. *Standard form: Ax + By = C*

standard form: $(\underline{\quad})x + 4y = -12$

x-intercept: $(\underline{\quad})x + 4(\underline{\quad}) = -12;$ *y*-intercept: $(\underline{\quad})x + 4y = -12$

$$(\underline{\quad})x = \underline{\quad}$$ $$4y = \underline{\quad}$$

$$x = \underline{\quad}$$ $$y = \underline{\quad}$$

e. *Let x = hours jogged and y = hours biked. Substitute y = 0 and x = 0 to find the x- and y-intercepts.*

x-intercept: $6x + 12(\underline{\quad}) = 24$ *y*-intercept: $6(\underline{\quad}) + 12y = 24$

$$6x = 24$$ $$12y = 24$$

$$x = \underline{\quad}$$ $$y = \underline{\quad}$$

To go 24 miles by one method of transportation, Hirva could jog for _____ hours or bike for _____ hours.

1. Cross multiply.

$$-\frac{2.25}{x} = \frac{9}{6}$$

_____ $\cdot x = -2.25 \cdot$ _____

_____ $x =$ _____

$x =$ _____

2. Cross multiply.

$$\frac{y+2}{y+7} = \frac{11}{31}$$

___ $\cdot$ (_____) = ___ $\cdot$ (_____)

___ $y +$ (___)$7 =$ ___ $y +$ (___)2

___ $y -$ ___ $y =$ ___ $-$ ___

___ $y =$ ___

$y =$ ___

3. $2(f+3) + 4f = 6 + 6f$

2___ $+$ ___ $+ 4f = 6 + 6f$

___ $f -$ ___ $f = 6 -$ ___

___ $=$ ___

$f =$ _____

4. Combine like terms.

$$3x + 7 - 2x = 4x + 10$$

___ $x + 7 = 4x + 10$

___ $x -$ ___ $x + 7 =$ ___

___ $x =$ ___ $-$ ___

___ $x =$ ___

$x =$ ___

5. $(m+6) \div (2-5)$ for $m = 9$

$=$ _____

6. $-3(x + 12 \cdot 2)$ for $x = -8$

$=$ _____

7. $10y^3 + 5y - 4y^3$

$=$ _____

8. Order of variables within term does not matter.

Combine like terms.

$$10xy^2 - 5x^2y + 3y^2x$$

$=$ _____

9. *See page 1 in the* Student Reference Guide.

$\sqrt{7}$ belongs to the _____ and

_____ subsets of real numbers.

10. *Substitute y = 0 to find the x-intercept and x = 0 to find the y-intercept.*

x-intercept: $5x + 10(\underline{\quad}) = -20$

$$5x = -20$$

$$x = \underline{\quad}$$

y-intercept: $5(\underline{\quad}) + 10y = -20$

$$10y = -20$$

$$y = \underline{\quad}$$

11. *Substitute y = 0 to find the x-intercept and x = 0 to find the y-intercept.*

x-intercept: $-8x + 20(\underline{\quad}) = \underline{\quad}$

$$-8x = \underline{\quad}$$

$$x = \underline{\quad}$$

y-intercept: $-8(\underline{\quad}) + 20y = \underline{\quad}$

$$20y = \underline{\quad}$$

$$y = \underline{\quad}$$

12. Knowing the x- and y-intercepts helps to

graph an equation because they lie on the

_____- and _____-axis and therefore are easy

to _____ and _____.

13. *Substitute y = 0 to find the x-intercept.*

$15x + 9 \cdot \underline{\quad} = \underline{\quad}$

$$x = \underline{\quad}$$

Circle the answer.

A $(0, 3)$ B $(3, 0)$

C $(5, 0)$ D $(0, 5)$

14. Substitute values for x into the equation. Graph the function.

$y = 8x$

x	y
0	0
1	
2	
3	
4	
5	

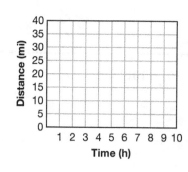

The number of miles the fish swims in 2.5

hours is _____ miles.

15. 34, 29, 24, 19, ...

Is this an arithmetic sequence? _____

If so, the common difference is _____.

next two terms: _____, _____

16. Student _____ is correcct. Student _____

subtracted the second term from the

_____ term instead of the first term

from the _____ term.

---

17. *Draw a sketch.*

x-intercept: $14x + 7$____ $= 56$

$14x = 56$

$x = $____

y-intercept: 14____ $+ 7y = 56$

$7y = 56$

$y = $____

Area $= \frac{1}{2} \cdot$ ____ $\cdot$ ____ $= $____

Let b = distance from origin to x-intercept: $b = $____

Let h = distance from origin to y-intercept: $h = $____

---

18. $a_n = a_{n+1} + d$

a. common difference: ____ a_1: ____

recursive formula: ____ $= $ ____ $+$ ____

b. $a_5 = 13.5 + $ ____ $= $ ____

$a_6 = $ ____ $+$ ____ $= $ ____

$a_7 = $ ____ $+$ ____ $= $ ____

19. $a_n = a_1 + (n - 1)d$

a. $a_1 = $ _____

The common difference is the difference between consecutive terms.

b. $d: = $ _____

c. $a_n = $ _____ $+ ($____ $- 1)($____$)$

---

20. *Determine if the outcome of the first event affects the outcome of the second event.*

The outcome of heads on the first flip

_____ affect the outcome of tails

on the second flip.

These are _____ events.

21. $a_n = a_1 + (n - 1)d$

$a_1:$ _____

$d:$ _____

$a_7 = $ _____ $+ ($____ $-$ ____$)($____$)$

$= $ _____

22. The first marble is drawn and not replaced.

P(two white marbles) = P(one white marble) · P(another white marble)

$$= \frac{3}{\square} \cdot \frac{\square}{\square} = \frac{\square}{\square} = \frac{\square}{\square}$$

---

23. *See page 5 in the* Student Reference Guide.

$$\frac{m^3n^{-10}p^5}{mn^0p^{-2}}$$

Circle the answer.

A $\dfrac{m^3p^3}{n^{10}}$ **B** $\dfrac{m^3p^7}{n^{10}}$

C $\dfrac{m^2p^3}{n^9}$ **D** $\dfrac{m^2p^7}{n^{10}}$

24. *See page 5 in the* Student Reference Guide.

_____, the base of _____ was raised to the

second power. The rule for _____

exponents _____ followed.

The solution is _____.

---

25. *Use a unit ratio.*

$$\frac{\square \text{ miles}}{1 \text{ hour}} \cdot \frac{\square \text{ h}}{\square \text{ min}}$$

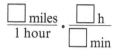

26. *Check for words that may be biased.*

Unbiased question: Do you prefer

_____

_____?

---

27. *The value of the dependent variable depends on the value of the independent variable.*

dependent variable: _____

independent variable: _____

28. $F = \frac{9}{5}(\underline{\quad}) + 32$

$F = \underline{\quad} + 32$

$F = \underline{\quad}$

---

29. d = number of days

$$f(d) = \underline{\quad} \bigcirc \underline{\quad}$$

30. Let f = total amount of fluid needed

Let h = # of hours

$f = \underline{\qquad\qquad}$

The relation _____ a function.

Writing and Solving Proportions page 223

New Concepts

- **Similar figures** have the same shape but may not be the same size. Corresponding angles are congruent. Corresponding sides may not be congruent but must be in proportion.
- The order of the letters in the similarity statement indicates which sides and angles correspond.

Example **Finding Measures in Similar Figures**

$PQRS \sim WXYZ$. Find $m\angle W$.

$\angle P$ and $\angle W$ and are corresponding angles.
So $\angle P \cong \angle W$ and $m\angle P = m\angle W$.

$m\angle W = \mathbf{120°}$

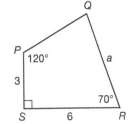

> **Math Language**
>
> A **scale factor** is the ratio of a side length of a figure to the side length of a similar figure.

Find the scale factor of $PQRS$ **to** $WXYZ$.

Use any two corresponding sides that have known dimensions.
$\dfrac{PS}{WZ} = \dfrac{3}{2}$ So, the scale factor is $\dfrac{3}{2}$.

Use the scale factor to find QR.

$\overline{QR}$ corresponds to $\overline{XY}$, and $\overline{SP}$ corresponds to $\overline{ZW}$.

$\dfrac{PS}{WZ} = \dfrac{QR}{XY}$ *Write a proportion.*

$\dfrac{3}{2} = \dfrac{QR}{5}$ *Substitute given lengths.*

$2 \cdot QR = 3 \cdot 5$ *Cross multiply to solve.*

$QR = 15 \div 2 = \mathbf{7.5}$ *Divide both sides by 2.*

- In a **scale drawing** of an object, all the object's dimensions are reduced or enlarged by a constant factor.

Example **Application: Scale Drawings**

In a scale drawing of a desk, the drawers are 4 cm wide. **If the scale of the drawing is 1 cm:7 cm, how wide will the actual drawers be?**

$\dfrac{\text{drawing width}}{\text{actual width}} = \dfrac{1}{7} = \dfrac{4}{x}$ *Write a proportion.*

$1 \cdot x = 7 \cdot 4$ *Cross multiply to solve.*

$x = \mathbf{28\ cm}$

---

a. $\triangle ABC \cong \triangle LKM$. Find $m\angle K$ and $m\angle C$.

Order of letters indicates correspondence.

$m\angle B \cong m\angle K$, so $m\angle K =$ _____

$m\angle C \cong m$_____, so $m\angle C =$ _____

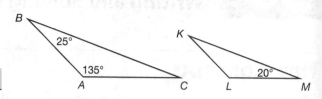

b. The triangles are similar. Find the scale factor. Use the scale factor to find x.

scale factor $= \dfrac{\boxed{} \text{ ft}}{3 \text{ ft}} = \dfrac{\boxed{}}{\boxed{}}$

$\dfrac{5}{3} = \dfrac{x \text{ ft}}{\boxed{} \text{ ft}}$

$3x =$ _____ • _____

$x = \dfrac{\boxed{}}{\boxed{}} \text{ ft}$

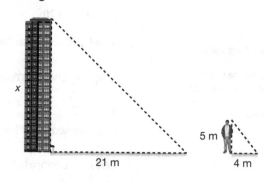

5 feet   3 feet   5 feet

c. The triangles are similar. How tall is the building?

Find x.

$\dfrac{\boxed{} \text{ m}}{4 \text{ m}} = \dfrac{x \text{ m}}{\boxed{} \text{ m}}$

_____ $x =$ _____ • _____

$4x =$ _____

$x =$ _____ m

x

21 m   5 m   4 m

d. In a scale drawing, a tabletop is 5 in. wide by 2.5 in. long. The scale factor is 1 in.:18 in. What are the table's dimensions?

$\dfrac{1}{18} = \dfrac{\boxed{}}{1}$

$l = 18 \cdot$ _____ $=$ _____ in.

$\dfrac{1}{18} = \dfrac{\boxed{}}{w}$

$w = 18 \cdot$ _____ $=$ _____ in.

e. Toy cars have a scale factor of 1 in.:64 in. What is the ratio of the areas of the toy car and the actual car?

If two similar figures have a scale factor of $\frac{a}{b}$, the ratio of their areas is $\frac{a^2}{b^2}$.

$\dfrac{1^2}{\boxed{}^2} = \dfrac{\boxed{}}{\boxed{}}$

ratio: _____ in.^{2} : _____

1. Cross multiply.

$$\frac{3}{4} = \frac{x}{100}$$

_____ $x =$ _____ $\cdot 100$

$x =$ _____

2. Cross multiply.

$$\frac{5.5}{x} = \frac{1.375}{11}$$

$x =$ _____

3. $2^2 + 6(8 - 5) \div 2$

$=$ _____

4. $\dfrac{(3 + 2)(4 + 3) + 5^2}{6 - 2^2}$

$=$ _____

5. $\dfrac{14 - 8}{-2^2 + 1}$

$=$ _____

6. Draw a sketch.

$=$ _____

7. In a function, for each x-value there is exactly one y-value.

Circle the answer: true or false?

8. $\dfrac{\square}{x} = \dfrac{16}{\square}$

_____ $x =$ _____ $\cdot$ _____

$x = \dfrac{\square}{\square} =$ _____

9. Since the triangles are similar, the shortest

side of the first triangle must correspond to the

_____ side of the second triangle.

Circle the answer.

A $\frac{1}{6}$ B $\frac{1}{3}$

C $\frac{1}{5}$ D $\frac{2}{3}$

10. a. *Draw similar triangles.*

b. $\dfrac{h}{\square} = \dfrac{\square}{2}$

_____ $h =$ _____ • _____

$h =$ _____

11. If similar figures have a scale factor of $\frac{a}{b}$, the ratio of their areas is $\frac{a^2}{b^2}$.

$$\dfrac{\square^2}{\square^2} = \dfrac{\boxed{}\,\text{sq. ft}}{\boxed{}\,\text{sq. ft}}$$

12. *Substitute y = 0 to find the x-intercept.*
Substitute x = 0 to find the y-intercept.

$2x + 3y = 24$

x-intercept = _____

y-intercept = _____

13. *Draw a sketch.*

$$\dfrac{\square}{\square} = \dfrac{x}{\square}$$

_____ $x =$ _____ • _____

$x =$ _____

14. *Substitute y = 0 to find the x-intercept.*

$11x - 33(\underline{}) = 99$

x-intercept = _____

15. *Substitute y = 0 to find the x-intercept.*

$-7(\underline{}) - 8y = 56$

y-intercept = _____

16. $11x - 4(\underline{}) = 22$ $\qquad$ $11(\underline{}) - 4y = 22$

$\qquad x =$ _____ $\qquad\qquad y =$ _____

Triangle vertices: $(0, 0)$, $(\underline{}, 0)$, and $(0, \underline{})$

Draw a sketch.

Find the area of the triangle.

$= \dfrac{1}{2} \cdot$ _____ $\cdot$ _____ $=$ _____

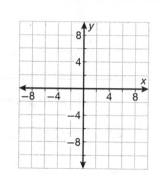

17. *Standard form: Ax + By = C*

a. _____ x + _____ $y = 280$

b. (_____)$x + 10y = 280$

$y =$ _____

If $x = 0$, then zero _____ are washed.

In that case, to earn $280, _____ SUVs would have to be washed.

c. $7x +$ (_____)$y = 280$

$x =$ _____

If $y = 0$, then zero _____ are washed.

In that case, to earn $280, _____ cars would have to be washed.

---

18. $0.1 - 0.4 =$ _____ $-0.2 - 0.1 =$ _____

$-0.5 - (-0.2) =$ _____

There _____ a constant difference between terms, so this _____ an arithmetic sequence.

Next two terms: _____ and _____

19. *Check for a common difference.*

Student _____ is correct. Student _____'s sequence does not have a constant

_____.

---

20. The girl's name is _____ of _____ names left in the hat.

The book is _____ of _____ prizes left.

$\frac{1}{\square} \cdot \frac{\square}{\square} = \frac{\square}{\square}$

21. *Set up a proportion.*

Let x = object's weight on the moon

$\frac{1}{6} = \frac{\square}{\square}$

About _____

---

22. *Odds: a ratio of m favorable outcomes to n unfavorable outcomes*

On the spinner, _____ of the sections are not B.

On the spinner, _____ of the sections are B.

Circle the answer.

A 1:2   B 1:3

C 2:1   D 3:1

23. a. Steve: _____ ◯ _____ w

Mario: _____ ◯ _____ w

b. Add the expressions. _____

c. *Substitute.* _____

---

24. The word *so* indicates "_____

_____" is the _____

clause. Therefore, "_____

_____" is the _____

clause.

25. The sum of the angle measures is 128°.

$x =$ _____

26. Let $x =$ the number of lessons

_____ + _____ = _____ • x

_____ lessons

27. *See page 5 in the* Student Reference Guide.

$$\frac{4x^2z^0}{2x^3z} = \frac{4}{2} \cdot \frac{x^2}{x^3} \cdot = \frac{\square}{\square}$$

$$= \frac{\square}{\square}$$

28. $T_V = T(1 + 0.61r)$

_____ = _____$(1 + 0.61r)$

_____ = _____ + _____$(0.61r)$

_____ = _____r

_____ = r

29. If smaller intervals are used, it will be easier

to see the _____ between the

heights of the five bars, which would show

Joe's measurements more precisely.

30. $34 - 2(x + 17) = 23x - 15 - 3x$

$34 \bigcirc$ _____ $x \bigcirc$ _____ $= 23x - 15 - 3x$ _____ Property.

_____$x =$ _____$x -$ _____   Combine like terms.

_____$x \bigcirc 20x =$ _____   _____ Property of _____.

_____$x =$ _____   _____.

$x =$ _____   _____ Property of _____.

New Concepts

Exploration page 230

Use your textbook to complete the exploration.

Example **Writing Numbers in Scientific Notation**

Write 856,000 in scientific notation.

Move the decimal point 5 places to the left. The number is greater than 1, so the exponent will be positive. Use 5 as the exponent.

$$856,000 = \mathbf{8.56 \times 10^5}$$

Write 0.0005 in scientific notation.

Move the decimal point 4 places to the right. The number is between 1 and 0, so the exponent will be negative. Use −4 as the exponent.

$$0.0005 = \mathbf{5 \times 10^{-4}}$$

Math Language

Scientific notation is a method of writing a number as a product of two factors. The first is greater than or equal to 1 and less than 10. The second is a power of 10.

Example **Multiplying Numbers in Scientific Notation**

Find the product. $(\mathbf{5.7 \times 10^5})(\mathbf{1.8 \times 10^3})$

$(5.7 \times 10^5)(1.8 \times 10^3)$

$= (5.7 \cdot 1.8) \cdot (10^5 \cdot 10^3)$ *Group the numbers and powers.*

$= 10.26 \times 10^8$ *Multiply the numbers and powers.*

$= 1,026,000,000 = \mathbf{1.026 \times 10^9}$ *Write in scientific notation.*

Example **Dividing Numbers in Scientific Notation**

Divide. $(\mathbf{1.2 \times 10^3})$ **by** $(\mathbf{9.6 \times 10^6})$

$\dfrac{1.2 \times 10^3}{9.6 \times 10^6}$

$= \dfrac{1.2}{9.6} \times \dfrac{10^3}{10^6}$ *Group the numbers. Group the powers.*

$= 0.125 \times 10^{-3}$ *Divide the numbers. Divide the powers.*

$= 0.000125 = \mathbf{1.25 \times 10^{-4}}$ *Write the quotient in scientific notation.*

Example Application: Speed of Light

The speed of light is 3×10^8 meters per second. If Earth is 1.47×10^1 meters from the sun, **how many seconds does it take light to reach Earth from the sun?** Write the answer in scientific notation.

$$\frac{\text{distance (m)}}{\text{speed (m/sec)}} = \frac{1.4 \times 10^{11}}{3 \times 10^8} = 0.49 \times 10^3$$

$$= 490 = 4.9 \times 10^2 \text{ seconds}$$

Lesson Practice 📖 page 233

Write each number in scientific notation.

a. 1,234,000

The number is greater than 1.
Move the decimal point 6 places to the left.

What exponent will you use for the 10? _____

$1,234,000 = $ _____ $\times$ _____

b. 0.0306

The number is between 0 and 1.
Move the decimal point 2 places to the right.

What exponent will you use for the 10? _____

$0.0306 = $ _____ $\times$ _____

c. $(5.82 \times 10^3)(6.13 \times 10^{11})$

$= (5.82 \cdot 6.13) \cdot (10^3 \cdot 10^{11})$

$= $ _____ $\times 10^{\square}$

The first factor must be a number greater than or equal to 1 and less than 10.

$= $ _____ $\times 10^{\square}$

d. $\dfrac{7.29 \times 10^{-2}}{8.1 \times 10^{-6}}$

$= \dfrac{7.29}{8.1} \times \dfrac{10^{-2}}{10^{-6}}$

$= $ _____ $\times$ _____

$= 9.0 \times$ _____

e. Simplify each expression.

$\dfrac{4.56 \times 10^9}{3 \times 10^5} = \dfrac{4.56}{3} \times \dfrac{10^9}{10^5} = 1.52 \times$ _____ $= 15,200$

$\dfrac{5.2 \times 10^8}{1.3 \times 10^5} = \dfrac{5.2}{1.3} \times \dfrac{10^8}{10^5} = $ _____ $\times 10^3 = $ _____

Compare: $\dfrac{4.56 \times 10^9}{3 \times 10^5} \bigcirc \dfrac{5.2 \times 10^8}{1.3 \times 10^5}$

f. $d = rt$, so $t = \dfrac{d}{r}$

$\dfrac{\text{distance}}{\text{rate}} = \dfrac{\square \times 10^{11}}{\square \times 10^8} = \dfrac{\square}{\square} \times 10^{\square} = $ _____ $\times$ _____ $= $ _____ $\times$ ▨

1. $18 \div 3^2 - 5 + 2$

   = _____

2. $7^2 + 4^2 + 3$

   = _____

3. $3[-2(8 - 13)]$

   = _____

4. $13b^2 + 5b - b^2$

   = _____

5. $-3(8x + 4) + \frac{1}{2}(6x - 24)$

   = _____

6. *The exponent is negative, so the decimal moves to the left.*

   7.4×10^{-9}

   standard form: _____

7. A number is in scientific notation if it has the form $a \times$ _____ ^{b}. The factor a must be greater than or equal to _____ and less than _____.

8. Scientific notation is a shorter way of writing very _____ or very _____ numbers.

9. $(3.4 \times 10^{10})(4.8 \times 10^5) = (3.4 \cdot 4.8) \cdot (10^3 \cdot 10^{11})$

   $= \underline{\hspace{1cm}} \times \underline{\hspace{1cm}}^{\square}$

   $= \underline{\hspace{1cm}} \times \underline{\hspace{1cm}}^{\square}$

   Circle the answer.

   A 1.632×10^{15} **B** 1.632×10^{16} **C** 16.32×10^{15} **D** 16.32×10^{16}

10. *The exponent is negative, so the decimal moves to the left.*

$$4 \times 10^{-5} =$$

standard notation: _____

11. *Corresponding sides of similar triangles have the same ratio.*

$$\frac{20}{18} = \frac{\square}{12}$$

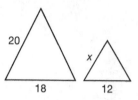

$$18 \cdot \underline{\quad} = 20 \cdot \underline{\quad}$$

$$x = \underline{\quad}$$

12. *The final grade of 90 is the average of the four test grades.*

Let x = last test grade

$$(79 + 88 + 94 + x) \div 4 = 90$$

$$x = \underline{\quad}$$

13. *Substitute $y = 0$ to find the x-intercept. Substitute $x = 0$ to find the y-intercept.*

$$50x - 100y = 300$$

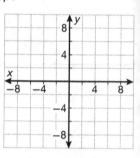

14. a. 3 cm to 6 cm = _____ to _____

b. $P_{smaller}$: _____ · _____ = _____

P_{larger}: _____ · _____ = _____

c. 12 cm to _____ = _____ to _____

d. $A_{smaller}$: _____ = _____

A_{larger}: _____ = _____

e. _____ cm² to _____ cm² = _____ to _____

15.

Student _____ is correct. Student _____ should have used the measure of angle ____ since this angle is congruent to $\angle F$.

16. scale factor $= \dfrac{1 \text{ in.}}{2 \text{ ft}}$

$$\frac{1 \text{ in.}}{2 \text{ ft}} = \frac{w \text{ in.}}{\boxed{} \text{ ft}}$$

$$\underline{\quad} w = \underline{\quad}$$

$$w = \underline{\quad} \text{ inches}$$

$$\frac{\boxed{} \text{ in.}}{\boxed{} \text{ ft}} = \frac{l \text{ in.}}{\boxed{} \text{ ft}}$$

$$\underline{\quad} l = \underline{\quad}$$

$$l = \underline{\quad} \text{ inches}$$

17. $\dfrac{(\text{smaller radius})^2}{(\text{larger radius})^2} = \dfrac{\square^2}{\square^2}$

$= \dfrac{\square}{\square}$

18. *Check for a common difference.*

$2\frac{2}{3} - \underline{\hspace{1cm}} = \underline{\hspace{1cm}}$

$\underline{\hspace{1cm}} - 2\frac{2}{3} = \underline{\hspace{1cm}}$

$\underline{\hspace{1cm}} - \underline{\hspace{1cm}} = \underline{\hspace{1cm}}$

The sequence is arithmetic because the data

have a common difference of _____.

19. *Determine if the outcome of the first event affects the outcome of the second event.*

After the first piece is eaten, there are

_____ pieces of fruit left in the box.

The events are _____.

20. Let x = total number of foxes in the forest

Write a proportion.

$\dfrac{\square}{13} = \dfrac{\square}{\square}$

21. *See page 9 in the* Student Reference Guide.

Circle the answer.

A the number of terms

B the first term

C the nth term

D the common difference

22. $x^{-n} = \dfrac{1}{x^n}$

10^{-9} to $10^{-7} = \dfrac{1}{\square}$ m to $\dfrac{1}{\square}$ m

23. *Proportion*   *Cross multiply.*   *Divide by the coefficient.*   *Simplify.*

$\dfrac{13}{14} = \dfrac{x}{10}$ $\longrightarrow$ $\underline{\hspace{0.5cm}} \cdot x = \underline{\hspace{0.5cm}} \cdot \underline{\hspace{0.5cm}}$ $\longrightarrow$ $\dfrac{\square}{\square}x = \dfrac{\square}{\square}$ $x = \underline{\hspace{1cm}}$

The solution x is between the whole numbers _____ and _____.

24.

Breed	Labrador Retriever	Yorkshire Terrier	German Shepherd	Golden Retriever	Beagle
Number	123,760	48,346	43,575	42,962	39,484

A _____ graph could be misleading because _____

_____.

25. A _____ graph would best allow the data to be displayed _____, and it would allow an easy _____ of the categories of data.

26. Let w = number of weight exercises.

$f(\underline{\hspace{0.5cm}})$ = amount of time for weight exercises + amount swim time

$f(\underline{\hspace{0.5cm}})$ = _____

27. *Round each number to the nearest power of 10.*

$89,678 \approx$ _____

= _____ = $10^{\square}$

$11,004,734 \approx$ _____

= _____ = $10^{\square}$

$10^{\square} \cdot 10^{\square} = 10^{\square}$

28.

$$7x + 9 = 2(4x + 2)$$

$$7x + 9 = \underline{\hspace{1cm}} \bigcirc \underline{\hspace{1cm}}$$ _____ Property

$$7x + 9 \bigcirc \underline{\hspace{1cm}} = 8x + 4 \bigcirc \underline{\hspace{1cm}}$$ _____ Property of _____

 Complete the solution. Justify the steps.

29. a. *There are 3 feet (f) in 1 yard (y).*

Complete the formula. $f =$ _____

b. Convert 27.5 yards to feet. $27.5y =$ _____

c. *There are 36 inches (n) in 1 yard.*

_____

30. *Draw a sketch.*

Let x = the width

a. $P =$ _____ = $38 + x$

b. Solve for x.

$x =$ _____

c. Length = _____$(\underline{\hspace{1cm}})$ − _____ = _____

LESSON

38

Simplifying Expressions Using the GCF page 236

New Concepts

Example Finding the Prime Factorization of a Number

Find the prime factorization of 120.

Use a factor tree.

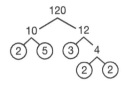

The prime factors are $2 \cdot 2 \cdot 2 \cdot 3 \cdot 5$.

Math Language

A **prime number** is a whole number that is only divisible by itself and 1.

An expression can be written as the product of prime factors. This is called the **prime factorization.**

- Prime factorization can be used when determining the greatest common factor (GCF) of monomials.

Example Determining the GCF of Algebraic Expressions

Find the GCF of $6a^2b^3 + 8a^2b^2c$.

Write the prime factorization for both terms. Circle the common factors.

$6a^2b^3 = 2 \cdot 3 \cdot a \cdot a \cdot b \cdot b \cdot b$
$8a^2b^2c = 2 \cdot 2 \cdot 2 \cdot a \cdot a \cdot b \cdot b \cdot c$

The GCF is $2 \cdot a \cdot a \cdot b \cdot b = 2a^2b^2$.

- Finding the GCF of a polynomial allows you to write the polynomial as a product of factors.

- Factoring a polynomial is the inverse of using the Distributive Property.

Example Factoring a Polynomial

Factor $6x^3 + 8x^2 - 2x$ completely.

Find the GCF of the terms. The GCF is 2x.

Write each term of the polynomial with the GCF as a factor.

$6x^3 + 8x^2 - 2x = (2x)(3x^2) + (2x)(4x) - (2x)(1)$

$2x(3x^2 + 4x - 1)$

Find the prime factorization.

a. $100 = 2 \cdot 50$

$\qquad = 2 \cdot 2 \cdot \underline{\hspace{1cm}}$

$\qquad = 2 \cdot 2 \cdot \underline{\hspace{1cm}} \cdot \underline{\hspace{1cm}}$

b. $51 = 3 \cdot \underline{\hspace{1cm}}$

Find the GCF of each expression.

c. $24m^3n^4 + 32mn^5p$

$24m^3n^4 = 2 \cdot \underline{\hspace{0.5cm}} \cdot \underline{\hspace{0.5cm}} \cdot \underline{\hspace{0.5cm}} \cdot m \cdot \underline{\hspace{0.5cm}} \cdot \underline{\hspace{0.5cm}} \cdot n \cdot \underline{\hspace{0.5cm}} \cdot \underline{\hspace{0.5cm}} \cdot \underline{\hspace{0.5cm}}$

$32mn^5p = \underline{\hspace{0.5cm}} \cdot \underline{\hspace{0.5cm}} \cdot \underline{\hspace{0.5cm}} \cdot \underline{\hspace{0.5cm}} \cdot \underline{\hspace{0.5cm}} \cdot m \cdot n \cdot \underline{\hspace{0.5cm}} \cdot \underline{\hspace{0.5cm}} \cdot \underline{\hspace{0.5cm}} \cdot \underline{\hspace{0.5cm}} \cdot p$

Circle the common factors.

GCF: _____

d. $5p^2q^5r^2 - 10pq^2r^2$

$5p^2q^5r^2 = 5 \cdot \underline{\hspace{0.5cm}} \cdot \underline{\hspace{0.5cm}} \cdot \underline{\hspace{0.5cm}} \cdot \underline{\hspace{0.5cm}} \cdot \underline{\hspace{0.5cm}} \cdot \underline{\hspace{0.5cm}} \cdot \underline{\hspace{0.5cm}} \cdot \underline{\hspace{0.5cm}} \cdot \underline{\hspace{0.5cm}}$

$10pq^2r^2 = \underline{\hspace{0.5cm}} \cdot \underline{\hspace{0.5cm}} \cdot \underline{\hspace{0.5cm}} \cdot \underline{\hspace{0.5cm}} \cdot \underline{\hspace{0.5cm}} \cdot \underline{\hspace{0.5cm}} \cdot \underline{\hspace{0.5cm}}$

GCF: _____

Factor each polynomial completely. *Divide each term by the GCF.*

e. $\qquad 8d^2e^3 \qquad + \qquad 12d^3e^2$

$= (4d^2e^2 \cdot \underline{\hspace{1cm}}) + (4d^2e^2 \cdot \underline{\hspace{1cm}})$

$= 4d^2e^2(\underline{\hspace{1cm}} + \underline{\hspace{1cm}})$

f. $\qquad 12x^4y^2z \qquad - \qquad 42x^3y^3z^2$

$= (\underline{\hspace{1cm}} \cdot 2x) - (\underline{\hspace{1cm}} \cdot 7yz)$

$= \underline{\hspace{1.5cm}}(\underline{\hspace{1cm}} - \underline{\hspace{1cm}})$

Factor each expression completely.

g. $\dfrac{6x + 18}{6} = \dfrac{6\left(x + \boxed{}\right)}{6} = x + \underline{\hspace{1cm}}$

h. $\dfrac{18x + 45x^3}{9x} = \dfrac{\boxed{}x\left(\boxed{} + \boxed{}\right)}{9x}$

$= \underline{\hspace{1cm}} + \underline{\hspace{1cm}}$

i. $h = -16t^2 + 60t + 4$

$= -\underline{\hspace{1cm}}(\underline{\hspace{1cm}} - 15t - \underline{\hspace{1cm}})$

1. Solve for j in $6 = hj + k$.

   $j =$ _____

2. Solve for a in $\frac{a+3}{b} = c$.

   $a =$ _____

3. A steady pace of growth can be shown by

   a _____ (line/curve) sloping

   _____(upward/downward).

   Draw and label a graph.

4. Rapid growth should have _____

   (steeper/less steep) slope than slow growth.

   Draw and label a graph.

5. A period at constant height should be

   shown by a _____ (horizontal/

   vertical) line.

   Draw and label a graph.

6. $\dfrac{144 \text{ pounds}}{30 \text{ books}} = \dfrac{x \text{ pounds}}{1 \text{ book}}$

   $x = \dfrac{\boxed{} \text{ lb}}{\text{book}}$

7. $\dfrac{\$43.45}{5.5 \text{ hours}} = \dfrac{\$x}{1 \text{ hour}}$

   $x = \dfrac{\$\boxed{}}{\text{hour}}$

8. The exponent is _____,

   so the decimal point shifts _____ places

   to the _____.

   $2 \times 10^6 =$ _____

9. *Cross multiply.*

$$\frac{p}{3} = \frac{18}{21}$$

(____)(p) = (____)(____)

$$p = \frac{\Box \cdot \Box}{\Box}$$

$$p = \frac{\Box}{\Box}$$

10. *Draw a factor tree.*

$140 = 2 \cdot$ ____ $\cdot$ ____ $\cdot$ ____

---

11. $\dfrac{10x + 5}{5} = \dfrac{\Box(\Box x + \Box)}{5}$

Circle the answer.

A $2x + 5$ **B** $2x + 1$

C $2x + 1$ **D** $5x$

12. The GCF of all the terms on the right side

of the equation is _____.

$h =$ ____(____ $-$ ____)

---

13. The Distributive Property uses

_____ to rewrite a product as a

polynomial.

Factoring _____ the GCF to write

a polynomial as a _____ of its factors.

They use _____ operations.

14. Algebraic fractions can be reduced only

if the numerator and denominator have a

common _____ in

every term.

---

15. The decimal point shifts _____ places to

the _____.

$0.000000002 =$ ___.____ $\times 10^{\Box}$

16. $\dfrac{1}{1,000,000,000} =$ _____

$= 1 \times 10^{\Box}$

---

17. The decimal point shifts _____ places to

the _____.

$78{,}000{,}000 =$ ___.____ $\times 10^{\square}$

18. $A = s^2$

$A = (6.04 \times 10^{-5}) \cdot ($ ___.___ $\times$ _____ $)$

$A = (6.04 \times$ _____ $) \times (10^{-5} \times 10^{\square})$

$A =$ _____ $\times 10^{\square}$

$A =$ _____ $\times 10^{\square}\, m^2$

19. *Write a proportion.*

$$\frac{x}{\square} = \frac{\square}{\square}$$

$x\,($ _____ $) = ($ _____ $)($ _____ $)$

$x =$ _____

20. a. $100{,}000{,}000{,}000 =$ _____ $\times 10^{\square}$

b. $3 \div \left($ _____ $\times 10^{\square}\right)$

$$= \frac{3}{10^{\square}}$$

$$= 3 \times 10^{\square}$$

21. The x-intercept is where $y =$ _____.

At this value for y, $x =$ _____.

The x-intercept is where $x =$ _____.

At this value for x, $y =$ _____.

Both the x-intercept and y-intercept are

located at the _____.

22. Odds are expressed as

favorable outcome:unfavorable outcome.

The odds in this situation are not being

a car: _____.

_____ : _____ = _____ : _____

23. 3^{-2} is the _____ 3^2.

$$3^{-2} = \frac{\square}{\square} = \frac{\square}{\square} \neq -6$$

24. sports books sold: _____

other books sold: _____

Yet on the graph, the Other bar is _____

times as tall as the Sports bar.

The graph is misleading because _____

_____.

25. $2 - \frac{5}{4} = $ _____ $\frac{11}{4} - 2 = $ _____ $\frac{7}{2} - \frac{11}{4} = $ _____

This _____ an arithmetic sequence.

$\frac{7}{2} + $ _____ $= $ _____   _____ $+ $ _____ $= $ _____

---

26. *See page 6 in the* Student Reference Guide.

Circle the answer.

A $y - 6 = 3(x + 4)$

B $y = -6x + 13$

C $10y = 12y + 25$

D $9x + 11y = 65$

27. on a stem-and-leaf plot, the stems show the _____ (tens/ones) digit and the leaves show the _____ (tens/ones) digit.

30 would be expressed as _____ | _____.

---

28. $n = $ number of visits per month

Barton Springs $= $ _____ $+ $ _____ n

Blue Danube $= $ _____ n

_____ $n = $ _____ $+ $ _____ n

_____ $n = $ _____

$n = $ _____

29. $p = $ original price of stock

(original price) decrease by ($5) then increase by (double the original price) ending at ($43):

$(p) - ($ _____ $) + ($ _____ $p) = (43)$

_____ $p = $ _____

$p = $ _____

---

30. a. 📝 Plot.

b. *See page 8 in the* Student Reference Guide.

The graph _____ a function because it passes the _____ line test.

c. You _____ predict what will happen in 3 hours because the graph is

not _____.

LESSON

39

Using the Distributive Property to Simplify Rational Expressions page 243

New Concepts

Math Language

A **rational expression** is an expression with a variable in the denominator.

- Rational expressions can be treated just like fractions.
- The denominator must not equal zero. Therefore, the value of the variable cannot cause the denominator to be equal to zero.
- The Distributive Property can be used to simplify rational expressions.

Example **Distributing Over Subtraction**

Simplify. $\frac{m}{z}\left(\frac{apx}{mk} - 2m^4p^4\right)$

$= \left(\frac{m}{z} \cdot \frac{apx}{mk}\right) - \left(\frac{m}{z} \cdot 2m^4p^4\right)$ *Distribute $\frac{m}{z}$.*

$= \frac{mapx}{zmk} - \frac{2m^5p^4}{z}$ *Multiply.*

$= \frac{apx}{zk} - \frac{2m^5p^4}{z}, z \neq 0, k \neq 0, m \neq 0$ *Simplify.*

Be sure to note that none of the variables in the denominator can equal zero. Include all variables found in the denominator of both the simplified expression and the original expression.

- When simplifying an expression, eliminate all negative exponents. Use the Product Property of Exponents: $a^{-n} = \frac{1}{a^n}$.

Example **Simplifying with Negative Exponents**

Simplify. $\frac{b^3}{d^{-3}}\left(\frac{2b^2}{d} - \frac{f^{-3}d}{b}\right)$

$= \frac{b^3d^3}{1}\left(\frac{2b^2}{d} - \frac{d}{bf^3}\right)$ *Product Property of Exponents*

$= \left(\frac{b^3d^3}{1} \cdot \frac{2b^2}{d}\right) - \left(\frac{b^3d^3}{1} \cdot \frac{d}{bf^3}\right)$ *Distribute $\frac{b^3d^3}{1}$.*

$= \frac{2b^5d^3}{d} - \frac{b^3d^4}{bf^3}$ *Multiply.*

$= 2b^5d^2 - \frac{b^2d^4}{f^3}, d \neq 0, b \neq 0, f \neq 0$ *Simplify.*

Simplify each expression.

a. $\dfrac{r^2}{q}\left(\dfrac{r^2}{q^3} + \dfrac{7q^3}{w}\right)$

Distribute.

$= \left(\dfrac{\square}{\square} \cdot \dfrac{r^2}{q^3}\right) + \left(\dfrac{\square}{\square} \cdot \dfrac{7q^2}{w}\right)$

$= \underline{\hspace{0.8cm}} + \underline{\hspace{0.8cm}},\ q \neq 0,\ \underline{\hspace{0.8cm}} \neq 0$

b. $\dfrac{t}{z}\left(\dfrac{uay}{tq} - 2t^3y^2\right)$

$= \left(\dfrac{\square}{\square} \cdot \dfrac{uay}{tq}\right) - \left(\dfrac{\square}{\square} \cdot \underline{\hspace{0.6cm}}\right)$

$= \underline{\hspace{0.8cm}} - \underline{\hspace{0.8cm}},$

$\underline{\hspace{0.8cm}} \neq 0,\ \underline{\hspace{0.8cm}} \neq 0,\ \underline{\hspace{0.8cm}} \neq 0$

c. $\dfrac{j^{-2}}{m}\left(\dfrac{j^{-3}}{m^{-2}} + \dfrac{9m^3}{k}\right)$

$= \dfrac{1}{j^2m}\left(\dfrac{\square}{\square} + \dfrac{9m^3}{k}\right)$

$= \left(\dfrac{1}{j^2m} \cdot \underline{\hspace{0.6cm}}\right) + \left(\dfrac{1}{j^2m} \cdot \underline{\hspace{0.6cm}}\right)$

$= \underline{\hspace{0.8cm}} + \dfrac{9m^3}{j^2km}$

$= \underline{\hspace{0.8cm}} + \dfrac{9m^{\square}}{j^2k},$

$j \neq 0,\ \underline{\hspace{0.8cm}} \neq 0,\ \underline{\hspace{0.8cm}} \neq 0$

d. $\dfrac{n^{-2}}{z}\left(\dfrac{v^{-2}cb}{nv^{-1}} - 4n^5b^{-3}\right)$

$= \dfrac{1}{\square z}\left(\dfrac{cb}{nv^{\square}} - \dfrac{4n^5}{b^3}\right)$

$= \left(\dfrac{1}{\square z} \cdot \dfrac{cb}{nv^{\square}}\right) - \left(\dfrac{1}{\square z} \cdot \dfrac{4n^5}{b^3}\right)$

$= \underline{\hspace{0.8cm}} - \underline{\hspace{0.8cm}}$

$\underline{\hspace{0.8cm}} \neq 0,\ \underline{\hspace{0.8cm}} \neq 0,\ \underline{\hspace{0.8cm}} \neq 0,\ \underline{\hspace{0.8cm}} \neq 0$

e. $\dfrac{fs}{d^4}\left(\dfrac{fhs}{d} + 2sk - \dfrac{7}{d^6}\right)$

$= \left(\dfrac{fs}{d^4} \cdot \dfrac{\square}{\square}\right) + \left(\dfrac{fs}{d^4} \cdot \underline{\hspace{0.6cm}}\right) - \left(\dfrac{fs}{d^4} \cdot \dfrac{\square}{\square}\right)$

$= \underline{\hspace{0.8cm}} + \underline{\hspace{0.8cm}} - \underline{\hspace{0.8cm}},\ \underline{\hspace{0.8cm}} \neq 0$

f. $\dfrac{zx}{w^{-2}}\left(\dfrac{zd^{-2}x}{w} + 5tz - \dfrac{2}{w^{-4}}\right)$

$= zxw^2\left(\dfrac{zx}{w^{\square}} + 5tz - 2\square\right)$

Distribute.

$= \underline{\hspace{0.8cm}} + \underline{\hspace{0.8cm}} - \underline{\hspace{0.8cm}},$

$\underline{\hspace{0.8cm}} \neq 0,\ \underline{\hspace{0.8cm}} \neq 0$

g. $\dfrac{t^2y}{z}\left(\dfrac{t^{-3}}{y^{-2}} + \dfrac{z^{-4}}{y^5t}\right)$

$= \dfrac{t^2y}{z}\left(\underline{\hspace{0.8cm}} + \underline{\hspace{0.8cm}}\right)$

Distribute.

$= \underline{\hspace{0.8cm}} + \underline{\hspace{0.8cm}},\ \underline{\hspace{0.8cm}} \neq 0,\ \underline{\hspace{0.8cm}} \neq 0,\ \underline{\hspace{0.8cm}} \neq 0$

1. $4\left(y + \frac{3}{2}\right) = -18$

$y = \underline{\hspace{1cm}}$

2. $x - 4 + 2x = 14$

$x = \underline{\hspace{1cm}}$

---

3. *See page 1 in the* Student Reference Guide.

Test values to look for a counterexample:

$4 \div -2 = \underline{\hspace{1cm}}$

$-2 \div 4 = \underline{\hspace{1cm}}$

Is the set of integers closed under division?

$\underline{\hspace{1cm}}$

4. A *sum* is the result of $\underline{\hspace{2cm}}$.

$a \underline{\hspace{1cm}} 3$

---

5. *More than* indicates $\underline{\hspace{2cm}}$.

$k \underline{\hspace{1cm}} 2.5$

---

6. *Less than* indicates $\underline{\hspace{2cm}}$.

$x \underline{\hspace{1cm}} 3$

7. A product is the result of $\underline{\hspace{2cm}}$.

More than indicates $\underline{\hspace{2cm}}$.

$\underline{\hspace{1cm}} y \underline{\hspace{1cm}} 2$

---

8. *List the values of the variables that are not permitted.*

$\dfrac{d^2}{s^2}\left(\dfrac{d^2}{s} + \dfrac{9s^3}{h}\right)$

$= \left(\dfrac{d^2}{s^2} \cdot \underline{\hspace{1cm}}\right) + \left(\dfrac{d^2}{s^2} \cdot \underline{\hspace{1cm}}\right)$

$= \dfrac{d^{\square}}{s^{\square}} + \dfrac{9d^{\square}s^{\square}}{hs^{\square}}$

$= \underline{\hspace{1cm}} + \underline{\hspace{1cm}}$,

$\underline{\hspace{1cm}} \neq 0, \underline{\hspace{1cm}} \neq 0$

9. Division implies that if $\frac{12}{3} = 4$, then

$3 \cdot \underline{\hspace{1cm}} = \underline{\hspace{1cm}}$. If $\frac{12}{0} = x$,

then $\underline{\hspace{1cm}} \cdot x = 12$, but this can never be

because zero times anything is $\underline{\hspace{1cm}}$.

This is a contradiction, so division by zero

is $\underline{\hspace{1cm}}$ allowed.

---

10. $\dfrac{x^{-2}}{n^{-1}}(2x^4 + n^{-3})$

$= \dfrac{\square}{\square}\left(\dfrac{2}{\square} + \dfrac{\square}{\square}\right)$ Rules of _____

$= \left(\dfrac{2n}{x^2} \cdot \text{\_\_\_\_}\right) + \left(\dfrac{2n}{x^2} \cdot \text{\_\_\_\_}\right)$ _____ Property

$= \dfrac{2n}{\square} + \dfrac{n}{\square}$ Multiply.

$= \dfrac{\square}{\square},$ ___ $\neq 0,$ ___ $\neq 0$ Rules of _____

---

11. $\dfrac{g^{-2}s}{b^2}\left(\dfrac{g^{-3}s^{-1}}{b^{-1}} + \dfrac{4}{b^3}\right)$

$= \dfrac{s}{b^2 g^{\square}}\left(\dfrac{\square}{g^{\square}s} + \dfrac{4}{b^3}\right)$

Distribute.

$= \dfrac{bs}{b^2 g^{\square}s} + \dfrac{4s}{b^{\square}g^2}$

Simplify.

$= \text{\_\_\_\_} + \text{\_\_\_\_}$

12. $\dfrac{w^2 p}{t}\left(\dfrac{4}{w^4} - \dfrac{t^2}{p^5}\right)$

Distribute.

$= \text{\_\_\_\_} - \text{\_\_\_\_}$

Simplify.

$\text{\_\_\_\_} - \text{\_\_\_\_},$

$\text{\_\_\_\_} \neq 0,$ $\text{\_\_\_\_} \neq 0,$ $\text{\_\_\_\_} \neq 0$

---

13. $918 = 2 \cdot$ _____

$= 2 \cdot 3 \cdot$ _____

$= 2 \cdot 3 \cdot$ _____ $\cdot$ _____

$= 2 \cdot 3 \cdot$ _____ $\cdot$ _____ $\cdot$ _____

14. Student _____ is correct.

Student _____ incorrectly factored

the _____ term in the polynomial.

$\dfrac{4x^3 y^2 z}{\square} = $ _____

---

15. $6a^2 b = 2 \cdot$ ____ $\cdot$ ____ $\cdot$ ____ $\cdot$ ____

$15ab = 3 \cdot$ ____ $\cdot$ ____ $\cdot$ ____

$GCF = $ _____

16. Side lengths of similar figures may be

_____ (congruent/similar) but must

be _____ (congruent/proportional).

Answer: _____

17. a. $24x^2y^3 = 2 \cdot$ _____

  $18xy^2 = 2 \cdot$ _____

  $6xy = 2 \cdot$ _____

  GCF = _____

b. $24x^2y^3 + 18xy^2 + 6xy =$ ____(_____)

18. Area of shaded rectangle = ____(_____)

  Area of entire rectangle = ___ · ___ = ___

  Probability = $\dfrac{\square}{\square}$

  $= \dfrac{\square}{\square}$

19. *Suppose the tank is 2 ft · 2 ft · 2 ft.*

  Volume of tank: _____ ft³

  Volume with all 3 dimensions doubled:

  $2(\underline{\quad}) \cdot 2(\underline{\quad}) \cdot 2(\underline{\quad}) =$ _____ ft³

  _____, if each dimension is doubled, the

  volume is not double but _____ times as

  large as the original volume.

20. At the x-intercept, $y =$ _____.

  $27x + 9(\underline{\quad}) = 54$

  $x =$ _____

  At the y-intercept, $x =$ _____.

  $27(\underline{\quad}) + 9y = 54$

  $y =$ _____

   Graph.

21. x-intercept: $5x + 8(\underline{\quad}) = 480$

  $x =$ _____

  y-intercept: $5(\underline{\quad}) + 8y = 480$

  $y =$ _____

22. $y =$ money won

  $x =$ number of questions answered correctly

  $y =$ _____ + _____x

  $y =$ _____ + _____(___)

  $y =$ _____ + _____

  $y =$ ▩_____

23. The decimal point shifts _____ places to

  the _____.

  $0.00608 =$ ___ . _____ $\times 10^{\square}$

24. Student _____ is correct.

  Student _____ shifted the decimal

  point too _____ places.

25. $\dfrac{1}{n-1} = \dfrac{4}{15}$

Cross multiply.

$4(\underline{} - \underline{}) = \underline{}$

Substitute $4\frac{3}{4}$ for n and simplify.

$\underline{} = \underline{}$

26. $\dfrac{x^2 y^{-2}}{z^2} = \dfrac{\boxed{}^2}{\boxed{}^2 \boxed{}^2}$

$= \left(\dfrac{\boxed{}}{\boxed{}\boxed{}}\right)^2$

$= \left(\dfrac{\boxed{}}{\boxed{}\boxed{}}\right)^2$

$= \left(\dfrac{\boxed{}}{\boxed{}}\right)^2$

$= \underline{}$

27. The odds of 3:7 mean that for every _____ favorable outcomes there are _____ unfavorable outcomes, which means there is a total of _____ outcomes. The probability of NOT winning a CD is _____ outcomes out of _____ possible outcomes, or $\dfrac{\boxed{}}{\boxed{}}$.

28. In a function, for every _____-value there is exactly one _____-value. Because there is more than one _____-value per _____-value in this problem, the ordered pairs represent a _____.

29. The vertical axis has a _____ scale, so the data appears to _____ dramatically. The employer may want it to appear that the candidate's pay will _____ quickly.

30. The table can be represented by the following situation. Susan has $0.50 in her piggy bank. She adds $0.50 each day.

g	0	1	2	3	4
$f(g)$	0.5	1.0	1.5	2.0	2.5

Let g = number of days

$f(g) = (\underline{})g + \underline{}$

LESSON 40

Simplifying and Evaluating Expressing Using the Powers Rule for Exponents page 249

New Concepts

Exploration page 249

Use your textbook to complete this exploration.

Power of a Power Property
If m and n are real numbers and $x \neq 0$, then $$(x^m)^n = x^{mn}.$$

Example **Simplifying a Power of a Power**

Simplify the expression. *Multiply the exponents.*

$$(a^6)^3 = a^{(6 \cdot 3)} = a^{18}$$

Power of a Product Property
If m is a real number with $x \neq 0$ and $y \neq 0$, then $$(xy)^m = x^m y^m.$$

Example **Simplifying a Power of a Product**

Simplify the expression.

$$(-2y^4)^3 = (-2)^3 \cdot (y^4)^3 \qquad \text{\textit{Raise each base to the power of 3.}}$$

$$= -8 \cdot y^{(4 \cdot 3)} \qquad \text{\textit{Multiply the exponents. Simplify }} (-2)^3.$$

$$= -8y^{12}$$

Power of a Quotient Property
If x and y are any nonzero real numbers and m is an integer, then $$\left(\frac{x}{y}\right)^m = \frac{x^m}{y^m}.$$

Example **Simplifying a Power of a Quotient**

Simplify the expression.

$$\left(\frac{-x^2}{3y^3}\right)^4$$

$$= \frac{(-x^2)^4}{3^4(y^3)^4} \qquad \text{\textit{Raise each base in the numerator and denominator to the power of 4.}}$$

$$= \frac{x^8}{81y^{12}} \qquad \text{\textit{Multiply the exponents. Simplify }} 3^4.$$

Simplify each expression.

a. *Use Power of a Power Property.*
Multiply the exponents.

$$(5^2)^2$$

$$= 5^{\square} \cdot {}^{\square}$$

$$= 5^{\square} = \underline{\hspace{2cm}}$$

b. $(b^4)^7 = b^{\square} \cdot {}^{\square} = \underline{\hspace{2cm}}$

c. *Use the Power of a Product Property.*
Raise each base to the power of 2.

$$(-3n^4)^2$$

$$(-3)^{\square}(n^4)^{\square} = \underline{\hspace{1.5cm}} \cdot \underline{\hspace{1.5cm}} = \underline{\hspace{1.5cm}}$$

d. $(9ab^{-2})^2(2a^2b^4)$

$$= (\underline{\hspace{0.8cm}})^2 \,{}^{|}\,{}^2(\underline{\hspace{0.8cm}}^{-2})^2(2a^2b^4) \qquad \text{Raise each factor in } (9ab-2)^2 \text{ to the power of 2.}$$

$$= (\underline{\hspace{0.8cm}})\,\underline{\hspace{0.6cm}}^2(\underline{\hspace{0.6cm}}^{-4})(2a^2b^4) \qquad \text{Simplify each power.}$$

$$= \underline{\hspace{0.8cm}} \left(b^{\square + \square}\right)\left(a^{\square + \square}\right) \qquad \text{Multiply the coefficients. To multiply the bases, add the exponents.}$$

$$= \underline{\hspace{0.8cm}} \left(b^{\square}\right)\left(a^{\square}\right) \qquad \text{Add the exponents.}$$

$$= \underline{\hspace{0.8cm}} (\underline{\hspace{0.8cm}}) \qquad \text{Any number, except 0, to the zero power is 0.}$$

e. *Use the Power of a Quotient Property.*

$$\left(\frac{3y^4}{4}\right)^3 = 3^{\square} y^{\square} \cdot \frac{\square}{4^{\square}} = \underline{\hspace{2.5cm}}$$

f. *Use the Power of a Quotient Property.*

$$\left(\frac{-x}{7y^5}\right)^2 = \frac{(-x)^{\square}}{7^{\square}} \cdot y^5 \cdot {}^{\square} = \frac{\square}{\square}$$

g. *Volume = s³*

$$(3x)^3 = 3^{\square} \cdot x^{\square} = \underline{\hspace{2cm}}$$

1.
$$\frac{3}{12} = \frac{-24}{m}$$

_____ $\cdot$ 12 = _____ m Write cross products.

_____ = _____ m Simplify.

_____ = m

2.
$$\frac{-4}{0.8} = \frac{2}{x-1}$$

$-4($_____$) = 0.8($_____$)$

_____ $x +$ _____ = _____

_____ $x =$ _____

$x =$ _____

3.
$$\frac{5}{12} = \frac{1.25}{k}$$

_____ $\cdot$ _____ = _____ $\cdot$ _____

_____ = _____

$k =$ _____

4. _See page 1 in the_ Student Reference Guide.

Circle the answer: true or false?

counterexample: _____

5. _Multiply powers._

$(4^4)^5$

$= 4^{\square} \cdot {}^{\square}$

$= 4^{\square}$

6. _See page 6 in the_ Student Reference Guide.

Circle the answer.

A $\left(-2x^2y\right)^2(6y)$ **B** $-2\left(x^2y\right)^2(6y)$

C $-\left(2x^2y\right)^2(6y)$ **D** $(-2xy)^3(3)$

7. $\dfrac{e^3}{r^5}\left(\dfrac{e^2}{4r} + \dfrac{r^9}{k}\right)$

Distribute

$\left(\dfrac{e^3}{r^5} \cdot \dfrac{\square}{\square}\right) + \left(\dfrac{e^3}{r^5} \cdot \dfrac{\square}{\square}\right)$

$=$ _____ $+$ _____

List the values of the variables that are not permitted.

_____ $\neq 0$ and _____ $\neq 0$

8. $A = \pi r^2$

$A_{\text{6 in. pizza}} =$ _____ $=$ _____ π

$A_{\text{12 in. pizza}} =$ _____ $=$ _____ π

The area of the pizza will be _____.

The area of the pizza with the radius

doubled is $A =$ _____ π

9. Let $a = 3$, $b = 4$, and $n = 2$.

$(3 + 4)^2 =$ _____ $=$ _____

$3^2 + 4^2 =$ _____ $=$ _____

_____ ◯ _____

The statement is _____ .

10. Add exponents when you are

_____ two powers

with the same base.

Multiply exponents when you are

raising a _____ to a _____ .

11. $\dfrac{wd^{-3}}{c}\left(\dfrac{d}{w^{-4}} + \dfrac{c^{-2}}{wd}\right)$

$= \dfrac{wd^{-3} \cdot \square}{c \cdot \square} + \dfrac{wd^{-3} \cdot \square}{c \cdot \square}$

$= \dfrac{w^{\square}}{cd^{\square}} + \dfrac{\square}{c^{\square}d^{\square}}$

12. $\dfrac{a^2}{a^2}\left(\dfrac{a^{-2}x}{d^{-1}} - \dfrac{2x}{d^{-3}}\right)$

$= \dfrac{a^2 \cdot \square}{d^2 \cdot \square} - \dfrac{a^2 \cdot \square}{d^2 \cdot \square}$

$= \dfrac{\square}{\square} - \dfrac{\square}{\square}$

$= \dfrac{\square}{\square} -$ _____ , _____ $\neq 0$, _____ $\neq 0$

13. *See page 4 in the* Student Reference Guide.

$\dfrac{g^5}{w^{-2}}\left(\dfrac{wx^2}{g^2} + \dfrac{gy^2}{w^2}\right)$

$= \dfrac{g^5 \cdot \square}{w^{-2} \cdot \square} + \dfrac{\square \cdot \square}{\square \cdot \square}$

$= \dfrac{\square}{\square} + \dfrac{\square}{\square} =$ _____

14. **a.** $\dfrac{rt}{w^3}\left(\dfrac{rty}{w} + 2ty - \dfrac{8}{w^2}\right)$

Distribute.

_____ $+$ _____ $-$ _____

b. *State the excluded values.*

_____ $\neq 0$

15. *Write the prime factorization of each term. Circle and multiply common factors.*

$4xy^2z^4 = 2 \cdot$ __ $\cdot x \cdot y \cdot$ __ $\cdot z \cdot$ __ $\cdot$ __ $\cdot$ __

$2x^2y^3z^2 = 2 \cdot$ __ $\cdot$ __ $\cdot y \cdot$ __ $\cdot$ __ $z \cdot$ __

$6x^3y^4z = 2 \cdot$ __ $\cdot x \cdot$ __ $\cdot$ __ $\cdot y \cdot$ __ $\cdot$

__ $\cdot$ __ $\cdot$ __

GCF: _____

16. Student _____ is correct. Student _____

did not _____ the numerator

before canceling. _____ of factors

cannot be canceled.

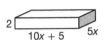

17. $V = lwh$

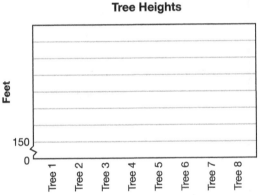

a. $2 \cdot$ _____ $\cdot$ _____

b. _____$(10x +$ ____$)$ *Simplify.*

($_____ +$ _____$)$ *Distribute.*

Find the GCF of the two terms.

_____$($____ $+$ ____$)$ *Factor.*

---

18. 0.78 of what number is 250?

"Of" means multiply.

$=$ _____

19. *The domain is the x-values. The range is the y-values.*

domain: {_____, _____, _____, _____}

range: {_____, _____, _____, _____}

---

20. Graph the tree heights on each of these graphs.

a.

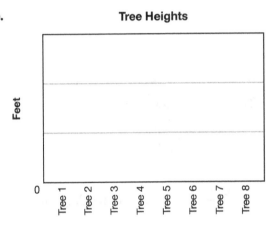

The y-axis is broken between 0 and 150.

c. The differences among the heights appears _____ in the graph with the broken scale.

The trees appear _____ in height on the graph with greater increments.

---

21. 1×10^{-4} is a _____ number, but it is greater than 0. So, it is _____ than -10.

22. *Divide the numbers. Then divide the powers.*

Circle the answer.

A 2.5×10^4 **B** 0.25×10^5

C 2.5×10^6 **D** 4×10^5

---

23. *The number is greater than 1, so the exponent will be positive.*

The decimal point moves _____ places to

the _____.

$3{,}480{,}000 = $ _____ $\times 10^{\square}$

24. *Use a proportion.*

$$\frac{\square}{12} = \frac{\square}{x}$$

_____ $x =$ _____

$x =$ _____

25. *Find and graph the x- and y-intercepts. Draw a line through them.*

$(11 \cdot \underline{\hspace{1cm}}) - 2y = 110$

$y = \underline{\hspace{1cm}}$

$11x - (2 \cdot \underline{\hspace{1cm}}) = 110$

$x = \underline{\hspace{1cm}}$

26. $2 - 0.2 = $ _____ $20 - 2 = $ _____

$200 - 20 = $ _____

_____ because the sequence does not have a

common _____ so it is not

an _____ sequence.

27.

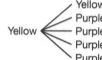

Yellow — Purple
Purple
Yellow — Purple
Purple
Purple

📓 Complete the tree diagram.

_____ ways

28. *See page 13 in the* Student Reference Guide.

_____ is the leaf.

29. *Use a unit ratio.*

$18 \text{ yd} \cdot \dfrac{\square \text{ ft}}{\square \text{ yd}} \cdot \dfrac{\square \text{ in.}}{\square \text{ ft}}$

$x = $ _____

30. If $x = 0$, then the rule could mean

$0^{-n} = \frac{1}{0^n}$, but $0^n = $ _____ and division by

_____ is _____, so the base x

cannot be zero.

Name _____

Using Deductive and Inductive Reasoning page 254

Math Language

A **premise** is the basis for an argument. It is the first statement in an argument.

A **conclusion** is a judgment that logically follows from the premise. It is the second statement in an argument.

Deductive reasoning bases a conclusion on laws or rules.

Inductive reasoning bases a conclusion on an observed pattern.

A **conditional statement** is a logical statement that can be written in "if-then" form. The "if" part is the **hypothesis**. The "then" part is the **conclusion**.

• An argument consists of a premise and a conclusion.

• An argument based on deductive reasoning is proven to be true.

• An argument based on inductive reasoning is supported by evidence, so if a counterexample can be found, it can be proven false.

Identify the type of reasoning used. Explain your answer.

1. _____ reasoning

   The conclusion is based on a _____, the student's past

   _____ on tests.

2. _____ reasoning

   The conclusion is based on the _____ of a rectangle, the fourth

   angle must also measure _____.

3. _____ reasoning

   The conclusion is based on the _____, established by the

   first five terms in the _____.

• A conditional statement can be either true or false.

Use the given hypothesis to write a true or false conditional statement.

4. True: If you stay in the sun too long, then you will get a _____.

5. True: If a student has a temperature higher than 101°, then the student

   should _____.

6. False: If a number is divisible by 5, then it is a _____ number.

Provide a counterexample for each statement.

7. Counterexample: _____ + _____ = _____
                 positive negative

   The sum of _____ and _____ = _____, which is a _____
   number.

8. Counterexample: A _____ -year old is a teenager, but _____
   14 years old.

Investigation Practice 📖 page 255

Identify the type of reasoning. Explain your answer.

Inductive reasoning is based on a pattern, deductive reasoning is based a law or rule.

a. My friend has an allergic reaction when he eats peanuts.

This statement uses _____ reasoning, based on an observed _____.

b. If a driver sees a red light, she should stop.

This statement uses _____ reasoning, based on a _____.

c. Use the given hypothesis to write a true conditional statement.

The game cannot be played in the rain.

If it rains today, then the game will be _____.

d. Use the given hypothesis to write a false conditional statement.

2 is a positive number.

If $x = 2$, then 2 is a _____ number.

Use the diagram to write a counterexample for each statement.

e. If an animal is a cat, then it is Siamese.

_____ are animals,

but not all cats are _____.

f. All female cats are Siamese.

Some _____ cats are not _____.

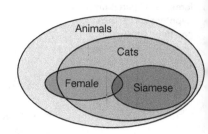

New Concepts

- A graph or a table can be used to find a rate of change.

 **Exploration** 📖 page 256

Use your textbook to complete this Exploration.

Math Language

A **rate of change** is a ratio that compares the change in one quantity to the change in another.

Example **Determining Rate of Change from a Graph**

Find the rate of change in the distance the car traveled at a constant speed.

Choose two points on the graph.

Find the ratio of the change in distance to the change in time.

$$\frac{\text{change in distance}}{\text{change in time}} = \frac{120 - 60}{2 - 1}$$

$$= 60$$

The rate of change is **60 miles per hour.**

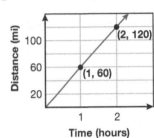

- The **slope** of a line is a rate of change. It is equal to the ratio of the vertical change (rise) to the horizontal change (run).

$$\text{slope} = \frac{\text{rise}}{\text{run}}$$

Example **Determining Slope from a Graph**

Find the slope of the line.

Choose two points on the line that also lie at the intersection of the grid lines.

Rise: From the point (4, 1) count to the point that is down 2 units

Run: From that point count left 4 units to the point (0, −1)

Write the ratio: $\frac{\text{rise}}{\text{run}} = \frac{\text{down 2 units}}{\text{left 4 units}} = \frac{(-2)}{(-4)} = \frac{1}{2}$

The slope of the line is $\frac{1}{2}$.

Note that you can also start at the point (0, −1) and count 4 units right, and from that point count 2 units up to the point (4, 1). The result is a rise of 2 and a run of 4, so the slope is $\frac{2}{4}$ or $\frac{1}{2}$.

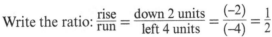

a. Use the graph to find the rate of change.

Find the change in 1 measure, then look at how many units the number of drum kicks has changed.

$$\frac{\boxed{}\text{ kicks}}{1 \text{ measure}} = \underline{\hphantom{xxx}} \text{ kicks per measure}$$

b. Use the table to find the rate of change.

The increase in the number of feet is the same amount for every two miles.

$$\frac{\text{change in feet}}{\text{change in miles}} = \frac{26{,}400 - 15{,}840}{5 - 3} = \frac{10{,}920}{2}$$

rate of change: _____ feet per mile

Find the slope of each line.

c. $Slope = \frac{rise}{run}$

rise: _____ run: _____

slope: _____

d. *A line that slopes down from left to right has a negative slope.*

rise: _____ run: _____

slope: _____

e. Find the slope of the horizontal line that passes through the points $(5, 3)$ and $(8, 3)$.

The quotient of zero and any number is zero: $\frac{0}{n} = 0$.

rise: $3 - 3 =$ _____   run: $8 - 5 =$ _____

slope $= \frac{rise}{run} =$ _____   The slope is _____.

f. Find the slope of the vertical line that passes through the points $(6, 5)$ and $(6, 10)$.

The quotient of any number and zero is undefined: $\frac{n}{0}$ is undefined.

rise: $10 - 5 =$ _____   run: $6 - 6 =$ _____

slope $= \frac{rise}{run} =$ _____   The slope is _____.

g. Use the table to find $\frac{rise}{run}$: $\dfrac{\text{change in number of drum kicks}}{\text{change in number of measures}} = \dfrac{8 - 4}{2 - 1} =$ _____

h. What does the rate of change mean in this problem?

During each _____, Iliana kicked the drum ____ times.

1. Solve for b.

$$-2(b + 5) = -6$$

_____ + _____ = -6

$$b = \_\_\_\_$$

2. Solve for y.

$$4(y + 1) = -8$$

$$y = \_\_\_\_$$

3. Solve for m.

$$\frac{5}{8} = \frac{2m + 3}{8}$$

$$m = \_\_\_\_$$

4. Start at the point $(-4, -3)$ and end at the point $(0, 2)$.

$$\frac{\text{rise}}{\text{run}} = \frac{\text{count } \boxed{} \text{ unit(s) up}}{\text{count } \boxed{} \text{ unit(s) right}} = \_\_\_\_\_$$

5. Start at the point $(3, -3)$ and end at the point $(0, -2)$.

$$\frac{\text{rise}}{\text{run}} = \frac{\text{count } \boxed{} \text{ unit(s) up}}{\text{count } \boxed{} \text{ unit(s) left}} = \_\_\_\_\_$$

6. $\frac{0}{n} = 0$

Find two points on line c.

$$(2, \_\_\_) \ (\_\_\_, -\tfrac{1}{2})$$

$$\frac{\text{rise}}{\text{run}} = \frac{\boxed{} - \boxed{}}{\boxed{} - \boxed{}} = \_\_\_\_\_$$

7. $\frac{n}{0}$ is undefined.

Find two points on line d.

$$(\_\_\_, 4) \ (5, \_\_\_)$$

$$\frac{\text{rise}}{\text{run}} = \frac{\boxed{} - \boxed{}}{\boxed{} - \boxed{}} = \_\_\_\_\_$$

8. Move the decimal point so the number is greater than 1 and less than 10.

110,400: _____._____

The number is greater than 1, so the exponent will be positive.

The decimal point moved _____ places.

$$110{,}400 = \_\_\,.\,\_\_\_\_ \cdot 10^{\boxed{}}$$

9. Write the prime factorization for both terms.

$$45a^3b^4c^2 + 30a^2bc^3$$

Circle the answer.

A $15a^2bc^2$ B $5a^2bc^2$

C $3a^3b^4c^3$ D $15a^3b^4c^3$

10. *List the factors of each term in the parentheses. Look for a common factor.*

$5x^3$: _____ $6x^2$: _____

$-3x$: _____

_____ because the terms in parentheses

have a common factor of _____.

If no, factor completely:

_____

11. rise: $_____   run: _____

$\dfrac{\text{rise}}{\text{run}} = \dfrac{\square}{\square} = $ _____

---

12. *Draw a sketch of a line with a negative slope.*

Mindy is _____ the mountain.

13. *Use the Power of a Power Property.*

$\left(b^3\right)^5 = b^{\square}$

---

14. *Use the Power of a Product Property.*

Student _____ is correct.

Student _____ incorrectly _____

_____

15. *Use the Power of a Product Property.*

$A = (4xy)^2$

$A = 4^{\square}x^{\square}y^{\square}$

$A = $ _____ $\cdot$ _____ $\cdot$ _____

$A = $ _____

---

16.   10 millimeters = 1 centimeter
$(10)^3$ cubic millimeters = 1 cubic centimeter

Use the Power of a Power Property.

a. 10^2 centimeters = 1 meter

_____$^{\square}$ cubic centimeters = 1 cubic meter

b. 10^3 millimeters = 1 meter

_____$^{\square}$ cubic centimeters = 1 cubic meter

---

17. $V = s^3$

$$(5ab)^\square = 5^\square a^\square b^\square = \underline{\quad} \cdot \underline{\quad} \cdot \underline{\quad} = \underline{\qquad}$$

---

18. Use the Product Property of Exponents.

$$\frac{fr}{d^3}\left(\frac{fsr}{d^2} + 3fs - \frac{8}{d}\right) = \frac{f^\square sr^\square}{d^\square} + \frac{\square}{\square} - \frac{\square}{\square}$$

19. $\dfrac{rt^{-2}}{g^{-3}h}\left(\dfrac{tg^4}{r^3h^{-2}} - \dfrac{r^3h}{g^{-2}r^{-2}}\right)$

Use the Product Property of Exponents.

$$= \left(\frac{rt^\square g^4}{g^\square r^3 h^\square} - \frac{r^\square t^{-2}h}{g^\square hr^{-2}}\right)$$

Use the Rule for Negative Exponents and simplify.

$$= \underline{\qquad}$$

---

20. Convert feet to inches.

Use the scale as one ratio in your proportion.

$$\frac{\square}{\square} = \frac{\square}{\square}$$

$$\underline{\qquad} = \underline{\qquad} \quad \text{Cross multiply.}$$

$$\underline{\qquad} = \underline{\qquad} \quad \text{Divide.}$$

height:

21. To find the x-intercept, look for the point on the line that has a 0 for the y-coordinate.

$(\underline{\quad}, 0)$ $\underline{\qquad}$ is the x-intercept.

To find the y-intercept, look for the point on the line that has a 0 for the x-coordinate.

$(0, \underline{\quad})$ $\underline{\qquad}$ is the y-intercept.

---

22. To write the formula in standard form, multiply to remove the fraction.

$$F = \frac{9}{5}C + 32$$

$$F(\underline{\quad}) = \left(\frac{9}{5}C\right)(\underline{\quad}) + 32(\underline{\quad})$$

$$\underline{\quad} = \underline{\quad} + \underline{\quad}$$

Standard form: $Ax + By = C$

$$\underline{\qquad} = \underline{\quad}$$

23. Write the starting number:

$$a_1 = \underline{\quad}$$

Let a_n = unknown number in sequence
Let a_{n-1} = previous term
Write the rule.

$$a_n = \underline{\qquad}$$

Write the next two terms.

$$\underline{\qquad}, \underline{\qquad}$$

24. Dependent events: The first event _____ affect the probability of the second event.

Independent events: The first event _____ affect the probability of the second event.

25. *Set up a proportion.*

$$\frac{\square}{\square} = \frac{\square}{\square}$$

Solve for x.

$x =$ _____

26. $y = f(x)$

$x =$ _____

$f(x) =$ the total cost

The cost is \$2.50 per square foot.

$f(x) =$ _____

27. *Use the vertical line test.*

Parabola A _____ a function.

Parabola B _____ a function.

28. $v = \dfrac{d}{t}$

$$v = \frac{\square}{\square} = \underline{\hspace{2cm}}$$

$E_k = \dfrac{1}{2}mv^2$

$E_k = \dfrac{1}{2} \cdot \underline{\hspace{1cm}} \cdot (\underline{\hspace{1cm}})^2 = \underline{\hspace{2cm}}$

29. $d = rt$

a. distance that Car 2 travels: _____

b. distance that Car 1 travels: ___(___ + ___)

c. *The cars traveled the same distance.*

_____ = _____

$x =$ _____

d. Evaluate the expression for either distance traveled by Car 1 or Car 2.

$d =$ _____

30. *Draw a sketch.*

Let $w =$ width   length = _____

width = _____   length = _____

LESSON 42

Solving Percent Problems page 263

New Concepts

- There are three parts to a percent equation:

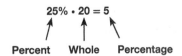

$$25\% \cdot 20 = 5$$

Percent   Whole   Percentage

Example Using an Equation to Find a Percentage

What number is 125% of 64?

percent · whole = percentage

$c = 125\% \cdot 64$ *Write an equation.*

$c = 1.25 \cdot 64$ *Change the percent to a decimal.*

$c = 80$ *Multiply.*

- A percent equation can be written as a proportion. One ratio of the proportion compares the part to the whole. The other ratio is the percent as written as a fraction.

Part ⟶
$$\frac{5}{50} = \frac{10}{100}$$ ⟵ Percent
Whole ⟶

Example Using a Proportion

What number is 125% of 48?

$\dfrac{c}{48} = \dfrac{125}{100}$ *Write a proportion.*

$c(100) = (48)(125)$ *Cross multiply.*

$c(100) = 6000$

$c = \dfrac{6000}{100}$ *Divide to solve for c.*

$c = 60$ *Simplify.*

a. What number is 35% of 70?

Change the percent to a decimal. Write and solve a percent equation: percent · whole = percentage.

$35\% = \underline{}.\underline{}$ $\underline{}.\underline{} \cdot 70 = \underline{}$

b. What number is 150% of 24?

Because the percent is greater than 100, the answer will be a number greater than 24.

$150\% = \underline{}.\underline{}$ $\underline{}.\underline{} \cdot 24 = \underline{}$

c. Use a proportion to find 315% of 21.

Set up a proportion. Cross multiply and solve.

$\dfrac{x}{\square} = \dfrac{315}{100}$ $100(x) = (\underline{})(\underline{})$ $x = \underline{}$

d. 59.5 is what percent of 17?

The number 59.5 is greater than 17, so the percent will be greater than 100%.

$\dfrac{59.5}{17} = \dfrac{x}{100}$ $17(x) = (\underline{})(\underline{})$ $x = \underline{}\%$

e. The driver reduces his car's miles per gallon by 33%. The car is supposed to get 32 miles per gallon. What is the mileage for this driver's car?

New rate = (100% − 33%) of original rate.

$100\% - 33\% = \underline{}\%$ $\underline{}\% = \underline{}.\underline{}$ $\underline{}.\underline{} \cdot 32 = \underline{}$ mpg

f. *Cross out information not needed.*

$\dfrac{x}{15{,}432} = \dfrac{45}{\square}$ $(x) = (\underline{})(\underline{})$ $x = \underline{}$

1. Solve for d.

$$5d - 8 = 3 + 7d$$

$$5d - \underline{\quad} - 8 = 3$$

$$\underline{\quad}d = 3 + \underline{\quad}$$

$$d = \underline{\quad}$$

2. Solve for t.

$$9 + 2.7t = -4.8t - 6$$

$$9 + 2.7t + \underline{\quad} = -6$$

$$\underline{\quad}t = -6 - \underline{\quad}$$

$$t = \underline{\quad}$$

3. Isolate the variable w.

$$V = \left(\frac{1}{3}\right)lwh$$

$$3V = \underline{\quad} \qquad \text{Multiply by 3.}$$

$$\frac{3V}{\square} = \underline{\quad} \qquad \text{Divide by } lh.$$

4. Isolate the variable t.

$$d = rt$$

$$\underline{\quad} = \underline{\quad}$$

5. *Find two perfect squares that are close to 42.*

$$\sqrt{36} = \underline{\quad}$$

$$\sqrt{49} = \underline{\quad}$$

$\sqrt{42}$ is between $\underline{\quad}$ and $\underline{\quad}$.

6. *Change the percent to a decimal.*

$$18\% = \underline{\quad}.\underline{\quad}$$

percent · whole = percentage

$$\underline{\quad} \cdot 340 = \underline{\quad}$$

7. *Change the percent to a decimal.*

$$270\% = \underline{\quad}$$

percent · whole = percentage

$$\underline{\quad} \cdot \underline{\quad} = \underline{\quad}$$

8. *Use the Power of a Power Rule.*

$$(6mn^3)^2 = 6^2 \cdot \underline{\quad}^2 \cdot \underline{\quad}^2$$

$$= \underline{\quad} \cdot \underline{\quad} \cdot \underline{\quad}$$

$$= \underline{\quad}$$

9. *Change the percent to a decimal.*

percent · whole = percentage

54% · _____ = _____

Circle the answer.

A 64.8   **B** 600   **C** 648   **D** 1254

10. *percent · whole = percentage*

Find 224% of $1.36.

224% · ____._____ = _____

new price: ▨_____ per gallon

---

11. Fractions, percentages, and decimals are all used to express a _____ of a whole.

---

12. a. *List the numbers in order.*

_____

b. greatest: _____

least: _____

Stem	Leaves
1	▢ , ▢
2	▢ , ▢ , ▢ , ▢ , ▢
3	▢ , ▢

Key: 1|9 means _____

---

13. *hours · $\frac{dollars}{hour}$ = total dollars*

_____ · _____ = _____

14. *To divide powers of 10, subtract the exponents.*

$$10^{12} \div 10^6 = 10^{\square}$$

$$= \rule{3cm}{0.4pt}$$

---

15. Simplify the equation. Is the solution correct? _____

$$6x + \frac{1}{4}(y) = 44 \quad \textit{Multiply each term by 4.}$$

$$4(6x) + 4\left(\frac{1}{4}\right)(y) = 4(44) \longrightarrow \rule{1.5cm}{0.4pt} + \rule{1.5cm}{0.4pt} = \rule{2cm}{0.4pt}$$

$$y = \rule{2.5cm}{0.4pt} \qquad \textit{Subtract to isolate y.}$$

---

16. a.

Number of pies (x)	2	4	
Cost (y)	$5		

b.

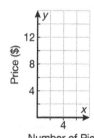

Number of Pies

The graph _____ a function.

c. $y = \rule{1.5cm}{0.4pt} x$ **d.** $y = $

---

17. To make the values on a line graph seem larger, draw the graph with a _____ axis.

---

18. a. $P(\text{Road 1}) =$ _____ $P(\text{Road 4}) =$ _____

$P(\text{Road 1, Road 4}) =$ _____ · _____ = _____

b. *Remember that Road 1 and Road 4 were already used, so they are eliminated.*

$P(\text{Road 2, Road 5}) =$ _____

---

19. *See page 9 in the* Student Reference Guide.

a. $a_1 =$ _____ $a_n =$ _____

b. $a_1 =$ _____ $a_2 =$ _____

$a_3 =$ _____ $a_4 =$ _____

c. _____, people _____ growing.

20. x-intercept: (_____, 0)

y-intercept: (0, _____)

---

21. Find the volume. Double the lengths and find the greater volume. Divide to compare.

$V =$ _____ · _____ · _____ = _____

double each length: _____, _____, _____

$V =$ _____ · _____ · _____ = _____

_____ ÷ _____ = _____

The volume will increase by _____ times.

22. *See page 2 in the* Student Reference Guide.

$14p^5qr^2 - 28p^2q^2r^3$

$GCF =$ _____

---

23. *Use the Distributive Property.*

Add or subtract the exponents to simplify.

$\dfrac{r^{-2}}{s^{-3}}\left(\dfrac{rs^{-2}}{sr^{-1}} - \dfrac{s^{-3}r^{-1}}{r^{-3}}\right) =$ _____ − _____ = _____ − _____ = _____

---

24. $0.002 =$ _____ $\cdot 10^{\square}$

$=$ _____

25. $\frac{n}{0}$ is undefined. Which variable is in the denominator of the expression?

$$\frac{pg^3}{s}\left(\frac{g^2p^3}{s^4} + \frac{9p}{s^2} - n\right)$$

Circle the answer.

A p **B** g **C** s **D** n

26. $Slope = \frac{rise}{run}$

$\dfrac{\text{change in miles}}{\text{change in gallons}} = \dfrac{\square - \square}{\square - \square} =$ _____

The rate of change is _____ miles per gallon.

27. Student _____ is correct because Student

_____ raised the base to the _____ power.

28. $Slope = \frac{rise}{run}$

$\dfrac{\text{change in miles}}{\text{change in inches}} = \dfrac{\square - \square}{\square - \square} =$ _____

The rate of change is _____ .

29.
a. $\dfrac{\text{change in cost}}{\text{change in days}} = \dfrac{\square - \square}{\square - \square} =$ _____

b. $days \cdot \dfrac{cost}{day} = total\ cost$

_____ $\cdot$ _____ $=$ _____

30. Picture the triangle on a coordinate plane.   *Height = rise*   *Base = run*

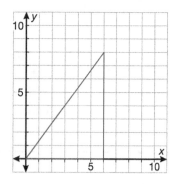

rise = _____

run = _____

slope = _____

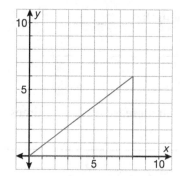

rise = _____

run = _____

slope = _____

Name _____

Simplifying Rational Expressions page 270

New Concepts

- Division by 0 is undefined. Therefore, the denominator of a rational expression cannot equal 0.

Example **Determining When an Expression is Undefined**

Determine the value for which the rational expression is undefined.

$$\frac{(2x + 1)}{(x - 4)}$$

Set the denominator equal to 0 and solve for the variable.

denominator $= x - 4$

$x - 4 = 0$ when $x = 4$

The expression is **undefined at $x = 4$.**

> **Math Language**
>
> A **rational expression** is a fraction with a variable in the denominator.

- Once you know the undefined value, you can simplify a rational expression. Use factoring to remove common factors.

Example **Simplifying Using a Common Factor**

Simplify. $\dfrac{(2x^2 - 10x)}{(4x^2 + 6x)}$

Determine undefined values.

GCF of numerator $= 2x$ *Find the numerator's GCF.*

GCF of denominator $= 2x$ *Find the denominator's GCF.*

$\dfrac{2x^2 - 10x}{4x^2 + 6x}$

$= \dfrac{2x(x - 5)}{2x(2x + 3)}; x \neq -\dfrac{3}{2}; x \neq 0$ *Factor. Determine undefined values.*

$= \dfrac{2\!\!\!/x(x - 5)}{2\!\!\!/x(2x + 3)}$ *Simplify by canceling monomials.*

$= \dfrac{x - 5}{2x + 3}; x \neq -\dfrac{3}{2}; x \neq 0$ *Include undefined values in the answer.*

Determine the values for which each rational expression is undefined.

Set the denominator equal to 0 and solve for x.

a. $\dfrac{16x - 7}{5x}$ $\qquad 5x = 0 \qquad\qquad\qquad x = \dfrac{0}{\boxed{}} =$ _____

For the expression $\dfrac{16x - 7}{5x}$, $x \neq$ _____

b. $\dfrac{1 + 3x}{x + 8}$ $\qquad$ _____ $= 0 \qquad x =$ _____

For the expression $\dfrac{1 + 3x}{x + 8}$, $x \neq$ _____

c. $\dfrac{11 - x}{6x - 42}$ $\qquad$ _____ $= 0 \qquad$ ___ $x =$ _____ $\qquad x =$ _____

For the expression $\dfrac{11 - x}{6x - 42}$, $x \neq$ _____

Simplify each rational expression. Determine undefined values.

Look for a common factor in all the terms.

d. $\dfrac{7x - 27}{5x}$ $\qquad$ Common factors: none $\qquad\qquad$ Simplified: _____

$\quad x \neq$ _____

e. $\dfrac{3x^2 - 3x}{9x^2 + 15x}$ $\qquad$ Common factors: 3, x $\qquad\qquad$ Simplified: _____

$\quad x \neq$ _____, $x \neq$ _____

f. $\dfrac{4x + 28}{3x^2 + 21x}$ $\qquad$ Common factors: _____ $\qquad$ Simplified: _____

$\quad x \neq$ _____, $x \neq$ _____

g. Simplify. $\dfrac{2\pi rh + 2\pi r^2}{\pi r^2 h}$

GCF of numerator: _____

factor: _____

Divide out common factors. _____

List undefined values: $r \neq$ _____, $h \neq$ _____

1. $f(x) = -2x$ for $x = -5$

$f(\underline{\quad}) = -2(\underline{\qquad})$

$= \underline{\qquad}$

2. $h(x) = 3x - 1$ for $x = 7$

$h(\underline{\quad}) = 3(\underline{\qquad}) - 1$

$= \underline{\qquad} - 1$

$= \underline{\qquad}$

3. Substitute the given ordinal for n. Simplify.

$a_{\square} = 16 + (\underline{\quad} - 1)(-0.5)$

$= 16 + (\underline{\quad})(-0.5)$

$= 16 + \underline{\qquad} = \underline{\qquad}$

4. Use the equation

$a_n = a_1 + (n - 1)(d)$.

Find the 100th term of the sequence.

$n = \underline{\quad}, a_1 = \underline{\quad}, d = \underline{\quad},$

$a_{\square} = \underline{\quad} + (\underline{\quad} - 1)(\underline{\quad}) = \underline{\quad}$

5. Set the denominator equal to 0 and solve for x.

$\underline{\qquad} = 0$

$x = \underline{\qquad}$

6. Set the denominator equal to 0 and solve for x.

$\underline{\qquad} = 0$

$x = \underline{\qquad}$

7. Change the percent to a decimal and multiply.

$14\% = \underline{\quad}.\underline{\qquad}$

$\underline{\quad}.\underline{\qquad} \cdot 120 = \underline{\qquad}$

8. Change the percent to a decimal and multiply.

$75\% = \underline{\quad}.\underline{\qquad}$

$\underline{\quad}.\underline{\qquad} \cdot 60 = \underline{\qquad}$

9. Use x for the amount of money the students need to raise.

amount donated from the store = $\underline{\qquad}$

$x + \underline{\qquad} = 2700$

$\underline{\qquad} = 2700$

$x = \underline{\qquad}$

10. a. Use 0.05n to represent the value of the nickels.

Value in dimes + value in nickels = total value

$\underline{\qquad} + \underline{\qquad} = \underline{\qquad}$

b. $\underline{\qquad} n = \underline{\qquad}$

$n = \underline{\qquad}$

11. *Think of the vertical line test for a function. Which values are important?*

Student _____ is correct. Student _____

confused the _____ and _____
values. If any x-values were the same the

relation would not be a _____ .

12. Use a _____ _____ test. If the _____

line passes through _____ than _____

point on the graph, the relation _____ a

function.

13. $\dfrac{1 \text{ in.}}{25 \text{ miles}} = \dfrac{\square}{\square}$

$1(\underline{\hspace{1cm}}) = 25(\underline{\hspace{1cm}})$

$\underline{\hspace{2cm}} = \underline{\hspace{2cm}}$

14. *Which denominator simplifies to 0?* _____

Circle the answer.

A $\dfrac{x-6}{12x+72}$ B $\dfrac{x}{2(x+12)}$

C $\dfrac{x+6}{72-12x}$ D $\dfrac{2x+12}{x}$

15. *Factor the numerator and simplify the fraction.*

$3z^2 + 2.7z = (\underline{\hspace{1cm}})(\underline{\hspace{1cm}})$

$\dfrac{\square(\square + \square)}{(z+0.9)(z-0.9)}$

$= \underline{\hspace{1.5cm}}; z \neq \underline{\hspace{1cm}}; z \neq \underline{\hspace{1cm}}$

16. $\dfrac{1}{n} \cdot \dfrac{n}{1} = 1$

The reciprocal of $\dfrac{8x}{2x+16}$ is _____ .

Set the denominator equal to zero and solve.

$\underline{\hspace{2cm}} = 0$

$x = \underline{\hspace{2cm}} = 0$

Undefined at $x = \underline{\hspace{2cm}}$

17. *There are 10 possible digits for the first number, and 9 possible digits for the second number.*

$\underline{\hspace{1.5cm}} \cdot \underline{\hspace{1.5cm}} = \underline{\hspace{2cm}}$

Since there is only one correct order for
the last two digits, the probability of

guessing correctly is $\dfrac{\square}{\square}$.

18. a. $a_n = a_1 + (n-1)d.$

$\underline{\hspace{5cm}}$

b. *Substitute the ordinal number for n in the equation and simplify.*

$4^{\text{th}}:$ $\underline{\hspace{2.5cm}} = \underline{\hspace{2.5cm}}$

$11^{\text{th}}:$ $\underline{\hspace{2.5cm}} = \underline{\hspace{2.5cm}}$

19.

$$y = -\frac{5}{6} - 2$$

$6y = \underline{\quad} - 12$ Multiply both sides by 6.

$5x + 6y = \underline{\quad}$ Add $\underline{\quad}$ to both sides.

---

20. Visualize one triangle flipped over to help you match the sides and angles.

The right angles ∠M and ∠K are corresponding angles.

Sides: _____

Angles: _____

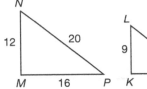

---

21. Multiply the numerical terms. Add the exponents of the 10s.

$1.6 \cdot 2.2 = \underline{\qquad}$

$10^{-5} \cdot 10^3 = 10^{(-5+3)} = 10^{\square}$

$= \underline{\qquad} \cdot \underline{\qquad}$

22. a. $A = lw$

$l = \underline{\qquad}$

$w = \underline{\qquad}$

$A = \underline{\qquad}$

b. $\underline{\qquad} = \underline{\qquad}$

---

23. $\left(10g^3h^{-4}\right)^2 = \underline{\qquad}$

$\left(3gh^6\right)^3 = \underline{\qquad}$

$\underline{\qquad} \cdot \underline{\qquad} = \underline{\qquad}$

Circle the answer.

A $2700g^9h^{10}$ B $180g^9h^{10}$

C $180g^5h^7$ D $2700g^{18}h^{16}$

24. Simplify the expression $(2x)^{-3}$.

$(2x)^{-3} = \underline{\qquad}$

Compare the expressions.

The expressions are _____

_____ of each other.

---

25. *Use the Distributive Property. Then simplify.*

$$\frac{k}{g}\left(\frac{rtw}{nk} - 5k^2w^6\right) = \frac{\square}{\square}\left(\frac{\square}{\square}\right) - \frac{\square}{\square}\left(\frac{\square}{\square}\right)$$

$$= \left(\frac{\square}{\square}\right) - \left(\frac{\square}{\square}\right)$$

$$= \underline{\qquad} - \underline{\qquad}$$

---

26. *Use the Distributive Property.*

$$\frac{r^2}{t}\left(\frac{t}{s} + \frac{s^2}{rt}\right) = \frac{\square}{\square}\left(\frac{\square}{\square}\right) + \frac{\square}{\square}\left(\frac{\square}{\square}\right)$$

$$= \left(\frac{\square}{\square}\right) + \left(\frac{\square}{\square}\right)$$

$$= \underline{\hspace{1cm}} - \underline{\hspace{1cm}}$$

---

27. *If you had one table, how many guests could be seated?*

$$\frac{\text{change in guests}}{\text{change in tables}}$$

$$= \frac{\square}{\square} = \underline{\hspace{1cm}}$$

rate of change: $\underline{\hspace{1cm}} \dfrac{\text{guests}}{\text{table}}$

28. a. Use the given heights to write a proportion.

$$\frac{x}{100} = \frac{\square}{\square}$$

b. Solve the proportion.

$$x(\underline{\hspace{1cm}}) = 100(\underline{\hspace{1cm}})$$

$$x = \underline{\hspace{1cm}} = \underline{\hspace{1cm}}$$

c. $320\% = \underline{\hspace{1cm}}$ times a number

$$42 \cdot \underline{\hspace{1cm}} = 134.4$$

---

29. *The word "about" tells you to estimate the answer.*

14.5 is about _____   10% of _____ is _____

_____ − _____ = _____   The tower now leans about _____ past center.

---

30. Measure of the side that corresponds to side x: _____

Change 130% to a decimal and multiply.

$$130\% = \underline{\hspace{0.5cm}}.\underline{\hspace{0.5cm}} \qquad x = \underline{\hspace{0.5cm}}.\underline{\hspace{0.5cm}} \cdot \underline{\hspace{1cm}} = \underline{\hspace{1cm}}$$

Finding Slope Using the Slope Formula page 275

New Concepts

• The slope m of a line that passes through points (x_1, y_1) and (x_2, y_2) is $m = \frac{y_2 - y_1}{x_2 - x_1}$.

Math Language

The **slope** is a measure of the steepness of a line.

Example **Determining Slope from Two Points**

Determine the slope of the line that contains the points $(-4, 4)$ and $(4, -2)$.

Decide which point will be point 1 and which will be point 2.

Point 1 will be $(-4, 4)$,   Point 2 will be $(4, -2)$,
so (x_1, y_1) is $(-4, 4)$.   so (x_2, y_2) is $(4, -2)$.

$m = \dfrac{y_2 - y_1}{x_2 - x_1}$ *Slope formula*

$m = \dfrac{-2 - 4}{4 - (-4)}$ *Substitute the x- and y-values.*

$m = -\dfrac{6}{8} = -\dfrac{3}{4}$ *Simplify.*

The slope of the line is $-\dfrac{3}{4}$.

Example **Determining Slope from a Table**

Determine the slope of the line that contains the given points shown in the table.

x	y
-5	6
10	0
40	-12

Choose any two points from the table.
Decide which point will be point 1 and which will be point 2.

$m = \dfrac{y_2 - y_1}{x_2 - x_1}$ *Slope formula*

$= \dfrac{0 - 6}{10 - (-5)}$ *(x_2, y_2) is $(10, 0)$ and (x_1, y_1) is $(-5, 6)$.*

$= -\dfrac{6}{15}$ *Subtract in the numerator and in the denominator.*

$= -\dfrac{2}{5}$ *Simplify.*

The slope of the line is $-\dfrac{2}{5}$.

Determine the slope of the line that contains the given points.

a. $(-3, -4)$ and $(3, 0)$ *Substitute the points into the slope formula and simplify.*

$(x_1, y_1) = (-3, -4)$ and $(x_2, y_2) = (3, 0)$

$$\frac{y_2 - y_1}{x_2 - x_1} = \frac{0 - (-4)}{\square - \square} = \frac{\square}{\square} = \underline{\qquad}$$

b. $(x_1, y_1) = (\underline{\quad}, \underline{\quad})$ and $(x_2, y_2) = (\underline{\quad}, \underline{\quad})$

$$\frac{y_2 - y_1}{x_2 - x_1} = \frac{\square - \square}{\square - \square} = \frac{\square}{\square} = \underline{\qquad}$$

c. $(x_1, y_1) = (\underline{\quad}, \underline{\quad})$ and $(x_2, y_2) = (\underline{\quad}, \underline{\quad})$

$$\frac{y_2 - y_1}{x_2 - x_1} = \frac{\square - \square}{\square - \square} = \frac{\square}{\square} = \underline{\qquad}$$

d. $(x_1, y_1) = (\underline{\quad}, \underline{\quad})$ and $(x_2, y_2) = (\underline{\quad}, \underline{\quad})$

$$\frac{y_2 - y_1}{x_2 - x_1} = \frac{\square - \square}{\square - \square} = \frac{\square}{\square} = \underline{\qquad}$$

Determine the slope of the line that contains the points shown in the table.

e. *Use any two points in the table and the formula for the slope of a line.*

$(x_1, y_1) = (\underline{\quad}, \underline{\quad})$ and $(x_2, y_2) = (\underline{\quad}, \underline{\quad})$

$$\frac{y_2 - y_1}{x_2 - x_1} = \frac{\square - \square}{\square - \square} = \frac{\square}{\square} = \underline{\qquad}$$

Determine the slope of the given line.

f. $m = \underline{\qquad}$

g. $m = \underline{\qquad}$

h. $m = \underline{\qquad}$

i. $m = \underline{\qquad}$

j. $55 - 10 = \underline{\qquad}$ seconds

Convert. 1 mile = 5,280 feet $\frac{1}{2}$ mile $= \frac{1}{2} \cdot \underline{\qquad} = \underline{\qquad}$ ft

$$\frac{\text{change in distance}}{\text{change in time}} = \underline{\qquad} \text{ feet per second}$$

1. *Negative exponent: decimal point ⟵*

$8.2 \cdot 10^{-9} =$ _____

2. *Positive exponent: decimal point ⟶*

$0.23 \cdot 10^6 =$ _____

3. *The given number is greater than 1, so the exponent is positive.*

$112,500 =$ _____ $\cdot 10^{\square}$

4. *The given number is between 0 and 1, so the exponent is negative.*

$0.00058 =$ _____ $\cdot 10^{\square}$

5. domain: {_____}

range: {_____}

6. domain: {_____}

range: {_____}

7. 3 hours = _____ minutes

_____ = _____ + _____

8. *Set up a proportion.*

$$\frac{\square}{520} = \frac{\square}{100}$$

_____

9. Write an equation to find 35% of 90.

$n = 35\% \cdot$ _____

$n =$ _____ $\cdot$ _____ = _____

Find 35% more than 90.

_____ + _____ = _____

10. $\frac{n}{0}$ *is undefined.*

_____ $= 0$

$x =$ _____

11. $m = \frac{y_2 - y_1}{x_2 - x_1}.$

(x_1, y_1) is (___, ___). (x_2, y_2) is (___, ___).

$m = \dfrac{\square - \square}{\square - \square} = \dfrac{\square}{\square}$

$m =$ _____

12. (x_1, y_1) is (___, ___). (x_2, y_2) is (___, ___)

$m = \dfrac{\square - \square}{\square - \square} = \dfrac{\square}{\square}$

$m =$ _____

13. $\frac{n}{0}$ = undefined

(x_1, y_1) is (___, ___). (x_2, y_2) is (___, ___).

$m = \dfrac{\square - \square}{\square - \square} = \dfrac{\square}{\square}$

The slope is _____.

14. $m = \dfrac{\text{change in length}}{\text{change in time}}$

1 year = _____ months

$\dfrac{\square - \square}{\square - \square}$

_____inches per _____

15. *Choose any two points from the table to find the slope.*

$m = \dfrac{\square - \square}{\square - \square}$

$m =$ _____

Use the slope formula and m to find y.

$\dfrac{}{} = \dfrac{6 - y}{1 - 0}$

$y =$ _____

16. *Write and solve an equation for the number of trees, y, in each row.*

_____ = _____

$y =$ _____

Find the number of trees in each orchard.

_____ trees

17. Let h = cost of the 12 lbs of hamburger
Let p = cost of the 3 lbs potato salad

Write and solve two proportions.

Find the total cost.

_____

18. *Use an arithmetic sequence formula to find the height of the eighth floor.*

_____

19. a. $2y - 500 = -20x \longrightarrow$ _____

b. *Substitute x = 0 to find the y-intercept.*

To earn all profits with only _____ sales, _____ must be sold.

$20x + 2y = 500 \longrightarrow 20(\underline{}) + 2y = 500 \longrightarrow$ _____ $\longrightarrow y =$ _____

c. *Substitute y = 0 to find the x-intercept.*

$20x + 2y = 500 \longrightarrow 20x + 2(\underline{}) = 500 \longrightarrow$ _____ $\longrightarrow x =$ _____

To earn all profits with only _____ sales, _____ must be sold.

---

20. a. *Convert the fractions to decimals.*

_____ $x =$ _____

b. First method for solving:

1. Multiply both sides by _____.

2. Isolate x by dividing by _____.

Second method for solving: _____

_____

_____

21. *Multiply the numbers, then multiply the powers of 10.*

$4.2 \cdot 3.14 =$ _____

$10^{12} \cdot 10^{-4} = 10^{\square} =$ _____

_____ $\cdot 10^{\square}$

Write the expression in scientific notation.

_____ $\cdot$ _____

---

22. *Find the prime factorization of each term.*

$3x^2y^2 =$ _____ $\qquad 3xy^3 =$ _____

$-6x^3y^6 =$ _____ $\qquad$ GCF $=$ _____

Divide each term by the GCF.

$=$ _____ (_____)

23. *Use the Power of a Power Property.*

$(-2^3)^3 = -2^{\square \cdot \square} =$ _____

---

24. a. *Use the Product Property of Exponents.*

$2^5 \cdot 2^{10} =$ _____

$=$ _____

b. *There is one way to get every question correct.*

P(every question correct) $=$ _____

---

25. $m = \dfrac{y_2 - y_1}{x_2 - x_1}$

$m = $ _____

Circle the answer.

A $-1\dfrac{2}{3}$ 　　　　　 B $-\dfrac{3}{5}$

C $\dfrac{3}{5}$ 　　　　　　 D $1\dfrac{2}{3}$

26. *Think of a situation in which one group of data values decrease as another group of data values increase.*

_____

_____

_____

27. $\dfrac{\text{weekends}}{\text{weekdays}} = $ _____

Factor the denominator, then divide out like factors.

$= $ _____

28. Student _____ is correct. Student _____

_____ when solving for

the undefined value.

29. a. *Multiply.*

total length of the 4 strands = _____(_____) = _____

b. *The total length of the rope is x^2.*

_____

c. Factor the denominator, then divide out like factors.

_____ = _____

30. *Find the numerator's GCF. Then factor the numerator.*

_____ (_____)

Divide out like factors in the numerator and denominator.

_____ = _____

Name _____

Translating Between Words and Inequalities page 282

New Concepts

Math Language

An **inequality** is a mathematical statement comparing quantities that are not equal.

The **inequality symbols** and their meanings are shown below:

$<$ less than
$>$ greater than
$\leq$ less than or equal to
$\geq$ greater than or equal to
$\neq$ does not equal

"At least" means that the value is the lowest possible, so the inequality will translate to "is greater than or equal to" ($\geq$).

Example Translating Sentences into Inequalities

Translate the sentence into an inequality.

The quotient of a number and 2 is less than or equal to 6.

The quotient	This is the answer to a division problem. A fraction can be used to show division.
of a number and 2	The first number n is the numerator of the fraction. The second number 2 is the denominator.
is less than or equal to	The correct sign will be $\leq$.
6.	6

Write the inequality: $\dfrac{n}{2} \leq 6$

Example Translating Inequalities into Words

Write each inequality as a sentence.

$-2x + 4 \geq -8$

Since there is no operation symbol between -2 and x, multiplication is implied.

$-2x$	the product of negative 2 and a number
$+4$	the sum of (some quantity) and 4
$\geq$	is greater than or equal to
-8	negative eight

Sentence: **The sum of the product of -2 and a number and 4 is at least -8.**

$3x - 6 \leq -30$

$3x$	3 times a number
-6	the difference of (some quantity) and 6
$\leq$	is less than or equal to
-30	negative thirty

Sentence: **The difference of 3 times a number and 6 is less than or equal to negative 30.**

Translate each sentence into an inequality.

Break each sentence into parts. Use symbols to represent each part.

a. The quotient of an unknown number and −2 is greater than the opposite of 9.

The quotient of an unknown number and −2	is greater than	the opposite of 9
$\dfrac{x}{-2}$	>	−9

inequality: _____

b. 0 is less than or equal to the difference of twice a number and 8.

0	is less than or equal to	the difference of twice a number and 8
0	_____	_____ − _____

inequality: _____

c. The sum of half a number and 3 does not equal 15.

The sum of half a number and 3	does not equal	15
_____	_____	_____

inequality: _____

d. The product of 11 and a number is less than 121.   inequality: _____

Write each inequality as a sentence.

Break each inequality into terms and operators. Use words to represent each term or operator.

e. $12b \geq -8$

12b	≥	−8
The _____ 12 and a number	_____	_____

f. The _____ of the product of 1.5 and _____ is _____.

g. Nine is greater than _____.

h. A number _____ by _____ is at most _____.

i. The temperature of the beef must be greater than or equal to 140°F.
Substitute into the formula, then change the equal sign to an inequality sign.

$\dfrac{9}{5}°C + 32 =$ _____ °F $\dfrac{9}{5}°C + 32$ ◯ _____

1. *Use unit ratios.*

1 in. = 2.54 cm

There are _____ cm in 42 ft.

2. *Use unit ratios.*

5,280 ft = 1 mi

There are _____ inches in two miles.

---

3. *Use the order of operations.*

$-2(-3-3)(-2-4) - (-3-2) + 3(4-2)$

$=$ _____

4. $\dfrac{5(-5+3) + 7(-5+9) + 2}{(4-2) + 3 + 5}$

$=$ _____

---

5. *Break the sentence into parts. Use symbols to represent each part.*

The product of 6 and an unknown number	is less than or equal to	15
_____	_____	_____

---

6. *Let x = number of hours that Josephine sleeps each night*

Answer: _____

---

7. $-4b \geq 7$

Break each inequality into terms and operators. Use words to represent each term or operator.

$-4b$	$\geq$	7
_____	_____	_____

---

8. $\dfrac{t}{7} - 4 < 8$

Break each inequality into terms and operators. Use words to represent each term or operator.

$\dfrac{t}{7}$	-4	$<$	8
	_____	_____	_____

---

9. Plot the points. Connect the points in order to form a quadrilateral.

$slope = \frac{rise}{run}$

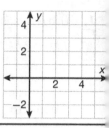

slope from (1, 3) to (3, 2) = _____   slope from (5, −1) to (2, 1) = _____

slope from (3, 2) to (5, −1) = _____   slope from (2, 1) to (1, 3) = _____

---

10. *Set up a proportion.*

$$\frac{24}{\square} = \frac{x}{\square}$$

Circle the answer.

  A 6.67%   **B** 15%

  C 136%   **D** 184%

11. *Use symbols to represent each part.*

4 more: _____

quotient of unknown and 9: _____

no less than: _____

inequality: _____

---

12. Let s = score in the third round

$s +$ _____ ◯ _____

13. Circle the answer.

  A $x + 5 \le 7$ **B** $x + 5 > 7$

  C $x − 5 \le 7$ **D** $x − 5 > 7$

---

14. $m = \frac{y_2 - y_1}{x_2 - x_1}$

(x_1, y_1) is (____, ____)

(x_2, y_2) is (____, ____)

$$m = \frac{\square - \square}{\square - \square}$$

$m = $ _____

15. **a.** *Find the point on the Stock A line for 9 days and for 0 days.*

(x_1, y_1) is (9, ___) and (x_2, y_2) is (0, ___)

$$m = \frac{\square}{\square} = \boxed{}$$ _____ per day

b. *Find the point on the Stock B line for 9 days and for 0 days.*

(x_1, y_1) is (9, ___) and (x_2, y_2) is (0, ___)

$$m = \frac{\square}{\square} = \boxed{}$$ _____ per day

c. Stock _____ was a better buy because

_____

---

16. (x_1, y_1) is (1962, 315)

(x_2, y_2) is (_____, _____)

$$m = \frac{\square}{\square} = $$ _____ parts per million per year

17. *Let the endpoints of the hypotenuse be (x_1, y_1) and (x_2, y_2).*

$$m = \frac{y_2 - y_1}{x_2 - x_1}$$

$$m = \frac{\square}{\square}$$

$m = $ _____

---

18. *Find the prime factorization of each term.*

$5m^2n^4 =$ _____

$10m^3n =$ _____

$GCF =$ _____

Divide each term by the GCF.

_____ (_____)

19. *Use the Distributive Property. Use the Product Property of Exponents.*

$$\frac{x^{-3}}{w^2}\left(\frac{4x^2}{w} - \frac{j^{-3}w}{x}\right) = \frac{x^{-3}}{w^2}\left(\frac{4x^2}{w}\right) - \frac{x^{-3}}{w^2}\left(\frac{j^{-3}w}{x}\right)$$

Answer: _____

20. *Substitute x = 0 to find the y-intercept.*
Substitute y = 0 to find the x-intercept.

$y = 4x + 12$

$y =$ _____

(_____ , _____)

$y = 4x + 12$

_____ $= x$

(_____ , _____)

21. *Use the scale factor $\frac{1}{16}$ to write and solve a proportion.*

a. $\dfrac{1}{16} = \dfrac{\square}{x}$

$x =$ _____

b. $\dfrac{1}{16} = \dfrac{\square}{\square}$

$x =$ _____

c. $\dfrac{1}{16} = \dfrac{\square}{\square}$ $x =$ _____

How many miles shorter is the shorter route?

_____ + _____ − _____ = _____

d. _____ because _____ may affect speed.

22. $r^2 = (1.75 \times 10^3)^2$

$A = 4\pi r^2$

$= 4 \cdot \pi \cdot ($ _____ $)^2$

$= 4\pi \cdot$ _____

$=$ _____

23. $rate = \dfrac{change\ in\ earnings}{change\ in\ time}$

$\dfrac{27 - \square}{4 - \square}$

The rate of change is _____

per _____ .

24. *There is a 25% increase in volume, so add the 25% to the original volume.*

$V =$ _____ $+ ($ _____ $)($ _____ $)$

$V =$ _____ $+$ _____

$V =$ _____ ▨

Draw a sketch.

25. Simplify.

$$\frac{24 + 9x}{x} = \underline{\hspace{2cm}}$$

Excluded values are those values that make the denominator equal zero.

$x \neq$ _____

26. Student _____ is correct. Student _____ did

not _____ the _____

_____ correctly.

27. *Find the points on the graph where x = 0, 1, −1, 2, and 4.*

x	0	1	−1	2	4
y					

28. a. $10^{\square} \div 10^{\square} = 10^{\square}$

$10^{\square} =$ _____ times longer

b. *Part **a** compared a kilometer to a centimeter. Part **b** compares a meter to a centimeter and then a kilometer to a meter.*

meter = centimeter · _____

kilometer = meter · _____   _____ · _____ = _____ = _____ times longer

The results are _____.

29. *There are 6 choices of names for the first name, but only 5 choices for the middle name.*

30. *Write each example in scientific notation. Compare the exponents to the number of zeros in the standard form.*

_____

_____

_____

Simplifying Expressions with Square Roots and Higher-Order Roots page 288

New Concepts

- A number has a positive square root and a negative square root.
  $3 \cdot 3 = 9$ and $-3 \cdot -3 = 9$. The square root of 9 would be 3 or -3.

Math Language

A **principal square root** is the positive root of a number.

Higher-Order Roots
If $a^n = b$, then the nth root of b is a, or $\sqrt[n]{b} = a$. The n to the left of the radical sign in the expression is the index of the radical. The index is an integer greater than or equal to 2.

Example **Simplifying Roots**

Simplify each expression.

$\sqrt[3]{-8}$

$\sqrt[3]{-8} = \sqrt[3]{(-2)^3}$

$= \sqrt[3]{(-2)(-2)(-2)} = -2$

$\sqrt[4]{81}$

$\sqrt[4]{81} = \sqrt[4]{3^4}$

$= \sqrt[4]{3 \cdot 3 \cdot 3 \cdot 3} = 3$

- When finding the root of a large number such as $\sqrt[4]{1296}$, it may be helpful to find the prime factorization of the radicand first.

  prime factorization of 1296: $2 \cdot 2 \cdot 2 \cdot 2 \cdot 3 \cdot 3 \cdot 3 \cdot 3$

  Since $1296 = 2^4 \cdot 3^4$, $\sqrt[4]{1296} = \sqrt[4]{2^4 \cdot 3^4} = 2 \cdot 3 = 6$.

- Roots can be written as fractional exponents.

Fractional Exponents
$\sqrt[n]{b} = b^{\frac{1}{n}}$

Example **Simplifying Expressions with Fractional Exponents**

Simplify each expression.

$(216)^{\frac{1}{3}}$

$(216)^{\frac{1}{3}} = \sqrt[3]{216}$

$= \sqrt[3]{6^3}$

$= 6$

$-256^{\frac{1}{4}} = \sqrt[4]{(-256)}$

$\sqrt[4]{(-256)}$ **has no real solution.**

Simplify each expression.

a. $\sqrt{196} = \sqrt{\underline{\quad} \cdot \underline{\quad}} = \underline{\qquad}$

b. $-\sqrt{64} = \sqrt{\underline{\quad} \cdot \underline{\quad}} = \underline{\qquad}$

c. $\sqrt{1} = \underline{\qquad}$

d. $\sqrt{(-64)} = \sqrt{\underline{\quad} \cdot \underline{\quad}} = \underline{\qquad}$

e. $\sqrt{\left(\frac{81}{144}\right)} = \frac{\sqrt{\square}}{\sqrt{\square}} = \frac{\square}{\square} = \frac{\square}{\square}$

f. prime factorization of 1728:

_____

$\sqrt[3]{1728} = \sqrt{\underline{\quad}^3 \cdot \underline{\quad}^3} = \underline{\qquad}$

g. prime factorization of 343:

_____

$\sqrt[3]{(-343)} = \sqrt[3]{\underline{\quad} \cdot \underline{\quad} \cdot \underline{\quad}} = \underline{\quad}$

h. $160{,}000 = 16 \cdot 10{,}000$

$\sqrt[4]{160{,}000} = \sqrt[4]{\underline{\quad} \cdot \underline{\quad} \cdot \underline{\quad} \cdot \underline{\quad}} = \underline{\qquad}$

i. $\sqrt[4]{(-16)} = \sqrt[4]{\underline{\quad} \cdot \underline{\quad} \cdot \underline{\quad} \cdot \underline{\quad}} = \underline{\qquad}$

j. $(125)^{\frac{1}{3}} = \sqrt[\square]{\underline{\quad}} = \sqrt{\underline{\quad} \cdot \underline{\quad} \cdot \underline{\quad}} = \underline{\qquad}$

k. $(-8)^{\frac{1}{3}} = \sqrt[\square]{\underline{\quad}} = \sqrt{\underline{\quad} \cdot \underline{\quad} \cdot \underline{\quad}} = \underline{\qquad}$

l. $(81)^{\frac{1}{4}} = \sqrt[\square]{\underline{\quad}} = \sqrt{\underline{\quad} \cdot \underline{\quad} \cdot \underline{\quad} \cdot \underline{\quad}} = \underline{\qquad}$

m. $(-625)^{\frac{1}{4}} = \sqrt[\square]{\underline{\quad}} = \sqrt{\underline{\quad} \cdot \underline{\quad} \cdot \underline{\quad} \cdot \underline{\quad}} = \underline{\qquad}$

n. A cube has a volume of 1728 cubic feet. What is the length of one side of the block?

$\sqrt[3]{1728} = \sqrt[3]{\underline{\quad} \cdot \underline{\quad} \cdot \underline{\quad}} = \underline{\quad}$ ft

1. $(p - x)(a - px)$ for $a = -3, p = 3, x = -4$

$(\underline{\quad} - \underline{\quad})(\underline{\quad} - \underline{\quad} \cdot \underline{\quad})$

$= (\underline{\quad})(\underline{\quad} - \underline{\quad})$

$= (\underline{\quad})(\underline{\quad})$

$= \underline{\quad}$

2. $-a[-a(x - a)]$ for $a = -2, x = 3$

$-(\underline{\quad})[-(\underline{\quad})(\underline{\quad} - (\underline{\quad}))]$

$= \underline{\quad}[\underline{\quad}(\underline{\quad})]$

$= \underline{\quad}(\underline{\quad})$

$= \underline{\quad}$

---

3. $\sqrt{(-10,000)}$

$= \sqrt{\underline{\quad} \cdot \underline{\quad}}$

$= \underline{\quad\quad}$

4. *Find the prime factorization of the radicand.*

$-\sqrt[4]{10,000}$

prime factorization of 10,000:

$\underline{\hspace{5cm}}$

$= \sqrt{\underline{\quad} \cdot \underline{\quad} \cdot \underline{\quad} \cdot \underline{\quad}}$

$= \underline{\quad}$

---

5. *Rearrange the factors.*

$xym^2 + 3xy^2m - 4m^2xy + 5mxy^2$

$\underline{\quad}m^{\square}xy + \underline{\quad}mxy^{\square}$

6. *Evaluate the numerator, then the denominator.*

$\sqrt[-3]{-\dfrac{27}{64}}$

$= \dfrac{\sqrt{\square \cdot \square \cdot \square}}{\sqrt{\square \cdot \square \cdot \square}} = \dfrac{\square}{\square}$

Answer: $\underline{\hspace{2cm}}$

7.

The opposite of 2	is less than or equal to	the difference of a number and 7.
$\underline{\quad}$	◯	$x - \underline{\quad}$

$\underline{\quad}$ ◯ $x - \underline{\quad}$

8.

A U.S. citizen	must be at least	35 years old in order to run for President.
$\underline{\quad}$	◯	$\underline{\quad}$

$\underline{\quad}$ ◯ $\underline{\quad}$

---

9. $\sqrt[3]{1500}$

$\sqrt[3]{1000} = \sqrt{\underline{\quad} \cdot \underline{\quad} \cdot \underline{\quad}} = \underline{\quad}$

$\sqrt[3]{1728} = \sqrt{\underline{\quad} \cdot \underline{\quad} \cdot \underline{\quad}} = \underline{\quad}$

$\underline{\qquad} < \sqrt[3]{1500} < \underline{\qquad}$

10. 1 mineral block for every 15 cows

independent variable:

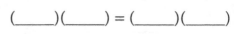
$\underline{\qquad\qquad} \cdot \underline{\qquad}$

dependent variable:

$\underline{\qquad\qquad\qquad\qquad}$

---

11. Use the ordered pairs to make a graph.

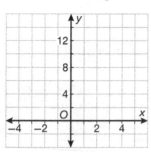

12. $\dfrac{5}{7} = \dfrac{h}{49}$

$(\underline{\quad})(\underline{\quad}) = (\underline{\quad})(\underline{\quad})$

$\underline{\qquad} = \underline{\qquad}$

$h = \underline{\qquad\qquad}$

---

13. *There are three choices: skirt OR pants, shirt, and tie OR vest.*

a. $\dfrac{\square}{\square} \times \dfrac{\square}{\square} \times \dfrac{\square}{\square} = \dfrac{\square}{\square}$

b. *Remember that two items are not replaced.*

$\dfrac{\square}{\square} \times \dfrac{\square}{\square} \times \dfrac{\square}{\square} = \dfrac{\square}{\square}$

---

14. *The product of $10 and a number is greater than or equal to $180.*

a. $\underline{\quad} \, y \, \bigcirc \, \underline{\qquad}$

b. Solve for y.

$y \, \bigcirc \, \underline{\qquad}$

---

15. *Distribute.*

$\dfrac{gt}{d^2}\left(\dfrac{gth}{d} - 3th + \dfrac{t}{5}\right)$

$= \dfrac{\square \cdot \square}{\square^2 \cdot \square} - \dfrac{\square \cdot 3th}{\square^2 \cdot 1} + \dfrac{\square \cdot \square}{\square^2 \cdot \square}$

$= \underline{\qquad} - \underline{\qquad} + \underline{\qquad}$

16. $\dfrac{(-8x^4)^2}{3}$

$= \dfrac{\square^2 \left(x^\square\right)^2}{3^\square}$

$= \dfrac{\square x^\square}{\square}$

17. $C = \pi \cdot d$

$\pi \cdot d \bigcirc$ _____

Solve for d.

$d \bigcirc$ _____

18. Set up a proportion.

$\dfrac{1}{10} = \dfrac{\square}{w}$ $\dfrac{1}{10} = \dfrac{\square}{l}$

(___)w = (___)(___)   (___)l = (___)(___)

$w =$ _____ $l =$ _____

The room is _____ inches by _____ inches.

---

19. $4.9 trillion is 4,900,000,000,000.

a. $4.9 trillion = _____ $\times 10^{\square}$

     300 million = _____ $\times 10^{\square}$

b. $\square \times \dfrac{10^{\square}}{\square} \times 10^{\square}$

     = about _____ $\times 10^{\square}$ per person

20. $27x^2y^3z + 12xy^2z$

prime factorization of $27x^2y^3z$:

_____

prime factorization of $12xy^2z$:

_____

The GCF is _____.

factored polynomial: _____(_____ + _____)

---

21. $\dfrac{\text{change in water}}{\text{change in time}} =$

$\dfrac{\square - \square}{\square - \square} =$ _____ gal per min

22. What is 120% of 250?

120% = _____

_____ $\times 250 =$ _____

---

23. Look for a common factor in the numerator, denominator, or both.

Circle the answer.

A $\dfrac{7x + 1}{5x^2 - x}$ **B** $\dfrac{x^2}{15 - x}$

C $\dfrac{x^2 + 1}{x^2 - 3x}$ **D** $\dfrac{8(2 - x)}{6 - 3x}$

24. Look for common factors.

$\dfrac{(6 - 6x)}{(9 - 9x)}$

$= \dfrac{\square(\square - x)}{\square(\square - x)}$

$= \dfrac{\square}{\square} = \dfrac{\square}{\square}$

I factored out a _____ in the numerator and a _____ in the denominator. Then I canceled the _____ binomial and simplified the remaining _____.

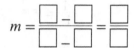

25. *Use any two points and the formula for slope.*

$$m = \frac{\square - \square}{\square - \square} = \frac{\square}{\square}$$

---

26. $m = \dfrac{\square - \square}{\square - \square}$

$= \dfrac{\square}{\square}$

$m = \underline{\hspace{2cm}}$

27. Student _____ is correct.

Student _____ incorrectly translated "at

most" as _____ or _____

instead of _____ or _____.

---

28. $P = 2l + 2w$

$2(\underline{\quad}) + 2(\underline{\quad}) \bigcirc \underline{\quad}$

$\underline{\quad} w \bigcirc \underline{\quad}$

29. $400 - \underline{\hspace{1.5cm}} = \underline{\hspace{1.5cm}}$

$\dfrac{\square}{\square} = \underline{\hspace{1cm}}$

Marcy needs to read about _____ pages.

---

30. *Solve for r. Then find the diameter of the can.*

$$V = \pi r^2 h$$

$$\frac{\square}{\square}\pi = \pi r^2(\underline{\quad})$$

$$\frac{\square}{\square}\pi \cdot \frac{\square}{\square} = \underline{\quad}\pi r^2 \cdot \frac{\square}{\square}$$

$$\frac{\square}{\square} = r^2$$

$$\sqrt{\frac{\square}{\square}} = r$$

$$\frac{\square}{\square} = r$$

$$d = 2 \times \underline{\hspace{1cm}} = \frac{\square}{\square} \text{ inches}$$

The diameter of a tennis ball is _____ inches.

LESSON 47

Solving Problems Involving the Percent of Change page 294

New Concepts

Math Language

The **percent of change** is the ratio of the amount of change compared to the original amount, expressed as a percent.

If the original amount is greater than the changed amount, it is a **percent of decrease.**

If the original amount is less than the changed amount, it is a **percent of increase.**

Example Finding the Percent of Increase or Decrease

Find the percent of change.

number of United States airports in 1985: 15,161
number of United States airports in 2005: 19,854

$19,854 - 15,161 = 4693$ The difference is positive, so the percent of change is a percent of increase.

$\dfrac{\text{amount of increase}}{\text{original amount}} = \dfrac{4693}{15,161} = 0.31,\text{ or } 31\%$

The percent of increase is 31%.

number of taxicabs in the United States in 2001: 31,800
number of taxicabs in the United States in 2002: 30,800

$30,800 - 31,800 = -1000$ The difference is negative, so the percent of change is a percent of decrease.

$\dfrac{\text{amount of increase}}{\text{original amount}} = -\dfrac{1000}{31,800} = -0.03 = -3\%$

The percent of decrease is 3%.

• You can use percent to find discount prices and markup prices.

Math Language

A **markup** results when a percent of increase is applied to a cost.

A **discount** results when a percent of decrease is applied to a cost.

Example Finding Markups and Discounts

A music store marks up the price of CDs they purchased at $9.00 each by 70%. **What is the markup and the new price of each CD?**

70% is the percent of increase in the $9.00 cost.

$n = 0.70 \cdot \$9$ Use an equation to find 70% of $9.
$n = 6.30$ **The markup is $6.30.**

$\$9 + \$6.30 = \$15.30$ **The new price of each CD is $15.30.**

A bookstore is having a sale of 40% off all items. **What is the discount and new price of a book that originally cost $12?**

40% is the percent of decrease in the $12.00 cost.

$0.40 \cdot \$12 = n$ Use an equation to find 40% of $12.
$n = \$4.80$ **The discount is $4.80.**

$\$12 - \$4.80 = \$7.20$ **The new price of the book is $7.20.**

Find the percent of change.

a. 2006 salary: $600 per week
2007 salary: $630 per week

630 − 600 = _____ $\dfrac{\boxed{}}{600}$ = _____

The percent of _____ is _____ %.

b. number of words in first draft: 1032
number of words in second draft: 774

1032 − 774 = _____ $\dfrac{\boxed{}}{1032}$ = _____

The percent of _____ is _____%.

c. markup: $44.00 · _____ = $_____

cost of new boots: $_____ + $44.00 = $_____

d. discount: $344,000 · _____ = $_____

$344,000 − $_____ = $_____

e. A weightlifter can lift 90 pounds. After six months he can lift 125 pounds. What is the percent of increase in the amount of weight he can lift?

125 − _____ = _____ $\dfrac{\boxed{}}{\boxed{}}$ = _____%

He can lift about _____% more weight than before.

f. Binders that originally sold for $4.95 each are now selling for $3.87 each. What is the percent of decrease in the price of the binders?

$3.87 − $_____ = $_____ $\dfrac{\$\boxed{}}{\$\boxed{}}$ = − _____%

There was about a _____% decrease in price.

1. $-(x-3) - 2(x-4) = 7$

$x = \dfrac{\square}{\square}$

 Check your answer.

2. $3p - 4 - 6 = -2(p-5)$

$p = \underline{\hspace{1cm}}$

Check your answer.

3. $k + 4 - 5(k+2) = 3k - 2$

$k = \dfrac{\square}{\square}$

Check your answer.

4. The product of 3.6 and an unknown number is greater than 18.

$\underline{\hspace{1cm}} x \bigcirc \underline{\hspace{1cm}}$

5. Simplify $a^3x - |x^3|$ for $a = -3$ and $x = -2$.

$= \underline{\hspace{1cm}}$

6. *Write and simplify a ratio.*

$\underline{\hspace{2cm}}$ per box

7. Evaluate $\sqrt[3]{(-512)}$

Find a number that multiplied by itself three times is equal to −512.

$\sqrt{\underline{\hspace{0.5cm}} \cdot - \underline{\hspace{0.5cm}} \cdot - \underline{\hspace{0.5cm}}}$

$= \underline{\hspace{1cm}}$

8.
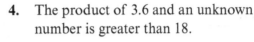
$\text{Percent of change} = \dfrac{\text{amount of change}}{\text{original amount}}$

$\$49 - \$\underline{\hspace{1cm}} = \underline{\hspace{1cm}}$

$\dfrac{\square}{\square} = \underline{\hspace{1cm}}$

$= \underline{\hspace{2cm}}$ increase

9.

$$\text{Percent of change} = \frac{\text{amount of change}}{\text{original amount}}$$

____ − ____ = ____

$$\frac{\boxed{}}{\boxed{}} = \text{\_\_\_\_} \approx \text{\_\_\_}\%$$

A 10% **B** 12% **C** 13% **D** 11%

10. It _____ (is/is not) possible to have a percent increase of more than 100%; this could be when _____

It _____ (is/is not) possible to have a percent of decrease more than 100%.

11. $\dfrac{12,000}{30,000}$ = _____ = _____ % $\dfrac{4800}{12,000}$ = _____ = _____ %

Each number after the first is ____% of the preceding number. The next two terms are _____ , _____ .

12. *A vertical line has an undefined slope.*

$m = \dfrac{y_2 - y_1}{x_2 - x_1}$

Circle the answer.

A $(-16, 8)$ and $(-1, 10)$
B $(-5, -15)$ and $(18, 6)$
C $(1, 1)$ and $(-1, -1)$
D $(-1, -4)$ and $(-1, 15)$

13. Rise over run refers to a change in the

_____ of a line divided by the corresponding change in the

_____

14. *Find 25% of $500.*

Sale price: $500 − $_____ = $_____

Find 25% of the sale price.

New price: Sale price + $_____ = $_____

$_____ − $_____ = $_____

The management _____ (is/is not) correct.

The _____ price is higher.

15. Student ____ is correct.

The expression is equal to the _____ root of 16, which is ____ .

16. $81\pi = \pi r^2$

$r^2 =$ ____ so $r =$ ____ and $2r =$ ____

$C = 2\pi r =$ _____

17. $\sqrt[3]{\text{\_\_\_} \cdot \text{\_\_\_} \cdot \text{\_\_\_} \cdot \text{\_\_\_}}$

= ____

18. *Let x = number of* _____   *Let 45 − x = number of* _____

There were _____ sparrows and _____ doves.

---

19. *Use the Negative and Zero Exponent Properties.*

$$\frac{3n^0}{m^{-2}} = \underline{\quad}m^{\square}$$

$$= 3(\underline{\quad})^2$$

$$= (\underline{\quad})(\underline{\quad})$$

$$= \underline{\quad}$$

20. a. $a_1 = \underline{\quad}$, $a_n = \underline{\quad}$

b. $a_1 = \underline{\quad}$, $a_2 = \underline{\quad}$,

$a_3 = \underline{\quad}$, $a_4 = \underline{\quad}$

---

21. Student _____ is correct.

Twice a number means ____ times the

_____. Student _____ added instead

of _____.

22. $m = \dfrac{y_2 - y_1}{x_2 - x_1}$

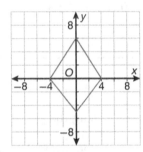

$$m = \pm\frac{\square}{\square}$$

---

23. $\frac{n}{0}$ *is undefined.*

The expression is _____ for _____ values of _____.

---

24. $\$3484.00 \cdot 15\% = \quad \$3484.00 \cdot \underline{\quad}.\underline{\quad} = \$\underline{\quad}$

_____ $\cdot$ ___% = _____ $\cdot$ ___.___ = $\underline{\quad}$

$\$\underline{\quad} - \$\underline{\quad} = \$\underline{\quad}$ more each month.

---

25. *Find the ratio of rise to run.*

$$\text{rate of change} = \frac{\Box}{\Box}$$

The rate of change is _____ eggs per omelet.

26. *Use the Power of a Product Property.*

$$(-4ab^2c^2)^3$$
$$= (-4)^{\Box}(a)^{\Box}(b^2)^{\Box}(c^2)^{\Box}$$
$$= \underline{}a^{\Box}b^{\Box}c^{\Box}$$

27. *For every nonzero number x, $x^{-n} = \frac{1}{x^n}$*

If $x = 0$, then $x^{-2} = \dfrac{\Box}{\Box}$

$$= \dfrac{\Box}{\Box}$$

$$= \underline{}$$

0 cannot be a _____.

28. $2.817939 \cdot 10^{-15}$

$$= \underline{}$$

29. a. The expression $2(2a + 2ab + 2bc)$ _____ (is/is not) a correct factorization of a polynomial.

Using the _____ Property, $2(2a + 2ab + 2bc) = \underline{}a + \underline{}ab + \underline{}bc$, which is the original polynomial.

b. The expression $2(2a + 2ab + 2bc)$ _____ (does/does not) factor the polynomial completely.

The polynomial in parentheses, $(2a + 2ab + 2bc)$, still has a common factor of _____.

The complete factorization would be _____.

30. *Write and solve an equation.*

Let x = amount that Shari forgot to write down

The two deposits were each for _____.

Analyzing Measures of Central Tendency

New Concepts

- A **measure of central tendency** is a value that describes the center of the data set. Measures include the mean, median, and mode.

Math Language
A **mean** is the sum of values in a data set divided by the number of data values. The mean is also known as the **average**.
The **median** is the middle number of a data set when the numbers are arranged in numerical order.
The **mode** is the number that occurs most often in a data set. There may or may not be a mode.

Example Finding the Mean, Median, and Mode

Find the mean, median, and mode of the values in this data set rounded to the nearest whole number.

35, 36, 33, 38, 36, 34, 35, 35, 33

$$\text{mean} = \frac{35 + 36 + 33 + 38 + 36 + 34 + 35 + 35 + 33}{9}$$

$$= \frac{315}{9}$$

$$= 35 \longleftarrow \text{mean}$$

median: 33, 33, 34, 35, ⑶⑤, 35, 36, 36, 38
mode: The number **35** occurs more than any other number.

- The **range of the set of data** is the difference between the greatest and least values in the data set.

Example Comparing Data

The table lists the total points teams scored in the two divisions of the All-Star Football League for the 2006 regular season.

Total Points Scored in the 2006 Regular Season

North	398, 425, 355, 307, 427, 301, 282, 305, 413, 270, 292, 211, 335, 367, 298, 314
South	385, 316, 300, 260, 353, 373, 353, 238, 427, 324, 371, 267, 492, 331, 319, 168

Does the North or the South have a greater range of points?

Calculate the range of values for each data set by determining the greatest and least values in each set and finding the difference between them.

North   greatest value: 427; least value: 211 $427 - 211 = 216$
South   greatest value: 492; least value: 168 $492 - 168 = 324$

Compare the ranges of the two data sets: $324 > 216$.
The data for the South has a greater range of values.

• An **outlier** is a data value that is much greater than or less than the other values in the data set.

> **Example** **Analyzing the Effects of an Outlier**
>
> The following data show the high temperatures (°F) for 15 days.
>
> 75, 79, 81, 81, 84, 81, 81, 78, 76, 78, 89, 98, 81, 78, 86
>
> **Identify any outliers in the data set.**
>
> Write the data in numeric order and observe any patterns.
>
> 75, 76, 78, 78, 78, 79, 81, 81, 81, 81, 81, 84, 86, 89, 98
>
> **The outlier value of 98 is much greater than the other values in the data set.**

Lesson Practice 📖 page 301

a. *Arrange the values in numerical order first.*

_____, _____, _____, _____, _____, _____, _____, _____, _____

median: _____   mode: _____

mean: ____ + ____ + ____ + ____ + ____ + ____ + ____ + ____ + ____ = _____

_____ ÷ ____ = ____

b. *The range is the difference between the greatest value and the least value.*

trucks: _____ − _____ = _____

convertibles: _____ − _____ = _____

_____ had the greater range of sales.

c. Write the values in order: ____, ____, ____, ____, ____, ____, ____, ____, ____, ____,

____, ____, ____, ____, ____, ____, ____, ____, ____, ____

outliers: _____ and _____

d. The outliers _____ the mean age by about ____ years and the median by ____ years.

e. median: _____

The _____ is better for budgeting because it is specific to the particular city in which one lives.

1. Greatest common factors of:

4, 2, and 6: _____

a, a^2, and a^3: _____

b^2, b^3, and b^4: _____

c^4, c^2, and c: _____

GCF = _____

2. Greatest common factors of:

5, 10, and 15: _____

m^2, m^2, and m^2: _____

x^2, x, and x^2: _____

y^5, y^2, and y^4: _____

GCF = _____

3. *Distribute.*

$4x^2(ax - 2) =$ _____ $-$ _____

4. *Write the expression with positive exponents first.*

$$\frac{(6a^{-3}c^{-3})}{(a^{-2}cd)}$$

$$= \frac{\square a^{\square}}{a^{\square}c^{\square}d^{\square}}$$

$$= \frac{\square}{\square}$$

5. Multiply.

$$\frac{6}{8} \cdot \frac{\square}{\square}$$

= _____

6. Write the data in order.

___, ___, ___, ___, ___, ___,

___, ___, ___, ___, ___

median: _____ mode: _____ mean: _____

7. *A data set with 10 members and a mean of 19*

has a sum of ___ • ___ = _____.

To find the sum of the four identical values, subtract the sum of the 6-member data set from the sum of the 10-member data set:

$190 - (19 + 18 + 17 + 17 + 19 + 15) =$ _____

To find the value of one of the identical four, divide the sum by four:

_____ $\div 4 =$ _____

8. **a.** $\left(\dfrac{x}{y} - \dfrac{r}{x}\right)\left(\dfrac{\square}{\square} - \dfrac{\square}{\square}\right)$

b. $\dfrac{x^2}{y^2} - \dfrac{\square}{\square} - \dfrac{\square}{\square} + \dfrac{r^2}{x^2}$

or $\dfrac{x^2}{y^2} - \dfrac{\square}{\square} - \dfrac{\square}{\square} + \dfrac{r^2}{x^2}$

c. Add like terms:

$\dfrac{x^2}{y^2} - \dfrac{\square}{\square} + \dfrac{r^2}{x^2}$

9. It is true when the exponent is _____ and false when the exponent is _____.

   Why? _____

---

10. **a.** *The mean is found by dividing the sum of the data by the number of data values.*

    $$\underline{\hspace{1cm}} = \dfrac{\square}{\square}$$

    b. *Multiply both sides by the denominator.*

    (_____)(_____) = (_____)

    Simplify.

    _____ + _____ = _____

    _____ = _____

    $x = $ _____

    c. *Substitute in the expression $x + 12$.* _____ = _____

---

11. *Write the numbers in order.*

    median: _____   mode: _____

    mean: _____   range: _____

    Circle the answer.

    A mean   **B** median

    C mode   **D** range

12. _____, it is possible for the mode

    to be the lowest or the _____ of the

    data set.

---

13. *Find each balance in order, working from the prior balance.*

    a. $\$150 + (150 \cdot 15\%) = $ _____   _____ − (_____ $\cdot\, 8\%) = $ _____

    _____ + (_____ $\cdot\, 25\%) = $ _____

    b. *Difference between new balance and starting balance*   _____ − $\$150 = $ _____

    Divide difference by starting balance and multiply by 100.   _____ ÷ $\$150 \times 100 = $ ___% _____

---

14. $\$3474 - $ _____ = _____   _____ ÷ _____ = _____

    _____ of _____%

---

15. The sum of _____ and _____ is odd.

16. The mode of _____ may show that Juan missed _____ games, so it _____ a representative measure of central tendency.

17. outlier: _____

The outlier represents _____ who did very _____ during the season.

18. a. *Write the equation so the variables are on one side.*

$10y = 3x + 360$ _____ = _____

b. Substitute $x = 0$ and solve for y. $y = $ _____

If the phone is not used, the charge is still _____.

c. Substitute $y = 0$ and solve for x. $x = $ _____

To have a bill of $0, _____ minutes would be used. Possible? _____

19. Factor out the -2.

$h = -16t^2 + 12t + 2$

$h = (-2)(\underline{\quad\quad\quad})$

20. $\dfrac{\square}{100} = \dfrac{\square}{\square}$

_____ = _____

_____ = _____

21. *Factor the denominator and eliminate the decimal to simplify.*

$\dfrac{xl}{0.5(x^2 + 4x)}$

$= $ _____

22. $m = \dfrac{y_2 - y_1}{x_2 - x_1}$

$= $ _____

$= $ _____

$= $ _____

23.

The sum of $\frac{1}{2}$ an unknown number and the opposite of 4	is less than	6.

_____ + _____ ◯ _____

24. amount deposited after w months: _____

current balance: _____

resulting balance: _____

The resulting balance is calculated by

adding the _____

and the _____.

Answer: _____

---

25. $\sqrt[6]{m} =$ _____

---

26. *This expression can be written as $-(15)^{\frac{1}{4}}$.*

The exponent _____ apply to the

negative sign, so

$-15^{\frac{1}{4}} = ($____$)($____$)^{\frac{1}{4}} =$

$\underline{\quad}\,\sqrt[\square]{\underline{\quad}}$

Answer: _____

---

27. \$500 $\bigcirc$ \$400, so this is a percent

_____.

\$500 − 400 = \$_____

_____ ÷ _____ × 100 = _____%

---

28. Student _____ is correct.

Student _____ found the percent of

_____.

---

29. *Let $x =$ new side length*

new perimeter = old perimeter + 75% of
old perimeter

$($____$) x = ($____$)(2) + ($____$)($____$)(2)$

$($____$) x =$ ____ + ____

$($____$) x =$ ____

$x =$ ____ in.

 Draw a sketch.

---

30. The premise and conclusion use _____ reasoning.

The conclusion is based on a(n) _____ pattern.

Writing Equations in Slope-Intercept Form

page 307

New Concepts

| **Example** | Graphing an Equation of a Line in Slope-Intercept Form |

Graph $2x + y + 5 = 0$.

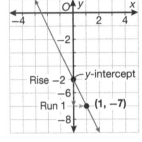

Write the equation in slope-intercept form.

$$2x + y + 5 = 0$$
$$y = -2x - 5$$

The slope $m = -2$.

The y-intercept $b = -5$.

Plot the y-intercept: $(0, -5)$.

Use the slope to find another point on the line.

$$m = -2 = \frac{-2}{1} = \frac{rise}{run}$$

From the y-intercept, $(0, -5)$, move 2 units down and 1 unit to the right. Plot that point, $(1, -7)$. Draw the line through the two points.

Math Language

The **slope-intercept form** of a linear equation is $y = mx + b$, where m is the slope of the line and b is the y-intercept.

The **y-intercept** is the y-value where a graph intersects the y-axis. It is usually represented by the variable b. The coordinate is $(0, b)$.

| **Example** | Writing the Equation of a Line from a Graph |

Write the equation of the graphed line in slope-intercept form.

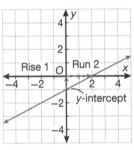

The line crosses the y-axis at $(0, -1)$, so $b = -1$.

Identify the slope by moving from the y-intercept to another point on the line such as $(2, 0)$.

$$m = \frac{rise}{run} = \frac{1 \text{ unit up}}{2 \text{ units right}} = \frac{1}{2}$$

Substitute the values for m and b into the slope-intercept form.

$$y = mx + b$$

$$y = \frac{1}{2}x - 1$$

Find the slope and the y-intercept of the equation.

a. $y = 0.7x - 4.9$

$m =$ _____

$b =$ _____

b. $-9x + 3y = 12$ *Isolate y.*

slope-intercept form: _____

$m =$ _____ $b =$ _____

Graph each line using the equation that is in slope-intercept form.

c. $y = \frac{3}{5}x$

y-intercept: $b =$ _____ or (0, ___)

slope: $m = \dfrac{\square}{\square}$

To find a second point, from (0, ___) move

_____ units _____ and ____ units to the

_____: (____, ____).

 Graph. Plot the y-intercept and the point. Then draw a line through the points.

d. $x - 4y - 20 = 0$

slope-intercept form: _____

y-intercept: _____ or (____, ____)

slope: $m = \dfrac{\square}{\square}$

second point: (____, ____)

 Graph.

Write the equation of the graphed line in slope-intercept form.

e. Line crosses y-axis at (0, ___), so $b =$ _____.

$m = \dfrac{\text{rise}}{\text{run}} = \dfrac{\square}{\square}$

equation: $y =$ ____ $x +$ ____

f. $b =$ _____

$m = \dfrac{\text{rise}}{\text{run}} = \dfrac{\square}{\square}$

equation: $y =$ _____

g. *The y-intercept is the starting value or constant amount. The slope is the rate of change.*

$b = \$$ _____ $m =$ _____ per mile

Point-slope equation: $y =$ ____ $x +$ ____

Plot the y-intercept. Then use the slope to find another point. Draw a line through the y-intercept and the new point.

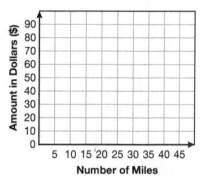

Car Rental Rates

1. $x^2y^3(3xy - 5y)$

$=$ _____

2. $-2x^3y^3(4x^2y - 3xy)$

$=$ _____

3. Evaluate x^2y^3z if $x = 3$, $y = -2$ and $z = 4$.

$=$ _____

4. Evaluate $-x^2 - y^3$ if $x = -3$ and $y = -2$.

$=$ _____

5. Find the x-intercept.

$3x + 2y - 10 = 0$

x-intercept $=$ (____ , ____)

6. Write the equation in slope-intercept form.

$2x - 5y - 6 = 0$

$-5y =$ _____

$y =$ _____

slope: $m =$ _____

y-intercept: $b =$ _____

7. y-intercept: $b =$ _____

slope: $m = \dfrac{\square}{\square} =$ _____

Circle the answer.

A $y = -\frac{1}{3}x + 3$ **B** $y = -\frac{1}{3}x - 3$

C $y = -3x + 3$ **D** $y = -3x - 3$

8. a. The y-intercept is the starting value or constant amount. The slope is the rate of change.

Let $x =$ number of _____

Let $y =$ total _____

$m =$ seconds per biscuits

$y =$ ____ $x +$ ____

b. y-intercept: _____ or (____ , ____)

The y-intercept has _____ meaning because you would not cook _____ biscuits for 75 seconds.

9. $F = y$ and $C = x$

slope: $m = $ _____

y-intercept: $b = $ _____

✎ Graph. Plot the y-intercept. Then use the slope to find another point. Draw a line through the y-intercept and the new point.

10. a. *Let y represent the amount of food and x represent the weight of the cat. Use the table and the slope formula to find the slope.*

$y = $ _____ x ◯ _____

b. The relationship _____ a linear equation. According to the table, a cat that weighs $1\frac{1}{2}$ lb should get _____ cups of food a day.

11. *See page 13 in the* Student Reference Guide.

mean: _____

median: _____

mode: _____

12. Student _____ is correct. Student _____ did not list the data _____ before finding the median.

13. mean: _____ median: _____ mode: _____

The next person he surveys _____ likely to have more than 4 pets. Because the data centers around _____, it is more likely that the next person surveyed _____.

14. *Factor out the GCG in the numerator and in the denominator.*

$$\frac{x^2 - 12x}{2x^2 - x} = \frac{\square(\square - \square)}{\square(\square - \square)}$$

$= $ _____

15. $\dfrac{22}{\square} = \dfrac{x}{\square}$

$22 \cdot$ _____ $= $ _____ $\cdot x$

_____ $= $ _____

_____ $\cdot$ ___ $= x$

16. *Choose two points on the line that are closest to the grid lines.*

$slope = \dfrac{rise}{run}$

rise $= $ _____   run $= $ _____

slope $= $ _____

17. *Write an equation and solve it.*

Let x = number of rides

Answer: _____ blocks

18. A deck of cards contains 15 cards, five of each number 1, 2, and 3.

odds of getting a 1:

_____ : _____ or _____ : _____

odds of NOT getting a 3:

_____ : _____ or _____ : _____

19. $a_1 =$ _____, $a_n = a_{n-1} + d$

$a_3 = a_2 +$ _____ $=$ _____ $+$ _____ $=$ _____

first four terms: _____, _____, _____, _____

$a_2 = a_1 +$ _____ $=$ _____ $+$ _____ $=$ _____

$a_4 = a_3 +$ _____ $=$ _____ $+$ _____ $=$ _____

20.

a. $\angle M$ corresponds to $\angle$ _____

b. $m\angle Q =$ _____

c. 6: _____ or _____ : _____

d. $\dfrac{\square}{\square} = \dfrac{\square}{\square}$

$x =$ _____

21. greatest value: _____ . _____ million

range = _____ . _____ $-$ _____ . _____ $=$ _____ . _____ million

least value: _____ . _____ million

22. *Add the number of visitors each year and then divide by the number of years.*

mean = _____

$$A = \frac{1}{2}b \cdot h$$

$$\underline{\hspace{1.5cm}} = \frac{1}{2}(\underline{\hspace{0.8cm}}) \cdot h$$

$$\underline{\hspace{1.5cm}} = \underline{\hspace{0.8cm}} \cdot h$$

$$\underline{\hspace{1.5cm}} = h$$

23. Student _____ is correct. Since the price decreased by 15%, the current price would be _____% of the original price.

24. $A = s^2$, so $\sqrt{A} = \sqrt{s^2}$

   a. $s^2 = 2116$ so $s_{table} =$ _____ $=$ ☐

   b. $s_{tablecloth} = s_{table} + 2($____$) =$ _____ ☐

      $A_{tablecloth} =$ _____ $\cdot$ _____ $=$ ☐

   c. _____ $- 2116 =$ _____ ☐

25. *Find the innermost root first, then find the outermost root.*

$\sqrt{256} =$ _____ $\sqrt[4]{256} =$ _____

 _____ $=$ _____ $\sqrt[4]{}$ _____ $=$ _____

$\sqrt[4]{\sqrt{256}}$ ◯ $\sqrt{\sqrt[4]{256}}$

26. $percent\ of\ change = \dfrac{amount\ of\ change}{original\ amount}$

amount of change in price $= \$$_____

 $= $ ____.____

The percent of _____ is _____.

27.

the sum of twice a number and $\frac{1}{3}$	is less than	$1\frac{2}{3}.$

inequality: _____

28. $average\ decay = m = \dfrac{y_2 - y_1}{x_2 - x_1}$

(x_1, y_1) is (____, ____).
(x_2, y_2) is (1996, 804).

average decay $=$ _____ ☐

29. The statement uses _____ reasoning because the conclusion is based on an observed _____.

30. $s = 2x$

   a. $A_{side} = s^2 =$ _____ $^2 =$ _____ ☐

   b. *The bottom is uncovered.*

      _____ $\cdot$ _____ $=$ _____ ☐

New Concepts

• An inequality can have more than one solution.

> **Example** **Identifying Solutions to Inequalities**
>
> Determine which of the values $\{0, 2, 4, 6\}$ are part of the solution set of the inequality $4y - 5 \geq 11$.
>
> $y = 0: 4(0) - 5 \geq 11 \longrightarrow -5 \geq 11$; false
> $y = 2: 4(2) - 5 \geq 11 \longrightarrow 3 \geq 11$; false
> $y = 4: 4(4) - 5 \geq 11 \longrightarrow 11 \geq 11$; true
> $y = 6: 4(6) - 5 \geq 11 \longrightarrow 19 \geq 11$; true
>
> The solution set for $4y - 5 \geq 11$ includes 4 and 6.

• A graph on a number line can represent the solution set of an inequality. An open or closed circle shows the endpoint and whether it is included. A heavy line and arrow show all values in the solution set.

Endpoint		Arrow	
$<, >, \neq$	$\leq, \geq$	$<, \leq$	$>, \geq$
open circle	closed circle	←	→

> **Example** **Graphing Inequalities**
>
> Graph each inequality.
>
> $g > 5.8$
>
> For $>$: Circle is open.
>   Arrow points right.
>
>
>
> $x \leq -2$
>
> For $\leq$: Circle is closed.
>   Arrow points left.
>
>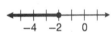

> **Example** **Writing an Inequality from a Graph**
>
> Write an inequality for each graph.
>
> *Identify the endpoint first. Determine if it is open or closed. Use the direction of the arrow to determine which inequality symbol to use.*
>
>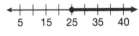
>
> endpoint: 25   sign: $\geq$ endpoint: $\frac{3}{4}$ sign: $<$
>
> $n \geq 25$ $r < \frac{3}{4}$

a. Determine which of the values $\{-2, 0, 5, 11\}$ are part of the solution set of $3x + 4 < 19$.

$x = -2$: $3(\underline{\quad}) + 4 < 19 \longrightarrow \underline{\quad} < 19$, $\underline{\hspace{2cm}}$ (*true, false*).

$x = 0$: $3(\underline{\quad}) + 4 < 19 \longrightarrow \underline{\quad} < 19$, $\underline{\hspace{2cm}}$ (*true, false*).

$x = 5$: $3(\underline{\quad}) + 4 < 19 \longrightarrow \underline{\quad} < 19$, $\underline{\hspace{2cm}}$ (*true, false*).

$x = 11$: $3(\underline{\quad}) + 4 < 19 \longrightarrow \underline{\quad} < 19$, $\underline{\hspace{2cm}}$ (*true, false*).

$\underline{\hspace{2cm}}$ and $\underline{\hspace{1.5cm}}$ make the inequality true.

Graph each inequality.

Determine if the circle is opened or closed. Determine the direction that the arrow points.

b. $u > -2$

<+—+—+—+—+—+—+—+—+—+>

c. $t \geq 2.5$

<+—+—+—+—+—+—+—+—+>

d. $y \leq 3\frac{1}{3}$

<+++++++++++++++++++>

e. $0 > v$

<+—+—+—+—+—+—+—+—+>

Write an inequality for each graph.

f. endpoint: $\underline{\hspace{1.5cm}}$ circle: $\underline{\hspace{2.5cm}}$

arrow points: $\underline{\hspace{1.5cm}}$ $x \bigcirc \underline{\hspace{1.5cm}}$

g. endpoint: $\underline{\hspace{1.5cm}}$ circle: $\underline{\hspace{2.5cm}}$

arrow points: $\underline{\hspace{1.5cm}}$ $x \bigcirc \underline{\hspace{1.5cm}}$

h. endpoint: $\underline{\hspace{1.5cm}}$ circle: $\underline{\hspace{2.5cm}}$

arrow points: $\underline{\hspace{1.5cm}}$ $x \bigcirc \underline{\hspace{1.5cm}}$

i. endpoint: $\underline{\hspace{1.5cm}}$ circle: $\underline{\hspace{2.5cm}}$

arrow points: $\underline{\hspace{1.5cm}}$ $x \bigcirc \underline{\hspace{1.5cm}}$

j. Water boils and becomes a gas at 100°C. Write an inequality to show all the temperatures at which water is a gas. Graph the solution set of the inequality.

At temperatures equal to and $\underline{\hspace{2cm}}$ 100°C, water is a gas.

inequality: $t \bigcirc \underline{\hspace{1.5cm}}$

80°C   90°C   110°C   120°C   130°C

1. $6k^5m^2 - 2k^3m - km$

= _____

2. $mx^4y^2 - m^2x^3y^3 + 5m^2x^6y^2$

= _____

3. $\left(\dfrac{2x}{3y^4}\right)^3 = \dfrac{\boxed{}^3 \cdot \boxed{}^3}{\boxed{}^3 \cdot \left(\boxed{}^4\right)^3}$

$= \dfrac{\boxed{}}{\boxed{}}$

4. $(2x^3y^2)^4$

$= (\text{_____})^4 \cdot (\text{_____})^4 \cdot (\text{_____})^4$

$= $ _____

5. The statement is _____.

If false, give a counterexample:

_____

_____

6. $m = \dfrac{y_2 - y_1}{x_2 - x_1}$

(x_1, y_1) is (__, __). (x_2, y_2) is (__, __).

$m = $ _____

7. *See page 6 in the* Student Reference Guide.

$5x - 2 = 6y$

standard form:

_____

8. $\sqrt[n]{b} = b^{\frac{1}{n}}$

$\sqrt[4]{y} = y^{\boxed{}}$

9.

$P(P) = \dfrac{\square}{\square}$

$P(E) = \dfrac{\square}{\square}$

$P(P \text{ and } E) = \underline{\hspace{3cm}}$

$= \dfrac{\square}{\square}$

10. odds that a family will be chosen:

$\underline{\hspace{1.5cm}} : \underline{\hspace{1cm}}$ or $\underline{\hspace{1.5cm}} : \underline{\hspace{1cm}}$

11. $a_n = a_1 + (n-1)^d$

$a_1 = \underline{\hspace{1.5cm}}, \ a_n = \underline{\hspace{1.5cm}} + (n-1)\,(\underline{\hspace{1cm}})$

$a_5 = \underline{\hspace{1.5cm}} + (\underline{\hspace{1cm}})(\underline{\hspace{1cm}}) = \underline{\hspace{1cm}}$

$a_{12} = \underline{\hspace{1.5cm}} + (\underline{\hspace{1cm}})(\underline{\hspace{1cm}}) = \underline{\hspace{1cm}}$

12. *Slope intercept form: $y = mx + b$*

Student $\underline{\hspace{1.5cm}}$ is correct. Student

$\underline{\hspace{2cm}}$ solved the equation $\underline{\hspace{1.5cm}}$

instead of for $\underline{\hspace{1.5cm}}$.

13. *Determine which values make the inequality true.*

for $y = -6$: $-2(\underline{\hspace{1cm}}) + 3 < 0 \longrightarrow \underline{\hspace{1.5cm}} < 0$

for $y = 0$: $-2(\underline{\hspace{1cm}}) + 3 < 0 \longrightarrow \underline{\hspace{1.5cm}} < 0$

for $y = 1$: $-2(\underline{\hspace{1cm}}) + 3 < 0 \longrightarrow \underline{\hspace{1.5cm}} < 0$

for $y = 6$: $-2(\underline{\hspace{1cm}}) + 3 < 0 \longrightarrow \underline{\hspace{1.5cm}} < 0$

$\underline{\hspace{1cm}}$ and $\underline{\hspace{1cm}}$ make the inequality true.

14. endpoint: $\underline{\hspace{2cm}}$ circle: $\underline{\hspace{2cm}}$

arrow points: $\underline{\hspace{2cm}}$

Circle the answer.

A $x \leq 7$ **B** $7 < x$

C $x \geq 7$ **D** $x > 7$

15. Draw a $\underline{\hspace{4cm}}$ and label

several numbers including the 12.

Draw a $\underline{\hspace{2.5cm}}$ circle at the 12.

Shade the section of the number line to

the $\underline{\hspace{2.5cm}}$ of the circle.

16. If $x \neq 2$, then the solution to the

inequality includes all values $\underline{\hspace{2.5cm}}$

than 2 and all values $\underline{\hspace{2.5cm}}$ than 2.

$x \bigcirc \underline{\hspace{1.5cm}}, \ x \bigcirc \underline{\hspace{1.5cm}}$

17. a. 12,756,000 = _____

695,900,000 = _____

b. Divide.

about _____ times larger

18. $E = mc^2 = ($____$)($____ $\cdot 10^{\square})^2$

= _____

---

19. *Use the marked points.*

a. $\dfrac{\boxed{}\ \text{pages}}{\boxed{}\ \text{min}} = $ _____

b. $\dfrac{\boxed{}\ \text{pages}}{\boxed{}\ \text{min}} = $ _____

20. *"Of" means multiply.*

36% of 212 = _____ = _____

$(212 \cdot 0.25) + (212 \cdot$ ____$) + (212 \cdot$ ____$) = $ ____

_____, Janice _____ use this method, because

of the _____ Property of _____ .

---

21. *Factor out the GCF in the numerator and in the denominator.*

$$\dfrac{6x + 30}{36x + 6} = \dfrac{(\boxed{})(\boxed{} - \boxed{})}{(\boxed{})(\boxed{} + \boxed{})}$$

$$= \dfrac{\boxed{}}{\boxed{}}$$

Any value for which the _____ would

equal _____ must be excluded: $x \neq$ _____ .

22. Let h = number of hours Ricardo babysits

_____ $h +$ _____ $\bigcirc$ _____

---

23. *See page 2 in the* Student Reference Guide.

$\dfrac{\boxed{} - \boxed{}}{\boxed{}} = $ ___._____

Circle the answer.

A 4%   **B** 8%

C 2%   **D** 6%

24. Kwami: $\dfrac{\boxed{} - \boxed{}}{\boxed{}} = $ ___._____

Lisa: $\dfrac{\boxed{} - \boxed{}}{\boxed{}} = $ ___._____

Kwami's video game collection increased by

_____, or _____%. Lisa's CD collection

increased by _____, or _____%.

25. List the jogging times in order from least to greatest.

_____, _____, _____, _____, _____, _____,

_____, _____, _____, _____, _____

The mean is the average.

mean: _____

The median is the middle data value.

median: _____

The mode occurs most often.

mode: _____

26. greatest value: _____

least value: _____

range: _____ – _____ = _____

27. If Doyle uses the _____ to

make the table and then plots the

_____ from the table of values,

he can check to see that the _____

lie on the _____.

28. *Slope intercept form: $y = mx + b$*

$y = $ _____ $x + $ _____ $ = $ _____

(____, ____), (____, ____), (____, ____)

29. a. *The y-intercept is the starting value or constant amount. The slope is the rate of change.*

$y = $ _____ $x \bigcirc$ _____

b. Graph.

c. *Find the lowest x-value for which $y > 0$.*

_____ candles

30. Under normal atmospheric conditions, water freezes at 32°F. Model the temperatures at which water freezes.

$t \bigcirc$ _____

Graph the inequality.

Name _____

Using Logical Reasoning page 320

• A conditional statement is written in the form "If..., then...."

If a figure is a triangle, then it has three sides.	
Hypothesis	Conclusion
a figure is a triangle	it has three sides

• Every conditional statement has a converse, an inverse, and a contrapositive.

Math Language

To **negate** a statement means to say the opposite, using the word "not."

Conditional	If a figure is a triangle, then it has three sides.
Converse	Reverses the order of the hypothesis and conclusion: If a figure has three sides, then it is a triangle.
Inverse	Negates the hypothesis and conclusion: If a figure is not a triangle, then it does not have three sides.
Contrapositive	Reverses the hypothesis and conclusion and negates both: If a figure does not have three sides, then it is not a triangle.

The four types of statements can be shown symbolically:

Let p = hypothesis
Let q = conclusion
~ means "not (or opposite)"

Conditional	If p, then q.
Converse	If q, then p.
Inverse	If $\sim p$, then $\sim q$.
Contrapositive	If $\sim q$, then $\sim p$.

1. Write the converse.
   If p, then q: If a number ends in 5, then it is a multiple of 5.

   If q, then p: _____

   False? _____

   Counterexample: _____

2. Write the contrapositive.
If p, then q: If two lines are parallel, then they do not meet.

If $\sim q$, then $\sim p$: _____

False? _____

Counterexample: _____

3. Write the inverse.
If p, then q: If it is Monday, then I will go to school.

If $\sim p$, then $\sim q$: _____

False? _____

Counterexample: _____

4. Write the inverse.
If p, then q: If a number is even, then it is divisible by two.

If $\sim p$, then $\sim q$: _____

False? _____

Counterexample: _____

5. Complete the table to compare the truth value of an original statement and its contrapositive.

Original	True or False	Contrapositive	True or False
If a figure is a square, then it is a rectangle.	_____	If a figure is not a rectangle, _____	_____
If a number is odd, then it is divisible by 2.	_____	If a number is not divisible by 2, _____	_____

6. If the original statement is true, the contrapositive is _____.

If the original statement is false, the contrapositive is _____.

7. To compare the truth values of the converse and inverse, complete the table for each original statement.

Original statement: If a figure is a square, then it is a rectangle.

		True or False
Converse	If a figure is a rectangle, _____	_____
Inverse	If a figure is not a square, _____	_____

Original statement: If an object has wheels, then it is a bicycle.

		True or False
Converse	If an object is a bicycle, _____	_____
Inverse	If an object does not have wheels, _____	_____

8. What is the relationship of the truth values of the converse and inverse of an original statement?

If the converse of the statement is true, the inverse is _____.

If the converse of the statement is false, the inverse is _____.

Investigation Practice 📖 page 321

Write the given statement in the form indicated.

Conditional statement: If p, then q. ⟶ If it is raining, then it is cloudy.

a. Contrapositive: If ~q, then ~p.

_____

_____

b. Converse: If q, then p.

_____

_____

c. Inverse: If ~p, then ~q.

_____

_____

d. If the original statement is true, what is the truth value of the contrapositive? That is, if p, then q is true. Is the contrapositive, if $\sim q$, then $\sim p$, true or false?

_____

e. If the converse of a statement is false, what is the truth value of the inverse of the statement? That is, if q, then p is false. Is the inverse, if $\sim p$, then $\sim q$, true or false?

_____

Identify statement 2 as the converse, the inverse, or the contrapositive. Tell the truth value of each statement.

f. Statement 1: If a figure is a rectangle, then it is not a triangle.
Statement 2: If a figure is a triangle, then it is not a rectangle.

_____

g. Statement 1: If a figure is not a polygon, then it is not a right triangle.
Statement 2: If a figure is a polygon, then it is a right triangle.

_____

Simplifying Rational Expressions with Like Denominators page 322

New Concepts

- Before simplifying rational expressions, exclude values that make a denominator zero.

  Example **Identifying Excluded Values**

  Find the excluded values for $\dfrac{3}{5m}$.

$5m = 0$	*Set the denominator equal to zero.*
$\dfrac{5m}{5} = \dfrac{0}{5}$	*Divide both sides by 5.*
$m = 0$	**The excluded value is 0.**

  When the $m = 0$, the denominator equals to 0 and the fraction is undefined. Therefore, $m \neq 0$.

- Factor to simplify rational expressions.

  Example **Simplifying Rational Expressions**

  Simplify. $\dfrac{2m - 6}{m - 3}$

  $= \dfrac{2(m - 3)}{m - 3}$ *Factor.*

  $= \dfrac{2(\overset{1}{\cancel{m - 3}})}{\underset{1}{\cancel{m - 3}}}$ *Divide out common factors $\dfrac{(m - 3)}{(m - 3)}$.*

  $= 2$ *Simplify.*

- When simplifying, look for like denominators.

  Example **Simplifying Expressions with Integer Exponents**

  Simplify. $pq^{-2} - \dfrac{7}{p^{-1}q^2}$

  $= \dfrac{p}{q^2} - \dfrac{7p}{q^2}$ *Write with positive exponents.*

  $= -\dfrac{6p}{q^2}$ *Subtract the numerators.*

Find the excluded values in each expression.

a. $\dfrac{9}{4h}$

$4h = \underline{\hspace{1cm}}$ *Set the denominator = 0.*

$\dfrac{4h}{4} = \dfrac{\square}{4}$

$h = \underline{\hspace{1cm}}$

$h \neq \underline{\hspace{1cm}}$ $\underline{\hspace{1cm}}$ is excluded.

b. $\dfrac{p+2}{p+4}$

$p + 4 = \underline{\hspace{1cm}}$ *Set the denominator = 0.*

$p = \underline{\hspace{1cm}}$

$p \neq \underline{\hspace{1cm}}$ $\underline{\hspace{1cm}}$ is excluded.

c. $\dfrac{g-5}{3g-15}$

$3g - 15 = \underline{\hspace{1cm}}$

$g = \underline{\hspace{1cm}}$ $g \neq \underline{\hspace{1cm}}$ $\underline{\hspace{1cm}}$ is excluded.

Simplify each rational expression, if possible. Identify any excluded values.

d. *Factor.*

$\dfrac{4a^3}{2a^2}$

$2a^2 = 0,\ a \neq 0$

$\dfrac{4a^3}{2a^2} = \underline{\hspace{1cm}}$

e. $\dfrac{d+1}{d}$

$d = \underline{\hspace{1cm}},\ d \neq \underline{\hspace{1cm}}$

$\underline{\hspace{1cm}}$ be simplified.

f. $\dfrac{3z^2 - 6z}{5z - 10}$

$5z - 10 = 0,\ z \neq \underline{\hspace{1cm}}$

Factor. Then divide out common factors.

$\dfrac{3z(z - \square)}{5(z - \square)} = \dfrac{\square}{\square}$

g. $\dfrac{5xy - 10x}{x^2y^2}$

$x^2y^2 = 0,\ x \neq 0,\ y \neq 0$

Factor. Then divide out common factors.

$\dfrac{5\square(y + \square)}{x^2y^2} = \dfrac{\square(y - \square)}{\square y^2}$

Simplify each rational expression, if possible.

h. $\dfrac{4f}{r^2} - \dfrac{2f}{r^2} = \dfrac{\square}{r^2}$

i. $6m^{-2}n^4 + \dfrac{3m^{-2}}{n^{-4}}$ *Write with positive exponents.*

$\dfrac{6n^4}{\square} + \dfrac{3n^4}{\square} = \dfrac{\square}{m^2} = 9m^{\square}n^{\square}$

j. $2\left(\dfrac{6-x}{\underset{2}{4y}}\right) + 2\left(\dfrac{2x+5}{\underset{2}{4y}}\right) = \dfrac{6-x}{\square} + \dfrac{\square + \square}{2y} = \dfrac{\square + \square}{2y}$

---

1. Find the prime factorization of the radicand.

$\sqrt[4]{81}$

$= \sqrt[4]{3 \cdot \underline{} \cdot \underline{} \cdot \underline{}}$

$= \underline{}$

2. The root is negative.

$\sqrt[3]{-27}$

$= \sqrt[3]{-3 \cdot \underline{} \cdot \underline{}}$

$= \underline{}$

---

3. Find the prime factorization of the radicand.

$\sqrt[3]{64}$

$= \sqrt[3]{\underline{} \cdot \underline{} \cdot \underline{}}$

$= \underline{}$

4. The root is negative.

$\sqrt[3]{-64}$

$= \sqrt[3]{-4 \cdot \underline{} \cdot \underline{}}$

$= \underline{}$

---

5. Standard form: $Ax + By = C$.

$7y = \frac{3}{8}x - 1$

$= \underline{}$

6. $4x$ is a factor.

$\dfrac{12x^2 - 16x}{16xy}$

$= \underline{}$

---

7. $\dfrac{dm^{-2}}{3} + \dfrac{5d}{m^2}$

$\dfrac{d}{3m^2} + \dfrac{\boxed{}d}{3m^2} = \dfrac{d + \boxed{}d}{\boxed{}} = \dfrac{\boxed{}d}{3\boxed{}}$

8. See page 4 in the Student Reference Guide.

$\dfrac{8h^{-6}}{y^2} + \dfrac{y^{-2}}{h^6} = \dfrac{8}{\boxed{}y^2} + \dfrac{1}{y^2h^6}$

$= \dfrac{\boxed{}}{\boxed{}h^6}$

---

9. Excluded value for $\frac{h+3}{2h-6}$ is

$2h - 6 = 0$

$h = \underline{}$

Circle the answer.

A $h \neq -2$ **B** $h \neq 0$

C $h \neq 2$ **D** $h \neq 3$

---

10. $P = 2l + 2w$

$$\frac{2(160 + 160f)}{f + 1} + \frac{2(360 + 360f)}{f + 1}$$

$$= \frac{320 + 320f}{f + 1} + \frac{\square + \square f}{f + 1} \quad \textit{Distribute.}$$

$$= \frac{\square + \square f}{\square} \quad \textit{Add.}$$

$$= \frac{\square(1 + \square)}{\square} \quad \textit{Factor.}$$

Divide out common factors.

$$= \underline{\hspace{2cm}} \text{ feet}$$

11. $\dfrac{5p}{p - 6}$

$p - 6 = 0$

$p \neq \underline{\hspace{1.5cm}}$. If $p = \underline{\hspace{1cm}}$, then the denominator would be equal to $\underline{\hspace{1.5cm}}$.

Division by $\underline{\hspace{2cm}}$ is undefined.

---

12. *See page 9 in the* Student Reference Guide.

21, 32, 43 ... $\quad a_1 = \underline{\hspace{1cm}} \quad d = \underline{\hspace{1cm}} \quad (n - 1) = 60 \div 5 = \underline{\hspace{1cm}}$

$a_n = a_1 + (n - 1)d$

$a_{12} = \underline{\hspace{1cm}} + (12)\underline{\hspace{1cm}}$ *Substitute.*

$a_{12} = \underline{\hspace{1cm}}$

---

13. Converse: If a number is a $\underline{\hspace{2.5cm}}$, number then the number is a $\underline{\hspace{2cm}}$ number.

Circle the answer: true false?

14. *Range = greatest − least*

Circle the answer.

A 7	**B** 10
C 60	**D** 62

---

15. Measure of corresponding angle:

$\underline{\hspace{2cm}}$

16. *change in y* / *change in x*

$$\frac{\text{change in cost}}{\text{change in weight}} = \frac{\square - \square}{\square - \square} = \underline{\hspace{1.5cm}}$$

---

17. cost of used bike = $8

cost of paint and parts = $150

total spent = $____ + $____ = $____

a. sale price: total cost + (285% of total cost)

$s =$ $____ + ($____ $\cdot$ 2.85)

b. $s =$ $____

18. A _____ expression is undefined only when the _____ is equal to zero. If the _____ is zero, and the denominator is not zero, then the value of the rational expression is _____.

19. $Slope = \dfrac{y_2 - y_1}{x_2 - x_1}$

Use the points $(-2, 6)$ and $(5, -3)$.

$x_1 =$ ____ $y_1 =$ ____

$x_2 =$ ____ $y_2 =$ ____

$m = \dfrac{\Box - \Box}{\Box - \Box}$

$= \_\_\_\_$

20. *See page 2 in the* Student Reference Guide.

original price: $7000

new price: $10,200

% of increase $= \dfrac{\text{new} - \text{original}}{\text{original}}$

$= \dfrac{10,200 - 7000}{\Box}$

% of increase $= \_\_\_\_$ %

21. Inductive or deductive? _____

The conclusion is based on the

_____ of a triangle.

22. Temperature greater than 5880 kelvins.

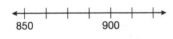

23. Let $x =$ area of sign

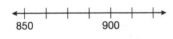

$x \le$ _____

24. a. To find the median:

List the numbers in _____.

Count to find that there are _____ data values.

Since the count is an even number, find the average of the tenth and the _____ data

values to determine the median.

b. median: _____

---

25. *Slope-intercept form: y = mx + b*

$5x + 3y = 9$

$y = $ _____ $+$ _____

26. *Use slope-intercept form.*

slope: $-\frac{1}{2}$ *y*-intercept: -3

Circle the answer.

A $4x + 2y + 3 = 0$ **B** $3x + 6y + 6 = 0$

C $5x + 10y + 30 = 0$ **D** $6x + 2y + 1 = 0$

---

27. *Solve for x. Then substitute.*

$x - 1 \geq 4$

$x \leq$ _____

Are any of these values $\{-1, 0, 1, 2\}$

solutions? _____

28. Student _____ is correct.

Student _____ graphed numbers _____

than 9. "At least 9" means numbers

_____ or _____ 9.

---

29. a. f _____

b. The temperature is _____

than or equal to _____.

30. *Let l = each lot*

$1\frac{1}{2}$ acres or more

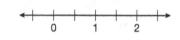

$1 \geq$ _____

LESSON
52

Determining the Equation of a Line Given Two Points page 329

New Concepts

• You can graph a line if you know its slope and one point on the line.

Example Using Slope and a Point to Graph

Graph a line that has a slope of 4 and passes through point (3, 5).

Graph point (3, 5).

Start at (3, 5). Count 4 units up and 1 unit right. Draw a point.

Draw a line through the points.

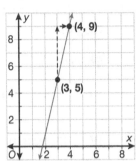

• If you know two points on a line, you can write its equation.

Example Writing an Equation Using Two Points

A line passes through points (1, −3) and (4, 5).
Write an equation of the line in slope-intercept form.

First find the slope.

$$m = \frac{y_2 - y_1}{x_2 - x_1}$$ *Use the formula for slope.*

$$m = \frac{5 - (-3)}{4 - 1}$$ *Substitute.*

$$m = \frac{8}{3}$$ *Simplify. The slope is $\frac{8}{3}$.*

$$y - y_1 = m(x - x_1)$$ *Use the point-slope formula.*

$$y - 5 = \frac{8}{3}(x - 4)$$ *Substitute a point and the slope.*

$$3(y - 5) = 3 \cdot \frac{8}{3}(x - 4)$$ *Multiply by 3 to eliminate fraction.*

$$3y - 15 = 8x - 32$$ *Distribute.*

$$3y = 8x - 17$$ *Add 15 to both sides.*

$$y = \frac{8}{3}x - \frac{17}{3}$$ *Solve for y.*

a. Graph a line that has a slope of 2 and passes through the point (5, 6).

Graph (5,6).

Count up 2 units and 1 unit right.

Draw the line.

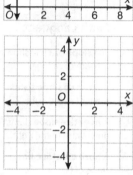

b. Graph a line that has a slope of 0 and passes through the point (−1, 1).

Graph (−1,1).

A line with slope 0 is horizontal.

c. Write the equation of a line that has a slope of 6 and passes through the point (7, 9) in point-slope form.

Substitute. $y_1 = 9$, $x_1 = 7$, $m = 6$

$$y - y_1 = m(x - x_1)$$

$$y - \underline{} = \underline{}(x - \underline{})$$

d. Write the equation of a line that passes through the points (2, −3) and (7, 4) in slope-intercept form.

First find the slope.

$$m = \frac{y_2 - y_1}{x_2 - x_1}$$

$$m = \frac{\square - \square}{\square - \square}$$

$$= \frac{\square}{\square}$$

$$y - y_1 = m(x - x_1)$$

$$y - \underline{} = \underline{}(x - \underline{})$$

$$y - \underline{} = \underline{}x - \underline{}$$

$$y = \underline{}x - \underline{}$$

e. *Use (1, −1) and (2, −5) to find the slope of the linear equation. Since Trevor begins the game with 3 points, the y-intercept is 3. Once the equation of the line has been determined, substitute $x = 3$ into the equation to find the number of points after 3 minutes.*

$$b = \underline{}$$

$$m = \frac{y_2 - y_1}{x_2 - x_1}$$

$$m = \frac{\square - \square}{\square - \square}$$

$$= \underline{}$$

$$y = mx + b$$

$$y = \underline{}x + \underline{}$$

$$= \underline{}(\underline{}) + \underline{}$$

$$= \underline{} + \underline{}$$

$$= \underline{}$$

1. *Substitute for x.*

$f(x) = 3x - 5$; domain: $\{0, 1, 2, 3\}$

$f(0) = 3(\underline{}) - 5 = \underline{}$

range: $\{\underline{}, \underline{}, \underline{}, \underline{}\}$

2. *Solve for f(x).*

$f(x) = \frac{1}{2}x + 3$; domain: $\{-2, 0, 2, 4\}$

$f(-2) = \frac{1}{2}(\underline{}) + 3 = \underline{}$

range: $\{\underline{}, \underline{}, \underline{}, \underline{}\}$

3. *More than 3 years.*

$x \; \bigcirc \; \underline{}$

4. *Pay was $5.15 or more.*

$x \; \bigcirc \; \underline{}$

5. *See page 4 in the* Student Reference Guide.

$$\frac{(3 \times 10^{-9})}{(4.8 \times 10^{-1})}$$

$$= \frac{3}{4.8} \times \frac{10^{-9}}{10^{-1}}$$

$$= \underline{} \times 10^{\square}$$

$$= \underline{} \times 10^{\square}$$

6. *Graph the point.*

slope: $-1 = \dfrac{\square}{\square}$

point: $(3, 1)$

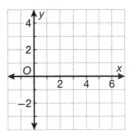

7. *Set up a proportion.*

Let x = actual distance

$x = \underline{}$ ▮

8. *Set up a proportion.*

Let y = actual length

$y = \underline{}$ ▮

9. a. $\dfrac{t^3}{y^4}\left(\dfrac{t^2}{y^2} + \dfrac{5y}{m}\right) =$ _____ + _____

   b. _____ $\neq 0$, _____ $\neq 0$

10. $6.95\% = 0.0695$

$I = prt$

$p = \$$_____, $r =$ _____%, $t =$ ____ years

Substitute

$I =$ _____ $\cdot$ _____ $\cdot$ _____

  $=$ _____

11. a. $15x^2 - 75x = 0$

   _____ $(x - 5) = 0$

   $15x = 0$, $x =$ _____

   $x - 5 = 0$, $x =$ _____

   The denominator is 0 at $x =$ ___

   and at $x =$ _____

  b. $x - 5 = 0$; $x =$ _____

   The numerator is 0 at $x =$ _____

  c. The expression is undefined at

   $x =$ ___ and at $x =$ _____

12. $m = 3$, $y_1 = -2$, $x_1 = -1$, $x_2 = 4$

$m = \dfrac{y_2 - y_1}{x_2 - x_1}$

Substitute.

_____ $= \dfrac{\square - \square}{\square - \square}$

$y_2 =$ _____

13. *x subtracted from −4 is less than or equal to 0.*

_____ − _____ ◯ _____

14. *See page 4 in the* Student Reference Guide.

$x = \dfrac{25}{16}$

Substitute.

$-\sqrt{x} =$ _____ $=$ _____

15. *Profit = sales price − production cost − materials cost*

$\$$_____ $= \$$____$x - \$$_____ $- \$$____x

Solve for x.

$x =$ _____ bags

16. *See page 13 in the* Student Reference Guide.

Weights in pounds from greatest to least:

___, ___, ___, ___, ___, ___, ___, ___,

___, ___

mean: _____   median: _____

mode: _____

17. *y = total cost, m = cost per game*
x = number of games, b = rental fee

y = mx + b

a. $y = \underline{\quad} + \underline{\quad}$

b. *Substitute.*

$y = \underline{\quad\quad}$

18. *total cost = shoe fee × number of people*
+ lane fee

y = mx + b

a. $y = \underline{\quad} x + \underline{\quad}$

b. *Substitute.*

$y = \underline{\quad\quad}$

---

19. *The dot shows the least number.*

$y \bigcirc \underline{\qquad}$

20. Student ____ is correct.

Student ____ graphed b as _____ than

2.5 rather than graphing _____ as
greater than b.

---

21. $\dfrac{b^5}{b^3}$

$b^3 = 0$ when $b = \underline{\quad}$, which is when the
expression is undefined.

22. *Add one length and one width.*

Simplify.

$$\frac{525x + 100}{5x + 1} + \frac{400x + 85}{5x + 1}$$

$$= \frac{\square x + \square}{5x + \square}$$

$$= \frac{\square(\square x + \square)}{5x + \square}$$

$$= \underline{\qquad\qquad}$$

---

23. If a _____ does not have _____

_____ then it is not a

_____.

Circle the answer: true   false?

If false, write a counterexample:

_____

24. Student _____ is correct. Student

_____ did not write each term with

_____ exponents, so the
expressions did not appear to be

_____ terms.

25. Factor.

$$\frac{4x + 8}{x^2 + 2x}$$

$$= \frac{\square(\square + \square)}{\square(\square + \square)} = \frac{\square}{\square}$$

26. $\dfrac{6a}{3a - 1} + \dfrac{4}{3a - 1} + \dfrac{6a}{3a - 1}$

$$= \frac{\square + \square}{3a - 1} \; \blacksquare$$

27. The points are: (1, 4), (2, 7).

$$m = \frac{y_2 - y_1}{x_2 - x_1} = \frac{\square - \square}{\square - \square}$$

$$= \frac{\square}{\square} = \underline{\quad}$$

$$y - y_1 = m(x - x_1)$$

$$y - \underline{\quad} = \underline{\quad}(x - \underline{\quad})$$

$$y = \underline{\quad} x + \underline{\quad}$$

Answer: _____

28. The y-values are the same. (−1, 2), (3, 2)

$$m = \frac{y_2 - y_1}{x_2 - x_1} = \frac{\square - \square}{\square - \square}$$

A _____ line has a slope

of _____ .

29. $y = 72$ in., $m = 8$ in. per day, $x = $ number of days, $b = 24$ in.

Use the slope intercept form.

$$y = mx + b$$

a. $y = \underline{\quad} x + \underline{\quad}$

 b. Solve for x.

c. _____

30. $d = 500 - 65t$, $t = 4$ hours

 a. Complete the table.

t	
0	
1	
2	
3	
4	
5	

b. Substitute.

$$d = \underline{\qquad\qquad}$$

New Concepts

Math Language

The **degree** of a term is the sum of the exponents of the variables. A constant has a degree of zero.

The **leading coefficient** is the coefficient of the greatest degree term. For $5x^3y^3 + 8xy^2 - 9$, the leading coefficient is 5.

• To write a polynomial in standard form, arrange the terms from greatest degree to least degree.

Example **Writing a Polynomial in Standard Form**

Write $8xy^2 - 9 + 5x^3y^3z$ in standard form.

$$8x \quad y^2 - 9 + 5x^3 \quad y^3 \quad z$$

$$\downarrow \quad \downarrow \quad \downarrow \quad \downarrow \quad \downarrow \quad \downarrow$$

$$1 + 2 \quad 0 \quad 3 + 3 + 1 \qquad \text{Add exponents to find degree.}$$
$$= 3 \qquad\qquad = 7$$

$$5x^3y^3z + 8xy^2 - 9 \qquad \text{Arrange the terms in order.}$$

The leading coefficient is 5.

Exploration 📖 page 337

Use your textbook to complete the exploration.

• To add or subtract polynomials, combine like terms. Add or subtract horizontally or vertically.

Example **Adding Polynomials**

Add. $(-8x^3 + 4x^2 + x + 1) + (3x^3 - 2x^2 + 7)$

$$\begin{array}{l} -8x^3 + 4x^2 + x + 1 \qquad \text{Line up like terms.} \\ +\ 3x^3 - 2x^2 \quad\ \ + 7 \\ \hline -5x^3 + 2x^2 + x + 8 \qquad \text{Add like terms.} \end{array}$$

• To subtract, add the opposite of each term.

Example **Subtracting Polynomials**

Subtract. $(x^2 + 4x - 9) - (4x^2 - 5x + 11)$

$$(x^2 + 4x - 9) - (4x^2 - 5x + 11)$$
$$= x^2 + 4x - 9 - 4x^2 + 5x - 11 \qquad \text{Distribute negative.}$$
$$= (x^2 - 4x^2) + (4x + 5x) + (-9 - 11) \qquad \text{Collect like terms.}$$
$$= -3x^2 + 9x - 20$$

Find the degree of each monomial. *Add the exponents of the variables.*

a. $3x^2yz^6$

$3x^2$ y z^6

↓   ↓   ↓

___ + ___ + ___ = ___

b. $-2^3xy\,z$

-2^3x y z

↓   ↓   ↓

$1 +$ ___ + ___ = ___

c. $4^2xy^2z^3$ ___ + ___ + ___ = ___

Write each polynomial in standard form. Then find the leading coefficient.
Order the terms from greatest degree to least degree.

d. $3w^2$ $-$ $2w^4$ $-2w^4 +$ _____

       ↓   ↓   ↓

    degree 2   degree 4   Leading coefficient is _____.

e. $5ab^2 + 3a^2b^2 + 8ab - 1$ _____ + ___ + _____ $-$ ___

    ↓   ↓   ↓   ↓

      3   ___   ___   ___   Leading coefficient is _____.

f. $2ab - 7 - 5a^2b$ _____

    ↓   ↓   ↓

    ___   ___   ___   Leading coefficient is _____.

Add the polynomials. Write each answer in standard form.

g. $(2x^2 + x + 8) + (x^2 + 4)$

    $= (2x^2 +$ ___$) + (x) + (8 +$ ___$)$

    $=$ ___ $x^2 + x +$ _____

h. $3n^2 + 7n - 1$

    $+ (-2n^2) - \quad n + 1$

    ―――――――――――――

    ___ $+$ ___

Subtract the polynomials. Write each answer in standard form.

i. $(12y^3 + 10) - (18y^3 - 3y^2 + 5)$

    $= 12y^3 + 10$ ___ $18y^3$ ___ $3y^2$ ___ $5)$

    $= (12y^3 - 18y^3) + (3y^2) + (10 - 5)$

    $=$ ___ $+ 3y^2 +$ ___

j. $(c^2 + 6c - 2) - (c^2 - 2c + 6)$

    $= c^2 + 6c - 2$ ___ c^2 ___ $2c$ ___ 6

    $= (c^2 +$ ___$) + (6c +$ ___$) + (-2 +$ ___$)$

    $=$ _____

k. *Subtract.*
$(-16t^2 + 22t + 4) - (16t^2 + 17t + 6)$

    $=$ _____ $+$ _____

    $=$ _____

1. $18 - 12 + 4^2$

= _____ = _____

2. $-2[7 + 6(3 - 5)]$

= _____

3. Graph $x \leq 8$.

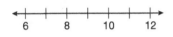

4. *An open circle shows the number is not included.*

x ◯ _____

5. *Write 0.00304 as a power of 10.*

0.00304 ◯ 3.04×10^{-4}

$3.04 \times 10^{-\square}$ ◯ 3.04×10^{-4}

6. GCF = _____

$18a^2b^3c - 45ab^6c$

= _____(_____ − _____)

7. *The GCF of 16, 80, and 8 is* _____.

$h = -16t^2 + 80t + 8$

$h = -$____(_____)

8. *See page 5 in the* Student Reference Guide.

$(3a)(6a^2b)^3$

= _____

9. *Factor. Cancel.*

$$= \frac{40 + 6t}{20 + 10t}$$

$$= \frac{\boxed{}(\boxed{} + \boxed{})}{\boxed{}(\boxed{} + \boxed{})}$$

$$= \underline{\hspace{2cm}}$$

10. *Use points (1, 2.08%) and (6, 2.69%).*

a.

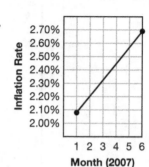

Month (2007)

b. $m = \dfrac{y_2 - y_1}{x_2 - x_1}$

$$= \frac{\boxed{} - \boxed{}}{\boxed{} - \boxed{}} = \underline{\hspace{2cm}}$$

c. If the line continues, what is the point

for $\frac{7}{2007}$? (____, ____)

rate = _____

11. *Replace the symbol ≥ with words.*

≥ : _____

_____

12. $\sqrt[n]{b} = \frac{b^1}{n}$

$-\sqrt{b} = $ _____

13. *See page 13 in the* Student Reference Guide.

$$\text{mean} = \frac{88 + 225 + \boxed{} + \boxed{} + \boxed{} + \boxed{} + \boxed{} + \boxed{}}{8}$$

$$= \underline{\hspace{3cm}}$$

$$\text{median} = \underline{\hspace{0.5cm}} + \frac{\boxed{}}{2}$$

$$= \underline{\hspace{3cm}}$$

14. *Eliminate answers with an open dot.*

$-3 \leq y$ has the same meaning as

$y \bigcirc$ _____

Circle the answer.

A ←—+—+—+—●—+—+—+→
    −6 −4 −2   0

B ←—+—+—+—○—+—+—+→
    −6 −4 −2   0

C ←—+—+—+—●—+—+—+→
    −6 −4 −2   0

D ←—+—+—○—+—+—+→
      −4 −2   0

15. If the number is on the part of the number

line that is _____, then it is

part of the _____ set.

16. Amount of change = original price − new

price = _____ − _____ = _____

$$\frac{\text{amount of change}}{\text{original amount}} = \frac{\boxed{}}{\boxed{}}$$

$$= \underline{\hspace{3cm}}$$

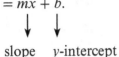

17. Write as: $y = mx + b$.

$$\downarrow \qquad \downarrow$$

slope y-intercept

$y = $ _____

$m = $ _____

$b = $ _____

18. $\dfrac{2k + 6}{k + 2} = \dfrac{\square(\square + \square)}{\square + \square}$

$k \ne$ _____

---

19. $P = 2(l + w)$

$2\left(\dfrac{50x + 150}{3x + 5} + \dfrac{40x}{3x + 5}\right)$

$= 2\left(\dfrac{\square x + \square}{\square + \square}\right)$

$= 2\left(\dfrac{\square(\square x + \square)}{\square + \square}\right)$

$=$ _____

20. Student _____ is correct.

Student _____ canceled parts of a

_____.

Only _____ can be canceled.

21.

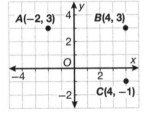

ordered pair for D: (_____, _____)

slope: _____

equation of diagonal: $y =$ _____

22. $y =$ unharvested area
$x =$ number of days
$50 =$ acres harvested per day
800 acres $=$ area of larger field
600 acres $=$ area of smaller field

a. $y = -50x +$ _____

b. $y =$ _____

Substitute in the equations.

c. larger field: _____

smaller field: _____

---

23. *Use the point-slope form.*

$$y - y_1 = m(x - x_1)$$

$$y \underline{\quad} = \underline{\quad}(x - \underline{\quad})$$

$$y = \underline{\hspace{2cm}}$$

24. *A monomial has* \underline{\hspace{2cm}} *exponents.*

Circle the answer.

A $-12b$ **B** $x^2 + x^{-1}$

C $y^2 - y + 6$ **D** -60

---

25. *Add.*

$$59x^2 - \quad 262x + \quad 3{,}888$$
$$\underline{-33x^3 + \quad 611x^2 - \quad 1433x + 28{,}060}$$

$$\underline{\quad}x^3 + \underline{\quad}x^2 - \underline{\quad}x + \underline{\quad}$$

26. *Find the degree of the greatest degree term.*

Find the sums of the exponents.

degree of $-a^2b^2c^3$: \underline{\hspace{2cm}}

degree of $5x^5$: \underline{\hspace{2cm}}

degree of $-a^2b^2c^3 + 5x^5$: \underline{\hspace{2cm}}

---

27. *See page 7 in the* Student Reference Guide.

  a. *Point slope:* $y - y_1 = m(x - x_1)$

$$y - \underline{\quad} = \underline{\quad}(x - \underline{\quad})$$

  b. *Slope-intercept:* $y = mx + b$

$$y = \underline{\quad} + \underline{\quad}$$

  c. Graph.

  d. $(\underline{\quad}, 4)$

     $(3, \underline{\quad})$

28. $(3, 1), m = -1$

Point slope: $y - y_1 = m(x - x_1)$

$$y - \underline{\quad} = \underline{\quad}(x - \underline{\quad})$$

---

29. Is $4 = 4x^0$?

$$x^0 = \underline{\hspace{2cm}} \text{ and } 4 \times \underline{\hspace{2cm}} = \underline{\hspace{1cm}}$$

Circle the answer: yes or no?

30. *To get −6, subtract the other terms.*

$$3x^2 + \quad 7x \quad - 6$$

$$\underline{\underline{\quad - \underline{\quad} - \underline{\quad}}}$$

$$-6$$

Displaying Data in a Box-and-Whisker Plot page 345

New Concepts

Math Language

A **box-and-whisker plot** displays data divided into four groups.

Example Displaying Data in a Box-and-Whisker Plot

Make a box-and-whisker plot of this data.

312, 210, 422, 323, 358, 511, 689, 722, 333, 301, 298, 755, 213, 245, 356

Follow these steps:

1. Arrange the data in order.
2. Find the median.
3. Find quartiles by finding the median of each half.
4. Draw the box-and-whisker plot.

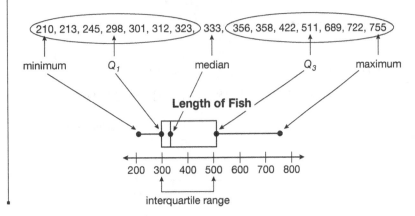

Length of Fish

Example Analyzing a Box-and-Whisker Plot

Use the interquartile range to identify outliers.

Math Language

The **interquartile range** (IQR) is the difference between the third quartile (Q_3) and the first quartile (Q_1). Half of the data is in the interquartile range.

Outliers are values that are more or less than 1.5 times the interquartile range.

first quartile (Q_1): 70
third quartile (Q_3): 90

interquartile range (IQR):
$90 - 70 = 20$

$1.5(IQR) = (1.5)20 = 30$

$Q_1 - 1.5(IQR)$

$= 70 - 30 = 40$

$Q_3 + 1.5(IQR)$

$= 90 + 30 = 120$

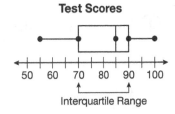

Test Scores

Interquartile Range

No values are less than 40 or greater than 120, so there are **no outliers.**

a. *Outlier $< Q_1 - 1.5(IQR)$ or Outlier $> Q_3 + 1.5(IQR)$*

$Q_1 = 31$ $\qquad$ $Q_3 = 51$ $\qquad$ $IQR = 51 - 31 =$ _____

outlier $<$ _____ $- 1.5 \cdot$ _____ $= 1$ $\qquad$ outlier $>$ _____ $+ 1.5 \cdot$ _____ $= 81$

Outliers are numbers less than _____ or greater than _____. There are _____ outliers.

b. State Test Scores:
387, 411, 459, 475, 477, 484, 496, 504, 507, 507, 508, 529, 585, 586, 589, 605

State Test Scores

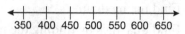

350 400 450 500 550 600 650

Half of the data lies within the IQR.

Half of the scores are between _____ and _____.

c. *Outlier $< Q_1 - 1.5(IQR)$ or Outlier $> Q_3 + 1.5(IQR)$*

Number of Yards Run: 1, 18, 19, 19, 21, 22, 23, 27, 28, 34, 37, 43, 44, 89

Number of Yards Run

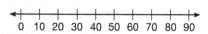

0 10 20 30 40 50 60 70 80 90

Q_1: _____ $\qquad$ Q_3: _____ $\qquad$ IQR: _____

Outlier $<$ _____ $- 1.5 \cdot$ _____ $=$ _____ Outlier $>$ _____ $+ 1.5 \cdot$ _____ $=$ _____

d. Populations in order:

0.6, _____, _____, _____, _____, _____, 0.8, 0.9, _____, _____, _____, _____, 1.5, _____, _____, _____, _____

Q_1: _____ $\qquad$ Q_3: _____ $\qquad$ IQR: _____

Outlier $<$ _____ $- 1.5 \cdot$ _____ $=$ _____ Outlier $>$ _____ $+ 1.5 \cdot$ _____ $=$ _____

Outliers are: _____ and _____.

e. The plot with the _____ represents the data better. There are no values between 3.8

and 8.1. A _____ makes it look like data are distributed throughout that range.

Identifying an outlier shows that most of the data are _____ 3.

1. *Combine like terms. Solve for x.*

$$\frac{1}{2} + \frac{3}{8}x - 5 = 10\frac{1}{2}$$

$x =$ _____

2. *Combine like terms. Solve for x.*

$$0.02x - 4 - 0.01x - 2 = -6.3$$

$x =$ _____

3. *Combine like terms. Solve for x.*

$$x - 5x + 4(x - 2) = 3x - 8$$

$x =$ _____

4. *Factor. Divide out common factors.*

$$\frac{2x^2 - 10x}{2x} = \frac{\boxed{}(\boxed{} - \boxed{})}{\boxed{}} = \underline{}$$

5. *Eliminate negative exponents.*

$$\frac{b^2}{d^{-3}}\left(\frac{db^{-2}}{4} - \frac{3f^{-3}d^2}{b^{-2}}\right) = \underline{} - \underline{}$$

6. $(6.02 \times 10^{15})(10^x)^2 = (6.02 \times 10^{15})\left(10^{\boxed{}x}\right) = \left(6.02 \times 10^{15 + \boxed{}}\right)$

Since $10^{23} = 10^{15 + \boxed{}}$, $23 = 15 +$ _____. Therefore $x =$ _____.

7. a. Use the formula $C = \frac{5}{9}(F - 32)$ to find C.

°F	−4	32	50	77
°C				

b.

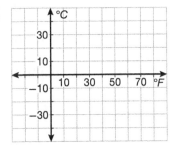

c. $m =$ _____

8. median: _____

$Q_3 =$ upper quartile: _____

$Q_1 =$ lower quartile: _____

maximum = upper extreme: _____

minimum = lower extreme: _____

$IQR = Q_3 - Q_1$

IQR: _____ − _____ = _____

9. median: _____

   Q_3 = upper quartile: _____

   Q_1 = lower quartile: _____

   maximum = upper extreme: _____

   minimum = lower extreme: _____

   $IQR = Q_3 - Q_1$

   IQR: _____ − _____ = _____

10. minimum: 62

    Q_1: 70

    median: 84

    Q_3: 86

    maximum: 95

    sample data set:

    _____

11. What information can be gathered from a box-and-whisker plot?

    You know the maximum and minimum.

    Circle the answer.

    A the mode   **B** the range
    C the mean   **D** the number of
                                data values

12. Distances in millions of miles:
    36, 67, 93, 142, 484, 887, 1765, 2791

    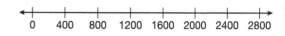

    There are _____ outliers.

13. *See page 2 in the* Student Reference Guide.

    original price: $2175.00
    new price: $2392.50

    difference: _____

    $\dfrac{\text{difference}}{\text{original}}$ = _____ = 0._____ = _____%

    Circle the answer: increase or decrease?

14. The _____ of 90, or the

    _____ 91, represents the center

    of the data. There is more than one

    _____ so it is not appropriate.

15. y = number of skateboards

m = 115 skateboards per hour

x = number of hours

b = 467 skateboards in stock

y = _____

16. −6 is the greatest number, so

$x \bigcirc -6$

17. $m = \dfrac{y_1 - y_2}{x_1 - x_2}$

$\dfrac{y_1 - y_2}{x_1 - x_2} = \dfrac{\square - \square}{10,000}$

= _____ mm/mi

18. a. The statement is _____.

A truck can be a vehicle and not

_____.

b. The statement is _____.

19. The square root of a negative number

is not a _____ number.

The square root of 1 is _____.

20. You must factor all three _____

of the expressions. The GCF is _____.

21. *Identify equivalent answers.*

$3rd^{-1} - \dfrac{6}{r^{-1}d}$

$= \dfrac{3r}{\square} - \dfrac{6\square}{d}$

$= \dfrac{3r - \square}{d}$

$= \dfrac{\square}{d}$

Circle the answer.

A $-3rd^{-1}$ **B** $\dfrac{-3r}{d}$

C $\dfrac{-3d}{r}$ **D** $\dfrac{-3}{r^{-1}d}$

22. b = 500 min, m = −25 min, x = 9 wk

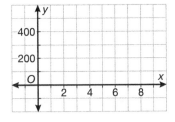

Plot (0, 500) and (___, ___).

Use the point-slope formula.

$y - y_1 = m(x - x_1)$

equation: _____

time left after 9 weeks: _____

23. $(1, 6), (3, -4)$

$m = \dfrac{y_2 - y_1}{x_2 - x_1}$

$m = \underline{\hspace{1cm}}$

24. The line that passes through $(-1, 1)$ and has zero slope is a

$\underline{\hspace{4cm}}$ line.

25. *Find the slope first.*

$(14, -3), (-6, 9) \qquad m = \dfrac{y_2 - y_1}{x_2 - x_1}$

$y = mx + b$

$y = \underline{\hspace{3cm}}$

26. Student $\underline{\hspace{1cm}}$ is correct.

Student $\underline{\hspace{1cm}}$ combined terms that are

not $\underline{\hspace{2cm}}$ terms.

27. $P = s_1 + s_2 + s_3$

$(2x + 6) + (4x + 3) + (3x + 7)$

Combine like terms.

$P = \underline{\hspace{4cm}}$

28. $P = 2l + 2w$

$2(3x - 16) + 2(5x + 21)$

$= \underline{\hspace{3cm}}$

29. *Replace Doug's savings with Jane's.*

$D = 300g^3 + 400g^2 + 200g + 25$

a. $J = \underline{\hspace{5cm}}$

b. $D + J = \underline{\hspace{4cm}}$

30. *Combine like terms.*

$(9x^3 + 12) + (16x^3 - 4x + 2)$

$= \underline{\hspace{2cm}} - \underline{\hspace{1.5cm}} + \underline{\hspace{1.5cm}}$

Name _____

Solving Systems of Linear Equations by Graphing page 354

New Concepts

• The point where two graphs intersect is a solution of both equations.

Example **Solving by Graphing**

Solve the system by graphing.

Plot the y-intercept. Find the next point on a line using the slope. Connect the points.

$$y = x + 3$$
$$y = 2x + 1$$

The lines cross at $(2, 5)$. **$(2, 5)$ is a solution of the system.**

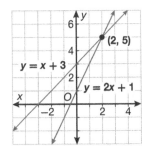

Example **Solving with a Graphing Calculator**

Use a graphing calculator to solve the system.

$$2x + y = -2$$
$$y = -3x - 5$$

Write $2x + y = -2$ in slope intercept form.

$$2x + y = -2$$
$$\underline{-2x \qquad = -2x}$$
$$y = -2x - 2$$

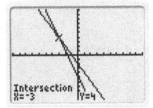

Enter the equation into the Y=Editor. Then use the intersection command to find **the intersection point $(-3, 4)$.**

Lesson Practice page 357

Tell whether the ordered pair is a solution of the given system.

a. *Substitute 1 for x, 3 for y.*

$(1, 3)$
$$2x + y = 5 \qquad\qquad 2x + 2y = 8$$
$$2(1) + (3) \stackrel{?}{=} 5 \qquad 2(1) + 2(3) \stackrel{?}{=} 8$$

____ ◯ 5 ____ ◯ 8

$(1, 3)$ _____ a solution to _____ equation(s).

---

b. (3, 4)

$$2x + y = 5 \qquad\qquad 2x + 2y = 8$$
$$2(3) + (4) \stackrel{?}{=} 5 \qquad\qquad 2(3) + 2(4) \stackrel{?}{=} 8$$

_____ ◯ 5 _____ ◯ 8

(3, 4) _____ a solution to _____ equation(s).

Solve each system by graphing. Then check your solution.

c. *Use x- and y-intercepts.*

$$y = 2x - 5$$
$$y = x - 3$$

Solution: (___ , ___)

 Check the solution.

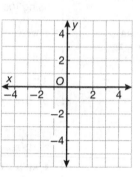

d. *Write 3x + y = 15 in slope-intercept form.*

$$y = 2x - 5$$

$$3x + y = 15 \longrightarrow y = \underline{}x + 15$$

Solution: (___ , ___)

 Check the solution.

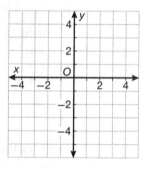

e. *Write 2x + 3y = 6 in slope-intercept form.* $y = \underline{}\, x + 2$

                                         $y = x - 12$ Solution: (___ , ___)

 Check the solution.

f. *The slope is the amount of the deposit per week. The y-intercept is the current amount in the account.*

Let x = number of weeks and let y = total amount in the account after x weeks

Jill: $y = \underline{}x + \underline{}$ Jose: $y = \underline{}x + \underline{}$

Find the point of intersection. _____ weeks; $_____

1. Solve $39.95 + 0.99d = 55.79$ for d.

$d =$ _____

Substitute to check.

2. Solve $12.6 = 4p + 1$ for p.

$p =$ _____

Substitute to check.

3. Solve $2(b - 4) = 8b - 11$ for b.

$b =$ _____

Substitute to check.

4. Solve $1.8r + 9 = -5.7r - 6$ for r.

$r =$ _____

Substitute to check.

5. *See page 4 in the* Student Reference Guide.

$\dfrac{k^{-4}}{2} =$ _____

6. *Write with positive exponents.*

$10r^{-3}t^4 =$ _____

7. $\dfrac{p^{-9}q^{-4}}{r^2s^{-3}} =$ _____

8. a. _____

_____?

b. _____?

c. _____

_____?

9. $\dfrac{rs}{z^2}\left(\dfrac{pr^{-5}s^4}{z^{-7}} - 7p^{-2}s^{-1} + \dfrac{5}{z^{-3}}\right)$

= _____

10. *Use the Power of a Product Property.*

$(2ab^2)^2(-2b^2)^2$

= _____

11. *The slope is the rate of change.*

1 foot for every 12 feet $= \dfrac{\square}{\square}$

12. **a.** Let $x =$ fraction of the hike already completed

$\dfrac{\square}{620} = x$

b. _____%

c. Round to the nearest hundred. 272.8 rounds to _____, 620 rounds to _____.

_____ ÷ _____ = _____ %. So, my answer is _____.

13. *Let m = number of miles walked*

_____ ◯ _____

14. $V = s^3$

$\dfrac{1}{2}V = 5324$ cubic inches

a. $V =$ _____

b. $s^3 =$ _____

$3\sqrt{s^3} = 3\sqrt{\underline{\hphantom{XX}}}$

$s =$ _____

15. *Round to the nearest percent.*

$\dfrac{48}{60} =$ _____

$\dfrac{47}{60} =$ _____

difference: _____

16. *Order the data. Find the mean, median, and mode.*

7, 5, 13, 5, 7, 10, 5, 5, 8

mean: _____   median: _____   mode: _____

The _____ value of _____ is best. It represents half of the values that

fall below the _____ of _____.

17. *The slope is the rate of change. The y-intercept is the original or constant amount.*

a. $y = $ _____

b. $2005 - 1997 = $ ____

Substitute.

estimated enrollment = _____

18. $m = \dfrac{y_2 - y_1}{x_2 - x_1}$

Circle the answer.

A $(0, 0)\ (0, 4)$ B $(0, 4)\ (6, 4)$

C $(4, 0)\ (6, 4)$ D $(6, 1)\ (2, 4)$

19. *Write $2x - 7y + 5 = 0$ in slope-intercept form.*

$y = $ _____

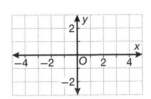

20. *13,468 is the lowest score.*

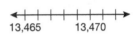

13,465   13,470

x ◯ _____

21. Simplify.

$\dfrac{5f^9}{20f^4} = \dfrac{\square}{\square}$

Identify any excluded values.

Excluded values cause the denominator in the original or simplified fraction to equal zero.

$f \neq $ ____

22. Student ____ is correct.

Student ____ found the _____ of all

of the _____ in all of the

terms.

23. $h = -16t^2 + 100t$

h_3:

____

h_5:

____

24. $(3n^3 + 2n - 7) - (n^3 - n - 2)$

Use a vertical form to find the difference.
Add the opposite of the 2nd polynomial.

$3n^3 + 2n - 7$

$+ \underline{\quad} n^3 \underline{\quad} n \underline{\quad} 7$

$\underline{\quad} n^3 \underline{\quad} n \underline{\quad}$

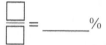

25. median: _____

Q₃ = upper quartile: _____

Q_3 = upper quartile: _____

Q_1 = lower quartile: _____

maximum = upper extreme: _____

minimum = lower extreme: _____

IQR: _____

26. *The interquartile range consists of half of the data.*

$$\frac{\square}{\square} = \underline{\hspace{1cm}}\%$$

---

27. $y = -\frac{1}{2}x + 4$ $\qquad$ $y = \frac{1}{4}x - 2$

$x =$ ____ $\qquad\qquad$ $y =$ ____

Substitute the point into both equations to check.

____ $\overset{?}{=} -\frac{1}{2}(\underline{\hspace{0.7cm}}) + 4$

____ $\overset{?}{=} \frac{1}{4}(\underline{\hspace{0.7cm}}) - 2$

28. Graph the equations on a coordinate grid.

$$y = \frac{3}{4}x + 1 \qquad\qquad y = -\frac{1}{4}x - 3$$

Circle the answer.

A $(4, -2)$ $\qquad\qquad$ **B** $(-2, 4)$

C $(-4, -2)$ $\qquad\qquad$ **D** $(4, 0)$

---

29. Talk-A-Lot = \$0.25 per minute + \$1.25

Save-N-Talk = \$0.50 per minute

Let x = number of minutes

a. Talk-A-Lot: $y =$ _____

Save-N-Talk: $y =$ _____

b. point of intersection: _____

c. Both phone companies will charge

_____ at ____ minutes of use.

30. a. **Fat Grams in Meat**

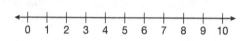

b. The upper _____ is missing because the values are contained in the _____ quartile.

Identifying, Writing, and Graphing
Direct Variation page 361

New Concepts

 Exploration 📖 page 361

Use your textbook to complete the Exploration.

Math Language
Direct variation is represented by an equation in which one variable is equal to a constant times another variable.
In the equation, $y = kx$, k is a nonzero **constant of variation** that shows the direct variation between x and y.
k is also the **slope** of the line $y = kx$

- Direct variation can be described with an equation, a graph, or words.
- The constant of variation can be found by solving $y = kx$ for k.

Example Identifying Direct Variation from an Equation

Tell whether each equation represents a direct variation. If it does, find the constant of variation, k.

$y + 8x = 0$
$\quad y = -8x$
This is a direct variation.
The constant of variation, k, is **−8.**

$xy = 6$
Change to $y = kx$ form.
$\quad y = \dfrac{6}{x}$
This is not a direct variation.

Example Identifying Direct Variation from Ordered Pairs

Tell whether the set of ordered pairs represents a direct variation.

$(2, -14), (5, -35), (-3, 21)$

Calculate $\frac{y}{x}$.

$\dfrac{-14}{2} = -7$

$\dfrac{-35}{5} = -7$

$\dfrac{21}{-3} = -7$

Yes, it is a direct variation because $\frac{y}{x}$ is a constant, -7.

$(2, 4), (3, 5), (5, 7)$

Calculate $\frac{y}{x}$.

$\dfrac{4}{2} = 2$

$\dfrac{5}{3} = \dfrac{5}{3}$

$\dfrac{7}{5} = \dfrac{7}{5}$

No, it is not a direct variation because $\frac{y}{x}$ is not a constant.

Lesson Practice page 365

Tell whether each equation represents a direct variation. If the equation is a direct variation, find the constant of variation.

a. $y - 12 = x$

$y = x +$ _____

Calculate $\frac{y}{x}$.

Direct variation? _____ If yes, $k =$ _____

b. $\dfrac{y}{-3} = x$

$y =$ _____x

Calculate $\frac{y}{x}$.

Direct variation? _____ If yes, $k =$ _____

c. $2xy = 8$

$y = \dfrac{\square}{\square x} = \dfrac{\square}{\square}$

Calculate $\frac{y}{x}$.

Direct variation? _____ If yes, $k =$ _____

d. $3y = x$

$y = \dfrac{\square}{x}$

Calculate $\frac{y}{x}$.

Direct variation? _____ If yes, $k =$ _____

Tell whether each set of ordered pairs represents a direct variation.

e. (3, 10), (12, 40), (9, 30)

Write as $k = \frac{y}{x}$.

$k = \dfrac{\square}{3}; k = \dfrac{40}{\square}; k = \dfrac{30}{\square}$

Simplify.

$= \dfrac{\square}{\square} \overset{?}{=} \dfrac{\square}{\square} \overset{?}{=} \dfrac{\square}{\square}$

Direct variation? _____

f. (10, 4), (12, 6), (14, 8)

Write as $k = \frac{y}{x}$.

$k = \dfrac{\square}{10}; k = \dfrac{6}{\square}; k = \dfrac{\square}{14}$

Simplify.

$= \dfrac{\square}{\square} \overset{?}{=} \dfrac{\square}{\square} \overset{?}{=} \dfrac{\square}{\square}$

Direct variation? _____

g. Write an equation for a direct variation that goes through the point (6, 48).

$48 =$ _____ x *Substitute 48 for y and 6 for x.*

_____ $= k$ *Solve for k.*

$y =$ _____ x *Substitute k into $y = kx$.*

h.

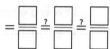   *Use a proportion.*

_____ • _____ $= 6b$ *Cross multiply.*

_____ $= 6b$ *Simplify.*

_____ $= b$ *Solve.*

i. $k = \dfrac{\square}{\square}$

Graph the points (4, 29)

and (_____ , _____)

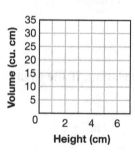

$\dfrac{\square}{\square} = \dfrac{y}{3}$

$3 \cdot$ _____ $=$ _____ y

_____ $=$ _____ y

_____ $= y$

Volume of a 3 cm tall box: _____

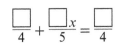
1. Convert to improper fractions.

$$\frac{\square}{4} + \frac{\square x}{5} = \frac{\square}{4}$$

Find a common denominator.

$x =$ _____

2. $0.3x - 0.02x + 0.2 = 1.18$

$x =$ _____

3. $7p + 3w = w - 12 - 3p$

$p =$ _____

4. 315

$=$ _____

5. $\frac{88}{160} = \frac{x}{100}$ Use a proportion.

$160x =$ _____   Cross multiply.

$x =$ _____

6. $\frac{c}{70} = \frac{140}{100}$

$c =$ _____

7. $20\% \cdot n = 18$

$n =$ _____

8. $\frac{y}{11} = x$

$y =$ _____ x Write as $y = kx$.

direct variation? _____

9. $3y = x$

$y =$ _____ x Write as $y = kx$.

direct variation? _____

10. $\left(\frac{10x^3}{y}\right)^2 \cdot \left(-2x^2y^2\right)^3$

$=$ _____

---

11. $63\% \cdot \underline{\hspace{2cm}}$

Change the percent to a decimal.

$= \underline{\hspace{2cm}} \cdot \underline{\hspace{2.5cm}}$

$= \underline{\hspace{2cm}}$

---

12. a. $A = \pi r^2$

$A = \pi \underline{\hspace{1.5cm}}^2 = \underline{\hspace{2cm}} \pi$

b. *side of square = 2 times radius of circle*

$A = s^2$

$A = (2 \cdot \underline{\hspace{1.5cm}})^2$

$A = (\underline{\hspace{1.5cm}})^2 = \underline{\hspace{1.5cm}}$

c. $\dfrac{\text{Area}_{\text{circle}}}{\text{Area}_{\text{square}}} = \dfrac{\square \pi}{\square} = \dfrac{\square}{\square}$

---

13. The origin $(0, 0)$ will always make the

equation $y = kx$ $\underline{\hspace{3cm}}$.

---

14. *Write as $y = kx$.*

Circle the answer.

A $y = 2 - x$ **B** $x + 3 = y$

C $xy = -2$ **D** $3y = -2x$

---

15. *Use a proportion.*

$$\frac{5}{\square} = \frac{\square}{e}$$

$\underline{\hspace{1.5cm}} \cdot \underline{\hspace{1.5cm}} = 5e$ *Cross multiply.*

$\underline{\hspace{2.5cm}} = 5e$

$e = \underline{\hspace{1.5cm}}$

---

16. *Slope-intercept form: $y = mx + b$*

$-4y + x = 2$

$-4y = \underline{\hspace{1.5cm}} x + 2$

$$y = \frac{\square}{\square} x - \frac{\square}{\square}$$

---

17. endpoint: $\underline{\hspace{1.5cm}}$

inequality: $\underline{\hspace{1cm}}$

$z \bigcirc \underline{\hspace{2cm}}$

---

18. $V = \frac{1}{3}Bh; \ B = s^2$

$\underline{\hspace{2cm}} = \frac{1}{3}(s^2 \cdot 6)$

$\underline{\hspace{2cm}} = \underline{\hspace{1cm}} s^2$

$\underline{\hspace{2cm}} = s^2$

$\sqrt{\underline{\hspace{1.5cm}}} = s$

$\underline{\hspace{2cm}} = s$

---

19. 9 is the mean so the _____ of the

terms divided by the _____

of terms must equal ____ .

9 is the median so it must occur in the

_____ of the set.

12 is the mode so it must occur

_____ _____ .

🖋 Create a data set that fits these
criteria.

20. $P = 2(l + w)$

$$P = 2\left(\frac{150x + 200}{2x + 4} + \frac{60x + 220}{2x + 4}\right)$$

$$P = 2\left(\frac{(\boxed{}x + \boxed{})}{2x + 4}\right)$$

$$P = 2\left(\frac{\boxed{}(x + 2)}{(x + 2)}\right)$$

$$P = 2(\underline{})$$

$$P = \underline{}$$

---

21. *Point-slope form:* $y - y_1 = m(x - x_1)$

$y - \underline{} = \underline{}(x - \underline{})$

22. The degree of a polynomial is the degree of

the _____ with the _____

degree.

---

23. degree of a^2b^3: _____

degree of a^3b^4: _____

degree of $2ab$: _____

term with the greatest degree: _____

Circle the answer.

A 14   B 2

C 7   D 5

24. Order data from _____ to _____ .

66, _____, _____, 75, _____, _____,

88 _____, _____, _____, 103, 105

minimum: _____ maximum: _____

median: _____

Q_1: from _____ to _____

Q_3: from _____ to _____

1st Quartile: _____

3rd Quartile: _____

🖋 Draw your box-and-whisker plot.

25. 201, _____, _____, 239, _____, _____,

245, _____, _____, 270, _____

minimum: _____ maximum: _____

median: _____

Q_1: from _____ to _____

Q_3: from _____ to _____

1st Quartile: _____

3rd Quartile: _____

 Draw your box-and-whisker plot.

_____ is an outlier.

26. Outlier $< Q_1 - 1.5(IQR)$ Outlier $> Q_3 + 1.5(IQR$

Student _____ is correct. Student _____

used the _____ instead of

the _____ in the outlier
formula.

27. $4s = 3(\underline{\hspace{2cm}})$

$4s = \underline{\hspace{0.8cm}} s + \underline{\hspace{0.8cm}}$

$s = \underline{\hspace{0.8cm}}$

28. Student _____ is correct. The solution of

Student _____ only satisfies _____ of
the equations.

29. $x + y + 81° = \underline{\hspace{1cm}}$

$\underline{\hspace{0.8cm}} x + \underline{\hspace{0.8cm}} y = \underline{\hspace{1cm}}$

Change equations to slope-intercept form.

$y = \underline{\hspace{0.8cm}} x + \underline{\hspace{1.2cm}}$

$y = \underline{\hspace{0.8cm}} x + \underline{\hspace{1.2cm}}$

Graph.

Intersection: (_____, _____);

$x = \underline{\hspace{1cm}}, y = \underline{\hspace{1cm}}$

30. a. $t = m + \underline{\hspace{0.8cm}}$

$t = \underline{\hspace{0.8cm}} + 3$

b. $m + \underline{\hspace{0.8cm}} = \underline{\hspace{0.8cm}} + 3$

$m = \underline{\hspace{0.8cm}}$

$t = \underline{\hspace{0.8cm}} + \underline{\hspace{0.8cm}} = \underline{\hspace{0.8cm}}$

c. $7 - 5 = \underline{\hspace{0.6cm}}$, which is _____'s age.

$7 - 3 = \underline{\hspace{0.6cm}}$, which is ___ · Miguel's age.

LESSON

57

Finding the Least Common Multiple page 368

New Concepts

Finding the Least Common Multiple
1. Write each number as a product of prime factors.
2. Use every factor of the given numbers as a factor of the LCM. Use each factor the greatest number of times it is a factor of any of the numbers or expressions.

Example Identifying the LCM of a Set of Numbers

Find the LCM of 11, 12, and 18.

$11 = 11 \cdot 1$
$12 = 2 \cdot 2 \cdot 3$
$18 = 2 \cdot 3 \cdot 3$

Use each factor the greatest number of times it is a factor of any of the numbers or expressions.

The LCM is $2 \cdot 2 \cdot 3 \cdot 3 \cdot 11$ or **396**

- In algebraic expressions, the number of times a variable appears in the LCM is the greatest number of times it appears in any of the factors of an algebraic expression.

Finding the Least Common Multiple of Algebraic Expressions
1. Write each expression as a product of prime factors and factors with an exponent of 1.
2. Use every factor of the given numbers as a factor of the LCM. Use each factor the greatest number of times it is a factor of any of the numbers or expressions.

Example Identifying the LCM of Three Monomials

Find the LCM of $6p^2s^3$, $2m^2s^2$, and $8m^3p$.

$6p^2s^3 = 2 \cdot 3 \cdot p \cdot p \cdot s \cdot s \cdot s$
$2m^2s^2 = 2 \cdot m \cdot m \cdot s \cdot s$
$8m^3p = 2 \cdot 2 \cdot 2 \cdot m \cdot m \cdot m \cdot p$

Each variable with the largest exponent is the LCM. Use this to check your work.

The LCM is $2 \cdot 2 \cdot 2 \cdot 3 \cdot m \cdot m \cdot m \cdot p \cdot p \cdot s \cdot s \cdot s$ or $\mathbf{24m^3p^2s^3}$.

> **Example** **Identifying the LCM of Polynomials**
>
> **Find the LCM of $(60x^3 + 24x)$ and $(45x^4 + 18x^2)$.**
>
> $60x^3 + 24x = 2 \cdot 2 \cdot 3 \cdot x(5x^2 + 2)$
> $45x^4 + 18x^2 = 3 \cdot 3 \cdot x \cdot x(5x^2 + 2)$
>
> **The LCM is $2 \cdot 2 \cdot 3 \cdot 3 \cdot x \cdot x(5x^2 + 2)$ or $36x^2(5x^2 + 2)$.**

Lesson Practice 📖 page 372

a. 16 and 42

$16 = $ ____ $\cdot$ ____ $\cdot$ ____ $\cdot$ ____

$42 = $ ____ $\cdot$ ____ $\cdot$ ____

The LCM is ____ .

b. 8, 12, and 17

$8 = $ ____ $\cdot$ ____ $\cdot$ ____

$12 = $ ____ $\cdot$ ____ $\cdot$ ____

$17 = $ ____ $\cdot$ ____

The LCM is ____ .

c. $6c^2d^7$ and $15c^5d$ *Each variable with the largest exponent is the LCM. Use this to check your work.*

$6c^2d^7 = $ ___ $\cdot$ ___ $\cdot$ ___ $\cdot$ ___ $\cdot$ ___ $\cdot$ ___ $\cdot$ ___ $\cdot$ ___ $\cdot$ ___ $\cdot$ ___

$15c^5d = $ ___ $\cdot$ ___ $\cdot$ ___ $\cdot$ ___ $\cdot$ ___ $\cdot$ ___ $\cdot$ ___ $\cdot$ ___   The LCM is _____ .

d. $4k^4p^3n^2$, $5k^2p^3$, and $20n^4k^3$

✎ Find the LCM.   The LCM is _____ .

e. $(3x + 5)$ and $(2x - 7)$ *The binomials are prime. Their only factors are 1 and themselves.*

The LCM is _____ .

f. $(15c^2 - 3c)$ and $(35c - 7)$

$15c^2 - 3c = $ ___ $\cdot$ ___ $($ ___ $c - $ ___ $)$ $35c - 7 = $ ____ $($ ___ $c - $ ___ $)$

The LCM is ___ $\cdot$ ___ $\cdot$ ___ $($ ___ $c - $ ___ $)$ or ___ $c($ ___ $c - $ ___ $)$.

g. $(8f^5 - 24f^2)$ and $(18f^3 - 54f^4)$

✎ Find the LCM.   The LCM is _____ .

h. ✎ Find the LCM of 24, 36, and 60.   The LCM is ____ .

_____ backpacks

1. $s + 4t = r$ for s

$s = $ _____

2. $3m - 7n = p$ for m

$m = $ _____

3. $\dfrac{3}{4} = \dfrac{a+5}{21}$

$a = $ _____

4. $\dfrac{3}{y-3} = \dfrac{1}{9}$

$y = $ _____

5.

50 to 20 is a ____% _____

6.

12 to 96 is a ____% _____

7. The GCF uses only the _____ that appear in _____ numbers.

The LCM uses _____ (all/no) factors the _____ (greatest/least) number of times they appear in _____ number(s).

8. 24 and 84

24 = ___ • ___ • ___ • ___

84 = ___ • ___ • ___ • ___

LCM: ___ • ___ • ___ • ___ • ___

or _____

9. 24 and 84

GCF: ____

10. Draw a horizontal and vertical line through the point (6, 5).

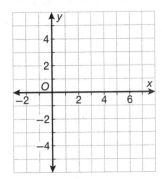

11. a. temp. change from 6 a.m. to noon:

change per hour: $\dfrac{\Box}{\Box}$ = _____ °F

b. temp. change from noon to 2 p.m.:

change per hour: $\dfrac{\Box}{\Box}$ = _____ °F

c. temp. at 6 a.m.: _____ °F

temp. at 4 p.m.: _____ °F

temp. change per hour from
6 a.m. − 4 p.m.:

_____ − $\dfrac{\Box}{\Box}$ or _____ °F

12. a. Place an X over each number on the line
plot that corresponds to a data point.

```
├┼┼┼┼┼┼┼┼┼┼┼┼┼┼┼┼┼┼┼┼┼┼┼┼┤
 26  28  30  32  34  36  38  40  42  44  46  48  50
```

b. The overall shape of a line plot is a

_____.

c. Most of the students could hop on

one leg for _____ to _____ seconds.

13. *Use the amount of change between new data
value and the original data value.*

= _____

14. *Write in standard form. Use placeholders if necessary.*

$(-9z^3 - 3z) = -9z^3 + \_\_\_\_ z^2 - 3z$

$13z - 8z^2 = \_\_\_ z^3 - 8z^2 + 13z$

Write in vertical form:

$$
\begin{array}{r}
-9z^3 + \_\_\_\_ z^2 - 3z \\
\underline{\_\_\_ z^3 - 8z^2 + 13z} \\
\_\_\_ z^3 - \_\_\_ z^2 + \_\_\_ z
\end{array}
$$

15. a. The domain is minutes which are

_____ numbers. The range is

money, so it consists of _____

numbers ≥ _____.

b. *The slope is the rate of change. The
y-intercept is the constant or starting
value.*

$y = \_\_\_ x + \_\_\_\_\_$

16. $\dfrac{k - 3}{7k - 21}$

$= \dfrac{k - 3}{\Box(k - \Box)}$

$= \dfrac{\Box}{\Box}$

*Excluded values cause the denominator in the original
or simplified fraction to equal zero.*

$k \neq \_\_\_$

17. *Use ≤ or ≥ if the circle is closed.*

n ◯ _____

18. $\text{mileage} = \dfrac{\text{mile gain}}{\text{wk}} + \dfrac{\text{miles}}{\text{wk}}$

Let m = weekly mileage

$m =$ _____$w +$ _____

$60 <$ _____$w +$ _____

_____ $<$ _____w

_____ $< w$

19. *Make a box-and-whisker plot.*

$x > Q_3 + 1.5\ (IQR)$

_____ $+ 1.5($_____$) =$ _____

221 ◯ _____

_____ _____(is/is not) an outlier.

20. *The upper extreme is the maximum data value.*

Circle the answer.

A 5   **B** 6

C 7   **D** There is none.

21. a. Stephen: $y =$ _____$x + 16$

Robert: $y =$ _____$x + 14$

Graph to solve the system of equations.

b. _____ shots

c. 3rd quarter total: _____ points

22. For Y1: $2x + 3y = 12$

$y = \dfrac{\square}{\square}x +$ ____

For Y2: $-3x + 2y = 8$

$y = \dfrac{\square}{\square}x +$ ____

Solution: (___, ___).

---

23. *The equation $y = kx$, $k \neq 0$, shows a direct variation.*

$7 + y = x$

$y = x - \underline{\quad}$

$7 + y = x$

Direct variation? $\underline{\quad\quad}$

24. *Use number of centimeters/number of inches.*

Set up a proportion.

$\underline{\quad\quad}$ cm

---

25. Student $\underline{\quad}$ is correct.

Student $\underline{\quad}$ substituted $\underline{\quad}$ months

instead of $\underline{\quad\quad}$.

26. *Use circumference/radius.*

Write and solve a proportion.

$c = \underline{\quad\quad}$

---

27. $k = \dfrac{\text{fluid pressure}}{\text{depth}}$

a. $k = \dfrac{\square}{\square} = \underline{\quad}$

$y = \underline{\quad} x$, where $x =$ feet below surface and $y =$ pressure in pounds per square foot

b. Amount of pressure exerted on an object 9 feet below the surface is about

$\underline{\quad\quad}$ pounds per square foot

c. *Find the intersection of the graphs of $y = 312$ and your equation.*

$d = \underline{\quad\quad}$

---

28. The LCM is the $\underline{\quad\quad\quad}$ $\underline{\quad\quad\quad}$ $\underline{\quad\quad\quad}$ of the fractions.

---

29. *Find the prime factorization of each number. Use each factor the greatest number of times it is a factor of any of the numbers or expressions.*

The LCM of $15k^{11}$ and $36k^6$ is:

A $3k^6$ **B** $180k^6$

C $180k^{11}$ **D** $540k^{17}$

30. *Find the LCM.*

$4x^3y^6$, $2xy^2$, and $6x^4y$

Each variable with the largest exponent is the LCM.

LCM: $\underline{\quad} x^{\square} y^{\square}$

Multiplying Polynomials page 375

New Concepts

Exploration  page 376

Use your textbook to complete this exploration.

Example **Using the Distributive Property**

Find the product. $(x + 7)(x + 3)$

$(x + 7)(x + 3)$

$x(x + 3) = x^2 + 3x$ *Multiply the first term in the first binomial by the second binomial.*

$7(x + 3) = 7x + 21$ *Multiply the second term in the first binomial by the second binomial.*

$x^2 + 3x + 7x + 21$ *Add the two products.*

$x^2 + 10x + 21$ *Simplify.*

- See The FOIL Method on  page 377.
- The FOIL Method is used to multiply two binomials.

Example **Using the FOIL Method**

Find the product. $(2a + 5)(3a + 1)$

$(2a)(3a) = 6a^2$ *Find the product of the First terms.*
$(2a)(1) = 2a$ *Find the product of the Outer terms.*
$(5)(3a) = 15a$ *Find the product of the Inner terms.*
$(5)(1) = 5$ *Find the product of the Last terms.*

$\quad\quad$ F $\quad\quad$ O $\quad\quad$ I $\quad\quad$ L
$(2a)(3a) + (2a)(1) + (5)(3a) + (5)(1)$ *Add the four products.*
$\quad 6a^2 \quad + \quad 2a \quad + \quad 15a \quad + \quad 5$ *Simplify.*

$6a^2 + 17a + 5$

Example **Multiplying a Binomial and Trinomial**

Find the product of $(3x + 4)(x^2 - 4x - 6)$. Use vertical multiplication.

$$\begin{array}{r} x^2 - 4x - 6 \\ 3x + 4 \\ \hline 4x^2 - 16x - 24 \\ + 3x^3 - 12x^2 - 18x \\ \hline 3x^3 - 8x^2 - 34x - 24 \end{array}$$

Align terms with like powers.

Math Language

A **binomial** has two terms and a **trinomial** has three terms. A **polynomial** is an expression with two or more terms.

Find each product.

a. $3x(x^2 + 3x - 7)$

$= \underline{\quad}x^{\square} + \underline{\quad}x^{\square} - \underline{\quad}x$

b. $-4x(x^2 + 2x - 3)$

$= \underline{\quad}x^{\square} \bigcirc \underline{\quad}x^{\square} \bigcirc \underline{\quad}x$

Find each product using the Distributive Property.

c. $(x + 4)(x + 3)$

$= (x)(x + 3) + (\underline{\quad})(x + 3)$

$= \underline{\quad}x^{\square} \bigcirc \underline{\quad}x \bigcirc \underline{\quad}x \bigcirc \underline{\quad}$

$= x^{\square} \bigcirc \underline{\quad}x \bigcirc \underline{\quad}$

d. $(x - 5)(x - 2)$

$= (\underline{\quad})(x - 2) + (-5)(x - 2)$

$= \underline{\quad}x^{\square} - \underline{\quad}x \bigcirc \underline{\quad}x \bigcirc \underline{\quad}$

$= x^{\square} \bigcirc \underline{\quad}x \bigcirc \underline{\quad}$

Find each product using the FOIL Method.

e. $(x + 6)(x + 4)$

First: $(\underline{\quad})(\underline{\quad})$ Outer: $(\underline{\quad})(\underline{\quad})$

Inner: $(\underline{\quad})(\underline{\quad})$ Last: $(\underline{\quad})(\underline{\quad})$

Simplify: $x^{\square} \bigcirc \underline{\quad}x \bigcirc \underline{\quad}$

f. $(x - 8)(x - 1)$

First: $(\underline{\quad})(\underline{\quad})$ Outer: $(\underline{\quad})(-1)$

Inner: $(-8)(\underline{\quad})$ Last: $(\underline{\quad})(\underline{\quad})$

Simplify: $x^{\square} \bigcirc \underline{\quad}x \bigcirc \underline{\quad}$

g. Multiply using the Distributive Property. $(2x + 2)(x^2 - 3x - 2)$

$= (2x)(x^2 - 3x - 2) + (2)(x^2 - 3x - 2)$

$= 2x^{\square} - \underline{\quad}x^{\square} - \underline{\quad}x + \underline{\quad}x^{\square} - \underline{\quad}x - \underline{\quad}$

$= \underline{\quad}x^{\square} \bigcirc \underline{\quad}x^{\square} \bigcirc \underline{\quad}x \bigcirc \underline{\quad}$

h. Multiply using vertical multiplication.

$(5x - 2)(x^2 - 3x - 2)$

$$
\begin{array}{r}
x^2 - \quad 3x - 2 \\
5x - 2 \\
\hline
-2x^2 + \underline{\quad}x + \underline{\quad} \\
\underline{\quad}x^{\square} - \underline{\quad}x^{\square} - \underline{\quad}x \\
\hline
\underline{\quad}^{\square} + \underline{\quad}^{\square} - \underline{\quad} + \underline{\quad}
\end{array}
$$

i. $l = (x + 6)$ in. $w = (x^2 + 4x - 2)$ in.

$A = lw$ *Use the Distributive Property to find the area.*

$A = (\underline{\qquad})(\underline{\qquad})$

$= x^{\square} + \underline{\quad}x^{\square} + \underline{\quad}x - \underline{\quad}$ in.^{2}

1. *Use a closed circle for ≤ or ≥.*

Graph $x \leq 2$ on a number line.

2. *Use an open circle for < or >.*

Graph $x > 2$ on a number line.

---

3. Solve.

$4(2x - 3) = 3 + 8x - 11$

$x =$ _____

4. $-5m + 2 + 8m = 2m + 11$

$m =$ _____

---

5. *Use FOIL or the Distributive Property.*

Circle the answer.

A $(6x + 1)(x - 7)$
B $(2x - 1)(3x + 2)$
C $(-6x + 1)(-x + 7)$
D $(-2x + 1)(-3x + 2)$

6. height: $3x^2 + 6x + 4$; width: $x + 5$

$A = ($ _____ $)($ _____ $)$

Use the Distributive Property or vertical multiplication.

_____

---

7. *Use FOIL.*

$(x - 2)(x + 3)$

first: _____   outer: _____

inner: _____   last: _____

$($ __ $)x^{\square} \bigcirc ($ __ $)x \bigcirc$ __

8. *Use the Distributive Property.*

$(2x - 3)(2x + 3)$

$(2x)(2x + 3) + (-3)(2x + 3)$

$=$ __ $x^{\square} \bigcirc$ __ $x \bigcirc$ __ $x \bigcirc$ __

$=$ __ $x^{\square} \bigcirc$ __

---

9. _____, because Monroe _____

the exponents rather than _____

them.

10. $5(x^2 + 3x - 7)$

$=$ __ $x^{\square} + ($ __ $\cdot$ __ $)x - ($ __ $\cdot$ __ $)$

$=$ __ $x^{\square} \bigcirc$ __ $x \bigcirc$ __

---

11. $35 = \underline{} \cdot \underline{}$

$60 = \underline{} \cdot \underline{} \cdot \underline{} \cdot \underline{}$

$100 = \underline{} \cdot \underline{} \cdot \underline{} \cdot \underline{}$

Use each factor the greatest number of times it is a factor of any of the numbers or expressions.

LCM = $\underline{} \cdot \underline{} \cdot \underline{} \cdot \underline{} \cdot \underline{} \cdot \underline{}$

LCM = $\underline{}$

12. 8 feet = $\underline{}$ in.

$16 = \underline{} \cdot \underline{} \cdot \underline{} \cdot \underline{}$

$96 = \underline{} \cdot \underline{} \cdot \underline{} \cdot \underline{} \cdot \underline{} \cdot \underline{}$

LCM = $\underline{}$ = $\underline{}$

There is a seam and a stud every $\underline{}$ feet

or $\underline{}$ inches.

13. Student $\underline{}$ is correct.

Student $\underline{}$ used only the factors that

both expressions have in $\underline{}$

which is the $\underline{}$, not the $\underline{}$.

14. Counterexample:

The angles in a $\underline{}$ add up to 360 degrees, but it is not a rectangle.

15. a. $10 = \underline{} \cdot \underline{}$

$15 = \underline{} \cdot \underline{}$

$24 = \underline{} \cdot \underline{} \cdot \underline{} \cdot \underline{}$

LCM: $\underline{}$ = $\underline{}$

b. $\dfrac{\square}{\square} = \underline{}$ or

$\underline{}$ complete shoes

16. *In a direct variation, $k = \frac{y}{x}$.*

Find k.

1st pair: $\dfrac{6}{9} = \dfrac{\square}{\square}$

2nd pair: $\dfrac{\square}{\square}$ 3rd pair: $\dfrac{\square}{\square}$

The ordered pairs $\underline{}$ (do/do not) show a direct variation.

17. $k = \dfrac{\textit{number of seconds}}{\textit{number of kilometers}}$

$\dfrac{\square}{\square} = \underline{}$

$51 = k \cdot d$

The lightning is $\underline{}$ away.

18. Student $\underline{}$ is correct.

Student $\underline{}$ reversed the $\underline{}$-

and $\underline{}$- values in the equation.

19. minimum = LE: ___

maximum = UE: ___

median: ___

Q_1: ___

Q_3: ___

IQR: ___

20. 81 is what percent of 108?

= ___

21. $\dfrac{9x - 81}{4x^2 - 36x}$

= _____

Excluded values cause the denominator in the original or simplified fraction to equal zero.

$x \neq$ ___ $x \neq$ ___

22. $\dfrac{(x - 4)(2x - 3)}{7x - 28}$

= _____

$x \neq$ ___

23. *The rational expression is undefined when the denominator is undefined.*

The rational expression is undefined when

$\dfrac{v^2}{c^2} =$ ___ or when the velocity

_____ the speed of light.

24. Let n = amount of apricot juice

a. $5\frac{1}{2} + \dfrac{\square}{\square}$ ___ ◯ ___

b. _____

_____

_____

25. Fargo mean amount: _____ in.

St. Paul mean amount: _____ in.

_____ receives less snow over the winter on average.

26.

x	y

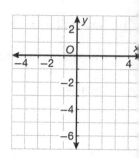

The pairs of values in the _____

satisfy the _____
and form coordinates that are

points on the _____ of the line.

27. *Add the polynomials vertically.*

$A =$ _____ $t^2 \bigcirc$ _____ $t \bigcirc$ _____

28. Write ordered pairs.

$(8, 9)$ and $(\_\_\_, \_\_\_)$

Find the slope. $\dfrac{\square}{\square} =$ _____

Use one point and the slope to write the equation in point-slope form.

equation: _____
Substitute to find what $- 8$ means.

When Kami says -8, she means _____.

29. *Factor the numerator and the denominator. Then divide out like factors.*

$\dfrac{\square(m - \square)}{\square(m - \square)}$

$\dfrac{\square}{\square} =$ _____

Excluded values cause the denominator in the original or simplified fraction to equal zero.

$m \neq$ _____

30. _____ or fewer guests could come.

The number line shows all the _____
number solutions for an inequality, and
because the number of guests must be a

_____ number, the graph

shows too many possible solutions.

Solving Systems of Linear Equations by Substitution page 382

New Concepts

- To be a solution to a system of equations, an ordered pair must make both equations true.

Steps for Solving by Substitution
1. Isolate x or y in one of the equations.
2. Substitute the expression from Step 1 into the other equation. Solve for the variable.
3. To find the value of the other variable, substitute the solution from Step 2 into one of the original equations. Solve.
4. Write the values identified for x and y as an ordered pair.

Example **Using the Distributive Property**

Solve the system of equations: $12x - 6y = 12$ and $x = -2y + 11$. Check your answer.

$12x - 6y = 12$	*Write the first equation.*
$12(-2y + 11) - 6y = 12$	*Substitute $-2y + 11$ for x.*
$-24y + 132 - 6y = 12$	*Distribute.*
$-30y + 132 = 12$	*Combine like terms.*
$-30y = -120$	*Subtract 132 from both sides.*
$y = 4$	*Divide both sides by −30.*

Now find x by substituting 4 for y in either of the original equations. The resulting value for x will be the same.

First Equation	**Second Equation**
$12x - 6y = 12$	$x = -2y + 11$
$12x - 6(4) = 12$	$x = -2(4) + 11$
$12x - 24 = 12$	$x = -8 + 11$
$12x = 36$	$x = 3$
$x = 3$	

The solution to the system is (3, 4).

To check, substitute the values for x and y into both of the original equations.

Solve by substitution.

a. $y = 4x - 3$ and $y = 3x - 5$

_____$x -$ _____ $= 3x - 5$

$x =$ _____

Substitute.

$y = 4($_____$) - 3 =$ _____

Solution: (_____, _____)

📓 Check your solution in both equations.

b. $x = 3y - 11$ and $5x + 2y = -4$

$5($_____$) + 2y = -4$

_____$y -$ _____ $+ 2y = -4$

_____$y =$ _____ ⟶ $y =$ _____

Substitute.

$x = 3($_____$) - 11 =$ _____

Solution: (_____, _____)

📓 Check your solution in both equations.

c. $4x + 3y = 2$ and $2x + y = 6$

Isolate a variable in one of the equations. Use the variable with a coefficient of 1 or −1, if possible.

$y =$ _____$x + 6$

$4x + 3($_____$x + 6) = 2$

_____$x +$ _____ $= 2$

_____$x =$ _____ ⟶ $x =$ _____

Substitute.

$4($_____$) + 3y = 2$

Solution: (_____, _____)

📓 Check your solution in both equations.

d. $4x + 3y = 19$ and $7x - 6y = -23$

Isolate a variable in one of the equations.

$3y =$ _____$x + 19$ ⟶ $y =$ _____$x +$ _____

$7x - 6($_____$x +$ _____$) = -23$

_____$x -$ _____ $= -23$

_____$x =$ _____ ⟶ $x =$ _____

Substitute.

$7($___$) - 6y = -23$ ⟶ $y =$ ___

Solution: (_____, _____)

📓 Check your solution in both equations.

e. Solve for b and p by substitution: $5b + 10p = \$36$ and $2b + 40p = \$18$.

$2b =$ _____$p + 18$

$b =$ _____$p +$ _____

Substitute.

$5($_____$p +$ _____$) + 10p = 36$

$p =$ _____

pencils: ▨ _____

Substitute.

$2b + 40($_____$) = 18$

$b =$ _____

books: ▨ _____

---

1. $-[-(-k)] - (-2)(-2 + k) = -k - (4k + 3)$

   $k = \underline{\hspace{1cm}}$

2. $\frac{1}{3} + 5\frac{1}{3}k + 3\frac{2}{9} = 0$

   $k = \underline{\hspace{1cm}}$

---

3. Simplify $\sqrt{9} + \sqrt{16} - \sqrt{225}$.

   $= \underline{\hspace{1cm}}$

4. Give an example of a rational number that is not an integer.

   Answer: $\underline{\hspace{1cm}}$

---

5. *The number $\sqrt{49}$ is a rational number.*

   Circle the answer: true or false?

6. $y = 3x - 5$
   $y = -2x + 15$
   Solve by substition.

   $3x - 5 = \underline{\hspace{1cm}}x + \underline{\hspace{1cm}}$

   $\underline{\hspace{1cm}}x = \underline{\hspace{1cm}} \longrightarrow x = \underline{\hspace{1cm}}$

   Substitute.

   $y = 3(\underline{\hspace{1cm}}) - 5 = \underline{\hspace{1cm}}$

   Solution: $(\underline{\hspace{1cm}}, \underline{\hspace{1cm}})$

---

7. $y = -8x + 21$
   $y = -3x + 6$
   Solve by substition.

   $-8x + 21 = \underline{\hspace{1cm}}x + \underline{\hspace{1cm}}$

   $\underline{\hspace{1cm}}x = \underline{\hspace{1cm}} \longrightarrow x = \underline{\hspace{1cm}}$

   Substitute.

   $y = -3(\underline{\hspace{1cm}}) + 6 = \underline{\hspace{1cm}}$

   Solution: $(\underline{\hspace{1cm}}, \underline{\hspace{1cm}})$

8. A point is a solution to a system of

   equations if it makes $\underline{\hspace{2cm}}$

   equation in the system a $\underline{\hspace{2cm}}$
   statement.

---

9. *If an ordered pair is a solution to a system, it will satisfy both equations.*

$4x + 9y = 75$
$8x + 6y = 66$

Circle the answer.

A $(3, 7)$ **B** $(0, 11)$

C $(10, 4)$ **D** $(12, -5)$

---

10. $a + b = $ _____ $a - b = $ _____

Isolate a variable in one of the equations.

$a = $ _____ $- b$

Substitute the result into the other equation.

$($ _____ $- b) - b = $ _____

$b = $ _____

Substitute. $a + $ _____ $= $ _____

$a = $ _____

The two numbers are _____ and _____.

---

11. Student _____. Student _____

multiplied the _____

instead of _____ them.

---

12. total length = _____ $x + $ _____ $+ $ _____

total width = $x + $ _____ $+ $ _____

$A = ($ _____ $x + $ _____ $)(x + $ _____ $)$

$= $ _____ $x^2 + $ _____ $x + $ _____

---

13. a. $A = ($ _____ $)($ _____ $)$

$= $ _____ $x^2 + $ _____ $x + $ _____

b. $V = ($ _____ $x^2 + $ _____ $x + $ _____ $)($ _____ $)$

$= $ _____ $x^3 + $ _____ $x^2 + $ _____ $+ $ _____

---

14. $= \frac{1}{2} \cdot ($ _____ $) \cdot ($ _____ $)$

$= \frac{1}{2} \cdot ($ _____ $)$

$= $ _____ $x^{\square} + $ _____ $x^{\square} + $ _____ $x - $ _____

---

15. $4x($ _____ $) \bigcirc 4x($ _____ $) \bigcirc 4x($ _____ $)$

$= $ _____ $\bigcirc$ _____ $\bigcirc$ _____

---

16. *See page 6 in the* Student Reference Guide.

equation: _____

---

17. *The degree of a polynomial is the degree of the greatest-degree term in the polynomial.*

degree of $12x^4x^3$ _____

degree of $6xy$: _____

degree of $41x^2y^3$: _____

degree of expression: _____

18. *Order the numbers from least to greatest.*

min: _____   max: _____

Q_1: _____   median: _____

Q_3: _____   IQR: _____

Make box-and-whisker plot.

Use 0.1 as the interval on the number line.

Outlier > Q_3 + 1.5 (IQR) or outlier < Q_1 − 1.5 (IQR)

There _____ outlier(s).

19. $\dfrac{cost}{length}$

cost of 14-inch chain ≈ \$_____

$k \approx \dfrac{\square}{14} \approx$ _____

$y =$ _____ x

$y = ($_____$)18 =$ _____

20. *In a direct variation k = $\frac{y}{x}$.*

$k = \dfrac{\square}{\square} =$ _____

Circle the answer.

A $(4, -8)$ **B** $(4, -7)$

C $(4, -12)$ **D** $(4, -16)$

21. $16c^6 =$ _____ • _____ • _____ • _____ c^6

$24c^3 =$ _____ • _____ • _____ • _____ c^3

The variable with the largest exponent is the LCM.

LCM = _____

22. *Find the LCM.*

_____ turns

23. $300d^2 = 2 \cdot$ _____

$90d^4 = 3 \cdot$ _____

LCM = _____

$=$ _____

24. $\dfrac{\text{first line}}{\text{second line}}$

Factor the numerator and denominator. Divide out like terms.

$=$ _____

---

25. *See page 6 in the* Student Reference Guide.

$m =$ _____

26. If an animal has wings, then the animal is an insect.

counterexample: _____

_____

---

27. a. $V_{cylinder} = A_{base \cdot height}$

$A_{base} = A_{circle} =$ _____

$V_{cylinder}: 28\pi =$ _____ $\cdot$ _____

b. $r^2 = \dfrac{\square}{\square}$

$r^2 =$ _____

$r =$ _____ $=$ _____

28. $\dfrac{\text{weight on Jupiter}}{\text{weight on Earth}} = \dfrac{\square}{\square}$

slope: _____

$x =$ _____ at the y-intercept: _____.

slope-intercept equation: _____

---

29. If a number is an integer, then it is a rational number.

converse: If _____

_____, then

_____.

counterexample: The number _____

is a(n) _____

but it is not a(n) _____.

30. An excluded value is the value of the

_____ that makes the _____

of the original or simplified rational

expression equal _____. It is excluded

because division by _____ is

_____.

Finding Special Products of Binomials page 390

New Concepts

Exploration 📖 Multiplying Binomials, page 390

Use your textbook to complete this exploration.

Special Product of Binomials	
Square of a Binomial	
Pattern	**Example**
$(a + b)^2 = a^2 + 2ab + b^2$	$(x + 5)^2 = x^2 + 10x + 25$
$(a - b)^2 = a^2 - 2ab + b^2$	$(2x - 4)^2 = 4x^2 - 16x + 16$
Sum and Difference	
Pattern	**Example**
$(a + b)(a - b) = a^2 - b^2$	$(3x - 2)(3x + 2) = 9x^2 - 4$

Example **Squaring Binomials in the Form $(a + b)^2$**

Find the product: $(2x + 4)^2$.

$(a + b)^2 = a^2 + 2ab + b$ *Factoring pattern.*

$(2x + 4)^2 = (2x)^2 + 2(2x)(4) + (4)^2$ *Apply the pattern.*

$= 4x^2 + 16x + 16$ *Simplify.*

Example **Squaring Binomials in the Form $(a - b)^2$**

Find the product: $(2x - 7)^2$.

$(a - b)^2 = a^2 - 2ab + b^2$ *Factoring pattern.*

$(2x - 7)^2 = (2x)^2 - 2(2x)(7) + (7)^2$ *Apply the pattern.*

$= 4x^2 - 28x + 49$ *Simplify.*

Example **Finding Products in the Form $(a + b)(a - b)$**

Find the product: $(5x + 4)(5x - 4)$.

$(a + b)(a - b) = a^2 - b^2$ *Factoring pattern.*

$(5x + 4)(5x - 4) = (5x)^2 - (4)^2$ *Apply the pattern.*

$= 25x^2 - 16$ *Simplify.*

Find each product.

a. $(x + 9)^2$

Use a factoring pattern.

$(a + b)^2 = \underline{}^2 \bigcirc \underline{} + \underline{}^2$

$(x + 9)^2$

$= (\underline{})^2 \bigcirc 2(\underline{})(\underline{}) + (\underline{})^2$

$= \underline{}x^2 + \underline{}x + \underline{}$

b. $(3x + 5)^2$

Use a factoring pattern.

$(a + b)^2 = \underline{}^2 \bigcirc \underline{} + \underline{}^2$

$(3x + 5)^2$

$= (\underline{})^2 \, 2(\underline{})(\underline{}) + (\underline{})^2$

$= \underline{}x^2 + \underline{}x + \underline{}$

c. $(x - 1)^2$

Use a factoring pattern.

$(a - b)^2 = \underline{}^2 \bigcirc \underline{} + \underline{}^2$

$(x - 1)^2$

$= (\underline{})^2 \bigcirc 2(\underline{})(\underline{}) + (\underline{})^2$

$= \underline{}x^2 \underline{}x + \underline{}$

d. $(8x - 6)^2$

Use a factoring pattern.

$(a - b)^2 = \underline{}^2 \underline{} + \underline{}^2$

$(8x - 6)^2$

$= (\underline{})^2 \bigcirc 2(\underline{})(\underline{}) + (\underline{})^2$

$= \underline{}x^2 \bigcirc \underline{}x + \underline{}$

e. $(x + 8)(x - 8)$

Use a factoring pattern.

$(a + b)(a - b) = \underline{}^2 \bigcirc \underline{}^2$

$(x + 8)(x - 8) = (\underline{})^2 \bigcirc (\underline{})^2$

$= \underline{}x^2 - \underline{}$

f. $(3x + 2)(3x - 2)$

Use a factoring pattern.

$(a + b)(a - b) = \underline{}^2 \bigcirc \underline{}^2$

$(3x + 2)(3x - 2) = (\underline{})^2 \bigcirc (\underline{})^2$

$= \underline{}x^2 - \underline{}$

g. Use mental math to find 28^2.

$28^2 = (30 - \underline{})^2$

$= 30^2 - 2(30)(\underline{}) + (\underline{})^2$

$= \underline{} - \underline{} + \underline{} = \underline{}$

h. Use mental math to find $58 \cdot 62$.

$58 \cdot 62 = (60 - \underline{})(\underline{} + \underline{})$

$= (\underline{})^2 - (\underline{})^2$

$= \underline{} - \underline{} = \underline{}$

i. Find the area of a rectangle with a length of $(x - 6)$ and a width of $(x + 6)$.

$A = l \cdot w = (\underline{})(\underline{})$

Use a factoring pattern.

$(a + b)(a - b) = \underline{}^2 \bigcirc \underline{}^2$

$A = (\underline{})^2 \bigcirc (\underline{})^2 = \underline{} - \underline{}$

1. k^2 terms: _____

  k terms: _____

  constants: _____

  _____k^2 + _____k + _____

2. *Combine like terms.*

  $(-2m + 1) + (6m^2 - m - 2)$

  = _____

3. *Use FOIL.*

  $(x + 4)(x - 5)$

  = _____

4. *Distribute.*

  $(x + 2)(6x^2 + 4x + 5)$

  = _____

5. *Use a factoring pattern.*

  $(a - b)^2 =$ ____^{2} ◯ ____ + ____^{2}

  $(3t - 1)^2$

  $= (\_)^2 ◯ 2(\_)(\_) + (\_)^2$

  = _____

6. *Use a factoring pattern.*

  $(a + b)^2 =$ ____^{2} ◯ ____ + ____^{2}

  $(3t + 1)^2$

  $= (\_)^2 ◯ 2(\_)(\_) + (\_)^2$

  = _____

7. length of side with border: _____

  $A = ($_____$)^2$

  Use a factoring pattern.

  $(a + b)^2 =$ _____

  $A =$ _____ + _____ + _____

8. Solve by substitution.

  $y = 2x - 9$
  $8x - 6y = 34$

  $8x - 6($_____$) = 34$

  $8x -$ _____ + _____ = 34

  _____$x =$ _____ ➝ $x =$ _____

  Substitute.

  $y = 2($_____$) - 9 =$ _____

  Solution: (_____, _____)

9. *Use a factoring pattern.*

$(a + b)^2 =$ _____

Circle the answer.

A　$36x^2 + 42x + 49$

B　$12x^2 + 84x + 49$

C　$36x^2 + 84x + 49$

D　$36x + 84x + 49$

10. Solve by substitution.

$y = 2x - 4$
$y = x + 5$

_____ $= 2x - 4$

____$x =$ ____　　⟶　$x =$ ____

Substitute.

$y =$ ____ $+ 5 =$ ____

Solution: (____ , ____)

11. The product of two binomials takes the

form $(a + b)($ _____ $)$.

After finding the product by using the special-product pattern, you can check your work by doing the actual multiplication, using the

_____ method.

12. *Use a factoring pattern.*

$(9x + 8)(9x + 8) = (9x + 8)^2$

The statement is _____ .

13. width $= w$　　　length $=$ ____ $w +$ ____

$P = 2$____ $+ 2($ _____ $) = 78$

$= 2$____ $+$ _____ $+$ ____ $= 78$

____ $w =$ ____　　⟶　$w =$ _____

$l =$ ____ $($ ____ $) + 3 =$ _____

14. Student ____ is correct. Student ____

did not use the _____ Property

to multiply the ____ by _____ .

15. 1st floor: ____ $n +$ ____ $c = 23$

2nd floor: ____ $n +$ ____ $c = 25$

Solve one equation for n or c. Substitute into the other equation.

$c =$ _____　　　　$n =$ _____

16. ____ $g +$ ____ $b = 169$

$b = 1 +$ ___ g

____ $g +$ ____ $(1 +$ ____ $g) = 169$

____ $g +$ ____ $+$ ____ $g = 169$

___ $g =$ ____　　⟶　$g =$ ____

$b = 1 + ($ ____ $)($ ____ $) =$ ____

In 10 years: $g =$ ____　　$b =$ ____

17. width $= w$ length $=$ _____ $w -$ _____

_____ $w +$ _____ (_____ $w -$ _____) $= P$

_____ $w +$ _____ $w -$ _____ $= 24$

_____ $w -$ _____ $= 24$

_____ $w =$ _____

$w =$ _____

$l =$ _____ (_____) $- 4 =$ _____

18. $Q_1 =$ __.___ *median of lower half*

$Q_3 =$ __.___ *median of upper half*

IQR $=$ __._____ $-$ __._____ $=$ __._____

outlier $< Q_1 - 1.5$ *(IQR)*   *outlier* $> Q_3 + 1.5$ *IQR*

_____ and _____ are outliers.

🗒 Draw box-and-whisker plot.

19. $6f^4 = 2 \cdot$ _____

$4f^2 = 2^2 \cdot$ _____

LCM: (___)^2 (___)$f^{\square} =$ _____

20. $4x^4 - 14x^3 =$ _____ $\cdot$ (___ $x -$ ___)

$6x^2 - 21x = 3x \cdot$ (___ $x -$ ___)

LCM: _____ $x^3 \cdot$ (_____)

Answer: _____

21. $(2, 8): k = \dfrac{8}{2} =$ _____

$(4, 16): k = \dfrac{\square}{\square} =$ _____

$(7, 28): k = \dfrac{\square}{\square} =$ _____

These ordered pairs _____ show direct variation.

22. $A = ($ ___ $x +$ ___ $)($ ___ $x +$ ___ $)$

Use FOIL.

$A =$ ___ $x^2 +$ _____ $x +$ _____

23. $m = \dfrac{\square - \square}{\square - \square}$

$= \dfrac{\square}{\square}$

The slope is _____ because the

_____ is _____.

24. *Use FOIL.*

$(x + 2)(x + 9)$

$=$ _____

25. The _____ between a

_____ and

2.5 is _____ than 4.7.

26. Let x = number of José's cards.

_____ x ◯ 79

x ◯ _____

José could have _____ cards.

27. a. *Base the percent decrease for each week on the number of players at the beginning of that week.*

$\dfrac{\square}{85} \approx$ ____._____ = _____ ▨

$\dfrac{\square}{\square} =$ ____._____ = _____ ▨

b. $\dfrac{\square}{\square} =$ ____._____ = _____ ▨

28. The graph should include only _____

numbers because _____

_____

_____

29. $P = 2\left(\dfrac{\square}{\square - \square}\right) + 2\left(\dfrac{\square - \square}{\square - \square}\right)$

$=$ _____ + _____

$=$ _____

$=$ _____ ▨

30. The equation of the line is already in

__-_____ form. The slope m is

the _____ of x: _____. The

y-intercept is the constant b: _____.

Name _____

Transforming Linear Functions page 396

- A **family of functions** share common features.

- A **parent function** is the simplest function in a family of functions.

- A **translation** or "slide" shifts every point in a figure the same amount in the same direction.

For example, $f(x) = x - 4$ is a translation of the parent function $f(x) = x$.

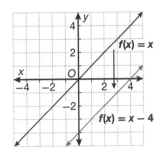

1. Graph $f(x) = x$, $f(x) = x + 3$, and $f(x) = x - 2$ on the coordinate grid.

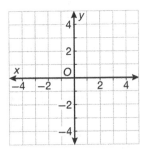

2. Compare the graphs of $f(x) = x + 3$ and $f(x) = x - 2$.

The y-intercept of $f(x) = x + 3$ shifts _____ units from $f(x) = x$.

Each point on the graph of $f(x) = x + 3$ shifts _____ units from $f(x) = x$.

The y-intercept of $f(x) = x - 2$ shifts _____ units from $f(x) = x$.

Each point on the graph of $f(x) = x - 2$ shifts _____ units from $f(x) = x$.

- A stretch or compression of a linear function changes its slope.

For example, $f(x) = 5x$ is a "stretch" of the parent function $f(x) = x$.

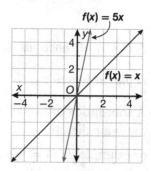

3. Graph $f(x) = x$, $f(x) = 3x$, and $f(x) = \frac{1}{3}x$ on the coordinate grid.

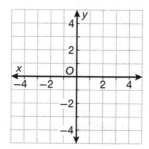

4. As the slope of the line _____, the line becomes

steeper. As the slope of the line _____, the line becomes
less steep.

5. _____ because when $m > 1$, the line is _____ than the

parent function. When $0 < m < 1$, the line is not as _____
as the parent function.

- A reflection produces a "mirror image" of a function.

For example, $f(x) = -\frac{1}{2}x$ is a reflection of $f(x) = \frac{1}{2}x$.

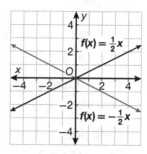

6. Graph $f(x) = 4x$ and $f(x) = -4x$ on the coordinate grid.

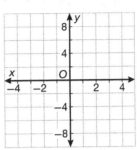

7. Graphing the original line with the _____ slope

results in a _____ of the line over the ____-axis.

• Some functions involve more than one transformation of the parent function.

For example $f(x) = \frac{1}{2}x - 4$ is not as steep as $f(x) = x$ and shifts the graph down from the graph of $f(x) = x$.

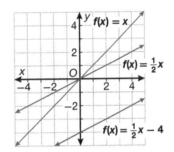

8. Graph $f(x) = x$ and $f(x) = 3x + 2$ on the coordinate grid.

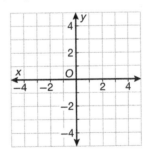

Compare the y-intercepts of the graphs to determine the shift.

9. The graph of $f(x) = 3x + 2$ is _____ than the graph of

$f(x) = x$, and is shifted _____.

Graph each function on a coordinate plane with the parent function $f(x) = x$. **Then describe the transformation.**

a.

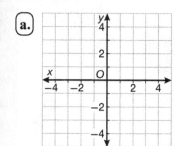

The graph of $f(x) = x$ is shifted _____.

b.

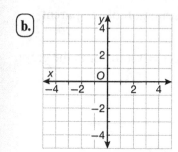

The graph of $f(x) = x$ is reflected _____.

c.

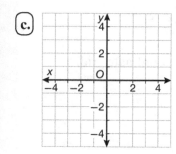

The graph of $f(x) = \frac{1}{2}x$ is not as _____ as the graph of $f(x) = x$.

d.

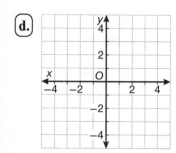

The graph of $f(x) = 4x - 2$ is _____ times as _____ as the graph of $f(x) = x$ and is

shifted _____ units.

LESSON
61

Simplifying Radical Expressions page 398

New Concepts

Math Language

The **radicand** is the expression or number inside or "under" the radical sign.

- A **radical expression** is an expression that contains a radical.
- The Product of Radicals Rule can be used to simplify radical expressions.

Product Property of Radicals
If a and b are non-negative real numbers, then $\sqrt{a}\,\sqrt{b} = \sqrt{ab}$ $\quad$ and $\quad$ $\sqrt{ab} = \sqrt{a}\,\sqrt{b}$.

- Radical expressions can be simplified by factoring products that include perfect squares.

Example **Simplifying with Perfect Squares**

Simplify using perfect squares.

$\sqrt{72}$

$= \sqrt{9 \cdot 8}$ $\qquad$ *Find a perfect square that is a factor of 72.*

$= \sqrt{9 \cdot 4 \cdot 2}$ $\qquad$ *Find all perfect squares that are factors of 72.*

$= \sqrt{9} \cdot \sqrt{4} \cdot \sqrt{2}$ $\qquad$ *Product Property of Radicals*

$= 3 \cdot 2\sqrt{2}$ $\qquad$ *Simplify.*

$= 6\sqrt{2}$ $\qquad$ *Multiply.*

Exploration 📖 page 399

Use your textbook to complete the Exploration.

Example **Simplifying with Prime Factors**

Simplify using prime factorization.

$\sqrt{180}$

$= \sqrt{18 \cdot 10}$ $\qquad$ *Find factors.*

$= \sqrt{(2 \cdot 9) \cdot (2 \cdot 5)}$ $\qquad$ *Factor further.*

$= \sqrt{2 \cdot 2 \cdot 3 \cdot 3 \cdot 5}$ $\qquad$ *Find the prime factorization.*

$= \sqrt{2} \cdot \sqrt{2} \cdot \sqrt{3} \cdot \sqrt{3} \cdot \sqrt{5}$ $\qquad$ *Product Property of Radicals*

$= 2 \cdot 3\sqrt{5}$ $\qquad$ *Simplify.*

$= 6\sqrt{5}$ $\qquad$ *Multiply.*

> **Example** **Simplifying with Variables**
>
> **Simplify.**
>
> $\sqrt{81x^4y^3}$
>
> $= \sqrt{81} \cdot \sqrt{x^4} \cdot \sqrt{y^3}$ *Product Property of Radicals*
>
> $= 9x^2y\sqrt{y}$ *Simplify and multiply.*

Lesson Practice page 401

Simplify with perfect squares.

a. $\sqrt{75}$

$= \sqrt{\underline{\quad} \cdot \underline{\quad}}$

$= \sqrt{\underline{\quad}} \cdot \sqrt{\underline{\quad}} = \underline{\quad}\sqrt{\underline{\quad}}$

b. $\sqrt{63}$

$= \sqrt{\underline{\quad} \cdot \underline{\quad}}$

$= \sqrt{\underline{\quad}} \cdot \sqrt{\underline{\quad}} = \underline{\quad}\sqrt{\underline{\quad}}$

c. Simplify using prime factorization.

$\sqrt{363} = \sqrt{\underline{\quad} \cdot \underline{\quad} \cdot \underline{\quad}} = \sqrt{\underline{\quad}} \cdot \sqrt{\underline{\quad}} \cdot \sqrt{\underline{\quad}} = \underline{\quad}\sqrt{\underline{\quad}}$

d. Simplify using powers of ten.

$\sqrt{1,000,000} = \sqrt{10^{\square}} = \sqrt{\underline{\qquad\qquad}} = 10^{\square}$ or $\underline{\qquad}$

Simplify.

e. $\sqrt{90b^2c^4}$

$= \sqrt{(\underline{\quad} \cdot \underline{\quad} \cdot b^{\square} \cdot c^{\square})}$

$= \sqrt{\underline{\quad}} \cdot \sqrt{\underline{\quad}} \cdot \sqrt{b^{\square}} \cdot \sqrt{c^{\square}}$

$= \underline{\quad}b^{\square}c^{\square}\sqrt{\underline{\quad}}$

f. $\sqrt{25x^3y^7}$

$= \sqrt{(\underline{\quad} \cdot x \cdot x^{\square} \cdot y \cdot y^{\square})}$

$= \sqrt{\underline{\quad}} \cdot \sqrt{x} \cdot \sqrt{x^{\square}} \cdot \sqrt{y} \cdot \sqrt{y^{\square}}$

$= \underline{\quad}x^{\square}y^{\square}\sqrt{xy}$

g. area of a square room $= 80$ square meters $= s^2$

side $= \sqrt{\underline{\quad}} = \sqrt{(\underline{\quad} \cdot \underline{\quad})} = \sqrt{\underline{\quad}} \cdot \sqrt{\underline{\quad}} = \underline{\quad}\sqrt{\underline{\quad}}$

length of room's sides: $\underline{\quad}\sqrt{\underline{\quad}}$ m

1. $\sqrt{12} = \sqrt{\underline{}} \cdot \sqrt{\underline{}}$

$= \underline{}\sqrt{\underline{}}$

2. $\sqrt{200} = \sqrt{\underline{}} \cdot \sqrt{\underline{}}$

$= \underline{}\sqrt{\underline{}}$

3. _____ because there is no real number a such that $a^4 = -16$.

4. $x^{\frac{1}{3}}$ when $x = 343$

$= \sqrt[\square]{x}$

$= \underline{}$

5. F: _____

O: _____

I: _____

L: _____

6. $P = 2(l + w)$

$P = 2(\underline{} + \underline{})$

$= 2(\underline{})$

Factor and simplify.

$\dfrac{2(\square)(\square + \square)}{\square + \square} = \underline{}$

7. Student _____ is correct.

Student _____ squared _____

instead of _____.

8. $A = lw$ $x =$ width of picture

Draw a diagram. Label dimensions.

length $= \underline{} \cdot x + \underline{}$

width $= x + \underline{}$

$A = (\underline{} \cdot x + \underline{})(x + \underline{})$

Circle the answer.

A $(2x)(x)$ **B** $(2x + 4)(x + 2)$

C $(2x + 8)(x + 8)$ **D** $(-2x + 6)(6 + 2)$

9. $-5x + 8y = 7$
$3y = -2x - 9$

Solution: (____, ____)

10. $2x - 3y = 3$
$x = 4y - 11$

Substitute for x:

$$2(\underline{\hspace{2cm}}) - 3y = 3$$

$$\underline{\hspace{1cm}}y - \underline{\hspace{1cm}} - 3y = 3$$

$$\underline{\hspace{1cm}}y = \underline{\hspace{1.5cm}}$$

$$y = \underline{\hspace{0.8cm}}$$

Substitute for y: $x = 4(\underline{\hspace{0.8cm}}) - 11 = \underline{\hspace{1cm}}$

Solution: (____, ____)

11. $V_{sphere} = \frac{4}{3}\pi r^3$

half $V_{sphere} = \underline{\hspace{1cm}}\pi r^3$

igloo volume: $1728\pi = \underline{\hspace{1cm}}\pi r^3$

Solve for r: $r^3 = \underline{\hspace{2cm}}$

$r \approx \underline{\hspace{1.5cm}}$ ft, so

$d = \underline{\hspace{0.8cm}} \cdot \underline{\hspace{0.8cm}} \approx \underline{\hspace{1cm}}$ ft

12. a. mean = _____

b. The outlier _____ the mean

attendance value to _____

13. *Use a special product pattern.*
$(a - b)^2 = a^2 - 2ab + b^2$
$(4b - 3)^2$

= _____

14. *Use a special product pattern.*
$(a + b)^2 = a^2 + 2ab + b^2$
$(-2x + 5)^2$

= _____

15. Let c = number of cars

Let s = number of SUVs

_____ $c +$ _____ $s = 1700$

$c + s =$ _____ or $c =$ _____ $- s.$

Substitute, simplify, and solve for s, then c.

_____ $\cdot ($ _____ $- s) +$ _____ $s = 1700$

_____ $s =$ _____ or

$s =$ _____ SUVs

$c =$ _____ $- s =$ _____ $-$ _____

$=$ _____ cars

16. a. $m = \dfrac{y_2 - y_1}{x_2 - x_1}$

$= \dfrac{(\square - \square)}{(\square - \square)} =$ _____

b. ✎ Graph the line.

c. $y - y_1 = m(x - x_1)$

$y -$ _____ $=$ _____ $(x -$ _____ $)$

d. Simplify part **c:** $y =$ _____ $x -$ _____

e. $-3 =$ _____ $x -$ _____ or $x =$ _____

$y =$ _____ $(-2) -$ _____ or $y =$ _____

17. w_m = weight on moon

$\dfrac{60}{9} = \dfrac{\square}{w_m}$ *Set up a proportion.*

$9($ _____ $) = 60w_m$ *Cross multiply.*

$w_m = \dfrac{\square}{\square} =$ _____

18. $y =$ _____ $x + 3$

Use substitution.

$3x + 8($ _____ $x + 3) = 24$

Circle the answer.

A $(1, 8)$ **B** $(0, 0)$

C $(0, 3)$ **D** $(4, 1.5)$

19. Write the _____ using prime

factorization: $\sqrt{(\square \cdot \square^2 \cdot \square^2)}.$

Since 3^2 and a^2 are _____,

they can be written outside the _____

sign: _____ $\sqrt{2}.$

20. $A = \frac{1}{2}bh$

$= \frac{1}{2}($ _____ $)($ _____ $) = \frac{1}{2}($ _____ $-$ _____ $)$

$= \dfrac{(\square - \square)}{2}$

21.

$$x^2 \quad + \quad 5x \quad + \quad 1$$

$$+ \underline{\quad} \bigcirc \underline{\quad} \bigcirc \underline{\quad}$$

$$\overline{\quad 4x^2 \qquad\qquad - \quad 3}$$

22. $21 = \underline{\quad} \cdot \underline{\quad}$; $33 = \underline{\quad} \cdot \underline{\quad}$;

$13 = \underline{\quad} \cdot \underline{\quad}$

LCM: $\underline{\quad} \cdot \underline{\quad} \cdot \underline{\quad} \cdot \underline{\quad}$

$= \underline{\qquad}$

23. *Use exponents.*

$8 = \underline{\quad}^{\square}$ $\qquad 32 = \underline{\quad}^{\square}$

$12 = \underline{\quad} \cdot \underline{\quad}^{\square}$

LCM: $\underline{\quad} \cdot \underline{\quad} = \underline{\quad}$

24. a. area of whole region $= lw = \underline{\quad}$

b. area of shaded region $= lw = \underline{\quad}$

c. area of non-shaded region $=$ area of whole region $-$ area of shaded region

$= \underline{\quad} - \underline{\quad}$

25. patio length *without* border: $8x - \underline{\qquad}$

square area $=$ length$^2 = (8x - \underline{\qquad})^2$

Use FOIL.

area $= \underline{\qquad\qquad}$

26. a. $A = \pi r^2$

$$r^2 = \frac{\square}{\square}$$

$$r = \sqrt{\left(\frac{\square}{\square}\right)}$$

b. If $A = 20\pi$, $r = \sqrt{\left(\frac{\square}{\square}\right)}$

$$= \sqrt{\underline{\quad}} = \sqrt{(\underline{\quad} \cdot \underline{\quad})} = \underline{\quad}$$

27. The $\underline{\qquad}$ of a number and $\underline{\quad}$

plus $\underline{\quad}$ is $\underline{\qquad}$ or

$\underline{\qquad}$ 5.

28. The $\underline{\qquad}$ of a number and

3 $\underline{\qquad}$ 4 is $\underline{\qquad}$ -2.

29. tangential velocity $= \sqrt{ar} = \sqrt{(\underline{\quad})(\underline{\quad})}$

How can 60 be factored to make a perfect square with 15?

$$\sqrt{(\underline{\quad} \cdot \underline{\quad} \cdot 15)}$$

$$= \sqrt{(\underline{\quad}^2)}\sqrt{(\underline{\quad}^2)}$$

$$= (\underline{\quad}) \cdot (\underline{\quad}) = \underline{\quad}$$

30. List the numbers in order.

$\underline{\qquad\qquad\qquad}$

$LE = \underline{\quad}$ $\qquad UE = \underline{\quad}$

Median $= Q_2 = \underline{\quad}$

$Q_1 = \underline{\quad}$ $\qquad Q_3 = \underline{\quad}$

📖 Draw a box-and-whisker plot.

Displaying Data in Stem-and-Leaf Plots and Histograms page 406

New Concepts

Example Making a Stem-and-Leaf Plot

Create a stem-and-leaf plot of the temperature data.

70, 83, 84, 77, 66, 67, 53, 55, 64, 69, 82, 78, 80, 81, 66, 71, 75, 76, 80, 78, 78, 81, 83, 83 , 82, 81, 80, 85, 87, 87

Step 1: Organize the data by tens values. Write in order from least to greatest.

50's: 53, 55
60's: 64, 66, 66, 67, 69
70's: 70, 71, 75, 76, 77, 78, 78, 78
80's: 80, 80, 80, 81, 81, 81, 82, 82, 83, 83, 83, 84, 85, 87, 87

Step 2: The tens digits are stems and the ones digits are leaves. Create a key for the plot.

High Temperatures (°F)
April 2007 for New Orleans, LA

Stem	Leaves
5	3, 5
6	4, 6, 6, 7, 9
7	0, 1, 5, 6, 7, 8, 8, 8
8	0, 0, 0, 1, 1, 1, 2, 2, 3, 3, 3, 4, 5, 7, 7

Key: 5 | 3 = 53°F

Example Analyzing a Stem-and-Leaf Plot

Find the following.

a. median
Average the two middle values, 78 and 80.
$$\frac{78 + 80}{2} = 79$$

b. mode
The most frequently-occurring numbers are **78, 80, 81,** and **83.**

c. range
greatest − least = 87 − 53 = **34**

d. relative frequency of 80
Value 80 occurs 3 times in a set of 30 values. The relative frequency is $\frac{3}{30} = 0.1 = $ **10%.**

a. Write the data in ascending order before creating a stem-and-leaf plot.

_____

_____

_____

Low Temperatures (°F)
April 2007 New Orleans LA

Stem	Leaves
4	____,____
5	____,____,____,____,____,____
6	____,____,____,____,____,____
7	____

Key: 5 | 6 = ____ °F

b. Create a histogram with the data.

intervals: _____   width: _____

data points in the following ranges:

40 to 49: _____   50 to 59: _____

60 to 69: _____   70 to 79: _____

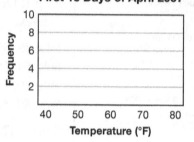

Low Temperatures in New Orleans
First 15 Days of April 2007

c. median = _____

mode = _____, _____, _____, _____

range = _____ − _____ = _____ °F

Low Temperatures (°F) Last 15 Days
April 2007 for New Orleans, LA

Stem	Leaves
4	5
5	4, 6, 7, 8, 9, 9
6	0, 3, 3, 4, 4, 8, 8
7	1

Key: 5 | 6 = 56°F

d. temperature 64°F: _____ times   total readings: _____

relative frequency of 64°F = $\dfrac{\square}{\square}$ = _____ = _____ %

e. Create a histogram of the data in **c.**

1. *Median = middle value*

median: _____

2. *Mode = value that occurs the most*

mode: _____

3. *Range = greatest − least*

range: _____

4. number of times 41 occurs in data set: _____

total number of values: _____

relative frequency of 41: $\dfrac{\square}{\square}$

$= \dfrac{\square}{\square} = $ _____ $ = $ _____

5. $\sqrt{88} = \sqrt{(\underline{\quad}) \cdot (\underline{\quad})}$

$= \sqrt{(\underline{\quad})} \cdot \sqrt{(\underline{\quad})}$

$= \underline{\quad} \cdot \sqrt{\underline{\quad}}$

6. $\sqrt{720} = \sqrt{(\underline{\quad})^4 \cdot (\underline{\quad})^2 \cdot \underline{\quad}}$

$= \sqrt{(\underline{\quad})^4} \cdot \sqrt{(\underline{\quad})^2} \cdot \sqrt{\underline{\quad}}$

$= \underline{\quad} \cdot \underline{\quad} \cdot \sqrt{\underline{\quad}}$

$= \underline{\quad} \cdot \sqrt{\underline{\quad}}$

7. $\sqrt{180} = \sqrt{(\underline{\quad})^2 \cdot (\underline{\quad})^2 \cdot \underline{\quad}}$

$= \sqrt{(\underline{\quad})^2} \cdot \sqrt{(\underline{\quad})^2} \cdot \sqrt{\underline{\quad}}$

$= \underline{\quad} \cdot \underline{\quad} \cdot \sqrt{\underline{\quad}}$

$= \underline{\quad} \cdot \sqrt{\underline{\quad}}$

8. Graph the point (_____, _____) for the y-intercept.

Then, use the slope of _____ to graph the point that is _____ unit down and _____ units to the right. Repeat this process to obtain a third point to verify you have drawn the correct line.

Draw a _____ between the points.

9. Student _____ is correct. Student _____

mistakenly used the _____ of two

squares pattern incorrectly.

10. Solution: (4, 6)

Add y to $3x$ to form a linear equation.

Then substitute (4, 6), and find the result.

$3x + y = 3(\underline{}) + \underline{} = \underline{}$

Write the equation.

$3x + y = \underline{}$

11. Substitute $x = 2$ and $y = -2$ into choices
A, B, C, and **D.** Do the substitutions make
a valid statement?

Circle the answer.

A $x + y = 0$
$\quad 2x - 3y = -2$

B $5x - 3y = 16$
$\quad 4x + 9y = 10$

C $9x - 2y = 22$
$\quad 3x + 6y = -6$

D $x + 2y = -2$
$\quad 2x + y = -2$

12. $-4(x^2 + 4x - 1)$

$= (\underline{})x^2 + (\underline{})(\underline{}) + (\underline{})(-1)$

$= \underline{} - \underline{} + \underline{}$

13. *Use a special product pattern.*

$(a - b)^2 = a^2 - 2ab + b^2$

$(b - 8)^2 = \underline{}b^2 - \underline{}b + \underline{}$

14. first: $(\underline{})(\underline{}) = \underline{}$

outer: $(\underline{})(\underline{}) = \underline{}$

inner: $(\underline{})(\underline{}) = \underline{}$

last: $(\underline{})(\underline{}) = \underline{}$

Add. $\underline{} + \underline{} + \underline{} + \underline{}$

$= \underline{} + \underline{} + \underline{}$

15. Mother's Day: $152 million
Father's Day: $95 million

$152 - 95 = \underline{}$, or a _____

of $\underline{}$ million from Mother's Day to

Father's Day.

$\dfrac{152}{(\square + \square)} \approx \underline{} = \underline{}$

16. The median diameter is the _____

number which is _____.

circumference $= \pi \cdot d$

$= \underline{} \cdot \underline{}$

$= \underline{}$

17. Write the second equation in slope-intercept form.

$y = \underline{\quad} + 6$

Graph the equations.

Solution: (\underline{\quad}, \underline{\quad})

18. The whiskers in a box-and-whisker plot represent the \underline{\qquad} and \underline{\qquad} quartiles of the data set.

---

19. Write data in ascending order. Make a stem-and-leaf plot.

place value(s) for stem:

\underline{\hspace{4cm}}

place value for leaves: \underline{\hspace{2cm}}

key: \underline{\quad} | \underline{\quad} means \$\underline{\quad}.

20. $p = 30n - 400$ is in \underline{\qquad} form.

y-intercept = \underline{\quad}

slope = \underline{\quad}

Plot the y-intercept and use the slope to graph the line.

For $n = 50$,

$p = \underline{\quad} - 400 = \underline{\quad}$.

---

21. *Use the Power of Powers Rule.*

$\sqrt[4]{x^2} = (x^2)^{\square} = x^{\square}$

Evaluate when $x = 9$.

$9^{\square} = \underline{\quad}$

22. *Use the Power of Powers Rule.*

$\sqrt[3]{x^6} = (x^6)^{\square} = x^{\square}$

Evaluate when $x = 2$.

$2^{\square} = \underline{\quad}$

---

23. *Direct variation:* $y = kx$

Substitute $x = 10$ and $y = -90$. Solve for k.

$\underline{\quad} = k(\underline{\quad})$

$k = \dfrac{\square}{\square} = \underline{\quad}$, so

$y = \underline{\quad} x$

24. a. *Add. Combine like terms.*

$500 + 1000r + 500r^2 + 600 + 600r$

$= 500r^2 + \underline{\qquad} r + \underline{\qquad}$

b. $500(\underline{\quad})^2 + \underline{\quad}(\underline{\quad}) + \underline{\quad}$

$= 500(\underline{\quad}) + \underline{\quad} + \underline{\quad}$

$= \underline{\qquad}$

---

25. original price: $68

29% increase: 29% of $68 = _____

new price: $68 + _____ = $ _____

26. original price: x

original price − 15% decrease = new price

Write an equation and solve for x.

$x =$ ▨ _____

---

27. *Factor each team. Then find LCM.*

running: (____)$(r - s)$

swimming: (_____)$(r - s)$

biking: (_____)$(r - s)$

LCM of numbers: ____

LCM of variables: _____ and _____

LCM: ____ · _____ · _____

after _____ days

28. *Convert each choice to a radical and compare.*

Circle the answer.

A $10\sqrt{28} = \sqrt{} \cdot \sqrt{28} = \sqrt{}$

B $2\sqrt{700} = \sqrt{} \cdot \sqrt{700} = \sqrt{}$

C $20\sqrt{7} = \sqrt{} \cdot \sqrt{7} = \sqrt{}$

D $40\sqrt{7} = \sqrt{} \cdot \sqrt{7} = \sqrt{}$

---

29. total side length: $9x$

garden side without border:

$9x -$ ____ $-$ ____

area of flower garden = side^2

$= ($ _____ $-$ _____ $)^2$

Use a special product pattern.

$(a - b)^2 = a^2 - 2ab + b^2$

area of garden without border

$=$ _____ ▨

30. area of square on grid paper: 25 units^2

area of square = side^2, so

side $= \sqrt{} =$ ____

Start at the origin $(0, 0)$ as the first point.

A point ____ units to the right of the origin is (____, 0).

A point up ____ units from the origin is $(0,$ ____$)$.

The fourth point is (____, ____).

LESSON
63

Solving Systems of Linear Equations by Elimination page 412

New Concepts

Example **Adding Equations**

Solve the system $5x + 2y = 9$ and $-5x + 6y = 7$.

Add the two equations to eliminate x. Solve for y.

$$\begin{array}{r} 5x + 2y = 9 \\ +(-5x + 6y = 7) \\ \hline 8y = 16 \\ y = 2 \end{array}$$

         Add equations. Combine like terms.

         Divide both sides by 8.

Substitute y and solve for x.

$$\begin{array}{l} 5x + 2y = 9 \\ 5x + 2(2) = 9 \\ 5x + 4 = 9 \\ 5x = 5 \\ x = 1 \end{array}$$

     Substitute 2 for y.

     Multiply.

     Subtract 4 from both sides.

     Divide both sides by 5.

The solution is $(1, 2)$.

Example **Subtracting Equations**

Solve the system $7x + 3y = -5$ and $2x + 3y = 5$.

Subtract to eliminate y. Solve for x.

$$\begin{array}{r} 7x + 3y = -5 \\ -(2x + 3y = 5) \\ \hline 5x = -10 \\ x = -2 \end{array}$$

         Subtract the equations. Combine like terms.

         Divide both sides by 5.

Substitute x and solve for y.

$$\begin{array}{l} 2x + 3y = 5 \\ 2(-2) + 3y = 5 \\ -4 + 3y = 5 \\ 3y = 9 \\ y = 3 \end{array}$$

     Substitute −2 for x.

     Multiply.

     Add 4 to both sides.

     Divide both sides by 3.

The solution is $(-2, 3)$.

Example **Multiplying Two Equations**

Solve the system $4x - 3y = 15$ and $6x + 5y = -25$.

Multiply the first equation by 3 and the second equation by -2 so the x coefficients are opposites. Add the two equations to eliminate x

$$12x - 9y = 45$$
$$+(-12x - 10y = 50)$$

$$\begin{aligned} -19y &= 95 \qquad & \text{\textit{Add and combine like terms.}} \\ y &= -5 \qquad & \text{\textit{Divide both sides by} -19.} \end{aligned}$$

Substitute y in the second equation, and solve for x.

$$\begin{aligned} 6x + 5(-5) &= -25 \qquad & \text{\textit{Substitute} -5 \textit{for} y.} \\ 6x - 25 &= -25 \qquad & \text{\textit{Multiply.}} \\ 6x &= 0 \qquad & \text{\textit{Add 25 to both sides.}} \\ x &= 0 \qquad & \text{\textit{Divide both sides by 6.}} \end{aligned}$$

The solution is **$(0, -5)$.**

Lesson Practice 📖 page 415

a. Add the equations.

$$\begin{aligned} 7x - 4y &= -3 \\ -3x + 4y &= -1 \end{aligned}$$

_____$x =$ _____

$x =$ _____

Substitute to find y:

$7(\underline{}) - 4y = -3$

$- 4y =$ _____

$y =$ _____

Solution: (_____, _____)

b. Subtract the second equation.

$$\begin{aligned} 11x + 6y &= 21 \\ -(11x + 4y &= 25) \end{aligned}$$

_____$y =$ _____

$y =$ _____

Substitute to find x:

$11x + 6(\underline{}) = 21$

$11x =$ _____

$x =$ _____

Solution: (_____, _____)

c. Multiply the first equation by 3 and add the second equation

_____$x +$ _____$y =$ _____
$\overline{ 6x \quad - \quad 2y \quad = \quad 34}$

_____$y =$ _____

$y =$ _____

Substitute to find x:

$6x - 2(4) = 34$

$6x =$ _____

$x =$ _____

Solution: (_____, _____)

d. $2(-8x - 3y = 26) =$ _____

$-3(-5x - 2y = 16) =$ _____

Add and solve for x: _____

Substitute x and solve for y.

Solution: (_____, _____)

e. total tickets: $a + c = 540$

total sales: _____$a +$ _____$c = 3060$

Multiply top equation by _____ and add to the second equation. Solve for a.

_____ adult tickets are sold.

1. $\sqrt{256} = \sqrt{(\underline{\quad})^2} = \underline{\quad}$

2. $\sqrt{108} = \sqrt{\underline{\quad} \cdot \underline{\quad}}$

$= \sqrt{(\underline{\quad})^2} \cdot \sqrt{\underline{\quad}}$

$= \underline{\quad} \sqrt{\underline{\quad}}$

3. $\sqrt{294} = \sqrt{\underline{\quad} \cdot \underline{\quad}}$

$= \sqrt{(\underline{\quad})^2} \cdot \sqrt{\underline{\quad}}$

$= \underline{\quad} \sqrt{\underline{\quad}}$

4. Simplify each variable.

for r: $\left(\frac{r^{-3}}{r}\right)^2 = \left(r^{\square}\right)^{\square} = r^{\square} = \frac{1}{r^{\square}}$

for g: $\left(\frac{1}{g^4}\right)^2 = \frac{1}{g^{\square}}$

for t: $\left(\frac{t^{\frac{1}{2}}}{t^{\frac{3}{2}}}\right)^2 = \left(t^{\square}\right)^2 = t^{\square} = \frac{1}{t^{\square}}$

for e: $(e)^2 = \underline{\quad}$

Multiply the terms: _____

5. $\frac{t^3 n^{-2} s}{f^7 t b^5}\left(\frac{t^{-2}}{ns^3} - \frac{f^6 t^{-1}}{b}\right)$

6. *Range = greatest − least*

$= \underline{\quad\quad\quad}$

range: _____

7. $y = kx$
$12 = k \cdot 5$

$k = \underline{\hspace{1cm}}$

$7.2 = k \cdot 3$

$k = \underline{\hspace{1cm}}$

$16.8 = k \cdot 7$

$k = \underline{\hspace{1cm}}$

The values of k show the three ordered

pairs $\underline{\hspace{1cm}}$ represent direct variation.

8. $2t^3sv^5 = \underline{\hspace{0.6cm}} \cdot \underline{\hspace{0.6cm}} \cdot \underline{\hspace{0.6cm}} \cdot \underline{\hspace{0.6cm}}$

$6v^3t^4 = \underline{\hspace{0.6cm}} \cdot \underline{\hspace{0.6cm}} \cdot \underline{\hspace{0.6cm}} \cdot \underline{\hspace{0.6cm}}$

$10v^8s^4 = \underline{\hspace{0.6cm}} \cdot \underline{\hspace{0.6cm}} \cdot \underline{\hspace{0.6cm}} \cdot \underline{\hspace{0.6cm}}$

LCM of numbers: $\underline{\hspace{0.6cm}} \cdot \underline{\hspace{0.6cm}} \cdot \underline{\hspace{0.6cm}}$

LCM of variables: $\underline{\hspace{0.6cm}} \cdot \underline{\hspace{0.6cm}} \cdot \underline{\hspace{0.6cm}}$

LCM: $\underline{\hspace{2cm}}$

9. $14dv^3 = \underline{\hspace{0.6cm}} \cdot \underline{\hspace{0.6cm}} \cdot \underline{\hspace{0.6cm}} \cdot \underline{\hspace{0.6cm}}$

$7s^2v = \underline{\hspace{0.6cm}} \cdot \underline{\hspace{0.6cm}} \cdot \underline{\hspace{0.6cm}} \cdot \underline{\hspace{0.6cm}}$

$28s^7v^5 = \underline{\hspace{0.6cm}} \cdot \underline{\hspace{0.6cm}} \cdot \underline{\hspace{0.6cm}} \cdot \underline{\hspace{0.6cm}}$

LCM of numbers: $\underline{\hspace{0.6cm}} \cdot \underline{\hspace{0.6cm}} \cdot \underline{\hspace{0.6cm}}$

LCM of variables: $\underline{\hspace{0.6cm}} \cdot \underline{\hspace{0.6cm}} \cdot \underline{\hspace{0.6cm}}$

LCM: $\underline{\hspace{2cm}}$

10. *Use a special product pattern.*

$(x + 5)(x - 5)$

$= \underline{\hspace{3cm}}$

Circle the answer.

A $x^2 - 25$ **B** $x^2 + 25$

C $x^2 - 5x + 25$ **D** $x^2 - 10x + 25$

11. height of cherry tree in x years:

$\underline{\hspace{1.5cm}}$ in. $+ \underline{\hspace{2cm}} x$

height of crabapple tree in x years:

$\underline{\hspace{1.5cm}}$ in. $+ \underline{\hspace{2cm}} x$

height of cherry = height of crabapple

$\underline{\hspace{1cm}} + \underline{\hspace{1cm}} x = \underline{\hspace{1cm}} + \underline{\hspace{1cm}} x$

$\underline{\hspace{1cm}} x = \underline{\hspace{1cm}}$

$x = \underline{\hspace{2cm}}$

12. $6x - 2(\underline{\hspace{4cm}}) = 12$

$6x + \underline{\hspace{1.5cm}} x - 20 = 12$

$\underline{\hspace{1.5cm}} x = \underline{\hspace{1.5cm}}$

$x = \underline{\hspace{1cm}}$

Substitute to find y:

$y = -5(\underline{\hspace{1cm}}) + 10$

$y = \underline{\hspace{1cm}}$

Solution: $(\underline{\hspace{1cm}}, \underline{\hspace{1cm}})$

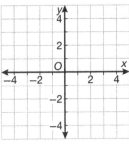

13.
$$6x + 4y = 22$$
$$+(-6x + 2y = -16)$$

$$\underline{}y = \underline{}$$

$$y = \underline{}$$

Substitute y to find x:

$$6x + 4(\underline{}) = 22$$

$$6x = \underline{}$$

$$x = \underline{}$$

Solution: (_____, _____)

14. Graph the equations.

Put both equations into slope-intercept form. Use the slope and y-intercept to graph each line. Find the point of intersection.

Solution: (_____, _____)

Check with your graphing calculator.

15. $p = 2 \cdot (l + w)$

$$= 2 \cdot (\underline{} + \underline{})$$

$$= 2 \cdot (\underline{}x - \underline{})$$

$$= \underline{}x - \underline{}$$

16. Eliminate y by multiplying the first equation by _____. Then, _____ the first equation to the second equation and solve for x. Substitute your answer into either original equation to find y.

Circle the answer.

A $\left(-\frac{2}{3}, 2\right)$ **B** $\left(2, \frac{2}{3}\right)$

C $\left(2, -\frac{2}{3}\right)$ **D** $\left(-2, \frac{2}{3}\right)$

17. To check solutions of a system of linear equations solved by linear combination, _____ the values of the variables into both _____ equations to be sure they give _____ statements.

18. min.: _____ Q_1: _____

median: _____ Q_3: _____

max.: _____

a.   Draw a box-and-whisker plot.

b. _____

19. area of a square = side^2

$$\text{side} = \sqrt{\text{area}}$$

$$\text{side} = \sqrt{\underline{}}$$

$$= \underline{}$$

20. $A = l \cdot w$

$$= (\underline{})(\underline{})$$

$$= \underline{}$$

21. 38% of $1527 = $_____

$1527 − $_____ = ▨_____

22. 1.5% of $25,720 = $_____

$25,720 + $_____ = ▨_____

23. 215% of $10.25 = $_____

new price: $10.25 + $_____ = ▨_____

24. $(a + b)^2 = $ ____ $+$ _____ $+$ ___

$(a − b)^2 = $ ____ $−$ _____ $+$ ___

25. area = side^2 = (_____)^2

Use a special product pattern.

area = _____ ▨

26. $\sqrt{76g^6}$

$$= \sqrt{\underline{\quad}} \cdot \sqrt{\underline{\quad}^{\square}}$$

$$= \sqrt{\underline{\quad} \cdot \underline{\quad}} \cdot \sqrt{\underline{\quad}}$$

$$= \underline{\quad} \cdot \sqrt{\underline{\quad}} \cdot g^{\square}$$

$$= \underline{\quad} \sqrt{\underline{\quad}}$$

Circle the answer.

A $2g^3\sqrt{19}$ **B** $2g^4\sqrt{19}$

C $6g^3\sqrt{2}$ **D** $6g^4\sqrt{2}$

27. Student _____ is correct. Student _____

found the _____ with the most data

points.

28. The second equation is the first equation

multiplied by _____. The equations

would be the _____ on a

graph, so there are an infinite number of

solutions.

29. The absolute value of the slope of a

function that vertically stretches the

parent function is _____ 1.

30. number working 0 − 5 hr: ____

number working 5 − 10 hr: ____

number working 10 − 15 hr: ____

number working 15 − 20 hr: ____

total students: _____

$$P(5 − 10 \text{ hr}) = \frac{\square}{\square}$$

$$= \frac{\square \cdot \square}{\square \cdot \square}$$

$$= \frac{\square}{\square} = \underline{\quad} ▨$$

LESSON 64

Identifying, Writing, and Graphing
Inverse Variation page 418

New Concepts

Math Language

Inverse variation occurs when the product of two variables is a constant. The equation $xy = k$, where $k \neq 0$, defines an inverse variation between x and y.

The variables x and y are said to **vary inversely** if $xy = k$.

 **Exploration** 📖 page 418

Use your textbook to complete this Exploration.

- Direct variation: $y = kx$
- Inverse variation: $y = \dfrac{k}{x}$

Example **Identifying an Inverse Variation**

Tell whether each relationship is an inverse variation. Explain.

$$\frac{y}{6} = x$$

Solve for y: $y = 6x$

No, this relationship is not an inverse variation. $y = kx$. y is equal to the product of the constant of variation k and x. This relationship is direct variation.

$$xy = 5$$

Solve for y: $y = \dfrac{5}{x}$

Yes, this is relationship is an inverse variation. $y = \dfrac{k}{x}$. y is equal to the quotient of the constant of variation k and x. This relationship is direct variation.

Product Rule for Inverse Variation
If (x_1, y_1) and (x_2, y_2) are solutions of an inverse variation, then $x_1 y_1 = x_2 y_2$.

Example **Using the Product Rule**

If y varies inversely as x and $y = 3$ when $x = 12$, find x when $y = 9$.

$$x_1 y_1 = x_2 y_2$$

$(12)(3) = x_2(9)$ *Substitute the 12 for x_1, 3 for y_1, and 9 for y_2.*

$36 = 9x_2$ *Multiply.*

$4 = x_2$ *Divide both sides by 9.*

When $y = 9$, $x = 4$.

Tell whether each relationship is an inverse relationship variation. Explain.

a. $4y = x$ — Solve for y: $y = \dfrac{\square}{\square}$

This _____ inverse variation, because $y = \dfrac{\square}{\square}$ _____ match the form for inverse variation, $y = \frac{k}{x}$.

b. $3xy = 9$ — Solve for y: $y = \dfrac{\square}{\square}$

This _____ inverse variation, because $y = \dfrac{\square}{\square}$ _____ match the form for inverse variation, $y = \frac{k}{x}$.

c. Given: y varies inversely with x and $y = 3.5$ when $x = 20$.
Find x when $y = 10$.

$$x_1 y_1 = x_2 y_2$$

$$(\underline{})(\underline{}) = (x_2)(\underline{})$$

$$\underline{} = \underline{}(x_2) \qquad x = \underline{}$$

d. Write an inverse relationship if $x = 8$ and $y = \frac{1}{2}$.

Find k. $xy = k$, so $k = (\underline{}) \cdot (\underline{}) = \underline{}$.

So, $xy = \underline{}$, $y = \dfrac{\square}{\square}$

Use the equation to make a table of values.

x	-4	-2	-1	0	1	2	4
y	-1			Undefined			

Graph the inverse relationship. Plot the points.
Then connect them with a smooth curve.

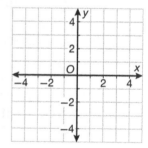

e. Use the product rule for an inverse variation.
7 hr at $8 per hour. How many hours at $10 per hour?

$$x_1 y_1 = x_2 y_2$$

$$(7)(\underline{}) = (x_2)(10)$$

$$x = \underline{}$$

1. $8mn^4 = $ ___ • ___ • ___ • m • n^4

$12m^5n^2 = $ ___ • ___ • ___ • m^5 • n^2

$LCM = $ ___ • $m^\square$ • $n^\square$

$= $ _____

2. The LCM is the least number that is evenly divisible by each of the given numbers.

$LCM = $ ___ • $w^\square$ • $x^\square$

$= $ _____

3. Inverse variation: $y = \frac{k}{x}$

$y = \frac{x}{11} = $ _____ • x

Inverse variation? _____

4. Inverse variation: $y = \frac{k}{x}$

$y = \frac{3}{x}$

Inverse variation? _____

5. $x_1y_1 = x_2y_2$

$(99)($ ___ $) = ($ ___ $)(y_2)$

$y \approx$ _____

6. Write the data in numeric order.

minimum: _____ maximum: _____

7. Write two ordered pairs where $x = $ the charge and $y = $ the number of minutes.

$($ ___ , ___ $)$ and $($ ___ , ___ $)$

The slope is the charge per minute. Use the points to find the slope.

$m = $ _____

Choose one of the points and write an equation in point-slope form. Then substitute 0 for x to find the monthly fee.

Monthly fee: _____

8. Use a special product pattern.

$(b + 2)^2 = ($ ___ $)^2 \bigcirc 2($ ___ $)($ ___ $) + ($ ___ $)^2$

$= $ ___ $x^2 + $ ___ $x + $ ___

9. first: _____ outer: _____

inner: _____ last: _____

Add and simplify:

_____

10. a. $A = side^2$; $side = \sqrt{\rule{1cm}{0pt}}$

b. $\sqrt{\rule{1.5cm}{0pt}}$

c. _____

d. unit of measurement: _____

11. Let t = time in hours

Joseph: ____miles + 4 mph • _____

Maya: ____miles + 6 mph • _____

Joseph's distance = Maya's distance

_____ = _____

$t =$ _____

Substitute t into one of the original equations to find the distance.

distance = _____

12. $x_1y_1 = x_2y_2$

$(9)(\underline{\quad}) = (\underline{\quad})(y_2)$

Circle the answer.

A 3   **B** 5.3   **C** 27   **D** 108

13. mean waste generated: _____

mean materials recovered: _____

On average, the U.S. generates about

_____ million tons of waste a year after

_____.

14. Length of trim = perimeter

Write and simplify an expression for the perimeter. Divide out common factors.

= _____

15. Median = middle value

median: _____

16. Mode = value that occurs most often

mode: _____

17. Range = greatest − least

range: _____

18. Relative frequency = number of times the event occurs/total events

relative frequency of $22,000:

about _____

19. Order the data. Make a box-and-whisker plot. Determine if there is an outlier.

Outlier $< Q_1 - 1.5(IQR)$ or
Outlier $> Q_3 + 1.5(IQR)$

outlier(s): _____

20. Statement 2 is the _____ of Statement 1. The original statement and the _____ are _____.

21. variance $= 24$

standard deviation $= \sqrt{\text{variance}}$

Find the perfect squares that are factors of 24.

standard deviation: _____

22. *The radical can be expressed as $\frac{5}{3}\sqrt{\frac{3}{5}}$ or as $\frac{1}{3}\sqrt{15}$.* The two ways depend on whether the _____ under the _____ is simplified.

23. Student _____ is correct. Student _____ _____ to eliminate the variable x, but then _____ the other terms in the equation.

24. Let $A =$ area of rectangle A

Let $B =$ area of rectangle B

Write a system of equations and solve them by elimination.

$$A + B = \underline{\quad\quad}$$

$$\underline{\quad}A + \underline{\quad}B = \underline{\quad\quad}$$

$A = \underline{\quad\quad}$ $B = \underline{\quad\quad}$

25. *Use slope-intercept form.*

$9x - 1.5y + 12 = 0$

$y = \underline{\quad}x + \underline{\quad}$

Graph the equation on a coordinate grid.

26. *Add the two equations.*

$\underline{\quad}x = \underline{\quad}$ so $x = \underline{\quad}$

Substitute.

$-3(\underline{\quad}) + 2y = -6$

$2y = \underline{\quad}$ so $y = \underline{\quad}$

Solution: $(\underline{\quad}, \underline{\quad})$

27. a.

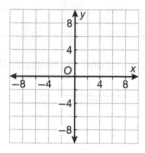

b. Solution: $(\underline{\quad}, \underline{\quad})$

c. Check.

$2(\underline{\quad}) - \underline{\quad} \stackrel{?}{=} 14$

$\underline{\quad} + 4(\underline{\quad}) \stackrel{?}{=} -2$

28. The volume of a sample of gas is inversely related to its pressure if the temperature remains constant.

Let p = pressure
Let v = volume

$p_1 v_1 = p_2 v_2$

$(95)(\underline{\quad}) = (\underline{\quad})(v)$

$= \underline{\quad}$

29. The number of points made in a football game _____ with the number of touchdowns.

30. *Use a graphing calculator to graph $y = \frac{1}{x}$ and $y = -\frac{1}{x}$. Compare the results.*

positive k:

graphs in quadrants \underline{\quad}, \underline{\quad}

negative k:

graphs in quadrants \underline{\quad}, \underline{\quad}

LESSON

65

Writing Equations of Parallel and Perpendicular Lines page 424

New Concepts

Math Language

Parallel lines are lines that are in the same plane but do not intersect.

Slopes of Parallel Lines

Two nonvertical lines are parallel if they have the same slope and are not the same line.

Any two vertical lines are parallel.

Example $y = 2x + 7$ and $y = 2x - 1$

Parallel lines have the same slope and different y-intercepts.

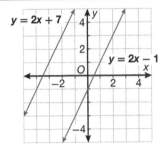

Example Determining if Lines are Parallel

Determine if the equations represent parallel lines.

$y = -\frac{4}{3}x + 5$ and $4x + 3y = 6$

Write the second equation in slope-intercept form:

$$4x + 3y = 6$$
$$\underline{-4x \qquad = -4x} \qquad \textit{Subtract 4x from both sides.}$$
$$3y = -4x + 6$$
$$\frac{3}{3}y = \frac{-4}{3}x + \frac{6}{3} \qquad \textit{Divide both sides by 3.}$$
$$y = -\frac{4}{3}x + 2 \qquad \textit{Simplify.}$$

Compare the slopes: $m_1 = -\frac{4}{3}$; $m_2 = -\frac{4}{3}$; $m_1 = m_2$

Compare the y-intercepts: $b_1 = 5$; $b_2 = 2$; $b_1 \neq b_2$

The slopes are equal and the y-intercepts are not, so **the lines are parallel.**

Math Language

Perpendicular lines are two lines that intersect at right angles.

The **reciprocal** of a number n is $\frac{1}{n}$.

The product of a number and its reciprocal is 1.

Slopes of Perpendicular Lines

Any two lines are perpendicular if their slopes are negative reciprocals of each other. A vertical and horizontal line are also perpendicular.

Example $y = 3x - 7$ and $y = \frac{-1}{3}x + 3$

The slopes of perpendicular lines are negative reciprocals.

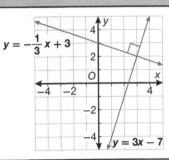

Example **Writing Equations of Perpendicular Lines**

Write the equation of line that passes through $(-2, -3)$ and is perpendicular to $y = -3x + 1$.

The slopes of perpendicular lines are negative reciprocals.

slope of the given line: -3 negative reciprocal of -3: $\frac{1}{3}$

Use $(-2, -3)$ and $\frac{1}{3}$ to write an equation in slope-intercept form.

$$y - y_1 = m(x - x_1)$$

$y - (-3) = \frac{1}{3}(x - (-2))$ *Substitute.*

$y + 3 = \frac{1}{3}(x + 2)$ *Simplify.*

$y = \frac{x}{3} + \frac{2}{3} - 3$ *Distribute. Subtract 3 from both sides.*

$y = \frac{1}{3}x - 2\frac{1}{3}$ *Simplify.*

Lesson Practice 📖 page 426

a. Write $\frac{3}{2}x + y = 1$ in slope intercept form. $y = \underline{\quad} x + \underline{\quad}$

Compare the slopes: $m_1 = \underline{\quad}$, $m_2 = \underline{\quad}$.

The lines _____ parallel.

b. *Parallel lines have the same slope.* $m = \underline{\quad}$
Use $(-3, 2)$ and the slope to write an equation of the new line in slope-intercept form.

$y - 2 = \underline{\quad}(x - (-3))$

$y = \underline{\quad}x + \underline{\quad}$

c. *Use $m = \frac{y_2 - y_1}{x_2 - x_1}$* $m_1 = \underline{\quad}; m_2 = \underline{\quad}$

The lines are _____.

d. *The slopes of perpendicular lines are negative reciprocals.* $m = \underline{\quad}$
Use $(-1, 3)$ and the slope to write an equation of the new line in slope-intercept form.

$y - 3 = \underline{\quad}(x - (-1))$

$y = \underline{\quad}x + \underline{\quad}$

e. slope $\overline{AB} = \underline{\quad}$ slope $\overline{BC} = \underline{\quad}$
The product of the slopes of perpendicular lines is -1.

$(\underline{\quad}) \cdot (\underline{\quad}) = -1$ so $\overline{AB} \underline{\quad} \overline{BC}$ and $\triangle ABC$ is a right triangle.

1. *Find the perfect squares that are factors of 360.*

$$\sqrt{360} = \sqrt{\underline{\hspace{2cm}}}$$

$$= \underline{\hspace{2cm}}$$

2. *Use prime factorization to simplify.*

$$\sqrt{252} = \sqrt{\underline{\hspace{2cm}}}$$

$$= \underline{\hspace{2cm}}$$

3. *Use prime factorization to simplify.*

$$\sqrt{384} = \sqrt{\underline{\hspace{2cm}}}$$

$$= \underline{\hspace{2cm}}$$

4. Use FOIL. Then combine like terms.

$$(x^2 + 5)^2 = (\underline{\hspace{2cm}}) \cdot (\underline{\hspace{2cm}})$$

$$= \underline{\hspace{3cm}}$$

5. Use FOIL. Then combine like terms.

$$(x - 2)(x - 9)$$

$$= \underline{\hspace{3cm}}$$

6. $c \geq -5$

7. *(x − 5) is a single factor.*
Use each factor the most times it occurs in either term.

LCM: _____

8. $2 \mid 9 = 2.9$ cm $7 \mid 4 = \underline{\hspace{1.5cm}}$ cm

   ↑   ↑   ↑   ↑

stem leaf   stem leaf

Circle the answer.

A 4.7 cm   **B** 7.4 cm

C 47 cm   **D** 74 cm

9. *List the data in order. Include a key.*

Complete the stem and leaf plot.

Stem	Leaves
203	2, 6, 9

10. initial cost for parking: $_____

cost for x hours: $_____ x

total cost: $y = $ _____ ◯ _____

Cost for 9 hours: ☐_____

11. *Inverse variation:* $y = \frac{k}{x}$

Student _____ is correct. Student _____

wrote a(n) _____ variation

equation.

12. *Write a system of equations and solve it by elimination. Eliminate y.*

Let $x = $ # of 7-cm pieces

Let $y = $ # of 3-cm pieces

$x + y = $ _____

___$x + $ ___$y = 108$ $x = $ _____

$7\text{ cm} \cdot x = 7 \cdot$ _____ $= $ _____ cm

$0.8\text{ m} = $ _____ cm

He needs _____ cm of wood for _____

pieces that are 7 cm each.

_____ cm are not enough.

13.

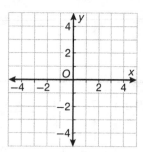

Solution: (_____ , _____)

14. *Subtract to eliminate y.*

$5x + 7y = 41$
$3x + 7y = 47$

Solution: (_____ , _____)

15. *Isolate y in* $9x + y = 12$.

Substitute: $5x - 2($ _____ $) = 22$

$x = $ _____

Substitute the x value to solve for the y value.

Solution: (_____ , _____)

16. *Let w = number of weeks*

Ryan's amount: _____ $+$ _____w

Kathy's amount: _____w

Kathy's amount = Ryan's amount

_____$w = $ _____ $+$ _____w

$w = $ _____

17. *Order the data.*

   a. The range of the data is_____, so

     create ___ intervals that are ___ points

     apart.

   b. 📝 Create a histogram using the

     intervals from part **a.**

   c. A _____ is better

     because the data is very

     _____.

18. *Find the slope.*

   x-intercept: (____, 0)

   y-intercept: (0, ____)

   Use slope-intercept form.

   m = _____

   Write the equation in the form $y = mx + b$:

   $y =$ ____x ◯ ____

19. *Use a special product pattern.*

  $(x - 11)^2 = ($__$)^2$ ◯ $2($__$)($__$) + ($__$)^2$

  $(x - 11)^2 =$ ____x^2 ◯ ____$x +$ ____

  _____ dollars

20. total area: _____ • _____

   border: 2 • _____ ft

   side without border: $7x -$ _____ ft

   total area without border:

   $(7x -$ _____$) \cdot (7x -$ _____$)$

   Use a special product pattern.

   = _____

21. *Parallel lines have the same slope.*

   $WXYZ$ is a _____.

   Slopes of $\overline{WX}$ and $\overline{YZ}$ are _____.

   So $\overline{WX}$ ____ $\overline{YZ}$.

   Slopes of $\overline{WZ}$ and $\overline{XY}$ are _____.

   So $\overline{WZ}$ ____ $\overline{XY}$.

22. *Inverse variation:* $y = \frac{k}{x}$

   Solve $5xy = 40$ for y.

   $y =$ _____

   The equation _____ inverse

   variation.

23. Choose two points on line a and two on line b. Find the _____ between the corresponding points on each line. Use this point and the _____ of lines a and b to create a line of _____ _____.

24. There are a(n) _____ number of lines parallel to the line given by the equation with a slope of _____, or for any given _____.

25. Write $6x + 3y = 36$ in slope-intercept form.

$y =$ _____$x +$ _____

Parallel lines have the same slope.

slope of a parallel line = _____

26. a. 📓 Graph $(-4, 0)$ and $(4, 2)$ on a coordinate grid and draw a line through them.

b. $m =$ _____ y-intercept: _____

$y =$ _____

c. slope of line in part b: $m =$ _____

slope of $y = -\frac{1}{4}x - 3$: $m =$ _____

The lines _____ parallel.

27. Student _____ is correct. Student _____ added _____ terms.

28. Let $x =$ # seconds spent racing in 1st phase

Let $y =$ # seconds spent racing in 2nd phase

_____ + _____ = 18.1

_____$x +$ _____$y = 100$

📓 Solve the system using elimination. Eliminate x. Substitute the y value into the 2nd equation and solve for $2.7x$.

Distance at 2.7 m/s: ≈ _____

29. *Inverse variation:* $x_1y_1 = x_2y_2$

$h_1 B_1 = h_2 B_2$

$(6)(\underline{\quad}) = (\underline{\quad})(B_2)$

$= \underline{\quad}$

30. Let $s =$ speed and and let $t =$ time

8 is the constant of variation.

📓 Find the time it took to get to his friend's house and then find the time it took to get home. Subtract.

$s \cdot t = 8$ _____

LESSON

66

Solving Inequalities By Adding or Subtracting page 430

New Concepts

• Add to solve inequalities just like you add to solve equations.

Math Language

Addition Property of Inequality: If the same number is added to both sides of an inequality, the inequality remains true.

Example Checking Solutions

Solve $x - 3 \geq 5$. Then graph and check the solution.

$x - 3 \geq 5$

$\underline{+3 \quad +3}$ *Addition Property of Inequality*

$x \geq 8$ *Simplify.*

Look at the inequality sign to determine if the endpoint is an open or closed circle.

Check the endpoint.   Check the direction of the inequality.

Substitute a number greater than 8.

$x - 3 = 5$ $x - 3 > 5$

$8 - 3 \overset{?}{=} 5$ $9 - 3 \overset{?}{>} 5$

$\quad 5 = 5$ True $\quad 6 \geq 5$ True

The solution is $x \geq 8$.

• Subtract to solve inequalities just like you subtract to solve equations.

Math Language

Subtraction Property of Inequality: If the same number is subtracted from both sides of an inequality, the inequality remains true.

Example Using Subtraction

Solve $x + 2 > 3$. Then graph and check the solution.

$x + 2 > 3$

$\underline{-2 \quad -2}$ *Subtraction Property of Inequality*

$x > 1$ *Simplify.*

Look at the inequality sign to determine if the endpoint is an open or closed circle.

Check the endpoint.   Check the direction of the inequality.

Substitute a number greater than 1.

$x + 2 = 3$ $x + 2 > 3$

$1 + 2 \overset{?}{=} 3$ $2 + 2 \overset{?}{>} 3$

$\quad 3 = 3$ True $\quad 4 > 3$ True

The solution is $x > 1$.

Solve and graph.

a. $x - \frac{1}{2} > 3$

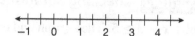

$\underline{\quad} \quad \underline{\quad}$

$x > \underline{\quad}$

b. $z - 2 \geq \frac{1}{2}$

$\underline{\quad} \quad \underline{\quad}$

$z \geq \underline{\quad}$

Check your solution.   *Substitute the endpoint and a number greater than* $\underline{\quad}$.

$z - 2 \geq \frac{1}{2}, z = \underline{\quad}$

$\underline{\quad} - 2 \overset{?}{\geq} \frac{1}{2}$

$\underline{\quad} \geq \frac{1}{2}$

$z - 2 \geq \frac{1}{2}, z = \underline{\quad}$

$\underline{\quad} - 2 \overset{?}{\geq} \frac{1}{2}$

$\underline{\quad} \geq \frac{1}{2}$

c. $y + 1.1 \leq 3.2$

$\underline{\quad} \quad \underline{\quad}$

$y \leq \underline{\quad}$

Check your solution.   *Substitute the endpoint and a number less than* $\underline{\quad}$.

$y + 1.1 \leq 3.2$

$\underline{\quad} + 1.1 \overset{?}{\leq} 3.2$

$\underline{\quad} \leq 3.2$

$y + 1.1 \leq 3.2$

$\underline{\quad} + 1.1 \overset{?}{\leq} 3.2$

$\underline{\quad} \leq 3.2$

d. A number (x) plus 2.5 feet is at least 4.4 feet.
At least 4.4 feet means equal to or greater than 4.4 feet.

Check:

Substitute the endpoint and a number greater

$x + \underline{\quad} \geq \underline{\quad}$

than the $\underline{\quad\quad}$.

$\underline{\quad} \quad \underline{\quad}$

$x \geq \underline{\quad}$

Rebecca will crochet at least $\underline{\quad}$ feet more.

1. Add the numerators, then divide out like terms.

$$\frac{11p}{6s^4} + \frac{p}{6s^4}$$

$$= \underline{\qquad}$$

2. $\frac{4x}{5w^4} - \frac{5x}{5w^4}$

$$= \underline{\qquad}$$

3. $\frac{7y}{3x^4 + 1} + \frac{5y}{3x^4 + 1}$

$$= \underline{\qquad}$$

4. Use the Subtraction Property of Inequality.

$$z + 10 \geq 3$$

$$z \geq \underline{\qquad}$$

5. Use the Addition Property of Inequality.

$$x - 4 \leq 9$$

$$x \leq \underline{\qquad}$$

6. Determine if the circle is opened or closed.
Determine the direction that the arrow points.

7. The inequality $x > 5$ _____ include 5.

The inequality $x \geq 5$ _____ include 5.

The graph of $x > 5$ has a(n) _____

circle.

The graph of $x \geq 5$ has a(n) _____

circle.

8. The parent function is $f(x) = x$.

$$f(x) = \underline{\quad} \bigcirc \underline{\quad}$$

9. *Times less than 21.64 seconds could beat Popov's record.*

```
 ←+++++++++++++++++→
   0   4   8   12  16  20  24
```

The graph includes only _____

numbers because the time cannot be a

_____ number.

10. *Set up a proportion.*

$$\frac{14}{\square} = \frac{\square}{x}$$

$x = $ _____

11. $P - F = M$

   a. $M = ($_____$) - ($_____$)$

      $= $ _____

   b. *Substitute.*

      $M = $ _____

      $= $ _____

12. *Combine like terms on each side of the inequality, then solve for z.*

$3z + 2 \le z - 4 + 2 + z$

Circle the answer.

A $z \le -4$ **B** $z \le 0$

C $z \le 3$ **D** $z \le 4$

13. *A line of symmetry divides a figure into two mirror image halves.*

Use $\overline{AB}$ and $\overline{EF}$.

Slopes of perpendicular lines are negative reciprocals.

slope of a line perpendicular to

$\overline{AB}$ and $\overline{EF}$: _____

   Use the midpoint of $\overline{AB}$ and the slope to write the equation of the line of symmetry and the perpendicular bisector of the two sides.

$y = $ _____

14. *Find the LCM.*

   a. $12 = $ _____ • _____ • _____

      $16 = $ _____ • _____ • _____ • _____

      $28 = $ _____ • _____ • _____

      LCM $= $ _____

   b. *Divide.*

      _____ $\div$ _____ $= $ _____

15. *Substitute 10y − 2 for x in the second equation. Solve for y.*

$2(\underline{\hspace{3cm}}) - 18y = 8$

$y = \underline{\hspace{1.5cm}}$

Substitute to solve for the x-value.

$2x - 18(\underline{\hspace{1cm}}) = 8$

$x = \underline{\hspace{1.5cm}}$

Solution: (\underline{\hspace{1cm}}, \underline{\hspace{1cm}})

16. $\sqrt{\dfrac{\boxed{} \cdot \boxed{}}{\boxed{}}}$

$= \sqrt{\dfrac{\boxed{}}{\boxed{}}}$

$= \sqrt{\underline{\hspace{1.5cm}}}$

$= \underline{\hspace{1cm}} \sqrt{\underline{\hspace{1cm}}\ \blacksquare}$

---

17. 📓 Solve by elimination. Eliminate x.

Circle the answer.

A $2x + 5y = 16$
$2x + y = -4$

B $2x + 5y = 19$
$x - 5y = -13$

C $2x + 5y = -4$
$-2x + y = -8$

D $2x + 5y = 11$
$x - 5y = -17$

18. Multiply the first equation by _____.

Multiply the second equation by _____.

_____ the _____ equation

from the _____ to eliminate x. Solve

for _____. Substitute the _____-value

into one of the equations to solve for _____.

---

19. *See page 16 in the* Student Reference Guide.

$\overline{EF} \parallel \overline{GH}$ because they have _____

slopes of _____, so *EFGH* has one pair

of _____ sides. *EFGH* is

a _____.

20. Student _____ is correct.

Student _____ _____ write down the

product rule correctly.

---

21. *Direct variation:* $y = kx$

Solve for k.

$y = \underline{\hspace{2cm}}$

22. *Inverse variation:* $y = \dfrac{k}{x}$

Solve for k.

$y = \underline{\hspace{2cm}}$

---

23. *Use a special product pattern.*

$(2x - 3)(2x - 3)$

= ___ ◯ ___ ◯ ___

24. *Use a special product pattern.*

$(t - 12)(t + 12)$

= ___ ◯ ___

25. *Use a special product pattern.*

$(y^3 - 4)^2$

= ___ ◯ ___ ◯ ___

26. Distribute:

$(2y)($ _____ $) =$ ___ + ___

$(4)($ _____ $) =$ ___ + ___

$=$ ___ + ___ + ___

FOIL: ___ + ___ + ___ + ___

$=$ ___ + ___ + ___

27. *Inverse variation: k = xy*

Let $x =$ heart rate
Let $y =$ life span
Solve for k.

$k = ($ _____ $)($ _____ $)$

$k =$ _____

Find the life span with a heart rate of 450

beats per minute. *Inverse variation: y = $\frac{k}{x}$*

$y = \dfrac{\square}{\square}$　　$y =$ ___▢

28. *Show that two sides of the triangle are perpendicular.*

The slope of $\overline{PQ}$ is _____.

The slope of $\overline{PR}$ is _____.

$\overline{PQ}$ and $\overline{PR}$ are _____.

Therefore triangle PQR is a _____ triangle.

29. $y = \frac{x}{3} - 1$　$m =$ ___

$-4 = 12x + 4$　$m =$ ___

The statement is _____. The slopes are

_____.

The lines are _____.

30. John will run at least 5 more miles than

25 miles.

At least means equal to or greater than.

x ◯ ___ ◯ ___

x ◯ ___▢

LESSON
67

Solving and Classifying Special Systems
of Linear Equations page 436

New Concepts

Example Solving Inconsistent Systems of Equations

Solve.

$$-3x + y = -4$$
$$y = 3x$$

$$-3x + 3x = -4 \quad \textit{Substitute 3x for y in } -3x + y = -4.$$

$$0 = -4$$

This statement is false, so the system has no solution. **It is an inconsistent system.**

> **Math Language**
>
> An **inconsistent system** has no solution.

Example Classifying Systems of Equations

Classify this system.

$$x - \frac{1}{4}y = \frac{3}{4} \longrightarrow y = 4x - 3 \quad \textit{Solve each equation for y.}$$
$$2x + y = 1 \longrightarrow y = -2x + 1$$

$$-2x + 1 = 4x - 3 \qquad \textit{Substitute y = -2x + 1 for y in the first equation.}$$

$$-6x = -4$$
$$x = \frac{2}{3} \qquad \textit{Solve for x.}$$

$$y = -2\left(\frac{2}{3}\right) + 1 \qquad \textit{Substitute } \frac{2}{3} \textit{ for x in the second equation.}$$

$$y = -\frac{4}{3} + 1 = -\frac{1}{3} \qquad \textit{Solve for y.}$$

> **Math Language**
>
> A **consistent system** has at least one solution.
>
> A **consistent and independent system** has exactly one solution.

The solution is $\left(\frac{2}{3}, -\frac{1}{3}\right)$.

There is one solution, so the system is **consistent and independent**.

Lesson Practice 📖 page 439

Solve.

a. _____ $= \frac{1}{2}x + 7$ *Substitute $\frac{1}{2}x + \frac{1}{2}$ for y in the second equation.*

 ___ ◯ ___

The statement is _____. There _____ solution(s).

b. $x + y = 10 \longrightarrow y = \underline{\hspace{1cm}} + \underline{\hspace{1cm}}$

Substitute your answer for y in the second equation and solve for x.

$-x - (\underline{\hspace{1cm}} + \underline{\hspace{1cm}}) = -10$

$\underline{\hspace{0.5cm}} \bigcirc \underline{\hspace{0.5cm}}$

If all the variables are eliminated and the last equation is true, there are $\underline{\hspace{3cm}}$

$\underline{\hspace{3cm}}$ solutions.

Determine if the system of equations is consistent and independent, consistent and dependent, or inconsistent.

c. $4y = 4x + 4 \longrightarrow y = \underline{\hspace{1cm}} + \underline{\hspace{1cm}}$

$-4y = -4x - 4 \longrightarrow y = \underline{\hspace{1cm}} + \underline{\hspace{1cm}}$

If the equations are identical, the system is $\underline{\hspace{3cm}}$ and $\underline{\hspace{3cm}}$.

There are $\underline{\hspace{3cm}}$ solutions.

d. $-2x + y = 3 \longrightarrow y = \underline{\hspace{1.5cm}} + \underline{\hspace{1cm}}$

$y = -x - 2$

$\underline{\hspace{1.5cm}} + \underline{\hspace{1cm}} = -x - 2 \qquad y = -(\underline{\hspace{1cm}}) - 2$

$x = \underline{\hspace{2cm}} \qquad\qquad y = \underline{\hspace{1.5cm}}$

$\underline{\hspace{3cm}}$ and $\underline{\hspace{3cm}}$ systems have exactly one solution.

The solution is ($\underline{\hspace{1cm}}$, $\underline{\hspace{1cm}}$).

e. Plan X: $y = \underline{\hspace{1.5cm}}x$; Plan Y: $y = \underline{\hspace{1.5cm}}x + 40$

$\underline{\hspace{1.5cm}}x = \underline{\hspace{1.5cm}}x + 40$

$x = \underline{\hspace{1cm}} \qquad\qquad \underline{\hspace{1cm}}$ service calls

$y = 22(\underline{\hspace{1cm}}) = \underline{\hspace{1.5cm}} \qquad$ Both plans cost $\underline{\hspace{2cm}}$ at $\underline{\hspace{1cm}}$ service calls.

1. Use a special product pattern.

$(2b - 3)^2$

$= \underline{} \bigcirc \underline{} \bigcirc \underline{}$

$= \underline{}$

2. Use a special product pattern.

$(-b^3 + 5)^2$

$= (\underline{})^2 \bigcirc 2(\underline{}) \bigcirc (\underline{})^2$

$= \underline{}$

3. $\sqrt{mn} = \sqrt{m} \cdot \sqrt{n}$

$\sqrt{25x^4} = \sqrt{\underline{}} \cdot \sqrt{\underline{}}$

$= \underline{}$

4. See page 4 in the Student Reference Guide.

$\sqrt{144x^6y} = \sqrt{\underline{}} \sqrt{\underline{}} \sqrt{\underline{}}$

$= \underline{} \sqrt{\underline{}}$

5. See page 4 in the Student Reference Guide.

$\dfrac{3x}{y^2} + xy^{-2}$

$= \dfrac{3x}{y^2} + \dfrac{\square}{\square}$

$= \dfrac{\square}{\square}$

6. Let $x = \#$ of hours   Let $y = \#$ of pages

$(\underline{}, \underline{})(\underline{}, \underline{})$

Use the points to find the slope.

$m = \underline{}$

Substitute one of the points and the slope to find the y-intercept.

$\underline{} = \underline{}(\underline{}) + b$

$b = \underline{}$

$y = \underline{}$

Substitute 6 for x.

$y = \underline{}(6) + \underline{} = \underline{}$ pages

7. Use the Addition Property of Inequality.

$z - 3 \geq 10$

$z \geq \underline{}$

8. $z - 5 < -2$

$z < \underline{}$

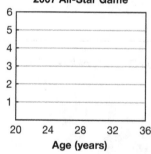

9. *Mode = value that occurs the most*

mode(s): _____

10. *Find the LCM.*

44 = _____

28 = _____

LCM = _____

= _____

---

11. Order the data: 25, 25, 25, 25, 50, ...

a.

```
←┼──┼──┼──┼──┼──┼──┼──┼──┼──┼──→
  0  10 20 30 40 50 60 70 80 90 100
```

b. LE: _____ Q_1: _____

Median: _____

Q_3: _____   UE: _____

12. Statement 2 is the _____ of

Statement 1. The original statement is

_____, but the

_____ is _____.

---

13. Student _____ is correct.

Student _____ did not _____

2 from each side to eliminate 2 from the

_____ side.

14. *Order the data. Use 4 intervals of 4 years.*

**Ages of Players on Eastern
Conference Team for NBA
2007 All-Star Game**

```
6
5
4
3
2
1
   20   24   28   32   36
        Age (years)
```

15. a. *Use a special product pattern.*

$(2x + 2)^2 = $ ____ ◯ ____ ◯ ____

   b. *Use distribution.*

$(2x + 2)($_____$)$

_____

16. *Substitute 20 for x and 15 for y.*

$5($_____$) - 2($_____$) = 70$

_____ $= 70$

$3($_____$) + 4($_____$) = 120$

_____ $= 120$

---

17. *A line of symmetry divides a figure into two mirror image halves.*

$y = $ ____ and $x = $ ____ are lines of symmetry.

$y = $ ____ is perpendicular to _____

and _____. $x = $ ____ is perpendicular

to _____ and _____.

18. Let $x = $ his base salary

Let $y = $ his base salary plus a bonus

Company A: $y = $ _____ $x + $ _____

Company B: $y = $ _____ $x + $ _____

  ✎ Use elimination to solve for x.

$x = $ _____

---

19. If a number is added to an equation, its

solution _____ be equal

to the solution of the original equation.

The system is _____ .

20. *Parallel lines have the same slopes. The slopes of perpendicular lines are negative reciprocals.*

slope of $y = 3x + 12$: ____

slope of $y + 9 = 3x$: ____

The lines are _____ .

---

21. *Subtract the equations. Solve for y.*

$2x - 3y = -17$

$2x - 9y = -47$

$x = $ ____

Substitute.

$2($____$) - 3y = $ _____

$y = $ ____

Solution: (____, ____)

22. *Substitute x − 5 for y in the second equation.*

_____ $= -2x + 1$

$x = $ ____

Substitute.

$y = $ ____ $- 5 = $ ____

Solution: (____, ____)

23. *Inverse variation: xy = k, where k ≠ 0.*

Circle the answer.

A 0   B 0.67   C 1.5   D 37.5

24. *Inverse variation: xy = k, where k ≠ 0.*

_____, the value of x can never be

equal to _____ because that would mean

the _____ of x and y would

equal _____.

25. *Inverse variation: xy = k*

Let x = # students   Let y = # items

_____ • 3 = _____

k = total number of prizes

P(graphing calculator) = _____

26. _____ + _____ > x

$x <$ _____

27. *Let x = odometer reading at the end of the trip*

a. $x -$ _____ < _____ + _____ + _____

b. $x -$ _____ < _____

$x <$ _____

c. x ◯ _____

28. Student _____ is correct.

Student _____ did not classify the

lines as _____ and

the system as having _____

solution.

29. $y = 65x + 15$

$13x - \dfrac{1}{5} = -3 \longrightarrow y =$ _____ $x -$ _____

The equations are _____.

_____ is faster. These

equations form a set of _____

and _____ equations.

30. *Substitute 8x − 7 for y in the first equation.*

$2($_____$) = 4x + 1$

$x =$ _____

Substitute the x-value into y = 8x − 7 to find the
y-value.

Solution: (_____, _____)

LESSON

68

Mutually Exclusive and Inclusive Events page 443

New Concepts

• It is not possible to roll both a sum of 6 and a sum of 11 on the same roll of two number cubes. The events are **mutually exclusive.**

Example **Finding the Probability of Mutually Exclusive Events**

If you roll two number cubes, what is the probability of rolling a sum of 6 or a sum of 11?

The table shows the possible sums for rolling two number cubes.

Find the probability of each event. Add the probabilities.

$$P(A \text{ or } B) = P(A) + P(B)$$
$$P(6 \text{ or } 11) = P(6) + P(11)$$
$$= \frac{5}{36} + \frac{2}{36} = \frac{7}{36}$$

Roll of Cube 2

	1	2	3	4	5	6
1	2	3	4	5	6	7
2	3	4	5	6	7	8
3	4	5	6	7	8	9
4	5	6	7	8	9	10
5	6	7	8	9	10	11
6	7	8	9	10	11	12

Roll of Cube 1

• It is possible to roll at least one odd number and also a sum of 8. The two events are **inclusive.**

Example **Finding the Probability of Inclusive Events.**

If you roll two number cubes, what is the probability of rolling at least one odd number or a sum of 8?

The circled numbers in the table show the ways to roll at least one odd number. The shaded oval shows the ways to roll a sum of 8. The shaded circles show the ways to roll a sum of 8 with at least one odd number.

Roll of Cube 2

	1	2	3	4	5	6
1	2	3	4	5	6	7
2	3	4	5	6	7	8
3	4	5	6	7	8	9
4	5	6	7	8	9	10
5	6	7	8	9	10	11
6	7	8	9	10	11	12

Roll of Cube 1

For inclusive events, subtract the probability of all events that can occur at the same time from the sum of the probabilities of each event.

$$P(A \text{ or } B) = P(A) + P(B) - P(A \text{ and } B)$$
$$P(\text{odd or sum of 8}) = P(\text{odd}) + P(\text{sum of 8}) - P(\text{odd and sum of 8})$$
$$= \frac{27}{36} + \frac{5}{36} - \frac{2}{36}$$
$$= \frac{30}{36} = \frac{5}{6}$$

a. *See the table showing the sums for rolling two number cubes on* 📖 *page 443.*

$P(\text{sum of 2 or sum of 10}) = P(\text{sum of 2}) + P(\text{sum of 10})$

$$= \frac{\square}{36} + \frac{\square}{36}$$

$$= \frac{\square}{36} = \frac{\square}{\square}$$

b. *"At least one even number" includes combinations in which both numbers are even.*

$P(\text{one even number or sum of 3}) = P(\text{one even}) + P(\text{sum of 3}) - P(\text{one even and sum of 3})$

$$= \frac{\square}{36} + \frac{\square}{36} - \frac{\square}{36}$$

$$= \frac{\square}{36} = \frac{\square}{\square}$$

c. *Selecting a rock song or selecting an alternative song are mutually exclusive events.*

$\text{Total songs} = \underline{\quad} + \underline{\quad} + \underline{\quad} + \underline{\quad} = \underline{\quad}$

$P(\text{rock or alternative}) = P(\text{rock}) + P(\text{alternative})$

$$= \frac{\square}{\square} + \frac{\square}{\square}$$

$$= \frac{\square}{\square}$$

d. *She assumes that 10,000 people over 75 are employed. The events are inclusive.*

$P(\text{employed or older than 75}) = P(\text{employed}) + P(\text{over 75}) - P(\text{employed and over 75})$

$$= \frac{\square}{\square} + \frac{\square}{\square} - \frac{\square}{\square}$$

$$= \frac{\square}{\square}$$

$$= \frac{\square}{\square}$$

Multiply the probability by the number of people surveyed. Round to the nearest whole number.

$200 \cdot \dfrac{\square}{\square} \approx \underline{\qquad} \text{ people}$

1. To find the degree of a monomial, add the exponents of the variables.

degree: _____

2. The degree of a polynomial is the degree of the greatest-degree term.

degree of 1st term: _____

If a variable has no exponent, its exponent is 1.

degree of 2nd term: _____

degree of 3rd term: _____

degree of the polynomial: _____

3. degree of 1st term: _____

degree of 2nd term: _____

degree of the polynomial: _____

4. Find the perfect square in the denominator.

$$\sqrt{\frac{1}{48}} = \sqrt{\frac{1}{\boxed{} \cdot \boxed{3}}}$$

$$= \frac{1}{4}\sqrt{\frac{1}{\boxed{}}}$$

5. Find the perfect squares in the numerator and in the denominator.

$$\sqrt{\frac{4}{24x^4}} = \frac{\boxed{}}{\boxed{}x^2}$$

6. Inverse variation: $y = \frac{k}{x}$

$$y = \frac{5}{x}$$

Inverse variation? _____

7. Inverse variation: $y = \frac{k}{x}$

$$y = \frac{1}{2}x$$

Inverse variation? _____

8. Use the Subtraction Property of Inequality.

$$x + 1 > 1.1$$

$$x > \text{\_\_\_\_}$$

9. Use the Addition Property of Inequality.

$x - 2.3 \le 7.6$

$x \le$ _____

10. See table showing the sums for rolling two number cubes on 📖 page 443.

$P(\text{sum 7 or sum 11}) = P(\text{sum 7}) + P(\text{sum 11})$

$$= \frac{\square}{\square}$$

11. $P(\text{impossible event}) = 0$

$P(\text{sum 1 or sum 13}) =$ _____

12. Find P(fork or red handle).

$P(\text{fork}) + P(\text{red handle}) - P(\text{fork and red handle})$

$=$ _____

$=$ _____

13. Let m = rate per mile

Let b = flat fee

Use slope-intercept form.

$y =$ _____

Substitute.

$y = ($____$)(100) +$ ____ $=$ ▢

14. The y-intercept is given.

Use $(0, -8)$, $(4, -9)$ to find the slope.

Let A = Liquid A

Let B = Liquid B

$m =$ _____

$B = mA + ($____$) =$ ____$A -$ ____

Substitute to find the temperature of B if A has a temperature of $-4°F$.

$=$ ____▢

15. The point where the lines cross is the solution.

a.

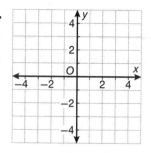

b. Solution: (____, ____)

16. Use FOIL.

$l = 2x + 5$

$w = x + 6$

$A =$ _____

17. Let g = girl's age and let b = boy's age

____b + ____g = ____

____ = ____b − ____

 Solve using the substitution

method.

$g =$ ____; $b =$ ____

Find their ages 5 years ago.

$b - 5 =$ ____

$g - 5 =$ ____

18. Justify.

$$(a + b)(a + b) = a^2 + b^2$$

Example:

$$(x + 2)(x + 2) \overset{?}{=} x^2 + 2^2$$

____ ⃝ ____ ⃝ ____ $\overset{?}{=}$ ____ + ____

_____ ⃝ _____

So, the statement is _____.

19. Let c = # of chairs and let t = # of tables.

____c + ____t = _____

____ + ____ = 20

 Solve using the elimination method.

$c =$ ____ $t =$ ____

20. Student ____ is correct.

Student ____ mixed up the values of

x and y when _____.

21. The slopes of perpendicular lines are negative reciprocals.

Line 1: (0, −4), (5, −2)   Line 2: (−2, 5), (0, 1)

a.

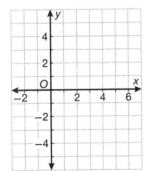

b. Line 1: $y =$ _____

Line 2: $y =$ _____

c. The lines _____ perpendicular. The

slopes _____ negative reciprocals.

22. The highest price minus $2 must be less than $14.99.

$x - 2$ ⃝ 14.99   so x ⃝ ____

23. *Use the Addition Property of Inequality.*

Student _____ is correct.

The solution is x ◯ _____ .

---

24. *Use substitution.*

$$y = \frac{3}{4} + 3$$

$$y = x$$

Solution: (_____ , _____)

---

25. *The number of stations must be a whole number.*

a. *Let y = 15 and then solve for x.* $y = \$10 + 1.5x$ $x =$ _____

b. Circle the answers: consistent   inconsistent   dependent   independent

c. The algebraic systems have a _____ solution. However, the solution to the

word problem is not a _____ number, so the plans _____ have a common solution.

d. _____ because the plans_____ cost the same amount.

---

26. *The systems have one common solution.*

They are _____ and _____ .

---

27. *See the table showing the sums for rolling two number cubes on* 📖 *page 443.*

$P(\text{sum } 7 \text{ or sum } 11) = P(\text{sum } 7) + P(\text{sum } 11)$

$=$ _____

Multiply by 100 to predict the number of times that a 7 or 11 will be rolled.

about _____

28. *Mutually exclusive events can not both occur in the same trial.*

Answer: _____

---

29. P (freezing rain or snow) $=$

P (freezing rain) $+ P$ (snow) $=$ _____

30. *Inclusive events can occur at the same time.*

The probability of A or B is higher if A

and B _____ .

LESSON

69

Adding and Subtracting Radical Expressions

page 449

New Concepts

Math Language

A **radicand** is the number or expression under the radical symbol.

Like radicals have the same radicand.

Unlike radicals have different radicands.

- When adding or subtracting radical expressions, treat radicals like variables.

- In order to add or subtract radical expressions, they must have like radicals.

- Unlike radicals expressions cannot be added or subtracted.

Example **Combining Like Radicals**

Simplify.

$2\sqrt{7} + 4\sqrt{7}$

$(2 + 4)\sqrt{7}$ *Factor.*

$6\sqrt{7}$ *Add.*

Simplify.

$6\sqrt{2} + 8\sqrt{11}$ *The radicands are not alike. You can not simplify.*

- To determine if the radical expressions are like radicals, simplify the radicals and compare the radicands.

Example **Simplifying Before Combining**

Simplify.

$c\sqrt{75c} - \sqrt{27c^3}$

$c\sqrt{25 \cdot 3c} - \sqrt{9 \cdot c^2 \cdot 3c}$ *Factor the radicands.*

$c\sqrt{25} \cdot \sqrt{3c} - \sqrt{9} \cdot \sqrt{c^2} \cdot \sqrt{3c}$ *Factor out squares.*

$5c \cdot \sqrt{3c} - 3c \cdot \sqrt{3c}$ *Find the square roots.*

$(5c - 3c)\sqrt{3c}$ *Factor out the common factor.*

$2c\sqrt{3c}$ *Subtract.*

Simplify.

a. $9\sqrt{5} + 8\sqrt{5} = ($ _____ $+$ _____ $)\sqrt{5} =$ _____

b. $11\sqrt{ab} - 23\sqrt{ab} = ($ _____ $-$ _____ $)\sqrt{ab} =$ _____

c. $5\sqrt{7} + 3\sqrt{2} =$ _____

d. $\dfrac{3\sqrt{2x}}{5} + \dfrac{2\sqrt{2x}}{5} - \dfrac{\sqrt{2x}}{5} = ($ _____ $+$ _____ $-$ _____ $)\dfrac{\sqrt{2x}}{5} = \dfrac{\Box\sqrt{\Box}}{5}$

e. $4\sqrt{3c^2} - 8\sqrt{2c^2} = 4\sqrt{3 \cdot c^2} - 8\sqrt{2 \cdot c^2}$

$\qquad\qquad = 4\sqrt{3} \cdot \sqrt{c^2} - 8($ _____ $) \cdot$ _____ *Factor the radicands.*

$\qquad\qquad =$ _____ $-$ _____

f. $-11\sqrt{10a} + 3\sqrt{250a} + \sqrt{160a}$

$\qquad = -11\sqrt{10a} + 3\sqrt{25} \cdot$ _____ $+$ _____ $\cdot \sqrt{10a}$

$\qquad = -11\sqrt{10a} + 3 \cdot$ _____ $+$ _____

$\qquad = -11\sqrt{10a} +$ _____ $+$ _____

$\qquad =$ _____

g. $P = \sqrt{12} + \sqrt{48} + 2\sqrt{15}$

$\qquad =$ _____ $\cdot \sqrt{3} +$ _____ $\cdot \sqrt{3} + 2\sqrt{15}$

$\qquad =$ _____ $+$ _____ $+ 2\sqrt{15}$

$\qquad =$ _____ $+ 2\sqrt{15}$ ▨

h. $P = 2\sqrt{27a^2} + 2\sqrt{75a^2}$

$\qquad = 2\sqrt{3} \cdot$ _____ $\cdot \sqrt{a^2} + 2\sqrt{3} \cdot$ _____ $\cdot \sqrt{a^2}$

$\qquad = 2\sqrt{3} \cdot$ _____ $\cdot$ _____ $+ 2\sqrt{3} \cdot$ _____ $\cdot$ _____

$\qquad =$ _____ $+$ _____

$\qquad =$ _____ ▨

1. *Add coefficients.*

$$-6\sqrt{2} + 8\sqrt{2} = (\underline{\quad} + \underline{\quad})\sqrt{2}$$
$$= \underline{\quad}\sqrt{2}$$

2. *Subtract coefficients.*

$$-4\sqrt{7} - 5\sqrt{7} = (\underline{\quad} + \underline{\quad})\sqrt{7}$$
$$= \underline{\quad}\sqrt{7}$$

3. *Add coefficients.*

$$2\sqrt{3} + 5\sqrt{3} = \underline{\quad}\sqrt{3}$$

4. *If a variable has no exponent its exponent is 1.*

degree of $9x$: _____

5. *A whole number has degree 0.*

degree of term 1: _____

degree of term 2: _____

degree of term 3: _____

degree of the greatest term: _____

6. *Add the exponents of the variables.*

degree of term 1: _____

degree of term 2: _____

degree of the greatest term: _____

7. *See table showing the sums for rolling two number cubes on* page 443.

$$P(2 \text{ or } 12) = P(2) + P(12) = \underline{\quad}$$

8. *The probability of a certain event is 1.*

$$P(\text{sum} > 1) = \underline{\quad}$$

9. *Add.*

$$\begin{array}{r} -4.3t^2 + 7.7t + 1.4 \\ -3.0t^2 + 5.0t + 6 \\ \hline \end{array}$$

10. 3, 3, 4, 4, 4, 5, 5, 7, 8, 8, 9, 12, 18

Hours a Candle Burns

outlier: _____

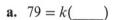
11. $y = kx$, x = number of inches, y = number of miles.

a. $79 = k(\underline{\quad})$ $k = \underline{\quad}$

b.

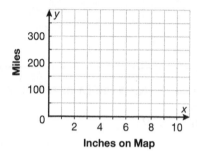

c. $y = (\underline{\quad})(\underline{\quad})$

$\approx \underline{\quad\quad}$ ▨

12. 📖 Solve the system for a and b.

$\$0.10b + \$0.25a = \$6.80$

$a + b = 35$

Substitute the second equation into the first.

$a = \underline{\quad}$ $b = \underline{\quad}$

13. $A = s^2$

a. $A_1 = x \cdot x = \underline{\quad}$

b. *The fence adds 5 ft to each side of the length and the width.*

$A_2 = (5 + x + 5)(\underline{\quad\quad})$

$= (x + 10)(\underline{\quad\quad})$

c. $A_2 = x^2 + \underline{\quad\quad\quad}$ *Use FOIL.*

d. $A_2 - A_1 = \underline{\quad\quad\quad}$

$= \underline{\quad}x + \underline{\quad\quad}$ ▨

14. Explain why $\sqrt{x^2} = -x$.

Let $x = -4$

$\sqrt{(-4)^2} = |-4| = \underline{\quad}$

$\underline{\quad}$ is the opposite of the original value $x = -4$.

15. *Multiply the second equation by 5 to eliminate the y-terms.*

$6x + 15y = 15 \longrightarrow 6x + 15y = 15$

$7x - 3y = -3 \longrightarrow 35x - \underline{\quad}y = \underline{\quad}$

$x = \underline{\quad}$

 Substitute x to solve for y.

Solution: $(\underline{\quad}, \underline{\quad})$

16. x = number of people

y = cost per person

Indirect variation: $y = \frac{k}{x}$

$180 = \dfrac{k}{\square}$

$k = \underline{\quad}$

$y = \dfrac{\square}{x}$

$y = \dfrac{\square}{\square}$

$y = \underline{\quad}$ ▨

17. *Use slope-intercept form.*

$y = -\frac{3}{2}x + 8\frac{1}{2}$

$y =$ _____

So the lines are _____ .

18. $\frac{(T_1 + T_2 + T_3)}{3}$ *must be greater than or equal to 90.*

$x \geq$ _____

19. Graph $x + 5 > 3$ and $x - 6 \leq -8$.

(number line marked −7 −5 −3 −1 0 1)

Together they include all _____ numbers, but they have no _____ in common.

20. *Solve for x.*

$x + 6 \geq 2x - 12$

Circle the answer.

A (number line marked −12 −10 −8 −6 −4)

B (number line marked 12 14 16 18 20)

C (number line marked −12 −10 −8 −6 −4)

D (number line marked −20 −18 −16 −14 −12)

21. Solve the system using substitution.

$$-\frac{1}{4}x + y = -2 \longrightarrow y = \frac{1}{4}x - 2$$

$$-x + 4y = -8$$

$-x + 4(_____) = -8$ *Substitute y from the first equation into the second.*

$-x + x - \_\_\_\_ = \_\_\_\_$ *Distribute.*

$\_\_\_\_ = \_\_\_\_$ *This is always a true statement.*

Any ordered pair (x, y) that satisfies the equation _____ is a solution.

22. Student _____ is correct.

Student _____ did not interpret the

_____ correctly.

23. *Multiply the second equation by 5.*

The equations are _____ so

the truck _____ on schedule.

24. Student _____ is correct.

Student _____ multiplied the two

probabilities instead of _____

them.

25. Total servings $= 36 + 24 + 30 + 28$

$= \underline{\hspace{1cm}}$

a. $\dfrac{24}{\square} = \dfrac{\square}{\square}$

b. $\dfrac{\square}{118} = \dfrac{\square}{\square}$

c. $\dfrac{\square}{118} + \dfrac{\square}{118} = \dfrac{\square}{\square} = \dfrac{\square}{\square}$

26. *A space can be both black and worth 10 points.*

black $= \dfrac{\square}{8}$ 10 points $= \dfrac{\square}{8}$ black and 10 points $= \dfrac{\square}{8}$

$P(\text{black or 10 points}) = \underline{\hspace{1.5cm}}$

27. If n is an _____ number greater than

or equal to _____, the radical will be

eliminated.

If n is an _____ number greater than

_____, an x will remain under the radical.

The statement is _____.

28. Student _____ is correct.

The radicals have different

_____ and cannot be

simplified. Therefore, they cannot be

_____.

29. *Look for square numbers that are close to the radicands.*

$\sqrt{51} + \sqrt{63} + \sqrt{83} + \sqrt{104}$

$7 + \underline{\hspace{0.7cm}} + \underline{\hspace{0.7cm}} + \underline{\hspace{0.7cm}} = \underline{\hspace{0.7cm}}$

30. $756 = 2 \cdot 2 \cdot 3 \cdot 3 \cdot 3 \cdot 7$

$P = 4 \cdot \sqrt{756} = 4\sqrt{4 \cdot 9 \cdot 3 \cdot 7}$

$= 4 \cdot 2 \cdot 3\sqrt{3 \cdot 7}$

$= 24\sqrt{\underline{\hspace{1cm}}}$

$= \underline{\hspace{1cm}}$

LESSON
70

Solving Inequalities by Multiplying or Dividing page 455

New Concepts

- When multiplying or dividing an inequality by a positive number, the order of the inequality does not change. This means the direction of the inequality symbol remains the same, and the inequality remains true.

Example **Multiplying by a Positive Number**

Solve, graph, and check the solution for the inequality $\frac{1}{2}x \le 8$.

$$\left(\frac{1}{2}\right)x \le 8$$

$$2\left(\frac{1}{2}\right)x \le 2 \cdot 8$$

$$x \le 16$$

Graph $x \le 16$.

Check the endpoint.   Check the direction.

$$\frac{1}{2}x \overset{?}{=} 8;\ x = 16 \qquad\qquad \frac{1}{2}x \overset{?}{\le} 8;\ x = 14$$

$$\frac{1}{2}(16) \overset{?}{=} 8 \qquad\qquad\qquad \frac{1}{2}(14) \overset{?}{\le} 8$$

$$8 = 8 \ \checkmark \qquad\qquad\qquad\qquad 7 \le 8 \ \checkmark$$

Both statements are true, so the solution is correct.

- When multiplying or dividing an inequality by a negative number, reverse the direction of inequality symbol. The inequality remains true.

Example **Dividing by a Negative Number**

Solve and graph the inequality $-4m \ge 7$.

$$-4m \ge 7$$

$$\frac{-4m}{-4} \le \frac{7}{-4} \qquad \textit{Reverse the direction of the inequality symbol.}$$

$$m \le 1\frac{3}{4}$$

Graph the solution on a number line.

Solve, graph, and check the solution for each inequality.

a. $\frac{1}{3}n < 2$

$3 \cdot \frac{1}{3}n < 2 \cdot$ ____

$n <$ ____

```
<+++++++++++>
 -2  0  2  4  6
```

Check.

$n =$ ____ $n =$ ____

$\frac{1}{3}(\underline{}) \overset{?}{=} 2$ $= \frac{1}{3}\underline{} \overset{?}{<} 2$

____ $\overset{?}{=} 2$ ✓   ____ $\overset{?}{<} 2$ ✓

b. *Reverse the direction of the symbol.*

$-\frac{x}{4} < 8$

____ $\cdot -\frac{x}{4} > 8 \cdot$ ____

$x >$ ____

```
<+++++++++>
 -32 -30 -28
```

Check.

$x =$ ____ $x =$ ____

$-\frac{\square}{4} \overset{?}{=} 8$ $-\square \overset{?}{<} 8$

____ $\overset{?}{=} 8$ ✓   ____ $\overset{?}{<} 8$ ✓

c. $6w \le 57$

$\frac{6w}{\square} \le \frac{57}{\square}$

$w \le$ ____

```
<+++++++++++>
 6  7  8  9  10
```

Check.

$w =$ ____ $w =$ ____

$6(\underline{}) \overset{?}{=} 57$ $6(\underline{}) \overset{?}{\le} 57$

____ $\overset{?}{=} 57$ ✓   ____ $\overset{?}{\le} 57$ ✓

d. *Reverse the direction of the symbol.*

$\frac{1}{2} \ge -4a$

____ $\cdot \frac{1}{2} \bigcirc -4a \cdot$ ____

____ $\bigcirc a$

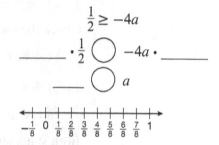

Check.

$a =$ ____ $a =$ ____

$\frac{1}{2} \overset{?}{=} -4(\underline{})$ $\frac{1}{2} \overset{?}{\ge} -4(\underline{})$

$\frac{1}{2} \overset{?}{=} \underline{}$ ✓ $\frac{1}{2} \overset{?}{\le} \underline{}$ ✓

e. $\frac{0.04x}{\square} \ge \frac{750}{\square}$

$x \ge$ _____

Barney must sell at least _____

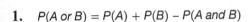
1. $P(A \text{ or } B) = P(A) + P(B) - P(A \text{ and } B)$

$P(\text{heads}) = \underline{\quad}$

$P(3) = \underline{\quad}$

These events are $\underline{\hspace{4cm}}$

$P(\text{heads or } 3) = \underline{\quad} + \underline{\quad} - \underline{\quad} = \underline{\quad}$

2. $P(A \text{ or } B) = P(A) + P(B) - P(A \text{ and } B)$

$P(\text{tails}) = \underline{\quad}$

$P(< 4) = \underline{\quad}$

These events are $\underline{\hspace{4cm}}$

$P(\text{tails or } 3) = \underline{\quad} + \underline{\quad} - \underline{\quad} = \underline{\quad}$

3. $P(A \text{ and } B) = P(A) \cdot P(B)$

$P(\text{tails}) = \underline{\quad}$

$P(> 6) = \underline{\quad}$

$P(\text{tails and } >6) = \underline{\quad} \cdot \underline{\quad} = \underline{\quad}$

4. $y - 2 < \frac{1}{2}$

$y < \underline{\quad} + \underline{\quad}$

$y < \underline{\quad}$

5. $y + \frac{3}{2} < \frac{1}{4}$

$y < \underline{\quad} - \underline{\quad}$

$y < \underline{\quad}$

6. *Combine coefficients.*

$18\sqrt{3y} + 8\sqrt{3y}$

$= (\underline{\quad} + \underline{\quad})\sqrt{\underline{\quad}}$

$= \underline{\quad}\sqrt{\underline{\quad}}$

7. *Combine coefficients.*

$\sqrt{3x} + 2\sqrt{3x}$

$= (\underline{\quad} + \underline{\quad})\sqrt{\underline{\quad}}$

$= \underline{\quad}\sqrt{\underline{\quad}}$

8. *Inverse variation:* $y = \frac{k}{x}$

Substitute 18 for x and 4.5 for y to find k.

$4.5 = \frac{k}{x}$

$k = \underline{\quad} \cdot \underline{\quad} = \underline{\quad}$

$\underline{\quad} = \dfrac{\square}{\square}$

9. To isolate the variable, divide by a

_____ number.

reverse direction of the sign? _____

$$-\frac{2a}{\boxed{}} \bigcirc -\frac{5}{\boxed{}}$$

$$a \bigcirc \underline{}$$

10. a. IQR = _____ − _____ = _____

1.5(_____) = _____

Q_1: _____ − _____ = _____

Q_3: _____ − _____ = _____

Outlier(s): _____

b. Make two box-and-whisker plots.

c. About _____ points. Excluding the

outlier, both the _____ and the

_____ of the scores are

_____ points.

11.

Ages at a Family Party

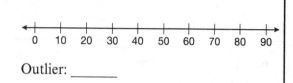

Outlier: _____

12. Solution: (_____, _____)

13. a. *Find the LCM.*

The first ball to have 3 patterns was

the ____th ball.

b. *List multiples of each number.*

15, _____, _____, _____, _____, _____

18, _____, _____, _____, _____

30, _____, _____

Look for common multiples.

balls with 2 designs: _____

14. $A = s^2$

$s = 8x + 18$

$A = (\underline{})^2$

$= \underline{} + \underline{} + \underline{}$

15. *Substitute.*

$\underline{} + \underline{}(\underline{})$

$= \underline{}$

16. a. **Customers Served Per Day**

Stem	Leaves

Key: 9 | 0 = 90 customers

b. The data is not distributed _____ ; it is

clustered at the _____ and

_____ extremes.

This means the restaurant is either extremely

_____ or relatively _____ .

---

17. *Multiply the second equation by 2.*

$$-8x - 5y = -52$$

$$+ \underline{\quad}x + \underline{\quad}y = \underline{\quad\quad}$$

$$y = \underline{\quad}$$

$$4x + 3(\underline{\quad}) = 28$$

$$4x + \underline{\quad\quad} = 28$$

$$4x = \underline{\quad\quad}$$

$$x = \underline{\quad}$$

Solution: (_____ , _____)

18.

$$I = \frac{k}{d^2}$$

$$0.1 = \frac{k}{1^2}$$

$$k = \underline{\quad}$$

$$0.0001 = \frac{\square}{d^2}$$

$$0.0001 d^2 = \square$$

$$d^2 = \frac{\square}{\square}$$

$$d = \sqrt{\underline{\quad}} \approx \underline{\quad}$$

---

19. Complete the proof.

Slope of $\overleftrightarrow{AB}$ = _____ , slope of $\overleftrightarrow{CD}$ = _____ ,

so $\overleftrightarrow{AB}$ is _____ $\overleftrightarrow{CD}$. Slope of $\overleftrightarrow{AD}$ = _____ ,

slope of $\overleftrightarrow{BC}$ = _____ , so $\overleftrightarrow{AD}$ is _____ $\overleftrightarrow{BC}$.

$\overleftrightarrow{AB}$ _____ $\overleftrightarrow{AD}$ _____ $\overleftrightarrow{CD}$ _____ $\overleftrightarrow{BC}$ _____ $\overleftrightarrow{AB}$

Therefore, $ABCD$ is a rectangle.

20. Which one of the following systems has only one common solution?

Circle the answer.

A $y = 21x + 6$
$y = -7x$

B $5x - 2y = 0$
$\frac{5}{2}x - y = 0$

C $-y = 13x - 6$
$-2y = 26x + 9$

D $x - 7y = 14$
$\frac{1}{4}x - \frac{7}{4}y = \frac{7}{2}$

---

21. The system is _____ and

_____ because both

equations are the graph of the

_____ line.

22. Student _____ is correct. Student _____

treated the events as _____

_____ .

---

23. Total number of players: _____

$P(\text{offense}) = $ _____

$P(\text{special teams}) = $ _____

$P(\text{offense or special teams})$

$= $ _____ $+$ _____ $= $ _____

24. $P = 4s$

$4(2\sqrt{9}) = $ ____ $\sqrt{}$

$= $ ____ $\cdot$ ____

$= $ ____

25. The absolute value of the coefficient

would be between ____ and ____.

26. $P = 2(l + w)$

1 flag: $P = 2(6\sqrt{4} + 5\sqrt{4})$

$= 2(\underline{} + \underline{})$

$= 2(\underline{})$

$= \underline{}$ and

8 flags $= 8(\underline{}) = \underline{}$

27. $5f > -10$

$\dfrac{5f}{\square} > -\dfrac{10}{\square}$

$f > $ ____

Circle the answer.

A
number line with $-4\ -2\ \ 0\ \ 2\ \ 4\ \ 6\ \ 8$

B number line with $-54\ -52\ -50\ -50$

C number line with $-4\ -2\ \ 0\ \ 2$

D number line with $-54\ -52\ -50\ -48$

28. _____ both sides by

$-\dfrac{\square}{\square}$ and _____ the

direction of the inequality sign.

29. Let $s = $ price of 1 gift

$4s \bigcirc$ _____

$s \bigcirc$ _____

The solutions are between _____ and

_____ and are _____

numbers to the _____ place.

30. Let $b = $ number of burgers

_____$b \bigcirc$ _____

$b \bigcirc$ _____

She can make at most _____ burgers.

Comparing Direct and Inverse Variation page 462

- A direct variation is a relationship between two variables whose ratio is constant.

- A constant of variation is a value k that remains constant in a direct variation or an inverse variation equation.

- The equation $y = kx$, where k is a nonzero constant, shows direct variation between variables x and y.

Identify the constant of variation, given that y varies directly with x. Then write the equation of variation.

1. y is 10 when x is 2.

$$y = kx$$

$$10 = k(2)$$

_____ $= k$ *Solve for k.*

$y = ($_____$)x$ *Substitute for k.*

2. y is 3 when x is 6.

$$y = kx$$

_____ $= k($_____$)$

_____ $= k$

$y = ($_____$)x$

- The formula $d = rt$ can represent either direct or inverse variation depending on the variable that is held constant.

Alex walks at a rate of 3 miles per hour. If he walks at that rate for twice as long, he will travel twice as far. The ratio of the distance and time is always the same.

3. Identify the constant of variation.

Distance = rate · time is a direct variation equation.

The constant is the _____, so $k =$ _____ miles per hour.

4. Write a direct variation equation that relates Alex's time to distance traveled. *Distance = 3 miles per hour · time*

$$d = ($$_____$$)t \text{ or } \frac{d}{t} =$$ _____

- An inverse variation describes a relationship between two variables whose product is a constant.

- The equation $xy = k$, where k is a nonzero constant, defines an inverse variation between x and y.

Identify the constant of variation, given that _y_ varies inversely with _x_. Then write the equation of variation.

The inverse variation equation can also be expressed as $y = \frac{k}{x}$.

5. _y_ is 1 when _x_ is 3.

$$y = \frac{k}{x}$$

$$\underline{\quad} = \frac{k}{\square}$$

$$\underline{\quad} = k$$

$$xy = \underline{\quad}$$

6. _y_ is 4 when _x_ is $\frac{1}{2}$.

$$y = \frac{k}{x}$$

$$\underline{\quad} = \frac{k}{\square}$$

$$\underline{\quad} = k$$

$$xy = \underline{\quad}$$

• In inverse variation, when _x_ increases, _y_ decreases.

Alex lives 4 miles from school. If he walks at a slower rate than normal, it will take him longer to reach his destination. In other words, the more time he spends walking home, the slower he is actually walking. This situation is represented by an inverse variation.

7. The constant in the situation above is the _____.

8. Write an inverse variation equation relating the time (_t_) it takes Alex to walk to school to his rate of speed (_r_).

$$r = \frac{\square}{t} \text{ or } r \cdot t = \underline{\quad}$$

(**Exploration**) 📖 page 463

Use your textbook to complete this exploration.

For problems 9–11, circle the answer.

9. $y = 3x$:

	direct	inverse
	linear	nonlinear
_x_-intercept:	(0, 0)	none

10. $y = \frac{1}{x}$:

	direct	inverse
	linear	nonlinear
_x_-intercept:	(0, 0)	none

11. A direct variation graph is: linear   nonlinear

      An inverse variation graph is: linear   nonlinear

      Graph contains origin: inverse   direct

      Graph never intersects _x_-axis: inverse   direct

Make a graph to determine whether the data show variation. If so, indicate the type of variation and write an equation of variation.

12. Graph the values in the table.

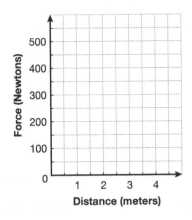

The graph shows _____ variation.

$$F = \dfrac{\square}{d}$$

13. Graph the values in the table.

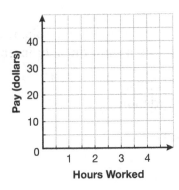

The graph shows _____ variation.

$$p = (\underline{\quad})h$$

Identify the constant of variation. Then write the equation of variation.

a. y varies directly with x; $y = 14$ when $x = 2$.

$y = kx$

$\underline{\hspace{1cm}} = k(\underline{\hspace{1cm}})$

$\underline{\hspace{1cm}} = k$

$y = (\underline{\hspace{1cm}})x$

b. w varies inversely with z; $w = -8$ when $z = 3$.

$w = \frac{k}{z}$

$\underline{\hspace{1cm}} = \frac{k}{\square}$

$\underline{\hspace{1cm}} = k$

$w = \frac{\square}{z}$

c. 3 tomatoes (t) make 9 servings (s) of salsa. *This is a direct variation relationship, s = kt.*

Write the direct variation equation.

$s = kt$

$\underline{\hspace{1cm}} = k(\underline{\hspace{1cm}})$

$\underline{\hspace{1cm}} = k$

$s = (\underline{\hspace{1cm}})t$

How many servings can 5 tomatoes make?

$s = (\underline{\hspace{1cm}})\underline{\hspace{1cm}}$

$s = \underline{\hspace{1cm}}$

d. The table compares the pressure P in atmospheres to the volume of oxygen V in liters at 0°C. Make a graph to determine whether the data show direct or inverse variation. If so, find the equation of variation.

Does the data show direct or inverse variation?

As the pressure gets greater, the volume decreases.

$\underline{\hspace{3cm}}$ variation

Write an equation for P, pressure, in terms of V volume.

Substitute an easy point, for example use (100, 0.7).

$P = \frac{k}{V}$

$0.7 = \frac{k}{\square}$

$\underline{\hspace{1cm}} = k$

$P = \frac{\square}{V}$

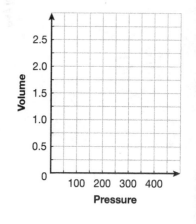

New Concepts

• Scatter plots relate two sets of (x, y) data points plotted on a coordinate plane. The line of best fit can be used to predict the value of one coordinate if the corresponding coordinate is known.

Math Language

A **trend line** is a line on a scatter plot that models the relationship between two sets of data.

A trend line that shows the most accurate relationship between two sets of data is the **line of best fit**.

A **correlation** is a measure of the strength and direction of the relationship between two sets of data. A **positive correlation** exists when both variables increase together. A **negative correlation** exists when one variable increases while the other decreases. **No correlation** exists when there is no pattern between the variables.

Example Graphing a Scatter plot and a Trend Line

Use the data in the table.

x	1	2	3	4	5	6
y	4	10	12	18	23	29

Make a scatter plot of the data. Then draw a trend line on the scatter plot.

Plot the points on a coordinate plane. Then draw a straight line as close to as many of the points as possible.

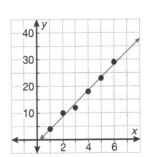

Find an equation for the trend line.
Use two points on or near the trend line to write an equation of the line.

$$m = \frac{y_2 - y_1}{x_2 - x_1}$$

$$= \frac{29 - 4}{6 - 1} = 5 \qquad \text{Find the slope of the line; use (1, 4) and (6, 29).}$$

$y - y_1 = m(x - x_1)$ Write the equation for the line.

$y - 4 = 5(x - 1)$ Substitute $m = 5$ and $(1, 4)$ for (x_1, y_1).

$y = 5x - 1$ Solve for y.

Example Identifying Correlations

State whether there is a positive correlation, a negative correlation, or no correlation between the data values.

x	10	9	8	7	6	5	4	3	2
y	60	63	72	75	77	81	83	89	92

As x-values decrease, the y-values increase.
There is a negative correlation.

Use the data in the table.

a. Make a scatter plot.
Then draw a trend line.

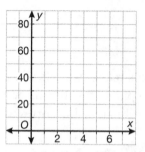

b. *Use two points on or near the line to find the approximate slope.*

Write an equation in slope-intercept form.

$$\frac{y_2 - y_1}{x_2 - x_1} = \frac{\square - \square}{\square - \square} = \frac{\square}{\square} = \underline{\hspace{1cm}} \qquad y\text{-intercept: } \underline{\hspace{2cm}}$$

The equation is _____.

c. Find the equation of the line of best fit for the data in the table.

The line of best fit is _____.

State whether there is a positive, negative, or no correlation between the data values.

d. The y-values decrease as the x-values _____. correlation: _____

e. The y-values _____ as the x-values _____. correlation: _____

f. As the temperature increases, the sale of sweaters _____. correlation: _____

g. As height increases, hair color _____. correlation: _____

Match each situation to the scatter plot that models it best.

h. As you exercise more, you burn _____ calories. Graph _____

i. As you use more detergent, the level in the bottle goes _____. Graph _____

j. As the population grows, the number of states _____. Graph _____

k. Draw the scatter plot and trend line.

l. predicted population in 2010 from trend line: _____

m. y = _____ + _____

n. predicted population in 2010 from line of best fit: _____

1. Make a scatter plot from the data in the table.

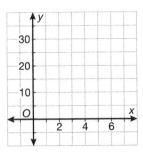

2. $y = 7 - x$

$y = \frac{1}{5}x + 1$

Substitute.

$(5 , 2)$ _____ a solution.

---

3. $5y - x = 5$

$y = 2x - 8$

Substitute.

$(5 , 2)$ _____ a solution.

4. *Since the radicals are the same, you can subtract the coefficients.*

$31\sqrt{5} - 13\sqrt{5} = $ ____$\sqrt{}$

---

5. *Simplify each radical.*

$\sqrt{27} = \sqrt{9 \cdot 3} = \sqrt{9} \cdot \sqrt{3} = $ ___$\sqrt{}$

$\sqrt{12} = \sqrt{4 \cdot 3} = \sqrt{} \cdot \sqrt{3} = $ ___$\sqrt{}$

Subtract.

___$\sqrt{}$ $-$ ___$\sqrt{}$ $= $ ___

6. *Add the equations to eliminate one variable. Solve for the other variable.*

$-y = x + 8$

$+(y = -x + 1)$

Since ____ = ____ ,

_____.

---

7. *Simplify the first equation.*

$6y - x = 12$

$6y = x + 12$

$y = $ ___$x + $ ____

Subtract first equation.

Since ____ = ____ ,

_____.

8. *Substitute the values for x and y into the equation:*

$y = \frac{k}{x}$.

Solve for k.

Substitute the value for k into $y = \frac{k}{x}$.

$y = \dfrac{\square}{\square}$

---

9. *Substitute the values for x and y into the equation: $y = \frac{k}{x}$.*

Solve for k.

Substitute the value for k into $y = \frac{k}{x}$.

$$y = \frac{\Box}{\Box}$$

10. Student _____ is correct. Student _____

divided the _____ side by _____

instead of _____.

11. 📝 *Make a simple sketch of the three correlations and test each one to see which one fits this situation.*

Circle the answer.

A positive   B negative

C constant   D none

12. a. 📝 Make a scatter plot.

b. *Look for a line of best fit. Is there a trend?*

_____

13. As one set of data values increases, the

other set of data values _____.

14. Student _____ is correct. Student _____ made

a calculation error in finding the

_____.

15. *Simplify each radical, if possible, then add or subtract as appropriate.*

$$\sqrt{27} \qquad \sqrt{3} \qquad \sqrt{12}$$

= _____ = _____ = _____

_____ − _____ + _____

= _____

16. *Look for two events that have a solution in common.*

Circle the answer.

A rolling a sum of 5 or a sum of 4 with two number cubes

B rolling a sum of 3 or a factor of 6 with two number cubes

C rolling two 5's or a sum of 8 with two number cubes

D two 4's or a sum of 9 with two number cubes

17. The probability of getting a heads or tails

is _____, because the only possible

outcomes are _____ or _____ and

they are mutually _____.

18. Let x = number of grams Paolo still needs to consume

$$x + \_\_\_\_ + \_\_\_\_ + \_\_\_\_ \bigcirc \_\_\_\_$$

$$x \bigcirc \_\_\_\_$$

19. *Find the slope of each line.*

$$\frac{y_2 - y_1}{x_2 - x_1} = \frac{\square - \square}{\square - \square} = \frac{\square}{\square} = \underline{\hspace{2cm}}$$

$$\frac{y_2 - y_1}{x_2 - x_1} = \frac{\square - \square}{\square - \square} = \frac{\square}{\square} = \underline{\hspace{2cm}}$$

The slopes are multiplicative inverses, so

the lines are _____.

20. Draw a scatter plot.

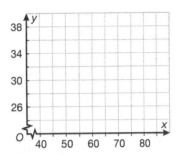

21. *When multiplying or dividing by a negative number, reverse the inequality sign.*

$11b < 5$

$b \bigcirc \dfrac{\square}{\square}$

In the solution, were both sides of the inequality

multiplied or divided by a negative number? _____.

The inequality sign _____ reversed.

22. The sides of an equilateral

triangle are _____.

$P = 3s$

$3s \bigcirc$ _____

$s \bigcirc$ _____

23. a. Use *s* for the amount of sales. Change the percent to a decimal.

_____ *s* $\bigcirc$ 250,000

b. *s* $\bigcirc$ _____

c. To spend $250,000 on marketing, the company needs to earn at least _____.

24. You could eliminate the variable that has the same _____ in both equations, or

eliminate the variable that has the same _____ in both equations but different signs.

You could also eliminate the variable whose coefficient in one equation is a _____

of the coefficient of the same variable in the other equation.

25. As the x-values increase, the y-values _____.

This shows a _____ correlation.

26. _____, a histogram _____ show exact values but rather shows how exact values are distributed within intervals. Thus, it _____ possible to find the mode from a histogram.

27. *Substitute and solve.*

$$2\pi\sqrt{\frac{1}{g}}$$

$$= 2\pi\sqrt{\frac{\square}{\square}}$$

$$= 2\pi\sqrt{\underline{\quad}}$$

$$= \underline{\quad}$$

28. *Write both equations in the form $y = ax + b$, where a is the annual increase and b is the starting population.*

a. $y =$ _____ $x +$ _____

$y =$ _____ $x +$ _____

b. Solve the system of equations.

The populations would be equal in _____.

29. Write the equation for direct variation.

Find k.

Substitute k into the equation for direct variation.

equation: _____

30. a. *Use FOIL.*

$(5x + 1)(2x + 2) =$ _____ + _____ + _____ + _____ = _____

b. *Multiply each term of the trinomial by each term of the binomial.*

$(6x + 4)($ _____ $) =$ _____ + _____ + _____ + _____ + _____

$=$ _____

Name _____

Factoring Trinomials: $x^2 + bx + c$ page 474

New Concepts

 **Exploration** 📖 page 474

Use your textbook to complete the exploration.

Math Language

A **binomial** is a polynomial with two terms.

- Many, but not all, trinomials can be factored.
- To factor a trinomial that is written in the standard form $x^2 + bx + c$, write it as the product of two binomials.

Example Factoring when *c* is Positive

Factor $x^2 + 9x + 18.$ $b = 9$ and $c = 18$

Because b is positive, it must be the sum of two positive numbers that are factors of c. Three pairs of positive numbers have a product of 18.

$(1)(18) = 18$ $(2)(9) = 18$ $(3)(6) = 18$

Only one pair of these numbers has a sum of 9.

$(1) + (18) = 19$ $(2) + (9) = 11$ $(3) + (6) = 9$

The constant terms in the binomials are 3 and 6.

The sum of the constant terms is 9 and their product is 18.

The factored form of $x^2 + 9x + 18$ is $(x + 3)(x + 6).$

Math Language

The **constant terms** of a binomial of the form $(x + a)(x + b)$ are **a** and **b.**

Example Factoring when *c* is Negative

Factor $x^2 + 3x - 10.$ $b = 3$ and $c = -10$

Four pairs of positive and negative numbers have a product of -10.

$(-1)(10)$ $(1)(-10)$ $(-2)(5)$ $(2)(-5)$

Only one pair of these numbers has a sum of 3.

$(-1) + 10 = 9$ $1 + (-10) = -9$

$(-2) + 5 = 3$ $(2)(-5) = -3$

The constant terms in the binomials are -2 and 5.

The sum of the constant terms is 3 and their product is -10.

$x^2 + 3x - 10 = (x - 2)(x + 5)$

Factor each trinomial.

a. *The constant terms have a product of 2.*

factors of 2: _____
The constant terms have a sum of 3.

____ + ____ = 3

factors of $x^2 + 3x + 2$: $(x + $___$)(x + $___$)$

b. *The constant terms have a product of 16.*

factors of 16: _____
The constant terms have a sum of −10.

____ + ____ = −10

factors of $x^2 - 10 + 16$: (_____)(_____)

c. *The constant terms have a product of −12.*

factors of −12: _____
The constant terms have a sum of 4.

____ + ____ = 4

factors of $x^2 + 4x - 12$: (_____)(_____)

d. *The constant terms have a product of −36.*

factors of −36: _____
The constant terms have a sum of −36.

____ + ____ = −36

factors of $x^2 - 5x - 36$: (_____)(_____)

e. *The constant terms have a product of $20y^2$.*

factors of $20y^2$: $1y \cdot 20y$, $20y \cdot 1y$, $2y \cdot 10y$, $10y \cdot 2y$, $4y \cdot 5y$, and $5y \cdot 4y$

$= b$ _____ + _____ $= 9y$ factors: $(x + $_____$)(x + $_____$)$

In f–g, find the factors that have a product of c and a sum of b.

f. $x^2 - xy - 12y^2$

(_____)(_____)

g. $12x + 20 + x^2$

(_____)(_____)

h. $7x + x^2 - 44$

(_____)(_____)

i. Evaluate $x^2 + x - 6$ and its factors for $x = 4$.

The factors of $x^2 + x - 6$ are (_____) and (_____).

Evaluate: $x^2 + x - 6$

____$^2 +$ ____ $- 6 =$ ____

(_____)(_____)

_____ = ____

1. $x + 2 + 3 > 6$

$x + \_\_\_\_ > 6$

$x \bigcirc \_\_\_\_$

$\begin{array}{ccccccc} \ & \ & \ & \ & \ \\ -2 & \ & 0 & \ & 2 & \ & 4 & \ & 6 \end{array}$

2. *The events are mutually exclusive.*

total outcomes (all letters): _____

number of vowels (v): ____

number of consonants (c): _____

$P(v \text{ or } c) = P(v) + P(c)$

$P(v \text{ or } c) = \_\_\_\_ + \_\_\_\_ = \_\_\_\_$

3. total number of outcomes: _____

\# of outcomes that are multiples of

4 (m): ____

\# of outcomes that are doubles (d): ____

The events are inclusive.

$P(m \text{ or } d) = P(m) + P(d) - P(m \text{ and } d)$

$P(\text{sum is multiple of } 4 \text{ or doubles}) =$

$\_\_\_\_ + \_\_\_\_ - (\_\_\_\_) = \_\_\_\_$

4. *The constant terms in the binomials have a product of 24 and a sum of 11.*

$x^2 + 11x + 24 = (_____)(_____)$

5. *Find the factors of −40 whose sum is −3.*

$k^2 - 3k - 40 = (_____)(_____)$

6. *Find the factors of 20 whose sum is 9.*

$m^2 + 9m + 20 = (_____)(_____)$

7. *Write in standard form.*

$x^2 + 33 + 14x = _____$

$= (_____)(_____)$

8. Student ____ is correct. Student ____

incorrectly _____ −6 and then

_____ instead of adding to get b.

9. *Factor. Then substitute.*

$x^2 + 15x + 54 = (_____)(_____)$

$x + \_\_\_\_ = 11 + \_\_\_\_ = _____$

$x + \_\_\_\_ = 11 + \_\_\_\_ = _____$

Answer: _____ × _____

10. Make a list of all the possible factors of 36.

_____ pairs of possible factors

11. *Factor.*

The shaded rectangles each represent the

term _____.

12. Graph the data.

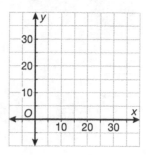

13. Student _____ is correct. The line _____ have to go through _____.

14. a. Graph the data.

b. Use two points that are on or close to the trend line. Use the slope, one of the points used to find the slope, and point-slope form to write an equation.

$$\frac{y_2 - y_1}{x_2 - x_1} = \frac{\boxed{}}{\boxed{}} = \underline{\hspace{1.5cm}}$$

equation: _____

c. The slope is close to _____ and the y-intercept is close to _____, so the equation is

_____ to the formula for the circumference of a circle.

15. *Visualize extending the line. Estimate the slope.*

a. When $x = 18$, $y \approx$ _____.

b. When $y = 50$, $x \approx$ _____.

16. _____ a perfect square _____

have a negative root because the product

of two _____ is _____.

17. *Multiply the second equation so it matches the form $y = bx + c$. Then compare.*

$$(\underline{\hspace{0.6cm}})\tfrac{1}{2}y = (\underline{\hspace{0.6cm}})\,3x + 1$$

$$y = \underline{\hspace{2.5cm}}$$

The airplane _____ be able to land

because _____.

18. Each system of paired equations will be

_____ and

_____.

19. *Parallel lines have the same slope. The slopes of perpendicular lines are negative reciprocals.*

slope of line 1: _____   slope of line 2: _____

The slopes are _____.   The lines are _____.

---

20. *Think of factors of 100.* Make a table.

---

21. Let x = the number of dimes and let y = the number of quarters.

The number of dimes plus the number of quarters is 124.

_____ + _____ = 124

The value of the dimes plus the value of the quarters is \$20.50.

0.1_____ + 0.25_____ = 20.50

Use elimination to solve the system.
Multiply the second equation by 10.

Solve for x and y. $x =$ _____ $y =$ _____

extra quarters: _____

---

22. *Factor the binomials, if possible, to find common factors.*

LCM: _____

23. *Combine the coefficients of like radicals.*

$20\sqrt{7} - 12\sqrt{7} + 2\sqrt{7} =$ _____

Answer: _____

---

24. median: _____

---

25. Let x = the larger number and let y = the smaller number.

The sum of the numbers is 36. $x + y =$ _____

The difference of the numbers is 8.   _____

Use substitution to solve.

$x =$ _____ $y =$ _____

$x \cdot y =$ _____

---

26. *In a direct variation, y = kx. Solve for k, then write the equation.*

$k =$ _____

equation: _____

27. *Find the constant of variation.*

$$y = kx$$

$$y = \underline{\quad}(\underline{\quad})$$

$$\underline{\quad} = k(\underline{\quad})$$

$$\underline{\quad} = k$$

object will travel _____

28. *When multiplying or dividing by a negative number, reverse the inequality sign.*

$$2 < -4a$$

a ◯ _____

29.

$$\frac{-1}{3} < \frac{-1}{9}p$$

$$(\underline{\quad})\frac{-1}{3} < (\underline{\quad})\frac{-1}{9}p$$

p ◯ _____

30. *Twenty percent of the cost of the house cannot be more than $35,000.*

Let x = cost of house

_____ x ◯ _____

x ◯ _____

The house must cost ≤ _____.

Name _____

Solving Compound Inequalities page 481

New Concepts

- A compound inequality is two inequalities combined with the word AND or OR.

Example Solving Conjunctions

Solve the conjunction as a statement with two inequality signs.

$$30 \leq 10 + 0.10x \quad \text{AND} \quad 10 + 0.10x \leq 40$$

$$20 \leq 0.10x \qquad \text{AND} \qquad 0.10x \leq 30$$

$$200 \leq x \qquad \text{AND} \qquad x \leq 300$$

The solution is $\mathbf{200 \leq x \leq 300}$. Between 200 and 300 minutes, inclusive, can be used monthly.

Example Solving Disjunctions

Solve the disjunction. $x - 3 < -5$ OR $-2x < -6$

Solve the two inequalities separately.

$$x - 3 < -5 \qquad \text{OR} \qquad -2x < -6$$

$$x < -2 \qquad \text{OR} \qquad x > 3$$

The solution is $\boldsymbol{x < -2}$ **OR** $\boldsymbol{x > 3}$.

Example Writing a Compound Inequality from a Graph

Write a compound inequality that describes the graph.

Because there is an open circle on $x = -1$, that value is not included in the solution.

Unlike $x = -1$, there is a filled circle on $x = 5$, so that value is included in the solution.

The compound inequality is $\boldsymbol{-1 < x \leq 5}$ **or** $\boldsymbol{x > -1}$ **AND** $\boldsymbol{x \leq 5}$.

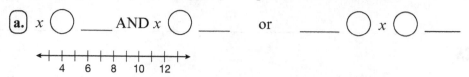

Lesson Practice 📖 page 483

Write and graph a compound inequality to represent each statement.

a. $x \bigcirc$ ____ AND $x \bigcirc$ ____   or   ____ $\bigcirc$ $x \bigcirc$ ____

<!-- number line 4 6 8 10 12 -->

b. ____ $\leq t \leq$ ____

<!-- number line 16 18 20 22 -->

c. ____ $\leq 20 + 0.05x \leq$ ____ ; ____ $\leq x \leq$ ____

d. $x <$ ____ OR $x >$ ____

<!-- number line 0 2 4 6 8 10 -->

e. $x \leq$ ____ OR $x \geq$ ____

<!-- number line -2 0 2 4 6 8 -->

f. $5x > -5$ OR $6x < -18$

$x \bigcirc$ ____ OR $x \bigcirc$ ____

Write a compound inequality that describes each graph.

g. $x \leq$ ____ OR $x >$ ____

h. $8 \bigcirc x \bigcirc 12$

or $x \bigcirc$ ____ AND $x \bigcirc 12$

1. *Multiply the first equation by 2 to eliminate the fraction. Add the equations to solve for y.*

$$(2)\left(-\tfrac{1}{2}x\right) + (2)y = (2)5 \longrightarrow \underline{\hspace{3cm}} = \underline{\hspace{1.5cm}}$$

$$x + \quad y = 5 \longrightarrow +(\quad x + \quad y = \quad 5)$$

$$\underline{\hspace{3cm}} = \underline{\hspace{1.5cm}}$$

$$y = \underline{\hspace{1.5cm}}$$

Substitute y to solve for x.

$$x + y = 5 \longrightarrow x + \underline{\hspace{0.7cm}} = 5 \longrightarrow x = \underline{\hspace{1cm}}$$

The equations are $\underline{\hspace{3cm}}$ and $\underline{\hspace{3cm}}$.

---

2. *Write the second equation in slope-intercept form.*

The equations are $\underline{\hspace{3cm}}$.

---

3. $x + 2 - 3 \le 6$

$x \underline{\hspace{1.5cm}} \le 6$

$x \bigcirc \underline{\hspace{0.8cm}}$

4. $z + 5 \ge 1.5$

$z \bigcirc \underline{\hspace{1.5cm}}$

---

5. *Solve two separate inequalities.*

$$-15 \le 2x + 7 \le -9$$

$$-15 \le 2x + 7 \qquad 2x + 7 \le -9$$

$$\underline{\hspace{1cm}} \le 2x \qquad\qquad 2x \le \underline{\hspace{1cm}}$$

$$\underline{\hspace{1cm}} \bigcirc x \qquad\qquad x \bigcirc \underline{\hspace{1cm}}$$

$$\underline{\hspace{1cm}} \le x \le \underline{\hspace{1cm}}$$

6. $x - 3 \ge 4 \qquad$ OR $\quad x + 2 < -5$

$x \ge \underline{\hspace{1cm}} \qquad$ OR $\quad x \bigcirc \underline{\hspace{1cm}}$

$\underline{\hspace{2cm}}$ OR $\underline{\hspace{2cm}}$

---

7. Graph. $-4 \le x \le 5$

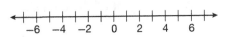

8. *"No more than" and "no less than" include the numbers they refer to.*

$x \bigcirc \underline{\hspace{1cm}}$ OR $x \bigcirc \underline{\hspace{1cm}}$

---

9. *Since the lines of the solution are heading in opposite directions, the inequality is a disjunction, which implies OR.*

Circle the answer.

A $x < -1$ OR $x > 3$

B $x > -1$ OR $x < 3$

C $x < -1$ AND $x > 3$

D $x > -1$ AND $x < 3$

10. cannot hear below 0:

_____

pain above 120:

_____

inequality: _____

11. AND shows the _____ of two inequalities. OR shows the _____ of two inequalities.

12. *When the constants are either both positive or both negative, the middle term determines the sign.*

$x^2 - 12x + 32 = ($_____$)($_____$)$

13. *The indices and radicands are the same, so add the coefficients.*

$x\sqrt[3]{xy} + x\sqrt[3]{xy} =$ _____

14. *A = lw. Factor the trinomial to find the binomial length and width of the rectangle.*

$x^2 + 12x + 27 = ($_____$)($_____$)$

15. *Combine like terms first. Then factor.*

$8x + x^2 - 4 - 5x =$ _____

$= ($_____$)($_____$)$

16. *Look for a first term and a third term that are both perfect squares.*

Circle the answer.

A $(x^2 + 7x - 8)$ **B** $(x^2 + 6x + 9)$

C $(x^2 + 9x + 8)$ **D** $(x^2 + 7x + 12)$

17. *Use two points on the line to find the slope.*

$\dfrac{y_2 - y_1}{x_2 - x_1} = \dfrac{\square - \square}{\square - \square} =$ _____

y-intercept: _____

$y =$ _____

18. Student _____ is correct. Student _____ did not arrange the x data in ascending order so that the corresponding values in the other set would also _____. A scatter plot of the data shows a _____ correlation even though the data values are not in increasing order.

19. *Round the weights to the nearest whole number.*

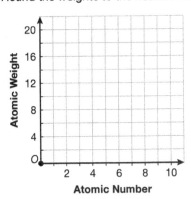

20. *Attach the negative sign in the fraction to the 12, not the n. When multiplying by a negative, reverse the inequality sign.*

Circle the answer.

A $n < -432$ **B** $n > -432$

C $n < 432$ **D** $n > 432$

21. In both cases, _____ to solve.

In the inequality, _____

because you are dividing by a _____

_____ .

22. *Add the probabilities.*

$$\frac{\square}{20} + \frac{\square}{10}$$

$$= \frac{\square}{20} + \frac{\square}{20} = \frac{\square}{\square}$$

23. *Find the multiples of 2 and 3.*

1 2 3 4 5 6 7 8 9 10 11 12 13 14 15 16 17 18 19 20

$$= \frac{\square}{20}$$

24. a. ✎ Draw the coordinate grid and graph the lines.

b. Find the slope and the *y*-intercept of each line.

slope of Line 1 =   slope of Line 2 =

$$\frac{y_2 - y_1}{x_2 - x_1} = \frac{\square - \square}{\square - \square} = \underline{\hspace{1cm}} \qquad \frac{y_2 - y_1}{x_2 - x_1} = \frac{\square - \square}{\square - \square} = \underline{\hspace{1cm}}$$

Use point-slope form to get equations of lines.

equation of Line 1: _____   equation of Line 2: _____

c. *Check whether the slopes are negative reciprocals.*

The lines _____ perpendicular, because _____

_____

_____ .

25. *Solve for k. Then substitute.*

$$F = \frac{k}{d^2} \qquad\qquad F = \frac{k}{d^2}$$

$$\underline{\hspace{2cm}} = \frac{k}{\square^2} \qquad\qquad \underline{\hspace{2cm}} = \frac{\square}{d^2}$$

$$\underline{\hspace{1.5cm}}(\underline{\hspace{1cm}})^2 = k \qquad\qquad \underline{\hspace{1.5cm}}d^2 = \underline{\hspace{1cm}}$$

$$\underline{\hspace{2cm}} = k \qquad\qquad d^2 = \underline{\hspace{1.5cm}} \div \underline{\hspace{1.5cm}}$$

$$d = \underline{\hspace{2cm}}$$

---

26. *Multiply the first equation by 9.*   *Subtract to solve for g.*   *Substitute.*

$$n + g = 0.7 \qquad \longrightarrow$$

$$9n + 19g = 10.3 \qquad \longrightarrow \qquad \underline{\hspace{3cm}}$$

$$-(9n + 19g = 10.3)$$

$$\underline{\hspace{1cm}}g = \underline{\hspace{1.5cm}}$$

$$g = \underline{\hspace{1.5cm}}$$

$$n + \underline{\hspace{1.5cm}} = 0.7$$

$$n = \underline{\hspace{1cm}}$$

$$\underline{\hspace{2cm}} \text{ of gold, } \underline{\hspace{2cm}} \text{ of nickel}$$

---

27. $A = l \cdot w = (\underline{\hspace{2cm}})(\underline{\hspace{2cm}})$

$$= \underline{\hspace{3cm}}$$

28. Distribute.

$$(\underline{\hspace{0.5cm}})(\underline{\hspace{1.5cm}}) + (\underline{\hspace{0.5cm}})(\underline{\hspace{1.5cm}})$$

$$= \underline{\hspace{5cm}}$$

$$= \underline{\hspace{5cm}}$$

---

29. *Factor each expression.*

$$24r - 6d = (\underline{\hspace{0.8cm}})(\underline{\hspace{1.5cm}})$$

$$20r - 5d = (\underline{\hspace{0.8cm}})(\underline{\hspace{1.5cm}})$$

$$LCM = (\underline{\hspace{0.6cm}} \cdot \underline{\hspace{0.6cm}})(\underline{\hspace{0.8cm}})$$

$$= \underline{\hspace{1.5cm}}$$

30. *Factor each term to find the LCM.*

$$14bn = \underline{\hspace{3cm}}$$

$$38b^9n = \underline{\hspace{3cm}}$$

$$LCM = \underline{\hspace{3cm}} \text{ books}$$

Name _____

Solving Absolute-Value Equations page 487

New Concepts

- An absolute-value equation is an equation with one or more absolute-value expressions.

- The equation $|x| = 5$ or $= |x - 0| = 5$ translates to:

  the distance between a number x and 0 is 5.

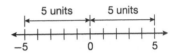

The distance between -5 and 0 equals 5 units and the distance between 5 and 0 equals 5 units. Therefore $x = -5$ or $x = 5$.

- The equation $|x + 2| = 6$ or $|x - (-2)| = 6$ translates to:

  the distance between a number x and -2 is 6.

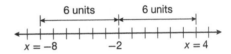

The distance between -8 and -2 equals 6 units and the distance between 4 and -2 equals 6 units. Therefore $x = -8$ or $x = 4$.

> **Math Language**
>
> **Absolute value** is the distance of a number from zero on the number line. Since distance cannot be a negative value, an absolute value expression is always positive.

Example **Isolating the Absolute Value**

Solve $4|x - 2| = 80$.

Isolate the absolute value.

$\dfrac{4|x - 2|}{4} = \dfrac{80}{4}$ *Division Property of Equality*

$|x - 2| = 20$ *Simplify.*

Write $|x - 2| = 20$ as two equations.

$x - 2 = 20$	or	$x - 2 = -20$
$x = 22$ *Add 2 to both sides.*		$x = -18$

The solution is **{22, −18}**.

Solve.

a. $|x| = 11$

$x = 11$ or $x = -11$

{_____, _____}

b. $|q + 3| = 6$

$q + 3 = 6$ or $q + 3 = -6$

$q = 3$ or $q =$ _____

{3, _____}

c. $4|y| = 24$

$\dfrac{4|y|}{4} = \dfrac{24}{\square}$

$y = 6$ or $y =$ _____

{_____, _____}

d. $5|z - 3| = 20$

$\dfrac{5|z - 3|}{5} = \dfrac{20}{\square}$

$|z - 3| =$ _____

$z = 7$ or $z =$ _____   {_____, _____}

e. $|x - 5| + 3 = 3$

$|x - 5| =$ _____

$x =$ _____   {_____}

f. $|x - 5| = -1$

_____ because the value cannot be

_____.

g. $|x -$ _____ $| =$ _____

$x =$ _____ or $x =$ _____

_____ or _____

The distance between a number and 30 is 0.4

Set up and solve the two equations.

Practice page 490

1. *The third term is negative.*

$x^2 + 12x - 28 = ($ _____ $)($ _____ $)$

2. $ax^2 + bx + c$ *form*

$15x + 50 + x^2 =$ _____

$= ($ _____ $)($ _____ $)$

3. $18 + x^2 + 11x =$ _____

$= ($ _____ $)($ _____ $)$

4. $3x - 18 + x^2 =$ _____

$= ($ _____ $)($ _____ $)$

---

5. *Solve both equations.*

$|n| = 13$

_____ = _____ or _____ = _____

Solution: {_____, _____}

6. $|x + 7| = 3$

$x + 7 =$ _____ $x + 7 =$ _____

$x =$ _____ or $x =$ _____

Solution: {_____, _____}

---

7. *Multiply the second equation by 2.*

$-2y + 3x = 4 \longrightarrow -2y + 3x = 4$

$2\left(-y + \frac{3}{2}x = 2\right) \longrightarrow -\square y + \square x = \square$

Solution: $y =$ _____

8. *The distance from a number and 12 is 2.*

$|x - \underline{\quad}| = \underline{\quad}$

$x - \underline{\quad} = \underline{\quad}$ or $x - \underline{\quad} = -\underline{\quad}$

$h = \underline{\quad}$ or $h = \underline{\quad}$

---

9. When the equation is evaluated for

$x = -3$, the right side of the equation

equals _____. This is impossible because

_____.

10. 📖 Graph.

Solve $|x - 3| = 5$.

The distance between a number x and 3 is 5.

Solution: {_____, _____}

11. a. $C = \pi d \qquad d_{\text{old}} = 10 \text{ cm}$

$C_{\text{new}} = d_{\text{old}} \pi \pm 5 = 10\pi \pm 5$

$C_{\text{new}} = \pi d_{\text{new}} \qquad \underline{\quad} \pi \pm 5 = \pi d_{\text{new}}$

Substitute for C_{new}. Then solve for d_{new}.

$d_{\text{new}} = \underline{\quad} \pm \frac{5}{\pi}$

Since there is $\pm$, isolate the $\pm$constant and set up an absolute value statement.

$|d_{\text{new}} - \underline{\quad}| = \underline{\quad}$

b. 📖 Determine the new diameters by

solving the absolute value statement.

$d_{\text{new}} = \underline{\quad}$ or $d_{\text{new}} = \underline{\quad}$

12. Graph the compound inequality.

$x \geq 5$ or $x < 0$

13. $6x < 12$ OR $3x > 15$

$x \bigcirc \underline{\quad}$ OR $x \bigcirc \underline{\quad}$

14. Student $\underline{\quad}$ is correct. Student $\underline{\quad}$

incorrectly wrote the term $\underline{\qquad}$

as $\underline{\quad}$.

15. difference of two sides: $\underline{\qquad}$

sum of two sides: $\underline{\qquad}$

$\underline{\quad} < x < \underline{\quad}$

16. **a.** $3x > 45$ OR $-2x \geq 24$

$x \bigcirc \underline{\quad}$ OR $x \bigcirc \underline{\quad}$

b. Graph the solution.

17. *The third term is negative, so the second term of one binomial must be negative.*

$x^2 - 3x - 40$

$= (x + \underline{\quad})(x - \underline{\quad})$

18. **a.** $x^2 + 9x + 20 = (\underline{\qquad})(\underline{\qquad})$

$x^2 + 21x + 20 = (\underline{\qquad})(\underline{\qquad})$

b. The $\underline{\qquad}$ set because the dimensions described by the $\underline{\qquad}$ are

much longer than they are $\underline{\qquad}$.

19. *See page 14 in the* Student Reference Guide.

A $\underline{\qquad}$ is a graph made up of separate, disconnected points.

Circle the answer.

A discrete graph   **B** continuous graph   **C** trend graph   **D** linear graph

20. When multiplying or dividing by a negative number, reverse the inequality.

$-\frac{2}{3}c \le 6$

$c \bigcirc$ _____

_____, $c \bigcirc -9$

21. $s = \sqrt{144}$

$=$ _____

$P = 4s$

$P =$ _____ ▨

---

22. Circle the sums of 9. Then circle all the other outcomes in which one or both addends are odd numbers.

Roll of Cube 2

	1	**2**	**3**	**4**	**5**	**6**
1	2	3	4	5	6	7
2	3	4	5	6	7	8
3	4	5	6	7	8	9
4	5	6	7	8	9	10
5	6	7	8	9	10	11
6	7	8	9	10	11	12

(Roll of Cube 1 along the left)

$P(\text{odd or } 9) = P(\text{odd}) + P(9) - P(\text{odd and } 9)$

$=$ _____ $+$ _____ $-$ _____

$=$ _____

$=$ _____ *Simplify.*

---

23. a. $d = 10$

$y = \$0.25d + \$0.05$

$y =$ ____(____) $+$ ____

$y =$ ____ $+$ ____

$y =$ ▨ _____

b. $d = 30$

$y = \$0.25d + \$0.05$

$y =$ ____(____) $+$ ____

$y =$ ____ $+$ ____

$y =$ ▨ _____

c. The equations are

_____ and

_____.

---

24. Compare the numerators and the denominators.

$\frac{x}{y} \bigcirc \frac{a}{b}$ because ____ will have

a _____ numerator and a

_____ denominator than ____.

25. When $x = 40$, then $y \approx$ _____.

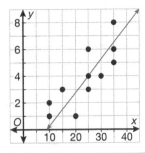

---

26. Write the second equation in slope intercept form.

$y = \frac{x}{4} - 2$

$4y = x + 8 \;\longrightarrow\; y =$ _____

_____, the lines are _____

because the slopes are _____ and the

y-intercepts are_____.

27. *Write an inverse variation and solve.*

y = number of people
x = number of days

$k = yx$ $\qquad k = $ _____

$y = \dfrac{\square}{x}$

$y = \dfrac{\square}{5}$

$y = $ _____

It would take _____ people 5 days to build the house.

28. $A = s^2$, *since s is positive* $s = \sqrt{A}$.

a. $\sqrt{800} = \sqrt{} \cdot \sqrt{}$

$= $ _____

b. $\sqrt{2}$ *is about 1.4.*

$= \underline{}\sqrt{} \approx \underline{}$ cm

_____ cm ◯ 30 cm

_____ cm ◯ 25 cm

c. The book _____ fit because

_____.

29. *Solve for y in terms of x.*

$3x + y = 13$

$y = $ _____

Substitute the expression and solve for x.

$2x - 4y = 4$

$2x - 4(\underline{}) = 4$

$x = $ _____

Substitute x and solve for y.

$3x + y = 13$

$3(\underline{}) + y = 13$

$y = $ _____

Solution: (_____, _____)

30. *Distribute.*

$(x + 8)(6x^2 + 6x + 6) = \underline{}(6x^2 + 6x + 6) + \underline{}(6x^2 + 6x + 6)$

$= \underline{} + \underline{}$

$= \underline{}$

Name _____

Factoring Trinomials: $ax^2 + bx + c$ page 493

New Concepts

- When the coefficient of the x^2 term of a trinomial is greater than 1, the first term must also be used to find the factors.

Example **Factoring when b and c are Positive**

Factor completely. $2x^2 + 7x + 5$

Since $2x^2$ is the product of $(2x)$ and (x), write $(2x \quad)(x \quad)$.

The third term of the trinomial, 5, is the product of the last terms in the binomials. List the pairs of numbers that give a product of 5.

$(1)(5) \qquad (5)(1) \qquad (-1)(-5) \qquad (-5)(-1)$

Because the middle term, $7x$, is positive, eliminate the pairs of negative numbers. Check the other pairs to see which results in $7x$.

$(2x + 1)(x + 5) \qquad\qquad (2x + 5)(x + 1)$

$\qquad\quad 1x \qquad\qquad\qquad\qquad\quad 5x$

$\qquad \underline{+ 10x} \qquad\qquad\qquad\qquad \underline{+ 2x}$

$\qquad\quad 11x \qquad\qquad\qquad\qquad\quad 7x$

$2x^2 + 7x + 5$

$= (2x + 5)(x + 1)$

Example **Factoring when c is Negative**

Factor completely. $4x^2 + 4x - 3$

The first term of the trinomial, $4x^2$, is the product of $(4x)(x)$ and $(2x)(2x)$. So, write $(4x \quad)(x \quad)$ and $(2x \quad)(2x \quad)$.

The trinomial has a negative last term, -3. One of the constants in the binomials is negative.

$(1)(-3) \qquad (-1)(3) \qquad (3)(-1) \qquad (-3)(1)$

Check each pair to see which results in the middle term, $4x$.

Possibilities	Middle Term	Possibilities	Middle Term
$(4x + 1)(x - 3)$	$-11x$	$(4x - 3)(x + 1)$	x
$(4x + 3)(x - 1)$	$-x$	$(2x + 1)(2x - 3)$	$-4x$
$(4x - 1)(x + 3)$	$11x$	$(2x + 3)(2x - 1)$	$4x$ ✓

$4x^2 + 4x - 3$

$= (2x + 3)(2x - 1)$

Factor completely.

a. $9x^2 + 38x + 8$

All the terms are positive so the factors will be positive.

possible factors:

first term: $(1x)(9x)$ or (____)(____)

last term: $(1)(8)$ or (____)(____)

Find two pairs of terms whose products when added equal the middle term.

1 and 9   3 and 3   9 and 1
⟩⟨ $8 + 9 = 17$ ⟩⟨ $12 + 6 = 18$ ⟩⟨ $36 + 2 = 38$
1 and 8   2 and 4   2 and 4

Write the binomial factors: (____$x +$ ____)(____$x +$ ____)

b. $10x^2 - 23x + 12$

The trinomial has a negative middle term and a positive last term. Both constants in the binomial factors are negative.

(____$x -$ ____)(____$x -$ ____)

c. $3x^2 + 5x - 2$

The trinomial has a negative last term. One of the constants in the binomial factors is negative.

(____$x +$ ____)(____$x -$ ____)

d. $6x^2 - 5x - 4$

The trinomial has a negative last term. One of the constants in the binomial factors is negative.

(_____)(_____)

e. $6x^2 + 11xy + 4y^2$

The trinomial has two variables. Include both variables in the binomial factors.

(____$x +$ ____y) (____$x +$ ____y)

f. *Write in standard form. Then factor.*

$-13x + 14x^2 + 3$

= _____

= (_____)(_____)

1. List the factors of the first and last terms. Find two pairs of terms whose products add to equal the middle term of the expression.

$6x^2 + 13x + 6 = ($ _____ $)($ _____ $)$

2. The trinomial has a negative last term. One of the constants in a binomial is negative.

$3x^2 - 14x - 5 = ($ _____ $)($ _____ $)$

3. Write in standard form.

$18 - 15x + 2x^2 =$ _____

$= ($ _____ $)($ _____ $)$

4. $-15 + 7x + 2x^2 =$ _____

$= ($ _____ $)($ _____ $)$

5. Factor out the common radical.

$22c\sqrt{de} - 9\sqrt{de}$

$= ($ _____ $)$ _____

6. Combine coefficients of like radicals.

$8\sqrt{7} - 4\sqrt{11} - 3\sqrt{7} + 7\sqrt{11} =$ _____

7. Since the coefficient of x^2 is not _____,

b is found by _____ the

_____ of the factors of c and

the factors of a.

8. There are four possible factor pairs. Show it is impossible to have a middle term of $-12x$.

$($ _____ $)($ _____ $) =$ _____

$($ _____ $)($ _____ $) =$ _____

$($ _____ $)($ _____ $) =$ _____

$($ _____ $)($ _____ $) =$ _____

9. Substitute.

Circle the answer.

A 2   **B** 10   **C** 42   **D** 50

10. Think of a graph of a direct variation that you made. Describe the graph. Remember $y = kx$.

The graph is a _____.

11. Find the numbers that are 5 units from zero.

$|z| = 5$ $z =$ _____ or $z =$ _____

Solution set: $\{$ ____ , ____ $\}$

12. *All four sides of the square must change at the same time, so the difference between the maximum (or minimum) perimeter and the set perimeter is 4 times 1.5.*

   a. $|x - 36| = $ _____ (_____)

   b. $x - 36 = $ _____ $x - 36 = -$_____

            $x = $ _____ $x = $ _____

       Solution set: {_____, _____}

---

13. a. $|x + 2| + 6 = 17$

          $|x + 2| = $ _____

   b. _____ = _____   _____ = $-$_____

   c. Solution set: {_____, _____}

---

14. *The difference between the maximum length (or the minimum length) and the new length is a 0.12% increase or decrease of the current length.*

$|x - $ _____ $| = $ _____ (L)

15. *Isolate x in the center of the inequality by performing the same operation on each part of the inequality.*

$-14 \leq -3x + 10 \leq -5$

_____ ◯ x ◯ _____

---

16. Student _____ is correct. Student _____

shaded in the part of the number line

that _____ included in the

solution set.

17. *There are two ways to write the inequality.*

_____ ◯ x ◯ _____

x ◯ _____ AND x ◯ _____

---

18. Factor.

$x^2 + 5x - 6 = ($ _____ $)($ _____ $)$

Answer: _____

19. *Substitute.*

$x < 3$ $x > 6$

____ < 3 ____ > 6

_____   _____
    (True or false)

2 is a solution of the compound inequality

because the inequality uses the word _____

The solution needs to be true for

_____.

---

20. *Choose two points on the line to find the slope. Then use the slope, one of the points, and point-slope form to write the equation.*

$y =$ _____

21. Let $x =$ number of servings

____x ◯ ____

He can make _____ servings or

_____.

---

22. Let $x =$ # of minutes per lap

____x ◯ ____

x ◯ ____

____ $\cdot 60 =$ ____ _____ than _____

23. *Distance = rate · time*

equation: _____

_____ variation

_____ is the constant.

---

24. *The events are inclusive.*

$P(odd \ or \ 1) = P(odd) + P(1) - P(odd \ and \ 1)$

$\dfrac{\square}{\square} + \dfrac{\square}{\square} - \dfrac{\square}{\square}$

$=$ ____

25. *Use substitution to solve the system.*

$y = 250 + 50w$
$y = 800$

_____ $= 250 + 50w$

_____

---

26. *Draw a sketch on a coordinate grid.*

The equations have _____ point(s) in

common, so they are _____

and _____.

27. a. (____)$a +$ (____)b ◯ _____

   b. She _____ buy 4 from each bin.

   c. $7($____$) + 5(b)$ ◯ 45

           b ◯ ____

---

28. a. Complete the histogram.

b. The histogram reports only days with

rainfall. It does not account for

_____.

It _____ the best representation

for the data.

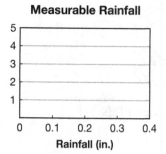

Measurable Rainfall

29. *Use the patterns of special products. Notice that the first and last terms are the same in each binomial.*

$(4y - 4)(4y + 4)$

$=$ _____

30. *Choose one equation to simplify.*

$8x + 4y = 4$

$4y =$ _____

$y =$ _____

Substitute into the other equation and solve.

$5x + 3($ _____ $) = 1$

$5x +$ _____ $= 1$

_____ $x +$ _____ $= 1$

_____ $x =$ _____

$x =$ _____

Substitute into the first equation to find y.

$8x + 4y = 4$

$8($ _____ $) + 4y = 4$

_____ $+ 4y = 4$

$4y =$ _____

$y =$ _____

Solution set: { _____ , _____ }

New Concepts

• Radical expressions can sometimes be simplified by using the Product Property of Radicals.

Product Property of Radicals
The square root of a product equals the product of the square roots of the factors. $$\sqrt{ab} = \sqrt{a} \cdot \sqrt{b} \text{ where } a \geq 0 \text{ and } b \geq 0.$$

• For example, $\sqrt{(8)(2)} = \sqrt{8} \cdot \sqrt{2}$.

Example **Simplifying Radical Expressions**

Simplify.

$6\sqrt{2} \cdot 4\sqrt{3}$

$= 6 \cdot 4\sqrt{2 \cdot 3}$ *Product Property of Radicals*

$= 24\sqrt{6}$ *Simplify.*

Simplify.

$\left(6\sqrt{3}\right)^2$

$= (6)^2\left(\sqrt{3}\right)^2$ *Power of a Product Property*

$= 36\sqrt{9}$ *Square each factor.*

$= 36 \cdot 3 = 108$ *Simplify. Multiply.*

Example **Applying the Distributive Property**

Simplify.

$\sqrt{2}\left(3 + \sqrt{6}\right)$

$= 3\sqrt{2} + \sqrt{12}$ *Distribute.*

$= 3\sqrt{2} + 2\sqrt{3}$ *Simplify.*

Example **Multiplying Binomials with Radicals**

Simplify.

$\left(4 + \sqrt{9}\right)\left(2 - \sqrt{6}\right)$

$= 8 - 4\sqrt{6} + 2\sqrt{9} - \sqrt{54}$ *Use FOIL.*

$= 8 - 4\sqrt{6} + 6 - 3\sqrt{6}$ *Simplify the radicals.*

$= 14 - 7\sqrt{6}$ *Combine like terms.*

Simplify.

a. $\sqrt{5} \cdot \sqrt{3}$

$= \sqrt{(5)(\underline{\hspace{1cm}})}$

$= \sqrt{\underline{\hspace{1cm}}}$

b. $3\sqrt{7} \cdot 2\sqrt{3}$

$= 3 \cdot \underline{\hspace{0.5cm}} \cdot \sqrt{(\underline{\hspace{0.5cm}})(3)}$

$= \underline{\hspace{0.5cm}}\sqrt{\underline{\hspace{0.5cm}}}$

c. $(3\sqrt{6})^2$

$= (3)^2 \cdot (\underline{\hspace{0.5cm}})^2$

$= \underline{\hspace{0.5cm}} \cdot \underline{\hspace{0.5cm}} = \underline{\hspace{0.5cm}}$

d. $3\sqrt{3x} \cdot \sqrt{2x}$

$= \underline{\hspace{0.5cm}} \cdot \sqrt{(\underline{\hspace{0.5cm}}x)(\underline{\hspace{0.5cm}}x)}$

$= 3 \cdot \sqrt{\underline{\hspace{0.5cm}}x^2} = \underline{\hspace{0.5cm}}x\sqrt{\underline{\hspace{0.5cm}}}$

e. $\sqrt{7}(2 + \sqrt{4})$

$= \sqrt{7}(2 + \underline{\hspace{0.5cm}})$

$= \sqrt{7}(\underline{\hspace{0.5cm}}) = \underline{\hspace{0.5cm}}\sqrt{7}$

f. $\sqrt{5}(\sqrt{4} - \sqrt{3})$

Distribute.

$= \underline{\hspace{0.5cm}}\sqrt{5} - \sqrt{(5 \cdot \underline{\hspace{0.5cm}})}$

$= \underline{\hspace{0.5cm}}\sqrt{5} - \sqrt{\underline{\hspace{0.5cm}}}$

g. $(5 + \sqrt{9})(4 - \sqrt{6})$

$= (5 + \underline{\hspace{0.5cm}})(4 - \sqrt{6})$

$= \underline{\hspace{0.5cm}}(4 - \sqrt{6})$

$= \underline{\hspace{0.5cm}} - \underline{\hspace{0.5cm}}\sqrt{6}$

h. $(4 - \sqrt{7})^2$

$= (4 - \sqrt{7})(\underline{\hspace{0.5cm}} - \sqrt{\underline{\hspace{0.5cm}}})$

Use FOIL.

$= 16 - \underline{\hspace{0.5cm}}\sqrt{\underline{\hspace{0.5cm}}} - 4\sqrt{7} + \underline{\hspace{0.5cm}}$

$= \underline{\hspace{0.5cm}} - \underline{\hspace{0.5cm}}\sqrt{7}$

i. The side length of a square dance floor is $32 + \sqrt{13}$. What is the area of the dance floor?

$A = s^2 = (\underline{\hspace{0.5cm}} + \sqrt{\underline{\hspace{0.5cm}}})^2$

$(a + b)^2 = a^2 + 2ab + b^2$

$(32 + \sqrt{13})^2 = 1024 + 2(\underline{\hspace{0.5cm}})(\sqrt{\underline{\hspace{0.5cm}}}) + \underline{\hspace{0.5cm}}$

$= \underline{\hspace{0.5cm}} + \underline{\hspace{0.5cm}}\sqrt{\underline{\hspace{0.5cm}}}$

1. When multiplying or dividing by a negative number, reverse the inequality sign.

$$\frac{5}{6} \le -2p$$

$$\frac{5}{6} \cdot \boxed{} \bigcirc p$$

2. $|x + 4| = 5$

$x + 4 = $ _____ or $x + 4 = -$_____

$x = $ _____ or $x = $ _____

Solution set: {_____, _____}

3. The last term is positive, and the middle term is negative. Both constants in the binomial factors are negative.

$$12x^2 - 25x + 7$$

factors of 12: _____

factors of 7: _____ and _____

(_____x $\bigcirc$ _____)(_____x $\bigcirc$ _____)

4. $x^2 + 10x - 39$

factors of 39: _____ and _____

Factors of 39 whose difference is 10.

(x $\bigcirc$ _____)(x $\bigcirc$ _____)

5. $5z^2 + 2z - 7$

The last term is negative. One of the constants in the binomial factors is negative.

factors of 5: _____ and _____

factors of 7: _____ and _____

(_____x $\bigcirc$ _____)(_____x $\bigcirc$ _____)

6. $3x^2 + 25x - 18$

factors of 3: _____ and _____

factors of 18: _____

(_____x $\bigcirc$ _____)(_____x $\bigcirc$ _____)

7. Product of numbers outside the radical:

_____ · _____ · _____ · _____ = _____

Product of radicands:

$$\sqrt{\underline{} \cdot \underline{} \cdot \underline{} \cdot \underline{}} = \sqrt{\underline{}}$$

$$= \underline{} \sqrt{\underline{}}$$

Product of the products:

$$\underline{} \cdot \underline{} \sqrt{\underline{}} = \underline{} \sqrt{\underline{}}$$

8. Simplify.

$$-17\sqrt{7s} - 4\sqrt{7s}$$

$$= \underline{} \sqrt{7s}$$

9. $\left(4\sqrt{5}\right)^2$

$= \left(\underline{\quad}\sqrt{\underline{\quad}}\right)\left(\underline{\quad}\sqrt{\underline{\quad}}\right)$

$= \underline{\quad} \cdot \underline{\quad} \cdot \sqrt{\underline{\quad} \cdot \underline{\quad}}$

$= \underline{\quad} \cdot \sqrt{\underline{\quad}}$

$= \underline{\quad}$

10. $3\sqrt{2} \cdot 4\sqrt{12} - 6\sqrt{54}$

$= \underline{\quad}\sqrt{\underline{\quad}} - 6\sqrt{54}$

$= \underline{\quad}\sqrt{\underline{\quad}} - \underline{\quad}\sqrt{\underline{\quad}}$

$= \underline{\quad}\sqrt{6}$

11. $\sqrt{\dfrac{x^3}{60}} = \dfrac{\sqrt{x^{\square}x}}{\sqrt{\square \cdot 15}} = \dfrac{\square\sqrt{x}}{\square\sqrt{15}} = \dfrac{}{\underline{\quad}} = \sqrt{\dfrac{\square}{15}}$

12. $17 \cdot 23$

$= (20 - 3)(20 + 3)$

$= 400 + \underline{\quad} + \underline{\quad} + \underline{\quad}$ *FOIL*

$= \underline{\quad}$

13. $A = s^2 = \left(8 - \sqrt{4}\right)^2$

$= (8 - \underline{\quad})^2$

$= (\underline{\quad})^2 = \underline{\quad\quad}$

14. $\sqrt{2}\left(\sqrt{3} - \sqrt{8}\right)$

$= \sqrt{(2 \cdot \underline{\quad})} - \sqrt{(2 \cdot \underline{\quad})}$ $\underline{\quad\quad}$

$= \sqrt{(\underline{\quad})} - \sqrt{(\underline{\quad})}$ Multiply.

$= \sqrt{(\underline{\quad})} - \underline{\quad}$ Simplify.

15. $\sqrt{12} \cdot \sqrt{(\underline{\quad})} = \sqrt{36} = (\underline{\quad})^2$

$\sqrt{12}, \sqrt{(\underline{\quad})}$

16. Which expression does not equal $\sqrt{48}$?

Circle the answer.

A $\sqrt{3 \cdot 16}$ **B** $16\sqrt{3}$

C $\sqrt{4^2 \cdot 3}$ **D** $4\sqrt{3}$

17. $46x^2 - 9x + 95$

$= \underline{\quad\quad\quad}$

18. ✎ *FOIL each set of binomials. Compare your answers with theirs.*

Student ____ is correct. Student ____'s trinomial would have a middle term of

_____, not _____.

---

19. $16x^2 - 40x + 25$

factors of 16: _____

factors of 25: _____

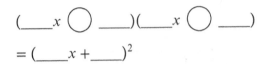

$= (\underline{}x + \underline{})^2$

square root: _____

20. **a.** *Substitute x = 12.*

$2x^2 + 3x - 27$

$= 2(\underline{})^2 + 3(\underline{}) - 27 =$ _____

b. factors of 2: ____, ____

factors of 27: _____

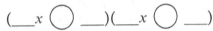

---

21. Solve $|3x| = 6$.

$3x = 6$ $3x = -$ _____

$x = \dfrac{6}{\square} =$ _____ $x = -\dfrac{\square}{3} =$ _____

Student ____ is correct. Student ____ isolated the absolute-value term by _____

the coefficient 3 instead of _____ it.

---

22. $|w - \underline{}| = \underline{}$

max: $w - \underline{} = \underline{}$

$w = \underline{}$

min: $w - \underline{} = -\underline{}$

$w = \underline{}$

23. *Closed circle means included.*

$-3 \bigcirc x \bigcirc 1$

Circle the answer.

A $-3 < x < 1$ **B** $-3 \leq x < 1$

C $-3 < x \leq 1$ **D** $-3 \leq x \leq 1$

24. Graph $x > 3$ or $x < 5$.

```
 ←──┼──┼──┼──┼──┼──┼──┼──→
    −1  0  2  3  4  5  6
```

The solution set is _____ because _____.

---

25. a. Make a scatter plot.

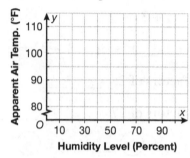

b. *See page 14 in the* Student Reference Guide.

_____ correlation

26.  Make a scatter plot.

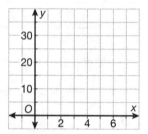

---

27. *Find 2 categories of chapters whose probability adds up to $\frac{8}{25}$.*

$P(\text{certain type}) = \dfrac{\square}{\square} + \dfrac{\square}{\square} = \dfrac{8}{25}$

certain type: _____

28. a. $20 + \underline{\quad} = 32$

$x = \underline{\quad}$ services

b. regular fee services:

$y = \underline{\quad} + \underline{\quad} x$

c.  Solve and classify the system.

_____

---

29. $20.5 + x < 23.5$

$x < \underline{\quad}$

_____ than _____ inches could have

fallen to maintain the record in 1947.

30.  Solve the system using elimination.

$K + D = \underline{\quad}$

$\underline{\quad} K - \underline{\quad} D = 5$

Find César's age.

$C = K - 5 = \underline{\quad}$ years old

Solving Two-Step and Multi-Step Inequalities

New Concepts

> **Example** Solving Two-Step Inequalities
>
> **Solve $9 - 3m > 21$. Graph the solutions.**
>
> $9 - 3m > 21$
>
> $-3m > 12$ *Subtract 9 from both sides.*
>
> $m < -4$ *Divide both sides by −3.*
>
> The inequality sign is <, so −4 is not included in the solution. Draw an open circle at −4.
>
> The solutions are less than −4, so draw an arrow pointing left.
>
>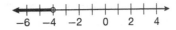

- Ways to simplify inequalities:
  1. Use the order of operations.
  2. Distribute.
  3. Combine like terms.
  4. For fractions, multiply by the LCM of the denominators.

> **Example** Solving Multi-Step Inequalities
>
> **Solve $\frac{3}{4}y + \frac{1}{2} < \frac{7}{10}$. Graph the solutions.**
>
> $$\frac{3}{4}y + \frac{1}{2} < \frac{7}{10}$$
>
> $$\left(\overset{5}{\cancel{20}} \cdot \frac{3}{4}y\right) + \left(\overset{10}{\cancel{20}} \cdot \frac{1}{2}\right) < \left(20 \cdot \frac{7}{10}\right)$$ *Multiply by the LCM 20.*
>
> $$15y + 10 < 14$$ *Simplify.*
>
> $$15y < 4$$ *Subtract 10 from both sides.*
>
> $$y < \frac{4}{15}$$ *Divide both sides by 15.*
>
> The inequality sign is <, so $\frac{4}{15}$ is not included in the solution. Draw an open circle at $\frac{4}{15}$.
>
> The solutions are less than $\frac{4}{15}$, so draw an arrow pointing left.
>
>

Solve and graph.

a. $4x + 29 \leq 25$

$$4x \leq \underline{\hspace{1cm}}$$

$$x \leq \underline{\hspace{1cm}}$$

b. *When multiplying or dividing by a negative number, reverse the inequality sign.*

$$-36 - 7k < 6$$

$$-7k < \underline{\hspace{1cm}}$$

$$k \bigcirc \underline{\hspace{1cm}}$$

c. *Simplify the left side of the inequality before using opposite operations to isolate the variable.*

$$-18 + (-3) < -4f + 11$$

$$\underline{\hspace{1cm}} < -4f + 11$$

$$\underline{\hspace{1cm}} < -4f$$

$$\underline{\hspace{1cm}} \bigcirc f$$

d. *Distribute −5 first.*

$$-5(10 - 5p) > (-10)^2$$

$$\underline{\hspace{1cm}} + \underline{\hspace{1cm}}p > \underline{\hspace{1cm}}$$

$$\underline{\hspace{1cm}}p > \underline{\hspace{1cm}}$$

$$p \bigcirc \underline{\hspace{1cm}}$$

e. $\frac{1}{12}y + \frac{2}{3} \geq \frac{5}{6}$

LCM of denominators: $\underline{\hspace{1cm}}$

$$(\underline{\hspace{1cm}} \cdot y) + \left(\underline{\hspace{1cm}} \cdot \frac{2}{3}\right) \geq \underline{\hspace{1cm}} \cdot \frac{5}{6}$$

$$y + \underline{\hspace{1cm}} \geq \underline{\hspace{1cm}}$$

$$y \bigcirc \underline{\hspace{1cm}}$$

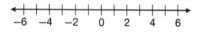

f. $180 - 5t \leq 150$

$$t \bigcirc \underline{\hspace{1cm}}$$

In $\underline{\hspace{1cm}}$ weeks, her time will be at most 150 seconds.

1. The median is the _____ value in a set of data.

_____

2. The mode is the value that occurs _____ in a set of data.

_____

3. Factor 2 out of the trinomial. Then factor the resulting trinomial.

$2(3x^2 - 5x - 2)$

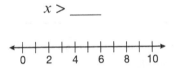
$= 2(\underline{\quad}x \bigcirc \underline{\quad})(x \bigcirc \underline{\quad})$

4. Use the Division Property of Inequality.

$\dfrac{9}{\square} > \dfrac{0.3r}{\square}$

$\underline{\quad} \bigcirc r$

5. $5 + 4x > 37$

$x > \underline{\quad}$

6. When multiplying or dividing by a negative number, reverse the inequality sign.

$\dfrac{x}{-3} - 2 \le 1$

$x \bigcirc \underline{\quad}$

7. $-3x + 2 \le 1$

$x \bigcirc \underline{\quad}$

8. $\dfrac{x}{5} - 4 > 9$

$x \bigcirc \underline{\quad}$

9. Isolate r in the center of the inequality by performing the same operation on each part of the inequality.

$-5 < r - 6 < -2$

$\underline{\quad} < r < \underline{\quad}$

10. $\sqrt{ab} = \sqrt{a} \cdot \sqrt{b}$ where $a \ge 0$ and $b \ge 0$.

$4\sqrt{\underline{\quad}x \cdot \underline{\quad}x}$

$= 4\sqrt{\underline{\quad}}$

$= \underline{\quad}\sqrt{\underline{\quad}}$

11. *Find the perfect squares that are factors of 400 and g^6.*

$$\sqrt{400} = \underline{\quad} \cdot \underline{\quad}$$

$$\sqrt{g^6} = \underline{\quad} \cdot \underline{\quad}$$

$$\sqrt{400g^6} = (\underline{\quad})(\underline{\quad}) = \underline{\quad}$$

12. The only difference is remembering to

_____ the _____

sign when multiplying or dividing

both sides by a _____ number.

---

13. $6 - 7y < 48$

$y \bigcirc \underline{\quad}$

Circle the answer.

A $y < -6$ **B** $y > -6$

C $y > -48$ **D** $y < -48$

14. $2(18) + 2b \le 42$

$b \le \underline{\quad}$

The bottles can cost at _____ each.

---

15. *Find the square roots of the height and weight before substituting them into the formula.*

$H = \underline{\quad}$ $W = \underline{\quad}$

Substitute.

16. *Factor 2 out of the trinomial. Then factor the resulting trinomial.*

$2(6x^2 - x - 2)$

$= 2(\underline{\quad}x - \underline{\quad})(\underline{\quad}x + \underline{\quad})$

---

17. Student ____ is correct. Student ____

did not simplify _____ correctly.

18. a. $S = \sqrt{(\underline{\;\cdot\;}) \cdot (\underline{\quad})}$

$= \sqrt{(\underline{\;\cdot\;}) \cdot (\underline{\quad})^3}$

$= \sqrt{(\underline{\quad}) \cdot (\underline{\quad})^2}$

$= \underline{\quad}\sqrt{(\underline{\quad}) \cdot (\underline{\quad})}$

$= \underline{\quad}\sqrt{\underline{\quad}}$

b. *Substitute. Evaluate.*

$= \underline{\quad\quad}$

19. $A = \frac{1}{2}bh$

Let $b = 3 + \sqrt{15}$ inches

Let $h = 5 - \sqrt{20}$ inches

Substitute.

_____

20. *Use FOIL to check the factors that Student A and B found.*

Student _____ is correct. Student _____'s

trinomial would have a middle term of

_____, not _____.

21. $|x - 3| + 2 = 0$

Isolate the absolute value expression.

$|x - 3| =$ _____

Circle the answer.

A $\{5, 1\}$ **B** $\{4, -1\}$

C $\{1\}$ **D** $\varnothing$

22. $|x + 11| + 3 = 1$

$|x + 11| =$ _____

An absolute value cannot _____

_____.

23. *Factor the trinomial. The binomial factors represent the length and width of the rug.*

$(x \bigcirc \underline{\quad})(x \bigcirc \underline{\quad})$

Substitute 40 for x.

$(40 \bigcirc \underline{\quad}) = \underline{\quad}$

$(40 \bigcirc \underline{\quad}) = \underline{\quad}$

dimensions: _____ × _____

24. *Visualize the line of best fit.*

The correlation is _____ because

as the _____-values increase,

the y-values _____.

25. *Since the actual width of the screw must be within 0.03 millimeters of the desired width, the compound inequality is a conjunction.*

___ ⃝ x ⃝ ___

26. $3gh\sqrt{275g^7h^9}$

$= 3gh\sqrt{275} \cdot \sqrt{g^7} \cdot \sqrt{\rule{1cm}{0.4pt}}$

$= 3gh\sqrt{\rule{0.5cm}{0.4pt} \cdot \rule{0.5cm}{0.4pt}} \cdot \sqrt{g^6 \cdot \rule{0.5cm}{0.4pt}} \cdot \sqrt{\rule{0.5cm}{0.4pt} \cdot \rule{0.5cm}{0.4pt}}$

$= 3gh \cdot \rule{0.5cm}{0.4pt}\sqrt{\rule{0.5cm}{0.4pt}} \cdot \rule{0.5cm}{0.4pt}\sqrt{\rule{0.5cm}{0.4pt}} \cdot \rule{0.5cm}{0.4pt}\sqrt{\rule{0.5cm}{0.4pt}}$

$= \rule{0.5cm}{0.4pt}\sqrt{\rule{0.5cm}{0.4pt}}$

27. a. total coins: _____

dimes and quarters: _____

$P(\text{dime or quarter}) = \dfrac{\square}{\square}$

b. quarters: _____

other coins greater than 5 cents: _____

$P(\text{q or} > 5\cent) = P(\text{q}) + P(> 5\cent) - P(\text{q and} > 5\cent)$

$= \dfrac{\square}{\square}$

c. The answers are the _____. The same set of outcomes are described in

_____.

28. *Solve the system of equations.*

$p = 6x + 24$
$p = 8x + 20$

Because the system of equations has _____ solution(s), the equations are _____ and _____.

29. *The problem describes a direct variation.*

$x_1y_1 = x_2y_2$

$12 \cdot 3 = \rule{0.8cm}{0.4pt} \cdot \rule{0.8cm}{0.4pt}$

_____ bricks wide by _____ bricks long

30. Student _____ is correct. Student _____ removed the _____-square factor instead of the _____ of that factor.

New Concepts

Math Language

A **rational function** is a function that can be given as a rational expression, which has a variable in the denominator. The parent function for a rational function is $y = \frac{1}{x}$.

An **excluded value** is a value of a variable in a function or an expression that makes the function undefined. The parent function is undefined at $x = 0$.

Example Determining Asymptotes

Identify the asymptotes.

$$y = \frac{2}{x - 8}$$ *The rational function is in the form $y = \frac{a}{x-b} + c$, where $a = 2$, $b = 8$, and $c = 0$*

Since $b = 8$, the equation of **the vertical asymptote is $x = 8$.**
Since $c = 0$, the equation of **the horizontal asymptote is $y = 0$ or the** ***x*-axis.**

$$y = \frac{4}{x + 10} + 3$$

Since $b = -10$, the equation of **the vertical asymptote is $x = -10$.**
Since $c = 3$, the equation of **the horizontal asymptote is $y = 3$.**

Math Language

A rational function is a **discontinuous function** because it has a break or jump in the graph. A break or jump can be due to an asymptote.

An **asymptote** is a boundary line that the graph of a function approaches but never touches or crosses.

Example **Graphing Using Asymptotes**

Identify the asymptotes and graph the function.

$$y = \frac{1}{x - 4} - 2$$

1. Identify vertical and horizontal asymptotes. $a = 1$, $b = 4$, $c = -2$
   The equation of the vertical asymptote is $x = 4$. The equation of the horizontal asymptote is $y = -2$.

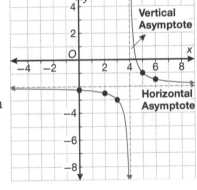

2. Graph the asymptotes using dashed lines.

3. Make a table of values.

x	0	2	3	5	6
y	$-2\frac{1}{4}$	$-2\frac{1}{2}$	-3	-1	$-1\frac{1}{2}$

4. Plot and connect the points with smooth curves.

Find the excluded values.

a. $y = \dfrac{4}{6m}$

$6m = $ ____

$m = $ ____ is the excluded

value, so $m \neq$ ____

b. $y = \dfrac{6m}{m + 2}$

$m + 2 = 0$

$m = $ ____ is the excluded

value, so $m \neq$ ____

c. $y = \dfrac{m - 3}{4m - 8}$

$4m - 8 = $ ____

$m = $ ____ is the excluded

value, so $m \neq$ ____

Identify the asymptotes.

d. $y = \dfrac{4}{x + 1}$. Compare to $y = \dfrac{a}{x} - b + c$.

$a = $ ____ $b = $ ____ $c = $ ____

vertical asymptote: $x = $ ____

horizontal asymptote: $y = $ ____

e. $y = \dfrac{2}{x + 7} + 6$

$a = $ ____ $b = $ ____ $c = $ ____

vertical asymptote: $x = $ ____

horizontal asymptote: $y = $ ____

Find the asymptotes and graph the function.

f. $y = \dfrac{6}{x + 4}$

vertical asymptote: $x + 4 = $ ____, $x = -4$

horizontal asymptote: $y = $ ____

Graph the asymptotes. Make a table.

x	−10	−6	−1	2
y				

Plot and connect the points.

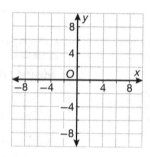

g. $y = \dfrac{1}{x - 6} - 5$

vertical asymptote: $x - 6 = $ ___, $x = $ ____

horizontal asymptote: $y = $ ____

Graph the asymptotes. Make a table.

x	5	5.5	6.5	7
y				

Plot and connect the points.

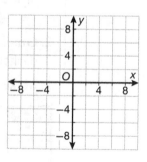

h. vertical asymptote: $x = b$, so $x = $ ____   horizontal asymptote: $y = c$, so $y = $ ____

i. Substitute. $\dfrac{5500}{\square} + 5 = $ ____ $+ 5 = $ ____

If each club is $100, he will receive _____ clubs.

1. $3x - 2y = 17$
   $-4x - 3y = 17$

   Solution: (____, ____)

2. $y = 2x + 4$
   $-x - 3y = 9$

   Solution: (____, ____)

3. *Use factors of 21.*

   $x^2 + 10xy + 21y^2$

   $= (x + \underline{} y)(x + \underline{})$

4. *Write in standard form.*

   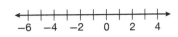

   $= (x + \underline{})(x - \underline{})$

5. $7m = \underline{}$

   $m = \underline{}$ is the excluded value, so $m \neq \underline{}$

6. $m + 3 = \underline{}$

   $m = \underline{}$ is the excluded value, so $m \neq \underline{}$

7. $a = \underline{}, b = \underline{}, c = \underline{}$

   vertical asymptote at $x = \underline{}$

8. $3 - 9m < 30$

   $m \bigcirc \underline{}$

   ```
   ←—+——+——+——+——+——+——+——+——+——+——+——→
     -6    -4    -2    0     2     4
   ```

9. $5(\underline{} + \underline{})$

   $= \underline{} + \underline{}$

   $= \underline{}$

10. vertical asymptote: $x = \underline{}$

   horizontal asymptote: $y = \underline{}$

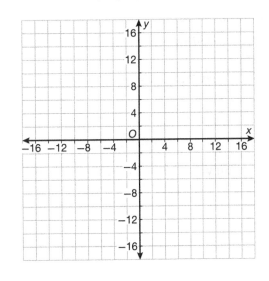

11. $y = \frac{1}{x} + 5$

  _____ $= \frac{1}{x} + 5$

  _____ $= \frac{1}{x}$

  There is no value x such that $\frac{1}{x} =$ _____ .

12. $a =$ _____ , $b =$ _____ , $c =$ _____

  vertical asymptote at $x =$ _____

  horizontal asymptote at $y =$ _____

13. $a =$ _____ , $b =$ _____ , $c =$ _____

  Circle the answer.

  A $x = 3.1$ **B** $x = 1.5$

  C $x = -1.5$ **D** $x = 6.1$

14. $30 + 15 \geq 12 + 3c$

  _____ $\geq 3c$

  _____ $\bigcirc$ c

  You can spend at most $\$$_____ on each CD

15. Student _____ is correct.

  Student _____ did not _____

  the inequality sign when dividing

  by _____ .

16. $(4g + 10) + (3g - 13) > 46$

  _____$g +$ _____ > 46

  $g >$ _____

17. $2.5(h - 1) \geq 15$

  _____$h -$ _____ ≥ 15

  _____$h \geq$ _____

  $h \geq$ _____

  You will hike for at least _____ hours.

18. Student _____ is correct.

  Student _____ multiplied a

  _____ and a

  _____ number.

19. *Use FOIL.*

$$A = \left(7 + \sqrt{\underline{}}\right)\left(\underline{} + \sqrt{\underline{}}\right)$$

$$= \underline{} + \underline{}\sqrt{\underline{}} + \underline{}\sqrt{\underline{}} + \underline{}\sqrt{\underline{}}$$

$$= \underline{} + \underline{}\sqrt{\underline{}} \text{ square inches}$$

20. *Factor and check. Use FOIL.*

$$10x^2 - 11xy - 6y^2 = (2x - 3y)(5x - 2y)$$

$$= \underline{}x^{\square} + \underline{}xy + \underline{}xy + \underline{}y^{\square}$$

$$= \underline{}x^{\square} + \underline{}xy + \underline{}y^{\square}$$

21. *Multiply each choice using FOIL and compare.*

Circle the answer.

A $(10x + 3)(2x + 3)$
B $(20x + 3)(x + 3)$
C $(5x + 1)(4x + 9)$
D $(5x + 9)(4x + 1)$

22. *Substitute $x = -3$ and simplify.*

$$4(\underline{})^2 - 16(\underline{}) + 16$$

$$= \underline{} + \underline{} + 16$$

$$= \underline{} \text{ square inches}$$

23. *The absolute value of a non-zero number is positive.*

$$n = \underline{} \text{ or } n = \underline{}$$

24. $x \bigcirc \underline{}$ OR $x \bigcirc \underline{}$

25. The data does not appear to fall in a linear

pattern, so the data shows \underline{}

correlation.

26.

$$\frac{n}{5} \le -3$$

$$\frac{n}{5} \cdot \underline{} \bigcirc \underline{} \cdot -3$$

$$n \bigcirc \underline{}$$

27. large sq. area $= 216x^2$

large sq. side $= \sqrt{(\underline{})}$

$= x \cdot \sqrt{(\underline{})(\underline{})}$

$= \underline{}x\sqrt{\underline{}}$

large sq. perimeter $= 4 \cdot \underline{}x\sqrt{\underline{}}$

$= \underline{}x\sqrt{\underline{}}$

small sq. area $= 125x^2$

small sq. side $= \sqrt{(\underline{})}$

$= x \cdot \sqrt{(\underline{})(\underline{})}$

$= \underline{}x\sqrt{\underline{}}$

small sq. perimeter $= 4 \cdot \underline{}x\sqrt{\underline{}}$

$= \underline{}x\sqrt{\underline{}}$

large perimeter + small perimeter

$= \underline{}x\sqrt{\underline{}} + \underline{}x\sqrt{\underline{}}$

28. *Find values when rolling three number cubes.*

total number of outcomes $= \underline{}$

number of same number outcomes $= \underline{}$

number of odd sum outcomes $= \underline{}$

P(same number on 3 cubes) $+$

P(outcome is odd) $-$

P(same number on 3 cubes is also odd)

$= \underline{} + \underline{} - \underline{}$

$= \underline{}$

29. *Write the equation in slope-intercept form. Identify the slope.*

$y = \underline{}x + \underline{}$

Circle the answer.

A $-\dfrac{1}{3}$ **B** $\dfrac{1}{3}$

C 3 **D** -3

30. Show the data on the graph.

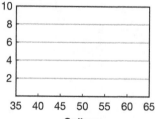

Average Milk Production

Factoring Trinomials by using the GCF page 517

New Concepts

To completely factor a polynomial, factor out the GCF of its terms.

Example **Factoring Trinomials with Positive Leading Coefficients**

Factor completely.

$4x^3 - 4x^2 - 80x$

$4x(x^2 - x - 20)$ *Factor out the GCF.*

$4 \cdot -5 = -20$ and $4 + (-5) = -1$ *Find two numbers: product −20, sum −1*

$4x(x + 4)(x - 5)$ *Factor the trinomial.*

• When the leading coefficient is negative, factor out a -1.

Example **Factoring Trinomials with Negative Leading Coefficients**

Factor completely.

$-3x^3 - 6x^2 + 72x$

$-3x(x^2 + 2x - 24)$ *Factor out the GCF and −1.*

$-4 \cdot 6 = -24$ and $-4 + 6 = 2$

$-3x(x - 4)(x + 6)$ *Factor the trinomial.*

Example **Factoring Trinomials with Two Variables**

Factor completely.

$bx^4 + 9bx^3 + 20bx^2$

$bx^2(x^2 + 9x + 20)$ *Factor out the GCF.*

$bx^2(x + 4)(x + 5)$ *Factor the trinomial.*

Example **Rearranging Terms Before Factoring**

Factor completely.

$-105k - 14pk + 7p^2k$

$7p^2k - 14pk - 105k$ *Write the polynomial in standard form.*

$7k(p^2 - 2p - 15)$ *Factor out the GCF.*

$7k(p + 3)(p - 5)$ *Factor the trinomial.*

Factor completely.

a. $p^5 + 13p^4 + 12p^3$

Factor out the GCF: ____

____(____ + 13____ + ____)

____(p ◯ ____)(p ◯ ____)

b. $6n^4 - 6n^3 - 12n^2$

Factor out the GCF: ____

____(____ ◯ ____ ◯ ____)

____(n ◯ ____)(n ◯ ____)

c. $-r^2 + r + 30$

Factor out ____.

-(____ - ____ - ____)

-(r ◯ ____)(r ◯ ____)

d. $-5d^3 - 25d^2 - 20d$

Factor out ____.

-____(____ ◯ ____ ◯ ____)

-____(d ◯ ____)(d ◯ ____)

e. $y^3x + 3y^2x - 54yx$

Factor out the GCF: ____

____(____ + 3____ - ____)

____(y ◯ ____)(y ◯ ____)

f. $5bx^3 - 5bx^2 - 60bx$

Factor out the GCF: ____

____(____ ◯ ____ ◯ ____)

____(x ◯ ____)(x ◯ ____)

g. $18fh - 240h + 6f^2h$

Write in standard form:

_____ + ____ - ____

Factor out the GCF: ____

____(____ ◯ ____ ◯ ____)

____(f ◯ ____)(f ◯ ____)

h. $90x^3 + 450x^2 + 540x$

Factor out the GCF: ____

____(____ ◯ ____ ◯ ____)

____(x ◯ ____)(x ◯ ____)

1. *Use the product rule for inverse variation.*

If $y = 6$ and $x = 9$, what is y, when $x = 12$?

$y =$ _____

2. *Write each equation in standard form. Solve by elimination.*

$x =$ _____

Substitute to find y.

$5(\underline{\hspace{0.5cm}}) - 2y = 10$

Solution: (_____ , _____)

3. *Write each equation in standard form. Solve by elimination.*

$x - y = 2$

$y + 2x = 1$

Solution: (_____ , _____)

4. $3b - 2 < -8$ OR $4b + 3 > 11$

$3b <$ _____ OR $4b >$ _____

$b <$ _____ OR $b >$ _____

5. $x^2 - 4x - 45$

___ • ___ = 45 and ___ + ___ = −4

$(x \bigcirc \underline{\hspace{0.5cm}})(x \bigcirc \underline{\hspace{0.5cm}})$

6. *Factor out the GCF.*

___(_____ + ___ + ___)

___ • ___ = ___ and ___ + ___ = ___

___$(k +$ ___$)(k +$ ___$)$

7. $5x^2 + 3x - 2$

_____ • _____ = _____ and _____ + _____ = _____

(___x ◯ ___)(x ◯ ___)

8. $2x^3 + 16x^2 + 30x$

Factor out the GCF: _____

_____(_____ + _____ + _____

_____($x +$ _____)($x +$ _____)

9. $abx^2 - 5abx - 24ab$

Factor out the GCF: _____

_____(_____ − _____ − _____)

_____(x ◯ ___)(x ◯ ___)

10. $15mx^2 + 9mx - 6m$

Factor out GCF: _____

_____(_____ + _____ − _____)

_____(x ◯ ___)(x ◯ ___)

11. _Set the denominator equal to zero._

$m + 3 =$ _____

$m =$ _____

$m \neq$ _____

12. $16 + (-6) \geq 2(d + 4)$

_____ $\geq$ ___$d +$_____

d ◯ _____

Graph the solution.

13. The GCF _____ be factored out after factoring a trinomial because the answer will be the _____.

14. _FOIL, then multiply by the GCF._

$3(x + 4)(x + 11)$

$3(x + 11)(x + 4)$

By the _____ Property of Multiplication, the order of the _____ does not matter.

15. *If a binomial has any terms with common factors, then it is not factored completely.*

Answer: _____

16. $-16x^2 + 32x - 16$

Factor out the GCF: _____

_____(_____ ◯ _____ ◯ _____)

_____(x ◯ _____)(x ◯ _____)

---

17. *In a function of the form $y = \frac{a}{x-b} + c$, the vertical asymptote occurs at $x = b$ and the horizontal asymptote occurs at $y = c$.*

Student _____ is correct.

Student _____ wrote the _____

asymptote.

18. **a.** _____ = _____

b. _____ = _____

c. *Substitute.*

$$\frac{50,000}{\Box} + 1$$

He will receive _____ instruments.

---

19. **a.** _____ = _____

b. _____ = _____

c. $\dfrac{1350}{\Box} + 15$

The planner will receive _____ dinners.

20. $\dfrac{5}{\Box} = \dfrac{y}{\Box}$

_____ = y

---

21. $7 + 3g \le 20$

$3g \le$ _____

$g \le$ _____ or $g \le$ _____

He can buy up to _____ gallons.

22. Student _____ is correct.

Student _____ reversed the _____

sign when dividing by a _____

number.

---

23. Use the _____ method, simplify

the _____, and then

combine _____ terms.

24. *Find square root of the nearest perfect square greater than 124 and the nearest perfect square less than 124.*

Answer: _____

---

25. $A = s^2$

$(\underline{\hspace{1cm}})^2$

$= (\underline{\hspace{1cm}})^2 \times \left(\sqrt{\underline{\hspace{0.5cm}}}\right)^2$

$= \underline{\hspace{1cm}} \times \underline{\hspace{1cm}}$

The area of the sandbox is $\underline{\hspace{2cm}}$ ▪.

26. *The difference between the maximum angle of inclination (or the minimum angle of inclination) and the current angle of inclination is 8°.*

$|x - \underline{\hspace{1cm}}| = \underline{\hspace{1cm}}$

maximum angle: $\underline{\hspace{1.5cm}}$ ▪

minimum angle: $\underline{\hspace{1.5cm}}$ ▪

27. The trend line for a positive correlation

$\underline{\hspace{2cm}}$ from left to right.

The trend line for a $\underline{\hspace{3cm}}$

correlation falls from left to right.

There is no $\underline{\hspace{2cm}}$ line when there is

no correlation.

28. Let n = number of videos rented

  a. Total expenses of the store: $\$\underline{\hspace{2cm}}$

  b. DVD sales = number of DVDs $\times$

  charge inequality:

  $\$\underline{\hspace{1.5cm}} n \bigcirc \$\underline{\hspace{1.5cm}}$

  c. $n \bigcirc \underline{\hspace{2cm}}$

  d. At least $\underline{\hspace{1.5cm}}$ DVDs need to be

  rented a month to make a profit.

29. *Simplify the radicals before finding the perimeter.*

$\underline{\hspace{2cm}}$ ▪

30. Let x = additional weight that the elevator can carry

  a. $\underline{\hspace{2cm}} + x \bigcirc 750$

  $x \bigcirc \underline{\hspace{2cm}}$

  b. Alicia $\underline{\hspace{2cm}}$ bring all the weight up

  in one elevator trip.

  The total weight of the weights is $\underline{\hspace{1.5cm}}$

  pounds. This would mean that Alicia

  could weigh no more than $\underline{\hspace{1.5cm}}$

  pounds, which is not reasonable.

New Concepts

- **Discrete events** have a finite number of outcomes.
- A **compound event** consists of two or more simple events.
- A **frequency distribution** shows how often events of the same type occur. Tables, graphs, tree diagrams, and lists are used to show frequency distributions.

Math Language

Frequency is how often something happens.

A **fair coin** has an equally likely chance of coming up heads or tails.

Exploration 📖 page 523

Use your textbook to complete the Exploration.

Example Using Experimental Probability.

Make a bar graph of the data. Find the experimental probability of each outcome.

Out	Walk	Single	Double	Triple	Home Run
30	36	20	9	3	1

Total times at bat: $30 + 36 + 20 + 9 + 3 + 1 = 99$

Probability of each outcome:

$$P(\text{out}) = \frac{30}{99} = \frac{10}{33} \qquad P(\text{walk}) = \frac{36}{99} = \frac{4}{11}$$

$$P(\text{single}) = \frac{20}{99} \qquad P(\text{double}) = \frac{9}{99} = \frac{1}{11}$$

$$P(\text{triple}) = \frac{3}{99} = \frac{1}{33} \qquad P(\text{home run}) = \frac{1}{99}$$

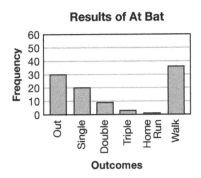

Results of At Bat

a.

Bowling

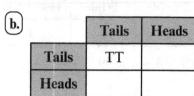

Frequency / Number of Pins on the First Try

5 games · 10 turns per game = _____ outcomes

$P(0) = \dfrac{\square}{\square}$ $P(1) = \dfrac{\square}{\square} =$ ____

$P(2) = \dfrac{\square}{\square} =$ ____ $P(3) = \dfrac{\square}{\square} =$ ____

$P(4) = \dfrac{\square}{\square}$ $P(5) = \dfrac{\square}{\square} =$ ____

$P(6) = \dfrac{\square}{\square} =$ ____ $P(7) = \dfrac{\square}{\square} =$ ____

$P(8) = \dfrac{\square}{\square}$ $P(9) = \dfrac{\square}{\square} =$ ____

$P(10) = \dfrac{\square}{\square}$

A student flips two coins.

b.

	Tails	Heads
Tails	TT	
Heads		

c. *P(TH) = P(HT)*

$P(TT) = \dfrac{\square}{4}$ $P(TH) = \dfrac{\square}{\square}$

$P(\underline{\ \ }) = \dfrac{\square}{\square}$ $= \dfrac{\square}{\square}$

d.

Soup Cans

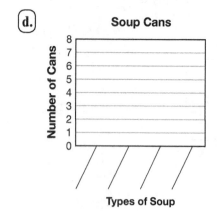

Number of Cans / Types of Soup

e. total outcomes:

6 + ____ + ____ + ____ = ____

$P(\text{clam}) = \dfrac{\square}{\square}$ $P(\text{tomato}) = \dfrac{\square}{\square}$

$P(\text{potato}) = \dfrac{\square}{\square}$ $= \dfrac{\square}{\square}$

$= \dfrac{\square}{\square}$ $P(\text{vegetable}) = \dfrac{\square}{\square}$

$= \dfrac{\square}{\square}$

1. *Write the equation in slope-intercept form.*

$2y = -10x - 36$

$y = \underline{\quad} x - \underline{\quad}$; So, $m = \underline{\quad}$

Parallel lines have the same \underline{\qquad}.

Use point-slope form: $y - y_1 = m(x - x_1)$

$y - \underline{\quad} = \underline{\quad}(x + \underline{\quad})$

$y = \underline{\qquad\qquad}$

2. *Use the product rule for inverse variation: If (x_1, y_1) and (x_2, y_2) are solutions to an inverse variation, then $x_1 y_1 = x_2 y_2$*

$3(\underline{\quad}) = \underline{\quad} x$

$\underline{\quad} = \underline{\quad} x$

$x = \underline{\quad}$

3. *Use the product rule for inverse variation: If (x_1, y_1) and (x_2, y_2) are solutions to an inverse variation, then $x_1 y_1 = x_2 y_2$*

$(\underline{\quad})(\underline{\quad}) = \underline{\quad} x$

$\underline{\quad} = \underline{\quad} x$

$x = \underline{\quad}$

4. In a rational function of the form:

$y = \frac{a}{x - b} + c$, the horizontal asymptote

occurs at $y = \underline{\quad}$.

horizontal asymptote: $y = \underline{\quad}$

5. In a rational function of the form:

$y = \frac{a}{x - b} + c$, the horizontal

asymptote occurs at $y = \underline{\quad}$.

horizontal asymptote: $y = \underline{\quad}$

6. $11|x| = 55$

$|x| = \underline{\quad}$

$x = \{\underline{\quad}, \underline{\quad}\}$

7. $x - 5 \geq 0$ \qquad OR \quad $x + 1 < -2$

$x \geq \underline{\quad}$ \qquad OR \qquad $x < \underline{\quad}$

8. Factor out the GCF: \underline{\qquad}

$\underline{\quad}(\underline{\qquad} + \underline{\qquad} c + 24)$

Factor the trinomial.

$\underline{\quad}(c + \underline{\quad})(c + \underline{\quad})$

9. Factor out the GCF: \underline{\qquad}

$\underline{\quad}(\underline{\quad} x^2 - \underline{\quad} x - \underline{\quad})$

Factor the trinomial.

$\underline{\quad}(\underline{\quad} x - \underline{\quad})(\underline{\quad} x + \underline{\quad})$

10. Factor out a \underline{\quad} and the GCF, \underline{\quad}.

$\underline{\quad}(\underline{\quad} + \underline{\qquad} + \underline{\quad})$

$\underline{\quad}(\underline{\quad} + \underline{\quad})(\underline{\quad} + \underline{\quad})$

11. GCF: _____

(_____)($x^2 +$ _____ + _____)

(_____)(_____)(_____)

12. Complete the table.

	Red	Blue	Yellow	Green
1	R1			
2				
3			Y3	
4				
5				
6				

13. Use a _____ to organize data for

further _____. Use a

_____ to display data.

14. $P(A \text{ and } B) = P(A) \cdot P(B)$

Circle the answer.

A $P = \dfrac{4}{5} \cdot \dfrac{5}{6} \cdot \dfrac{4}{2}$ 　　**B** $P = \dfrac{1}{6} \cdot \dfrac{1}{6} \cdot \dfrac{1}{2}$

C $P = \left(\dfrac{1}{6}\right)^2 \cdot \left(\dfrac{1}{2}\right)^4$ 　　**D** $P = \left(\dfrac{1}{3}\right)^3 \cdot \left(\dfrac{1}{2}\right)^4$

15. Complete the table.

	Chemical	Physical
Success		
Failure		

16. $P(A, B, \text{ and } C) = P(A) \cdot P(B) \cdot P(C)$

$P(\text{red}) = \dfrac{\text{number of red}}{\text{total marbles}} = \dfrac{\square}{\square}$

$P(\text{red, red, red}) = \dfrac{\square}{\square} \cdot \dfrac{\square}{\square} \cdot \dfrac{\square}{\square}$

$= \left(\dfrac{\square}{\square}\right)^{\square} = \dfrac{\square}{\square}$

17. Factor out _____.

_____ ($x^2 -$ _____ $x -$ _____)

Factor the trinomial:

_____ (_____ $-$ _____)(_____ $+$ _____)

18. Student _____ is correct. Student _____

did not factor out the _____, _____.

19. Factor out the GCF, _____.

_____(____ + _____ + ____)

Factor the perfect square trinomial.

_____(____ − ____)(____ − ____) =

(_____)² · (_____)²

$A = \text{side}^2$, so side = $\sqrt{\rule{2cm}{0pt}}$

side = $\sqrt{(\rule{1cm}{0pt})^2 \cdot (\rule{2cm}{0pt})^2}$

= _____(_____)

20. a. GCF: _____.

_____(____ + ____ − ____) =

_____(____ − ____)(____ + ____)

b. If each factor is a _____ length,

the dimensions are:

(_____) by (_____) by (_____)

21. Student _____ is correct. Student _____

did not change the sign when

_____ 3 from both sides

after setting the _____

equal to _____.

22. For, $y = \frac{a}{x-b} + c$, the asymptotes

are $x =$ ____ = ____, and,

$y =$ ____ = ____

Complete the table.

x	−30	−20	−10	0	10	20	30
y							

 Graph the function.

23. In the first inequality, solve by

_____ both sides by ____.

In the second inequality, solve by _____

_____ both sides by ____.

The direction of the sign for the first

inequality is not reversed because the

divisor was a _____ number

rather than a _____ number.

24. *Distribute. Then collect like terms and solve for m.*

Circle the answer.

A $m \le -10$ **B** $m \ge -10$

C $m \le 10$ **D** $m \ge 10$

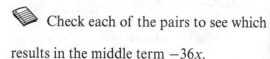

25. *Simplify.*

$$\sqrt{4} = \underline{\quad}$$

$$\underline{\quad}\left(\underline{\quad} + \sqrt{\underline{\quad}}\right)$$

Distribute.

$$= \underline{\quad} \cdot \underline{\quad} + \underline{\quad}\sqrt{\underline{\quad}}$$

$$= \underline{\quad} + \underline{\quad}\sqrt{\underline{\quad}}$$

26. *Factor the first term.*

$$9x^2 = 3x \cdot \underline{\quad}$$

List the factor pairs of −13.

$(1)(\underline{\quad\quad})$, $(\underline{\quad\quad})(13)$,

$(13)(\underline{\quad\quad})$, $(\underline{\quad\quad})(\underline{\quad\quad})$

Check each of the pairs to see which

results in the middle term $-36x$.

$(\underline{\quad\quad\quad})(\underline{\quad\quad\quad})$

27. The sum of $\underline{\quad\quad} + \underline{\quad\quad}$ does not

contain a factor of $\underline{\quad\quad}$, which is

necessary for the coefficient b, $\underline{\quad\quad}$.

28. a. $y = \underline{\quad\quad}x + \underline{\quad\quad}$

  b. The $\underline{\quad\quad\quad\quad}$ of the line is

$\underline{\quad\quad\quad\quad}$, so there is a

$\underline{\quad\quad\quad\quad}$ correlation.

29. $6.5\% = \underline{\quad\quad\quad}$

6.5% of each house sold: $\underline{\quad\quad\quad}h$

For "at least," use the $\underline{\quad}$ symbol.

$0.065h \bigcirc 20{,}000$

$h \bigcirc \$\underline{\quad\quad\quad}$

30. a. *Solve second equation for d.*

$$\tfrac{1}{4}d = 10t + 3$$

$$d = \underline{\quad}t + \underline{\quad}$$

Compare this with the first equation.

The equations are $\underline{\quad\quad\quad}$,

so they are $\underline{\quad\quad\quad}$ and

$\underline{\quad\quad\quad}$.

b. $\underline{\quad\quad\quad}$ train travels farther;

they both travel the $\underline{\quad\quad\quad}$

distance because the equations are

$\underline{\quad\quad\quad}$.

Identifying and Writing Joint Variation page 529

Math Language

Joint variation is when a quantity varies directly as the product of two or more other quantities.

- In $y = kxz$, k is the constant of variation and $k \neq 0$, y varies jointly with x and z.

- When y varies jointly with a set of variables, y is directly proportional to each variable taken one at a time.

- The table illustrates the relationship between the variables a, b, and c in the joint variation $b = 3ac$.

a	b	c
1	3	1
2	6	1
1	6	2
2	12	2

1. Doubling a causes b to change by a factor of _____.

2. Look at the rows where a stays the same.

_____ c causes b to change by a factor of 2.

3. The statements above are true because b is _____

proportional to a, and b is directly proportional to _____.

4. Doubling both _____ and _____ causes _____ to quadruple.

- In the equation $y = kxz$, y varies jointly with x and z.

5. Set up an equation in the form $y = kxz$ using the given values:

$y = 20 \qquad x = 5 \qquad z = 2$.

$20 = k \cdot$ _____ $\cdot$ _____

6. Solve for k. _____ $= k \cdot$ _____ ; $k =$ _____

7. Use the value of k to write an equation of joint variation that relates x, y, and z.

$y =$ _____

8. Find y when $x = 8$ and $z = 3$.

$y = 2 \cdot$ _____ $\cdot$ _____ $=$ _____

Math Language

The amount of substance of gas is *n* moles.

- The ideal gas law relates the absolute pressure (P) in atmospheres, the volume (V) of the vessel containing n moles of gas, and the temperature (T) in kelvins of the gas.

- The ideal gas law is the formula $PV = nRT$.
  R is the gas constant and equals 0.08206.

Use the ideal gas law to answer the questions.

9. constant of variation: $R =$ _____

10. Solve for n.

$$n = \frac{PV}{\square}$$

$P = 2.3$ atmospheres, $V = 120$ liters, $T = 340$ K, $R = 0.08206$

$$n = \frac{(\square) \cdot (\square)}{(\square) \cdot (\square)} = \frac{\square}{\square}$$

$n \approx$ _____ moles of gas

11. Find P if $n = 45$ moles, $T = 473.15$ K, and $V = 50$ liters.

$$P \cdot (\underline{\quad}) = (\underline{\quad})(\underline{\quad})(\underline{\quad})$$

$$P = \frac{(\square) \cdot (\square) \cdot (\square)}{\square} = \frac{\square}{\square}$$

$\approx$ _____ atmospheres

12. Solve $PV = nRT$ for P.

$$P = \frac{\square}{\square} = \frac{0.08206\square}{\square}$$

- In $y = \frac{kx}{z}$, y varies jointly with x ($y = kx$) and inversely with z.

13. The absolute pressure is _____ proportional to

the number of _____ of gas and the

_____, and _____ proportional to

the _____ of the vessel.

• The load P in pounds that a horizontal beam can safely carry varies jointly with the product of its width W in feet and the square of its depth D in feet, and inversely with its length L in feet.

14. *Put variables that vary jointly in the numerator and variables that vary inversely in the denominator.*

$$P = \frac{\square \cdot \square \cdot \square^2}{\square}$$

15. L is in the denominator so it varies _____ with P.

When L is doubled, P, the load the beam can safely support, is

_____.

16. *Try a specific example.*

Use $W = 2$, $D = 2$, and $L = 1$.   Use $W = 1$, $D = 1$, and $L = 1$.

$$P = \frac{k \cdot \square \cdot \square}{1} = \underline{\quad}$$ $$P = \frac{k \cdot \square \cdot \square}{1} = \underline{\quad}$$

The load the beam can safely support is divided by ____.

Investigation Practice page 531

a. $k = 4$, $s = \underline{\quad} \cdot \underline{\quad} \cdot \underline{\quad} = \underline{\qquad}$

b. $k = \frac{1}{3}$, $m = \underline{\quad} \cdot \underline{\quad} \cdot \sqrt{\underline{\quad}} = \underline{\qquad}$

The value of y varies jointly with w and x and inversely with z.
If $w = 12$, $x = 9$, $z = 15$, then $y = 36$.

c. Use variables to write an equation for the given relationship.

If y is isolated, joint variation variables are in the numerator and inverse variation variables are in the denominator.

$$y = \frac{k(\square)(\square)}{\square} = \underline{\qquad}$$

d. *Isolate k. Substitute the given values of the variables and solve for k.*

$$k = \frac{(\square)(\square)}{(\square)(\square)} = \frac{\square}{\square} = \underline{\quad}$$

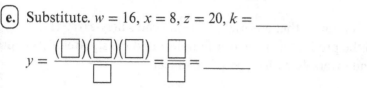
e. Substitute. $w = 16$, $x = 8$, $z = 20$, $k =$ _____

$$y = \frac{(\square)(\square)(\square)}{\square} = \frac{\square}{\square} = \underline{\quad}$$

The ideal gas law is $PV = 0.08206nT$.

Isolate n.

f. Solve for n. $n = \dfrac{\square}{0.08206(\square)}$

Substitute. $V = 30$ liters, $T = 300$ K, $P = 200$ atmospheres

$$n = \frac{\square . \square}{\square . \square} = \frac{\square}{\square}$$

$$\approx \underline{\qquad\qquad}$$

g. $V = \dfrac{\square}{\square}$

P is in the _____. It varies _____ with V.

n and T are in the _____. They vary _____ with V.

The volume V of a right circular cone varies jointly with the square of the radius of the base r and the height of the cone h.

h. $V = k \cdot (\underline{\quad})^2 \cdot (\underline{\quad}) = \underline{\qquad\qquad}$

i. Substitute. $r = 2$ cm, $h = 4$ cm, $V = 16.76$ cubic cm

$$\underline{\qquad\qquad} = k(\underline{\quad})^2(\underline{\quad})$$

$$k = \frac{\square}{\square^2 . \square} = \underline{\qquad\qquad} \approx \underline{\qquad\qquad}$$

j. Substitute. Use the constant of variation found in part **i** and the measurements from the diagram.

$$V = (\underline{\quad})(\underline{\quad})^2(\underline{\quad})$$

$$= (\underline{\quad})(\underline{\quad})(\underline{\quad})$$

$$= \underline{\qquad\qquad} \text{ cubic centimeters}$$

Solving Inequalities with Variables on Both Sides page 532

New Concepts

- To solve an inequality with a variable on both sides, begin by isolating the variable on one side of the inequality.

Example **Solving Inequalities with Variables on Both Sides**

Solve and graph the inequality.

$2x + 7 > -5x + 21$
$7x + 7 > 21$ *Add 5x to both sides.*
$7x > 14$ *Subtract 7 from both sides.*
$x > 2$ *Divide both sides by 7.*

Graph the inequality on a number line.

- Use the distributive property and combine like terms before moving the variable to one side of the inequality.

Example **Simplifying Each Side Before Solving**

Solve and graph the inequality.

$2(x - 8) - 3x > 6 - 3(2x + 4)$
$2x - 16 - 3x > 6 - 6x - 12$ *Use the Distributive Property.*
$-x - 16 > -6x - 6$ *Combine like terms.*
$5x - 16 > -6$ *Add 6x to both sides.*
$5x > 10$ *Add 16 to both sides.*
$x > 2$ *Divide both sides by 5.*

Graph the inequality on a number line.

Lesson Practice 📖 page 534

Solve and graph each inequality.

a. $4x - 8 > -2x + 4$

     ___$x - 8 > 4$ *Add 2x to both sides.*

     ___$x >$ ___   *Add 8 to both sides.*

     $x >$ _____   *Division Property of Inequality*

b. $-\dfrac{3a}{5} + \dfrac{7}{10} \geq \dfrac{2a}{5} - \dfrac{9}{10}$

$\dfrac{\square a}{5} + \dfrac{7}{10} \geq -\dfrac{9}{10}$ *Isolate the variable on one side of the inequality.*

$-a \geq -\underline{\hspace{1cm}}$ *Subtraction Property of Inequality*

$a \leq \underline{\hspace{1cm}}$ *Division Property of Inequality*

c. $4(x - 1) - 2x \leq 6 - 5(x + 2)$

$4x - \underline{\hspace{0.8cm}} - 2x \leq 6 - \underline{\hspace{0.4cm}}x - \underline{\hspace{0.8cm}}$ *Distributive Property*

$\underline{\hspace{0.6cm}}x - \underline{\hspace{0.5cm}} \leq -\underline{\hspace{0.4cm}}x - \underline{\hspace{0.6cm}}$ *Combine like terms.*

$\underline{\hspace{0.6cm}}x - \underline{\hspace{0.8cm}} \leq -\underline{\hspace{0.8cm}}$ *Isolate the variable on one side of the inequality.*

$\underline{\hspace{0.6cm}}x \leq \underline{\hspace{1cm}}$ *Isolate the constant on one side of the inequality.*

$x \leq \underline{\hspace{0.8cm}}$ *Division Property of Inequality*

Determine whether each inequality is always true, sometimes true, or never true.

d. $x + 5 + 3x > 4x + 19$

$\underline{\hspace{0.6cm}}x + 5 > 4x + 19$ *Combine like terms.*

$\underline{\hspace{1cm}} > 19$ *Subtraction Property of Inequality*

The inequality is $\underline{\hspace{3cm}}$ true.

e. $x + 5 > x - 3$

$\underline{\hspace{1cm}} > \underline{\hspace{1cm}}$ *Subtraction Property of Inequality*

The inequality is $\underline{\hspace{3cm}}$ true.

f. Ara: $\underline{\hspace{1.5cm}} + 500x$

Lexi: $\underline{\hspace{1.5cm}} - 500x$

Ara's minutes $\geq$ Lexi's minutes

$\underline{\hspace{2cm}} + 500x \geq \underline{\hspace{2cm}} - 500x$

$\underline{\hspace{2.5cm}}x \geq \underline{\hspace{1cm}}$

$x \geq \underline{\hspace{1cm}}$

If $x = 0$ represents January, $x = \underline{\hspace{1cm}}$ represents the month of $\underline{\hspace{2.5cm}}$, which is when Ara's average minutes will be equal to or greater than Lexi's.

---

1. $w^2 - 13w + 36$

$= (\underline{\quad})(\underline{\quad})$

---

2. Factor out −1.

$= -q^2 + q + 42$

$= -\underline{\quad}(\underline{\qquad\qquad})$

$= -\underline{\quad}(\underline{\quad})(\underline{\quad})$

---

3. $30x^2 - 7xy - 2y^2$

$= (\underline{\quad}x - \underline{\quad}y)(\underline{\quad}x + \underline{\quad}y)$

---

4. Combine like terms before factoring.

$x^2 - 11 + 6x - 44$

$= \underline{\qquad\qquad}$

$= (\underline{\quad})(\underline{\quad})$

---

5. $|x - 3| = 14$

$x - 3 = \underline{\qquad} \qquad x - 3 = \underline{\qquad}$

$x = \underline{\qquad} \qquad\qquad x = \underline{\qquad}$

Solution: $\{\underline{\quad}, \underline{\quad}\}$

---

6. $|x + 4| = 7.5$

$x + 4 = \underline{\qquad} \qquad x + 4 = \underline{\qquad}$

$x = \underline{\qquad} \qquad\qquad x = \underline{\qquad}$

Solution: $\{\underline{\quad}, \underline{\quad}\}$

---

7. When multiplying or dividing by a negative number, reverse the inequality sign.

$-5 - \dfrac{n}{8} \geq -6$

$-\dfrac{n}{8} \geq \underline{\qquad}$

$-n \geq \underline{\qquad}$

$n \bigcirc \underline{\qquad}$

---

8. When multiplying or dividing by a negative number, reverse the inequality sign.

$12 - 3d \leq -3$

$-3d \leq \underline{\qquad}$

$d \bigcirc \underline{\qquad}$

---

9. Isolate the variable on one side of the inequality.

$6v + 5 > -2v - 3$

$\underline{\quad}v + 5 > -3$

$\underline{\quad}v > \underline{\qquad}$

$v > \underline{\qquad}$

---

10. See page 10 in the Student Reference Guide.

$y + 4.5 < 10$

$y < \underline{\qquad}$

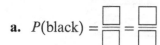

11. The slope of $y = 2x + 6$ is _____.

The slope of the line perpendicular to

$y = 2x + 6$ is _____.

$y - (\underline{\ \ }) = \dfrac{\square}{\square}(x - \underline{\ \ })$

$y =$ _____

12. The slope of $y = -x + 4$ is _____.

The slope of the line parallel to $y = -x + 4$

is _____.

$y - (\underline{\ \ }) = \underline{\ \ }(x - \underline{\ \ })$

$y =$ _____

---

13. *See page 13 in the* Student Reference Guide.

a. $P(\text{black}) = \dfrac{\square}{\square} = \dfrac{\square}{\square}$

b. $P(10) = \dfrac{\square}{\square}$

c. The events are _____

_____

d. $P(\text{black or 10})$

$= \dfrac{\square}{\square} + \dfrac{\square}{\square}$

$= \dfrac{\square}{\square} = \dfrac{\square}{\square}$

14. Make a scatter plot of the data.

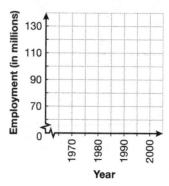

---

15. Because OR is contained in the compound inequality, the solution needs to be true for only

_____ inequality. Since _____ < 3, the compound inequality has _____ as a solution.

---

16. $A = s^2$

$s =$ _____

$A = (\underline{\quad\quad})^{\square}$

$=$ _____ + _____ square inches

17. $x + (x + 13) + (2x + 12) > 81$

_____ $x +$ _____ > 81

_____ $x >$ _____

$x >$ _____

---

18. Changes to the value of b affect the position of the vertical _____.

---

19. *See page 13 in the* Student Reference Guide.

$$P(2) = \frac{\square}{\square} = \frac{\square}{\square} \qquad P(3) = \frac{\square}{\square} = \frac{\square}{\square}$$

$$P(4) = \frac{\square}{\square} = \frac{\square}{\square} \qquad P(5) = \frac{\square}{\square} = \frac{\square}{\square}$$

$$P(6) = \frac{\square}{\square} = \frac{\square}{\square} \qquad P(7) = \frac{\square}{\square} = \frac{\square}{\square}$$

$$P(8) = \frac{\square}{\square} = \frac{\square}{\square} \qquad P(9) = \frac{\square}{\square} = \frac{\square}{\square}$$

20. Circle the horizontal asymptote for the rational expression $y = \frac{7}{x-2} + 4$.

A $y = -2$ **B** $y = 4$

C $y = -4$ **D** $y = 7$

21. $-5t^2 + 25t - 30$

$$= -\underline{}(\underline{})$$

$$= -\underline{}(\underline{})(\underline{})$$

22. Student _____ is correct. Student _____ did not include the _____ in the final factoring.

23. See 📖 page 443 for a table of sums for rolling two number cubes.

$$P(\leq 7) = P(\underline{}) + P(\underline{}) + P(\underline{}) + P(\underline{}) + P(\underline{}) + P(\underline{})$$

$$= \frac{\square}{\square} + \frac{\square}{\square} + \frac{\square}{\square} + \frac{\square}{\square} + \frac{\square}{\square} + \frac{\square}{\square}$$

$$= \frac{\square}{\square} = \frac{\square}{\square}$$

24. *See page 13 in the* Student Reference Guide.

$$P(\text{one } 3) = \frac{1}{\square}$$

$$P(\text{five } 3s) = \left(\frac{\square}{\square}\right)^{\square}$$

$$= \underline{}$$

25. Student _____ is correct.

Student _____ included the sum of

_____ but the question asked for

_____ 6.

26. *See page 13 in the* Student Reference Guide.

a.
Sum of Two Spins

	1	2	3	4	5	6	7	8
1								
2								
3								
4								
5								
6								

b. $P(> 8) = P(\underline{\quad}) + P(\underline{\quad}) + P(\underline{\quad}) + P(\underline{\quad}) + P(\underline{\quad}) + P(\underline{\quad})$

$$= \frac{\square}{\square} + \frac{\square}{\square} + \frac{\square}{\square} + \frac{\square}{\square} + \frac{\square}{\square} + \frac{\square}{\square}$$

$$= \frac{\square}{\square}$$

$$= \frac{\square}{\square}$$

---

27. Circle the first step in solving the inequality $2(x + 5) > x + 12$.

  A Combine the variables.

  B Use the Addition Property of Inequality.

  C Apply the Distributive Property.

  D Use the Multiplication Property of Inequality.

28. $40 < 24 + 0.16m$

  $\underline{\quad} < 0.16m$

  $\underline{\quad} < m$

over $\underline{\quad}$ miles per day

---

29. Distribute $\underline{\quad}$ through the

parentheses on the right side.

Then add $\underline{\quad}$ to both sides.

Subtract $\underline{\quad}$ from both sides.

$\underline{\quad\quad\quad}$ both sides by 5.

The solution is $x > \underline{\quad}$.

30. Malcolm's change in rate: $\underline{\quad\quad}$

Frederico's change in rate: $\underline{\quad\quad}$

$\underline{\quad} + \underline{\quad}y > \underline{\quad} + \underline{\quad}y$

$y > \underline{\quad}$

Frederico will have a better average than

Malcolm in their $\underline{\quad}$ and $\underline{\quad}$ years.

Solving Multi-Step Compound Inequalities

Name _____

New Concepts

A **compound inequality** is two inequalities joined by the word **AND** or the word **OR**.

Math Language
If joined by **AND** the solution must satisfy both inequalities.
If joined by **OR** the solution must satisfy one of the inequalities.

Example **Solving Multi-Step Compound Inequalities**

Solve and graph the inequality.

$4x - 7 < 3$ OR $2x - 19 > -7$ If a compound inequality is joined by OR, solve each part of the inequality separately.

$\quad\quad 4x < 10 \quad\quad\quad\quad 2x > 12$ Add.

$\quad\quad x < 2\frac{1}{2}$ OR $\quad\quad x > 6$ Divide.

Graph both inequalities:

 0 1 2 3 4 5 6 7

Example **Simplifying Before Solving Inequalities**

Solve the inequality. Justify each step.

$$-15 \le 3(2x - 1) \le 39$$
$$-15 \le \quad 6x - 3 \quad \le 39 \quad\quad \textit{Distributive Property}$$
$$\underline{+3 \quad\quad\quad +3 \quad +3} \quad\quad \textit{Addition Property of Inequality}$$
$$-12 \le \quad 6x \quad\quad \le 42 \quad\quad \textit{Simplify.}$$
$$\tfrac{1}{6} \cdot -12 \le \quad 6x \cdot \tfrac{1}{6} \quad \le 42 \cdot \tfrac{1}{6} \quad \textit{Division Property of Inequality}$$
$$-2 \le \quad\quad x \quad\quad \le 7 \quad\quad \textit{Simplify.}$$

Lesson Practice 📖 page 540

Solve and graph each inequality.

a. $2x + 9 < 8$ OR $3x + 3 > 12$

$\quad\quad 2x < \underline{\quad}$ OR $3x > \underline{\quad}$ ←++++++++++→

$\quad\quad x < \underline{\quad}$ OR $x > \underline{\quad}$

b. $\quad 24 \le 2x + 8 < 36$

$\quad\quad 16 \le \quad 2x \quad < \underline{\quad}$ ←++++++++++→

$\quad\quad \underline{\quad} \le \quad x \quad < \underline{\quad}$

Solve the inequality. Justify each step.

c. $6 \le 2(x + 12) < 12$

$6 \le 2x +$ _____ < 12 _____ Property

$\underline{-24} \qquad \underline{-24} \quad \underline{-24}$ _____ Property

_____ $\le 2x \qquad\qquad < $ _____ _____

$\dfrac{\square}{2} \le \dfrac{2x}{2} \qquad < \dfrac{\square}{2}$ _____ Property of Inequality

_____ $\le x \qquad\qquad <$ _____ _____

d. $-16 > 2(x - 2)$ OR $27 < 3(x + 2)$

$-16 >$ ___$x -$ _____   OR $27 <$ ___$x +$ _____ _____ Property

$\underline{+4} \qquad\qquad \underline{+4} \qquad\qquad \underline{-6} \qquad\qquad \underline{-6}$ _____ Property of Inequality

$-12 >$ ___x OR   _____ $< 3x$ _____

$\dfrac{\square}{2} > \dfrac{\square}{2}$ OR $\dfrac{\square}{3} < \dfrac{3x}{3}$ _____ Property of Inequality

_____ $> x$ OR   _____ $< x$ _____

e. Of the 4 babies born at night, 3 have the following weights: 5.2 pounds, 6.3 pounds, and 7.5 pounds. What weight could the fourth baby be if the average of all their weights falls within 6 and 8 pounds?

The sum of the four weights divided by 4 is greater than or equal to 6 pounds and less than or equal to 8 pounds.

$$6 \le \frac{(5.2 + 6.3 + 7.5 + x)}{4} \le 8$$

_____ $\le 5.2 + 6.3 + 7.5 + x \le 32$

_____ $\le$ _____ $+ x \le$ _____

_____ $\le \qquad x \le$ _____

The fourth baby could weigh between _____ and _____ pounds.

1. $2x^2 + 9xy + 7y^2$

   $= (2x + \underline{\quad})(x + \underline{\quad})$

2. $-4m^2 + 8mn + 5n^2$

   $= (\underline{\quad} + n)(\underline{\quad} + 5n)$

3. *Use FOIL.*

   $(\sqrt{3} - 12)^2$

   $= \left(\sqrt{\underline{\quad}} - \underline{\quad}\right)\left(\sqrt{\underline{\quad}} - \underline{\quad}\right)$

   $= \underline{\quad} - \underline{\quad} - \underline{\quad} + \underline{\quad}$

   $= \underline{\quad} - \underline{\quad}$

4. $(2x + \sqrt{3})(2x - \sqrt{3})$

   $= \underline{\quad} - \underline{\quad} + \underline{\quad} - \underline{\quad}$

   $= \underline{\quad} - \underline{\quad}$

5. *Set the denominator equal to zero.*

   $\dfrac{m - 6}{2m - 10}$

   $2m - 10 = 0$

   $2m = \underline{\quad}$

   $\dfrac{2m}{2} = \dfrac{\square}{\square}$

   $m \neq \underline{\quad}$

6. $\dfrac{y + 4}{-2y - 6}$

   $-2y - 6 = 0$

   $-2y = \underline{\quad}$

   $\dfrac{2y}{-2} = \dfrac{\square}{\square}$

   $y \neq - \underline{\quad}$

7. *See pages 10 and 11 in the* Student Reference Guide.

   $2z - 6 \leq z$

   $z \leq \underline{\quad}$

8. *Isolate the variable.*

   $2x + 9 > -x + 18$

   $x > \underline{\quad}$

9. *See page 8 in the* Student Reference Guide.

$y = 10x - 2 \qquad y = 10x + 8$

This is a _____ statement.

Therefore, the system of equations is

_____ .

10. *See page 8 in the* Student Reference Guide.

$y = 3x \qquad 2y = 6x$

This is a _____ statement.

The system of equations is _____

_____ .

11. $P = 4s$

$48 = 4s$

Each side of the perimeter is _____ feet.

One possible way to express the answer

as a radical number is _____ .

12. *Factor first.*

$l \cdot w = (x^2 + 7x + 12)$

$= (x + \underline{\quad})(x + \underline{\quad})$

Substitute $x = 20$ into the longer side.

$(x + \underline{\quad})$

$= (\underline{\quad}, \underline{\quad})$

$= \underline{\quad\quad}$

13. a. $x \bigcirc \underline{\quad}$ OR $x \bigcirc \underline{\quad}$

b. ⟵┼┼┼┼┼┼┼┼┼┼┼⟶

14. $|q - 24.9| = 5.1$

$q - 24.9 = 5.1 \qquad q - 24.9 = -5.1$

$q = \underline{\quad\quad} \qquad q = \underline{\quad\quad}$

The lesser value of q is _____ .

15. *Round the answer down.*

$10 + 0.3m \leq 20$

$0.3m \leq \underline{\quad\quad}$

$m \leq \underline{\quad\quad}$

You can talk at most _____ minutes.

16. *See page 13 in the* Student Reference Guide.

$y = \dfrac{\text{number of red}}{\text{total}} = \dfrac{\square}{\square}$

17. *Factor.*

$-8u^5y + 56u^4y - 80u^3y$

$= -8u^{\square}y(u^{\square} - \underline{\quad} + \underline{\quad})$

$= -8u^{\square}y(u - \underline{\quad})(u - \underline{\quad})$

18. *Find the GCF.*

Circle the expression that is the complete

factored form.

A $3x^4(x - 3)(x + 5)$

B $x^4(3x - 9)(x + 5)$

C $x^4(x - 3)(3x - 15)$

D $(3x - 9)(x^5 + 5x^4)$

19. $P(A) = \dfrac{\square}{\square} = \dfrac{\square}{\square}$ $\qquad$ $P(B) = \dfrac{\square}{\square} = \dfrac{\square}{\square}$

$P(C) = \dfrac{\square}{\square}$ $\qquad$ $P(D) = \dfrac{\square}{\square}$

$P(F) = \dfrac{\square}{\square}$

20. The possibility that the plant will be short

is _____. The combination labeled "tt,"

_____ occur on the chart.

21. Student _____ is correct.

Student _____ found the probability of

rolling a 2 or a 3 to be $\dfrac{\square}{\square} \cdot \dfrac{\square}{\square} = \dfrac{\square}{\square}$,

when it is actually $\dfrac{\square}{\square} = \dfrac{\square}{\square}$.

22. a. $\underline{\quad} + \underline{\quad}p < \underline{\quad} + \underline{\quad}p$

  b. $p < \underline{\quad}$

  c. The solution set is all _____

  numbers less than _____ since

  Veejay can invite only whole people

  and at _____ the costs are equal.

23. $7 - \underline{\quad}d \bigcirc 1 + \underline{\quad}d$

$\underline{\quad} \bigcirc \underline{\quad}d$

$\underline{\quad} \bigcirc d$

It will take _____ days.

24. Solve $5x - 2 < 4x + 7$.　　　　$x < \underline{\quad}$

---

25. Student _____ is correct because $-2 + x > x + 3$ is an inequality that will _____

be true. Student _____ wrote an inequality that is _____ true.

26.　$-17 > -2x - 7$　　　OR　　　$27 > 3(x + 6)$

　　　$-17 > -2x - \underline{\quad}$　　OR　　　$27 > \underline{\quad}x + \underline{\quad}$　　　_____ Property

　　　$\underline{+\quad}$　　　$\underline{+\quad}$　　　$\underline{-18}$　　　$\underline{-18}$　　　_____ Property of Inequality

　　　$-10 < -\underline{\quad}x$　　OR　　$\underline{\quad} > \underline{\quad}x$　　　_____ Property of Inequality

　　　　　　Division Property of Inequality

　　　$\underline{\quad} < x$　　　OR　　$\underline{\quad} > x$　　　_____

　　　$x > \underline{\quad}$　　　OR　　$x < \underline{\quad}$　　　_____

---

27. *Check inequality signs to eliminate answers.*

Circle the solution to $32 < 7x + 11 < 39$.

A $21 > x > 28$　　　**B** $3 < x > 4$

C $3 < x < 4$　　　**D** $3 > x > 4$

28.　$\underline{\quad} \le \dfrac{(45 + 52 + 60 + c)}{4} \le 60$

　$\underline{\quad} \le \dfrac{(\square + c)}{4} \le 60$

　$\underline{\quad} \le \underline{\quad} + c \le 240$

　$\underline{\quad} \le c \le \underline{\quad}$

---

29. *Students' scores that studied: greater than or equal to 90. Students' scores that did not study: less than 70.*

$x \bigcirc \underline{\quad}$ OR $x \bigcirc \underline{\quad}$

30.　$90 \le \dfrac{(94 + 88 + 91 + x)}{4} \le \underline{\quad}$

　$90 \le \dfrac{(\square + x)}{4} \le \underline{\quad}$

　$360 \le \underline{\quad} + x \le \underline{\quad}$

　$\underline{\quad} \le x \le \underline{\quad}$

Felipe must score between _____ and

_____ on his final test.

New Concepts

• See "Perfect-Square Trinomials" on 📖 page 543.

Math Language

A **perfect-square trinomial** is a polynomial that is the square of a binomial.

Example **Factoring Perfect-Square Trinomials**

Determine whether each polynomial is a perfect-square trinomial. If it is, factor the trinomial.

$x^2 + 6x + 9$

$= x^2 + 2 \cdot 3x + 3^2$ *Write in perfect-square trinomial form.*

$= (x + 3)^2$ *It is a perfect-square trinomial.*

In a perfect-square trinomial, $a^2 + 2ab + b^2$, squaring the quotient of the middle term and 2 will always result in the last term. In the previous example, $\left(\frac{6}{2}\right)^2 = 9$.

$x^2 - 2x + 4$

The square of the quotient of -2 and 2 equals 1, not 4. That is, $\left(-\frac{2}{2}\right)^2 \neq 4$. **It is not a perfect-square trinomial.**

• See "Difference of Two Squares" on 📖 page 545.

Example **Factoring the Difference of Two Squares**

Determine whether each binomial is a difference of two squares. If so, factor the binomial.

$4x^2 - 25$

$= (2 \cdot 2)(x \cdot x) - (5 \cdot 5)$ *Factor each term.*

$= (2x)^2 - 5^2$ *Write as the difference of two squares.*

$= (2x + 5)(2x - 5)$ *Factor.*

In a difference of two squares, the first and last terms are always perfect squares.

$x^2 - 8$

Since 8 is not a perfect square, **this is not a difference of two squares.**

Determine whether the polynomial is a perfect-square trinomial. If so, factor the trinomial.

A perfect-square trinomial is in the form $a^2 + 2ab + b^2$ or $a^2 - 2ab + b^2$

a. $x^2 + 14x + 49$

$= \underline{\hspace{1cm}} + 2(7x) + \underline{\hspace{1cm}}$

It _____ a perfect square trinomial.

$(\underline{\hspace{0.5cm}} + \underline{\hspace{0.5cm}})^2$

b. $6n^4 - 12n^2 + 6$

Factor out the GCF.

$= \underline{\hspace{0.5cm}}(n^4 - 2n^2 + 1)$

$\underline{\hspace{0.5cm}}(\underline{\hspace{0.8cm}})^2 - 2(n^2)(1) + \underline{\hspace{0.5cm}}^2$

It _____ a perfect square trinomial.

$\underline{\hspace{0.5cm}}(\underline{\hspace{0.8cm}} - 1)^2$

c. $3g^2 + 9g + 9$

$= \underline{\hspace{0.5cm}}(g^2 + 3g + 3)$

In a perfect-square trinomial, squaring the quotient of the middle term and 2 will always result in the last term. $\left(\frac{3}{2}\right)^2 \neq 3$

It _____ a perfect square trinomial.

d. *Factor to determine by how much the radius increased.*

$= \underline{\hspace{0.5cm}}(r^2 + \underline{\hspace{1cm}} + \underline{\hspace{1cm}})$

$= \underline{\hspace{0.5cm}}(r^2 + 2(\underline{\hspace{1cm}}) + \underline{\hspace{1cm}})$

$= \underline{\hspace{0.5cm}}(\underline{\hspace{1.2cm}})^2$

The radius increased by _____ miles.

Determine whether the binomial is a difference of two squares. If so, factor the binomial.

e. $25x^2 - 4$

In a difference of two squares, the first and last terms are always perfect squares.

It _____ a difference of two squares.

$(5x + \underline{\hspace{0.5cm}})(5x - \underline{\hspace{0.5cm}})$

f. $9b^2 - 100a^2$

It _____ a difference of two squares.

$= (\underline{\hspace{0.3cm}}b \bigcirc \underline{\hspace{0.3cm}}a)(\underline{\hspace{0.3cm}}b \bigcirc \underline{\hspace{0.3cm}}a)$

g. $x^2 - 14$

It _____ a difference of two squares.

h. $-81 + x^{10}$

Write the terms in descending order.

$\underline{\hspace{3cm}}$

$x^{10} = (\underline{\hspace{0.5cm}})^2 \qquad 81 = (\underline{\hspace{0.5cm}})^2$

It _____ a difference of two squares.

$= (\underline{\hspace{1.5cm}})(\underline{\hspace{1.5cm}})$

i. Area of the border: 34^2
Area of the pool: s^2

Difference $= \underline{\hspace{1cm}} - \underline{\hspace{1cm}}$

$= (\underline{\hspace{0.5cm}} + \underline{\hspace{0.5cm}})(\underline{\hspace{0.5cm}} - \underline{\hspace{0.5cm}})$

1. Use FOIL.

___ ◯ ___ ◯ ___ ◯ ___

Simplify radicals if possible.

___ ◯ ___ ◯ ___ ◯ ___

Combine like terms. Like radicals have the same radicand.

= _____

2. Use FOIL.

$(x + \sqrt{12})(x - \sqrt{3})$

= _____

---

3. Isolate the variable.

$\dfrac{-b}{4} + \dfrac{3}{8} \geq \dfrac{3b}{4} - \dfrac{5}{8}$

$\dfrac{\square}{4} \geq \dfrac{\square}{8}$

$b \leq$ _____

4. See pages 10 and 11 in the Student Reference Guide.

$11h + 9 \leq 5h - 21$

____$h \leq$ _____

$h \leq$ _____

---

5. Factor out the GCF.

_____(_____ − _____ − _____)

= _____(_____)(_____)

6. Factor out −1. In the binomial, write the opposite of every term.

GCF: _____

= _____(____ ◯ ____)

---

7. In a perfect-square trinomial, squaring the quotient of the middle term and 2 will always result in the last term.

$\left(\dfrac{10}{2}\right)^2 =$ _____

perfect-square trinomial? _____

= (_____ + _____)²

8. perfect-square trinomial? _____

= (_____ + _____)²

---

9. *The slopes of perpendicular lines are negative reciprocals.*

$m_{\overline{TU}} =$ _____ $m_{\overline{UV}} =$ _____

_____ · _____ = _____; so $\overline{TU}$ _____ $\overline{UV}$,

therefore $\angle TUV$ _____ a right triangle.

10. *The factored form of the difference of two squares is $(a + b)(a - b)$.*

$(-7 + 2y)($ _____ $)$

$=$ _____ $+$ _____ $+$ _____ $+$ _____

$= ($ _____ $)$

11. *Write an inequality.*

_____ ◯ _____

12. *Put the second equation in standard form.*

$y =$ _____

The equations have the _____ slope.

The system is _____ .

13. *Solve each equation for y.*

$y =$ _____

$y =$ _____

The equations _____ have the same slope. The equations _____ identical. The system is _____

_____ .

14. *The events are inclusive.*

$P(\text{sum of } 10) =$ _____

$P(\text{doubles}) =$ _____

$P(\text{sum of 10 or doubles}) =$

$P(10) + P(\text{doubles}) - P(10 \text{ and doubles})$

$=$ _____ $+$ _____ $-$ _____

$=$ _____

Simplify.

$=$ _____

15. *0.03 times the amount deposited is greater than or equal to $60.*

a. _____ d ◯ _____

b. d ◯ _____

c. at least ▓ _____

d. ◁—+++++++++—▷
     1000   2000   3000

16. $x = 8 -$ _____ $=$ _____

$x = 8 +$ _____ $=$ _____

_____ ◯ x ◯ _____

The inequality may also be written:

x ◯ _____ AND x ◯ _____

17. a. $\dfrac{|x+3|}{4} = 6$ *Multiply.*

$|x+3| =$ _____

b. $x + 3 =$ _____ or

$x + 3 =$ _____

c. $x =$ _____ or

$x =$ _____

{_____ , _____}

18. Given a trinomial in the form $ax^2 + bx + c$,

if c is _____ , then both terms

have the same sign as b: either both are

_____ , or both are

_____ . If c is

_____ , then they have

_____ signs.

19. For $y = \dfrac{a}{x-b} + c$, the vertical asymptote is at $x = b$; the horizontal asymptote is at $y = c$.

a. $y =$ _____

b. $x =$ _____

c. $x = 5$

$y =$ _____ toys

20. Factor the trinomial and take the square root of the result.

$c^2 = 16m^6 + 320m^5 + 1600m^4$

$c^2 =$ _____$(m^2 + 20m +$ _____$)$

$c^2 =$ _____$($_____$)($_____$)$

$c =$ _____$($_____$)$

21. In independent events, $P(A \text{ and } B) = P(A) \cdot P(B)$

$P(\text{heads, heads}) = ($___$) \cdot ($___$)$

$=$ ___

22. $P(A \text{ or } B) = P(A) + P(B)$

The table shows that there are ____

favorable outcomes and a total of ____

possible outcomes.

Circle the answer.

A $\dfrac{1}{3}$ **B** $\dfrac{1}{6}$ **C** $\dfrac{1}{18}$ **D** $\dfrac{1}{1944}$

23. The expression is a difference of _____ .

Factor as (_____ + _____)(_____ − _____) which equals

_____ · _____ = _____ .

24. *Solve the inequality.*

_____, the inequality is only true

if x is _____ or _____.

25. Let $x =$ amount each is paid per hour

____$x >$ ____$x + 50$

____$x > 50$

$x >$ ____

more than ▨____ an hour

---

26. Student _____ is correct. Student _____ did not change the _____ of the

inequality symbol when using the _____ Property of Inequality.

---

27. *No more than means less than or equal to.*

a. _____ ◯ F ◯ _____

b. _____ ◯ $\dfrac{35 + \Box + \Box + \Box + x}{\Box}$ ◯ _____

_____ ◯ x ◯ _____

---

28. $28 <$ $2(x + 3)$ < 42

$28 <$ _____ $+$ ____ < 42 _____ Property of Inequality

_____ $<$ ____x $<$ _____   _____ Property of Inequality

_____ $<$ x $<$ _____   _____ Property of Inequality

---

29. $a^2 + 2ab + b^2$ or $a^2 - 2ab + b^2$

Circle the answer.

A $9x^2 + 49$

B $64x^2 - 100$

C $6x^2 + 48x - 96$

D $49x^2 - 28x + 4$

30. *Draw a sketch.*

painted area $= A_{\text{deck}} - A_{\text{shed}}$

$=$ ____$^2 -$ ____^{2}

$=$ ____$^2 -$ _____

Factor the expression.

$=$ (_____)(_____)

New Concepts

• A quadratic function must have a quadratic term. It may also have a linear and/or a constant term.

$$f(x) = ax^2 + bx + c, \text{ where } a \neq 0$$

quadratic   linear   constant
term   term   term

Example **Identifying Quadratic Functions**

Determine whether each function represents a quadratic function.

$y + 7x = 4x^2 - 6$

$y = 4x^2 - 7x - 6$ *Solve for y.*

It can be written in standard form. **It is a quadratic function.**

$y = 5 + 2x$

There is no quadratic term. **It is not a quadratic function.**

$-2x^3 + y = -5x^3 + x^2$

$y = -3x^3 + x^2$ *Solve for y.*

There is a cubic term, $-3x^3$. **It is not a quadratic function.**

The graph of $f(x) = x^2$ is known as the quadratic parent function. Graph the parent function by making a table of values. It forms a smooth U-shaped curve called a **parabola.**

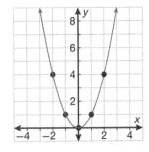

x	−4	−2	0	1	2
y	16	4	0	4	16

Direction of a Parabola
For a quadratic function in standard form, $y = ax^2 + bx + c$:
If $a < 0$, the parabola opens downward.
If $a > 0$, the parabola opens upward.

Determine whether each function represents a quadratic function.
See if each function can be written in the form $y = ax^2 + bx + c$, $a \neq 0$.

a. $4 - y = x - 2x^2 - 3$

$- y = -2x^2 + x -$ ____

$y = 2x^2 - x +$ ____

Quadratic function? _____

b. $x = -x^2 + y$ ____ $+ x = y$

The equation lacks a _____ term,

but c _____ be equal to 0.

Quadratic function? _____

c. $4 = y$

Is there a quadratic term? _____   Quadratic function? _____

Use a table of values to graph $f(x) = 4x^2 - 3$.

d. $f(-2) = 4(\_\_\_)^2 - 3$

$= 4(\_\_\_) - 3$

$= \_\_\_$

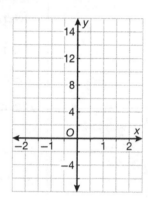

x	-2	-1	0	1	2
y	13				

Determine whether the graph of each function opens upward or downward.

e. $f(x) = 2x^2 - 4$

coefficient of x^2: $a =$ ____, which is

_____ 0.

The graph opens _____.

f. $f(x) = 2x - 5x^2$

$= _____$ *Write in standard form.*

$a = \_\_\_ \bigcirc 0$

The graph opens _____.

g. The equation $h = -16t^2 + 16$ describes the height of an acorn that has fallen for t seconds.

Find h when $t = 0.5$.

$h = -16(\_\_\_)^2 + 16$

$= -16(\_\_\_) + 16$

$= \_\_\_ + 16$

$= \_\_\_$

1. polynomial type:

_____

$q^2 + 18q + 81$

$= (q \; \bigcirc \; \underline{\quad})(q \; \bigcirc \; \underline{\quad})$

$= \underline{\hspace{4cm}}$

2. polynomial type:

_____

$36x^2 - 144$

$= (x \; \bigcirc \; \underline{\quad})(x \; \bigcirc \; \underline{\quad})$

---

3. $\sqrt{12} + \sqrt{48} - \sqrt{27}$

$= \underline{\quad}\sqrt{\underline{\quad}} + \underline{\quad}\sqrt{\underline{\quad}} - \underline{\quad}\sqrt{\underline{\quad}}$

$= \underline{\quad}\sqrt{\underline{\quad}}$

---

4. $\sqrt{18} + \sqrt{32} + \sqrt{50}$

$= \underline{\quad}\sqrt{\underline{\quad}} + \underline{\quad}\sqrt{\underline{\quad}} + \underline{\quad}\sqrt{\underline{\quad}}$

$= \underline{\quad}\sqrt{\underline{\quad}}$

---

5. $2p + 7 > p - 10$

$\underline{\quad}p + 7 > -10$

$p > \underline{\quad}$

6. $16 < 2x + 8$ OR $15 > 7x + 1$

$\underline{\quad} < 2x$ $\underline{\quad} > 7x$

$\underline{\quad} < x$ OR $\underline{\quad} > x$

$x > \underline{\quad}$ OR $x < \underline{\quad}$

---

7. *Isolate y on one side. Write terms in descending order of powers.*

$x + 15x^2 - y = 4$

$y = \underline{\hspace{4cm}}$

8. $P(\text{blue or B}) = P(\underline{\quad}) + P(\underline{\quad}) - P(\underline{\quad})$

$= \underline{\quad} + \underline{\quad} - \underline{\quad}$

$= \underline{\quad}$

---

9. $P(\text{gray or D}) = P(\underline{\quad}) + P(\underline{\quad}) -$

$\quad P(\underline{\quad})$

$\quad = \underline{\quad} + \underline{\quad} - \underline{\quad}$

$\quad = \underline{\quad\quad}$

10. $P(\text{white or C}) = P(\underline{\quad}) + P(\underline{\quad}) - P(\underline{\quad})$

$\quad = \underline{\quad} + \underline{\quad} - \underline{\quad}$

$\quad = \underline{\quad\quad}$

11. The events are $\underline{\quad\quad\quad\quad}$

$\quad P(\text{A or B}) = P(\text{A}) + P(\text{B})$

$\quad = \underline{\quad} + \underline{\quad}$

$\quad = \underline{\quad}$

12. a. *Use slope-intercept form.*

$\quad$ points: $(3, \underline{\quad})(8, \underline{\quad})$

$\quad m = \dfrac{\square - \square}{\square - \square} = \underline{\quad}$

$\quad b = \underline{\quad}$

$\quad y = \underline{\quad\quad}$

b. *See page 14 in the* Student Reference Guide.

$\quad$ It is a $\underline{\quad\quad}$ correlation.

13. $\left| W - \underline{\quad} \right| = \underline{\quad}$

$\quad W - \underline{\quad} = \underline{\quad}$ or $W - \underline{\quad} = \underline{\quad}$

$\quad W = \underline{\quad}$ or $W = \underline{\quad}$

14. a. *Substitute $x = 2$.*

$\quad$ answer $= \underline{\quad\quad}$

b. GCF: $\underline{\quad}$

$\quad \underline{\quad}(\underline{\quad\quad\quad})$

$\quad = \underline{\quad}(\underline{\quad})(\underline{\quad})$

15. $\sqrt{14} \cdot \sqrt{21} = \sqrt{\underline{\quad} \cdot \underline{\quad}}$

$\quad = \underline{\quad}\sqrt{\underline{\quad}}$

16. At the vertical asymptote, the value of the function is undefined because the

$\underline{\quad\quad\quad}$ equals $\underline{\quad\quad}$.

This occurs at $x = \underline{\quad}$.

17. $-5t^2 + 40t - 35$

Factor out the GCF.

$-\underline{\hspace{1cm}}(\underline{\hspace{3cm}})$

$= -\underline{\hspace{1cm}}(\underline{\hspace{2cm}})(\underline{\hspace{2cm}})$

18.

Student Committee

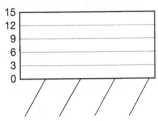

19. Complete the bar graph.

Salad Request

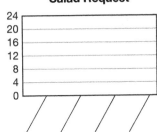

20. *See page 6 in the* Student Reference Guide.

$\underline{\hspace{1cm}} = k(\underline{\hspace{1cm}})(\underline{\hspace{1cm}})$

$\underline{\hspace{1cm}} = k$

$a = \underline{\hspace{1cm}} bc$

21. $\underline{\hspace{1cm}}x + \underline{\hspace{1cm}} - 14 > \underline{\hspace{1cm}}x + 7$

$\underline{\hspace{1cm}}x + \underline{\hspace{1cm}} > \underline{\hspace{1cm}}x + 7$

$\underline{\hspace{1cm}} > \underline{\hspace{1cm}}x$

$\underline{\hspace{1cm}} > x$

$x < \underline{\hspace{1cm}}$

22. Circle the answer.

A Combine the variable.

B Addition Property of Inequality

C Distributive Property of Inequality

D Multiplication Property of Inequality

23. $\underline{\hspace{1cm}} \leq \dfrac{\left(210 + \square + \square + \square + x\right)}{5} \leq \underline{\hspace{1cm}}$

$\underline{\hspace{1cm}} \leq \dfrac{\left(\square + x\right)}{5} \leq \underline{\hspace{1cm}}$

$\underline{\hspace{1cm}} \leq \square + x \leq \underline{\hspace{1cm}}$

$\underline{\hspace{1cm}} \leq x \leq \underline{\hspace{1cm}}$

24. *See page 12 in the* Student Reference Guide. *Check that the factored form is equal to the polynomial.*

Student _____ . Student _____ did

not put the trinomial in the form

_____ .

25. a. GCF: _____

_____(____r^2 − ____r + ____)

_____(____ ◯ ____)^2

b. $V_{cylinder} = \pi r^2 h$

_____ ▨

c. _____ ▨

---

26. $A_{square} = s^{\square}$

$S_{cube} = $ _____$s^{\square}$

Factor.

$6x^2 + 36x + 54$

$s = $ _____

27. *Substitute the value for x into the function and verify that the equation is satisfied for y.*

Circle the answer.

A $y = x + 8$

B $y = -x^2 + 12$

C $y = x^2 + 2$

D $y = -x^2 - 3x + 4$

---

28. *See page 12 in the* Student Reference Guide.

function of degree one:

$f(x) = $ _____

function of degree two:

$f(x) = $ _____

29. In $y = x^2$, the coefficient of x^2 is

_____, which means the graph is a

parabola that opens _____.

In $y = -x^2$, the coefficient of x^2 is

_____, which means the graph is a

parabola that opens _____.

---

30. $A_{circle} = \pi r^2$

$A_{large\ circle} = $ _____ $A_{small\ circle} = $ _____

$A_{pool} = $ _____ − _____

$= $ _____ − _____

$= $ _____

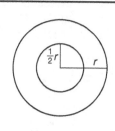

Solving Problems Using the Pythagorean Theorem page 556

New Concepts

- The Pythagorean Theorem states:

  If a triangle is a right triangle with legs of length a and b and hypotenuse of length c, then $a^2 + b^2 = c^2$.

  ┌─ **Exploration** 📖 page 556

  │ Justifying the Pythagorean Theorem

- Use the Pythagorean Theorem to identify an unknown side length of a right triangle.

┌─ **Example** **Calculating Missing Side Lengths**

Use the Pythagorean Theorem to find t to the nearest tenth.

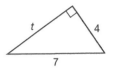

$a^2 + b^2 = c^2$	*Pythagorean Theorem*
$4^2 + t^2 = 7^2$	*Substitute 4 for a, t for b, and 7 for c.*
$16 + t^2 = 49$	*Simplify.*
$t^2 = 33$	*Subtract 16 from each side.*
$t = \sqrt{33}$	*Take the positive root of each side.*
$t \approx 5.7$	*Estimate and round.*

- The **Converse of the Pythagorean Theorem** states that for a triangle with sides a, b, and c, if $a^2 + b^2 = c^2$, then the triangle is a right triangle.

- Use the Converse of the Pythagorean Theorem to prove (or disprove) that 3 given side lengths form a right triangle.

Math Language

A **Pythagorean Triple** is three *nonzero whole numbers* that are side lengths of a right triangle.

Examples:
3, 4, 5
5, 12, 13

┌─ **Example** **Determining a Right Triangle**

Determine whether the given side lengths form a Pythagorean triple.

9, 40, 41

$9^2 + 40^2 \stackrel{?}{=} 41^2$	*Use the Converse of the Pythagorean Theorem.*
$81 + 1600 \stackrel{?}{=} 1681$	*Simplify.*
$1681 = 1681$	*The equation is true.*

This is a Pythagorean triple.

7, 11, $\sqrt{170}$

$\sqrt{170}$ is not a whole number. **This is not a Pythagorean triple.**

Use the Pythagorean Theorem to find the missing side lengths.

a. Find side length c.

$$a^2 + b^2 = c^2$$

$$12^2 + \underline{\hspace{0.6cm}}^2 = c^2$$

$$\underline{\hspace{0.8cm}} + 256 = c^2$$

$$\underline{\hspace{0.8cm}} = c^2$$

$$\sqrt{\underline{\hspace{0.8cm}}} = c \longrightarrow \underline{\hspace{0.8cm}} = c$$

b. Find side length m to the nearest tenth.

$$a = \underline{\hspace{0.8cm}} \qquad b = \underline{\hspace{0.8cm}} \qquad c = \underline{\hspace{0.8cm}}$$

$$2^2 + m^2 = \underline{\hspace{0.8cm}}^2$$

$$\underline{\hspace{0.8cm}} + m^2 = \underline{\hspace{0.8cm}}$$

$$m^2 = \underline{\hspace{0.8cm}}$$

$$m = \sqrt{\underline{\hspace{0.8cm}}} = \underline{\hspace{0.6cm}}.\underline{\hspace{0.6cm}}$$

c. Find side length r.

$$(\underline{\hspace{0.8cm}})^2 + r^2 = \left(\sqrt{\underline{\hspace{0.8cm}}}\right)^2$$

$$\underline{\hspace{0.8cm}} + r^2 = \underline{\hspace{0.8cm}}$$

$$r^2 = \underline{\hspace{0.8cm}} \longrightarrow r = \sqrt{\underline{\hspace{0.8cm}}} = \underline{\hspace{0.8cm}}$$

d. Find side length s in simplest radical form.

$$(\underline{\hspace{0.8cm}})^2 + (\underline{\hspace{0.8cm}})^2 = s^2$$

$$\underline{\hspace{0.8cm}} + \underline{\hspace{0.8cm}} = s^2$$

$$\underline{\hspace{0.8cm}} = s^2 \longrightarrow \underline{\hspace{0.8cm}}\sqrt{\underline{\hspace{0.8cm}}} =$$

Determine whether the given side lengths form a Pythagorean triple.

e. 5, 9, 11

$$5^2 + 9^2 \stackrel{?}{=} (\underline{\hspace{0.8cm}})^2$$

$$\underline{\hspace{0.8cm}} + 81 \stackrel{?}{=} \underline{\hspace{0.8cm}}$$

$$\underline{\hspace{0.8cm}} \bigcirc \underline{\hspace{0.8cm}} \qquad \text{Triple?} \underline{\hspace{1.2cm}}$$

f. 8, 15, 17

$$8^2 + \underline{\hspace{0.6cm}}^2 \stackrel{?}{=} (\underline{\hspace{0.8cm}})^2$$

$$\underline{\hspace{0.8cm}} + 225 \stackrel{?}{=} \underline{\hspace{0.8cm}}$$

$$\underline{\hspace{0.8cm}} \bigcirc \underline{\hspace{0.8cm}} \qquad \text{Triple?} \underline{\hspace{1.2cm}}$$

g. 4, $\sqrt{65}$, 13   Triple? \underline{\hspace{1.2cm}}

h. A ladder's base is 8 ft from a wall. Its top touches the wall 32 ft up.

Find the ladder's length to the nearest tenth.

$$(\underline{\hspace{0.8cm}})^2 + (\underline{\hspace{0.8cm}})^2 = c^2$$

$$\underline{\hspace{0.8cm}} + \underline{\hspace{0.8cm}} = c^2$$

$$\underline{\hspace{0.8cm}} = c^2$$

$$\underline{\hspace{0.8cm}} = c \longrightarrow \underline{\hspace{0.8cm}} = c$$

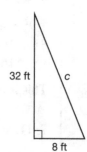

32 ft c

8 ft

1. $3\sqrt{45} - \sqrt{5}$

   $= \underline{\quad}\sqrt{\underline{\quad}} - \sqrt{5}$

   $= \underline{\quad}\sqrt{\underline{\quad}}$

2. All exponents should be positive.

   $\dfrac{p^{-1}}{w}\left(\dfrac{wx}{cp^{-2}q^{-4}} + 5pq^{-3}\right)$

   $= \underline{\hspace{3cm}}$

3. $-3t^3 - 27t^2 - 24t$

   $= \underline{\quad}(\underline{\quad}t^2 + \underline{\quad}t + \underline{\quad})$

   $= \underline{\quad}(\underline{\quad}t + \underline{\quad})(\underline{\quad}t + \underline{\quad})$

4. $4x^4 - 16x^2$

   $= \underline{\quad}(\underline{\quad}x^2 + \underline{\quad})$

   $= \underline{\quad}(\underline{\quad}x - \underline{\quad})(\underline{\quad}x + \underline{\quad})$

5. $2x^2 + 14 - 9x - x^2$

   $= x^2 - \underline{\quad} + \underline{\quad}$

   $= (x - \underline{\quad})(x - \underline{\quad})$

6. $3g^2 - 12$

   $\underline{\quad}(\underline{\quad}g^2 + \underline{\quad})$

   polynomial type? $\underline{\hspace{3cm}}$

   $\underline{\hspace{4cm}}$

   $\underline{\quad}(\underline{\quad}g - \underline{\quad})(\underline{\quad}g + \underline{\quad})$

7. $9x^2 - 24x + 16$

   polynomial type? $\underline{\hspace{2.5cm}}$

   $\underline{\hspace{4cm}}$

   $(\underline{\quad}x - \underline{\quad})^2$

8. $4 + y = -8 + 16x$

   $\underline{\hspace{3cm}}$

   quadratic term? $\underline{\quad}$

   quadratic function? $\underline{\quad}$

---

9. *Simplify.*

$$y + x^2 = 3x^2 - 10x + 12$$

_____

quadratic term? _____

quadratic function? _____

---

10. $0.7 + 0.05y = 0.715$

$0.05y =$ ___._____

$y = \dfrac{\square}{\square}$

$y =$ ___._____

---

11. LCM of the denominators: _____

Multiply every term by the LCM.

$$(\underline{})\tfrac{1}{2} + (\underline{})\tfrac{3}{4}x = (\underline{})\tfrac{1}{6}x + (\underline{})2$$

$$\underline{} + \underline{}x = \underline{}x + 24$$

$$x = \dfrac{\square}{\square}$$

$$x = \underline{}$$

---

12. *When dividing an inequality by a negative number, reverse the sign.*

$$-1.2x \geq -4.8$$

$x \bigcirc$ _____

←+++++++++++++++++→

---

13. slope of given line: _____

$$y - y_1 = m(x - x_1)$$

The parallel line has a slope of _____

and passes through $(1, 5)$.

$y =$ _____

---

14. width: $2\sqrt{4} =$ _____

length: $\sqrt{25} =$ _____

$$P = 2w + 2l$$

$P =$ _____

$=$ _____ feet

---

15. $\dfrac{x}{-5} + 6 \leq 10$

$\dfrac{x}{-5} \leq$ _____

$x \bigcirc$ _____

---

16. $a^2 + b^2 = c^2$

$$(\underline{})^2 + (\underline{})^2 = c^2$$

$$\underline{} = c^2$$

$$\sqrt{\underline{}} = c$$

$$\underline{}\sqrt{\underline{}} = c$$

---

17. To find the vertical asymptote, set the

_____ of the rational

expression equal to zero.

$x + 4.5 =$ _____

$x =$ _____

A vertical asymptote occurs at $x =$ _____.

18. *See page 6 in the* Student Reference Guide.

$y = \frac{k}{x}$

$k = y(\underline{\quad})$

$k = (\underline{\quad})(\underline{\quad}) =$ _____

19.

rate of change in ND: $\dfrac{7000 \text{ people}}{5 \text{ yrs}} = 1400$

rate of change in WY: $\dfrac{\boxed{} \text{ people}}{\boxed{} \text{ yrs}}$

Let y equal the number of years since 2005.

$509,000 +$ _____ $y \bigcirc 635,000 - 1400y$

 Solve for y. Calculate year.

20. $a^2 + b^2 = c^2$

$27.5^2 + 10^2 = c^2$

_____ $+$ _____ $= c^2$

_____ $= c^2$

$\sqrt{\underline{}} = c$

The leach edge is about _____ ft long.

21. **a.** ____ $\bigcirc$ c $\bigcirc$ ____

b. 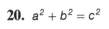 Solve $5 \le \frac{5}{9}(f - 32) \le 60$.

Distribute first.

____ $\bigcirc$ f $\bigcirc$ ____

c. $f \bigcirc$ ____ OR $f \bigcirc$ ____

22. $24 < 2x + 6 < 36$

____ $< 2x <$ ____

____ $< x <$ ____

This is an _____ inequality since the

entire solution falls within a specific range.

23. Student _____ is correct because the

polynomial is a difference of

_____.

24. $A_{circle} = \pi r^2$

$A_{whole\ tire} =$ _____

$A_{without\ rim} = \pi r^2 - 81\pi$

$A_{rim} = A_{whole\ tire} - A_{without\ rim}$

= _____ − (_____) = _____

$A_{rim}:$ _____ = πr^2

$r^2 =$ _____

$r =$ _____

$d = 2r =$ _____

---

25. area of each face = _____   number of faces: _____ $S =$ _____

📓 Graph.

x	0	1	2	3
S				

---

26. The Pythagorean Theorem only applies to _____.

---

27. $a = x$ $b = 2x$ $c = \sqrt{45}$

(____)² + (____)² = (____)²

_____ + ____x^2 = _____

____x^2 = _____

$x^2 =$ _____

$x =$ _____

$a =$ _____ $b =$ _____

28. $a^2 + b^2 = c^2$

📓 Solve $5^2 + x^2 = 13^2$.

$x =$ _____

$P = 13 + 5 +$ _____ = _____

Circle the answer.

A 212 inches   **B** 30 inches

C 32 inches   **D** 12 inches

---

29. $6x^2 + 5x - 38$

a. (_____)(_____)

Substitute $x = 4$.

b. _____

30. $A = ($ _____ $)($ _____ $)$ Use FOIL.

$A =$ _____

$A =$ _____ square meters

Name _____

Calculating the Midpoint and Length of a Segment page 563

New Concepts

- The Pythagorean Theorem can be used to derive the Distance Formula. The distance d between two points (x_1, y_1) and (x_2, y_2) is

$$d = \sqrt{(x_2 - x_1)^2 + (y_2 - y_1)^2}.$$

Example **Finding the Distance Between Two Points**

Find the distance between $(3, -2)$ and $(6, 4)$.

Use the distance formula.
Substitute $(3, -2)$ for (x_1, y_1) and $(6, 4)$ for (x_2, y_2).

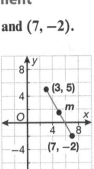

$d = \sqrt{(x_2 - x_1)^2 + (y_2 - y_1)^2}$

$= \sqrt{(6 - 3)^2 + (4 - (-2))^2}$

$= \sqrt{3^2 + 6^2}$ *Simplify.*

$= \sqrt{9 + 36}$ *Simplify powers.*

$= \sqrt{45}$ *Add.*

$= 3\sqrt{5}$ *Simplify the radical.*

The distance between $(3, -2)$ and $(6, 4)$ is $3\sqrt{5}$.

- The **midpoint** of a line segment with endpoints (x_1, y_1) and (x_2, y_2) can be found using the Midpoint Formula.

$$M = \left(\frac{x_1 + x_2}{2}\right), \left(\frac{y_1 + y_2}{2}\right)$$

Example **Finding the Midpoint of a Segment**

Find the midpoint of the segment between $(3, 5)$ and $(7, -2)$.

Use the midpoint formula.

$M = \left(\frac{x_1 + x_2}{2}\right), \left(\frac{y_1 + y_2}{2}\right)$

$= \frac{3 + 7}{2}, \frac{5 + (-2)}{2}$ *Substitute.*

$= \left(\frac{10}{2}, \frac{3}{2}\right) = \left(5, \frac{3}{2}\right)$ *Simplify.*

The midpoint of the line segment is $\left(5, \frac{3}{2}\right)$.

a. Use the diagram from the first example. What is the direct distance from C St. and 2nd Ave. to the corner of D St. and 5th Ave.?

distance from C St. to D St.: ____ block(s)

distance from 2nd to 5th Ave.: ____ block(s)

Substitute in the Pythagorean Theorem.

$$\sqrt{\underline{}^2 + \underline{}^2} = \sqrt{\underline{}} \approx \underline{} \text{ blocks}$$

b. Find the distance between $(-3, -2)$ and $(4, 2)$.

$$\text{distance} = \sqrt{(\underline{} - \underline{})^2 + (\underline{} - \underline{})^2} = \sqrt{\underline{} + \underline{}} = \sqrt{\underline{}}$$

c. Is $PQRS$ a rhombus? $P(\underline{}, \underline{})$, $Q(\underline{}, \underline{})$, $R(\underline{}, \underline{})$, $S(\underline{}, \underline{})$

$$d_{PQ} = \sqrt{(\underline{} - \underline{})^2 + (\underline{} - \underline{})^2} = \sqrt{\underline{}}$$

$$d_{RS} = \sqrt{(\underline{} - \underline{})^2 + (\underline{} - \underline{})^2} = \sqrt{\underline{}} = \underline{}$$

$$d_{QR} = \sqrt{(\underline{} - \underline{})^2 + (\underline{} - \underline{})^2} = \sqrt{\underline{}}$$

$$d_{PS} = \sqrt{(\underline{} - \underline{})^2 + (\underline{} - \underline{})^2} = \sqrt{\underline{}}$$

The distances show that the figure _____ a rhombus.

d. Find the midpoint of the line segment between $(-2, 3)$ and $(4, 7)$.

$$\text{midpoint} = \frac{\square + \square}{2}, \frac{\square + \square}{2} = (\underline{}, \underline{})$$

e. Find the distance a pass travels from a point $(20, 33)$ on the 20-yard line to a point $(58, 15)$ on the opponent's 58-yard line.

$$d = \sqrt{(\underline{} - \underline{})^2 + (\underline{} - \underline{})^2}$$

$$= \sqrt{\underline{}^2 + \underline{}^2}$$

$$= \sqrt{\underline{}} = \sqrt{\underline{}} \approx \underline{} \text{ yds.}$$

1. $15y < 60$

$y <$ _____

$$\begin{array}{c} \leftarrow\!\!+\!\!+\!\!+\!\!+\!\!+\!\!+\!\!+\!\!+\!\!+\!\!+\!\!+\!\!+\!\!\rightarrow \\ \begin{matrix} -2 & 0 & 2 & 4 & 6 & 8 & 10 \end{matrix} \end{array}$$

2. $16 < 6x + 10$ OR $-16 > 6x - 10$

_____ $< x$ OR   _____ $> x$

$$\begin{array}{c} \leftarrow\!\!+\!\!+\!\!+\!\!+\!\!+\!\!+\!\!+\!\!+\!\!\rightarrow \\ \begin{matrix} -2 & 0 & 2 & 4 \end{matrix} \end{array}$$

3. Factor out _____ and the GCF _____.

Then factor the trinomial.

_____$(g^2 \bigcirc$ _____ $g \bigcirc$ _____$)$

$=$ _____$(g \bigcirc$ _____$)(g \bigcirc$ _____$)$

4. factors of 20: _____

factors of -5: _____

Combine factors to give 21:

$($ ___$)($ ___$) + ($ ___$)($ ___$) = 21$

Factor:

$($ ___$b \bigcirc$ ___$)($ ___$b \bigcirc$ ___$)$

5. Factor out _____.

_____$(13w^2 \bigcirc 38w \bigcirc 25)$

factors of 13: _____

factors of 25: _____

Combine factors to give -38:

$($ ___$)($ ___$) + ($ ___$)($ ___$) = -38$

Factor:

_____$($ ___$w \bigcirc$ ___$)(w \bigcirc$ ___$)$

6. *Isolate the y.*

$y =$ _____$x^2 +$ _____x

7. This equation cannot be written in

standard form because there is no _____

variable.

8. $d = \sqrt{(\underline{\quad} - \underline{\quad})^2 + (\underline{\quad} - \underline{\quad})^2}$

$= \sqrt{\underline{\quad} + \underline{\quad}} = \sqrt{\underline{\quad}} = \underline{\quad\quad}$

9. *The amount of cash back on purchases is 4% · p.*

"At least" $100 cash back means

_____ than or _____ $100,

so _____ p ◯ _____ .

Solve for p:

p ◯ ▢ _____

10. *There is a positive correlation when the data values for both variables increase. There is a negative correlation when the data values for one variable increase while the data values for the other variable decrease.*

The correlation is _____ .

---

11. a. x is "at most" 13: x ◯ 13

x is "at least" 5: x ◯ 5

b. _____ ◯ x ◯ _____

c.

12. $A = ($_____$)($_____$)$

Simplify the radicals before multiplying.

$($_____$)($_____$)$

$=$ _____ ▢

---

13. *Isolate C.*

$120 - $_____ $\geq \frac{9}{5}C$

The temperature in Texas has never been above _____ ▢ .

14. The value of c determines whether the graph shifts _____ or _____ .

---

15. Fill in the table.

	Turkey	Ham	Chicken
Lettuce	TL		
Tomato			
Cucumber		HC	
Onion			CO
Peppers			

16. *Write and solve an inequality for the number of games, g.*

_____ $+$ _____ g ◯ _____ g

_____ games or _____

17. Let s = side length of third square

$$\text{\_\_\_\_} < s^2 < \text{\_\_\_\_}$$

$$\sqrt{\text{\_\_\_\_}} < s < \sqrt{\text{\_\_\_\_}}$$

$$\text{\_\_\_\_} < s < \text{\_\_\_\_}$$

18. *Factor the difference of two squares.*

Circle the answer.

A $2(4x + 5y)^2$

B $2(4x - 5y)^2$

C $2(4x + 5y)(4x - 5y)$

D $2(16x + 25y)(16x - 25y)$

---

19. Multiply $(y + 5)(y - 5)$: _____

Multiply $(x + 4)^2$: _____

Subtract the polynomials.

$(\text{_____}) - (\text{_____})$

20. Student _____ is correct. Student _____

did not use the _____

Property correctly.

---

21. Since the coefficient of the quadratic

term is negative, the graph opens

_____. If the price is too

_____, more will be sold, but the

company will make _____ profit

due to expenses. If the price is too

_____, fewer will be sold.

22. $a^2 + b^2 = c^2$

$$(\text{\_\_\_\_})^2 + n^2 = (\text{\_\_\_\_})^2$$

$$n^2 = (\text{\_\_\_\_})^2 - (\text{\_\_\_\_})^2$$

$$n^2 = \text{\_\_\_\_\_} - \text{\_\_\_\_\_}$$

$$n^2 = \text{\_\_\_\_\_}$$

$$n = \text{\_\_\_\_}$$

---

23. $c^2 = a^2 + b^2$

  a. $(\text{\_\_\_})^2 + (\text{\_\_\_})^2 = \text{\_\_\_\_}$

  $c = \sqrt{\text{\_\_\_\_}} = \text{\_\_\_}\sqrt{\text{\_\_\_}}$

  b. $(\text{\_\_\_})^2 + (\text{\_\_\_})^2 = \text{\_\_\_\_}$

  $c = \sqrt{\text{\_\_\_\_}} = \text{\_\_\_}\sqrt{\text{\_\_\_}}$

  c. Substitute a for the leg length:

  $c = \text{\_\_\_}\sqrt{\text{\_\_\_}}$

24. Student _____ is correct.

Student _____ used _____

as the hypotenuse,

but the length of the hypotenuse is _____.

---

25. A St. to E St.: ____

2nd Ave. to 4th Ave.: ____

Substitute. $\sqrt{(\underline{\quad})^2 + (\underline{\quad})^2}$

= _____ or about _____ city blocks

26. a. _____ $= h^2 +$ _____

$h = \sqrt{(\underline{\quad})^2 + (\underline{\quad})^2}$

$=$ _____ ▨

b. ____ $+$ ____ $=$ _____ ▨

27. The $x_2 - x_1$ and $y_2 - y_1$ values will be substituted in reverse but the result will be the

_____ because the _____ of the values are _____.

28.

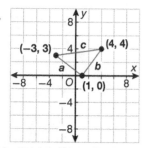

 Find the lengths of a, b and c.

$d = \sqrt{(x_2 - x_1) + (y_2 - y_1)}$

$a =$ _____

$b =$ _____

$c =$ _____

$a^2 + b^2 \stackrel{?}{=} c^2$

It _____ a right triangle because the

sides satisfy the Pythagorean Theorem.

29. $M = \left(\dfrac{x_1 + x_2}{2}, \dfrac{y_1 + y_2}{2}\right)$

Answer: ____

30. 📖 *Plot the points on a coordinate grid.*

$d = \sqrt{(\underline{\quad} - \underline{\quad})^2 + (\underline{\quad} - \underline{\quad})^2}$

$= \sqrt{\underline{\quad\quad} + \underline{\quad\quad}}$

$= \sqrt{(\underline{\quad\quad})} \approx$ _____ ▨

LESSON
87

Factoring Polynomials by Grouping page 570

New Concepts

Math Language

Factoring is the opposite of multiplying. Check factoring by multiplying the factors. Their product should be the original polynomial.

• Polynomials can be factored by grouping. If the polynomial has four terms, make two groups of two terms each where each group has a greatest common factor. Factor out the greatest common factor from each group. You may be able to factor one more time.

• The trinomial $ax^2 + bx + c$ can be factored by grouping. Write the middle term as a sum of two terms and factor by grouping.

Example **Factoring Four-Term Polynomials**

Factor.

$2x^2 + 4xy + 7x + 14y$

$= (2x^2 + 4xy) + (7x + 14y)$ *Group terms with common factors.*

$= 2x(x + 2y) + 7(x + 2y)$ *Factor out GCFs.*

$= (x + 2y)(2x + 7)$ *Factor out $(x + 2y)$.*

Example **Factoring with the Greatest Common Factor**

Factor out the GCF, regroup, and factor completely.

$45a^3b - 15a^3 + 15a^2b - 5a^2$

$= 5a^2(9ab - 3a + 3b - 1)$ *Factor out GCF.*

$= 5a^2[(9ab - 3a) + (3b - 1)]$ *Group into two binomials.*

$= 5a^2[(3a)(3b - 1) + 1(3b - 1)]$ *Factor out GCF of each.*

$= 5a^2(3b - 1)(3a + 1)$ *Factor out $(3b - 1)$.*

Example **Factoring with Opposites**

Factor completely.

$3a^2b - 18a + 30 - 5ab$

$= (3a^2b - 18a) + (30 - 5ab)$ *Group into two binomials.*

$= 3a(ab - 6) + 5(6 - ab)$ *Factor out GCF of each.*

$= 3a(ab - 6) + 5(-1)(ab - 6)$ *Multiply by -1.*

$= 3a(ab - 6) - 5(ab - 6)$ *Simplify.*

$= (ab - 6)(3a - 5)$ *Factor out $(ab - 6)$.*

Example **Factoring a Trinomial**

Factor with grouping.

$x^2 - 7x - 44$

$= x^2 - 11x + 4x - 44$ Replace $-7x$ with $(-11x + 4x)$.

$= (x^2 - 11x) + (4x - 44)$ Group into two binomials.

$= x(x - 11) + 4(x - 11)$ Factor out the GCF of each.

$= (x - 11)(x + 4)$ Factor out $(x - 11)$.

Lesson Practice 📖 page 573

Factor completely.

a. $3y^2 + 6yz + 4y + 8z$

$= \_\_y(y + \_\_z) + \_\_(y + \_\_z)$

$= (y + \_\_z)(\_\_y + \_\_)$

b. $3y^2 - 4y^3 + 3 - 4y$

$= \_\_(3 - 4y) + \_\_(3 - 4y)$

$= (3 - 4y)(\_\_ + \_\_)$

c. $99x^3y - 33x^3 + 33x^2y - 11x^2$

$= \_\_\_\_\_(\_\_xy - \_\_x + \_\_y - \_\_)$

$= \_\_\_\_\_[\_\_x(\_\_y - \_\_) + \_\_(\_\_y - \_\_)]$

$= \_\_\_\_\_(\_\_y - \_\_)(\_\_x + \_\_)$

d. $3a^2b - 4ab + 20 - 15a = \_\_\_\_(3a - 4) + \_\_\_\_(4 - 3a)$

Notice that $3a - 4 = -(4 - 3a)$, so $= \_\_\_\_(3a - 4) + \_\_\_\_(4 - 3a)$

$= \_\_\_\_(3a - \_\_\_\_) - \_\_\_\_(3a - 4)$

$= (3a - 4)(\_\_\_\_ - \_\_\_\_)$

Factor the trinomials by grouping.

e. $x^2 - 4x - 77$

$= x^2 - 11x + \_\_\_\_x - 77$

$= \_\_\_(x - 11) + \_\_\_(x - 11)$

$= (x - 11)(\_\_\_\_ + \_\_\_\_)$

f. $6a^2 - 1a - 15$

$= 6a^2 - 10a + 9a - 15$

$= \_\_\_a(3a - 5) + \_\_\_(3a - 5)$

$= (3a - 5)(\_\_\_a + \_\_\_)$

1. factors of -54: ____, ____, or

____, ____, or ____, ____, or

____, ____, or ____, ____, or ____, ____

factors that add up to $+3$: ____ and ____

$(x \bigcirc \underline{\quad})(x \bigcirc \underline{\quad})$

2. *Factor out a GCF from the first two terms and the last two terms.*

$$\underline{\quad}(\underline{\quad}b - a) + \underline{\quad}(2a^2b - \underline{\quad})$$

3. *Simplify both sides.*

$9 - \underline{\quad}g < \underline{\quad} + 6g$

Isolate the variable and solve.

$\underline{\quad} < \underline{\quad}g$ or $\underline{\quad} < g$

4. *Distribute.*

$\underline{\quad}k - \underline{\quad} > 3k - 26$

Isolate the variable and solve.

$\underline{\quad}k > \underline{\quad}$ or $k > \underline{\quad}$

5. $P(4 \text{ on a number cube}) = \underline{\quad}$

$P(4 \text{ on two number cubes}) = (\underline{\quad})^2$

$P(\text{heads on a coin}) = \underline{\quad}$

$P(4 \text{ on two number cubes and heads})$

$= \left(\dfrac{\Box}{\Box}\right)^2 \cdot \underline{\quad} = \underline{\quad}$

6. $P(n < 4 \text{ on a number cube}) = \underline{\quad}$

$P(n < 4 \text{ on two number cubes}) = (\underline{\quad})^2$

$P(\text{heads on a coin}) = \underline{\quad}$

$P(n < 4 \text{ on two number cubes and heads})$

$= \left(\dfrac{\Box}{\Box}\right)^2 \cdot \underline{\quad} = \underline{\quad}$

7. difference of _____ _____

$100 - c^6 = (\underline{\quad})^2 - (\underline{\quad})^2$

$= (\underline{\quad} + \underline{\quad})(\underline{\quad} - \underline{\quad})$

8. $2 \cdot \underline{\quad} \cdot \underline{\quad} = 20$, so it is a

perfect _____ _____.

$4x^2 + 20x + 25 = (\underline{\quad}x + \underline{\quad})^2$

9. $d = \sqrt{(\underline{\quad} - \underline{\quad})^2 + (\underline{\quad} - \underline{\quad})^2}$

$= \sqrt{\underline{\quad} + \underline{\quad}} = \underline{\quad}$

10. $d = \sqrt{(\underline{\quad} - \underline{\quad})^2 + (\underline{\quad} - \underline{\quad})^2}$

$= \sqrt{\underline{\quad} + \underline{\quad}} = \sqrt{\underline{\quad} \cdot \underline{\quad}}$

$= \underline{\quad}\sqrt{\underline{\quad}}$

11. positive correlation: As one variable

_____, the other variable

_____.

negative correlation: As one variable

_____, the other variable

_____.

hours of practice and _____

12. Graph the dates.

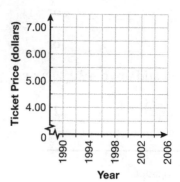

13. a. A case will not be accepted if the difference between its weight and the 50 pound requirement is +0.5 pounds or −0.5 pounds. This difference can be thought of as the "distance" between the actual weight of the box and the 50 pound requirement.

Thus, $|x - 50| =$ _____

b. Solve for x.

$x - 50 =$ _____ or $x =$ _____

$x - 50 =$ _____ or $x =$ _____

Thus, the minimum is _____ and

the maximum is _____.

14. *Isolate the variable.*

$2m \leq$ _____ or $m \leq$ _____ hours

She can hike at _____ more hours.

15. a. horizontal asymptote: $y = c$,

so $y =$ _____

b. vertical asymptote: $x = b$, so $x =$ _____

c. $y = \dfrac{3000}{\square} + 100$

= _____ + 100 = _____ books

16. There are no _____ factors that

can be factored out of any grouped

_____.

17. Let b = number of big walls

Let s = number of small walls

If all big walls:

___$b + 20 \leq 2420$

$b \leq$ ___

If all small walls:

___$s + 20 \geq 2420$

$s \geq$ ___

18. $A = \pi r^2 = \pi(9x^2 - 6x + 1)$

$= \pi($___$x - 1)^2$

Thus, $r^2 = ($___$x - 1)^2$, and $r = ($___$x - 1)$.

diameter $= 2($___$x - 1) = $___$x - $___

If 1 cm = 500 m, diameter

$=$ ___$($___$x - $___$)$

$=$ ___$x - $___

---

19. Solve for y term. If the coefficient of

the x^2 term is ___ than zero, the

graph opens downward.

Circle the answer.

A $-8y + 3x^2 = 4 + 7x$

B $-12x^2 + 15y = 18$

C $-y + 36x = x^2 + 40$

D $-15 + 9y = 45x^2 - 3x$

20. Rewrite the equation in the

___ form for a quadratic

function. Make a ___ of

values. ___ the points on a

graph. Draw a ___ through

the points.

---

21. $x^2 + $ ___ $= $ ___ ^{2}

$x^2 = $ ___ $^2 - $ ___ ^{2}

$= $ ___ $- $ ___

$= $ ___

22. $10^2 = $ ___; $\left(5\sqrt{5}\right)^2 = $ ___; $15^2 = $ ___

___ $+ $ ___ $\overset{?}{=}$ ___, so the sides

___ form a right triangle.

---

23. $24^2 = $ ___; $32^2 = $ ___; $42^2 = $ ___

___ $+ $ ___ $\overset{?}{=}$ ___, so the sides

___ form a right triangle.

24. Student ___ is correct. In calculating

$(x_2 - x_1)$, Student ___ subtracted ___

instead of ___ from the 4.

25. a. midpoint of PQ

$$\left(\frac{x_1 + x_2}{2}, \frac{y_1 + y_2}{2}\right) = \left(\frac{3 + \square}{2}, \frac{2 + \square}{2}\right)$$

$$= (\underline{}, \underline{})$$

midpoint QR:

$$\left(\frac{x_1 + x_2}{2}, \frac{y_1 + y_2}{2}\right) = \left(\frac{3 + \square}{2}, \frac{8 + \square}{2}\right) = (\underline{}, \underline{})$$

b.

$$d_{MN} = \sqrt{(\underline{} - \underline{})^2 + (\underline{} - \underline{})^2}$$

$$= \sqrt{(\underline{} + \underline{})^2} = \sqrt{\underline{}}$$

$$= \underline{}\sqrt{\underline{}}$$

$$d_{PR} = \sqrt{(\underline{} - \underline{})^2 + (\underline{} - \underline{})^2}$$

$$= \sqrt{(\underline{} + \underline{})^2} = \sqrt{\underline{}}$$

$$= \underline{}\sqrt{\underline{}}$$

Thus, $MN = \dfrac{\square}{\square} PR$.

26. a. $d_{1st} = \sqrt{(30 - 25)^2 + (\underline{} - \underline{})}$

$$= \sqrt{(5^2 + \underline{}{}^2} = \sqrt{\underline{}}$$

$$\approx \underline{}$$

b. $d_{2nd} = \sqrt{(\underline{} - \underline{})^2 + (20 - 10)}$

$$= \sqrt{(\underline{}{}^2 + 10^2} = \sqrt{\underline{}}$$

$$\approx \underline{}$$

c. $d_{1st} \bigcirc d_{2nd}$, thus, the receiver at

$(\underline{}, \underline{})$ is closer to the

quarterback.

27.

a. $A = \dfrac{1}{2}\underline{} \cdot \underline{}$

b. $A = \dfrac{1}{2}(\underline{})h = x^2 + 2x$

$(\underline{})h = 2(x^2 + 2x)$

c. $(\underline{})h = 2\underline{}(x + 2)$

d. $h = \underline{}$

28. $\underline{}$, any number of

$\underline{}$

expressed as a sum or difference is

a $\underline{}$.

29. 1st book: $20 + n$

2nd book: $(20 + n)(n - 5)$

both books: $\underline{} + \underline{}$

factor out $(20 + n)$: $\underline{}(\underline{} + n - 5)$

simplify: $(\underline{})(n - \underline{})$

30. 1st group of five: $y^2 + 5$

2nd and 3rd groups of five: $\underline{}(y + 1)$

total cost for 15:

$\underline{} + \underline{}(y + 1)$ ▨

LESSON

88

Multiplying and Dividing Rational Expressions page 576

New Concepts

- The procedures for multiplying and dividing rational expressions are the same as those for multiplying and dividing fractions.

Multiplying Rational Expressions	Dividing Rational Expressions
If a, b, c, and d are nonzero polynomials, $\frac{a}{b} \cdot \frac{c}{d} = \frac{ac}{bd}$.	If a, b, c, and d are nonzero polynomials, $\frac{a}{b} \div \frac{c}{d} = \frac{a}{b} \cdot \frac{d}{c} = \frac{ad}{bc}$.

Example **Multiplying a Rational Expression by a Polynomial**

Multiply.

$$\frac{9}{3x - 15} \cdot (x^2 - 2x - 15)$$

$$= \frac{9}{3x - 15} \cdot \frac{(x^2 - 2x - 15)}{1} \qquad \textit{Write the polynomial with a denominator of 1.}$$

$$= \frac{9}{3(x - 5)} \cdot \frac{(x - 5)(x + 3)}{1} \qquad \textit{Factor.}$$

$$= \frac{{}^3\cancel{9}}{{}^1\cancel{3}\cancel{(x - 5)}} \cdot \frac{\cancel{(x - 5)}(x + 3)}{1} \qquad \textit{Divide out like factors.}$$

$$= 3(x + 3) \qquad \textit{Simplify.}$$

$$= 3x + 9 \qquad \textit{Distribute.}$$

Example **Dividing Rational Expressions**

Find the quotient.

$$\frac{5st^4}{4s^2t} \div \frac{15s^2t}{2s^3t^2}$$

$$\frac{5st^4}{4s^2t} \cdot \frac{2s^3t^2}{15s^2t} \qquad \textit{Write as multiplication by the reciprocal.}$$

$$\frac{10s^4t^6}{60s^4t^2} \qquad \textit{Multiply the numerators and denominators.}$$

$$\frac{{}^1\cancel{10}\,\cancel{s^4}t^{\cancel{6}4}}{{}^6\cancel{60}\,\cancel{s^4}\,\cancel{t^2}} \qquad \textit{Divide out like factors.}$$

$$\frac{t^4}{6} \qquad \textit{Simplify.}$$

Find each product.

a. $\dfrac{4z^5q^8}{14qz^7} \cdot \dfrac{14qz^4}{3q^4z}$

$= \dfrac{4q^{\square}}{z^{\square}} \cdot \dfrac{z^{\square}}{3q^{\square}}$

$= \dfrac{\square q^{\square} z^{\square}}{3}$

b. $\dfrac{5x^2}{7y^4} \cdot \dfrac{4x^2}{9y^3}$

$= \dfrac{\square x^{\square}}{\square y^{\square}}$

Multiply. Simplify your answer.

c. $\dfrac{6}{2x-18} \cdot (x^2 - 6x - 27)$

$= \dfrac{6}{2(x - \square)} \cdot (x - \square)(x + \square)$

$= \underline{\quad}(x + \underline{\quad})$

d. $\dfrac{8m + 6m^2n}{12} \cdot \dfrac{8m}{24m + 8mn}$

$= \dfrac{\square(\square + \square mn)}{12} \cdot \dfrac{8m}{\square(\square + n)}$

$= \dfrac{\square(\square + \square mn)}{\square(\square + n)}$

Find each quotient.

e. $\dfrac{8j^2k^7}{15k^7j^4} \div \dfrac{6j^3k}{5kj^6} = \dfrac{8j^2k^7}{15k^7j^4} \cdot \dfrac{\square kj^{\square}}{\square j^{\square}k}$

$= \dfrac{8}{15j^{\square}} \cdot \dfrac{5j^{\square}}{6}$

$= \underline{\quad}$

f. $\dfrac{x^2 + 7x + 12}{x + 5} \div (x + 3)$

$= \dfrac{(x + \square)(x + \square)}{(x + 5)} \cdot \dfrac{1}{(x + 3)}$

$= \dfrac{x + \square}{x + \square}$

g. $\dfrac{x^2 + 5x + 6}{x + 2} \div \dfrac{x + 3}{y^2}$

$= \dfrac{(x + \square)(x + \square)}{x + 2} \cdot \dfrac{y^2}{\square}$

$= \underline{\quad}$

h. $\dfrac{x^2}{20x^2 + 10x} \cdot (x^2 + 9x + 20)$

$= \dfrac{x^2}{\square(\square + \square)} \cdot (\square + \square)(\square + \square)$

$= \dfrac{\square(\square + \square)(\square + \square)}{\square(\square + \square)}$

1. Simplify each side before solving.

_____$x +$ _____ $- 4x >$ _____ $+ x$

Isolate x and solve.

x ◯ _____

2. Distribute 2 in the first equation.

$4 \geq$ _____ $x +$ _____

Solve each inequality.

_____ $\geq$ _____ x OR $23 < 8x + 7$

_____ $\geq 2x$ OR   _____ $< 8x$

$x \leq$ _____   OR $x >$ _____

3. Distribute the x and solve for y.

_____ $- 2$ _____ $= 18x^2$

_____ $=$ _____ x^2

$y =$ _____ x

This _____ a quadratic function.

4. Distribute the 2 and solve for y.

_____ $y -$ _____ $x = 6x^2$

$y =$ _____ x^2 ◯ _____ x

This _____ a quadratic function.

5. $d = \sqrt{(x_2 - x_1)^2 + (y_2 - y_1)^2}$

$d = \sqrt{(\_\_◯\_\_)^2} + \sqrt{(\_\_◯\_\_)^2}$

$= \sqrt{\_\_ + \_\_}$

$= \sqrt{\_\_} = \_\_\sqrt{\_\_}$

6. $d = \sqrt{(\_\_◯\_\_)^2} + \sqrt{(\_\_◯\_\_)^2}$

$= \sqrt{\_\_ + \_\_}$

$= \sqrt{\_\_} = \_\_\sqrt{\_\_}$

7. $M = \left(\dfrac{x_1 + x_2}{2}, \dfrac{y_1 + y_2}{2}\right)$

$\left(\dfrac{\Box + \Box}{2}, \dfrac{\Box + \Box}{2}\right) = (\_\_\_, \_\_\_)$

8. $\left(\dfrac{\Box + \Box}{2}, \dfrac{\Box + \Box}{2}\right) = (\_\_\_, \_\_\_)$

9. *Factor and simplify.*

$$\frac{\boxed{}\,y\left(\boxed{}+\boxed{}\right)}{y+5}\cdot\frac{\boxed{}}{x^{\boxed{}}}$$

$$=\frac{\boxed{}\,y}{x^{\boxed{}}}$$

10. $\dfrac{6y}{x}\cdot\dfrac{\boxed{}}{\boxed{}}$

$$=\frac{\boxed{}\,y^{\boxed{}}}{\boxed{}+\boxed{}}$$

11. $\dfrac{7x}{y}\cdot\dfrac{\boxed{}}{\boxed{}}$

$$=\frac{\boxed{}}{\boxed{}}$$

12. *Write the trinomial in standard form.*

$$\underline{\quad\quad}+7x-60$$

Factors of -60: _____

Factors of -60 that add up to 7: _____

$(x\,\bigcirc\,\underline{\quad})(x\,\bigcirc\,\underline{\quad})$

13. *Factor out the GCF.*

$$\underline{\quad\quad}(8ab-4a+2b-1)$$

Factor by grouping.

Factor $8ab-4a$: _____$(2b-1)$

$\underline{\quad}[\underline{\quad\quad}(2b-1)+1(2b-1)]$

$=\underline{\quad}(2b-1)(\underline{\quad\quad}+1)$

14. *Assume that the product of the pattern's two dimensions equals the trinomial.*

Factor to find the dimensions.

$(x\,\bigcirc\,\underline{\quad})\cdot(x\,\bigcirc\,\underline{\quad})$

15. Right of an open circle at _____ means

$x\,\bigcirc\,\underline{\quad\quad}$

Left of an open circle at _____ means

$x\,\bigcirc\,\underline{\quad\quad}$

Combine.

$\underline{\quad}\,\bigcirc\,x\,\bigcirc\,\underline{\quad}$

16. *For $y=\dfrac{a}{x-b}+c$, the vertical asymptote is at $x=b$; the horizontal asymptote is at $y=c$.*

a. horizontal asymptote: $y=$ _____

b. vertical asymptote: $x=$ _____

c. *Substitute.*

_____ uniforms

d. _____, because the company would not give away free uniforms unless some were purchased.

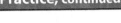

17. a. *Factor out* $\frac{1}{2}$. $5 = \dfrac{\square}{2}$

$\frac{1}{2}(x^2 + \underline{\quad}x + \underline{\quad})$

$= \frac{1}{2}(x + \underline{\quad})(x + \underline{\quad})$

b. *Substitute.* $\frac{1}{2}(\underline{\quad})(\underline{\quad}) = \underline{\quad}$

18. Tables and graphs are _____ to read than a long list of _____.

19. *Find the dimensions of the parking lot. Use the pattern for a perfect-square trinomial.*

dimensions$_{\text{lot}} = (\underline{\quad}s + \underline{\quad})^2$

length of parking lot $= \underline{\quad}s + \underline{\quad}$

Area$_{\text{building}} = s^2$, so the length of the building is _____.

side length $_{\text{lot}}$ − side length $_{\text{building}}$

$= \underline{\quad}s + \underline{\quad}$

The width of the parking lot on one side of the building is half of this difference.

_____

20. a. left to right:

$\triangle 1: c^2 = \underline{\quad}^2 + \underline{\quad}^2 = \underline{\quad}$, so $c = \sqrt{\underline{\quad}}$

$\triangle 2: c^2 = \underline{\quad}^2 + (\underline{\quad})^2 = \underline{\quad}$, so $c = \sqrt{\underline{\quad}}$

$\triangle 3: c^2 = \underline{\quad}^2 + (\underline{\quad})^2 = \underline{\quad}$, so $c = \sqrt{\underline{\quad}}$

$\triangle 4: c^2 = \underline{\quad} + \underline{\quad} = \underline{\quad}$, so $c = \sqrt{\underline{\quad}}$

b. The length of the 10th triangle's

hypotenuse is $\sqrt{\underline{\quad}}$.

21. $c^2 = a^2 + b^2$

Circle the answer.

A 3, 4, 6   **B** $\sqrt{13}$, 5, 12

C $\sqrt{15}$, 7, 8   **D** 6, 8, 12

22. Student _____ is correct. Student _____

_____ the x-coordinates instead of

_____ them.

23. $d = \sqrt{(\underline{\quad} - \underline{\quad})^2 + (\underline{\quad} - \underline{\quad})^2}$

$= \sqrt{\underline{\quad}} \approx \underline{\quad}$

24. Draw a sketch.

new area: 50   new length: $x + \underline{\quad}$

$50 = x(x + \underline{\quad})$

$x^2 + \underline{\quad}x - \underline{\quad} = 0$

factors: $(x + \underline{\quad})(x - \underline{\quad})$ so $x = \underline{\quad}$

length: _____   width: _____

25. $(12x^2 + 3y)(6x^2 + y)$

Factor out the GCF from the first binomial.

$= \underline{\quad}(\underline{\quad}x^2 + y)(6x^2 + y)$

$= \underline{\quad}(\underline{\quad}x^4 + \underline{\quad}x^2y + y^2)$

It is simpler to express the area as

_____ without multiplying

them.

26. *The expression is a difference of two squares.*

Circle the answer.

A $25(x + 9)(x - 9)$

B $5x \cdot 5x - 81$

C $5^2x^2 - 9^2$

D $(5x + 9)(5x - 9)$

27. *See page 4 in the* Student Reference Guide.

_____ exponents when multiplying,

and _____ exponents when

dividing.

28. Factor and simplify.

$$\frac{(y + \square)(y + \square)}{y^2} \cdot \frac{y}{y + 1}$$

Circle the answer.

A $\dfrac{y + 5}{y^2}$ B $\dfrac{y + 5}{y}$

C $\dfrac{(y + 1)(y + 5)}{y^2}$ D $y(y + 5)$

29. Factor the trinomial: $(c + \underline{\quad})(c + \underline{\quad})$

Multiply it by $\frac{1}{c+5}$. *Divide out like factors.*

$$\frac{(c + \square)(c + \square)}{1} \cdot \frac{1}{c + 5}$$

Price $= \$10 \cdot (\underline{\qquad})$

$= \underline{\quad}\ c + \underline{\quad}$

30. a. *The expression is a perfect square trinomial.*

$(\underline{\quad}x \bigcirc \underline{\quad})(\underline{\quad}x \bigcirc \underline{\quad})$

b.   It is the product of an expression

_____ by itself.

Name _____

Identifying Characteristics of Quadratic Functions page 585

New Concepts

Math Language

The **minimum of a function** is its least possible y-value. The **maximum of a function** is its greatest possible y-value. The minimum and maximum values always occur at the vertex of a parabola.

• The **vertex of a parabola** is the highest or lowest point on its graph.

Example **Identifying the Vertex and the Maximum or Minimum**

Give the coordinates of the vertex, the minimum or maximum value of the function, and its domain and range.

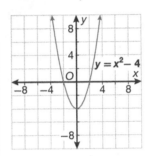

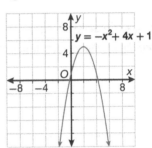

This vertex occurs at the parabola's lowest point.

vertex: $(0, -4)$

minimum: -4

This vertex occurs at the parabola's highest point.

vertex: $(2, 5)$

maximum: 5

Domain: x-values; Range: y-values

domain: $\{x \mid \text{all real numbers}\}$
range: $\{y \mid y \geq -4\}$

domain: $\{x \mid \text{all real numbers}\}$
range: $\{y \mid y \leq 5\}$

• A **zero of a function** is the value(s) of x that make(s) $f(x) = 0$ or $y = 0$. The zeros are the same as the x-intercepts of the graph of the function.

Example **Finding Zeros from the Graph**

Find the zeros from the graph.

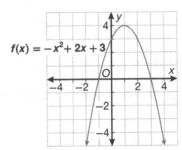

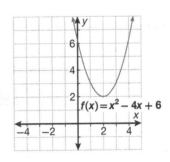

The zeros are at -1 and 3, where $y = 0$.

There are **no real zeros** since the graph does not intersect the x axis.

Give the coordinates of the vertex, the minimum or maximum value of the function, and its domain and range.

a. vertex: _____

    Max or min: y-value only

    minimum or maximum: _____

    D: $\{x \mid$ _____$\}$

    R: $\{y \mid y \bigcirc$ _____$\}$

b. vertex: _____

    minimum or maximum: _____

    D: $\{x \mid$ _____$\}$

    R: $\{y \mid y \bigcirc$ _____$\}$

Find the zeros of each function.

The zeros are the x-intercepts of the graph of the function.

c. zero(s): _____

d. zero(s): _____

e. zero(s): _____

Find the axis of symmetry for each graph.

Add the zeros and divide by 2 to find the equation of the axis of symmetry.

f. zeros at $x =$ _____ and _____

    axis of symmetry: $x =$ ____

g. zeros at $x =$ _____ and _____

    axis of symmetry: $x =$ _____

Find the axis of symmetry for the graph of each quadratic function.

The equation of the axis of symmetry for the graph of a quadratic equation $y = ax + bx + c$ is $x = -\frac{b}{2a}$.

h. $x = -\frac{b}{2a}$ $a =$ _____, $b =$ _____

    $x = -\dfrac{\square}{\square} =$ _____

i. $x = -\frac{b}{2a}$ $a =$ _____, $b =$ _____

    $x = -\dfrac{\square}{\square} =$ _____

j. The time of maximum height is the t coordinate of the vertex (t, y).

    Since the axis of symmetry passes through the vertex, use $x = -\frac{b}{2a}$ to find the t-coordinate of the vertex.

    t-coordinate of the vertex: $t = -\dfrac{b}{2a} = -\dfrac{\square}{\square} =$ _____

    The parabola opens downward since a is negative, so the function has a maximum value.

    The maximum height reached is the y-coordinate of the vertex. Substitute the t-coordinate of the vertex.

    height reached: $y = -16($____$)^2 + 680($____$) + 12{,}447$

    $=$ _____

1. *Isolate the absolute value expression.*

$$-2|r + 2| = -30$$

Solution: {_____ , _____}

2. $3|r + 6| = 15$

$r + 6 =$ _____ or $r + 6 =$ _____

Solution: {_____ , _____}

---

3. Solve for x in each inequality.

Distribute.

$$35 < 3x + 8 \quad \text{OR} \quad 72 \geq \underline{}x + \underline{}$$

$$\underline{} < x \quad\quad \text{OR} \quad \underline{} \geq x$$

4. *Factor out the GCF.*

$$\underline{}(\underline{}y^2 - \underline{}y + \underline{})$$

Factor $(\underline{}y^2 - \underline{}y + \underline{})$

$(5y \bigcirc \underline{})(\underline{} \bigcirc \underline{})$

Factor completely.

$$\underline{}(\underline{} \bigcirc \underline{})(\underline{} \bigcirc \underline{})$$

kind of polynomial: _____

---

5. $81x^2 - 1$

$\sqrt{81} =$ _____

$\sqrt{1} =$ _____

$(\underline{}x \bigcirc \underline{})(\underline{}x \bigcirc \underline{})$

kind of polynomial: _____

_____

6. $\sqrt{9c^2} =$ _____ $\sqrt{49} =$ _____

$2 \cdot \sqrt{9c^2} \cdot \sqrt{49} =$ _____

$a^2 + 2ab + b^2$ or $a^2 - 2ab + b^2$

$(\underline{}x \bigcirc \underline{})(\underline{}x \bigcirc \underline{})$

or $(\underline{} \bigcirc \underline{})^2$

---

7. $d = \sqrt{(x_2 - x_1)^2 + (y_2 - y_1)^2}$

$$d = \sqrt{(\underline{} - \underline{})^2 + (\underline{} - \underline{})^2}$$

$$= \sqrt{\underline{} + \underline{}} = \sqrt{\underline{}}$$

$$= \underline{}\sqrt{\underline{}}$$

8. *Factor and multiply by the reciprocal.*

$$\frac{\square(\square a + b)}{5ab} \cdot \frac{1}{\square}$$

Divide out like factors.

$$= \underline{}$$

---

9. Factor and multiply by the reciprocal.

$$\frac{\square(x+\square)}{1} \cdot \frac{\square}{\square}$$

$$= \underline{\hspace{2cm}}$$

10. $-\dfrac{b}{2a} = -\dfrac{\square}{\square} = -\underline{\hspace{1cm}},$

so $x = \underline{\hspace{1.5cm}}$

11. $-\dfrac{b}{2a} = -\dfrac{\square}{\square} = \underline{\hspace{1.5cm}},$ so $x = \underline{\hspace{1.5cm}}$

12. Use the formula for the _____ and sketch it on a graph. Substitute

the x-value of the _____ to find the _____ -value of the vertex. Plot the

_____. Make a table of values to find values to the _____ or _____ side of the

axis of symmetry to find the points that are _____ images of those points.

13. no faster than 65: $s \bigcirc 65$

no slower than 45: $s \bigcirc 45$

Combine.

$45 \bigcirc s \bigcirc 65,$

or $s \bigcirc 45$ AND $s \bigcirc 65$

14. $x \bigcirc \underline{\hspace{1cm}}$

$x \bigcirc \underline{\hspace{1cm}}$

So, $\underline{\hspace{1cm}} \bigcirc x \bigcirc \underline{\hspace{1cm}},$

or $x \bigcirc \underline{\hspace{1cm}}$ AND $x \bigcirc \underline{\hspace{1cm}}$

15. $A_{trapezoid} = \frac{1}{2} \cdot h \cdot (b_1 + b_2)$

$A = \frac{1}{2}(\underline{\hspace{0.5cm}})(\underline{\hspace{1.5cm}} + \underline{\hspace{1.5cm}})$

$= (\underline{\hspace{0.5cm}} + \underline{\hspace{0.5cm}}) + (\underline{\hspace{0.5cm}} + \underline{\hspace{0.5cm}})$

$= \underline{\hspace{0.5cm}} + \underline{\hspace{0.5cm}} = \underline{\hspace{1cm}}$

16. Factor out the GCF.

$\underline{\hspace{0.5cm}}(x^2 \bigcirc \underline{\hspace{0.5cm}}x \bigcirc \underline{\hspace{0.5cm}})$

$\underline{\hspace{0.5cm}}(x \bigcirc \underline{\hspace{0.5cm}})(x \bigcirc \underline{\hspace{0.5cm}})$

17. a. $P(\text{brown}) = \dfrac{\text{brown outcomes}}{\text{total outcomes}}$

$$= \dfrac{\Box}{\Box} = \underline{\quad}$$

$P(\text{red}) = \dfrac{\text{red outcomes}}{\text{total outcomes}}$

$$= \dfrac{\Box}{\Box} = \underline{\quad}$$

$P(\text{yellow}) = \dfrac{\text{yellow outcomes}}{\text{total outcomes}}$

$$= \dfrac{\Box}{\Box} = \underline{\quad}$$

b. Draw a spinner that shows the theoretical probabilities that you found.

18. Let m = number of minutes

plan 1: _____ + 0.09m

plan 2: $45 +$ _____ m

Solve for m.

For how many minutes is Plan 1 more expensive?

_____ $+ 0.09m$ ◯ $45 +$ _____ m

m ◯ _____

Plan 1 is more expensive after _____.

---

19. $2x + 8 > 2 + 5x + 6$

$2x + 8 > 5x +$ _____

_____ $>$ _____ x or $x <$ _____

Substitute.

$2(0) + 8 > 2 + 5(0) + 6$

_____ $\overset{?}{>}$ _____

$2(\underline{\quad}) + 8 > 2 + 5(\underline{\quad}) + 6$

_____ $\overset{?}{>}$ _____

20. Use a table to graph the function.

x	-9	-3	0	3	9
y					

Find the distance between the zeros.
Each unit on the graph represents 1 foot.

$=$ _____

---

21. $V_{cylinder} = \pi(r^2 h)$

$V_{cylinder} = \pi(\underline{\quad})^2(\underline{\quad})$

$V_{prism} = (s^2 h)$

$V_{prism} = (\underline{\quad})^2(\underline{\quad})$

📖 Graph the volumes.

The volume of the _____

increases faster than the _____.

22. $c^2 = a^2 + b^2$

$(\underline{\quad})^2 = (\underline{\quad})^2 + (\underline{\quad})^2$

_____ $= \sqrt{\underline{\quad}}$

_____ $=$ _____

---

23. $M = \left(\dfrac{x_1 + x_2}{2}, \dfrac{y_1 + y_2}{2}\right)$

Answer: _____

24. *The parent function is* $f(x) = x.$

The function is _____

about the ____-axis and is _____

stretched by a factor of _____.

---

25. a. *Simplify the numbers and the variables.*

$$\dfrac{6r^{\square}h^{\square}}{4} \cdot \dfrac{8h^{\square}}{3r^{\square}} \cdot \dfrac{2r^{\square}}{h^{\square}}$$

_____$r^{\square}h^{\square}$ or _____

b. fraction $= \dfrac{V_{globe}}{V_{box}} =$

$$= \dfrac{4\pi rh}{3} \div \text{_____}$$

$$= \text{_____}$$

26. $A = \dfrac{3x^2 + x}{y} \cdot (x + 2y)$

$= $ _____

---

27. Student _____ is correct.

Student _____ did not multiply by the

_____ of $2s - 1$.

28. *Add the zeros and divide by 2 to find x-coordinate of the vertex.*

Circle the answer.

A −4   **B** 0   **C** 4   **D** 8

---

29. *The x-coordinate of the vertex is the time it takes the ball to reach the maximum height. The y-coordinate is the maximum height.*

✎ Use $x = -\dfrac{b}{2a}$ to find the x-coordinate

of the vertex. Substitute the answer into

$y = -5.5x^2 + 44x$ to find the y-coordinate

of the vertex.

$x = $ _____ , so $y = $ _____

30. If the value of a is _____ ,

the graph opens _____ and has a

_____. If the value of a is

_____ , the graph opens

_____ and has a _____.

Adding and Subtracting Rational Expressions

page 592

New Concepts

- To add or subtract rational expressions with the same denominator, add or subtract the numerators and keep the common denominator.

Example **Adding and Subtracting with Like Denominators**

Add or subtract. Simplify your answers.

$$\frac{3a - 2}{a + 2} - \frac{a - 6}{a + 2}$$

$$= \frac{3a - 2 - (a - 6)}{a + 2} \qquad \text{\textit{Subtract the numerators. Keep the denominator.}}$$

$$= \frac{3a - 2 - a + 6}{a + 2} \qquad \text{\textit{Distribute} } -1.$$

$$= \frac{2a + 4}{a + 2} \qquad \text{\textit{Combine like terms.}}$$

$$= \frac{2(a + 2)}{a + 2} \qquad \text{\textit{Factor and divide out common factors.}}$$

$$= 2 \qquad \text{\textit{Simplify.}}$$

- If the denominators are different, find the LCM of the denominators and use it as the LCD before simplifying.

Example **Subtracting with Unlike Denominators**

Subtract. Simplify your answers.

$$\frac{x + 3}{x - 4} - \frac{2}{x^2 + x - 20}$$

$$= \frac{x + 3}{x - 4} - \frac{2}{(x - 4)(x + 5)} \qquad \text{\textit{Factor the denominators.}}$$

$$= \frac{x + 3(x + 5)}{(x - 4)(x + 5)} - \frac{2}{(x - 4)(x + 5)} \qquad \text{\textit{Write each expression using the LCD.}}$$

$$= \frac{x^2 + 8x + 15}{(x - 4)(x + 5)} - \frac{2}{(x - 4)(x + 5)} \qquad \text{\textit{Multiply.}}$$

$$= \frac{x^2 + 8x + 13}{(x - 4)(x + 5)} \qquad \text{\textit{Subtract the numerators.}}$$

Since the numerator cannot be factored, the expression is in simplified form.

Add or subtract and simplify.

a. $\dfrac{4mn}{24m} + \dfrac{11mn}{24m}$

Like denominators, add the numerators.

$\dfrac{\boxed{}mn}{24m}$

Simplify.

$= \dfrac{\boxed{}n}{\boxed{}} = \underline{}$

b. $\dfrac{7y-2}{y+6} - \dfrac{y-38}{y+6}$

$\dfrac{7y-2-(y-38)}{y+6} = \dfrac{\boxed{}y\,\bigcirc\,\boxed{}}{y+6}$

Factor and simplify. $= \dfrac{\boxed{}\big(y\,\bigcirc\,\boxed{}\big)}{y+6}$

$= \underline{}$

c. Like denominators, add the numerators.

$\dfrac{d^4 + \boxed{}d^3}{d^2 - 5d - 36}$

Factor and simplify.

$\dfrac{\boxed{}\big(\boxed{} + 4\big)}{\big(d - \boxed{}\big)\big(d - \boxed{}\big)} = \dfrac{\boxed{}}{\boxed{}}$

d. LCD: $\underline{}$

Rewrite with the LCD, and simplify.

$\dfrac{\boxed{}p^{\boxed{}}}{6p^{\boxed{}}} + \dfrac{\boxed{}p^3}{6p^{\boxed{}}} = \dfrac{\boxed{}}{\boxed{}}$

$= \underline{}$

e. LCD: $(x + \underline{})(x + \underline{})$

Rewrite first term.

$\dfrac{x(x+2)}{\big(x + \boxed{}\big)\big(x + \boxed{}\big)}$

Add numerators.

$= \dfrac{\boxed{} + \boxed{}x - 3}{\big(x + \boxed{}\big)\big(x + \boxed{}\big)}$

Factor the numerator and simplify.

$= \dfrac{\big(x + \boxed{}\big)\big(x - \boxed{}\big)}{\big(x + \boxed{}\big)\big(x + \boxed{}\big)} = \dfrac{\big(x - \boxed{}\big)}{\big(x + \boxed{}\big)}$

f. Multiply the second term by $\frac{-1}{-1}$.

$\dfrac{(-1)}{(t^4 - 2)} + \dfrac{(-1)(t+9)}{(-1)(2 - t^4)} = \dfrac{-1}{t^4 - 2} + \dfrac{-\boxed{} - 9}{t^4 - \boxed{}}$

Add numerators.

$\dfrac{\boxed{} - \boxed{}}{t^4 - \boxed{}}$

g. distance = rate · time, or d = r · t, so time = $\frac{\text{distance}}{\text{rate}}$ = $\frac{\text{distance}}{\text{rate against current}} + \frac{\text{distance}}{\text{rate with current}}$

$d = \dfrac{5}{\boxed{} - c} + \dfrac{5}{\boxed{} + c}$

LCD: $(\underline{} - c)(\underline{} + c)$

Rewrite the fractions with the LCD.

$\dfrac{5\big(\boxed{} - c\big)}{\big(\boxed{} - c\big)\big(\boxed{} + c\big)} + \dfrac{5\big(\boxed{} + c\big)}{\big(\boxed{} - c\big)\big(\boxed{} + c\big)} = \dfrac{\boxed{}}{\big(\boxed{} - c\big)\big(\boxed{} + c\big)}$

1. $d = \sqrt{(\underline{\quad} - \underline{\quad})^2 + (\underline{\quad} - \underline{\quad})^2}$

   $= \sqrt{\underline{\quad} + \underline{\quad}} = \sqrt{\underline{\quad}}$

2. $d = \sqrt{(\underline{\quad} - \underline{\quad})^2 + (\underline{\quad} - \underline{\quad})^2}$

   $= \sqrt{\underline{\quad} + \underline{\quad}} = \sqrt{\underline{\quad}} = \underline{\quad}$

3. Write in standard form.

   $\underline{\quad}x^2 + \underline{\quad}x + \underline{\quad}$

   $(\underline{\quad}x + \underline{\quad})(\underline{\quad}x + \underline{\quad})$

4. Write in standard form.

   $\underline{\quad}t^2 + \underline{\quad}t - \underline{\quad}$

   $(\underline{\quad}t \bigcirc \underline{\quad})(\underline{\quad}t \bigcirc \underline{\quad})$

5. $\sqrt{9x^4} = \underline{\quad}$ $\sqrt{49y^2} = \underline{\quad}$

   $(\underline{\quad} \bigcirc \underline{\quad})(\underline{\quad} \bigcirc \underline{\quad})$

   It is a _____.

6. $\sqrt{x^6} = \underline{\quad}$ $\sqrt{64} = \underline{\quad}$

   $(\underline{\quad} \bigcirc \underline{\quad})(\underline{\quad} \bigcirc \underline{\quad})$

   It is a _____.

7. Make a table of values. Use x values of 0, ±2, ±4.

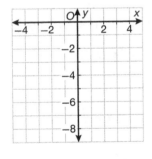

8. Factor. Then divide out like factors.

   $$\frac{\boxed{}(x - 8)}{6x^2} \cdot \frac{\boxed{}(y + \boxed{})}{\boxed{}(x - \boxed{})}$$

   $$= \frac{\boxed{} + \boxed{}}{\boxed{}}$$

9. Isolate the absolute value expression.

   $|n + 3| = \underline{\quad}$

   $n = \underline{\quad}$

10. $x = -\dfrac{b}{2a}$

    $x = -\dfrac{\boxed{}}{\boxed{}}$

    $x = \underline{\quad}$

11. *Same denominators, subtract the numerators.*

$$\frac{7x}{y} - \frac{2}{y}$$

= _____

12. LCD = _____

$$\frac{4y}{x} \cdot \frac{\square}{\square} - \frac{5y}{2x}$$

$$\frac{\square y - 5y}{2x} = \frac{\square y}{2x}$$

13. *The difference between the average length and the max or min length is 33mm.*

$| x - $ _____ $| = $ _____

longest sardine: $x - $ _____ $= +$ _____

= _____

shortest sardine: $x - $ _____ $= -$ _____

= _____

14. Multiply by both sides by _____, and solve for x.

$$75 + 90 + x \geq \underline{\qquad}$$

$$x \geq \underline{\quad}$$

His score must be _____ or better.

15. Complete the graph.

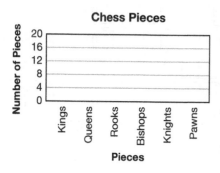

16. a. Let $d = $ number of days

add _____ ounces of adult food per day

remove _____ ounces of puppy food per day

total of 20 ounces of food per day

Write an inequality and solve for d.

_____ d $\bigcirc$ $20 - $ _____ d

d $\bigcirc$ _____

b. solution set: whole numbers > _____

After 4 days there will always be more

_____ food than _____ food.

17. "And" means that _____ inequalities must be _____ by the range of answers.

18. ✎ *Plot the points on a coordinate grid.*

a. vertical segment, (____, ____) to (____, ____), is _____ to the horizontal segment, (____, ____) to (____, ____).

b. $d_1 = $ _____

$d_2 = $ _____

c. $c = \sqrt{\underline{\quad}^2 + \underline{\quad}^2} = $ _____

19. *The hypotenuse c is the longest side of a right triangle.*

Does $(\underline{\quad})^2 = (\underline{\quad})^2 + (\underline{\quad})^2$?

_____ = _____ + _____

A right triangle _____ formed by the distances.

20. a. $A = s^{\square}$

b. $x^2 + 6x + 9$ *is a perfect square trinomial.*

$(x \bigcirc \underline{\quad})(x \bigcirc \underline{\quad})$

c. _____ $= (x + \underline{\quad})(x + \underline{\quad})$

d. _____ $=$ _____

21. *Joint variation:* $y = kxz$

$A_{\text{triangle}} = kbh$

_____ $= k(\underline{\quad})(\underline{\quad})$

$k = $ _____

Substitute.

$A = $ _____ bh

22. *Multiply* 1st *term by the reciprocal of the* 2nd. *Then simplify.*

$\dfrac{3mn^2}{4m^2n} \cdot \dfrac{\square}{\square}$

Answer: _____

23. *Factor the numerator and divide out like factors.*

$t = \dfrac{d}{r} = \dfrac{x^2 - 25}{\square + \square}$

$t = $ _____

24. Student _____ is correct. Student _____ did not take the _____ of b.

25. a. The function has a _____,

because the value of a is _____.

b. 📝 To find when the minimum
population occurred, find the x-coordinate
of the vertex using $x = -\frac{b}{2a}$. To find the
population, substitute x into the function
and solve for y.

population ≈ _____

_____ years (to the nearest whole

year) after 1900 or during _____

c. 📝 Let x = 2020 − 1900. Substitute
to find the population in 2020.

≈ _____ million people.

26. Find the x-coordinate of the vertex.

$$x = -\frac{b}{2a}$$

$$= -\frac{\Box}{2\Box} = \underline{\hspace{2cm}}$$

This value of x corresponds to the

_____ value for the area.

Substitute.

$$-(\underline{\hspace{1cm}})^2 + 35(\underline{\hspace{1cm}})$$

$$= \underline{\hspace{2cm}}$$

27. Same denominator, so subtract the numerators.

$$\frac{\Box}{9q^2}$$

Factor the new numerator and simplify.

Answer: _____

28. $\frac{winter\ and\ spring}{total}$

$$\frac{\left(x^2 + \Box + \Box\right) + \left(\Box + \Box\right)}{x^2 + \Box + \Box}$$

= _____

29. Multiplying by these expressions makes

each of the _____ equal to

the LCD _____.

30. _____ the denominator of the first term. Multiply the second term by

_____. Factor the_____ of the numerators into (___ + ___)(___ + ___).

_____ common factors cancel, so the answer is _____ = _____.

Name _____

Choosing a Factoring Method page 598

- Like whole numbers, many polynomials can be factored into prime factors.

- Unlike whole numbers, factors of polynomials are sometimes other polynomials.

- A polynomial is not factored completely until all the factors cannot be factored again.

- Factors can be checked by multiplying and simplifying. If this results in the original polynomial, the factors are correct.

- There are different methods for factoring different polynomials. These checklists help determine which method to use when more than one can be used.

Checklist Item 1: Factor out the GCF. Always do this first.

Factor $x^3y + 2xy^2$.

    1. Write the factors of each term.

        $x^3y =$ ____ · ____ · ____ · ____

        $2xy^2 =$ ____ · ____ · ____ · ____

    2. Greatest common factor: _____

    3. Factor out the greatest common factor from each term.

        _____(____) + _____(2____)

    4. Factor out the greatest common factor from the polynomial.

        _____(____ + 2____)

Checklist Item 2: Difference of Two Squares.

Factor $x^2 - 4$.

    5. Any common factors? _____ If yes, see Checklist Item 1.

    6. Are there only two terms being subtracted? _____

    7. Is it in the $a^2 - b^2$ form? _____

        $a =$ _____ $b =$ _____

8. Use $a^2 - b^2 = (a + b)(a - b)$ to factor the binomial.

(_____ + _____)(_____ − _____)

9. If the binomial was in the form $a^2 + b^2$, could you factor it the same way?

_____, because there is no rule for factoring the _____ of two squares

Checklist Item 3: Perfect-Square Trinomials.

Factor $x^2 + 16x + 64$.

$(a^2 + 2ab + b^2) = a^2 + b^2$

10. Any common factors? _____. If yes, see Checklist Item 1.

11. How many terms? _____

12. Are the first and last terms perfect squares? _____

What are their square roots? $a =$ _____ $b =$ _____

13. What is the value of a? _____ of b? _____

14. Use the formula $(a^2 + 2ab + b^2) = a^2 + b^2$ to factor the perfect-square trinomial.

_____

15. Is it possible to factor $x^2 + 8x + 32$ in a similar manner? Explain.

_____, the value of a is _____, but 32 is not a _____

_____.

Checklist Item 4: Other Trinomials.

Factor $x^2 + 8x + 15$.

16. Any common factors? _____. If yes, see Checklist Item 1.

17. Perfect-square trinomial? _____. If yes, see Checklist Item 3.

18. Is the trinomial of the form $x^2 + (j + k)x + jk$? _____

If so, find j and k so their product is 15 and their sum is 8.

$j =$ _____, $k =$ _____ or $j =$ _____, $k =$ _____

19. Factor the polynomial. $(x +$ _____$)(x +$ _____$)$

Checklist Item 5: Polynomials with Four Terms.

Factor $x^3 + 7x^2 + 2x + 14$.

20. Any common factors? _____ . If yes, see Checklist Item1.

21. How many terms? ____

22. Group first two and last two terms. (_____) + (_____)

23. Factor out the GCF in the first group. _____(_____ + 7)

24. Factor out the GCF in the second group. _____(x + _____)

25. Write the polynomial. _____(_____ + 7) + _____(x + _____)

26. Common factor: (_____ + _____)

27. Factor out the common factor. (_____ + _____)(_____ + _____)

Exploration 📖 page 600

Use your textbook to complete the Exploration.

Investigation Practice 📖 page 601

Factor.

a. $x^2 + 2x + 1$

First and last terms are _____ and _____.

$\sqrt{x^2}$ = _____, $\sqrt{1}$ = _____ factors are (_____ + _____)(_____ + _____) or (_____ + _____)^2

b. $3x^2 + xy - 12x - 4y$

_____ terms. Group. ___(3_____ + _____) − ___(3_____ + _____)

= (_____ − _____)(3_____ + _____)

c. $9y^4 - 1$

_____ terms, _____ of two _____

a = _____, b = _____

$a^2 - b^2 = (a - b)(a + b)$

$9y^4 - 1 = ($_____ + _____$)($_____ − _____$)$

Identify the first step needed to factor the polynomial. Use it to begin factoring. After this, list other methods to continuing factoring if applicable.

d. Factoring method: _____; _____(_____ − _____).

The remaining binomial is a _____ of two _____.

e. Factoring method: _____ _____ $a =$ _____, $b =$ _____

factors: (___ + ___)(___ + ___) or (___ + ___)^2

f. Factoring method: _____ of two _____ $a =$ _____, $b=$ _____

factors: (___ + ___)(___ − ___)

Sketch the arrangement of the tiles. Verify by factoring.

g. $3x^2 + 13x + 4$

GCF? _____. If so, factor it out.

positive factors of 3: ___,___; positive factors of 4: ___,___, or ___,___

(___$x +$ ___)(___$x +$ ___) *Use FOIL to check.*

h. $x^2 + 9x + 20$

GCF? _____. If so, factor it out.

positive factors of 20 that add to 9: _____,_____

$(x +$ ___$)(x +$ ___$)$. *Use FOIL to check.*

i. $2x^2 + 8x + 6$

GCF? _____. If so, factor it out. ____$(x^2 + 4x +$ ____$)$

positive factors of ___: ___,___, or ___,___

$(x +$ ___$)(x +$ ___$)$ *Use FOIL to check.*

Name _____

Solving Absolute-Value Inequalities page 602

New Concepts

• The absolute value of a number is the distance of that number from 0 on the number line. Since distance is always positive, the absolute value of any number is positive.

Example **Isolating the Absolute Value to Solve**

Solve and graph the inequality.

$\dfrac{|x|}{4} > 2$ *Isolate the absolute value.*

$\dfrac{|x|}{4} \cdot 4 > 2 \cdot 4$ *Multiplication Property of Inequalities*

$|x| > 8$ *Simplify.*

The inequality $|x| > 8$ translates to:

All real numbers whose distance from 0 is more than 8 units.

The solution is **$x > 8$ OR $x < -8$**

Rules for Solving Absolute-Value Inequalities
For an inequality in the form $|K| < a$, where K represents a variable expression and $a > 0$, solve $-a < K < a$ or $K > -a$ AND $K < a$.
For an inequality in the form $|K| > a$, where K represents a variable expression and $a > 0$, solve $K < -a$ OR $K > a$.
Similar rules are true for $|K| \le a$ or $|K| \ge a$.

Example **Solving Inequalities with Operations Inside Absolute-Value Symbols**

Solve the inequality and graph the solution.

Isolate the absolute value. Then set up an equivalent compound inequality.

$|x - 5| \le 3$

$x - 5 \ge -3$ AND $x - 5 \le 3$
$\underline{+5 \quad +5}$ $\underline{+5 \quad +5}$
    $x \ge -2$ AND $x \le 8$

$-2 \le x \le 8$

Graph the inequality.

Solve and graph each inequality.

a. $|x| < 12$ *All real numbers whose distance from 0 is less than 12 units.*

_____ $\bigcirc$ $x < 12$

b. $|x| > 19$ *All real numbers whose distance from 0 is greater than 19 units.*

_____ $\bigcirc$ x OR $x > 19$

c. $|x| + 2.8 \leq 10.4$ *Isolate the absolute value before writing the inequality.*

$|x| \leq$ _____

_____ $\leq x \leq$ _____

d. $\dfrac{|x|}{-5} < -1$

$|x|$ $\bigcirc$ _____

x $\bigcirc$ _____ OR x $\bigcirc$ _____

e. $|x - 10| \leq 12$

$|x| \leq$ _____

_____ $\leq x \leq$ _____

f. $|x + 12| > 18$

$|x|$ $\bigcirc$ _____

x $\bigcirc$ _____ OR x $\bigcirc$ _____

g. $|x| + 21 \leq 14$

$|x|$ $\bigcirc$ _____

_____

h. $|x| + 33 > 24$

$|x|$ $\bigcirc$ _____

_____

A machine part must be 15 ± 0.2 cm in diameter.

i. *All real numbers whose distance from 15 is less than or equal to 0.2 cm.*

Inequality of range of diameters:

$|x - 15|$ $\bigcirc$ _____

j. Write the equivalent compound inequality.

m _____ $\geq -$ _____ AND m _____ $\bigcirc$ _____

m $\bigcirc$ _____ m $\bigcirc$ _____

Inequality: _____ $\bigcirc$ m $\bigcirc$ _____

1. Axis of symmetry: $x = \dfrac{-b}{2a}$

$a =$ _____ $b =$ _____ $x = \dfrac{-\boxed{}}{\boxed{}} =$ _____   Axis of symmetry: $x =$ _____

---

2. Combine the terms. Divide out a common factor. Then simplify.

$$\frac{6rs}{r^2s^2} + \frac{18r}{r^2s^2} = \frac{6rs + \boxed{}}{r^2s^2} = \frac{\boxed{}\left(s + \boxed{}\right)}{r^2s^2} = \frac{\boxed{}\left(\boxed{} + \boxed{}\right)}{\boxed{}s^2}$$

---

3. Find the LCD.

$$\frac{b}{2b+1} \cdot \frac{\boxed{} - \boxed{}}{\boxed{} - \boxed{}} - \frac{6}{b-4} \cdot \frac{\boxed{} + \boxed{}}{\boxed{} + \boxed{}} = \frac{\left(b^2 - 4b\right) - \left(12b + \boxed{}\right)}{(2b+1)(b-4)} = \frac{b^2 - \boxed{}b - \boxed{}}{(2b+1)(b-4)}$$

---

4. First, factor out $-y$.

$-4y^4 + 8y^3 + 5y^2 - 10y$

$= -y(\underline{\hspace{3cm}})$

$= -y(\underline{\hspace{1.5cm}})(\underline{\hspace{1.5cm}})$

5. $3a^2 - 27$

$= \underline{\hspace{0.5cm}}(\underline{\hspace{2cm}})$

$= \underline{\hspace{0.5cm}}(\underline{\hspace{0.5cm}} + \underline{\hspace{0.5cm}})(\underline{\hspace{0.5cm}} - \underline{\hspace{0.5cm}})$

---

6. Factor $4x^2 + 6x - 4$.

$=$ _____

7. Factor $9x^2 - 2x + 32$.

$=$ _____

---

8. Write two equations to solve.

$x >$ _____   AND $x <$ _____

_____ $< x <$ _____

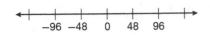

9. In $|x| \geq 54$, x can be any _____ that is 54 or _____ units from _____ on the number line.

---

10. Since absolute value is always _____, the absolute value of any real number x, in the inequality $|x| \geq -5$, will _____ be greater than _____.

---

11. *Use rules of absolute-value inequalities.*

Circle the answer represented by the graph.

A $|x| < 9$ **B** $|x| > 9$

C $|x| \leq 9$ **D** $|x| < -9$

12. $|t - 8.54| \leq 0.3$

$t - 8.54 \geq$ _____ $t - 8.54 \leq$ _____

$t \geq$ _____ $t \leq$ _____

_____ $\leq t \leq$ _____

8.24 8.44 8.64 8.84

13. Student _____ is correct. Student _____ multiplied the _____ by -1 but did not multiply the _____ of that expression by _____.

14. **a.** $\dfrac{land\ set\ aside}{total\ land} = \dfrac{x^2 + \square x - 8}{\square + 22x + \square}$

$= \dfrac{\left(x + \square\right)\left(x - \square\right)}{\left(x + \square\right)\left(x + \square\right)} = $ _____

b. $\dfrac{\square - 2}{\square + 18} \approx$ _____   The farmer set aside about _____ % of the field.

15. area of triangle $= \dfrac{1}{2}($ _____ $)($ _____ $) = $ _____

area of small rectangle $= ($ _____ $)($ _____ $) = $ _____

area covered $= $ _____ $+$ _____ $= $ _____

area of large rectangle $= ($ _____ $)($ _____ $) = $ _____

$\dfrac{area\ covered}{area\ of\ large\ rectangle} = \dfrac{\square x^2 - \square x}{\square x^2 - \square x} = \dfrac{\square x\left(x - \square\right)}{\square x\left(x + \square\right)} = \dfrac{\square\left(x - \square\right)}{\square\left(x + \square\right)}$

16. *Use the order of operations.*

$\left(\sqrt{4} - 6\right)^2 = ($ _____ $-$ _____ $)^2 = $ _____

17. It is necessary to understand factoring when dealing with rational expressions, because

factoring makes is easier to _____ complicated expressions.

---

18. *Factor each term before multiplying.*

a. $\dfrac{(x^2 + y)}{1} \cdot \dfrac{(4x + 2xy)}{(x^3 + xy)} = \dfrac{(x^2 + y)}{1} \cdot \dfrac{2x(\square + \square)}{x(\square + \square)} =$ _____

b. _____ $\times \dfrac{1}{2} =$ _____

---

19. Student _____ is correct. Student _____ used the wrong values for _____ and _____. The

equation in standard form is _____, so $a =$ _____ and $b =$ _____.

---

20. *Find x-coordinate of the vertex by using the formula for the axis of symmetry.*

Substitute the x-coordinate of the vertex into the function and solve for y.

$x = \dfrac{-b}{2a}$

$y = -13x^2 + 39x$

$x =$ _____ $=$ _____

$y =$ _____ $=$ _____

The ball reaches a maximum height of _____ feet in _____ seconds.

---

21. $D = \sqrt{(x_2 - x_1)^2 + (y_2 - y_1)^2}.$ $A(5, 3)$ and $B(7, 10)$

$d = \sqrt{(\underline{\quad} - \underline{\quad})^2 + (\underline{\quad} - \underline{\quad})^2} = \sqrt{(\underline{\quad})^2 + (\underline{\quad})^2} = \sqrt{(\underline{\quad}) + (\underline{\quad})} =$ _____

$d =$ _____ $\times$ _____ $=$ _____

---

22. $D = \sqrt{(x_2 - x_1)^2 + (y_2 - y_1)^2}.$ $(41, 37)$ and $(5, 2)$

$d = \sqrt{(\underline{\quad} - \underline{\quad})^2 + (\underline{\quad} - \underline{\quad})^2} = \sqrt{(\underline{\quad})^2 + (\underline{\quad})^2} = \sqrt{(\underline{\quad}) + (\underline{\quad})} =$ _____

$d =$ _____ $\times$ _____ $=$ _____ feet

---

23. *Use the Pythagorean Theorem.*

$t^2 = (\underline{\quad})^2 + (\underline{\quad})^2$

$t^2 =$ _____

$t =$ _____

24. 📝 Solve $34^2 = h^2 + 7^2$.

_____ feet tall ◯ 33 feet

The top of the ladder would touch

_____ the windowsill.

---

25. $y = 4x^2$

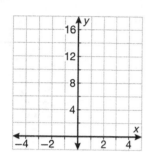

26. *Use a special factoring pattern.*

$a^{2m} + 2a^m b^n + b^2 n$

$= (a^m)^2 + 2a^m b^n + (b^n)^2$

$= (\underline{\quad})(\underline{\quad})$

27. Let x = number of CDs that Roger can buy

Roger will buy at least 3 CDs: $x \geq 3$

Roger will buy no more than \$40 worth of CDs: $\underline{\quad} x \bigcirc \$40$

Solve the compound inequality. $x \geq 3$ AND $\underline{\quad} x \bigcirc \$40$

$\underline{\quad} \bigcirc x \bigcirc \underline{\quad}$

28. *Rational equation:* $y = \frac{a}{x+b} + c$

a. The horizontal asymptote is $y = \underline{\quad}$

b. The vertical asymptote is $x = \underline{\quad}$

c. The program can receive $\underline{\quad}$ T-shirts.

29. $4x^2 + 9x + 2 = (\underline{\quad})(\underline{\quad})$

width = $(\underline{\quad} + \underline{\quad})$ and length = $(\underline{\quad} + \underline{\quad})$ OR

width = $(\underline{\quad} + \underline{\quad})$ and length = $(\underline{\quad} + \underline{\quad})$

30. *Simplify the radicals first.*

$6\sqrt{8} \cdot \sqrt{5} = 6(\underline{\quad})\sqrt{\underline{\quad}} \cdot \sqrt{\underline{\quad}} = \underline{\quad}\sqrt{(\underline{\quad})(\underline{\quad})} = \underline{\quad}\sqrt{\underline{\quad}}$

New Concepts

Math Language

A **complex fraction** is a fraction that contains one or more fractions in the numerator, denominator, or both.

Complex Fractions
There are two ways to write a fraction divided by a fraction.

$$\frac{\frac{a}{b}}{\frac{c}{d}} = \frac{a}{b} \div \frac{c}{d}, \text{ when } b \neq 0, c \neq 0, \text{ and } d \neq 0.$$

Example Simplifying by Dividing

Simplify the complex fraction by dividing.

$$\frac{\frac{a}{x}}{\frac{b}{a+x}} = \frac{a}{x} \div \frac{b}{a+x}$$ *Write the problem using a division sign.*

$$= \frac{a}{x} \cdot \frac{a+x}{b} = \frac{a(a+x)}{xb}$$ *Multiply by the reciprocal.*

Example Factoring to Simplify

Simplify the complex fraction by factoring.

$$\frac{\frac{3x}{6x+12}}{\frac{9}{x+2}}$$

$$\frac{3x}{6x+12} \div \frac{9}{x+2}$$ *Write using a division sign.*

$$\frac{3x}{6x+12} \cdot \frac{x+2}{9}$$ *Multiply by the reciprocal.*

$$\frac{\overset{1}{\cancel{3x}}}{6\cancel{(x+2)}} \cdot \frac{\cancel{x+2}}{\underset{3}{\cancel{9}}} = \frac{x}{18}$$ *Factor and cancel to simplify.*

Example Combining Fractions to Simplify

Simplify the complex fraction.

$$\frac{\frac{1}{x}}{1 - \frac{1}{x}}$$

Subtract in the denominator. Write with a division sign. Then, factor and cancel to simplify.

$$\frac{\frac{1}{x}}{\frac{x(1)}{x} - \frac{1}{x}} = \frac{\frac{1}{x}}{\frac{(x-1)}{x}} = \frac{1}{\cancel{x}} \cdot \frac{\cancel{x}}{(x-1)} = \frac{1}{x-1}$$

Simplify.

a. The reciprocal of $\frac{3(x-3)}{x}$ is $\dfrac{\square}{\square(\square-\square)}$.

$\dfrac{x}{4} \cdot \dfrac{\square}{\square(\square-\square)} = \underline{\hspace{3cm}}$

b. $\dfrac{\frac{b}{cd}}{\frac{2b}{c}} = \dfrac{b}{cd} \cdot \dfrac{\square}{\square} = \underline{\hspace{3cm}}$

c. $\dfrac{\frac{4x^2}{x-3}}{\frac{x}{3x-9}} = \dfrac{4x^2}{x-3} \cdot \dfrac{3(\square-\square)}{\square} = \underline{\hspace{3cm}}$

d. *Simplify the numerator and denominator. Then multiply by the reciprocal.*

$\dfrac{1}{m} + 5 = \dfrac{1}{m} + \dfrac{5m}{m} = \dfrac{\square+\square}{m}$ $\dfrac{2}{m} - \dfrac{x}{m} = \dfrac{2-x}{\square}$

$\dfrac{\frac{\square+\square}{m}}{\frac{2-x}{\square}} = \dfrac{\square+\square}{m} \cdot \dfrac{\square}{2-x} = \underline{\hspace{3cm}}$

e. It took Ariel $\dfrac{5x^2-45x}{5x}$ minutes to walk to school that was $\dfrac{3x-27}{x^3}$ miles away.

Find the rate in miles per minute. *Factor before simplifying.*

$\dfrac{\frac{3x-27}{x^3}}{\frac{5x^2-45x}{5x}} = \dfrac{\frac{\square(x-9)}{x^3}}{\frac{5x(\square-9x)}{5x}} = \dfrac{\square(x-9)}{x^3} \cdot \dfrac{5x}{5x(\square-9x)} = \underline{\hspace{2cm}}$

1. Factor each term first.

$$\frac{15x^4}{x-4} \cdot \frac{x^2 - 10x + 24}{3x^3 + 12x^2}$$

$$= \frac{\square x^2 \cdot \square x^2}{x-4} \cdot \frac{(\square - \square)(\square + \square)}{\square(\square + \square)}$$

$$= \underline{\hspace{3cm}}$$

2. $\dfrac{x^2 + 12x + 36}{x^2 - 36} \div \dfrac{1}{x-6}$

$$= \frac{(\square + \square)(\square + \square)}{(\square - \square)(\square + \square)} \div \frac{1}{x-6}$$

$$= \frac{(\square \bigcirc \square)}{(\square \bigcirc \square)} \cdot \frac{(\square \bigcirc \square)}{1}$$

$$= \underline{\hspace{2cm}}$$

3. When multiplying or dividing by a negative, reverse the inequality sign.

$$-3(r - 2) > -2(-6)$$

$$\underline{\hspace{1.5cm}} > \underline{\hspace{1.5cm}}$$

$$\underline{\hspace{1.5cm}} > \underline{\hspace{1.5cm}}$$

$$\underline{\hspace{1cm}} \bigcirc \underline{\hspace{1cm}}$$

4.
$$\frac{y}{4} + \frac{1}{2} < \frac{2}{3}$$

$$(\underline{\hspace{0.5cm}})\frac{y}{4} + (\underline{\hspace{0.5cm}})\frac{1}{2} < (\underline{\hspace{0.5cm}})\frac{2}{3}$$

$$\underline{\hspace{0.7cm}} + \underline{\hspace{0.7cm}} < \underline{\hspace{0.7cm}}$$

$$\underline{\hspace{0.7cm}} < \underline{\hspace{0.7cm}}$$

$$\underline{\hspace{0.7cm}} \bigcirc \underline{\hspace{0.7cm}}$$

5. Multiply by the reciprocal of the denominator.

$$\frac{\frac{5x}{10x + 20}}{\frac{15}{x + 2}} = \frac{5x}{\square + \square} \cdot \frac{\square + \square}{\square}$$

Factor.

$$= \frac{5x}{\square(\square + \square)} \cdot \frac{(\square + \square)}{\square}$$

$$= \underline{\hspace{3cm}}$$

6. Simplify the radical first.

$$8\sqrt{9} \cdot 2\sqrt{5}$$

$$= \underline{\hspace{0.5cm}}(\underline{\hspace{0.5cm}})(\underline{\hspace{0.5cm}})\sqrt{\underline{\hspace{1cm}}}$$

$$= \underline{\hspace{0.5cm}}\sqrt{\underline{\hspace{1cm}}}$$

7. A rational expression is undefined when the _____ equals _____.

8. Substitute a different number for each variable and simplify.

📝 Give an example.

9. $d = rt$, so $r = \frac{d}{t}$

$$r = \dfrac{\dfrac{2x}{8x-8} + \dfrac{x}{4x+12}}{\dfrac{15}{x^2+2x-3}}$$

Factor and multiply by reciprocal.

$$= \frac{2x}{8(x-1)} + \frac{x}{4(x+3)} \cdot \frac{(\square\bigcirc\square)(\square\bigcirc\square)}{15}$$

Using the LCD, combine the fractions in the numerator.

$$\frac{(\square)(\square+\square) + (\square)(\square-\square)}{(8)(x-1)(x+3)} \cdot \frac{(\square+\square)(\square+\square)}{15}$$

Simplify.

$$= \text{Jim's rate} = \frac{\square+\square}{\square} \text{ miles per minute}$$

10. $x^2 + 6x + 9 = (\underline{\hspace{1cm}})(\underline{\hspace{1cm}})$

$x^2 - 9 = (\underline{\hspace{1cm}})(\underline{\hspace{1cm}})$

$LCD = (\underline{\hspace{1cm}})(\underline{\hspace{1cm}})(\underline{\hspace{1cm}}) = (\underline{\hspace{1cm}})^2(\underline{\hspace{1cm}})$

Circle the least common denominator.

A $x^2 + 9$ **B** $x^2 + 6x + 9$ **C** $2x^2 + 9$ **D** $(x+3)^2(x-3)$

11. *x can never be equal to or greater than 65 units away from zero.*

$|x| < 65$

$\underline{\hspace{1cm}} < x < \underline{\hspace{1cm}}$

12. Student $\underline{\hspace{1cm}}$ is correct.

Student $\underline{\hspace{1cm}}$ did not realize that an

absolute value could never be less than

$\underline{\hspace{1cm}}$ because an $\underline{\hspace{1cm}}$ $\underline{\hspace{1cm}}$

by definition is always $\underline{\hspace{1cm}}$.

13. _____ $\bigcirc$ x $\bigcirc$ _____

14. *The "distance" from 80 (greater than and less than) is an absolute value.*

    a. $|x - 80|$ $\bigcirc$ 15

    b. *Write the equation without absolute value.*

      _____ $\bigcirc$ $x - 80$ $\bigcirc$ 15

      _____ $\bigcirc$ x $\bigcirc$ _____

15. Student _____ is correct. Student _____ did not distribute the _____

sign through the numerator of the _____ term.

16. $d = rt$, so $r = \frac{d}{t}$

total time: $\dfrac{\square}{6-c} + \dfrac{\square}{6+c}$

$\dfrac{\square}{6-c} \cdot \dfrac{(\square\bigcirc\square)}{(\square\bigcirc\square)} + \dfrac{\square}{6+c} \cdot \dfrac{(\square\bigcirc\square)}{(\square\bigcirc\square)}$

Simplify. $\dfrac{\square\bigcirc\square}{(\square\bigcirc\square)(\square\bigcirc\square)}$

17. *Positive coefficients of the x^2 term indicate graphs that open downward, thus having a maximum.*

    A $y = -5 + x^2$

    B $y = -x^2 + 5x$

    C $y = x^2 + 5$

    D $y = 5x^2 - 1$

18. One way to find the axis of symmetry is to use the _____ of the function. The axis of

symmetry goes through the _____ when there is 1 _____ because the y-value of the

vertex is zero. When there are _____ zeros, it goes through the average of the _____ zeros.

The second way is to use the formula $x = -\dfrac{\square}{2\square}$. This is the only way to find the axis of

symmetry when the function has no _____ .

19. *Use the standard form of a linear function and a quadratic function.*

    📝 Explain.

20. *Use the Pythagorean Theorem.*

    $a =$ _____ $\approx$ _____

21. *Subtract the numerators. Factor. Then simplify.*

$$\frac{5f + 6}{f^2 + 7f - 8} - \frac{f + 10}{f^2 + 7f - 8}$$

$=$ _____

22. *Use properties of parallelograms and the distance formula.*

✎ Use another sheet of paper for your calculations.

$AB =$ _____ $BC =$ _____

$CD =$ _____ $DA =$ _____

$ABCD$ _____ a parallelogram.

23. *Find the coordinates of Athens and Oneonta and then find the distance between the two points.*

Athens = (____, ____)

Oneonta = (____, ____)

$d = \sqrt{(85 - \underline{\quad})^2 + (\underline{\quad} - 10)^2}$

$= \sqrt{\underline{\qquad}}$

$\approx$ _____

24. Student _____ is correct.

Student _____ did not _____

the _____ sign correctly.

25. $P_{red} = \dfrac{\square}{\square + \square + \square}$

$= \dfrac{\square + \square}{\square + \square} = \dfrac{\square}{\square(\square + \square)} = \dfrac{\square}{\square}$

26. *All the coefficients are even numbers.*

a. $2x^2 - 8x + 6 =$ ____(____)(____)   b. length = _____   width = _____

27. _____ ◯ t ◯ _____

28. a. length: _____ + 2

$2(\underline{\quad} + 2) + 2w = 8x$, w = _____

b. $A = (\underline{\quad} + 2)(\underline{\quad}) = (\underline{\quad})$

c. $x^4 - (\underline{\quad}) = x^4 - \underline{\quad}^2 + \underline{\quad} = (\underline{\quad})^2$

29. height $= h = -16t^2 + vt + s$; $v = 0$, $s = 14{,}400$, so $h = -16\underline{\quad}^2 + \underline{\quad}$

Factor the expression: $16(-\underline{\quad}^2 + \underline{\quad}) = 16(\underline{\quad} - \underline{\quad}^2) = 16(\underline{\quad})(\underline{\quad})$

30. *y = kx represents joint variation and y = $\frac{k}{x}$ represents inverse variation.*

In the equation, _____ is jointly proportional to _____ and _____, and inversely proportional to ___.

Dividing Polynomials page 616

New Concepts

• Dividing polynomials is very much like dividing whole numbers.

> **Example** **Dividing a Polynomial By a Binomial**
>
> **Divide.** $(x^2 - 6x + 9) \div (x - 3)$
>
> $$= \frac{x^2 - 6x + 9}{x - 3} \qquad \text{Write as a rational expression.}$$
>
> $$= \frac{(x - 3)(x - 3)}{x - 3} \qquad \text{Factor the numerator.}$$
>
> $$= x - 3 \qquad \text{Simplify.}$$

> **Example** **Dividing a Polynomial Using Long Division**
>
> **Divide using long division.** $(-25x + 3x^2 + 8) \div (x - 8)$
>
> $3x^2 - 25x + 8$ *Write the polynomial in standard form.*
>
> $x - 8\overline{)3x^2 - 25x + 8}$ *Write in long-division form.*
>
> $\dfrac{3x}{x - 8\overline{)3x^2 - 25x + 8}}$ *Divide the first term of the dividend by the first term of the divisor: $3x^2 \div x = 3x$.*
>
> $\begin{array}{r} 3x \\ x - 8\overline{)3x^2 - 25x + 8} \\ -\,(3x^2 - 24x) \\ \hline -\,x + 8 \end{array}$
>
> *Multiply the first term of the quotient by the divisor: $3x \cdot (x - 8) = 3x^2 - 24x$.*
> *Subtract: $(3x^2 - 25x) - (3x^2 - 24x)$.*
> *Bring down the next term of the dividend, 8.*
>
> $\begin{array}{r} 3x - 1 \\ x - 8\overline{)3x^2 - 25x + 8} \\ -\,(3x^2 - 24x) \\ \hline -\,x + 8 \\ -(-x + 8) \\ \hline 0 \end{array}$
>
> *Repeat the steps to complete the division.*
> *The remainder is 0.*
>
> **The quotient is $(3x - 1)$ remainder 0.**

Hint

When the dividend is missing a term, insert a placeholder with 0 as the coefficient.

For example, if the dividend is $x^2 - 7$, rewrite it as: $x^2 + \mathbf{0x} - 7$.

• If there is a remainder, write it as the numerator of a fraction with the divisor as the denominator. Add the fraction to the end of the quotient.

Divide each expression.

a. $(7x^4 + 7x^3 - 84x^2) \div 7x^2$

$$\frac{(7x^4 + 7x^3 - 84x^2)}{7x^2} = \frac{7x^4}{7x^2} + \frac{\square}{7x^2} - \frac{\square}{7x^2} = x^2 + \underline{\hspace{0.5cm}} - \underline{\hspace{0.5cm}}$$

b. $(x^2 - 10x + 25) \div (x - 5)$

$$= \frac{(x^2 - 10x + 25)}{x - 5} = \frac{(x - \square)(x - \square)}{x - 5} = \underline{\hspace{0.5cm}} - \underline{\hspace{0.5cm}}$$

c. $(3x^2 - 14x - 5) \div (5 - x)$ *Rewrite the denominator.*

$$= \frac{(3x^2 - 14x - 5)}{(\square - \square)} = \frac{(\square + \square)(x - 5)}{-1(x - 5)} = \underline{\hspace{0.5cm}} - \underline{\hspace{0.5cm}}$$

Divide using long division.

d. $(8x^2 + x^3 - 20x) \div (x - 2)$

standard dividend: _____

$$x - 2 \overline{)x^3 + 8x^2 - 20x}$$
$$\overline{}^{\displaystyle x^2}$$
$$\underline{-(\square - \square x^2)}$$
$$10x^2$$

 Complete the division.

quotient: _____

e. $(-3x^2 + 6x^3 + x - 33) \div (-2 + x)$

standard dividend: _____

standard divisor: _____

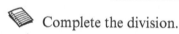 Complete the division.

remainder: _____

final term of quotient: $\dfrac{\square}{x - 2}$

quotient: _____

f. $(6x + 5x^3 - 8) \div (x - 4)$

dividend in standard form:

$$\underline{\hspace{0.5cm}}x^3 + 0x^2 + \underline{\hspace{0.5cm}}x - \underline{\hspace{0.5cm}}$$

Complete the division.

final term of quotient: $\dfrac{\square}{\square}$

quotient: _____

g. $(x^2 - 10x + 24) \div (x - 4)$

$$= \frac{x^2 - 10x + 24}{x - 4}$$

$$= \frac{(x - \square)(x - \square)}{x - 4}$$

$$= (\underline{\hspace{0.5cm}} - \underline{\hspace{0.5cm}}) \text{ ft}$$

1. $d = \sqrt{(x_2 - x_1)^2 + (y_2 - y_1)^2}$

$(-3, 2)$ and $(9, -3)$

$d =$ _____

2. $\frac{5}{6}y + \frac{3}{8} \geq \frac{1}{2}$

$y \geq \dfrac{\square}{\square}$

```
<--+--+--+--+--+--+--+--+--+--+--+-->
        -1        0        1
```

3. $2x^2 + 12x + 16$

$= \underline{\quad}(\underline{\qquad\qquad})$

$= \underline{\quad}(x \bigcirc \underline{\quad})(x \bigcirc \underline{\quad})$

4. $3x^3 - 5x^2 - 9x + 15$

$= (3x \bigcirc \underline{\quad})(x^2 \bigcirc \underline{\quad})$

5. $\dfrac{4x^3 + 42x^2 - 2x}{2x} = \dfrac{\square}{2x} + \dfrac{\square}{\square} - \dfrac{\square}{\square}$

$= 2x^2 + \underline{\quad} - \underline{\quad}$

6. *Axis of symmetry:* $x = -\dfrac{b}{2a}$

$a = \underline{\quad}$ $b = \underline{\quad}$ $x = -\dfrac{\square}{\square}$

Axis of symmetry: $x =$ _____

7. $= \dfrac{7x^4}{4x + 18} \div \dfrac{3x^2}{6x + 27} = \dfrac{7x^4}{4x + 18} \cdot \dfrac{\square + \square}{\square}$

✏️ Multiply. Simplify.

$=$ _____

8. $\dfrac{\frac{1}{x^3}}{\frac{1}{x^3} + \frac{1}{x^3}} = \dfrac{\frac{1}{x^3}}{\frac{\square}{x^3}} = \dfrac{1}{x^3} \div \dfrac{\square}{x^3} = \dfrac{1}{x^3} \cdot \dfrac{\square}{\square} = \dfrac{\square}{\square}$

9. Since division and _____ are inverse operations, multiply the divisor by the _____. The product should equal the _____.

$(5x + 6) \cdot (\underline{\qquad}) = 15x^2 + 13x - 6$

10. *Use a factoring pattern to divide.*

$\dfrac{x^2 - 4}{x + 2} = \dfrac{(x - \square)(x + \square)}{(x + 2)} =$ _____

 Then use long division to divide.

11. $l = \frac{A}{w}$

$$\frac{x^2 - 16x + 63}{\square - \square}$$

Simplify.

$l = $ _____

12. dividend in standard form:

____$x^3 + $ ____$x^2 - $ ____$x - $ ____

 Use long division.

Circle the answer.

A $x^2 - 7$ **B** $x^3 - 7$

C -3 **D** $\frac{x^2 - 7}{2x}$

---

13. Student _____ is correct. Student _____ did not write the solution in _____.

---

14. *Rate = distance ÷ time*

a. $\dfrac{7x - 42}{4x^2} \div \dfrac{8x^2 - 48x}{24x^5} = \dfrac{7x - 42}{4x^2} \cdot \dfrac{24x^5}{\square} = \dfrac{\square(x - \square)}{4x^2} \cdot \dfrac{24x^5}{\square x(\square - \square)} = \dfrac{\square x^2}{\square}$ mi per minute

b. $\dfrac{\square x^2}{\square} \div \dfrac{1}{x} = \dfrac{\square x^2}{\square} \cdot \dfrac{\square}{\square} = \dfrac{\square}{\square}$ mi per minute

---

15. $A = bh$

$b = \dfrac{A}{\square}$

$\dfrac{m + n}{5} \div \dfrac{\square + \square}{\square}$

$= \dfrac{m + n}{5} \cdot \dfrac{\square}{\square + \square} = $ _____ inches

16. $x \bigcirc 84$ OR $x \bigcirc -84$

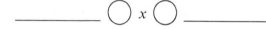

---

17. $|x - $ _____$| \bigcirc$ _____

 Solve.

_____ $\bigcirc \; x \; \bigcirc$ _____

18. Student _____ is correct.

Student _____ did not realize that all

_____ _____

are _____ than -15.

---

19. $\dfrac{1}{x^2 - 5x - 50} + \dfrac{1}{2x - 20} = \dfrac{1}{\left(x + \boxed{}\right)\left(x - \boxed{}\right)} \cdot \dfrac{\boxed{}}{\boxed{}} + \dfrac{1}{\boxed{}\left(x + \boxed{}\right)} \cdot \dfrac{\boxed{}}{\boxed{}} =$ _____

Circle the answer.

A 1　　　　　　　**B** 2　　　　　　　**C** $x + 5$　　　　　　**D** $x + 7$

20. _____ one of the expressions by $\dfrac{\boxed{}}{\boxed{}}$.

21. *Use the x^2-term to determine which functions have a minimum.*

number of functions that have a minimum: _____　　　total equations: _____

The first paper each student chooses is not replaced before he/she chooses a second.

$P(2 \text{ with minimums}) = \dfrac{\boxed{}}{\boxed{}} \cdot \dfrac{\boxed{}}{\boxed{}} = \dfrac{\boxed{}}{\boxed{}}$

22. Student _____ is correct.

Student _____ did not multiply by

the _____ of the divisor.

23. $6b + b^2 + (\underline{})(4b + b^2)$

= _____ dollars

24. *Rational equation:* $y = \dfrac{a}{x - b} + c$

$y = \dfrac{4}{x + 2} + 0$

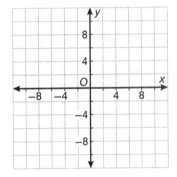

vertical asymptote: $x =$ _____

horizontal asymptote: $y =$ _____

25. side of tile: $4s^2 + 12s + 9$

= (____ + ____)(____ + ____) = (____ + ____)^2　*Factor.*

$A = s^2 \longrightarrow s = \sqrt{A}$　　side of tile $= \sqrt{(\underline{} + \underline{})^2} =$ _____

difference between side of tile and side of small square:

(____ + ____) − s = (____ + ____) ▪

26. a. $t = 1: h = -16(\underline{})^2 + 256 = \underline{} + \underline{} = \underline{}$

b. Graph $h = -16t^2 + 256$.

$t = 2: h = -16(\underline{})^2 + 256 = \underline{} + \underline{} = \underline{}$

$t = 3: h = -16(\underline{})^2 + 256 = \underline{} + \underline{} = \underline{}$

t	1	2	3
h			

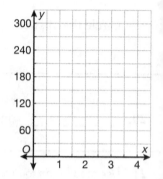

c. $h = \underline{}$ when the pencil hits the ground, $t = \underline{}$.

---

27. Graph the function using a table. Then find the time t for a 1-meter pendulum to make a complete swing.

$t = \underline{}$

---

28. Substitute $a = 5$, $b = \underline{}$, and $c = \underline{}$ into the equation $\underline{}$. If the equation is true, then the triangle $\underline{}$ a right triangle. If the equation is false, then the triangle $\underline{}$ a right triangle.

---

29. a. Graph the frequency distribution.

Marbles

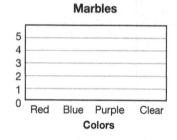

b.

$P(\text{red}) = \dfrac{\square}{\square}$

$P(\text{clear}) = \dfrac{\square}{\square}$

$P(\text{red or clear}) = \dfrac{\square}{\square} + \dfrac{\square}{\square}$

$= \dfrac{\square}{\square} = \dfrac{\square}{\square}$

---

30. If y varies directly with x and inversely with z, then the combined relationship is $y = \dfrac{(\square)k}{\square}$.

Substitute to find k.

$y = \dfrac{(\square)k}{\square}$ $k = \underline{}$

✎ Solve for the missing values using the equation.

y	x	z
1	1	3
3	2	
	4	2
9		2
2		12

Name _____

Solving Multi-Step Absolute-Value Equations

page 624

New Concepts

> **Math Language**
>
> The **absolute value** of a number is its distance from 0 on the number line. Since distance is positive, an absolute value is always positive.

- To solve absolute-value equations:

    1. Use inverse operations to isolate the absolute value on one side.

    2. Write the absolute value as two equations.

    3. Solve each equation, and write the solution set.

Example **Solving Equations with Two Operations**

Solve $\frac{|x|}{5} + 3 = 18$. Graph the solution.

$$\frac{|x|}{5} + 3 - 3 = 18 - 3 \qquad \textit{Subtract 3 from both sides.}$$

$$\frac{|x|}{5} = 15 \qquad \textit{Simplify.}$$

$$\frac{|x|}{5} \cdot 5 = 15 \cdot 5 \qquad \textit{Multiply both sides by 5.}$$

$$|x| = 75 \qquad \textit{Simplify.}$$

$$x = 75 \quad \text{or} \quad x = -75 \qquad \textit{Write two equations without absolute value.}$$

The solution set is $\{-75, 75\}$. Graph the solution on a number line.

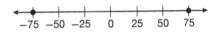

Example **Solving Equations with Operations Inside the Absolute-Value Symbols**

Solve $5\left|\frac{x}{3} - 2\right| = 15$.

$$\left|\frac{x}{3} - 2\right| = 3 \qquad \textit{To isolate the absolute value, divide both sides by 5.}$$

Write as two equations without the absolute value. Solve.

$$\frac{x}{3} - 2 = 3 \qquad\qquad or \qquad\qquad \frac{x}{3} - 2 = -3$$

$$\frac{x}{3} = 5 \qquad \textit{Add 2 to both sides.} \qquad \frac{x}{3} = -1$$

$$x = 15 \qquad \textit{Multiply both sides by 3.} \qquad x = -3$$

The solution set is $\{15, -3\}$.

Solve each equation. Then graph the solution.

a. $\dfrac{|x|}{7} + 10 = 18$

$-56 \quad -28 \quad 0 \quad 28 \quad 56$

$\dfrac{|x|}{7} = \underline{\quad} \longrightarrow |x| = \underline{\quad} \longrightarrow x = \underline{\quad}$ or $x = -\underline{\quad} \longrightarrow \{\underline{\quad}, \underline{\quad}\}$

b. $3|x| - 11 = 10$

$-7 \quad -3.5 \quad 0 \quad 3.5 \quad 7$

$3|x| = \underline{\quad} \longrightarrow |x| = \underline{\quad} \longrightarrow x = \underline{\quad}$ or $x = -\underline{\quad} \longrightarrow \{\underline{\quad}, \underline{\quad}\}$

Solve each equation.

c. $\dfrac{4|x|}{9} + 23 = 11$

$\dfrac{4|x|}{9} = \underline{\quad} \longrightarrow 4|x| = \underline{\quad} \longrightarrow |x| = \underline{\quad}$

An absolute value cannot be _____, so there are _____ solutions.

d. $\dfrac{|x| + 3}{2} - 2 = 1$

$\dfrac{|x| + 3}{2} = \underline{\quad} \longrightarrow |x| + 3 = \underline{\quad} \longrightarrow |x| = \underline{\quad} \longrightarrow x = \{\underline{\quad}, \underline{\quad}\}$

e. $|7x| + 2 = 37$

$\qquad |7x| = \underline{\quad}$

$\qquad 7x = \underline{\quad}$ or $7x = \underline{\quad}$

$\qquad x = \underline{\quad} \qquad\qquad x = \underline{\quad}$

$\qquad x = \{\underline{\quad}, \underline{\quad}\}$

f. $5|x + 1| - 2 = 23$

$\qquad 5|x + 1| = \underline{\quad} \longrightarrow |x + 1| = \underline{\quad}$

$\qquad x + 1 = \underline{\quad}$ or $x + 1 = \underline{\quad}$

$\qquad x = \underline{\quad} \qquad\qquad x = \underline{\quad}$

$\qquad x = \{\underline{\quad}, \underline{\quad}\}$

g. $9\left|\dfrac{x}{2} - 1\right| = 45$

$\qquad \left|\dfrac{x}{2} - 1\right| = \underline{\quad}$

$\qquad \underline{\quad\quad}$ or $\underline{\quad\quad}$

$\qquad x = \{\underline{\quad}, \underline{\quad}\}$

h. $|5x - 100| = 10$

$\qquad 5x - 100 = \underline{\quad}$ or $5x - 100 = \underline{\quad}$

least: _____ items

greatest: _____ items

1. *After subtracting, factor completely.*

$$\frac{\square - \square}{m-4} = \frac{(\square + \square)(\square - \square)}{m-4} = \underline{\hspace{2cm}}$$

---

2. $$\frac{-66}{(\square \bigcirc \square)(\square \bigcirc \square)} + \frac{w}{w-6} \cdot \frac{(\square \bigcirc \square)}{(\square \bigcirc \square)}$$

$$= \underline{\hspace{3cm}}$$

---

3. An absolute value cannot be _____ , so any absolute-value equation equal to a _____ number has no solution.

4. 📝 Substitute the solution set into each equation and verify it is true.

Circle the answer.

A $6\left|\frac{x}{4} - 1\right| = 42$ **B** $-2\left|\frac{x}{4} - 1\right| = 16$

C $8\left|\frac{x}{3} - 2\right| = 48$ **D** $-5\left|\frac{x}{6} - 4\right| = -30$

---

5. $(x + y)\left(\frac{400 + 100x}{y}\right) \cdot 0.30 = \frac{(\square + \square)(\square + \square x)}{y} \cdot 0.30$

$$= \frac{(\square x + \square x^2 + \square y + \square xy)}{y} \cdot 0.30 = \frac{\square(\square x^2 \square x + \square y + \square xy)}{y} \text{ dollars}$$

---

6. When the droplet hits the ground, the height $y = $ ____ .

📝 Factor and solve to explain when this will happen.

7. *Factor out the GCF.*

$(\underline{\hspace{1cm}})(\underline{\hspace{3cm}})$

Then factor by grouping.

$(\underline{\hspace{1cm}})(a + \underline{\hspace{1cm}})(a + \underline{\hspace{1cm}})$

---

8. GCF: _____

$(\underline{\hspace{1cm}})(\underline{\hspace{0.5cm}} - \underline{\hspace{0.5cm}} - \underline{\hspace{0.5cm}})$

$= (\underline{\hspace{1cm}})(x - \underline{\hspace{0.5cm}})(x + \underline{\hspace{0.5cm}})$

9. 2nd term factored: $(b + \underline{\hspace{1cm}})(b + \underline{\hspace{1cm}})$

Simplify. Then find the product.

product: _____

---

10. Student _____ is correct.

Student _____ did not write the terms of the dividend in _____ order

and did not insert _____.

---

11. $\dfrac{-1}{10x-10} \div \dfrac{x^5}{10x^2-10} = \dfrac{-1}{10x-10} \cdot \dfrac{\boxed{}\bigcirc\boxed{}}{\boxed{}}$

Factor. Simplify. Then multiply.

$$\dfrac{-1}{\boxed{}(\boxed{}\bigcirc\boxed{})} \cdot \dfrac{\boxed{}(\boxed{}\bigcirc\boxed{})}{\boxed{}}$$

$= \underline{\hspace{2cm}}$

---

12. $\dfrac{\boxed{}}{(\boxed{})(x+\boxed{})} \div \dfrac{\boxed{}}{(x+\boxed{})(x+\boxed{})}$

$= \underline{\hspace{4cm}}$

---

13. $\left|10 + (\underline{})x - \underline{}\right| = 20$

$10 + \underline{}x - \underline{} = \underline{}$ $\qquad\qquad$ $10 + \underline{}x - \underline{} = \underline{}$

$\underline{}x = \underline{}$ $\qquad\qquad\qquad$ $\underline{}x = \underline{}$

$x = \underline{}$ $\qquad\qquad\qquad\quad$ $x = \underline{}$

minimum: $\$\underline{}$ $\qquad\qquad\qquad$ maximum: $\$\underline{}$

---

14. *Write dividend in descending powers with placeholders.*

 Use long division.

Answer: _____

15. *Cancel common factors. Then factor completely.*

$$\dfrac{25x^3 + 20x^2 - 5x}{5x}$$

$= \underline{\hspace{2cm}}$

---

16. $\frac{|x|}{11} + 9 = 15$

$\frac{|x|}{11} =$ _____

$|x| =$ _____ $x = \{$___ , ___$\}$

17. Subtract ____ from both sides to get

_____ . Multiply both sides by

____ to get _____ . An absolute

value cannot be _____ , so

there are _____ solutions.

18. a. Dividend in standard form:

$x^3 -$ _____

📓 Divide. Use long division.

b. $x^2 - 36 = (x + 6)($_____$)$

The width is $($_____$)$ feet.

19. $A = \frac{1}{2}bh$

$10y^2 + 6y = \left(\frac{1}{2}\right)(5y + 3)h$

____ $y^2 +$ ____ $y = (5y + 3)h$

📓 Find h. Use factoring.

$h =$ _____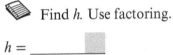

20. Student _____ is correct.

Student _____ did not multiply by the

_____ of the denominator.

21. $\frac{\text{miles}}{\text{minutes}} = \frac{x^2}{6x + 48} \div \frac{1}{x^2 + 3x - 40}$

$= \frac{x^2}{6x + 48} \cdot \frac{\Box + \Box - \Box}{\Box}$

📓 Factor. Simplify. Then multiply.

$=$ _____

22. *Substitute $x = 0$. Show that the statement is true.*

$|x - 14| < 30$

_____ ◯ _____

23. *Find the endpoints first.*

____ ◯ x ◯ ____

Circle the answer.

A $|x| \le -21$ **B** $|x| < 21$
C $|x| \le 21$ **D** $|x| > 21$

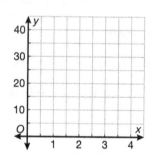

24. In a horizontal line, the _____-coordinate is constant, so (_____ − _____)² would equal zero.

---

25. $d = rt$ or $t = \frac{d}{r}$

    a. rate on difficult trails = r

       rate on easy trails = _____ r

       total hiking time

$$= \frac{\Box}{\Box_r} + \frac{3}{r}$$

$$= \frac{\Box}{\Box_r}$$

    b. Substitute $r = 2$.

       Total hiking time was _____ hrs.

26. $y = \frac{a}{x+b} + c$

    horizontal asymptote: $y =$ _____

    Denominator will equal zero if $x =$ _____.

    vertical asymptote: $x =$ _____

    Graph.

---

27. *Compare Plan A to Plan B.*

    a. _____ + _____ m ◯ _____ + _____ m

    b. Solve.

       m ◯ _____

       For Plan B to cost less than Plan A,

       Jenna must make _____ minutes

       of long-distance calls.

    c. ◄─┼┼┼┼┼┼┼┼┼┼┼┼┼┼─►

28. Graph $y = 1.9x^2$.

about _____

---

29. *Use Pythagorean Theorem to find length.*

    a. _____ $^2 + l^2 =$ _____ ^{2}

       $l =$ _____

    b. perimeter ≈ _____

30. The volume of the sphere is _____ proportional to the _____ of its radius. The constant of variation is equal to _____.

Combining Rational Expressions with Unlike Denominators page 631

New Concepts

Name _____

Math Language

A **least common denominator (LCD)** contains every factor of each denominator, used the greatest number of times it appears in any denominator.

• Just as with simple fractions, the denominators of rational expression must be alike before you can add or subtract.

Example **Using Equivalent Fractions to Add with Unlike Denominators**

Add.

$$\frac{6x^2}{x^2 - 16} + \frac{x - 1}{2x - 8}$$

$$= \frac{6x^2}{(x - 4)(x + 4)} + \frac{x - 1}{2(x - 4)} \qquad \text{Factor each denominator.}$$

Determine the LCD. Every factor of each denominator should be represented.

$$\text{LCD} = 2(x - 4)(x + 4)$$

If the denominator of a term does not have all of the factors of the LCD, then multiply the numerator and denominator of the term by that missing factor.

Multiply the numerator and denominator of the first fraction by 2. Multiply the numerator and denominator of the second fraction by x + 4.

$$= \frac{6x^2}{(x - 4)(x + 4)} \cdot \frac{2}{2} + \frac{x - 1}{2(x - 4)} \cdot \frac{(x + 4)}{(x + 4)}$$

$$= \frac{2(6x^2)}{2(x - 4)(x + 4)} + \frac{(x - 1)(x + 4)}{2(x - 4)(x + 4)} \qquad \text{Multiply the fractions.}$$

Both terms now have a common denominator.

$$= \frac{12x^2}{2(x - 4)(x + 4)} + \frac{x^2 + 3x - 4}{2(x - 4)(x + 4)} \qquad \text{Simplify the numerators.}$$

$$= \frac{12x^2 + (x^2 + 3x - 4)}{2(x - 4)(x + 4)} \qquad \text{Add the fractions.}$$

$$= \frac{13x^2 + 3x - 4}{2(x - 4)(x + 4)} \qquad \text{Simplify the numerator.}$$

Find the LCD for each expression.

a. *Write a duplicate factor only once.*

$$\frac{5x}{5x-45} - \frac{44}{x^2-81} = \frac{5x}{\square(x-\square)} - \frac{44}{(x-9)(x+\square)}$$ LCD = _____

b. $\dfrac{3x}{x+4} - \dfrac{12}{x^2+2x-8} = \dfrac{3x}{x+4} - \dfrac{12}{(x+4)(x-\square)}$ LCD = _____

c. $\dfrac{3x^2}{x^2-25} + \dfrac{x-1}{4x-20} = \dfrac{3x^2}{(x+\square)(x-\square)} + \dfrac{x-1}{\square(x-\square)}$ LCD = _____

$$= \frac{3x^2}{(x+\square)(x-\square)} \cdot \frac{\square}{\square} + \frac{x-1}{\square(x-\square)} \cdot \frac{(x+\square)}{(x+\square)} = \frac{\square x^2 + (x-\square)(x+\square)}{4(x-5)(x+5)}$$

$$= \frac{\square x^2 + \square x - \square}{4(x-5)(x+5)}$$

d. $\dfrac{2x^2}{6x-24} - \dfrac{3x-4}{x^2-16} = \dfrac{2x^2}{6(x-\square)} \cdot \dfrac{\square}{\square} - \dfrac{3x-4}{(x-\square)(x+\square)} \cdot \dfrac{\square}{\square}$

$$= \frac{2x^2\square - \square(3x-4)}{6(x-\square)(x+\square)} = \frac{2x^3 + \square x^2 - \square x + \square}{6(x-\square)(x+\square)} = \frac{\square + \square - \square + \square}{3(x-\square)(x+\square)}$$

e. $\dfrac{x-1}{x^2-1} + \dfrac{2}{5x+5} = \dfrac{x-1}{(x+\square)(x-\square)} + \dfrac{2}{\square(x+\square)}$ LCD = _____

 Complete the addition of the rational expressions.   Answer: _____

f. $\dfrac{2}{x^2-36} - \dfrac{1}{x^2+6x} = \dfrac{2}{(x+\square)(x-\square)} - \dfrac{1}{\square(x+\square)}$ LCD = _____

 Complete the addition of the rational expressions.   Answer: _____

g. $\dfrac{4x}{x^2-64} + \dfrac{12}{7x-56} = \dfrac{4x}{(x+\square)(x-\square)} + \dfrac{12}{7(x-\square)}$ LCD = _____

 Complete the addition of the rational expressions.   Answer: _____

1. $3x^3 - 9x^2 - 30x$

$= 3x(x^2 - \underline{\hspace{1cm}} - \underline{\hspace{1.5cm}})$

$= \underline{\hspace{0.8cm}}(\underline{\hspace{1cm}})(\underline{\hspace{1cm}})$

2. $8x^3y^2 + 4x^2y - 12xy^3$

$= 4xy(\underline{\hspace{1cm}} + \underline{\hspace{1cm}} - \underline{\hspace{0.8cm}})$

3. $32x^3 - 24x^4 + 4x^5$

$= \underline{\hspace{1cm}}(\underline{\hspace{0.8cm}} - \underline{\hspace{0.6cm}} + \underline{\hspace{0.6cm}})$

$= \underline{\hspace{1cm}}(\underline{\hspace{1.2cm}})(\underline{\hspace{1.2cm}})$

4. $mn^3 - 10mn^2 + 24mn$

$= \underline{\hspace{1cm}}(\underline{\hspace{0.8cm}} - \underline{\hspace{0.6cm}} + \underline{\hspace{0.6cm}})$

$= \underline{\hspace{1cm}}(\underline{\hspace{1.2cm}})(\underline{\hspace{1.2cm}})$

5. *Multiply by the reciprocal.*

$\dfrac{4m}{17r} \div \dfrac{12m^2}{5r} = \dfrac{4m}{17r} \cdot \dfrac{\square}{\square} = \dfrac{\square}{\square}$

6. *Factor, then divide.*

$\dfrac{x^2 - 16x + 64}{x - 8} = \dfrac{(x - \square)(x - \square)}{x - 8} = \underline{\hspace{1cm}}$

7. The parabola does not cross the

____-axis so it has _____ zeros.

8. $\dfrac{4}{x + 4} - \dfrac{8}{(x + \square)(x + \square)}$ *Factor.*

LCD = _____

9. ✎ Complete the addition of the rational expressions.

$\dfrac{2x}{2x^2 - 128} + \dfrac{5}{x^2 - 7x - 8} = \dfrac{2x}{\square(x - \square)(x + \square)} + \dfrac{5}{(x + \square)(x - \square)}$

LCD = _____   Answer: _____

10. $9|x| - 22 = 14$

$9|x| = \underline{\hspace{1cm}}$

$|x| = \underline{\hspace{1cm}}$

$x = \underline{\hspace{1cm}}$ or $x = \underline{\hspace{1cm}}$

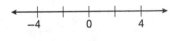

11. Student _____ is correct.

Student _____ did not distribute the

_____ all the way

through the second _____.

12. _____ each denominator. The LCD must contain every factor of each

_____ and use each factor the _____ number of times it

occurs in either _____.

---

13. $\dfrac{3x^2}{x^2 - 100} + \dfrac{x - 1}{2x - 20} = \dfrac{3x^2}{(x + \square)(x - \square)} + \dfrac{x - 1}{\square(x - \square)}$ LCD = _____

Multiply numerator and denominator of each term by its missing factor, if any.

$= \dfrac{3x^2}{(x + \square)(x - \square)} \cdot \dfrac{\square}{\square} + \dfrac{x - 1}{\square(x - \square)} \cdot \dfrac{\square}{\square}$

📎 Once the terms have a common denominator, complete addition of the rational expressions.

Answer: _____

---

14. a. *Find the sum of the rational expressions. Then simplify by dividing out common factors.*

$\dfrac{2x}{4x^2 - 196} + \dfrac{12x}{x^2 + x - 56} = \dfrac{2x}{\square(x + \square)(x - \square)} + \dfrac{12x}{(x - \square)(x + \square)} =$ _____

b. *Since $t = \frac{d}{r}$, divide the distance from part **a** by the rate to find how much time it took.*

📎 *Complete the division by multiplying by the reciprocal.*

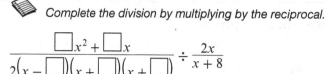

$\dfrac{\square x^2 + \square x}{2(x - \square)(x + \square)(x + \square)} \div \dfrac{2x}{x + 8}$

time: _____

---

15. Student _____ is correct.

Student _____ did not _____

the absolute value, and assumed that there

is no solution since the absolute

value would be equal to a

_____ number.

16. Solve $|P - 34| = 2$.

$P = 4s$

maximum: $s =$ _____ $\div\, 4 =$ _____

minimum: $s =$ _____ $\div\, 4 =$ _____

---

17. a. *Let x = cost of lunch*

$\left|5+\underline{\hspace{0.6cm}}x-\underline{\hspace{0.6cm}}\right|=\underline{\hspace{0.6cm}}$

b. $5+\underline{\hspace{0.6cm}}x-35=\underline{\hspace{0.6cm}}$ or $\underline{\hspace{0.6cm}}+\underline{\hspace{0.6cm}}x-35=-2$

$x=\underline{\hspace{1.2cm}}$ $x=\underline{\hspace{1.2cm}}$

---

18. Student _____ is correct.

Student _____ had _____

terms that were not _____

_____.

19. $w=\dfrac{A}{l}$

$\dfrac{x^3-18x^2+81x}{x-9}=\dfrac{\square(x-\square)(x-\square)}{x-9}$

$=\underline{\hspace{2cm}}$ feet

---

20. *Substitute a = 4, b = 2, c = 3, and d = 9.*

$\dfrac{4}{2}\cdot\dfrac{3}{9}=\underline{\hspace{0.6cm}}\cdot\dfrac{\square}{\square}=\dfrac{\square}{\square}$ and $\dfrac{4\cdot\square}{\square\cdot9}=\dfrac{\square}{\square}=\dfrac{\square}{\square}$

---

21. ✎ Factor and simplify each fraction first.

Circle the answer.

A 1   **B** $\dfrac{(x-3)^2}{(x-2)^2}$ **C** -1 **D** $\dfrac{(x-3)}{(x-2)}$

---

22. $|x|>17$

$x\bigcirc\underline{\hspace{0.8cm}}$ or $x\bigcirc\underline{\hspace{1cm}}$

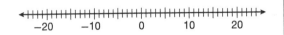

23. $|x-15.6|\le0.1$

$x-15.6\le0.1$ $x-15.6\le\underline{\hspace{1cm}}$

$x\le\underline{\hspace{1cm}}$ $x\le\underline{\hspace{1cm}}$

$\underline{\hspace{1cm}}\bigcirc\,x\,\bigcirc\underline{\hspace{1cm}}$

---

24. a. $165 - \underline{\hspace{1cm}} = \underline{\hspace{1cm}}°$ up

$100 - \underline{\hspace{1cm}} = \underline{\hspace{1cm}}°$ down

b. *Write and solve two equations.*

$t \le 45 + 1(\underline{\hspace{0.8cm}})$ $\qquad$ $t \ge 10 + 2(\underline{\hspace{0.8cm}})$

$t \le \underline{\hspace{1.5cm}}$ $\qquad$ $t \ge \underline{\hspace{1.5cm}}$

c. It is faster to $\underline{\hspace{2cm}}$ the stew.

25. *Use the Pythagorean Theorem.*

$c \approx \underline{\hspace{2.5cm}}$

26. a. Use the distance formula $d = \sqrt{(x_2 - x_1)^2 + (y_2 + y_1)^2}$ to find each distance.

$PQ \approx \underline{\hspace{1.5cm}}$ $\qquad$ $PR \approx \underline{\hspace{1.5cm}}$ $\qquad$ $QR \approx \underline{\hspace{1.5cm}}$

b. $\underline{\hspace{1.5cm}}, \underline{\hspace{1.5cm}}, \underline{\hspace{1.5cm}}$

27. *Work backwards. Multiply 4a and two or more binomials.*

$= 4a(\underline{\hspace{1.5cm}})(\underline{\hspace{1.5cm}})$

$= \underline{\hspace{4cm}}$

28. *Find the vertex.*

$t = -\dfrac{b}{2a} = \dfrac{\square}{2\square} = \underline{\hspace{2cm}}$

$y = -5x^2 + 10x + 260$

$y = -5(\underline{\hspace{1cm}})^2 + 10(\underline{\hspace{1cm}}) + 260$

$y = \underline{\hspace{2.5cm}}$

29. *If the total trip is 30 miles, then he travels 15 miles each way.*
Let r = rate in miles per hour

$\text{time} = \dfrac{\text{distance}}{\text{rate}}$ $\qquad$ $t_1 = \dfrac{15}{r}$ $\qquad$ $t_2 = \dfrac{15}{(r-5)}$

$\dfrac{15}{r} \cdot \dfrac{\square}{\square} + \dfrac{15}{r-5} \cdot \dfrac{\square}{\square} = \dfrac{\square \bigcirc \square \bigcirc \square}{r(r-5)} = \underline{\hspace{1cm}}$ hours

30. total possible outcomes: $\underline{\hspace{2cm}}$ $\qquad$ favorable outcomes: $\underline{\hspace{2cm}}$

$P(\text{blue shirt, khaki skirt}) = \underline{\hspace{3cm}}$

LESSON

96

Graphing Quadratic Functions page 638

New Concepts

• Follow the steps in the Example to graph a quadratic function.

Example **Graphing Quadratics of the Form** $y = ax^2 + bx + c$

Graph the function $y = 3x^2 + 18x + 13$.

Step 1: Find the axis of symmetry.

$$x = -\frac{b}{2a}$$ *Use the formula.*

$$= -\frac{18}{2(3)} = -3$$ *Substitute values for a and b.*

The axis of symmetry is $x = -3$

Step 2: Find the vertex.

$$y = 3x^2 + 18x + 13$$

$$= 3(-3)^2 + 18(-3) + 13 = -14$$ *Substitute x = −3 to find y-coordinate.*

The vertex is $(-3, -14)$.

Step 3: Find the y-intercept. The y-intercept is when $x = 0$ or c, which is 13.

Step 4: Find one point not on the axis of symmetry.

$$y = 3x^2 + 18x + 13$$

$$= 3(-1)^2 + 18(-1) + 13 = -2$$ *Substitute x = −1.*

A point on the curve is $(-1, -2)$.

Step 5: Graph.

Graph the axis of symmetry $x = -3$, the vertex $(-3, -14)$, the y-intercept $(0, 13)$. Reflect the point $(-1, -2)$ across the axis of symmetry to get the point $(-5, -2)$. Connect the points with a smooth curve.

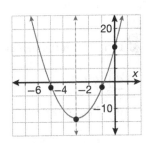

Graph each function.

Find the axis of symmetry, the vertex, the y-intercept, and a point on the curve.

Reflect the y-intercept and the point on the curve over the axis of symmetry.

a. $y = x^2 - 4x + 7$

$a = \underline{\quad}, b = \underline{\quad}, c = \underline{\quad}$

$x = -\dfrac{-4}{2 \cdot 1} = \underline{\quad}$ The axis of symmetry is $x = \underline{\quad}$.

$y = x^2 - 4x + 7, x = 2$

$y = (\underline{\quad})^2 - 4(\underline{\quad}) + 7 = \underline{\quad}$ The vertex is $(\underline{\quad}, \underline{\quad})$.

c is the y-intercept.   The *y*-intercept is $\underline{\quad}$.

$y = x^2 - 4x + 7$

$y = 1^2 - 4(1) + 7 = \underline{\quad}$ A point on the curve is $(1, \underline{\quad})$.

b. $y = 2x^2 - 16x + 24$

$x = -\dfrac{\boxed{}}{2 \cdot \boxed{}} = \dfrac{\boxed{}}{\boxed{}} = \underline{\quad}$ The axis of symmetry is $x = \underline{\quad}$.

$y = 2(\underline{\quad})^2 - 16(\underline{\quad}) + 24 = \underline{\quad}$ The vertex is $(\underline{\quad}, \underline{\quad})$.

            The *y*-intercept is $\underline{\quad}$.

$y = 2(1)^2 - 16(1) + 24 = \underline{\quad}$ A point on the curve is $(1, \underline{\quad})$.

c. $y = 2x^2 - 9$

$x = -\dfrac{\boxed{}}{2 \cdot \boxed{}} = \underline{\quad}$ The axis of symmetry is $x = \underline{\quad}$.

$y = 2(\underline{\quad})^2 - 9 = \underline{\quad}$ The vertex is $(\underline{\quad}, \underline{\quad})$.

            The *y*-intercept is $\underline{\quad}$.

$y = 2(1)^2 - 9 = \underline{\quad}$ A point on the curve is $(1, \underline{\quad})$.

Find the zeros of each function.

d. zeros: $\underline{\quad}$ **e.** zeros: $\underline{\quad}$ **f.** zeros: $\underline{\quad}$

g. *Find the axis of symmetry.*

$f(x) = -8x^2 + 24x$

$x = -\dfrac{\boxed{}}{2 \cdot \boxed{}} = \underline{\quad}$ The ball reaches maximum height in $\underline{\quad}$ seconds.

1. Find the x-intercepts. Check by substituting.

zeros: _____

2. LCD = _____

$$= \frac{\Box}{\Box} + \frac{\Box}{\Box}$$

= _____

3. An absolute-value expression cannot equal a negative number.

$$\frac{10|x|}{3} + 18 = 4$$

$$|x| = \underline{\hspace{1cm}}$$

_____ , _____

4. Multiply the equation by 100 to eliminate the decimals.

$$-0.3 + 0.14n = 2.78$$

_____ + _____ n = _____

$$n = \underline{\hspace{1cm}}$$

5. $\dfrac{6}{x-3} = \dfrac{3}{10}$

$$x = \underline{\hspace{1cm}}$$

6. Factor completely to determine LCD.

$$x + 6 = \underline{\hspace{3cm}}$$

$$x^2 + 8x + 12 = \underline{\hspace{3cm}}$$

$$\text{LCD} = (\underline{\hspace{1cm}})(\underline{\hspace{1cm}})$$

7. Each domain-value must have exactly one range-value.

The relation _____ a function.

8. Factor completely and simplify.

$$\frac{\frac{-x^5}{21x+3}}{\frac{5x^9}{28x+4}} = \frac{\Box}{\Box(\Box + \Box)} \cdot \frac{\Box(\Box + \Box)}{\Box}$$

= _____

9. $y = x^2 - 2x - 8$

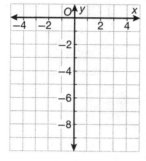

axis of symmetry:

$x = -\dfrac{b}{2a}$

$= $ _____

10. The second point will have the same

____-coordinate, but the ____-coordinate wil

be different. To determine that coordinate,

the _____ distance from the axis of

symmetry will be the same as the original

point, but the second point will be located

on the _____ side of the axis of

symmetry.

---

11. *The x-coordinate of the vertex is located at the axis of symmetry.*

$x = -\dfrac{b}{2a}$

$= \dfrac{\square}{\square} = $ _____

Substitute the x-coordinate into the equation to get the y-coordinate.

$4(\underline{\quad})^2 - 24(\underline{\quad}) + 9 = $ _____

12. *Substitute x = 6 in each equation.*

Circle the answer.

A $y = 6x^2 - 72x + 56$

B $y = 2x^2 - 8x + 48$

C $y = 3x^2 + 42x - 12$

D $y = 5x^2 - 5x + 43$

---

13. *Substitute v = 10 ft/sec, t = 0.5 sec, s = 6 ft into equation to find height.*

$h = -16t^2 + vt + s$

$h = $ ____ $+$ ____ $+$ ____

$= $ _____

14. *Factor completely to find LCD.*

$2x - 10 = $ _____

$2x^2 - 4x - 30 = $ _____

Circle the answer.

A $2(x - 5)(x + 3)$ **B** $(x - 5)(x + 3)$

C $(x + 5)(x - 3)$ **D** $\dfrac{2}{(x - 5)(x + 3)}$

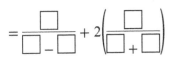

15. *Perimeter is the sum of all the side lengths.*

$$= \dfrac{\boxed{}}{\boxed{} - \boxed{}} + 2\left(\dfrac{\boxed{}}{\boxed{} + \boxed{}} \right)$$

Factor to find a common denominator. Add.

$$= \underline{}$$

16. *Subtract Jessie's measurement from Carrie's measurement.*

$$\text{Difference} = \dfrac{\boxed{}}{\boxed{} - \boxed{}} - \dfrac{\boxed{} - \boxed{}}{\boxed{} - \boxed{}}$$

Factor to find a common denominator. Subtract.

$$= \underline{}$$

17. $|x - 200| \le 110$

$$\underline{} \text{ AND } \underline{}$$

$$x \ge \underline{} \text{ AND } x \le \underline{}$$

$$\underline{} \le x \le \underline{}$$

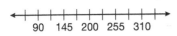
90   145   200   255   310

18. The placeholder helps line up _____ terms for the dividend and the quotient.

19. $x - 3 \overline{)\, 2x^2 - 5x - 3}$

Circle the answer.

A $2x - 1$ **B** $2x + 1$

C $\dfrac{x - 2}{2x}$ **D** $\dfrac{x^2 - 3}{5x}$

20. $|2x - 100| = 10$

$$2x - 100 = \underline{} \quad \text{or} \quad 2x - 100 = \underline{}$$

$$x = \underline{} \qquad\qquad x = \underline{}$$

minimum: _____

maximum: _____

21. Student _____ is correct.

Student _____ graphed all values _____ −9 and −1 in addition to the solution set.

22. 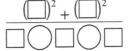 $\dfrac{\text{area of picture 1} + \text{area of picture 2}}{\text{area of frame}}$

$$\dfrac{\left(\boxed{}\right)^2 + \left(\boxed{}\right)^2}{\boxed{}\,\bigcirc\,\boxed{}\,\bigcirc\,\boxed{}}$$

$$= \underline{}$$

23. $\dfrac{3x^2 + 2x}{9y} \div \dfrac{y + 2}{y} = \dfrac{3x^2 + 2x}{9y} \cdot \dfrac{\square}{\square + \square}$

= _____

To check, substitute real numbers for x

and y before and after _____.

24. $6x^3 + 14x^2 + 4x$

a. $2x(\underline{\hspace{4cm}})$

b. $2x(\underline{\hspace{1.5cm}})(\underline{\hspace{1.5cm}})$

25. *See page 7 in the* Student Reference Guide.

Use two points.

$d = \sqrt{(\underline{\hspace{1.5cm}})^2 + (\underline{\hspace{1.5cm}})^2}$

= _____

26. a. If $a^2 - b^2 = a^2 - 16$, then $b = $ _____

b. $A = 36b^2 + 60b + 25 = (\underline{\hspace{1.5cm}})(\underline{\hspace{1.5cm}})$

So, side length $= (\underline{\hspace{1.5cm}})$

c. side length: _____

area: _____

27. $6x > 7x$

$6x - 6x > 7x - 6x$

____ > ____

For $x < $ ____, x must be _____. The

inequality is _____ true.

28. Total colors = _____

$P(\text{red}) = \dfrac{\square}{\square} = \dfrac{\square}{\square}$ $P(\text{blue}) = \dfrac{\square}{\square}$

$P(\text{green}) = \dfrac{\square}{\square} = \dfrac{\square}{\square}$ $P(\text{purple}) = \dfrac{\square}{\square}$

$P(\text{yellow}) = \dfrac{\square}{\square} = \dfrac{\square}{\square}$

$P(\text{orange}) = \dfrac{\square}{\square} = \dfrac{\square}{\square}$

29. *Write the equation and substitute values to solve for k.*

$d = \dfrac{k \cdot \square \cdot \square}{\square}$ $\square = \dfrac{k \cdot \square \cdot \square}{\square}$

$k = $ _____

Substitute with k. $d = $ _____

30. $(x + 10)(x - 2)$ _____ the correct

factorization for $x^2 - 8x - 20$. If

$(x + 10)(x - 2)$ is multiplied, the result is

_____. Changing the

signs to $(x \bigcirc 10)(x \bigcirc 2)$ will

produce the correct factorization.

Name _____

Graphing Linear Inequalities page 647

New Concepts

Exploration 📖 page 648
Use your textbook to complete the exploration.

Math Language

The graph of the equation is the **boundary line** for an inequality.

The boundary line is **solid** if the inequality symbol is ≤ or ≥. It is **dashed** if the inequality symbol is < or >.

An ordered pair that makes an inequality true is a **solution** of the inequality.

A **half-plane** is a region containing all of the points that are **solutions of a linear inequality.**

If the inequality symbol is > or ≥, the half-plane is **above** the boundary line. If the symbol is < or ≤, the half-plane is **below** the boundary line.

• To graph an inequality, graph the boundary line. Then decide which side to shade by testing a point.

Example **Graphing Linear Inequalities without Technology**

Graph $y \geq -\frac{3}{4}x - 3$.

Use the y-intercept, -3 and the slope, $-\frac{3}{4}$ to graph the boundary line. The inequality symbol is $\geq$ so the line is solid.

Test $(0, 0)$. Substitute $x = 0$, $y = 0$.

$$y \geq -\frac{3}{4}x - 3$$

$$0 \geq -\frac{3}{4}(0) - 3$$

$$0 \geq -3$$

The inequality is true, so shade the half-plane in which the point is located.

• To write an inequality for a graph, read the y-intercept. Then count squares or use two points and the slope formula to find the slope.

Example **Writing a Linear Inequality Given the Graph**

Write an inequality for the shaded region.

The boundary line is dashed and the shading is above the line, so the inequality symbol is >.

The y-intercept is -4.
The slope is 1.

The inequality is $y > x - 4$.

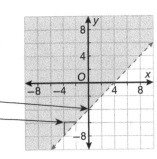

Determine if each ordered pair is a solution of the given inequality. Write _yes_ or _no_.

Substitute to see if the point makes the inequality true.

a. $(2,6); y > 3x - 2$

$6 > 3(2) - 2$

$6 > \underline{\hspace{1.5cm}}$

$\underline{\hspace{2.5cm}}$

b. $(4, 1); y < -4x + 1$

$\underline{\hspace{1.5cm}} < 4(\underline{\hspace{1cm}}) + 1$

$\underline{\hspace{1.5cm}} < \underline{\hspace{1.5cm}}$

$\underline{\hspace{2.5cm}}$

c. $(-6, 2); y \leq 5$

$\underline{\hspace{1.5cm}} \leq 5$

$\underline{\hspace{2cm}}$

 Graph each inequality.

Solve for y. Use the slope and y-intercept to graph the boundary line. Test a point.

d. $4x + 5y \geq -10$

$5y \geq \underline{\hspace{2cm}}$

$y \geq \underline{\hspace{1cm}} x - \underline{\hspace{1.5cm}}$

Test $(0, 0)$.

$y \geq \underline{\hspace{1cm}} x - \underline{\hspace{1cm}}$

$0 \geq \underline{\hspace{1cm}} (0) - \underline{\hspace{1cm}}$

$0 \geq \underline{\hspace{1.5cm}}$

e. $x < 6$ Test $(0, 0)$.

$\underline{\hspace{1.5cm}} < 6$

Graph each inequality using a graphing calculator.

f. $4x + 2y \leq 6$

$2y \leq \underline{\hspace{2cm}}$

$y \leq \underline{\hspace{2cm}}$

g. $y > 2x + 6$

Write an inequality for each region.

h. equation of the boundary line: $y = \underline{\hspace{3cm}}$

The boundary line is solid and the shading is below the line, so the inequality is $\underline{\hspace{2cm}}$.

i. The _y_-intercept is $\underline{\hspace{2cm}}$.   The slope is $\underline{\hspace{2cm}}$.

equation of the boundary line: $y = \underline{\hspace{3cm}}$

The boundary line is dashed and the shading is above the line, so the inequality is $\underline{\hspace{2cm}}$.

j. Let x = number of series and let y = number of books

$\underline{\hspace{2cm}} x + \underline{\hspace{2cm}} y \leq 25$

$\underline{\hspace{2cm}} y \leq \underline{\hspace{2cm}} x + 25$

$y \leq \underline{\hspace{2cm}} x + \underline{\hspace{1.5cm}}$

1. Eliminate negative exponents.

$$\frac{30x^{-2}y^{12}}{6y^{-5}} = \frac{30y^{\square}y^{\square}}{6x^{\square}} = \frac{\square y^{\square}}{x^{\square}}$$

2. $\sqrt{0.09q^2r} + q\sqrt{0.04r}$

$$= \sqrt{0.09} \cdot \sqrt{q^2} \cdot \sqrt{r} + q\sqrt{0.04} \cdot \sqrt{r}$$

$$= \underline{\quad\quad} + \underline{\quad\quad}$$

$$= \underline{\quad\quad}$$

3. Factor twice.

$$\frac{16g^4}{2g+3} - \frac{81}{2g+3} = \frac{\square\bigcirc\square}{\square\bigcirc\square}$$

$$= \frac{(\square + \square)(\square - \square)}{2g+3}$$

$$= \frac{(\square + \square)(\square - \square)(\square + \square)}{2g+3}$$

$$= (\underline{\quad\quad})(\underline{\quad\quad})$$

4.   oldest member's age = $\underline{\quad\quad}$

youngest member's age = $\underline{\quad\quad}$

range = $\underline{\quad\quad}$

5. Use FOIL.

$$(4x^2 + 8)(2x - 7)$$

$$= \underline{\quad\quad\quad}$$

6. Factor denominators to find LCD.

$$\frac{9}{9x - 36} + \frac{-24}{3x^2 - 48}$$

Write fractions with LCD. Add.

$$= \underline{\quad\quad\quad}$$

7. Factor denominators to find LCD. Subtract.

$$\frac{x}{x^2 + 2x + 1} - \frac{x + 2}{x + 1}$$

$$= \underline{\quad\quad\quad}$$

8. $(x^2 - 14x + 49) \div (x - 7)$

$$= (x - \underline{\quad})(x - \underline{\quad}) \div (x - 7)$$

$$= \underline{\quad\quad\quad}$$

9. *Isolate the variable.*

$13 \leq 2x + 7 < 15$

___ $\leq$ ___ $<$ ___

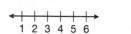

1 2 3 4 5 6

10. $\dfrac{|x|}{6} > 8$

$|x| >$ _____

$x <$ ____ or $x >$ ____

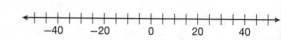

−40   −20   0   20   40

11. $3x - 4x \geq 6 - x + 8$

$-x \geq -x +$ _____

____ $\geq$ ____

The inequality is _____ true.

12. *Substitute (2, 6) into the inequality.*

$y > 3x - 2$

___ $>$ ___

(2, 6) _____ a solution.

13. $y = x^2 + 2x - 24$

$x = -\dfrac{b}{2a} =$ _____

vertex: _____

y-intercept: _____

a point not on the axis of symmetry: _____

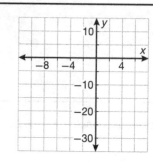

14. All of the points that are on a

_____ boundary line and

all the points that fall in the _____

half-plane satisfy the inequality.

15. Choose a test point and evaluate the

inequality for that point. If the point

satisfies the inequality, _____ the

half-plane that contains the point. If it does

not satisfy the inequality, shade the _____

half of the plane.

16. Boundary line is solid, line falls from left to right and shaded region is below the boundary line.

Circle the answer.

A $y \geq -\frac{2}{3}x + 2$ **B** $y \leq -\frac{2}{3}x + 2$

C $y \leq \frac{2}{3}x + 2$ **D** $y < -\frac{2}{3}x + 2$

17. Let x = number of adult tickets and let y = number of student tickets.

_____$x +$ _____$y \geq$ _____

18. Student _____ is correct.

Student _____ did not substitute the

x-value into the original equation to

find the _____ -value.

19. $0 = 3w^2 - 48$

$w =$ _____ or _____

Choose the positive zero.

$w =$ _____

20. If an equation has no c term the value of the c term is zero.

$y = -16x^2 + 49x$

a. y-intercept: _____

b. The ball's initial position is on the

_____.

c. After 5 seconds the height is _____.

d. There _____ be a negative height.

The ball _____ before 5 seconds.

21. Find the difference in miles between Tuesday and Monday. First factor to find LCD.

$$\frac{1}{x^3 - 2x^2} - \frac{1}{2x^2 - 4x}$$

$$= \frac{1}{x^2(\square - \square)} - \frac{1}{2x(\square - \square)}$$

$$= \frac{\square}{\square(\square - \square)} - \frac{\square}{\square(\square - \square)}$$

$$= \underline{\hspace{2cm}}$$

22. $\dfrac{3y + 2}{y + z} + \dfrac{4}{2(\square + \square)}$

$$= \frac{\square + \square + \square}{\square + \square}$$

$$= \underline{\hspace{2cm}}$$

Answer: _____

23. Substitute x = −11. Verify statement is true.

$$|3x| - 2 = 31$$

$$|3(\underline{\hspace{1cm}})| - 2 = 31$$

$$\underline{\hspace{1cm}} - 2 = 31$$

$$\underline{\hspace{1cm}} = 31$$

24. $4|x - 8| = 12$

$|x - 8| = $ _____

Circle the answer.

A $\{-5, 5\}$ **B** $\{11, -11\}$

C $\{5, 11\}$ **D** $\{-20, 20\}$

25. $r = \frac{d}{t}$. *Factor each fraction to find LCD.*

$$r = \frac{\dfrac{1}{45x - 5} + \dfrac{2x}{25x + 5}}{\dfrac{10}{45x^2 + 4x - 1}}$$

$= $ _____

26. $\left| x - 95\frac{5}{8} \right| \leq \frac{1}{32}$

_____ $\leq x - 95\frac{5}{8} \leq$ _____

_____ $\leq x \leq$ _____

27. When the vertex is on the x-axis, there is

_____ zero. When the vertex is above

the x-axis and opening upward or below

the x-axis opening downward, there are

_____ zeros. When the vertex is above the

x-axis and opening downward or below

the x-axis opening upward, there are

_____ zeros.

28. *Cancel like factors.*

$$P(\text{both}) = \frac{2x^4y^2}{15xy^3} \cdot \frac{5x^2y}{8x^3y^2}$$

$= $ _____

29. $\dfrac{(x^2 + 30x) \text{ oranges}}{1 \text{ hr}} \cdot \dfrac{\square \text{ hours}}{\square \text{ day}}$

$= $ _____ oranges per day

$$\frac{3000}{24(\square + \square)}$$

$= $ _____

30. a. $A = \pi r^2$

radius x: $A = $ _____

radius $3x$: $A = $ _____

c. The graph of the larger circle is

_____ than the smaller circle.

b.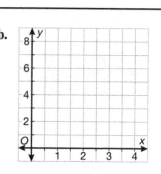

LESSON
98

Solving Quadratic Equations by Factoring

page 655

New Concepts

Math Language

The **roots** of a quadratic equation are the solution(s) of the equation.

The **Zero Product Property** states that if the product of two factors is zero, at least one of the factors is equal to zero.

• To find the roots of a quadratic equation, first write the equation so it is equal to zero. Factor the quadratic expression. Then apply the Zero Product Property to solve.

Example Solving Quadratic Equations by Factoring

Find the roots.

$$x^2 + 2x = 8$$

$x^2 + 2x - 8 = 0$	Subtract 8 from both sides.
$(x + 4)(x - 2) = 0$	Factor the quadratic expression.
$x + 4 = 0 \qquad x - 2 = 0$	Zero Product Property
$x = -4 \qquad x = 2$	Solve.

The roots are **−4 and 2.**

Example Finding the Roots by Factoring Out the GCF

Find the roots.

$$20 - 2x^2 = 70 - 20x$$

$0 = 2x^2 - 20x + 50$	Set the equation equal to zero.
$0 = 2(x^2 - 10x + 25)$	Factor out the GCF.
$0 = 2(x - 5)(x - 5)$	Factor.

Ignore the factor of 2 since 2 cannot equal 0.
The two other factors are the same.

$$x - 5 = 0$$

$$x = 5$$

The root is **5.**

Lesson Practice page 659

Solve.

a. $(x - 3)(x + 7) = 0$

$x - 3 = 0 \qquad\qquad x + 7 = 0$

$x = \underline{\hspace{1cm}} \qquad\qquad x = \underline{\hspace{1cm}}$

Find the roots.

b. $x^2 + 3x - 18 = 0$

$(x + \underline{\hspace{1cm}})(x - 3) = 0$

$x + \underline{\hspace{1cm}} = 0 \qquad x - 3 = 0$

$x = \underline{\hspace{1cm}} \qquad\qquad x = \underline{\hspace{1cm}}$

c. $2x^2 + 13x + 15 = 0$

$(2x + \underline{\hspace{1cm}})(x + \underline{\hspace{1cm}}) = 0$

$2x + \underline{\hspace{1cm}} = 0 \qquad x + \underline{\hspace{1cm}} = 0$

$2x = \underline{\hspace{1cm}} \qquad\qquad x = \underline{\hspace{1cm}}$

$x = \underline{\hspace{1cm}}$

Solve.

d. $5x^2 - 20x = 10x - 45$

$5x^2 - \underline{\hspace{1cm}} x = -45$

$5x^2 - \underline{\hspace{1cm}} x + \underline{\hspace{1cm}} = 0$

$5(x - \underline{\hspace{1cm}})(x - \underline{\hspace{1cm}}) = 0$

$x - \underline{\hspace{1cm}} = 0$

$x = \underline{\hspace{1cm}} \qquad \{\underline{\hspace{1cm}}\}$

e. $45x^2 = 27x$

$45x^2 - \underline{\hspace{1cm}} = 0$

$9x(5x - \underline{\hspace{1cm}}) = 0$

$9x = 0 \qquad\qquad 5x - \underline{\hspace{1cm}} = 0$

$x = \underline{\hspace{1cm}} \qquad\qquad 5x = \underline{\hspace{1cm}}$

$x = \underline{\hspace{1cm}}$

$\{\underline{\hspace{1cm}}, \underline{\hspace{1cm}}\}$

f. $25x^2 - 16 = 0$

$(\underline{\hspace{1cm}} x + \underline{\hspace{1cm}})(\underline{\hspace{1cm}} x - \underline{\hspace{1cm}}) = 0$

$\underline{\hspace{1cm}} x + \underline{\hspace{1cm}} = 0 \qquad \underline{\hspace{1cm}} x - \underline{\hspace{1cm}} = 0$

$\underline{\hspace{1cm}} x = -\underline{\hspace{1cm}} \qquad \underline{\hspace{1cm}} x = \underline{\hspace{1cm}}$

$x = \underline{\hspace{1cm}} \qquad\qquad x = \underline{\hspace{1cm}} \qquad\qquad \{\underline{\hspace{1cm}}, \underline{\hspace{1cm}}\}$

g. $w(3w + 6) = 360$

$3w^2 + \underline{\hspace{1cm}} = 360$

$3w^2 + \underline{\hspace{1cm}} - 360 = 0$

$3(w^2 + \underline{\hspace{1cm}} - \underline{\hspace{1cm}}) = 0$

$3(w + \underline{\hspace{1cm}})(w - \underline{\hspace{1cm}}) = 0$

$w + \underline{\hspace{1cm}} = 0 \qquad w - \underline{\hspace{1cm}} = 0$

$w = \underline{\hspace{1cm}} \qquad\qquad w = \underline{\hspace{1cm}}$

The width is \underline{\hspace{1cm}}. The length is \underline{\hspace{1cm}}.

1. $11 < 2(x + 5) < 20$

$11 < \underline{\quad} x + \underline{\quad} < 20$

$\underline{\quad} < x < \underline{\quad}$

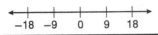

2. $|x| + 1.5 \leq 7.6$

$|x| \leq \underline{\quad}$

$\underline{\quad} \leq x \leq \underline{\quad}$

3. $a^2 - b^2 = (a + b)(a - b)$

$9x^2 - 121 = (\underline{\quad\quad})(\underline{\quad\quad})$

difference of two squares? $\underline{\quad}$

perfect square trinomial? $\underline{\quad}$

4. $y = 2x^2 + 8x + 6$

Solve $2x^2 + 8x + 6 = 0$ to find the x-intercepts. Find the axis of symmetry and two additional points.

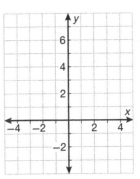

5. Add.

$A = 15x^3 + 17x - 20$
$O = 20x^3 + 11x - \underline{\ 4}$

$S = \underline{\quad\quad\quad}$

6. Slopes of perpendicular lines are negative reciprocals.

slope of new line: $\underline{\quad}$

$y - y_1 = m(x - x_1)$

$y = \underline{\quad\quad\quad}$

7. $\dfrac{4|x|}{9} + 3 = 11$

$\dfrac{4|x|}{9} = \underline{\quad}$

$|x| = \underline{\quad}$

Solution: $\{\underline{\quad}, \underline{\quad}\}$

8. Multiply by the reciprocal.

$\dfrac{3x + 6}{7x - 7} \cdot \dfrac{\square\bigcirc\square}{\square\bigcirc\square} =$

$\dfrac{3(x + \square)}{7(x - \square)} \cdot \dfrac{\square(\square\bigcirc\square)}{\square(\square\bigcirc\square)} = \underline{\quad}$

9. *See page 5 in the* Student Reference Guide.

$(5xyz)^2(3x^{-1}y)^2$

$=$ _____

10. $y < -5x + 4; y = 5, x = 5$

Substitute.

_____, $(5, 5)$ _____ satisfy

the inequality.

---

11. If two numbers are _____

and the product is 0, then at least one of

the numbers has to be _____.

12. The _____ Product Property states

that for every real number a and b,

if $ab = 0$, then $a =$ _____ and/or $b =$ _____.

---

13. $0 = (3x - 5)(x + 2)$

$0 = 3x -$ _____ $0 = x +$ _____

Circle the answer.

A $\left\{\frac{5}{3}, -2\right\}$ **B** $\left\{\frac{5}{3}, 2\right\}$

C $\left\{-\frac{5}{3}, -2\right\}$ **D** $\left\{-\frac{5}{3}, 2\right\}$

14. $m(m - 27) = 324$

$m^2 -$ _____$m -$ _____ $= 0$

$(m -$ ____$)(m -$ ____$) = 0$

$m =$ _____   or $m =$ _____

mother: _____

girl: _____

---

15. a. *Let x = jeans and let y = shorts*

_____$x +$ _____$y \le$ _____

b.

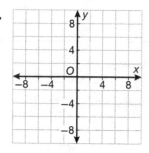

c. _____ pair(s) of jeans, _____ pair(s)

of shorts.

16. Solve for y. Then graph the inequality.

$4x + 2y > 8$

$2y >$ ____ $+ 8$

$y >$ ____ $+$ ____

17. $(x + 4)(x - 9) = 0$

$x + 4 = 0$ $x - 9 = 0$

$x =$ _____ $x =$ _____

18. Student _____ is correct.

Student _____ wrote an inequality using the symbol for "greater than or equal to", so the boundary line is _____.

---

19. $r = \frac{d}{t}$

 Divide to find the rate.

$$\frac{3x^2 - 15x}{3x} \div \frac{2x - 10}{2x^5}$$

$=$ _____

20. $A = \frac{bh}{2}$ $b = \frac{2A}{h}$

 Solve for b.

$$b = \frac{2(4x^2 - 2x - 6)}{(x + 1)}$$

$b =$ _____

---

21. $A = lw$ $l = \frac{A}{w}$

$$l = \frac{(20x + 5 + x^3)}{(x - 5)}$$

 Complete the long division.

$x - 5 \overline{)x^3 + 0x^2 + 20x + 5}$

$l =$ _____

22. Find the LCD in addition and _____ problems so that parts of equal size can be added or _____. Do not find the LCD to _____ or divide.

---

23. Find the LCD.

a. $\dfrac{4x}{3(x + 3)} + \dfrac{16}{(x + 9)\left(x + \Box\right)}$

$=$ _____

b. $d \div r = t$

 Divide.

$$\frac{\Box + \Box + \Box}{\Box(\Box + \Box)(\Box + \Box)} \div \frac{4x}{x + 3}$$

$t =$ _____

24. $h = -16t^2 + vt + s$
$s = 100,\ t = 2,\ v = 0$

Substitute. Then solve for h.

$h = -16t^2 + vt + s$

$h = -16(\underline{})^2 + (\underline{})(\underline{}) + (\underline{})$

$h =$ _____

---

25. Student _____ is correct. Student _____

found the _____.

26. a. $l_{picture} = 26 - (2 \times 1.5) =$ _____

$w_{picture} = 20 - (2 \times 1.5) =$ _____

b. *Use the Pythagorean Theorem.*

$c^2 =$ ____$^2 +$ ____^{2}

$c^2 =$ ____

27.

a. profit $= (x^2 + 6x + 5)\left(\dfrac{x^2}{100x}\right)$

$=$ ____

b. *Substitute.* $x = 50$

____

28. a. Area: $x($____ $-$ ____$) = 36$

The formula needs to be in

_____

$(ax^2 + bx + c = 0)$ to solve for x.

b. x^2 ◯ ____ ◯ ____ $=$ ____

$(x -$ ____$)(x +$ ____$) =$ ____

length: ____   width: ____

29. Steps for solving $\dfrac{x^2 - x - 30}{x + 5} - \dfrac{x - 6}{x + 5}$:

Step 1: Distribute the _____ sign

in the second term.

Step 2: Combine _____ terms in the

numerator to get _____.

Step 3: Try to factor out $(x +$ ____$)$ in the

numerator.

Step 4: Since the numerator _____ be

factored, the answer in simplest form is:

_____.

30. *Use FOIL.*

$A = (4x - 6)(8x + 7)$

$A =$ ____$x^2 +$ ____$x -$ ____$x -$ ____

$A =$ _____

_____, the expression is

_____.

Name _____

Solving Rational Equations page 662

New Concepts

- To solve equations that have one term on both sides, the easiest way is to use cross products.

Example **Solving a Rational Proportion**

Solve.

$\frac{x}{4} = \frac{3}{x-1}$

$$x(x-1) = 4(3) \qquad \text{Use cross products.}$$

$$x^2 - x = 12 \qquad \text{Distribute x over } (x-1).$$

$$x^2 - x - 12 = 0 \qquad \text{Subtract 12 from both sides.}$$

$$(x-4)(x+3) = 0 \qquad \text{Factor.}$$

$$x - 4 = 0, \ x + 3 = 0 \qquad \text{Use the Zero Product Property.}$$

$$x = 4 \quad \text{or} \quad x = -3 \qquad \text{Solve.}$$

- To solve a rational equation that includes more than two terms, multiply each term by the LCD.

Example **Using the LCD to Solve Subtraction Equations**

Solve.

$\frac{3}{x-1} - \frac{2}{x} = \frac{5}{2x}$ The LCD is $2x(x-1)$.

Multiply each term by the LCD.

$$2x(x-1) \cdot \frac{3}{x-1} - 2x(x-1) \cdot \frac{2}{x} = 2x(x-1) \cdot \frac{5}{2x}$$

$$6x - 4(x-1) = 5(x-1) \qquad \text{Simplify.}$$

$$6x - 4x + 4 = 5x - 5 \qquad \text{Distributive Property}$$

$$2x + 4 = 5x - 5 \qquad \text{Combine like terms.}$$

$$9 = 3x \qquad \text{Divide.}$$

$$3 = x$$

Solve each equation.

a. $\frac{6}{x} = \frac{7}{x-1}$

$\underline{\hspace{1cm}}(x-1) = 7x$

$\underline{\hspace{1cm}}x - 6 = 7x$

$\underline{\hspace{1cm}} = x$

b. $\frac{2}{x+4} = \frac{x}{6}$

$2(\underline{\hspace{1cm}}) = (x + \underline{\hspace{1cm}})x$

$\underline{\hspace{1cm}} = x^2 + \underline{\hspace{1cm}}$

$0 = x^2 + \underline{\hspace{1cm}} - \underline{\hspace{1cm}}$

$0 = (x + \underline{\hspace{1cm}})(x - \underline{\hspace{1cm}})$

$0 = x + \underline{\hspace{1cm}} \qquad 0 = x - \underline{\hspace{1cm}}$

$\underline{\hspace{1cm}} = x \qquad \underline{\hspace{1cm}} = x$

c. $\frac{12}{2x} + \frac{16}{4x} = 5$　　*Multiply by LCD.*

$\underline{\hspace{1cm}} = \underline{\hspace{1cm}}x$

$\underline{\hspace{1cm}} = x$

d. $\frac{4}{x-2} - \frac{2}{x} = \frac{1}{3}x$　　$LCD = \underline{\hspace{0.5cm}}(x-2)$

$3x(x-2)\left(\frac{4}{x-2}\right) - 3x(x-2)\left(\frac{2}{x}\right) = 3x(x-2)\left(\frac{1}{3}x\right)$

$\underline{\hspace{1cm}}x - (3x - \underline{\hspace{1cm}})(2) = \underline{\hspace{1cm}} - \underline{\hspace{1cm}}$

$\underline{\hspace{1cm}}x - \underline{\hspace{1cm}}x + \underline{\hspace{1cm}} = \underline{\hspace{1cm}} - \underline{\hspace{1cm}}$

$\underline{\hspace{1cm}}x + \underline{\hspace{1cm}} = \underline{\hspace{1cm}} - \underline{\hspace{1cm}}$

$\underline{\hspace{1cm}}x = \underline{\hspace{1cm}} \longrightarrow x = \underline{\hspace{1cm}}$

e. $\frac{x+5}{x+4} = \frac{x-2}{2x+8}$

$(x+5)(\underline{\hspace{1cm}} + \underline{\hspace{1cm}}) = (x+4)(\underline{\hspace{1cm}} - \underline{\hspace{1cm}})$

$\underline{\hspace{1cm}}x^2 + \underline{\hspace{1cm}}x + \underline{\hspace{1cm}} = x^2 + \underline{\hspace{1cm}}x - \underline{\hspace{1cm}}$

$\underline{\hspace{1cm}}x^2 + \underline{\hspace{1cm}}x + \underline{\hspace{1cm}} = 0$

$x + \underline{\hspace{1cm}} = 0 \qquad x + \underline{\hspace{1cm}} = 0$　📝 Check that the solutions are not extraneous.

$x = \underline{\hspace{1cm}} \qquad\qquad x = \underline{\hspace{1cm}}$

f. $\frac{1}{2}h + \frac{1}{3}h = 1$　　$LCD = \underline{\hspace{1cm}}$

$\underline{\hspace{1cm}} \cdot \frac{1}{2}h + \underline{\hspace{1cm}} \cdot \frac{1}{3}h = \underline{\hspace{1cm}} \cdot 1$

$\underline{\hspace{1cm}}h + \underline{\hspace{1cm}}h = \underline{\hspace{1cm}}$

$h = \underline{\hspace{1cm}}$　　　Together it will take them $\underline{\hspace{2cm}}$ hours.

1. $\dfrac{4}{x} = \dfrac{8}{x+4}$

_____$(x+4) =$ _____(8)

_____$= x$

2. $(x-13)(x+22) = 0$

$x - 13 =$ _____ $x + 22 =$ _____

$x =$ _____ $x =$ _____

$\{$_____, _____$\}$

---

3. $|10x - 20| = 2$

$x =$ _____

minimum: _____

maximum: _____

4.   Substitute.

$y \overset{?}{=} x^2 + x - 12$

_____ $\overset{?}{=}$ (_____$)^2 +$ (_____$) + 12$

_____ $\overset{?}{=}$ _____ ✓

---

5. $\dfrac{\dfrac{4x}{12x-60} + \dfrac{1}{4x-16}}{\dfrac{-2}{9x-20-x^2}}$

Factor and multiply by reciprocal.

$= \left(\dfrac{4x}{12(x-5)} + \dfrac{1}{4(x-4)} \right) \cdot \dfrac{(\square - \square)(\square - \square)}{-2}$

Using the LCD, combine the fractions.

Cancel, multiply, combine like terms.

$=$ _____

---

6.   Factor.

$x + 4x^2 - 5x$

standard form: _____

$=$ (_____ $+$ _____) (_____ $-$ _____)

7.   Let $y =$ Larry's weight and let $x =$ the number of months

$y =$ _____ $-$ _____x

Substitute.

$y =$ _____

---

8.   An extraneous solution is an answer that satisfies a transformed equation but not the _____ equation.

---

9. *Factor each denominator. The LCD contains the highest degree of every factor in the two denominators.*

$$\frac{2x}{2x^2 - 72} - \frac{12}{x^2 + 13x + 42}$$

$$= \frac{2x}{2(x + \square)(x - \square)} - \frac{12}{(x + \square)(x + \square)}$$

LCD: $2(x - \underline{})(x + \underline{})(x + \underline{})$

10. $y = -0.0003x^2 + 0.03x + 1.3$

$$x = -\frac{b}{2a} = \underline{}$$

$y = -0.0003(\underline{})^2 + 0.03(\underline{})x + 1.3$

vertex: ($\underline{}$, $\underline{}$)

The population was a $\underline{}$ of

about $\underline{}$ people in $\underline{}$.

11. *See page 7 in the* Student Reference Guide.

a. $M_1 = \left(\dfrac{x_1 + x_2}{2}, \dfrac{y_1 + y_2}{2}\right)$

$$= \left(\frac{\square + \square}{2}, \frac{\square + \square}{2}\right)$$

$$= (\underline{}, \underline{})$$

b. $M_2 = \left(\dfrac{\square + \square}{2}, \dfrac{\square + \square}{2}\right)$

$$= (\underline{}, \underline{})$$

12. *Use placeholders.*

$$\frac{6x^4 +}{x - 2\overline{\smash{\big)}6x^5 + 0x^4 + 0x^3 + 18x^2 - 120}}$$
$$\underline{-6x^5 - 12^4}$$

Answer: $\underline{}$

13. $V = s^3$

$$\frac{5^3}{3^3} = \underline{}$$

14. The solution is extraneous if it would cause one of the denominators to be $\underline{}$.

15. 📝 *Substitute solutions into the denominators.*

Circle the answer.

A $x = -1$ **B** $x = 0$

C $x = 1$ **D** $x = 5$

16. $\dfrac{1}{8}h + \dfrac{1}{6}h = 1$

$$\underline{} \cdot \frac{1}{8}h + \underline{} \cdot \frac{1}{6}h = \underline{} \cdot 1$$

$$\underline{} h + \underline{} h = \underline{}$$

$$h = \underline{}$$

17. Student _____ is correct.

Student _____ has incorrect _____

in both answers.

18. $A = \left(\frac{1}{2}\right)bh$

$\frac{1}{2}b(2b + 4) = 24$

$b = $ _____ $h = $ _____

19. $l = 2x,\ w = x$

a. $l = 2x - $ _____ , $w = x - $ _____

b. $144 = A$ $A = lw$

$144 = (2x - \_\_)\,(x - \_\_)$

$w = x = $ _____

c. $l = 2x = $ _____

20. There is no solution when the absolute

value ◯ zero because the absolute value

can not be a _____

number.

21.

$$x - 7\overline{)\ x^2 - 15x + 56}$$
$$-18x^2$$

with x above.

$w = $ _____

22. Solve $4x^2 + 28x - 72 = 0$ or substitute points in $4x^2 + 28x - 72$ until you find one that fits.

Circle the answer.

A $0, 4$ **B** $0, -4$

C $2, -9$ **D** $2, -76$

23. Let $x = $ number of adult tickets
Let $y = $ number of student tickets

$y = $ _____ + _____

$3x + $ _____ $\geq$ _____

24.

$$x + 4\overline{)\ 3x^3 + 0x^2 - 8x + 2}$$
$$-3x^3$$

with $3x^2$ above.

Answer: _____

25. Student _____ is correct.

Student _____ used a symbol that

did not include "or equal to",

so the boundary line is _____.

26. *Use slope-intercept form.*

$4x + 5y \geq -7$

$5y \geq$ _____ $- 7$

y ◯ _____

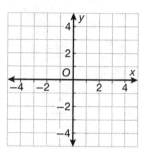

27. $t = \frac{d}{r}$

  a. riding time on the street $= \frac{12}{x}$

     riding time on dirt trails $= \frac{6}{.25x}$

     total time $= \dfrac{\square}{\square} + \dfrac{\square}{\square}$

            $= \dfrac{\square}{\square}$

  b. The $.25x$ will be replaced with _____.

28. *Solve for y and make a table of x and y values.*

$y - 3 = -x^2 + 3 \longrightarrow$ _____

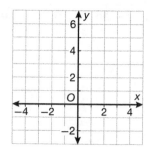

29. *Factor.* $A = s^2$

  Area $= x^2 + 16x + 64$

      $= ($_____$)^2$

  side length: _____

30. *Direct variation:* $y = kx$ *and indirect variation:* $y = \frac{k}{x}$

  $j =$ _____

LESSON

100

Solving Quadratic Equations by Graphing

page 669

New Concepts

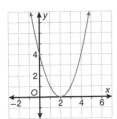
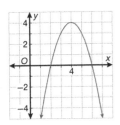
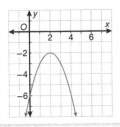
• You can follow these steps to graph a quadratic function and find the *x*-intercepts.

> **Example** Solving Quadratic Equations by Graphing
>
> **Solve the equation by graphing the related function.**
>
> $$x^2 - 36 = 0$$
>
> Step 1: Find the axis of symmetry.
>
> $x = -\dfrac{b}{2a}, a = 1, b = 0$
>
> $x = -\dfrac{0}{2(1)} = 0$ The axis of symmetry is $x = 0$.
>
> Step 2: Find the vertex.
>
> $f(x) = x^2 - 36, x = 0$
>
> $f(0) = 0^2 - 36$
>
> $f(0) = -36$ The vertex is $(0, -36)$.
>
> Step 3: Find the *y*-intercept.
>
> The *y*-intercept is *c*.   The *y*-intercept is -36.
>
> Step 4: Find two points that are not on the axis of symmetry.
>
> $f(5) = 5^2 - 36$ $f(7) = 7^2 - 36$
>
> $f(5) = 25 - 36$ $f(7) = 49 - 36$
>
> $f(5) = -11$ $f(7) = 13$
>
> One point is $(5, -11)$.   Another point is $(7, 13)$.
>
> Step 5: Graph.
>
> Graph $x = 0$, $(0, -36)$, $(5, -11)$, $(7, 13)$.
>
> Reflect $(5, -11)$, $(7, 13)$ over the axis of symmetry. Connect the points. The *x*-intercepts are 6, and -6.

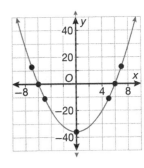

Solve each equation by graphing the related function.

Find the axis of symmetry, the vertex, the y-intercept, and two points on the curve.

Graph each function.

a. $3x^2 - 147 = 0$

$x = -\dfrac{b}{2a}, b = 0, a = 3$

$x = -\dfrac{\square}{2\square} = \underline{\hspace{1cm}}$

$f(0) = 3(\underline{\hspace{0.7cm}})^2 - 147 = \underline{\hspace{1.5cm}}$

$f(5) = 3(\underline{\hspace{0.7cm}})^2 - 147 = \underline{\hspace{1.5cm}}$

$f(10) = 3(\underline{\hspace{0.9cm}}) - 147 = \underline{\hspace{1.5cm}}$

The axis of symmetry is $x = \underline{\hspace{1cm}}$.

The vertex is $\underline{\hspace{1.5cm}}$.

The y-intercept is $\underline{\hspace{1.5cm}}$.

A point on the curve is $(\underline{\hspace{0.7cm}}, \underline{\hspace{0.7cm}})$.

A point on the curve is $(\underline{\hspace{0.7cm}}, \underline{\hspace{0.7cm}})$.

The x-intercepts are $\underline{\hspace{1cm}}$ and $\underline{\hspace{1cm}}$.

Solution: $\underline{\hspace{4cm}}$

b. $5x^2 + 6 = 0$

$x = -\dfrac{b}{2a}, b = \underline{\hspace{1cm}}, a = \underline{\hspace{1cm}}$

$x = -\dfrac{\square}{2\square} = \underline{\hspace{1cm}}$

$f(0) = 5\underline{\hspace{0.7cm}}^2 + 6 \quad (0, \underline{\hspace{1cm}})$

$f(3) = 5\underline{\hspace{0.7cm}}^2 + 6 \quad (3, \underline{\hspace{1cm}})$

$f(10) = 5\underline{\hspace{0.7cm}}^2 + 6 \quad (10, \underline{\hspace{1cm}})$

Solution: $\underline{\hspace{4cm}}$

c. $x^2 - 10x + 25 = 0$

$x = -\dfrac{b}{2a}, b = \underline{\hspace{1cm}}, a = \underline{\hspace{1cm}}$

$x = -\dfrac{\square}{2\square} = \underline{\hspace{1cm}}$

$f(0) = \underline{\hspace{0.7cm}}^2 - 10(\underline{\hspace{0.7cm}}) + 25$

$f(\underline{\hspace{0.7cm}}) = \underline{\hspace{0.7cm}}^2 - 10(\underline{\hspace{0.7cm}}) + 25$

$f(\underline{\hspace{0.7cm}}) = \underline{\hspace{0.7cm}}^2 - 10(\underline{\hspace{0.7cm}}) + 25$

Solution: $\underline{\hspace{4cm}}$

Solve problems d–g by graphing the related function for each equation on your graphing calculator.

d. $x^2 + 64 = 16x$

$x^2 - \underline{\hspace{2cm}} + 64 = 0$

$x = \underline{\hspace{1.5cm}}$

e. $x^2 + 4 = 2x$

$x^2 - \underline{\hspace{2cm}} + 4 = 0$

$\underline{\hspace{4cm}}$

f. Round to the nearest tenth:

$-7x^2 + 3x = -7$

$-7x^2 + 3x + \underline{\hspace{1.5cm}} = 0$

$x = \underline{\hspace{1.5cm}}$ and $\underline{\hspace{1.5cm}}$

g. Round to the nearest tenth:

$h = -16t^2 + 2t + 17$

$t = \underline{\hspace{1.5cm}}$ seconds

1. $x(2x - 11) = 0$

$x = 0$ or $2x - 11 = 0$

$x = \underline{\quad}, \dfrac{\square}{\square}$

2. *Use cross products.*

$\dfrac{12}{x - 6} = \dfrac{4}{x}$

$12x = \underline{\qquad}$

$x = \underline{\qquad}$

3. The ball's path creates a parabola that

opens _____. The vertex shows

the ball's maximum _____.

The positive zero shows the time when

the ball _____.

4. The graph does not cross the x-axis when

there is _____ solution. The graph

has its vertex on the x-axis when there is

_____ solution. The graph crosses

the x-axis two times when there are

_____ solutions.

5. *Substitute.*

$y = kx,\ x = 15,\ y = 30$

$k = \underline{\qquad}$

6. *Find the vertex and the positive solution.*

$h = -16t^2 + 7t + 7$

$t = -\dfrac{b}{2a}$

$h = \underline{\qquad}$ $t = \underline{\qquad}$

7. $y = \frac{1}{4}(x - 4)^2 + 5$

$= \frac{1}{4}(\underline{\quad})(\underline{\quad}) + \underline{\quad}$

$x = -\dfrac{b}{2a} = \underline{\qquad}$

Circle the answer.

A $x = 1$ **B** $x = 4$

C $x = 5$ **D** $x = -4$

8. Graph.

$-7x^2 - 10 = 0$

$x = -\dfrac{b}{2a} = \underline{\qquad}$

vertex $= (\underline{\quad}, \underline{\quad})$

graph opens _____

Solution: _____

9.
$$\frac{6}{x} = \frac{8}{x+7}$$

$$6(\underline{}) = 8x$$

$$x = \underline{}$$

10. *See page 13 in the* Student Reference Guide.

$$P \text{ (black, black, 6)} = \frac{\square}{\square} \cdot \frac{\square}{\square} \cdot \frac{\square}{\square}$$

$$= \frac{\square}{\square}$$

---

11. *Use cross products.*

$$\frac{x+5}{6} = \frac{6}{x}$$

$$x(\underline{}) = 36$$

$$x^2 + \underline{} = \underline{}$$

$$(x\underline{})(x\underline{}) = \underline{}$$

$$x = \underline{}\,\blacksquare$$

12. *Multiply by the LCD.*

a. Henry: $t + \underline{}$

b. $\frac{1}{4}\left(t + \frac{1}{2}\right) + \frac{1}{3}t = 1$

$$(\underline{})\left[\frac{1}{4}\left(t+\frac{1}{2}\right)\right] + (\underline{})\frac{1}{3}t = (\underline{})1$$

$$t = \underline{}\,\blacksquare \quad \underline{}\,\blacksquare$$

c. *Substitute.*

$$\underline{}\,\blacksquare$$

---

13. *Factor the numerator.*

$$\frac{a^2 + 10a - 24}{a - 2} = \frac{(a + \square)(a - \square)}{a - 2}$$

$$= \underline{}$$

14. *Factor the radicand into perfect squares.*

$$\sqrt{49y^5} = \underline{}$$

---

15. $\left|\underline{} - 270\right| = 30$

$$\underline{} - 270 = 30 \quad \text{or} \quad \underline{} - 270 = -30$$

$$x = \underline{} \quad \text{or} \quad x = \underline{}$$

max.: $\underline{}\,\blacksquare$

min.: $\underline{}\,\blacksquare$

16. $\left|\frac{1}{4}x - \underline{}\right| = 5$

$$\frac{1}{4}x - \underline{} = 5 \quad \text{or} \quad \frac{1}{4}x - \underline{} = -5$$

$$x = \underline{} \quad \text{or} \quad x = \underline{}$$

max.: $\underline{}\,\blacksquare$

min.: $\underline{}\,\blacksquare$

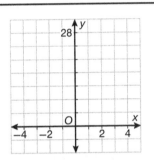

17. $|10x| - 3 = 87$

$\qquad |10x| = \underline{\hspace{2cm}}$

$\qquad\qquad 10x = \underline{\hspace{1.5cm}}$ or $10x = \underline{\hspace{1.5cm}}$

$\qquad \{\underline{\hspace{0.7cm}}, \underline{\hspace{0.7cm}}\}$

18. *Factor to help find LCD before subtracting.*

$$\frac{7x}{x^2 + 3x - 18} - \frac{2x + 1}{7x + 42}$$

$$= \frac{7x}{(x + \square)(x - \square)} - \frac{2x + 1}{7(x + \square)}$$

$= \underline{\hspace{5cm}}$

19. $y = 5x^2 - 10x + 5$

$x = -\dfrac{b}{2a}$

$f(\underline{\hspace{0.7cm}}) = 5\underline{\hspace{0.7cm}}^2 - 10(\underline{\hspace{0.7cm}}) + 5$

$f(\underline{\hspace{0.7cm}}) = 5\underline{\hspace{0.7cm}}^2 - 10(\underline{\hspace{0.7cm}}) + 5$

$f(\underline{\hspace{0.7cm}}) = 5\underline{\hspace{0.7cm}}^2 - 10(\underline{\hspace{0.7cm}}) + 5$

20. *Think of a number line.*

Shade the half-plane on the \underline{\hspace{3cm}}

side of the vertical line.

21. *Substitute.*

$x + 2y < 5$

Circle the answer.

A $(0, 0)$ \qquad\qquad **B** $(2, 1)$

C $(3, -4)$ \qquad\qquad **D** $(-1, 3)$

22. $\qquad b(b + \underline{\hspace{0.7cm}}) = \underline{\hspace{0.7cm}}$

$\qquad b^2 + \underline{\hspace{0.7cm}} - \underline{\hspace{0.7cm}} = 0$

$\qquad (\underline{\hspace{0.7cm}})(\underline{\hspace{0.7cm}}) = 0$

$\qquad\qquad boy = b = \underline{\hspace{1.5cm}}$

$\qquad\qquad father = b + 23 = \underline{\hspace{1.5cm}}$

23. Student \underline{\hspace{1.5cm}} is correct.

Student \underline{\hspace{1.5cm}} did not put the equation

in \underline{\hspace{3cm}} form

before factoring.

24. *A positive coefficient of the x^2-term indicates the parabola opens upward. When it is negative, the parabola opens downward.*

$y + 2x^2 = 12 + x$

$y = \underline{\hspace{1.5cm}} + x + 12$

coefficient: \underline{\hspace{2cm}}

graph opens: \underline{\hspace{2cm}}

25. $c^2 = a^2 + b^2$

$\underline{\hspace{1cm}}^2 \stackrel{?}{=} \underline{\hspace{1cm}}^2 + \underline{\hspace{1cm}}^2$

\underline{\hspace{1cm}}, 18, 80 and 82 \underline{\hspace{3cm}}

a Pythagorean triple.

---

26. $3x^3 + 12x^2 + 9x$

a. $3x(x^2 + \underline{\hspace{1.5cm}} + \underline{\hspace{1.5cm}})$

b. $3x(x + \underline{\hspace{1cm}})(x + \underline{\hspace{1cm}})$

c. dimensions are \underline{\hspace{1.5cm}}, \underline{\hspace{1.5cm}}

and \underline{\hspace{1cm}}

27. *$t = \frac{d}{r}$; Find the LCD. Then add and factor.*

$\text{Saturday} = t_1 = \frac{480}{x}$ and $\text{Sunday} = t_2 = \frac{300}{x - 10}$

$t_1 + t_2 = \dfrac{\square}{\square} \cdot \dfrac{480}{x} + \dfrac{\square}{\square} \cdot \dfrac{300}{x - 10}$

$= \dfrac{\square(\square - \square)}{\square(\square - \square)}$

---

28. *The absolute value of the difference between the guess and 120 is less than or equal to 5.*

a. $\left| x - \underline{\hspace{1cm}} \right| \leq \underline{\hspace{1cm}}$

b. $x - \underline{\hspace{1cm}} \leq \underline{\hspace{1cm}}$ or $x - \underline{\hspace{1cm}} \geq - \underline{\hspace{1cm}}$

$\underline{\hspace{1cm}} \leq x \leq \underline{\hspace{1cm}}$

29. If there are no common factors, then

the expression is in \underline{\hspace{3cm}}

form.

Example: $\dfrac{x^2 - \square}{x^2 + 6x + \square}$

$= \dfrac{(x + \square)(x - \square)}{(x + \square)(x + \square)}$

---

30. *Let x = original price*

$x - \underline{\hspace{2cm}} = \$227{,}500$

$\underline{\hspace{1cm}} x = \$227{,}500$

$x = \underline{\hspace{3cm}}$

Name _____

Transforming Quadratic Functions page 676

Math Language

The **quadratic parent function** is $f(x) = x^2$.

A transformation of the quadratic parent function can be written in the form: $f(x) = ax^2 + bx + c$, where $a \neq 0$ and $b = 0$. a makes the graph narrower or wider and c shifts the graph up or down.

Complete the table and graph the parent function.

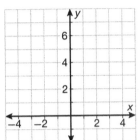

x	$f(x)$
-3	
-2	
-1	
0	
1	
2	
3	

Graph each transformation.

1. The graph of $y = 2x^2$ is _____ than the graph of $y = x^2$.

2. The graph of $y = \frac{1}{2}x^2$ is _____ than the graph of $y = x^2$.

3. The graph of $y = -x^2$ opens _____ while the graph of

   $y = x^2$ opens _____.

4. a makes the graph _____ or _____ and changes the

   _____ in which the parabola _____.

5. The graph of $f(x) = \frac{2}{3}x^2$ is _____.

6. The graph of $f(x) = -4x^2$ is _____ and

   opens _____.

7. Graph $f(x) = x^2$ and $f(x) = x^2 + 1$ on the same axes. The

   graph of $f(x) = x^2 + 1$ moved _____ 1 unit.

8. Graph $f(x) = x^2$ and $f(x) = x^2 - 2$ on the same set of axes. The

   graph of $f(x) = x^2 - 2$ moved _____ 2 units.

9. The graph of $f(x) = x^2 + 7$ moved _____ 7 units.

> Predict how each graph will compare to the graph of the quadratic parent function. Verify your answer with the graphing calculator.

10. The graph of $f(x) = -x^2 + 2$ moves _____ 2 units and open

_____ .

11. The graph of $f(x) = \frac{1}{2}x^2 - 3$ moves _____ 3 units and

is _____ .

Investigation Practice 📖 page 677

> Describe how the graph for the given values of a and c changes in relation to the graph of the quadratic parent function. Verify your answer with a graphing calculator.

a. $f(x) = ax^2 + c$ for $a = 2$ and $c = 1$

The graph is _____ and moved _____ unit(s) _____ .

b. $f(x) = ax^2 + c$ for $a = -3$ and $c = -2$

The graph is _____ , moved _____ unit(s) _____ and opens _____

c. $f(x) = ax^2 + c$ for $a = \frac{1}{2}$ and $c = 2$

The graph is _____ and moved _____ unit(s) _____ .

d. $f(x) = ax^2 + c$ for $a = -\frac{1}{2}$ and $c = -1$

The graph is _____ , moved _____ unit(s) _____ , and opens _____ .

Write an equation for the transformation. Graph the original function and the transformation on the same set of axes.

e. Shift $f(x) = 2x^2 - 4$ up 2 units.

$f(x) = $ _____

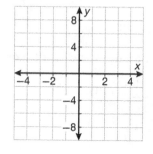

f. Shift $f(x) = 3x^2 + 5$ down 4 units and open it downward.

$f(x) = $ _____

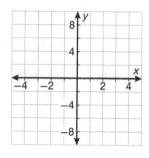

LESSON
101

Solving Multi-Step Absolute-Value
Inequalities page 678

New Concepts

- To solve an absolute-value inequality:
  1. Isolate the absolute-value expression.
  2. Write the inequality as a compound inequality.
  3. Solve the compound inequality.
- When an absolute-value inequality is "less than," the resulting compound inequality uses AND. When the absolute-value inequality is "greater than," it uses OR.

Example **Solving Inequalities with One Operation Inside Absolute-Value Symbols**

Solve and graph the inequality. $|x + 5| - 1 > 7$

Isolate the absolute-value expression $|x + 5|$.

$$|x + 5| - 1 > 7$$

$$|x + 5| > 8 \qquad \text{Add 1 to each side.}$$

$$x + 5 < -8 \quad \text{OR} \quad x + 5 > 8 \qquad \text{Write as a compound inequality.}$$
$$\text{Solve the compound inequality for } x.$$

$$x < -13 \quad \text{OR} \quad x > 3 \qquad \text{Subtract 5 from each side of}$$
$$\text{two inequalities.}$$

Example **Solving Inequalities with Two Operations Inside Absolute-Value Symbols**

Solve and graph the inequality.

$$\left|\frac{x}{3} - 2\right| + 12 \le 19$$

$$\left|\frac{x}{3} - 2\right| \le 7 \qquad \text{Subtract 12 from each side.}$$

$$\frac{x}{3} - 2 \ge -7 \quad \text{AND} \quad \frac{x}{3} - 2 \le 7 \qquad \text{Write as a compound inequality.}$$

$$\frac{x}{3} \ge -5 \quad \text{AND} \quad \frac{x}{3} \le 9 \qquad \text{Add 2 to each side.}$$

$$x \ge -15 \quad \text{AND} \quad x \le 27 \qquad \text{Multiply each side by 3.}$$

$$-15 \le x \le 27$$

Solve and graph each inequality.

a. $5|x| + 6 < 31$

$$5|x| < \underline{\hspace{1cm}}$$

$$|x| < \underline{\hspace{1cm}}$$

$$x > \underline{\hspace{1cm}} \quad \text{AND} \quad x < \underline{\hspace{1cm}}$$

$$\underline{\hspace{1cm}} < x < \underline{\hspace{1cm}}$$

b. $\frac{|x|}{7} - 3 \geq 1$

$$\frac{|x|}{7} \geq \underline{\hspace{1cm}}$$

$$|x| \geq \underline{\hspace{1cm}}$$

$$x \bigcirc \underline{\hspace{1cm}} \quad \text{OR} \quad x \bigcirc \underline{\hspace{1cm}}$$

c. *Reverse the inequality sign when dividing by a negative number.*

$$-4|x| + 9 > -1$$

$$-4|x| > \underline{\hspace{1cm}}$$

$$|x| \bigcirc \underline{\hspace{1cm}}$$

$$x \bigcirc \underline{\hspace{1cm}} \quad \text{AND} \quad x \bigcirc \underline{\hspace{1cm}}$$

$$\underline{\hspace{1cm}} \bigcirc x \bigcirc \underline{\hspace{1cm}}$$

d. $|x - 9| + 3 \leq 10$

$$|x - 9| \leq \underline{\hspace{1cm}}$$

$$x - 9 \geq \underline{\hspace{1cm}} \quad \text{AND} \quad x - 9 \leq \underline{\hspace{1cm}}$$

$$x \geq \underline{\hspace{1cm}} \quad \text{AND} \quad x \leq \underline{\hspace{1cm}}$$

$$\underline{\hspace{1cm}} \bigcirc x \bigcirc \underline{\hspace{1cm}}$$

e. $\left|\frac{x}{2} + 5\right| - 9 < -2$

$$\left|\frac{x}{2} + 5\right| < \underline{\hspace{1cm}}$$

$$\frac{x}{2} + 5 \bigcirc \underline{\hspace{1cm}} \quad \text{AND} \quad \frac{x}{2} + 5 \bigcirc \underline{\hspace{1cm}}$$

$$x \bigcirc \underline{\hspace{1cm}} \quad \text{AND} \quad x \bigcirc \underline{\hspace{1cm}}$$

$$\underline{\hspace{1cm}} \bigcirc x \bigcirc \underline{\hspace{1cm}}$$

f. $|5x - 5| - 12 > -2$

$$|5x - 5| > \underline{\hspace{1cm}}$$

$$5x - 5 \bigcirc \underline{\hspace{1cm}} \quad 5x - 5 \bigcirc \underline{\hspace{1cm}}$$

$$x \bigcirc \underline{\hspace{1cm}} \quad x \bigcirc \underline{\hspace{1cm}}$$

g. Write and solve the absolute-value inequality that models the required weight of a basketball used in NCAA men's basketball games. What is the largest acceptable weight?

$$|w - \underline{\hspace{0.5cm}}| \leq 1$$

$$w - 21 \bigcirc \underline{\hspace{1cm}} \quad \text{AND} \quad w - 21 \bigcirc \underline{\hspace{1cm}}$$

$$w \bigcirc \underline{\hspace{1cm}} \quad \underline{\hspace{0.5cm}} \quad w \bigcirc \underline{\hspace{1cm}}$$

$$\underline{\hspace{1cm}} \bigcirc w \bigcirc \underline{\hspace{1cm}}$$

The largest acceptable weight is _____.

1. $7|x| - 4 \geq 3$

$7|x| \geq$ _____

$|x| \geq$ _____

$x \bigcirc$ _____ OR $x \bigcirc$ _____

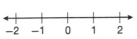

2. Student _____ is correct.

Student _____ did not isolate the

_____ - _____ expression

before _____ the absolute-value

bars.

3. (1) _____ from each side.

(2) _____ each side by _____.

(3) Rewrite as a _____ .

4. *Use rule of exponents.*

$$\frac{pt^{-2}}{m^3}\left(\frac{p^{-2}wt}{4m^{-1}} + 6t^4w^{-1} - \frac{w}{m^{-3}}\right)$$

$=$ _____

5. $-a|x - b| \geq -c$

$|x - b| \bigcirc$ _____

The solution of the compound inequality

will use _____ .

6. $|t - 475| \bigcirc 9$

$t - 475 \geq -9$ AND $t - 475 \leq$ _____

$t \geq$ _____ AND $t \leq$ _____

_____ $\bigcirc$ t $\bigcirc$ _____

highest possible temperature: _____

7. Student _____ is correct. Student _____ did

not remember that a parabola can cross

the x-axis _____, _____, or _____

times.

8. Graph $h(t) = -16t^2 + 2t + 9$.

  a. vertex (t, h): $h =$ _____

  b. When $h = 0$, $t =$ _____ .

  c. vertex (t, h): $t =$ _____

9. *See page 2 in the* Student Reference Guide.

$6w^3 - 48w^5 = 6w3\left(\underline{\quad} - 8w^{\square}\right)$

$9w - 72w^3 =$ _____ $\left(\underline{\quad} - \underline{\quad}w^2\right)$

LCM: _____

10. Graph $A(t) = -2t^2 + 5t + 125$.

When $A = 60$ feet^2, $t =$ _____.

---

11. Graph $f(x) =$ _____ + _____ + _____.

x-intercept(s): $x =$ _____

---

12. $|8x| + 4 = 28$

$|8x| =$ _____

$8x =$ _____ and $8x =$ _____

{_____ , _____}

---

13. *Multiply one expression by $\frac{-1}{-1}$.*

$$\frac{\square}{\square}\frac{4}{r-2} + \frac{r^2}{2-r} = \frac{-4}{\square - \square} + \frac{r^2}{2-r}$$

$$= \frac{r^2 - \square}{2-r} = \frac{(\square - 2)(r + \square)}{2-r}$$

$$= \frac{-1}{-1} \cdot \frac{(\square - 2)(r + \square)}{2-r}$$

$$= \frac{\square(\square - 2)(r + \square)}{r-2} =$$ _____ miles

---

14. $\dfrac{5}{x-3} \cdot \dfrac{(x - \square)}{(x - \square)} - \dfrac{2}{x-2} \cdot \dfrac{(x - \square)}{(x - \square)}$

$$= \frac{5x - \square}{(x-3)(x - \square)} - \frac{2x - \square}{(x-3)(x - \square)}$$

$$= \frac{5x - \square - \square + \square}{(x-3)(x - \square)}$$

$$=$$ _____

---

15. $t =$ _____   *Time*

$v =$ _____   *Initial velocity in ft/sec*

$s =$ _____   *Initial height in ft*

$h = -16t^2 + vt + s$

$h = -16(\_\_\_)^2 + (\_\_\_)(\_\_\_) + (\_\_\_)$

$h =$ _____

---

16. *Substitute 0 for y.*

$x^2 - 24x - 81 = 0$

$(x - \square)(x + 3) = 0$

$x =$ _____ , _____

_____

---

17. *Substitute.*

$y \le 3$

_____ ≤ 3

The ordered pair, $(-7, 2)$, _____
satisfy the inequality.

---

18. $\left(4\dfrac{\square}{\square} - 3\right)\left(5\dfrac{\square}{\square} + 7\right)$

$$= (\square - 3)\left(\frac{\square}{4}\right)$$

$$= \square\left(\frac{\square}{4}\right) =$$ _____

19. $x^2 - 10x - 39 = 0$

$(x + \underline{\quad})(x - 13) = 0$

$x + \underline{\qquad} = 0$ OR $x - 13 = 0$

$x = \underline{\quad}$ OR $x = \underline{\qquad}$

Circle the roots of the equation.

A 0, 39   **B** 10, 0

C 3, −13   **D** 13, −3

20. *Multiply both sides by LCD.*

$$\frac{x}{11} = \frac{6}{x - 5}$$

$$(\underline{\quad})\left(x - \square\right) \cdot \frac{x}{11} = (\underline{\quad})\left(x - \square\right) \cdot \frac{6}{x - 5}$$

$$x^2 - \square = 66$$

$$x^2 - \square - 66 = 0$$

$$(x - \underline{\quad})(x + \underline{\quad}) = 0$$

$$x = \underline{\quad}, \underline{\quad}$$

 Check your work

21. *Write in standard form.*

$-8x^2 - 12 = 3 - y$

$y = \underline{\hspace{5cm}}$

Since the coefficient of $8x^2$ is

$\underline{\hspace{3cm}}$, the graph opens $\underline{\hspace{2cm}}$.

22. Maria: 1 batch of copies per hour

Lucille: $\frac{1}{2}$ batch of copies per hour

Let h = hours worked

(Maria's rate)h + (Lucille's rate)$h = 1$

$(\underline{\quad})h + (\underline{\quad})h = 1$

$\underline{\quad}h = \underline{\quad}$

$h = \underline{\quad}$ hour(s)

23. Student $\underline{\qquad}$ is correct.

Student $\underline{\qquad}$ did not check to see that $\underline{\hspace{7cm}}$.

24. Since $3\sqrt{3} \bigcirc 6$, $\underline{\qquad}$ is the length

of the hypotenuse c.

$a^2 + b^2 = c^2$

$\underline{\hspace{2cm}} + \underline{\hspace{2cm}} = \underline{\hspace{2cm}}$

$\underline{\hspace{2cm}} = \underline{\hspace{2cm}}$

The side lengths $\underline{\hspace{2cm}}$ form a

Pythagorean triple.

25. $PQ = \sqrt{(\underline{\ } - \underline{\ })^2 + (\underline{\ } - \underline{\ })^2} = \underline{\quad}$

$QR = \sqrt{(\underline{\ } - \underline{\ })^2 + (\underline{\ } - \underline{\ })^2} = \underline{\quad}$

$RS = \sqrt{(\underline{\ } - \underline{\ })^2 + (\underline{\ } - \underline{\ })^2} = \underline{\quad}$

$PS = \sqrt{(\underline{\ } - \underline{\ })^2 + (\underline{\ } - \underline{\ })^2} = \underline{\quad}$

$PQRS$ $\underline{\hspace{2cm}}$ a rhombus.

26. **a.** $\dfrac{5x^2y^2}{3x^3y^3} \cdot \dfrac{9xy^2}{25xy^3} = \dfrac{45x^{\square}y^{\square}}{\square x^4y^{\square}} = \dfrac{\square}{\square xy^{\square}}$

b. $\dfrac{5x^2y^2}{3x^3y^3} \cdot \dfrac{9xy^2}{25xy^3} = \dfrac{\square}{3x^{\square}} \cdot \dfrac{9}{25^{\square}} = \dfrac{\square}{\square xy^{\square}}$

c. I prefer _____ because _____

_____.

---

27. $|x - 974.6| \le 0.1$

$x - 974.6$ ◯ ____ AND $x - 974.6$ ◯ ____

x ◯ ____ AND x ◯ ____

____ ◯ x ◯ ____

⟵————————————⟶

---

28. $Rate = \dfrac{distance}{time}$

a. $\dfrac{2x^2 - 4x}{7x^3} \div \dfrac{3x - 6}{9x} = \dfrac{2x^2 - 4x}{7x^3} \cdot \dfrac{9x}{3x - 6} = \dfrac{2x\left(\square - \square\right)}{7x^3} \cdot \dfrac{9x}{3\left(x - \square\right)} = $ ____ mi per hour

b. $\dfrac{\square}{\square x} \div \dfrac{1}{x^2} = \dfrac{\square}{\square x} \cdot \dfrac{x^2}{1} = $ ____ mi per hour

---

29. $\dfrac{remainder}{divisor}$

$= $ _____

30. parent quadratic function:

$f(x) = $ _____

Its graph is a _____, which opens

_____ with its vertex at the

_____, (____ , ____).

Solving Quadratic Equations Using Square Roots page 684

New Concepts

• To solve a quadratic equation in the form $x^2 = a$, take the square root of both sides.

Example **Solving $x^2 = a$**

Solve each equation.

$x^2 = 25$

$\sqrt{x^2} = \pm\sqrt{25}$ *Take the square root of both sides.*

$x = 5 \text{ or } x = -5$

$\mathbf{x = \pm 5}$ *Combine and use ± symbol.*

$x^2 = -16$

$\sqrt{x^2} = \pm\sqrt{-16}$ *Take the square root of both sides.*

$x \neq \pm\sqrt{-16}$ *No real number squared can be negative.*

There is no real-number solution.

• Numbers that are not perfect squares have irrational roots. Use a calculator to approximate their roots.

Example **Approximating Solutions**

Solve each equation.

$x^2 = 40$

$\sqrt{x^2} = \pm\sqrt{40}$ *Take the square root of both sides.*

$\sqrt{x^2} = \pm\sqrt{4 \cdot 10}$ *Simplify the radical number.*

$x = \pm 2\sqrt{10}$ *Product Property of Radicals*

$x \approx \pm 2 \cdot 3.16227766$ *Write the approximate value.*

$\mathbf{x \approx \pm 6.325}$ *Multiply.*

$8x^2 - 24 = 100$

$8x^2 = 124$ *Add 24 to both sides.*

$x^2 = 15.5$ *Divide both sides by 8.*

$\sqrt{x^2} = \pm\sqrt{15.5}$ *Take the square root of both sides.*

$x \approx \pm 3.937003937$ *Find the approximate square root.*

$\mathbf{x \approx \pm 3.937}$ *Round to the nearest thousandth.*

Solve each equation.

a. $x^2 = 81$

$\sqrt{x^2} = \pm\sqrt{\underline{}}$ $x = \pm\underline{}$

There _____ real-number solution.

b. $x^2 = -36$

$\sqrt{x^2} = \pm\sqrt{\underline{}}$

There _____ real-number solution.

c. $x^2 + 5 = 54$

$x^2 + 5 - \underline{} = 54 - \underline{}$

$x^2 = \underline{}$

$x = \pm\sqrt{\underline{}}$

$x = \underline{}$

d. $3x^2 - 75 = 0$

$3x^2 - 75 + \underline{} = 0 + \underline{}$

$3x^2 = \underline{}$

$\dfrac{3x^2}{\square} = \dfrac{\square}{\square}$

$x^2 = \underline{}$

$x = \pm\sqrt{\underline{}}$

$x = \underline{}$

e. $x^2 = 72$

$x = \pm\sqrt{\underline{}}$

$x = \pm\sqrt{\underline{} \cdot \underline{}}$

$x = \pm\underline{}\sqrt{\underline{}}$

$x \approx \pm\underline{}$

f. $5x^2 - 60 = 0$

$x^2 = \underline{}$

$x = \pm\sqrt{\underline{}}$

$x = \pm\sqrt{\underline{} \cdot 15}$

$x = \pm\underline{}\sqrt{\underline{}}$

$x \approx \pm\underline{}$

g. A golf ball is dropped from a height of 1600 feet. Use $16t^2 - 1600 = 0$ to find how many seconds t it takes for the ball to hit the ground.

$16t^2 - 1600 = 0$

$t^2 = \underline{}$

$t = \pm\underline{}$ *Time is always positive.*

It takes _____ for the ball to hit the ground.

1. Use the rules of exponents.

$4(2p^{-2}q)^2(3p^3q)^2$

$= 4\left(\underline{\quad}p^{\square}\underline{\quad}q^{\square}\right)\left(\underline{\quad}p^{\square}\underline{\quad}q^{\square}\right)$

$= \underline{\hspace{3cm}}$

2. $\left(7\sqrt{8}\right)^2$

$= 7^{\square}(\sqrt{8})^{\square}$

$= \underline{\quad\quad}(\underline{\quad\quad})$

$= \underline{\quad\quad}$

---

3. Student $\underline{\quad}$ is correct. Student $\underline{\quad}$ did not realize that a $\underline{\hspace{2cm}}$ measurement $\underline{\quad}$ possible in this situation.

---

4. a. Area of property $=$ area of yard $+$ area of house

$x =$ side length of property

$x^2 = \underline{\hspace{2cm}} + \underline{\hspace{2cm}}$

b. $x^2 = \underline{\hspace{2cm}}$

$\sqrt{\underline{\quad\quad}} = \pm\sqrt{\underline{\quad\quad}}$

$x = \underline{\hspace{2cm}}$

c. $P = 4x$

$P = 4(\underline{\hspace{1.5cm}}) = \underline{\hspace{2cm}}$

---

5. $1000(1 + r)^2 = 1123.6$

$(1 + r)^2 = \underline{\hspace{2.5cm}}$

$(1 + r) = \pm\sqrt{\underline{\quad\quad}}$

$r \approx \pm\underline{\hspace{1.5cm}} - \underline{\quad}$

$r \approx \underline{\quad}$ OR $r \approx \underline{\quad}$ $\underline{\quad}\%$

6. $8(\underline{\quad})^2 - 72 = 0$

$\underline{\quad} - \underline{\quad} = 0$ $\underline{\quad} = 0$

$8(\underline{\quad})^2 - 72 = 0$

$\underline{\quad} - \underline{\quad} = 0$ $\underline{\quad} = 0$

$x = \pm3$ is $\underline{\hspace{2cm}}$

---

7. $s^2 = \underline{\hspace{1.5cm}}$

$\sqrt{\underline{\quad\quad}} = \pm\sqrt{\underline{\quad\quad}}$

$s = \pm\sqrt{\underline{\quad\quad}} \cdot \underline{\quad}$

$s = \pm\underline{\quad}\sqrt{\underline{\quad}}$

$s \approx \underline{\hspace{1.5cm}}$

8. $\dfrac{|x|}{3} + 6 < 13$

$\dfrac{|x|}{3} < \underline{\hspace{1.5cm}}$

$|x| < \underline{\hspace{1.5cm}}$

$\underline{\hspace{2.5cm}}$ AND $\underline{\hspace{2cm}}$

$\underline{\quad}\bigcirc x \bigcirc\underline{\quad}$

---

9. **a.** $|x + 1| - 8 \le -4$

$|x + 1| \le$ _____

$x + 1 \le$ ____   AND $x + 1 \ge 4$

x ◯ ____   AND $x \le 3$

____ $\le x$ ◯ ____

b. $|y - 4| + 6 \le 9$

$|y - 4| \le$ _____

$y - 4$ ◯ ____ $y - 4 \le$ ____

y ◯ ____ $y \le$ ____

____ $\le y \le$ ____

c. $(-5, 1),$ (____, ____),

(____, ____), (____, ____)

10.

$$-7x^2 \qquad - x + 7$$
$$\underline{\times \qquad\qquad x - 7}$$
$$\Box x^2 + \Box x - 49$$
$$\underline{-7x^\Box - x^\Box + \Box x}$$

11. $y = 4x^2 + 6$

axis of symmetry: $x = -\dfrac{b}{2a} =$ _____

vertex: (____, ____)

2 other points: (____, ____), (____, ____)

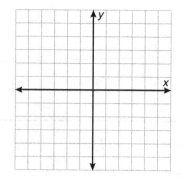

12. $h = -16t^2 + 30$

Substitute.

$h = -16(\text{____})^2 + 30$

$h =$ _____

13. **a.** $|t - (-187.65)| < 1.65$

$t + 187.65 >$ ____   AND $t + 187.65 < 1.65$

$t >$ ____   AND $t <$ ____

____ $< t <$ ____

b. boiling point: _____   melting point: _____

14. **a.** $x^2 + 10x + 25 = (x +$ _____$)(x +$ _____$) =$ _____

b. $x^2 - 25 = (x +$ _____$)(x -$ _____$)$

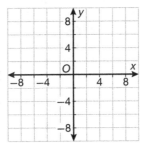

15. $5x + 4y > 20$

$4y >$ _____ + _____

$y >$ _____ + _____

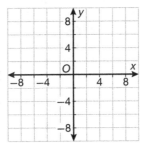

---

16. $x =$ *packs of paper* $y =$ *sets of paint*

_____ + _____ ≤ 40

 Graph.

---

17. $x(x + 12) = 0$

$x =$ _____   OR $x + 12 =$ _____

$x =$ _____

{ _____ , _____ }

---

18. *Substitute.*

$\dfrac{1}{x - 1} = \dfrac{3}{2x - 2}$

$\dfrac{1}{\square - 1} = \dfrac{3}{2(1) - 2}$

$\dfrac{1}{\square} = \dfrac{3}{\square}$

Since the fractions $\frac{1}{0}$ and $\frac{3}{0}$ are

_____ , this shows that _____ is

an _____ solution.

---

19. $\dfrac{2}{x - 3} = \dfrac{x}{9}$

extraneous solution: $x =$ _____

Find the cross products.

$$x(x - 3) = 2(\underline{\quad})$$

$$x^{\square} - 3 \underline{\quad} = \underline{\quad}$$

$$x^{\square} - 3 \underline{\quad} - \underline{\quad} = 0$$

$$(x - \underline{\quad})(x + 3) = 0$$

Circle the solution for the equation.

A $\{3, 6\}$ **B** $\{-3, 6\}$

C $\{3, -6\}$ **D** $\{6\}$

---

20. $\dfrac{m}{m^2 - 4} + \dfrac{2}{3m + 6} = \dfrac{m}{(m - \square)(m + \square)} + \dfrac{2}{3(m + \square)}$ LCD: _____(_____)(_____)

$\dfrac{\square}{\square} \cdot \dfrac{m}{(m - \square)(m + \square)} + \dfrac{(m - \square)}{(m - \square)} \cdot \dfrac{2}{3(m + \square)} = \dfrac{3m + \square m - \square}{\square(m - \square)(m + \square)}$

$= \dfrac{\square m - \square}{\square(m - \square)(m + \square)}$

---

21. Graph both functions.

 Student _____ is correct. Student _____ wrote an equation that forms a _____

that crosses the _____-axis _____ , so it has _____ solutions.

---

22. Graph $h(t) = -16t^2 + 4t + 10$.

vertex: (___, ___)

greatest value of h: _____

x-intercepts: _____ , _____

positive value of t: _____

23. axis of symmetry: $x = -\dfrac{b}{2a} =$ _____

vertex: (_____ , _____)

2 other points: (___ , ___), (___ , ___)

Graph the function.

Solution: _____

24. $\left(\dfrac{\square + \square}{2}, \dfrac{\square + \square}{2} \right)$

$= ($ _____ , _____ $)$

25. $-3y^3 - 9yz + 5y^2 + 15z$

$= -3y(\_\_ + \_\_) + \_\_(\_\_ + \_\_)$

$= (\_\_\_ + \_\_\_)(\_\_\_ + \_\_\_)$

26. a. $x =$ width; $x + 7 =$ length   Area: $($ ____ $)($ _____ $) =$ _____

To solve, the formula needs to be set in the form _____ in order to solve for _____.

b. $x^2 +$ _____ $-$ _____ $= 0$ Use the Quadratic Formula to solve.

$x =$ _____ OR $x =$ _____   width: _____   length: _____

27. $a^2 + b^2 = c^2$

_____ $+$ _____ $=$ _____

_____ $=$ _____

3, 7, and 8 _____ a

Pythagorean triple.

28. *Simplify the distance expression.*

Distance: _____

 *To find the rate divide the distance by the time.*

Rate: _____ $\dfrac{\text{miles}}{\text{minute}}$

29. a. $\dfrac{x^2 - 64}{x + 8} = \dfrac{(x - \square)(x + \square)}{x + 8} =$ ____

b. $x^3 - 2x^2 - 64x + 128$

$= \_\_(x - 2) - 64(x - \_\_)$

$=$ _____

$length = \dfrac{area}{width}$

$\dfrac{(x - \square)(x - \square)(x + \square)}{(x - \square)}$

$=$ _____ feet

30. When the operations are on the inside, write two _____ to represent the absolute-value equation and _____ each. When the operations are on the outside, first _____ the absolute value, then write two _____ to represent the absolute value equation and _____ each.

Name _____

Dividing Radical Expressions page 691

New Concepts

- To divide radical expressions, use the quotient Property of Radicals:
$$\sqrt[n]{\frac{a}{b}} = \frac{\sqrt[n]{a}}{\sqrt[n]{b}}, \text{ where } b \neq 0.$$

- A radical expression in simplest form CANNOT have:

  a fraction for a radicand, or

  a radical in the denominator.

Example **Rationalizing the Denominator**

Simplify $\sqrt{\frac{7}{3}}$.

$= \dfrac{\sqrt{7}}{\sqrt{3}}$ *Quotient Property of Radicals*

$= \dfrac{\sqrt{7}}{\sqrt{3}} \cdot \dfrac{\sqrt{3}}{\sqrt{3}}$ *Multiply by 1 to make the radicand in the denominator a perfect square.*

$= \dfrac{\sqrt{7 \cdot 3}}{\sqrt{3 \cdot 3}}$ *Multiplication Property of Radicals*

$= \dfrac{\sqrt{21}}{\sqrt{9}} = \dfrac{\sqrt{21}}{3}$ *Multiply. Simplify the square root.*

- When the denominator is a binomial containing a radical $(a + \sqrt{b})$, use the conjugate $(a - \sqrt{b})$ to rationalize the denominator.

Example **Using Conjugates to Rationalize the Denominator**

Simplify $\dfrac{3}{4 + \sqrt{5}}$.

$= \dfrac{3}{4 + \sqrt{5}} \cdot \dfrac{4 - \sqrt{5}}{4 - \sqrt{5}}$ *Use the conjugate of $4 + \sqrt{5}$.*

$= \dfrac{12 - 3\sqrt{5}}{16 - 4\sqrt{5} + 4\sqrt{5} - 5}$ *Use the Distributive Property and FOIL.*

$= \dfrac{12 - 3\sqrt{5}}{11}$ or $\dfrac{12}{11} - \dfrac{3\sqrt{5}}{11}$ *Combine like terms. Simplify.*

Simplify. All variables represent non-negative numbers.

a. *Rationalize the denominator.*

$$\sqrt{\frac{5}{3}} = \frac{\sqrt{5}}{\sqrt{3}} \cdot \frac{\sqrt{\square}}{\sqrt{3}} = \frac{\sqrt{\square}}{\square}$$

b. $\sqrt{\frac{11}{x}} = \frac{\sqrt{\square}}{\sqrt{x}} \cdot \frac{\sqrt{\square}}{\sqrt{\square}} = \frac{\sqrt{\square}x}{\square}$

c. *First, factor out perfect squares and then simplify.*

$$\frac{\sqrt{6x^6}}{\sqrt{27x}} = \frac{\sqrt{6 \cdot x^2 \cdot x^{\square} \cdot x^{\square}}}{\sqrt{9 \cdot \square \cdot x}} = \frac{x^{\square}\sqrt{6}}{\square\sqrt{\square}x}$$

Rationalize the denominator.

$$= \frac{x^{\square}\sqrt{6}}{\square\sqrt{\square}x} \cdot \frac{\sqrt{\square}x}{\sqrt{\square}x} = \frac{x^3\sqrt{\square}x}{\square x} = \frac{\square x^3\sqrt{2x}}{\square x} = \frac{x^{\square}\sqrt{2x}}{\square}$$

d. *The conjugate of $a + \sqrt{b}$ is $a - \sqrt{b}$. Multiply by the conjugate to rationalize the denominator.*

$$\frac{3}{5 - \sqrt{6}} \qquad \text{conjugate of } 5 - \sqrt{6}: \underline{\quad} \bigcirc \sqrt{\square}$$

$$= \frac{3}{5 - \sqrt{6}} \cdot \frac{\square + \sqrt{\square}}{\square + \sqrt{\square}} = \frac{15 + \square\sqrt{6}}{25 - \square\sqrt{6} + 5\sqrt{6} - \square} = \frac{15 + \square\sqrt{6}}{\square}$$

e. $\dfrac{3}{\sqrt{7} - 1} \qquad \text{conjugate of } \sqrt{7} - 1: \sqrt{\underline{\quad}} \bigcirc \underline{\quad}$

$$= \frac{3}{\sqrt{7} - 1} \cdot \frac{\sqrt{\square} \bigcirc \square}{\sqrt{\square} \bigcirc \square}$$

Multiply by the conjugate of $\sqrt{7} - 1$.

$$= \frac{3\sqrt{\square} \bigcirc \square}{\square \bigcirc \square}$$

Use the Distributive Property and FOIL to simplify.

$$= \frac{\square(\sqrt{\square} \bigcirc \square)}{\square}$$

Factor the numerator and divide out common factors.

$$= \frac{\sqrt{\square} \bigcirc \square}{\square}$$

Simplify.

1. Rationalize the denominator. Multiply the numerator and denominator by $\sqrt{7}$.

$$\frac{35}{\sqrt{7}} \cdot \frac{\sqrt{\Box}}{\sqrt{\Box}}$$

$$= \frac{35\sqrt{\Box}}{\Box} = \underline{\quad}\sqrt{\underline{\quad}}$$

2. Use cross products.

$$(x - 1)(\underline{\quad}) = (\underline{\quad})(\underline{\quad})$$

$$(x \bigcirc \underline{\quad})(x \bigcirc \underline{\quad}) = 0$$

$$x = \underline{\quad} \quad \text{OR} \quad x = \underline{\quad}$$

---

3. Student _____ is correct.

Student _____ did not use a _____ to _____ the denominator.

---

4. Substitute 150 for W. Then factor out perfect squares.

$$V = \sqrt{\frac{2 \cdot \Box}{0.0063}} = \frac{\Box\sqrt{\Box}}{\sqrt{\Box}}$$

Multiply the numerator and denominator by 10,000 to clear the decimal.

$$V = \frac{\Box\sqrt{\Box} \cdot 10,000}{\sqrt{\Box}}$$

Factor out perfect squares. Then rationalize.

$$V = \underline{\qquad\qquad}$$

5. Use a proportion to find 400% of 40.

$$\frac{x}{\Box} = \frac{\Box}{\Box}$$

$$x = \underline{\qquad}$$

---

6. _____ because the _____ in the

denominator needs to be _____.

7. $239 \div \sqrt{239} = \underline{\qquad}$

---

8. **a.** $s + \underline{\quad} = \underline{\quad}$ $\qquad s = \underline{\qquad}$

b. $A = \underline{\quad}^2 = \underline{\qquad}$

c. $9x^2 = \underline{\qquad}$

Linear measures must be positive.

$$x = \underline{\quad}$$

9. Isolate the variable and solve.

$$25t^2 = \underline{\qquad}$$

$$t = \pm\sqrt{\underline{\qquad}}$$

The number of seconds must be positive.

$$t \approx \underline{\qquad\qquad}$$

---

10. *Isolate y.*

$4x + 2y = 22$

$y = \underline{\hspace{0.8cm}}x + \underline{\hspace{0.8cm}}$

Substitute.

$6x - 5(\underline{\hspace{0.6cm}}x + \underline{\hspace{0.6cm}}) = 9$

$x = \underline{\hspace{1cm}}$

$(\underline{\hspace{0.6cm}}, \underline{\hspace{0.6cm}})$

---

11. $5x^2 = \underline{\hspace{1.5cm}}$

$x^2 = \underline{\hspace{1.5cm}}$

$x = \pm\sqrt{\underline{\hspace{1.5cm}}} = \pm\underline{\hspace{0.6cm}}\sqrt{\underline{\hspace{0.8cm}}}$

So, the given answer is $\underline{\hspace{2cm}}$.

12. $-6|x| + 20 \geq 2$

$-6|x| \geq \underline{\hspace{1.5cm}}$

$|x| \bigcirc \underline{\hspace{1.5cm}}$

$\underline{\hspace{1cm}} \bigcirc x \bigcirc \underline{\hspace{1cm}}$

```
<-+--+--+--+--+--+--+--+--+--+--+--+->
      -4  -2   0   2   4
```

---

13. *Isolate y.*

$2y > \underline{\hspace{1.5cm}}x + 6$

$y > \underline{\hspace{1.5cm}}x + \underline{\hspace{0.8cm}}$

📝 Graph the inequality on a coordinate grid.

14. Student $\underline{\hspace{1cm}}$ is correct. When dividing each side by $\underline{\hspace{1cm}}$, Student $\underline{\hspace{1cm}}$ did not $\underline{\hspace{2.5cm}}$ the inequality sign when $\underline{\hspace{2cm}}$ each side by $\underline{\hspace{1cm}}$.

---

15. *Isolate the absolute value expression.*

$\left|\dfrac{x}{7} + 6\right| \leq \underline{\hspace{1.5cm}}$

$\dfrac{x}{7} + 6 \bigcirc \underline{\hspace{1.5cm}}$

$x \bigcirc \underline{\hspace{1.5cm}}$

$\dfrac{x}{7} + 6 \bigcirc \underline{\hspace{1.5cm}}$

$x \bigcirc \underline{\hspace{1.5cm}}$

The length is the absolute value of the difference of the endpoints.

$|\underline{\hspace{1.5cm}} - \underline{\hspace{1.5cm}}| = \underline{\hspace{1cm}}$

length of segment: $\underline{\hspace{1.5cm}}$

---

16. $\left|d - \underline{\hspace{1.5cm}}\right| \leq \underline{\hspace{1.5cm}}$

greatest acceptable diameter: $\underline{\hspace{1.5cm}}$

17. $b = 0$

axis of symmetry: $x = -\dfrac{b}{2a} = \underline{\hspace{1.5cm}}$

vertex: $(\underline{\hspace{0.8cm}}, \underline{\hspace{0.8cm}})$

📝 Graph.

Find a point to the left or right of the axis of symmetry, then reflect it across the axis of symmetry.

18. When the ball is on the ground, $h =$ ___.

Substitute. Solve for t.

The ball is on the ground at _____ and _____.

---

19. $f(x) = x^2 - 170x + 7000$

$$= (x \bigcirc \underline{\quad})(x \bigcirc \underline{\quad})$$

Set each factor equal to 0 and solve for x.

roots: _____ and _____

20. What are other names for the x-intercept of a function?

_____ or _____

---

21. 📎 Plot $(0, 2)$, $(-2, 6)$, and $(6, 14)$. Sketch the graph.

The parabola opens _____, so the coefficient of x^2 must be _____.

Choice(s) _____ can be eliminated.

Substitute each point in the remaining choices and eliminate choices that are not satisfied by the point.

Answer: _____

---

22. *Factor by grouping.*

$$2x^2y + 4xy - 7xyz - 14yz = \underline{\quad}xy(\underline{\quad} + \underline{\quad}) \bigcirc \underline{\quad}yz(\underline{\quad} + \underline{\quad})$$

$$= (\underline{\quad}xy \bigcirc \underline{\quad}yz)(\underline{\quad} \bigcirc \underline{\quad})$$

---

23. $\dfrac{90}{24a} \cdot \dfrac{6a^2b^2}{25b}$

Divide out common factors.

$= $ _____

24. $a^2 + b^2 = c^2$

They _____ form a Pythagorean triple.

---

25. a. $D = rt$, so $t = \frac{d}{r}$

$t_{\text{west}} = \dfrac{\boxed{}}{\boxed{} + w}$ $\qquad$ $t_{\text{east}} = \dfrac{\boxed{}}{\boxed{} - w}$

The numerators represent

_____. The denominators

represent _____. Going with the

wind, _____ the wind speed to the

rate. Going against the wind,

_____ it.

b. Add and simplify.

_____

c. The simplified expression represents

_____

_____

_____

---

26. *Divide the area by the length to find the width.*

$$\frac{x^2 - 14x + 45}{x - 5}$$

The width of the garden is _____.

27. a. charge for 2 bikes for x hours:

_____(_____x + _____)

equation:

$\left| \underline{}(\underline{}x + \underline{}) - 66 \right| =$ _____

b. 📓 Solve.

min.: _____ $\qquad$ max.: _____

---

28. To find $\dfrac{4y - 5}{6}$ as the difference of two rational expressions, write each term in the

_____ separately over the _____. Simplify, if

possible, to get _____.

---

29. It _____ be factored.

The whole-number factors of 1 are _____.

_____ of the whole-number factors

of 1 will produce a _____ term

of x.

30. *Compare the graphs of $f(x) = x^2$ and $f(x) = 2x^2$.*

A vertically stretched parabola is

_____ than the parent function.

Solving Quadratic Equations by Completing the Square page 697

New Concepts

- To complete the square of $x^2 + bx$, add $\left(\frac{b}{2}\right)^2$ to the expression.

Math Language

Completing the square is a process used to form a perfect-square trinomial.

Exploration page 698

Use your textbook to complete the exploration.

Example Solving $x^2 + bx = c$ by Completing the Square

Solve $x^2 + 10x = 11$ by completing the square.

$$x^2 + 10x + \underline{\quad} = 11$$

$$x^2 + 10x + \left(\frac{10}{2}\right)^2 = 11 + \left(\frac{10}{2}\right)^2 \quad \textit{Add } \left(\frac{b}{2}\right)^2 \textit{ to both sides.}$$

$$x^2 + 10x + (5)^2 = 11 + (5)^2 \quad \textit{Simplify the fraction.}$$

$$x^2 + 10x + 25 = 11 + 25 \quad \textit{Simplify.}$$

$$(x + 5)^2 = 36 \quad \textit{Factor the left side. Simplify the right.}$$

$$\sqrt{(x + 5)^2} = \pm\sqrt{36} \quad \textit{Take the square root of both sides.}$$

$$x + 5 = \pm 6 \quad \textit{Simplify.}$$

$$x + 5 = 6 \quad \text{or} \quad x + 5 = -6 \quad \textit{Write as two equations.}$$

$$x = 1 \quad \text{or} \quad x = -11 \quad \textit{Subtract.}$$

- To use the completing-the-square method, the coefficient of the quadratic term (x^2) must be 1.

Example Solving $ax^2 + bx = c$ by Completing the Square

Solve $3x^2 - 12x = -54$ by completing the square.

$$\frac{3x^2 - 12x}{3} = -\frac{54}{3} \quad \textit{Divide both sides by coefficient of } x^2.$$

$$x^2 - 4x = -18 \quad \textit{Simplify.}$$

$$x^2 - 4x + \left(-\frac{4}{2}\right)^2 = -18 + \left(-\frac{4}{2}\right)^2 \quad \textit{Add } \left(\frac{b}{2}\right)^2 \textit{ to both sides.}$$

$$x^2 - 4x + 4 = -18 + 4 \quad \textit{Simplify.}$$

$$(x - 2)^2 = -14 \quad \textit{Factor the left side. Simplify the right.}$$

$$\sqrt{(x - 2)^2} = \pm\sqrt{-14} \quad \textit{Take the square root of both sides.}$$

$$x - 2 = \pm\sqrt{-14} \quad \textit{Simplify.}$$

$$x = 2 \pm\sqrt{-14} \quad \textit{Add 2 to both sides.}$$

No real number is the square root of a negative value.
There is no solution.

a. Complete the square: $x^2 + 24x$ $x^2 + 24x + \left(\dfrac{\square}{2}\right)^2 = x^2 + 24x +$ ____

Solve by completing the square.

b.
$$x^2 + 2x = 8$$
$$x^2 + 2x + \left(\dfrac{\square}{2}\right)^2 = 8 + \left(\dfrac{\square}{2}\right)^2$$
$$x^2 + 2x + \underline{\quad} = 8 + \underline{\quad}$$
$$(x + \underline{\quad})^2 = \underline{\quad}$$
$$\sqrt{(x - \underline{\quad})^2} = \pm\sqrt{\underline{\quad}}$$
$$x + \underline{\quad} = \pm\underline{\quad}$$
$$x = \underline{\quad} \text{ or } x = \underline{\quad}$$

c.
$$x^2 - 14x = 15$$
$$x^2 - 14x + (\underline{\quad})^2 = 15 + (\underline{\quad})^2$$
$$x^2 - 14x + \underline{\quad} = 15 + \underline{\quad}$$
$$(x - \underline{\quad})^2 = \underline{\quad}$$
$$\sqrt{(x - \underline{\quad})^2} = \pm\sqrt{\underline{\quad}}$$
$$x - \underline{\quad} = \pm\underline{\quad}$$
$$x = \underline{\quad} \text{ or } x = \underline{\quad}$$

d.
$$3x^2 + 24x = -27 \quad \textit{Divide both sides by coefficient of } x^2.$$
$$x^2 + \underline{\quad}x = \underline{\quad}$$
$$x^2 + 8x + \left(\dfrac{\square}{2}\right)^2 = -9 + \left(\dfrac{\square}{2}\right)^2$$
$$x^2 + 8x + \underline{\quad} = -9 + \underline{\quad}$$
$$(x + \underline{\quad})^2 = \underline{\quad}$$
$$\sqrt{(x + \underline{\quad})^2} = \pm\sqrt{\underline{\quad}}$$
$$x + \underline{\quad} = \pm\sqrt{\underline{\quad}}$$
$$x = \underline{\quad} + \sqrt{\underline{\quad}} \text{ or } x = \underline{\quad} - \sqrt{\underline{\quad}}$$

e.
$$2x^2 + 6x = -6$$
$$x^2 + \underline{\quad}x = \underline{\quad}$$
$$x^2 + 3x + \left(\dfrac{\square}{2}\right)^2 = -2 + \left(\dfrac{\square}{2}\right)^2$$
$$x^2 + 3x + \underline{\quad}.\underline{\quad} = -2 + \underline{\quad}.\underline{\quad}$$
$$(x + \underline{\quad}.\underline{\quad})^2 = -\underline{\quad}.\underline{\quad}$$
$$\sqrt{(x + \underline{\quad})^2} = \pm\sqrt{-\underline{\quad}.\underline{\quad}}$$
$$x + \underline{\quad}.\underline{\quad} = \pm\sqrt{-\underline{\quad}.\underline{\quad}}$$
There are _____ solutions because _____

_____ .

f. The area of a parallelogram is 20 cm. Its base is 8 cm more than its height. Find its dimensions.

height = h base = $h +$ ____

$A = h \cdot b = h(\underline{\quad\quad})$

Substitute. Complete the square.

$20 = h^2 + \underline{\quad}h$

$h^2 + \underline{\quad}h + \left(\dfrac{\square}{2}\right)^2 = \underline{\quad} + \left(\dfrac{\square}{2}\right)^2$

$h = \underline{\quad} \text{ or } h = \underline{\quad}$

Height must be a _____ value.

$h = \underline{\quad}$ ▨ $b = \underline{\quad}$ ▨

1. *Complete the square.*

$$c^2 + 100c + \left(\dfrac{\square}{\square}\right)^2$$

$$= c^2 + 100c + \underline{\hspace{1cm}}$$

2. $y^2 - 26y + \left(\dfrac{\square}{\square}\right)^2$

$$= y^2 - 26y + \underline{\hspace{1cm}}$$

---

3. $\left(\dfrac{\square}{2}\right)^2 = \underline{\hspace{1cm}}$

Circle the answer.

A −225   **B** −15

C 15   **D** 225

4. $6x^2 - 12x = \underline{\hspace{1cm}}$ Add $\underline{\hspace{0.6cm}}$ to both sides.

$$x^2 - \underline{\hspace{0.6cm}}x = \underline{\hspace{0.8cm}} \qquad \underline{\hspace{1cm}} \text{ both sides by } \underline{\hspace{0.6cm}}.$$

📓 Complete the solution. Justify each step.

---

5. $A_{\text{base}} = (\underline{\hspace{0.6cm}})(x + \underline{\hspace{0.6cm}}) = 24$

$$\underline{\hspace{1cm}} + \underline{\hspace{1cm}} = 24$$

📓 Solve for x by completing the square.

$$w = \underline{\hspace{1cm}} \qquad l = \underline{\hspace{1cm}} \qquad h = \underline{\hspace{1cm}}$$

6. $\dfrac{\sqrt{3}}{\sqrt{11}} \cdot \dfrac{\sqrt{\square}}{\sqrt{\square}}$

$$= \underline{\hspace{1.5cm}}$$

---

7. total cards for 1st pick: $\underline{\hspace{1cm}}$

total cards for 2nd pick: $\underline{\hspace{1cm}}$

$$P(\text{green then yellow}) = \dfrac{\square}{\square} \cdot \dfrac{\square}{\square}$$

$$= \dfrac{\square}{\square} = \dfrac{\square}{\square}$$

8. **a.** $A = \pi r^2$

$$r = \sqrt{\dfrac{\square}{\square}}$$

b. $r = \sqrt{\dfrac{\square}{\square}} = \sqrt{\dfrac{\square}{\square}}$

c. *Substitute $A = 6$ and simplify. Then rationalize the denominator.*

$$r = \sqrt{\dfrac{\square}{\square}} = \underline{\hspace{1.5cm}}$$

---

9. $D = \sqrt{(x_2 - x_1)^2 + (y_2 - y_1)^2}$

$AC = \sqrt{(\square - \square)^2 + (\square - \square)^2}$

$AC = \underline{\hspace{1cm}}$

10. *Draw a sketch. Label length and width.*

paper width $= 10 - 2(\underline{\hspace{0.3cm}} . \underline{\hspace{0.5cm}}) = \underline{\hspace{1cm}}$

paper length $= 8 - 2(\underline{\hspace{0.5cm}}) = \underline{\hspace{1cm}}$

image width $= \underline{\hspace{1cm}}$

image length $= \underline{\hspace{1cm}}$

11. $(18 \cdot \underline{\hspace{0.3cm}} . \underline{\hspace{0.5cm}})r^2 = 339.12$

$(\underline{\hspace{0.3cm}} . \underline{\hspace{0.5cm}})r^2 = 339.12$

$r^2 = \dfrac{339.12}{\square}$

$r = \pm\sqrt{\underline{\hspace{2cm}}}$

$r \approx \underline{\hspace{0.3cm}} . \underline{\hspace{1cm}}$

12. Student $\underline{\hspace{1cm}}$ is correct.

Student $\underline{\hspace{1cm}}$ did not correctly factor

$\underline{\hspace{2cm}}$ in the $\underline{\hspace{2cm}}$

denominator.

13. $\dfrac{x - 6}{x}$

undefined when $x = \underline{\hspace{1.5cm}}$

14. *Simplify. Set the equation equal to zero with the x^2-term positive. Factor.*

$32x - 3x = 24 - 4x^2$

$\underline{\hspace{0.5cm}}x^2 \bigcirc \underline{\hspace{0.5cm}}x \bigcirc \underline{\hspace{0.5cm}} = 0$

$(\underline{\hspace{0.5cm}}x - \underline{\hspace{0.5cm}})(\underline{\hspace{0.5cm}}x + \underline{\hspace{0.5cm}}) = 0$

$x = \underline{\hspace{1.5cm}}$ or $x = \underline{\hspace{1.5cm}}$

15. $x^2 = 100$

$x = \underline{\hspace{1.5cm}}$

16. When the ball hits the ground, $\underline{\hspace{1cm}} = 0$.

$-32t^2 + 12t + 2 = \underline{\hspace{1cm}}$

Divide each term by −2. Factor and solve.

$\underline{\hspace{0.5cm}}t^2 + \underline{\hspace{0.5cm}}t + \underline{\hspace{1cm}} = \underline{\hspace{0.5cm}}$

$(\underline{\hspace{1.5cm}})(\underline{\hspace{1.5cm}}) = \underline{\hspace{0.5cm}}$

The ball hits the ground in $\underline{\hspace{1cm}}$ second(s).

17. Pedro's rate: $\dfrac{1}{\square}$ fence/hr   Partner's rate: $\dfrac{1}{\square}$ fence/hr

Let h = hours to build fence together

$\dfrac{1}{\square}h + \dfrac{1}{\square}h = 1$ job   *Multiply by the LCD.*

____$h +$ ____$h =$ ____   ⟶ $h =$ ____

---

18. $x^2 -$ ____$x + 81 = 0$

axis of symmetry: $x = -\dfrac{b}{2a} =$ _____

vertex: (____ , ____)

two more points: (____ , ____) and (____ , ____)

 Solve by graphing.

$x =$ ____

19. *Cross multiply.*

$x($ ____ $) = (x - 20)($ ____ $)$

Distribute. Solve for x.

$x =$ ____

---

20. a. $-8|x + 7| \geq -24$

$|x + 7|\,\bigcirc$ _____

$x +$ ____ $\bigcirc$ _____ $x +$ ____ $\bigcirc$ _____

_____ $\bigcirc\ x\ \bigcirc$ _____

b. Choose two values in your solution. Verify.

---

21. $5x - 2\ \bigcirc$ ____ $5x - 2\ \bigcirc$ _____   Circle the answer.

Compare to the answer choices.

A $5x - 2 > -9$ **B** $5x - 2 > 9$

C $-9 < 5x - 2$ **D** $5x - 2 < 9$

---

22. Zeros occur when the graph crosses the

____-axis.

zero(s): _____

23. $\dfrac{49x^2 + 21xy}{5x^2} \cdot \dfrac{\square}{\square}$

 Factor completely. Divide out common factors. Multiply.

---

24. *Use FOIL and simplify.*

$(6y - 3)(6y + 3)$

$= \underline{\hspace{3cm}}$

25. GCF: \underline{\hspace{1cm}}

$4x^4 - 64 = \underline{\hspace{1cm}}(x^4 - \underline{\hspace{1cm}})$

$= \underline{\hspace{0.5cm}}(\underline{\hspace{1.5cm}})(\underline{\hspace{1.5cm}})$

$= \underline{\hspace{0.5cm}}(\underline{\hspace{1.5cm}})(\underline{\hspace{1.5cm}})(\underline{\hspace{1.5cm}})$

26. a. $\left| x - \underline{\hspace{1.5cm}} \right| \bigcirc \underline{\hspace{1cm}}$

   b. $x - \underline{\hspace{1.5cm}} \bigcirc \underline{\hspace{1cm}}$ $x - \underline{\hspace{1.5cm}} \bigcirc \underline{\hspace{1cm}}$

   $\underline{\hspace{1.5cm}} \bigcirc x \bigcirc \underline{\hspace{1cm}}$

27. $\text{Midpoint} = \left(\dfrac{x_1 + x_2}{2}, \dfrac{y_1 + y_2}{2} \right)$

$\text{Midpoint} = \left(\dfrac{\square + \square}{\square}, \dfrac{\square + \square}{\square} \right) = (\underline{\hspace{1cm}}, \underline{\hspace{1cm}})$

28. monthly cost for x minutes $= 10 + \underline{\hspace{0.3cm}}.\underline{\hspace{0.5cm}} x$

$\left| (10 + \underline{\hspace{0.3cm}}.\underline{\hspace{0.5cm}} x) - \underline{\hspace{0.5cm}} \right| \bigcirc \underline{\hspace{1cm}}$

$\left| \underline{\hspace{0.3cm}}.\underline{\hspace{0.5cm}} x - \underline{\hspace{0.5cm}} \right| \bigcirc \underline{\hspace{1cm}}$

$\underline{\hspace{0.3cm}}.\underline{\hspace{0.5cm}} x - \underline{\hspace{0.5cm}} \bigcirc \underline{\hspace{1cm}}$ $\underline{\hspace{0.3cm}}.\underline{\hspace{0.5cm}} x - \underline{\hspace{0.5cm}} \bigcirc \underline{\hspace{1cm}}$

$\underline{\hspace{1cm}} \bigcirc x \bigcirc \underline{\hspace{1cm}}$

minimum: \underline{\hspace{2cm}}   maximum: \underline{\hspace{2cm}}

29. To be able to add the numerators, you must first have common \underline{\hspace{4cm}}.

30. A quadratic function will have only one zero when the \underline{\hspace{2cm}} of its graph is on the \underline{\hspace{2cm}}.

Recognizing and Extending Geometric Sequences page 705

New Concepts

Math Language

A **sequence** is a list of numbers that often follows a rule. A **geometric sequence** has a constant ratio between consecutive terms. That ratio is the **common ratio**.

• To find the **common ratio** of a **geometric sequence**, divide any term by the previous term. You can use the common ratio of a geometric sequence to find more terms in the sequence.

Example **Extending Geometric Sequences**

Find the next four terms in the geometric sequence 2, 8, 32, 128, ...

Find the common ratio. Find the ratio of the first two terms. Then check by finding the ratio of other pairs of terms.

$$2 \longrightarrow 8 \longrightarrow 32 \longrightarrow 128$$

$$\frac{8}{2} = 4 \qquad \frac{32}{8} = 4 \qquad \frac{128}{32} = 4$$

The common ratio is **4.** Multiply by it to find the next four terms.

$$\times 4 \qquad \times 4 \qquad \times 4 \qquad \times 4$$

$$2, 8, 32, 128 \longrightarrow 512 \longrightarrow 2048 \longrightarrow 8192 \longrightarrow 32{,}768$$

Finding the nth Term of a Geometric Sequence

Let $A(n)$ equal the nth term of a geometric sequence, then
$$A(n) = ar^{n-1}$$
where a is the first term of the sequence and r is the common ratio.

Example **Finding the nth Term of a Geometric Sequence**

Find the 5th term of the geometric sequence 1.2, 7.2, 43.2, ...

Use the first two terms to find the common ratio.

$$\frac{7.2}{1.2} = 6$$

$A(n) = ar^{n-1}$ *Formula for the nth term of a geometric sequence*

$A(5) = 1.2(6)^{5-1}$ *Substitute 5 for n, 1.2 for a, and 6 for r.*

$A(5) = 1.2(6)^4$ *Simplify.*

$A(5) = \mathbf{1555.2}$ **5th term**

Find the common ratio for each geometric sequence.

a. $2 \longrightarrow 16 \longrightarrow 128 \longrightarrow 1024$

$\dfrac{16}{\square} =$ _____ $\qquad \dfrac{128}{\square} =$ _____ $\qquad \dfrac{\square}{\square} =$ _____ $\qquad$ common ratio: _____

b. $-162 \longrightarrow$ _____ $\longrightarrow$ _____ $\longrightarrow$ _____

$\dfrac{\square}{-162} =$ _____ $\qquad \dfrac{\square}{\square} =$ _____ $\qquad \dfrac{\square}{\square} =$ _____ $\qquad$ common ratio: $\dfrac{\square}{\square}$

c. $0.7 \longrightarrow$ _____ $\longrightarrow$ _____ $\longrightarrow$ _____

$\dfrac{\square}{\square} =$ _____ $\qquad \dfrac{\square}{\square} =$ _____ $\qquad \dfrac{\square}{\square} =$ _____ $\qquad$ common ratio: _____

Find the next four terms of each sequence.

d. common ratio: _____ $\div$ _____ $=$ _____

$\times$_____ $\qquad \times$_____ $\qquad \times$_____ $\qquad \times$_____

$5, -15, 45, -135,$ _____ _____ _____ _____

e. common ratio: _____ $\div$ _____ $= \dfrac{\square}{\square}$

$\times$_____ $\dfrac{\square}{\square} \qquad \times$_____ $\dfrac{\square}{\square} \qquad \times$_____ $\dfrac{\square}{\square} \qquad \times$_____ $\dfrac{\square}{\square}$

$336, 168, 84, 42,$ _____ _____ _____ _____

Use the formula $A(n) = ar^{n-1}$ to find the nth term of each sequence.

f. $n =$ _____, $a =$ _____, $r =$ _____

$A(\underline{}) =$ _____$(\underline{})^{\square - 1} =$ _____

g. $n =$ _____, $a =$ _____, $r =$ _____

$A(\underline{}) =$ _____$(\underline{})^{\square - 1} =$ _____

h. $n =$ _____, $a =$ _____, $r =$ _____

$A(\underline{}) =$ _____$(\underline{})^{\square - 1} =$ _____

i. $n =$ _____, $a =$ _____, $r =$ _____

$A(\underline{}) =$ _____$(\underline{})^{\square - 1} =$ _____

j. *Each minute, $\frac{1}{3}$ of the water is lost. So, after each minute, $\frac{2}{3}$ of the water remains. This is the common ratio.*

The first term (after 1 minute) $= \frac{9}{10} \cdot \frac{2}{3} = \dfrac{\square}{\square}$.

The fifth term is $A(5) = \dfrac{\square}{\square}\left(\dfrac{\square}{\square}\right)^{\square - 1} =$ _____

1. $-80 \longrightarrow 20 \longrightarrow -5 \longrightarrow 1\frac{1}{4}$

$\dfrac{\square}{\square} = $ _____ $\dfrac{\square}{\square} = $ _____ $\dfrac{\square}{\square} = $ _____ common ratio: _____

---

2. 4, 6, 9, 13.5, ... is a _____ sequence.

Circle the answer.

A $A(n) = 4(1.5)^n$

B $A(n) = 4(1.5)^{n-1}$

C $A(n) = 4(2)^{n-1}$

D $A(n) = 3(1.5)^n$

3. Let 2007 be the first term.

2012 is the _____ term.

common ratio: $100 - $ _____ $ = $ _____

$A(n) = ar^{n-1}$

$A(\underline{\quad}) = \underline{\qquad}(\underline{\quad})^{\square - 1}$

$\approx \underline{\qquad\qquad}$

---

4. _____, the formula to find the third term of a _____ series is

$A(3) = ar^2$. If the _____ term is not 0, the only way any term of

the series could equal 0 would be if _____ $= 0$. Since the second term is not _____, this

_____ be true. So the sequence _____ be geometric.

---

5. $a_n = a_{(n-1)} + d$

$a_n = a_{n-1} + $ _____

$a_1 = \dfrac{\square}{\square}$

$a_2 = a_1 + \dfrac{\square}{\square} = $ _____

$a_3 = a_{\square} + \dfrac{\square}{\square} = \underline{\quad}\dfrac{\square}{\square}$

$a_4 = a_{\square} + \dfrac{\square}{\square} = $ _____

6. $A(n) = ar^{n-1}$

$A(\underline{\quad}) = \underline{\quad}r^{\square - 1}$

$605 = \underline{\quad}r^{\square}$

$r^2 = $ _____

$r = \pm$ _____

possible rules: $A(n) = \underline{\quad}(\underline{\quad})^{n-1}$

$A(n) = \underline{\quad}(\underline{\quad})^{n-1}$

---

7. Complete the square by finding the missing term.

$= \left(\dfrac{\square}{\square}\right)^2 = (\underline{\quad})^2 = $ _____

8. _____, the correct value is $\underline{\quad}^2 = $ _____.

Dominic forgot to _____ the 14.

---

9. **a.** $A = lw$

$(\underline{\hspace{2cm}})(\underline{\hspace{2cm}}) = \underline{\hspace{1cm}}$

b. $x^2 + \underline{\hspace{1cm}} x = \underline{\hspace{1cm}}$

c. $\underline{\hspace{4cm}} = 0$

$(\underline{\hspace{1.5cm}})(\underline{\hspace{1.5cm}}) = 0$

$x = \underline{\hspace{1cm}}$ OR $x = \underline{\hspace{1.5cm}}$

width: $x = \underline{\hspace{1cm}}$

d. length: $2x = \underline{\hspace{2cm}}$

area of interior:

$(\underline{\hspace{0.7cm}})(\underline{\hspace{0.7cm}}) = \underline{\hspace{1.5cm}}$

area of border:

$\underline{\hspace{1.5cm}} - \underline{\hspace{1.5cm}} = \underline{\hspace{1.5cm}}$

10. $\dfrac{11x + 22}{22x^2 + 44x}$

$= \dfrac{\square(\square + \square)}{\square(\square + \square)}$

$= \dfrac{\square}{\square}, x \neq \underline{\hspace{0.8cm}}, \underline{\hspace{0.8cm}}$

11. $\dfrac{\sqrt{63}}{\sqrt{18}} = \dfrac{\sqrt{\overline{\square \cdot \square}}}{\sqrt{\overline{\square \cdot \square}}}$

$= \dfrac{\square\sqrt{\square}}{\square\sqrt{\square}}$

$= \dfrac{\square}{\square} \cdot \dfrac{\square}{\square} = \underline{\hspace{1.2cm}}$

12. $a^2 + b^2 = c^2$

$h^2 + (h + 14)^2 = \underline{\hspace{0.8cm}}^2$

$h^2 + h^2 + 28h + \underline{\hspace{0.8cm}} = \underline{\hspace{0.8cm}}$

$h^2 + 14h = \underline{\hspace{0.8cm}}$

$h^2 + 14h + \left(\dfrac{\square}{\square}\right)^2 = \underline{\hspace{0.8cm}} + \left(\dfrac{\square}{\square}\right)^2$

$h^2 + 14h + \underline{\hspace{0.8cm}} = \underline{\hspace{0.8cm}}$

$(h + \underline{\hspace{0.8cm}})(h + \underline{\hspace{0.8cm}}) = \underline{\hspace{0.8cm}}$

$h = \underline{\hspace{0.8cm}}$ or $h = \underline{\hspace{0.8cm}}$

height $= \underline{\hspace{1cm}}$; base $= \underline{\hspace{1cm}}$

13. Student $\underline{\hspace{0.8cm}}$ is correct. When rationalizing the denominator, Student $\underline{\hspace{0.8cm}}$ did not

$\underline{\hspace{4cm}}$ by an expression equivalent to $\underline{\hspace{0.8cm}}$.

14. $A_{cube} = 6s^2$

$$\sqrt{\dfrac{A}{6}} = \sqrt{\dfrac{\square}{6}}$$

$$= \dfrac{\sqrt{\square}}{\sqrt{\square}} \cdot \dfrac{\square}{\square} = \dfrac{\sqrt{\square}}{\square} = \underline{\quad\quad}$$

15. $14x^2 - 2x = 3 - 21x$

$$\underline{\hspace{4cm}} = 0$$

$$(\underline{\hspace{2cm}})(\underline{\hspace{2cm}}) = 0$$

$$(\underline{\hspace{1.5cm}}) = 0 \quad \text{or} \quad (\underline{\hspace{1.5cm}}) = 0$$

$$x = \underline{\hspace{1cm}} \quad \text{or} \quad x = \underline{\hspace{1cm}}$$

16. $\dfrac{\square}{\square}h + \dfrac{\square}{\square}h = 1$

Multiply by the LCD.

$$\dfrac{\square \cdot \square}{\square}h + \dfrac{\square \cdot \square}{\square}h = \square \cdot 1$$

$$\underline{\hspace{1.5cm}}h = \underline{\hspace{1.5cm}}$$

$$h = \underline{\hspace{1cm}}$$

17. $(a - b)^2 = a^2 - 2ab + b^2$

$$29^2 = (\underline{\hspace{1.5cm}} - \underline{\hspace{0.5cm}})^2$$

$$= \underline{\hspace{0.5cm}}^2 - 2(\underline{\hspace{0.5cm}})(\underline{\hspace{0.5cm}}) + \underline{\hspace{0.5cm}}^2$$

$$= \underline{\hspace{1.5cm}} - \underline{\hspace{1cm}} + \underline{\hspace{1cm}}$$

$$= \underline{\hspace{1cm}}$$

18. maximum value of $f(t)$: $\underline{\hspace{2cm}}$

zeros of function: $\underline{\hspace{2cm}}$

$t = \underline{\hspace{1.5cm}}$ when horseshoe hits

the ground.

19. $\underline{\hspace{1cm}} = 3t^2 + 8t - 70$

$3t^2 + 8t - \underline{\hspace{1cm}} = 0$

When $f(t) = 55$, $t \approx \underline{\hspace{2cm}}$.

20. $2|x| - 12 > -5$

$$2|x| > \underline{\hspace{1.5cm}}$$

$$|x| > \underline{\hspace{1.5cm}}$$

$$x \bigcirc \underline{\hspace{1cm}} \quad \text{or} \quad x \bigcirc \underline{\hspace{1cm}}$$

-4 -2   0   2   4

21. $4x^2 - 64 = 0$

$$\underline{\hspace{1cm}}(\underline{\hspace{2cm}}) = 0$$

$$(\underline{\hspace{1.5cm}})(\underline{\hspace{1.5cm}}) = 0$$

$$\underline{\hspace{2cm}} = 0 \quad \text{or} \quad \underline{\hspace{2cm}} = 0$$

$$x = \underline{\hspace{1.5cm}} \quad \text{or} \quad x = \underline{\hspace{1.5cm}}$$

Circle: true   false

22. Student $\underline{\hspace{1cm}}$ is correct. Student $\underline{\hspace{1cm}}$

added 460 to both sides of the equation

instead of subtracting.

23. vertex: ($\underline{\hspace{1cm}}$, $\underline{\hspace{1cm}}$)

The parabola has a $\underline{\hspace{3cm}}$

value, which is $\underline{\hspace{1cm}}$.

24. *Use the LCD.*

$$\frac{d}{d-10} + \frac{-1}{\Box} \cdot \frac{10}{10-d}$$

$$= \frac{d}{d-10} \bigcirc \frac{10}{\Box}$$

$$= \frac{\Box}{\Box} = \underline{\hspace{1cm}}$$

25. *Use the LCD.*

$$\Box \cdot \left(\frac{18}{2x} - 4\right) = \Box \cdot \frac{15}{3x}$$

$$\frac{\Box}{\Box} - \underline{\hspace{0.8cm}} = \frac{\Box}{\Box}$$

$$\underline{\hspace{0.8cm}} - \underline{\hspace{0.8cm}} = \underline{\hspace{0.8cm}}$$

$$x = \underline{\hspace{1cm}}$$

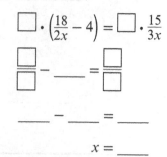 *Use substitution to check.*

26. **a.** $d = rt$, so $r = \dfrac{\Box}{\Box}$

$$r = \frac{\frac{4x-16}{x^3}}{\frac{\Box}{\Box}} = \frac{\Box}{\Box} \cdot \frac{\Box}{\Box} = \frac{\Box}{\Box} \,\blacksquare$$

b. $\dfrac{\frac{\Box}{\Box}}{\frac{\Box}{\Box}} = \frac{\Box}{\Box} \cdot \frac{\Box}{\Box} = \frac{\Box}{\Box}\,\blacksquare$

27. *Use the LCD.*

$$\frac{8x^2}{x^2 - 11x + 18} - \frac{2}{8x - 72}$$

$$= \frac{8x^2}{(\Box - \Box)(\Box - \Box)} - \frac{2}{\Box(\Box - \Box)}$$

$$= \frac{8x^2}{(\Box - \Box)(\Box - \Box)} \cdot \frac{\Box}{\Box} - \frac{1}{(\Box - \Box)} \cdot \frac{\Box}{\Box}$$

$$= \underline{\hspace{1.5cm}}\,\blacksquare$$

28. $\left(\dfrac{\Box + \Box}{2}, \dfrac{\Box + \Box}{2}\right) = (\underline{\hspace{0.8cm}}, \underline{\hspace{0.8cm}})$

29. **a.** $f(t) = -16t^2 + vt + 0$

$$f(2) = -16(\underline{\hspace{0.5cm}})^2 + (\underline{\hspace{0.5cm}})(\underline{\hspace{0.5cm}}) + 0$$

$$= \underline{\hspace{1cm}}\,\blacksquare$$

b. 0 feet represents the _____ the ball was thrown from.

c. −48 feet represents _____ below the _____ of the cliff.

30. _____ and _____ are graphed with dashed boundary lines and _____ and _____ are graphed with solid boundary lines.

LESSON

106

Solving Radical Equations page 712

New Concepts

Math Language

An equation with a variable in the radicand is a **radical equation**.

Inverse operations undo each other.

• Use inverse operations to solve radical equations.

Example Solving Simple Radical Equations

Solve $\sqrt{x + 2} = 12$.

$\left(\sqrt{x + 2}\right)^2 = 12^2$	*Square both sides.*
$x + 2 = 144$	*Simplify.*
$x + 2 - 2 = 144 - 2$	*Subtract 2 from both sides.*
$x = 142$	

• When both sides of an equation are squared to solve an equation, the resulting equation may have solutions that do not satisfy the original equation.

Example Determining Extraneous Solutions

Solve $\sqrt{x} + 5 = -2$.

First isolate the radical.

$\sqrt{x} + 5 = -2$	
$\sqrt{x} + 5 - 5 = -2 - 5$	*Subtract 5 from both sides.*
$\sqrt{x} = -7$	*Simplify.*
$(\sqrt{x})^2 = (-7)^2$	*Square both sides.*
$x = 49$	

Check: $\sqrt{x} + 5 = -2$ *Substitute 49 for x.*

$\sqrt{49} + 5 \overset{?}{=} -2$

$7 + 5 \overset{?}{=} -2$

$12 \neq -2$

Math Language

A solution that does not satisfy the original equation is called an **extraneous solution**.

The solution $x = 49$ is extraneous. There is no solution.

Lesson Practice page 717

Solve each equation.

a. $\sqrt{x} = 6$

$(\sqrt{x})^2 = 6^2$

$x =$ _____

b. $\sqrt{5x} = 15$

$\left(\sqrt{5x}\right)^2 = 15^2$

$x =$ _____

c. $\sqrt{x + 3} = 12$

$\left(\sqrt{x + 3}\right)^2 = 12^2$

$x =$ _____

Isolate the radical expression before squaring both sides of the radical equation.

d. $\sqrt{4x - 15} = 7$

$4x - 5 =$ _____

$x =$ _____

e. $\sqrt{x} - 8 = 5$

$\sqrt{x} =$ _____

$x =$ _____

f. $\sqrt{x} + 8 = 15$

$\sqrt{x} =$ _____

$x =$ _____

g. $6\sqrt{x} = 24$

$\sqrt{x} =$ _____

$x =$ _____

h. $\dfrac{\sqrt{x}}{3} = 15$

$\sqrt{x} =$ _____

$x =$ _____

i. $\sqrt{x + 4} = \sqrt{2x - 1}$

$\left(\sqrt{x + 4}\right)^2 = \left(\sqrt{2x - 1}\right)^2$

$x +$ _____ $=$ _____ $-$ _____

_____ $= x$

j. *Rewrite with the radical expressions on opposite sides of the equal sign.*

$\sqrt{x + 5} - \sqrt{6x} = 0$

$\sqrt{x + 5} =$ _____

$($ _____ $)^2 = ($ _____ $)^2$

_____ $+$ _____ $=$ _____

_____ $= x$

k. $\sqrt{x - 2} = x - 4$

$($ _____ $)^2 = (x - 4)^2$

$x - 2 = x^2 -$ _____ $x +$ _____

$0 = x^2 -$ _____ $x +$ _____

Factor the quadratic equation.

$0 = ($ __ $\bigcirc$ __ $)($ __ $\bigcirc$ __ $)$

Set each factor equal to zero. Solve for x. Check for extraneous solutions.

$x =$ _____

l. $\sqrt{x} + 8 = -3$

$x =$ _____

Check for extraneous solutions.

There _____ solution.

m. $42 = (\sqrt{x}) \cdot [(\sqrt{x}) + (7 - \sqrt{x})]$

$42 = x + 7\sqrt{x} -$ _____

$42 =$ _____

_____ $= x$

area of the planter $= 42 -$ _____ $=$ _____ yd^2

---

1. *There are two solutions, use the ± sign.*

$x^2 = 64 \qquad x = \underline{\hspace{2cm}}$

2. $x^2 - 9x + 20$

$= (x \bigcirc \underline{\hspace{1.5cm}})(x \bigcirc \underline{\hspace{1.5cm}})$

---

3. Translate the inequality $3z + 4 < 10$ into a sentence.

_____

_____

4. *Find the equation that uses the inverse of division.*

Answer: _____

---

5. $\sqrt{x - 1} = \sqrt{3x + 2}$

$\left(\sqrt{x-1}\right)^2 = \left(\sqrt{3x+2}\right)^2$

solution: _____

When $x = $_____, the radicand

is _____.

6. *Isolate the radical.*

$\dfrac{\sqrt{x}}{4} = 32$

$\sqrt{x} = $ _____ \qquad _____.

$x = $ _____ \qquad _____ both sides.

---

7. *Divide each term by the previous term.*

$\dfrac{-9}{18} = $ ___ \qquad $\dfrac{4\frac{1}{2}}{-9} = $ ___ \qquad $\dfrac{-2\frac{1}{4}}{4\frac{1}{2}} = $ ___

The common ratio is $\dfrac{\square}{\square}$.

8. $A(n) = ar^{n-1}$

$a = $ _____, $r = $ _____, $n = $ _____

6th term: _____

---

9. $A(n) = ar^{n-1}$

   a. _____ $\cdot \, 0.75 =$ _____

   b. $A(n) = 0.75(0.75)^{n-1}$

      The bases are the same, add the exponents.

      $A(n) = 0.75^{\square}$

   c. 6th bounce $= 0.75^{\square} =$ _____

10. *The sequence is 1, 4, 16, ...*

   $r =$ _____ $A(n) = ar^{n-1}$

   $A(9) =$ _____ (_____)$^{9-1}$

   $=$ _____

   The area of each figure is 5 times the number of squares.

   $\text{Area}_{\text{9th figure}} =$ _____

11. *Isolate the radical expression before squaring.*

   $2\sqrt{x-4} =$ _____

   $\sqrt{x-4} =$ _____

      $x =$ _____

12. *Eliminate the x-terms.*

   $-5x + 4y = -37 \longrightarrow 3(-5x + 4y = -37)$

   $3x - 6y = 33 \quad \longrightarrow \quad 5(3x - 6y = 33)$

   📝 Solve the system.

   (_____ , _____)

13. *The sequence is 1, 3, 9, ...*

   $A(n) = ar^{n-1}$

   $r =$ _____ $a =$ _____

   $A(6) =$ _____ (_____)$^{6-1}$

      $=$ _____

14. $x^2 + 9x = 4.75$

   $x^2 + 9x + \left(\dfrac{9}{\square}\right)^2 = 4.75 + \left(\dfrac{9}{\square}\right)^2$

   📝 Complete the solution.

   $x =$ _____   or $x =$ _____

15. Student _____ is correct.

   Student _____ did not _____

   all terms by 2 in the first step.

16. Complete the square to solve for u.

   $u^2 - 0.8u =$ _____

   $u^2 - 0.8u + \left(\dfrac{0.8}{2}\right)^2 =$ _____ $+ \left(\dfrac{0.8}{2}\right)^2$

   📝 Complete the solution.

   The number of 1000 units u must be positive.

   $1000u =$ _____

17. *Multiply each term by the LCD.*

$$\frac{60}{4x} + \frac{45}{5x} = 3$$

$$x = \underline{\quad}$$

 Check your answer.

18. *Square both sides.*

$$\sqrt{x} = 9$$

$$x = \underline{\quad}$$

Check your answer.

19. *Find the h-value at the vertex to find the maximum height.*

$$t = -\frac{b}{2a} \qquad h = \underline{\quad}$$

Use the Zero function to determine t when $h = 0$.

$$t = \underline{\quad}$$

20. Graph the related function $f(x) = x^2 - 16$ on a coordinate grid.

axis of symmetry: $x = \underline{\quad}$

vertex: ($\underline{\quad}$, $\underline{\quad}$)

y-intercept: $\underline{\quad}$

additional points: ($\underline{\quad}$, $\underline{\quad}$), ($\underline{\quad}$, $\underline{\quad}$)

Solution: $x = \underline{\quad}$ and $x = \underline{\quad}$

21. *The difference between the weight of the ball and $2\frac{1}{12}$ ounces is $\frac{1}{12}$ ounce.*

least acceptable weight: $\underline{\quad}$

22. *Simplify before rationalizing.*

Circle the answer.

A $\frac{3}{2}$ **B** 3

C $\frac{6\sqrt{7}}{\sqrt{28}}$ **D** $\frac{6\sqrt{7}}{7}$

23. $\sqrt{145}$ is close to $\sqrt{\underline{\quad}}$, so for the numerator, Anton should find the square root of $\underline{\quad}$. The numerator is $\underline{\quad}$. For the denominator he should find the square root of 9. That is $\underline{\quad}$. Multiply it by 2. The denominator is $\underline{\quad}$. He should then divide the numerator by the denominator to estimate that the quotient is $\underline{\quad}$.

24. *Factor the denominator of the second term. Then determine the LCD.*

$$\frac{2r}{r - 4} - \frac{6}{12 - 3r}$$

$$= \frac{2r}{r - 4} \bigcirc \frac{6}{3r - \square}$$

$$= \underline{\quad}$$

25. $|x - 16| \leq 12$

$x - 16 \leq$ _____ AND $x - 16 \leq$ _____

_____ $\leq x \leq$ _____

```
  0   10   20   30
```

26. Divide using long division.

$$x + 5\overline{)9x^2 + 44x - 5}$$

$l =$ _____

27. $t = 1$ second, $v = 23$ ft/sec, $s = 3$ feet

Substitute.

$h = -16t^2 + vt + s$

$h =$ _____

28. a. _____ ◯ _____

b.

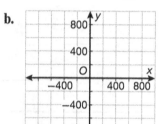

c. 📖 Check $(200, 400)$.

Answer: _____

29. The roots are the _____

of the constant term in each factor.

30. $f(x) = x^2 + bx + 3$

$x = -\dfrac{b}{2a}$

$4 = -\dfrac{b}{2 \cdot \square}$

$b =$ _____

New Concepts

• This is the graph of the absolute value parent function, $f(x) = |x|$. You can use the parent function to graph other absolute value functions

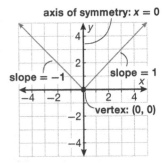

axis of symmetry: $x = 0$

slope = −1   slope = 1

vertex: (0, 0)

Example **Graphing Multiple Translations**

Graph the function $f(x) = |x - 4| + 1$ and give the coordinates of the vertex.

The graph is translated both vertically and horizontally.

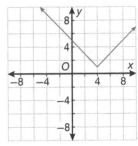

$$f(x) = |x - \textcircled{4}| + \textcircled{1}$$

Translate 4 units right.   Translate 1 unit up.
(4 > 0, so translate right.)   (1 > 0 so translate up.)

The vertex is (h, k). Since $h = 4$ and $k = 1$, **the vertex is (4, 1).**

• The absolute-value parent function can be reflected, stretched, or compressed by multiplying by a constant a.

Example **Reflecting, Stretching, and Compressing Absolute-Value Graphs**

Describe the graph of the function $f(x) = -0.2|x|$.

The parent function is multiplied by −0.2, so $a = -0.2$.

Since $-0.2 < 0$, the graph is reflected across the *x*-axis.

$|-0.2| = 0.2$

Since $0.2 < 1$, **the graph is compressed toward the *x*-axis.**

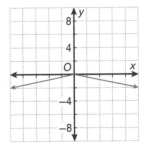

Graph each function and give the coordinates of the vertex.

a. $f(x) = |x| + 2$

x	−6	−2	0	2	6
y					

The vertex is (____, ____).

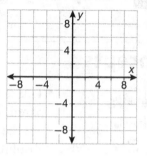

b. $f(x) = |x + 2|$

x	−8	−4	−2	4	8
y					

The vertex is (____, ____).

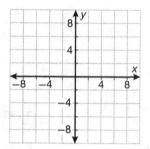

c. $f(x) = |x - 1| + 2$

Since h > 0 the graph of y = |x| translates 1 unit right.
Since k > 0, the graph of y = |x| translates 2 units up.

The vertex is (____, ____).

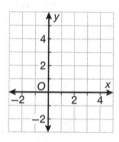

Describe the graph of each function.

d. $f(x) = 4|x|$ Since $|a| > 1$, the graph is _____ vertically.

e. $f(x) = -2|x|$ Since $a < 0$, the graph is reflected _____.

Since $|a| > 1$, the graph is _____ vertically.

f. $f(x) = -0.5|x|$ Since $a < 0$, the graph is _____.

Since $|a| < 1$, the graph is _____ vertically.

g. *In the equation f(t) = |t| + 25, a = 1, a is the rate.*

$f(t) = |t| + 25$ $f(t) = $ _____

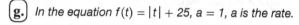

---

1. *For f(x) = |x| + k, the graph translates up if k > 0. It translates down if k < 0.*

$f(x) = |x| - 6$ shifts the parent function

_____.

2. $\sqrt{2x} = 14$

$2x =$ _____

$x =$ _____

Check the answer.

---

3. *See page 6 in the* Student Reference Guide.

$5y - 29 = -14x$

_____ = ____

4. *The graph of the parent function is reflected over the x-axis and stretched vertically.*

Circle the answer.

A $f(x) = 2|x|$ **B** $f(x) = 0.5|x|$

C $f(x) = -5|x|$ **D** $f(x) = -0.5|x|$

---

5. The sum of _____ times an unknown

number and _____ is greater than or

equal to _____.

6. *Find the vertex. Write the absolute value in the form f(x) = a|x - h| + k.*

$f(x) = \left|\frac{3}{5}x - 30\right| + 30$

$30 \div \frac{3}{5} =$ ____

$f(x) = \left|\frac{3}{5}(x - \underline{\quad})\right| + 30$

$f(x) = \underline{\quad}\left|(x - \underline{\quad})\right| + 30$

turning point: (____, ____)

---

7. The absolute-value function has a

minimum value that is the _____-value

at the vertex.

8. $4y = -3x - 4$

$4x + 6 = -5y$

(____, ____)

---

9. The length of a side $s = \sqrt{x}$ and $P = 20$.

$20 =$ _____

$x =$ _____ ▨

10. Student _____ is correct.

Student _____ _____ incorrectly and

should have _____

from each side first.

---

11. Factor the area.

$l = \dfrac{x^2 - 20x + 100}{(x - 10)}$

$= \dfrac{(\;\Box\;)(\;\Box\;)}{x - 10}$

$=$ _____ ▨

12. a. $l^2 = ($ _____ $)^2 + ($ _____ $)^2$

b. $l^2 =$ _____

_____ $=$ _____

c. Substitute 10 for l in the simplified equation.

$x =$ _____

---

13. Use substitution.

_____ $= \sqrt{x}$

Solve for y by substituting each value of x into $y = x$.

points: (_____ , _____) and (_____ , _____)

14. Divide each term by the previous term to find the common ratio.

$\dfrac{25}{125} =$ _____ $\dfrac{5}{25} =$ _____

next 3 terms: _____ , _____ , _____

---

15. $A(n) = ar^{n-1}$, $a = 50\%$, $r = \dfrac{1}{2}$, $n = 9$

Substitute.

$A(9) = ($ _____ $)($ _____ $)^{\Box}$

$\approx$ _____ ▨

16. Student _____ is correct.

Student _____ incorrectly multiplied by

_____ rather than using _____ as an

exponent.

---

17. Write the equation in standard form.

$$\underline{\hspace{4cm}} = 0$$

$x = \underline{\hspace{1cm}}$ and $x = \underline{\hspace{1cm}}$

18. Isolate the absolute value expression before squaring.

$|x - 4| + 15 \geq 21$

$x \leq \underline{\hspace{1cm}}$ OR $x \geq \underline{\hspace{1cm}}$

19. An absolute value cannot be negative.

$|x| + 45 \leq 34$

$|x| \leq \underline{\hspace{1.5cm}}$ $\{\underline{\hspace{0.8cm}}\}$

20. $|c - \underline{\hspace{1.5cm}}| \leq \underline{\hspace{1.5cm}}$

$\underline{\hspace{1.5cm}} \leq c \leq \underline{\hspace{1.5cm}}$

least acceptable circumference:

$c = \underline{\hspace{2cm}}$

21. a. $\pi(\underline{\hspace{2cm}})^2 = \underline{\hspace{2cm}}$

b.

$r = \underline{\hspace{2cm}}$

c. $d = \underline{\hspace{2cm}}$

22. Since $k > 0$, the graph of $f(x) = |x|$ translates up.

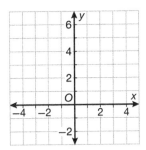

23. Write the equation in standard form.

Circle the answer.

A $x = -8$ or 0 **B** $x = -6$ or 2

C $x = 2$ or 6 **D** $x = 0$ or 8

24. $x^2 - 50x = c$

$x^2 - 50x + \left(\dfrac{b}{2}\right)^2 = c + \left(\dfrac{b}{2}\right)^2$

 Complete the square to find c. Substitute 50 for b.

$c \bigcirc \underline{\hspace{2cm}}$

25. Factor the denominators and divide out common factors.

$$\dfrac{\dfrac{4x}{2x + 12} + \dfrac{x}{3x + 18}}{\dfrac{8x^2}{x^2 + 8x + 12}}$$

= _____

26. Factor out perfect squares before rationalizing.

$$\sqrt{\dfrac{20}{3}}$$

= _____

27. Let x = number of items sold

a. $\left|\underline{\hspace{1cm}}x - \underline{\hspace{1cm}}\right| = \underline{\hspace{1cm}}$

b. Solve for x.

minimum: _____ items

maximum: _____ items

28. Write the inequality and then isolate y.

$\underline{\hspace{1cm}}x + \underline{\hspace{1cm}}y \bigcirc \underline{\hspace{1cm}}$

29. a. $l = \underline{\hspace{0.6cm}} + \underline{\hspace{0.6cm}}x$

$w = \underline{\hspace{0.6cm}} + \underline{\hspace{0.6cm}}x$

b. Solve for x.

$(\underline{\hspace{0.6cm}} + \underline{\hspace{0.6cm}}x)(\underline{\hspace{0.6cm}} + \underline{\hspace{0.6cm}}x) = 42$

$w = \underline{\hspace{1.5cm}}$

30. $\dfrac{x}{x - 3} = \dfrac{4}{x}$

Transform the equation by _____

_____.

Identifying and Graphing Exponential Functions page 727

New Concepts

Example Evaluating an Exponential Function

Evaluate $f(x) = 2(4)^x$ for $x = -1, 1,$ and 2.

Use the order of operations to evaluate an exponential function.

$$f(-1) = 2(4)^{-1} = 2 \cdot \frac{1}{4} = \frac{2}{4} = \frac{1}{2}$$

$$f(1) = 2(4)^1 = 2 \cdot 4 = \mathbf{8}$$

$$f(2) = 2(4)^2 = 2 \cdot 16 = \mathbf{32}$$

> **Math Language**
>
> An **exponential function** is a function in the form $f(x) = ab^x$, where a and b are nonzero constants and b is a positive number not equal to 1.

- For any exponential function, $f(x) = ab^x$, x changes by a constant amount, $f(x)$ changes by a constant factor.

For $f(x) = 4(2)^x$, as x increases by 1, $f(x)$ increases by a factor of 2.

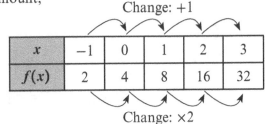

Change: +1

x	-1	0	1	2	3
$f(x)$	2	4	8	16	32

Change: ×2

Example Identifying an Exponential Function

Determine if the set of ordered pairs satisfies an exponential function.

$$\left\{(0, -3), \left(-2, -\tfrac{1}{3}\right), (1, -9), (-1, -1)\right\}$$

Arrange ordered pairs with x-values least to greatest.

$$\left\{\left(-2, -\tfrac{1}{3}\right), (-1, -1), (0, -3), (1, -9)\right\}$$

The x-values increase by a constant amount, 1.

Divide each y-value by the y-value before it.

$$-1 \div -\frac{1}{3} = -1 \cdot -3 = 3$$

$$-3 \div -1 = 3$$

$$-9 \div -3 = 3$$

The y-values decrease by a constant factor 3. **Because each ratio is the same, the ordered pairs satisfy an exponential function.**

Lesson Practice 📖 page 731

Evaluate each function for the given values.

a. $f(x) = 2^x$ for $x = -4, 0,$ and 5.

$$f(-4) = 2^{-4} \qquad f(0) = 2^0 \qquad f(5) = 2^5$$

$$f(-4) = \underline{\qquad} \qquad f(0) = \underline{\qquad} \qquad f(5) = \underline{\qquad}$$

b. $f(x) = -3(3)^x$, $x = -3, 1, 3$

$f(-3) = -3(3)^{-3}$　　　　　　$f(1) = -3(3)^1$　　　　　　　$f(3) = -3(3)^3$

$\quad = -3\left(\dfrac{1}{\square}\right)$　　　　　　$\quad = -3(\underline{\quad})$　　　　　　$\quad = -3(\underline{\quad})$

$f(-3) = \underline{\quad}$　　　　　　$f(1) = \underline{\quad}$　　　　　　$f(3) = \underline{\quad}$

Determine whether each set of ordered pairs satisfies an exponential function. Explain your answer.

c. Arrange ordered pairs with the x-values least to greatest.

$\{(3, -12), (6, -24), (\underline{\ }, \underline{\ }), (\underline{\ }, \underline{\ })\}$

The x-values increase by a constant amount

of _____.

Ratios of y-values:

$\dfrac{-24}{-12} = \underline{\quad}, \dfrac{\square}{-24} = \underline{\quad}, \dfrac{\square}{\square} = \underline{\quad}$

The y-values _____ a common ratio.

d. $\{(1, 12), (2, 36), (\underline{\ }, \underline{\ }), (\underline{\ }, \underline{\ })\}$

The x-values increase by a constant

amount of _____.

Ratios of y-values:

$\dfrac{36}{12} = \underline{\quad}, \dfrac{\square}{36} = \underline{\quad}, \dfrac{\square}{\square} = \underline{\quad}$

The y-values _____ a common ratio.

Graph each function by making a table of ordered pairs.

Plot the points on a coordinate grid and connect them with a smooth curve.

e. $y = 2(3)^x$

x	-2	-1	0	1	2
y					

f. $y = -4(2)^x$

x	-2	-1	0	1	2
y					

g. $y = 2\left(\dfrac{1}{4}\right)^x$

x	-2	-1	0	1	2
y					

Graph the functions on the same screen. Tell how the graphs are alike and how they are different.

h. alike: Both graphs are _____ the x-axis and symmetric about the _____.

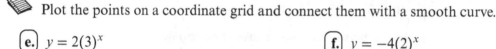

different: When $b = 3$, the y-values _____ as the x-values _____. When $b = \frac{1}{3}$

_____.

i. Tell how the graphs are alike and how they are different.

j. approximate population in 2006: _____ year population reaches 10 million: _____

1. $f(-2) = 2(5)^{-2} = 2 \cdot$ _____ = _____

$f(0) = 2(5)^{\square} =$ _____

$f(2) = 2(5)^{\square} =$ _____

2. $f(x) = |x - 2|$

$h > 0$ so $f(x) = |x|$ moves to the right.

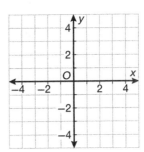

3. 1 raised to any power is _____. 4 would

be multiplied by _____ for every value

of x. The result is a linear function,

$f(x) =$ _____.

4. Compare the given graph to the graphs and their related functions in the example on page 729 of your textbook.

Circle the answer.

A $y = -\left(\frac{1}{2}\right)^{x}$ **B** $y = \left(\frac{1}{2}\right)^{x}$

C $y = -(2)^{x}$ **D** $y = 2^{x}$

5. If the year is 2010, $x = 10$.

population in 2010:

$20.85(1.0212)^{\square} =$ _____

population in 2020:

$20.85(1.0212)^{\square} =$ _____

Subtract.

_____

6. First order the pairs by increasing x-values.

(___, ___), (___, ___), (___, ___), (___, ___)

The x-values increase by the constant

amount of _____.

$\dfrac{\square}{\square} = \dfrac{\square}{\square} = \dfrac{\square}{\square} = \dfrac{4}{1}$

7. Draw a sketch.

$\overline{RS}$ and _____ $\angle R$ and _____

$\overline{ST}$ and _____ $\angle S$ and _____

$\overline{RT}$ and _____ $\angle T$ and _____

8. The reflection of $a|x|$ is $-a|x|$.

$k = 2$

$f(x) =$ _____

9. The graph does not have an _____ of _____ so it is not the graph of an absolute-value function.

10. *Substitute* $(-4)^3$ *for x.*

Answer: _____

11. *Compare* $|x|$ *and* $|-x|$ *for a few values of x.* The *y*-values for _____ and _____ are the same.

12. Student _____ is correct. Student _____ squared the number _____ within the radicand instead of squaring _____.

13. *Isolate the radical expression before squaring.*

$\sqrt{x} - 2 = 8$

$\sqrt{x} =$ _____

$x =$ _____

Check by substituting in the original equation.

14. *For* $f(x) = a|x - h| + k$, (h, k) *is the vertex and a is the slope of the right side of the V-shaped graph.*

$(h, k) = ($ ____ , ____ $)$

$a =$ _____

$f(x) =$ ____ $|x -$ ____ $| +$ ____

15. *See page 6 in the* Student Reference Guide.

$y =$ _____

16. $108 = 12\sqrt{x}$

$x =$ _____

17. *Isolate the absolute value.*

$$\frac{|x|}{8} - 10 < -9$$

$$|x| < \_\_\_\_\_$$

$$\_\_\_\_ < x < \_\_\_\_$$

18. $x^2 = -9$

$$x = \sqrt{\rule{1cm}{0pt}}$$

No real number squared can be negative.

_____ solution

19. $12|x + 9| - 11 = 1$

$$12|x + 9| = \_\_\_\_\_$$

$$|x + 9| = \_\_\_\_\_$$

$$x + 9 = \_\_\_\_\_ \quad \text{OR} \quad x + 9 = \_\_\_\_\_$$

$$x = \_\_\_\_ \quad \text{OR} \quad x = \_\_\_\_$$

$$\{\_\_\_\_, \_\_\_\_\}$$

20. $A = lw$

$$338 = x(\_\_\_\_)$$

_____ by _____

21. $\dfrac{\frac{24a^2b}{7c^2}}{\frac{8ab^2}{49c^2}} = \dfrac{24a^2b}{7c^2} \cdot \_\_\_\_\_$

$$= _____$$

22. *Complete the square.*

$$x^2 + 7x + \_\_\_\_\_$$

missing term: _____

23. Divide each term by the previous term.

Circle the answer.

A -2 **B** $-\frac{1}{2}$

C $\frac{1}{2}$ **D** 2

24. *Change the given dimensions to improper fractions.*

$$(\_\_\_\_)^2 + (\_\_\_\_)^2 = c^2$$

$$c = _____$$

25. *Divide each term by the previous term to determine is there is a common ratio.*

The absolute values of the terms have a common ratio of _____, but the _____ of the terms do not follow a geometric pattern, so the sequence _____ geometric.

26. *Write the numerator in standard form. Then factor completely.*

$$\frac{(36x + 12x^2 + 15)}{(2x + 1)}$$

= _____

27.

a. $\dfrac{7x^2}{x^2 - 49} + \dfrac{x - 1}{4x + 28}$

$= \dfrac{7x^2}{(x - \square)(x + \square)} + \dfrac{x - 1}{4(x + \square)}$

Find the LCD.

= _____

b. $t = \dfrac{d}{r}$

🔖 Divide the answer to part a by $\dfrac{7}{7x + 49}$.

$t = $ _____

28. Let $w = $ width

$A = lw$

_____ = (_____)w

Set the equation equal to zero and solve for x.

Linear measurement must be positive.

width = _____

length = _____

29. a. $9\dfrac{36}{60} = $ _____

Let K = Kim's time.

b. $9.6\left(\dfrac{1}{16}\right) + 9.6\left(\dfrac{1}{\square}\right) = $ ____

c.

$k = $ _____

30. It represents the _____ it takes the ball to reach that height.

Graphing Systems of Linear Inequalities

page 735

New Concepts

Math Language

A **system of linear inequalities** is a set of inequalities that have the same variables.

The **solution of a system of linear inequalities** is the point or set of points that satisfies all of the inequalities in the system.

Example Solving by Graphing

Graph the system.

For each inequality, graph the related line. Then shade.

$$y > \frac{1}{4}x - 3$$

$$y \le 3x + 4$$

All of the points in the overlapping section satisfy both inequalities and are solutions of the system.

You can check by substituting a point from the overlapping section into both inequalities. It will satisfy both inequalities.

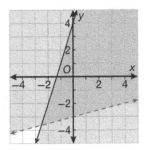

Example Solving Systems of Inequalities with Parallel Boundary Lines

Graph the system.

$$y \ge -\frac{2}{3}x - 2$$

$$y \ge -\frac{2}{3}x + 3$$

All of the solutions of $y \ge -\frac{2}{3}x + 3$ are solutions of $y \ge -\frac{2}{3}x - 2$. The solutions of the system are the same as the **solutions of $y \ge -\frac{2}{3}x + 3$.**

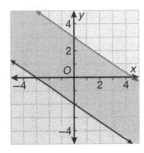

Lesson Practice page 738

Graph each system.

a. $y > -2x - 1, y \le \frac{1}{5}x + 4$

Use a dashed line for inequalities with > or <.
Use a solid line for inequalities with ≥ or ≤.

For the symbols > and ≥: shade above the line.
For the symbols < and ≤: shade below the line.

Lightly shade the two inequalities, then darken the shading
where the graphs overlap to clearly show the solutions.

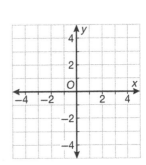

b. $6y + 6 > -2x,\ y < 2$

Isolate y in the inequality $6y + 6 > -2x$.

$6y > -2x$ ◯ _____

$y > -\underline{\quad}x$ ◯ _____

Darkly shade the region where the graphs overlap. This region contains the solutions that satisfy both inequalities.

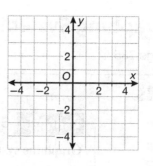

c. Graph the system $y \geq x - 6$ and $y \leq -x + 3$.

d. $y > \frac{1}{2}x - 4,\ y > \frac{1}{2}x$

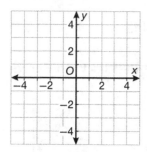

e. $y < \frac{1}{2}x - 4,\ y > \frac{1}{2}x$

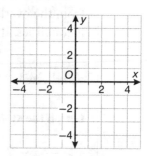

If the solutions sets do not overlap, the system has no solution.

f. $y > \frac{1}{2}x - 4,\ y < \frac{1}{2}x$

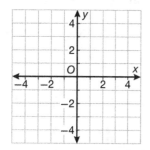

g. Let x = number of pounds of strawberries
Let y = number of pounds of pineapple

_____$x +$ _____$y \leq 30$

Isolate y.

$y \leq$ _____$x +$ _____

$x \geq$ _____

$y \geq$ _____

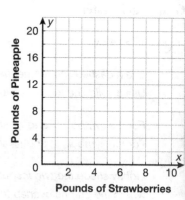

1. The dark blue region shows where the shading overlaps.

Circle the answer.

A $y \leq -0.5x + 3$
 $y \geq -0.5x - 1$

B $y \leq -0.5x + 3$
 $y \leq -0.5x - 1$

C $y \geq -0.5x + 3$
 $y \geq -0.5x - 1$

D $y \geq -0.5x + 3$
 $y \leq -0.5x - 1$

2. The axes are marked off in intervals of 0.25.

x ◯ 9

x ◯ _____

y ◯ _____

y ◯ _____

3. The graph of the parent function is reflected over the x-axis and stretched vertically.

$f(x) = -3|x|$

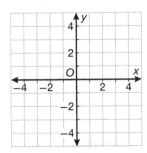

4. Graph $y = -3x + 4$ using a _____ line, and shade _____ the line.

On the same plane, graph $y = 2x - 1$ using a _____ line and shade _____ the line.

The solution is shown by the region where the shadings_____.

5. Plot the point $(1, -2)$ to show that it is not in the region of overlap.

$y \geq -x$
$y \leq 2x$

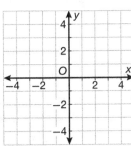

6. $f(x) = 3\left(\frac{1}{3}\right)^x$ for $x = -2, 0,$ and 2

$f(-2) = 3\left(\frac{1}{3}\right)^{\square} = \underline{\hspace{1cm}}$

$f(0) = 3\left(\frac{1}{3}\right)^{\square} = \underline{\hspace{1cm}}$

$f(2) = 3\left(\frac{1}{3}\right)^{\square} = \underline{\hspace{1cm}}$

7. Add the markup to the original price.

$x = \underline{\hspace{2cm}}$

8. Factor the radicands. Then simplify.

Answer: _____

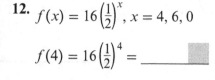

9. *Simplify the radicals before rationalizing the denominator.*

= _____

10. Student _____ is correct.

The _____-values do not increase by

a _____ amount.

---

11. *If the year is 2010, x = 10.*

value in 2005:

$4.8(1.25)^{\square} = $ _____

value in 2010:

$4.8(1.25)^{\square} = $ _____

Subtract.

_____

12. $f(x) = 16\left(\frac{1}{2}\right)^x, x = 4, 6, 0$

$f(4) = 16\left(\frac{1}{2}\right)^4 = $ _____

$f(6) = $ _____ = _____

$f(0) = $ _____ = _____

---

13. *Find the number of x-values that result in a value of f(x) that is between 100 and 1000.*

 Evaluate.

$f(x) = 7(5)^x$ for $x = 0, 1, 2, 3, 4, 5.$

$P(100 < x < 1000) = \dfrac{\square}{\square}$

14. *The graph of a quadratic function, or parabola, is curved at the vertex.*

The graph of the function _____

make a V-shape, so it _____

an absolute value function.

---

15. $y > \frac{1}{4}x + 3$

$y > -\frac{1}{4}x + 3$

Darkly shade the region where the graphs overlap.

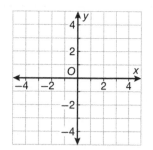

16. *Determine the direction that the vertex shifts.*

To find the vertex of $d = |90t - 120|$ and $d = |90t - 100|$, write each absolute value in the form $f(x) = a|x - h| + k$.

$120 \div 90 = $ _____ $d = \left|90(x - \text{\_\_\_})\right|$

Vertex: (_____, 0)

$100 \div 90 = $ _____ $d = \left|90(x - \text{\_\_\_})\right|$

Vertex: (_____, 0)

The graph would shift to the _____.

---

17. $48x^2 =$ _____

$x^2 =$ _____

$x =$ _____

The _____ tiles would work best.

18. *The object will strike the ground when y = 0.*

$-4.9t^2 - 53.9t = -127.4$

$-4.9t^2 - 53.9t +$ _____ $= 0$

$-4.9(t^2 +$ _____ $t +$ _____ $) = 0$

$t =$ _____

19. *Find the common ratio.*

$\dfrac{4.5}{5} =$ _____

Multiply by the common ratio to find the next three terms.

next 3 terms: _____,

_____, _____

20. *Check for extraneous solutions.*

Answer: _____

21. If the radical is isolated, _____

the equation eliminates the

_____.

22. *Divide the area by the length to find the width.*

$w =$ _____

23. *Isolate the absolute value expression.*

$4|x + 2| =$ _____

$|x + 2| =$ _____

$x + 2 =$ _____ or $x + 2 =$ _____

$x =$ _____ or $x =$ _____

Solution: { _____ , _____ }

24. *The square of a number is never negative.*

$x^2 = -49$

_____ solution

25. $2\left|\dfrac{x}{4} - 6\right| = 8$

{____, ____}

26. $h = -16t^2 + vt + s$

$h = -16t^2 + 47t + 5$

a. *Substitute: t = 1*

$h =$ _____

b. *The starting height of the object in feet is represented by s.*

$s =$ _____

c. *The initial height in feet/second is represented by v.*

$h =$ _____

---

27. *The sum of the amount of work done by both the boy and his sister is 1.*

Let $t =$ amount of time it takes them to weed the garden when working together

$\dfrac{\square}{\square}t + \dfrac{\square}{\square}t =$ ____

$t =$ _____

28. 📝 Use $h = -16t^2 + 31t + 7$.

a. *Find the x-coordinate, $-\dfrac{b}{2a}$, of the vertex.*

$t =$ _____

b. $0 = -16t^2 + 31t + 7$

$t =$ _____

c. *Substitute the x-coordinate of the vertex to find the y-coordinate of the vertex.*

$h =$ _____

---

29. In both cases, _____ 1 from

both sides and divide both sides

by _____. For $2|x| + 1 < 7$, do the

operations _____ removing

the absolute value bars. For

$|2x + 1| < 7$, do the operations

_____ writing as a compound inequality.

30. *Divide the area by the width to find the length.*

_____ $= l$

New Concepts

Math Language

Quadratic Formula

For the quadratic equation

$ax^2 + bx + c = 0$

$x = \dfrac{-b \pm \sqrt{b^2 - 4ac}}{2a}$

when $a \neq 0$.

Square Roots of Negative Numbers

If the quadratic formula produces an expression containing the square root of a negative number, the quadratic equation has no real solutions.

• The quadratic formula can be used to solve any quadratic equation. It is used when graphing, factoring, or completing the square are not possible or are too complicated. Substitute a, b, and c into the quadratic formula to find values of x.

Example **Rearranging Quadratic Equations before Solving**

Use the quadratic formula to solve for x.

$$-18x + x^2 = -32$$

$$x^2 - 18x + 32 = 0 \qquad \text{Write the equation in standard form.}$$

$$x = \frac{-b \pm \sqrt{b^2 - 4ac}}{2a} \qquad \text{Use the Quadratic Formula.}$$

$$= \frac{-(-18) \pm \sqrt{(-18)^2 - 4(1)(32)}}{2(1)} \qquad \text{Substitute.}$$

$$= \frac{18 \pm \sqrt{324 - 128}}{2}$$

$$= \frac{18 \pm \sqrt{196}}{2}$$

$$= \frac{18 \pm 14}{2}$$

$$= 9 \pm 7 \qquad \text{Simplify.}$$

$$= 9 + 7 \text{ and } 9 - 7$$

$$x = \textbf{16 and 2}$$

Example **Recognizing a Quadratic Equation With No Real Solutions**

Use the quadratic formula to solve for x.

$$2x^2 + 3x + 4 = 0$$

$$x = \frac{-b \pm \sqrt{b^2 - 4ac}}{2a}$$

$$= \frac{-3 \pm \sqrt{3^2 - 4(2)(4)}}{2(2)} \qquad \text{Substitute.}$$

$$= \frac{-3 \pm \sqrt{9 - 32}}{4}$$

$$= \frac{-3 \pm \sqrt{-23}}{4} \qquad \text{The expression contains a negative square root.}$$

There are **no real solutions**.

a. $x^2 + 3x - 18 = 0$

$x = \dfrac{-b \pm \sqrt{b^2 - 4ac}}{2a}$

$= \dfrac{-3 \pm \sqrt{3^2 - 4(1)(-18)}}{2(1)}$

$= \dfrac{-3 \pm \sqrt{\boxed{} + \boxed{}}}{\boxed{}}$

$= \dfrac{-3 \pm \boxed{}}{\boxed{}}$

$x = \underline{}$ and $x = \underline{}$

b. $-72 - 14x + x^2 = 0$

$x^2 - \underline{} x - \underline{} = 0$

$x = \dfrac{-b \pm \sqrt{b^2 - 4ac}}{2a}$

$= \dfrac{-\boxed{} \pm \sqrt{\boxed{}^2 - 4(\boxed{})(\boxed{})}}{2(\boxed{})}$

$= \dfrac{\boxed{} \pm \sqrt{\boxed{} + \boxed{}}}{\boxed{}}$

$= \dfrac{\boxed{} \pm \boxed{}}{\boxed{}}$ $x = \underline{}$ and $x = \underline{}$

c. $x^2 + 80 = 21x$

$x^2 - \underline{} x + 80 = \underline{}$

$x = \dfrac{-\boxed{} \pm \sqrt{\boxed{}^2 - 4(\boxed{})(\boxed{})}}{2(\boxed{})}$

$= \dfrac{\boxed{} \pm \sqrt{\boxed{} - \boxed{}}}{\boxed{}}$

$= \dfrac{\boxed{} \pm \boxed{}}{\boxed{}}$ $x = \underline{}$ and $x = \underline{}$

d. $9x^2 + 6x - 1 = 0$

$x = \dfrac{-\boxed{} \pm \sqrt{\boxed{}^2 - 4(\boxed{})(\boxed{})}}{2(\boxed{})}$

$= \dfrac{\boxed{} \pm \sqrt{\boxed{} + \boxed{}}}{\boxed{}}$

$= \dfrac{\boxed{} \pm \boxed{}}{\boxed{}}$

$x \approx \underline{}$ and $x \approx \underline{}$

e. $4x^2 + 5x + 3 = 0$

$x = \dfrac{-\boxed{} \pm \sqrt{\boxed{}^2 - 4(\boxed{})(\boxed{})}}{2(\boxed{})}$

$= \dfrac{\boxed{} \pm \sqrt{\boxed{} - \boxed{}}}{\boxed{}}$

_____

f. $-4.9t^2 + vt + s = 0$
$v = 6$ meters/sec, $s = 50$ meters

$-4.9t^2 + \underline{} t + \underline{} = 0$

$t = \dfrac{-b \pm \sqrt{b^2 - 4ac}}{2a}$

$= \dfrac{-\boxed{} \pm \sqrt{\boxed{}^2 - 4(\boxed{})(\boxed{})}}{2(\boxed{})}$

$= \dfrac{\boxed{} \pm \sqrt{\boxed{} + \boxed{}}}{\boxed{}} = \dfrac{\boxed{} \pm \boxed{}}{\boxed{}}$

The ball reaches the ground in about

_____ seconds

1. $x^2 - 2x - 35 = 0$

$$x = \frac{-b \pm \sqrt{b^2 - 4ac}}{2a}$$

$$= \frac{-(-2) \pm \sqrt{\boxed{}^2 - 4(1)(-35)}}{2(\boxed{})}$$

$$= \frac{\boxed{} \pm \sqrt{\boxed{} + \boxed{}}}{\boxed{}}$$

$x = $ _____ and $x = $ _____

2. $x^2 - 10x + 25 = 0$

$$x = \frac{-\boxed{} \pm \sqrt{\boxed{}^2 - 4(\boxed{})(\boxed{})}}{2(\boxed{})}$$

$$= \frac{\boxed{} \pm \sqrt{\boxed{} + \boxed{}}}{\boxed{}}$$

$= $ _____

3. $16h^2 + 25 = 40h$

a. $16h^2 - $ _____ $h + 25 = $ _____

b. $b^2 - 4ac$

$$= \boxed{}^2 - 4(\boxed{})(\boxed{}) = $$ ____

c. when $b^2 = $ _____

4. $12{,}000. = 1.2 \times 10^{\boxed{}}$

Convert scientific notation to standard notation.

$12{,}000$ $\bigcirc$ $1.2 \cdot 10^3$

5. $y = x^2 + 12x + 36$

$= (x + $ _____$)(x + $ _____$)$

$x = $ ____

6. The graph is a _____ in

quadrants I and _____ with the x- and

y-axes as asymptotes.

x and y must both be positive or

_____.

7. *Look at the pattern in the data set.*

outlier(s) : _____

8. Easy to factor? _____

Easy to complete the square? _____

The quadratic formula _____

necessary.

$= $ _____

9. *Use the quadratic formula.*

$$h = -4.9t^2 + v_0 t + h_0$$

$$v_0 = 7 \text{ m/s}, \ h_0 = 1.5 \text{ m}, \ h = 0$$

Solve for t.

$$t \approx \underline{\hspace{2cm}}$$

10. Student _____ is correct.

The ordered pair (____,____) is a solution
to both equalities; the ordered pair

(____,____) is a solution to only one of
the inequalities.

11. $y \le 2$
   $x \ge 2$

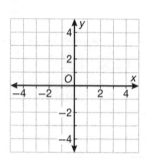

12. *Let x = basic washes*
   Let y = detail washes

$$\underline{\hspace{1.5cm}} x + \underline{\hspace{1.5cm}} y \bigcirc 300$$

$$\underline{\hspace{1.5cm}} x + \underline{\hspace{1.5cm}} y \bigcirc 480$$

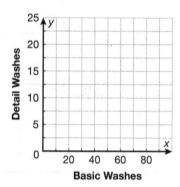

The student's goal will never be satisfied

because there is _____ solution.

13. $2x + 2y \bigcirc 50$

   $y \bigcirc 5$

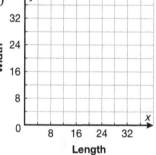

*Possible dimensions are solutions to the
inequalities.*

Possible dimensions for the rectangle are

length = _____ and width = _____.

14. $f(x) = -3(6)^x$

$$f(-2) = -3(6)^{-2} = \underline{\hspace{1cm}}$$

$$f(0) = -3(6)^{\square} = \underline{\hspace{1cm}}$$

$$f(2) = -3(6)^{\square} = \underline{\hspace{1cm}}$$

15. Student _____ is correct.

Student _____ should not multiply 2 by

3 because 3 is the _____ of the

exponent.

16. *Check the y-intercept using x = 0.*

Graph _____.

17. $\dfrac{\sqrt{15xy}}{3\sqrt{10xy^3}}$

$= \dfrac{\sqrt{15xy}}{3\square\sqrt{10x\square}}$

$= \dfrac{\sqrt{15xy}}{3\square\sqrt{10x\square}} \cdot \dfrac{\sqrt{\square}}{\sqrt{\square}}$

$= \dfrac{\sqrt{\square}}{\square}$

18. *Factor the denominators. Then find the LCD.*

$$\dfrac{5x^2}{10x - 30} - \dfrac{2x - 5}{x^2 - 9}$$

$$= \dfrac{5x^2}{10(\square - \square)} - \dfrac{2x - 5}{(x + \square)(x + \square)}$$

$$= \dfrac{\square \cdot \square \cdot \square \cdot \square}{\square(\square + \square)(\square - \square)}$$

$$= \underline{\hspace{3cm}}$$

19. $\sqrt{\dfrac{3\square}{2\square}} = \sqrt{\dfrac{\square}{\square}}$

$= \dfrac{\sqrt{\square}}{\sqrt{\square}} = \dfrac{\square\sqrt{\square}}{\square\sqrt{\square}} \cdot \dfrac{\sqrt{\square}}{\sqrt{\square}}$

$= \dfrac{\square\sqrt{\square}}{\square}$

20. *The absolute value graph is translated right if a positive constant is subtracted inside the absolute value bars.*

Circle the answer.

A $f(x) = |x + 2|$　　**B** $f(x) = |x - 2|$

C $f(x) = |x| + 2$　　**D** $f(x) = |x| - 2$

21. *Add $\left(\frac{b}{2}\right)^2$ to both sides.*

$$p^2 + 13p + \left(\dfrac{\square}{\square}\right)^2 = -50 + \left(\dfrac{\square}{\square}\right)^2$$

$$\left(p + \left(\dfrac{\square}{\square}\right)^2\right) = \sqrt{-50 + \left(\dfrac{\square}{\square}\right)^2} = \sqrt{-\square}$$

Since a square root of a negative number

is involved, there are _____

22. $A_n = P\left(1 + \dfrac{r}{n}\right)^{nt}$

$$= \underline{\hspace{1cm}}\left(1 + \dfrac{0.045}{\square}\right)^{1 \cdot \square} = \underline{\hspace{1.5cm}}$$

repeat for $t = 2, 3,$ and 4.

$t = 2$: _____

$t = 3$: _____

$t = 4$: _____

23. $\sqrt{x + 11} = 16$

$\left(\sqrt{x + 11}\right)^2 = \underline{\hspace{1cm}}^2$

$x = \underline{\hspace{1cm}}$

 Substitute to check.

24. _____ does not change the

absolute value like addition and subtraction

do, so the graphs _____ the same.

25. $9\left|\frac{x}{2} - 6\right| = 27$

$\left|\frac{x}{2} - 6\right| = \underline{\hspace{1cm}}$

$\frac{x}{2} - 6 = \underline{\hspace{1cm}}$ or $\frac{x}{2} - 6 = \underline{\hspace{1cm}}$

$x = \underline{\hspace{1cm}}$ or $x = \underline{\hspace{1cm}}$

26. $x^2 + 42 + 13x$

$= x^2 + \underline{\hspace{1cm}}x + 42$

$= (\underline{\hspace{0.5cm}} + \underline{\hspace{0.5cm}})(\underline{\hspace{0.5cm}} + \underline{\hspace{0.5cm}})$

27. Let x = number of books
Let y = number of magazines

a. _____ $x + $ _____ y ◯ _____

b.

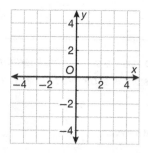

c. _____ book(s), _____ magazine(s)

28. $h = -16t^2 + 3t + 14$

maximum height $h = \underline{\hspace{1.5cm}}$

$t = \underline{\hspace{1.5cm}}$

29. $\left|t - (-247.35)\right|$ ◯ 1.25

a. $\left|t + \underline{\hspace{1.5cm}}\right|$ ◯ 1.25

___ ◯ t ◯ ___

-250   -248   -246

b. boiling point: _____

melting point: _____

30. $\pi r^2 - 165.05m^2 = 0$

$\pi r^2 = \underline{\hspace{1.5cm}}$

$r = \underline{\hspace{1.5cm}}$

$r \approx \underline{\hspace{1.5cm}}$

Name _____

Investigating Exponential Growth
and Decay page 749

1. Create a graph of the data in the table at the top of 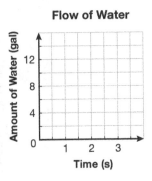 page 749.

Flow of Water

2. How many gallons of water flow from the pool in the fourth second?

_____ gallons

3. Complete the table of values below. Round each share to the nearest billion. $S = 39(1.2)^x$

x	S
0	39
2	56
4	
6	
8	
10	

Stocks Traded on the NYSE

4. Plot the coordinates on the graph above. Connect the points with a smooth curve.

5. Estimate the number of shares traded in 1997:

about _____ billion shares

6. Use the equation $S = 39(1.2)^x$ to calculate algebraically the exact number of shares traded in 1997.

_____ billion shares

Exploration 📖 page 750

Use your textbook to complete the Exploration.

Math Language

In an **exponential growth** situation, a quantity increases by the same percent in each period of time.

Exponential growth is modeled by the function $f(x) = k(b)^x$, where $k > 0$ and $b > 1$. These functions curve up to the right.

---

7. Plot the points from each of the data sets in the Exploration on 📖 page 750. Let $x =$ the number of folds and let $y =$ the number of regions. Connect the points for each set with a smooth curve.

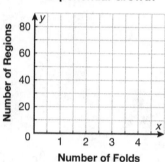

Exponential Growth

Compare the graphs of $f(x) = 2^x$, $g(x) = 3(2)^x$, $h(x) = 5(2)^x$.
All three functions are of the form $y = k(b)^x$.

8. What is the y-intercept of each function?

$f(x) = 2^x$ (____, ____) $g(x) = 3(2)^x$ (____, ____)

$h(x) = 5(2)^x$ (____, ____) $y = kb^x$ (____, ____)

9. How does changing the value of k affect the graph of the function?

The ____-intercept is k. _____ values of k cause the

graph to curve upward more sharply.

10. Every time the paper is folded in half, the number of regions

_____. b-value for each equation: ____

Write an equation in the form $y = kb^x$ to model situations in which

y doubles as x increases. _____

Math Language

The doubling time equation has the form $y = k(2)^x$.

---

11. For any function $y = kb^x$, what does k represent when $x = 0$?

k represents the _____ amount.

• The period of time required for a quantity to double in size or value is called **doubling time.**

• In an **exponential decay** situation, a quantity decreases by the same percent in each period of time.

Carbon-14 dating is used to find the amount of animal and plant material after it has decomposed. The half-life of carbon-14 is 5730 years. So, every 5730 years half of the carbon-14 in a substance decomposes. Find the amount remaining from a sample containing 100 milligrams of carbon-14 after four half-lives.

12. There are _____ years in four half-lives.

13. Complete the table below.

Number of Half-Lives	Number of Years	Amount of Carbon-14 Remaining (mg)
0	0	100
1	5730	
2	11,460	
3	17,190	
4	22,920	

14. Amount of the sample left after 22,920 years: _____ mg

• The **half-life** of a substance is the time it takes for one-half of the substance to decay into another substance.

Many diabetes patients take insulin. The exponential function $f(x) = 100\left(\frac{1}{2}\right)^x$ describes the percent of insulin in the body after x half-lives.

15. About what percent of insulin would be left in the body after 8 half-lives?

$$f(8) = 100\left(\frac{1}{2}\right)^{\square} = 100 \cdot \underline{\quad\quad} = \underline{\quad\quad\quad}$$

16. The effect that the b-value has on the amount of substance remaining as the number of half-lives x increases is that in each interval x, the

amount of y remaining decreases by _____.

17. Graph the functions $f(x) = 100\left(\frac{1}{2}\right)^x$ and $g(x) = 50\left(\frac{1}{2}\right)^x$.

x	$f(x)$	$g(x)$
0		
1		
2		
3		
4		
5		

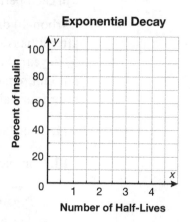

Exponential Decay

Compare the k-value in each equation to the y-intercept.

The _____ and the _____ are the same. The

exponential decay graphs have y-intercept (____, ____).

How does the k-value affect the graph of the function?

A larger k-value causes the graph to curve _____ more sharply.

Math Language

Exponential decay is modeled by the function $f(x) = k(b)^x$, where $k > 0$ and $0 < b < 1$.

Match the following exponential growth and decay equations to the graphs shown on 📖 page 752. Explain your choices.

18. $y = 2(0.5)^x$ Graph ____

The y-intercept is ____ because ____ = 2.

The value of b is ____, which is greater than zero and less than one, so the equation is exponential _____. As ____

increases, ____ decreases.

19. $y = 2(3)^x$ Graph ____

The y-intercept is ____ because ____ = 2.

The value of b is ____, which is greater than one, so the

equation is exponential _____. As ____ increases,

____ decreases.

20. $y = (0.25)^x$ Graph ____

The y-intercept is ____ because ____ $= 1$.

The value of b is ____, which is greater than zero and less

than one, so the equation is exponential _____. As

____ increases, ____ decreases.

21. $y = 0.25(2)^x$ Graph ____

The y-intercept is ____ because ____ $= 0.25$.

The value of b is ____, which is greater than one, so the equation

is exponential _____. As ____ increases, ____ decreases.

Investigation Practice page 752

a. $y = kb^x$

$k = 500, b = 2, x = \dfrac{32}{8} =$ _____ times

$y =$ _____ (_____)$^{\square}$

$y =$ _____

balance: ▨_____

b. $x = \dfrac{(24 \cdot 60)}{100} =$ _____ half-lives

$y = kb^x, k = 100, b = \dfrac{1}{2}$

$y =$ _____ (_____)$^{\square}$

$y =$ about _____▨

Use the equation $f(x) = \left(\frac{1}{2}\right)^x$ to answer each problem.

c. The value of b is _____, which is between _____ and 1, so the equation models

_____.

d. Both graphs have y-intercept (____, ____) and neither crosses the _____-axis.

Both graphs show exponential _____.

The graph of $g(x) = \left(\frac{1}{3}\right)^x$ curves downward _____ sharply than the graph of

$f(x) = \left(\frac{1}{2}\right)^x$.

e. Both graphs have y-intercept (____, ____) and neither crosses the _____-axis.

The graph of $f(x) = \left(\frac{1}{2}\right)^x$ represents exponential _____.

The graph of $h(x) = 2^x$ represents exponential _____.

The graphs are mirror images of each other reflected over the _____-axis.

Match the following exponential growth and decay equations to the graphs shown. Explain your choices.

Graph A	Graph B	Graph C	Graph D
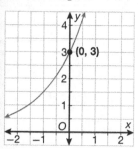	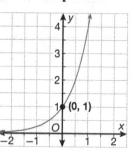	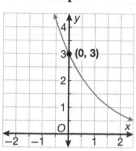	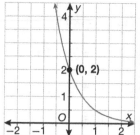

f. Graph _____. The y-intercept = _____

because $k =$ _____. The value of b is

_____, so the graph shows exponential

_____. As x_____,

y _____.

g. Graph _____. The y-intercept = _____

because $k =$ _____. The value of b is

_____, so the graph shows exponential

_____. As x_____,

y _____.

h. Graph _____. The y-intercept = _____

because $k =$ _____. The value of b is

_____, so the graph shows exponential

_____. As x_____,

y _____.

i. Graph _____. The y-intercept = _____

because $k =$ _____. The value of b is

_____, so the graph shows exponential

_____. As x _____,

y _____.

New Concepts

- The Fundamental Counting Principle can be used to determine the number of outcomes involving independent events.

Fundamental Counting Principle
If an independent event M can occur in m ways and another independent event N can occur in n ways, then the number of ways that both events can occur is $$m \cdot n.$$ Example: A restaurant offers 4 entrées and 5 vegetable dishes. How many meals with one entrée and one vegetable dish are possible? 20 meals may be ordered since $4 \cdot 5 = 20$.

Example Using the Fundamental Counting Principle

How many ways can a 1-topping pizza be ordered when there are 4 topping choices and 3 crust choices?

By the Fundamental Counting Principle, there are

4 topping choices $\cdot$ 3 crust choices = 12 possible ways.

See the tree diagram on 📖 page 755.

- An arrangement of objects or people in a certain way is called a **permutation.**
- The **factorial** operation can be used to find different ways to arrange a set of n items.

Math Language

The expression 8! is read **"8 factorial".**

Factorial
The factorial $n!$ is defined for any natural number n as $n! = n(n-1)$ ... $(2)(1)$. Zero factorial is defined to be 1. $0! = 1$ Example: $5! = 5 \cdot 4 \cdot 3 \cdot 2 \cdot 1$

Example Simplifying Expressions with Factorials

Find 7!

7!

$= 7 \cdot 6 \cdot 5 \cdot 4 \cdot 3 \cdot 2 \cdot 1 = \mathbf{5040}$

Find $\frac{9!}{4!}$

$\frac{9!}{4!}$

$= \dfrac{9 \cdot 8 \cdot 7 \cdot 6 \cdot 5 \cdot \cancel{4} \cdot \cancel{3} \cdot \cancel{2} \cdot \cancel{1}}{\cancel{4} \cdot \cancel{3} \cdot \cancel{2} \cdot \cancel{1}}$

$= 9 \cdot 8 \cdot 7 \cdot 6 \cdot 5 = \mathbf{15{,}120}$

Exploration   📖 page 756

Use your textbook to complete the Exploration.

Permutation
The number of permutations of n objects taken r at a time is given by the formula $_nP_r = \dfrac{n!}{(n-r)!}$.

Example   Finding the Number of Permutations

In how many ways can six classes finish in order from first to sixth?

6 things taken 6 at a time.

$$_nP_r = \frac{n!}{(n-r)!}$$

$$_6P_6 = \frac{6!}{(6-6)!} = \frac{6!}{0!}$$

$$= \frac{6 \cdot 5 \cdot 4 \cdot 3 \cdot 2 \cdot 1}{1}$$

$$= 720$$

In how many ways can six classes finish in first and second place?

6 things taken 2 at a time.

$$_nP_r = \frac{n!}{(n-r)!}$$

$$_6P_2 = \frac{6!}{(6-2)!} = \frac{6!}{4!}$$

$$= \frac{6 \cdot 5 \cdot \cancel{4} \cdot \cancel{3} \cdot \cancel{2} \cdot \cancel{1}}{\cancel{4} \cdot \cancel{3} \cdot \cancel{2} \cdot \cancel{1}}$$

$$= 30$$

Lesson Practice   📖 page 757

a. two departure times, four return times

total choices = ____ departure times · ____ return times = ____ choices

b. six choices *each* of hair, face, attitude and outfit; male or female choices

total choices = ___ for hair · ___ for face · ___ for attitude · ___ for outfit · ___ for gender

= _____ choices

c. $5! =$ ___ · ___ · ___ · ___ · ___ = ___

d. $\dfrac{6!}{3!} = \dfrac{\square \cdot \square \cdot \square \cdot \square \cdot \square \cdot \square}{\square \cdot \square \cdot \square}$

= ___ · ___ · ___ = ___

e. $_7P_\square = \dfrac{\square!}{(\square - \square)!} = \dfrac{\square}{\square} =$ _____

f. $_{10}P_\square = \dfrac{\square!}{(\square - \square)!} = \dfrac{\square}{\square} =$ _____

g. total possibilities $= {}_{10}P_\square = \dfrac{\square!}{(\square - \square)!} = \dfrac{\square}{\square} =$ _____

P(first 5 seasons arrive in order) $= \dfrac{\square}{\square}$

1. Write "H" or "T" in the circles.

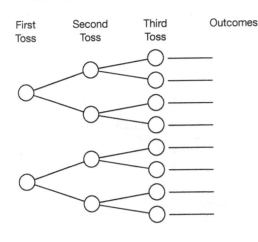

First Toss   Second Toss   Third Toss   Outcomes

2. $10! =$ ____ · ____ · ____ · ____ · ____

____ · ____ · ____ · ____ · ____

$=$ _____

Circle the answer.

A 3,628,800   **B** 362,880

C 55   **D** 9

3. drama · comedy · science fiction

$=$ ____ · ____ · ____

$=$ ____ choices

4. The denominators are _____, so subtract

the _____: ___d − ___d = ___d

Simplify: $\dfrac{\Box\, d}{\Box} =$ ____

5. Zeros occur when $y =$ ____.

$x^2 - 8x + 16 =$ ____

(_____)(_____) $=$ ____

(_____)$^2 =$ ____

$x =$ ____

6. *First divide each term by 3.*

$3x^2 + 36x - 39 =$ ____

____$x^2 +$ ____$x -$ ____ $= 0$

$(x +$ ____$)(x -$ ____$) = 0$

$x =$ ____ or ____

7. ✍ Draw a tree for each letter grade.

total outcomes

$=$ ____letter grades · ____ courses

$=$ _____

Check that the tree diagram has this number of outcomes.

8. Multiply ____ (the number of shirts)

by ____ (the number of pants) to get

____ outfits.

9. *See page 6 in the* Student Reference Guide.

$$c = \frac{-\square \pm \sqrt{\square^2 - 4(\square)(\square)}}{2(\square)}$$

$$= \frac{-\square \pm \sqrt{\square}}{2}$$

$$= -\underline{\quad} \pm \underline{\quad}$$

$$c = \underline{\quad} \text{ or } \underline{\quad}$$

Check: Does $(\underline{\quad})^2 + 16(\underline{\quad}) - 36 = 0$?

Does $(\underline{\quad})^2 + 16(\underline{\quad}) - 36 = 0$?

10. *Use the quadratic formula. Estimate the radical using the following facts:* $52^2 = 2704$, $51^2 = 2601$, $50^2 = 2500$, $49^2 = 2401$.

$$x^2 \underline{\qquad\qquad} = 0$$

$$x = \frac{-\square \pm \sqrt{\square^2 - 4(\square)(\square)}}{2(\square)}$$

$$= \frac{-\square \pm \sqrt{\square}}{2} = \frac{-\square \pm \sqrt{\square}}{2}$$

$$= \frac{-\square \pm \square}{2}$$

$$x \approx \underline{\quad} \text{ or } \underline{\quad}$$

11. The student should have made both lines

_____ because the points on the

_____ lines are ____ solutions.

12. *Rewrite the inequalities in terms of y.*

$y \bigcirc \underline{\quad} x - \underline{\quad}$

$y \bigcirc \underline{\quad} x + \underline{\quad}$

📓 Graph the lines represented by the inequalities. Shade the proper region as the inequalities indicate.

13. *To complete the square, find* $\left(\frac{b}{2}\right)^2$.

$$\left(\frac{b}{2}\right)^2 = \left(\frac{\square}{2}\right)^2 = \underline{\quad}$$

$$r^2 - 24r + \underline{\quad} = -144 + \underline{\quad}$$

$$(r - \underline{\quad})^2 = \underline{\quad}$$

$$r - \underline{\quad} = 0$$

$$r = \underline{\quad}$$

14. Student ____ is correct. Student ____ did not substitute the correct values for

____, ____, and ____ into the quadratic formula. The student also did not subtract the terms correctly to set the equation equal to _____.

15. _____, because the formula involves the initial _____ and the

initial _____, and that information has not been given.

---

16. $15 \text{ cm} \left(\dfrac{\boxed{} \text{ in.}}{\boxed{} \text{ cm}}\right) \le l \le 17 \text{ cm} \left(\dfrac{\boxed{} \text{ in.}}{\boxed{} \text{ cm}}\right) \rightarrow$ _____ $\le l \le$ _____

$9 \text{ cm} \left(\dfrac{\boxed{} \text{ in.}}{\boxed{} \text{ cm}}\right) \le w \le 11 \text{ cm} \left(\dfrac{\boxed{} \text{ in.}}{\boxed{} \text{ cm}}\right) \rightarrow$ _____ $\le l \le$ _____

---

17. _____ $= p^2 - 7p$

Set the equation equal to zero. Then solve the problem by completing the square.

$p^2 - 7p -$ _____ $= 0$

approximately _____ units

18. _Numerators are the same; denominators change._

$2187 \div$ _____ $= 729$; $729 \div$ _____ $= 243$;

$243 \div$ _____ $= 81$

next term: $\dfrac{1}{\left(\boxed{} \div \boxed{}\right)} = \dfrac{1}{\boxed{}}$

next two terms: $\dfrac{1}{\boxed{}}, \dfrac{1}{\boxed{}}$

---

19. $\dfrac{\underline{}}{} = \dfrac{\sqrt{x}}{6}$

$6 \cdot$ _____ $= \sqrt{x}$

$x = (6 \cdot$ ____$)^2 =$ _____

20. Make a table.

$f(x) = 3|x|$

x	0	± 1	± 2
y	___	___	___

📓 Sketch the graph.

---

21. _Exponential function form:_ $y = a^x$

Circle the answer.

A $y = 4(3)^x$ **B** $y = -4(3)^x$

C $y = 4^3 x$ **D** $y = 4\left(\dfrac{1}{3}\right)^x$

22. $y = (b)a^x$

To show that the _____ only

applies to _____ and not to the product of

_____ and _____.

---

23. set of numbers:

_____, _____ numbers

24. factors: $(x -$ ___$)(x -$ ___$)$

Evaluate $($___$)^2 - 8($___$) + 15 =$ ___

$($___ $+$ ___$)($___ $+$ ___$) = ($___$)($___$)$

---

25. $|t - 350| \leq$ _____

___ $\leq t - 350 \leq$ ___

___ $\leq t \leq$ ___

lowest possible temperature: _____

26. a. length: _____   width: _____

b. _____ • _____ = 110

$x^2 +$ ___ $x +$ ___ $= 110$

$x^2 +$ ___ $x -$ ___ $= 0$

$(x +$ ___$)(x -$ ___$) = 0$

$x =$ ___ or ___

_____ by _____

27. Let x = side length of property

a. area of property = house + yard

$x^2 =$ _____ + _____

b. $x^2 =$ _____

$x =$ _____ feet

c. _____ feet = _____ inches

_____ $\div 6 =$ ___ bulbs, plus ___

for the starting corner, for a total of

___ bulbs.

28. 1st step: Multiply the numerator and

denominator by the _____, or

$\sqrt{5} + 7$.

2nd step: Simplify the numerator using the

_____ Property, and simplify the

denominator using the _____ Method.

3rd step: Combine _____ terms and

simplify.

29. Factor the denominators to find LCD.

$$\frac{2x^2}{(\square)(\square)} - \frac{x - 7}{(\square)(\square)}$$

$$= \frac{2x^2(\square) - (x - 7)(\square)}{(x + \square)(x + \square)(x - \square)}$$

$$= \underline{\hspace{4cm}}$$

30. $y = a^x$

_____ represents exponential growth,

because $a \bigcirc 1$.

_____ represents exponential decay,

because $0 \bigcirc a \bigcirc 1$.

Name _____

Graphing and Solving Systems of Linear and Quadratic Equations page 761

New Concepts

• Systems of linear and quadratic equations can have three possible solutions as shown.

System A has two solutions.	**System B** has one solution.	**System C** has no solutions.

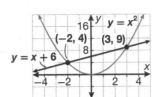 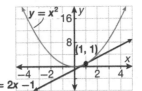 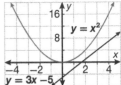

Example Solving by Graphing

Solve each system by graphing.

$y = 2x^2 - 9$
$y = 4x - 9$

Graph the parabola and the straight line.

(2, −1) and (0, −9)
There are 2 solutions.

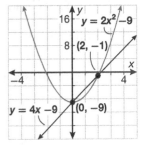

Example Solving Using Substitution

Solve using substitution.

$y = x^2 + 5x - 1$
$y = 5x + 3$

$$\begin{array}{rl} x^2 + 5x - 1 = & 5x + 3 \\ \underline{-5x - 3} & \underline{-5x - 3} \\ x^2 - 4 = & 0 \end{array}$$

Substitute $x^2 + 5x - 1$ for y into $y = 5x + 3$. Then simplify and set the equation to zero.

$(x + 2)(x - 2) = 0$ *Solve the equation by factoring.*
$x + 2 = 0$ and $x - 2 = 0$
    $x = -2$ $x = 2$

To determine the solution points, find the associated y-coordinate.

$\begin{array}{ll} y = 5x + 3 & y = 5x + 3 \\ y = 5(-2) + 3 & y = 5(2) + 3 \\ y = -7 & y = 13 \end{array}$ *Substitute each x-value into one of the original equations.*

Solutions to the system are **(−2, −7) and (2, 13).**

Solve each system by graphing.

a. Graph $y = x^2$ and $y = 16$.

The solutions are the intersection points: (___, ___) and (___, ___).

b. Graph $y = x^2$ and $y = 6x - 9$.

The solution is the intersection point: (___, ___).

c. Graph $y = x^2$ and $y = -2x + 3$.

The solutions are the intersection points: (___, ___) and (___, ___).

Solve using a graphing calculator.

d. Y1 = _____ and Y2 = _____.

Use TRACE and INTERSECT functions.

Solutions: (___, ___) and (___, ___)

e. Y1 = _____ and Y2 = _____.

Use TRACE and INTERSECT functions.

Solutions: (___, ___) and (___, ___)

Solve using substitution.

f. $x^2 - 3x - 17 = -3x + 8$

$x^2 -$ _____ $= 0$

(_____)(_____) $= 0$

$x =$ _____ or _____

$y = -3($___$) + 8 \qquad y = -3($___$) + 8$

$y =$ _____ $\qquad\qquad y =$ _____

Solutions: (___, ___) and (___, ___).

g. $x^2 + 7x + 5 = 2x - 1$

$x^2 +$ ___$x +$ ___ $= 0$

$(x +$ ___$)(x +$ ___$) = 0$

$x =$ ___ or _____

$y = 2($___$) - 1 \qquad y = 2($___$) - 1$

$y =$ ___ $\qquad\qquad y =$ ___

Solutions: (___, ___) and (___, ___).

h. $\dfrac{2x}{5} = -\dfrac{x^2}{25} + x$

$25\left(\dfrac{2x}{5}\right) =$ ___$\left(-\dfrac{x^2}{25} + x\right)$

$10x =$ _____

_____ $= 0$

$x($_____$) = 0$

$x =$ ____ or ____

Substitute the nonzero x-value into one of the original equations to determine the altitude (height) of the rock.

$y = \dfrac{2^{\square}}{5} =$ ____

Height of the rock is _____ feet.

1. Graph the equations.

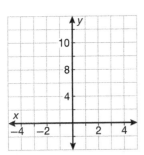

2. 🖎 Use substitution to solve each system. Circle the answer.

A $y = x^2 + 2$
   $y = 3$

B $y = x^2 - 2$
   $y = 3$

C $y = -x^2 + 2$
   $y = 3$

D $y = -x^2 - 2$
   $y = -3$

3. Write without negative exponents.

$$\frac{1}{\boxed{}} + \frac{6}{c^2 f^5} = \underline{\hspace{1cm}}$$

4. numbers greater than -4: $n \bigcirc -4$

numbers less than 8: $n \bigcirc 8$

$-4 \bigcirc n \bigcirc 8$

5. Use substitution.

$-x^2 + 4 = -2x + 5$

$x^2 - \underline{}x + \underline{} = 0$

$(x - \underline{})(x - \underline{}) = 0$

$x = \underline{}$

Substitute to find the y-coordinate.

$y = -2(\underline{}) + 5 = \underline{\hspace{1cm}}$

Solution: $(\underline{}, \underline{})$

6. Since two unique lines can only intersect at _____ point(s) and that point must also be the point of intersection with $y =$ _____, there can be only _____ point of _____ for all three equations. Therefore, the maximum number of ordered pairs in the solution set is _____ ordered pair(s).

7. There are _____ outcomes for each roll of the cube.

total outcomes for three rolls:

_____ • _____ • _____ = _____

8. Student _____ is correct. Student _____ is incorrect, because $0! = $ _____, not _____.

9. **a.** total combinations:

_____ • _____ = _____

b. not possible:

_____ triangle

_____ triangle

10. **a.** $_nP_r = \dfrac{n!}{(n-r)!} = $ _____

b. $P = \dfrac{\text{number of places}}{\text{sample space}} = \dfrac{\square}{\square}$

11. $a =$ _____ $b =$ _____ $c =$ _____

Quadratic Formula: $x = \dfrac{-b \pm \sqrt{b^2 - 4ac}}{2a}$

$x = \dfrac{-\square \pm \sqrt{\square^2 - 4\square\square}}{2\square}$

$= \dfrac{-\square \pm \sqrt{\square}}{\square}$

$=$ _____ $\pm$ _____ $x =$ _____ or _____

12. $a =$ _____ $b =$ _____ $c =$ _____

Quadratic Formula: $x = \dfrac{-b \pm \sqrt{b^2 - 4ac}}{2a}$

$a = \dfrac{-\square \pm \sqrt{\square^2 - 4\square\square}}{2\square}$

$= \dfrac{-\square \pm \sqrt{\square}}{\square} = $ _____ $\pm$ _____

Answer : _____

13. Since Cassandra is dealing with measurements, the _____ numbers are not relevant to the problem.

14. $2 \cdot (l + w) = 200$ feet $(l + w) = 100$ feet $l = 100 - w$

$\$5(\text{width of front}) + \$3(\text{length of side}) + \$3(\text{length of side}) + \$3(\text{width of back}) = \$720$

$\$5w + \$3(100 - w) + \$3(100 - w) + \$3w = \$720$

_____$w +$ _____ $= \$720$

$w =$ _____ $l = 100 - w =$ _____   dimensions: _____ by _____

15. $-0.032 \cdot r = 0.16$

$r =$ _____

5th term: $4r =$ _____

6th term: _____ $r =$ _____

7th term: _____ $r =$ _____

16. $2 \cdot r = 4\,r =$ _____

$A(n) = ar^{n-1}$

$A(12) = 2(\underline{\quad})^{12-1}$

$A(12) =$ _____

12th fold: _____ rectangles

17. Solve: Check:

$$\frac{\sqrt{x}}{6} = 12$$

$$\sqrt{x} = \underline{\hspace{1cm}}$$

$$x = \underline{\hspace{1cm}}$$

$$\frac{\sqrt{\square}}{6} \stackrel{?}{=} 12$$

$$\frac{\square}{6} \stackrel{?}{=} 12$$

$$\underline{\hspace{1cm}} = 12$$

18. *Use your calculator.*

$$x = \text{years after } 2000 = \underline{\hspace{1cm}}$$

$$y = 11.35 \cdot (\underline{\hspace{1cm}})^{\square}$$

$$= \underline{\hspace{1cm}} \text{ million people}$$

19. $f(-2) = -2 \cdot 4^{\square} = -2 \cdot \underline{\hspace{0.5cm}} = \underline{\hspace{0.5cm}}$

$f(0) = -2 \cdot 4^{\square} = -2 \cdot \underline{\hspace{0.5cm}} = \underline{\hspace{0.5cm}}$

$f(2) = -2 \cdot 4^{\square} = -2 \cdot \underline{\hspace{0.5cm}} = \underline{\hspace{0.5cm}}$

20. ✎ Draw a number line from -3 to 3 for each system.

Which system does not have any overlapping values?

Answer: \underline{\hspace{1cm}}

21. Graph the related lines and shade the area between the lines. Write the inequality symbols representing the shaded region.

$$y \,\square\, \frac{3}{5}x + 7$$

$$y \,\square\, \frac{3}{5}x + 1$$

22. *Write the related equation.*

$$x^2 - 6x - 72 = 0$$

$$(x - \underline{\hspace{0.5cm}})(x + \underline{\hspace{0.5cm}}) = \underline{\hspace{0.5cm}}$$

$$x = \underline{\hspace{0.5cm}} \text{ or } \underline{\hspace{0.5cm}}$$

23. ✎ Solve for y.

$$4x - y \le -5$$

$$-y \le \underline{\hspace{0.5cm}} - 5$$

$$y \,\bigcirc\, \underline{\hspace{0.5cm}} + 5$$

Graph the related equation. Then shade the correct region.

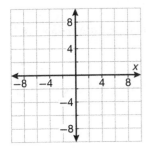

24.
  a. girl's rate: $\dfrac{1 \text{ job}}{4 \text{ hr}}$

  mom's rate: $\dfrac{1 \text{ job}}{\square \text{ hr}}$

  sister's rate: $\dfrac{1 \text{ job}}{\square \text{ hr}}$

  $$\frac{1}{4}t + \frac{\square}{\square}t + \frac{\square}{\square}t = 1$$

  b. ✎ Find the LCD and solve.

  \underline{\hspace{1.5cm}} hours

  c. \underline{\hspace{1cm}} hours $\cdot$ 60 $=$ \underline{\hspace{1cm}} minutes

25. Use the Pythagorean theorem.

$$x^2 = 49^2 + 81^2$$

$$x^2 = \underline{\hspace{1cm}}$$

$$x = \sqrt{\underline{\hspace{0.8cm}}}$$

$$\approx \underline{\hspace{3cm}}$$

26. The graph of $y = x^2 - 3$ is a parabola that opens _____ with a vertex at (____, ____).

Any line $y = a$, where $a >$ _____, will intersect the parabola in _____ place(s), and therefore the system will have two solutions.

27. a. $d = r \cdot t$ or $t = d \div r$

$$\square = \frac{\square}{\sqrt{10,800}}$$

b. *Rationalize the denominator.*

$$t = \frac{\square}{\sqrt{10,800}} = \frac{85}{\sqrt{3 \cdot 36 \cdot \square}} = \frac{85}{\square\sqrt{\square}} \cdot \frac{\sqrt{\square}}{\sqrt{\square}} = \frac{17\sqrt{\square}}{\square}$$

28. _____ each term of the quadratic equation by the _____ of the quadratic term. The coefficient of the quadratic term must be ____ to complete the square.

29. The graph is _____

across the x-axis, opens _____,

and is shifted _____ by _____

units.

30. This is exponential _____.

$$f(x) = \underline{\hspace{1.5cm}} \cdot 2^x$$

How many 7-year periods are in 48 years?

number of doubles: ____ ÷ ____ = ____

$$f(\underline{\hspace{0.8cm}}) = \underline{\hspace{1.5cm}} \cdot 2^{\square} = \$\underline{\hspace{1.5cm}}$$

LESSON

113

Interpreting the Discriminant page 769

New Concepts

- In the quadratic formula, the **discriminant** is the expression under the radical sign: $b^2 - 4ac$.

- The value of the discriminant tells how many real roots, or solutions, a quadratic equation has—one, two, or none.

Using the Discriminant
For the quadratic equation $ax^2 + bx + c = 0$ where $a \neq 0$, find the value of the discriminant, $b^2 - 4ac$, to determine the number of real solutions, which represents the number of x-intercepts of the graph of its related function.
If $b^2 - 4ac < 0$, then there are no real solutions and no x-intercepts.
If $b^2 - 4ac = 0$, then there is one real solution and one x-intercept.
If $b^2 - 4ac > 0$, then there are two real solutions and two x-intercepts.

Example **Finding the Number of Solutions Without Solving**

Use the discriminant to find the number of real solutions to the equation. Then state the number of x-intercepts of its graph.

$x^2 - 3x + 9 = 0$

Find $b^2 - 4ac$.

$(-3)^2 - 4(1)(9)$

$= 9 - 36$

$= -27$

Since $b^2 - 4ac < 0$, there are no real solutions, and **the graph has no x-intercepts.**

$2x^2 - 3x - 4 = 0$

Find $b^2 - 4ac$.

$(-3)^2 - 4(2)(-4)$

$= 9 + 32$

$= 41$

Since $b^2 - 4ac > 0$, there are two real solutions, and **the graph has two x-intercepts.**

$x^2 + 8x + 16 = 0$

Find $b^2 - 4ac$.

$8^2 - 4(1)(16)$

$= 64 - 64$

$= 0$

Since $b^2 - 4ac = 0$, there is one real solution, and **the graph has one x-intercept.**

Use the discriminant to find the number of real solutions to the equation. Then state the number of x-intercepts of the graph of the related function.

a. $b^2 - 4ac$ $a =$ _____ $b =$ _____ $c =$ _____

($\quad$)$^2 - 4($_____$)($_____$) =$ _____

_____ $\bigcirc$ 0, so

_____ solution(s) and _____ x-intercepts

b. $b^2 - 4ac$ $a =$ _____ $b =$ _____ $c =$ _____

($\quad$)$^2 - 4($_____$)($_____$) =$ _____

_____ $\bigcirc$ 0, so

_____ solution(s) and _____ x-intercept(s)

c. $b^2 - 4ac$ $a =$ _____ $b =$ _____ $c =$ _____

($\quad$)$^2 - 4($_____$)($_____$) =$ _____

_____ $\bigcirc$ 0, so

_____ solutions(s) and _____ x-intercepts

d. Substitute 45 for y.

$45 = -16t^2 + 60t + 2$

$0 = -16t^2 + 60t - 43$

discriminant: ($\quad$)$^2 - 4($_____$)($_____$) =$ _____,

which is $\bigcirc$ 0, so there are _____ solutions.

The maximum height occurs at $t = -\dfrac{b}{2a} = -\dfrac{\square}{2\square} =$ _____ seconds.

The maximum height $= -16($_____$)^2 + 60($_____$) + 2 =$ _____ feet

Therefore, the ball _____ reach a height of 45 feet.

1. *Discriminant = b² − 4ac*

$$(\underline{})^2 - 4(\underline{})(\underline{}) = \underline{}$$

2. perimeter = $2 \cdot (l + w)$ =

$$2(\underline{} + \underline{})$$

Answer: _____

3. *Isolate the absolute value and solve for z.*

$$|z - 3| = \underline{}$$

$z - 3 = \underline{}$ or $z - 3 = \underline{}$

Solution: {____, ____}

4. 8!

$$= (\underline{})(\underline{})(\underline{})(\underline{})(\underline{})(\underline{})(\underline{})(\underline{})$$

$$= \underline{}$$

5. Does the graph intersect the *x*-axis? _____

What is the sign of the discriminant? ___

Circle the answer.

A −5   B 0
C 3   D 5

6. If the sign of the discriminant is greater than zero there are _____ solutions

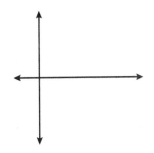

7. If a quadratic equation has two real roots, the value of the discriminant is _____.

8.

(graph with y-axis labeled 14, 12, 10, 8, 6, 4, 2, O, −2 and x-axis labeled −4, −2, 2, 4)

9. Student _____ is correct. Student _____

_____ the linear equation to the

quadratic equation instead of

_____ it for *y*.

10. *Use substitution, then set equal to zero.*

$(\underline{\hspace{0.5cm}})x^2 + (\underline{\hspace{0.5cm}})x + (\underline{\hspace{0.5cm}}) = 0$, so

$x = \underline{\hspace{0.8cm}}$ or $\underline{\hspace{0.8cm}}$

The altitude cannot be negative.

Substitute. $y = -(\underline{\hspace{0.8cm}}) + 14 = \underline{\hspace{1cm}}$

11. Enter equations.

Y1 = \underline{\hspace{3cm}}

Y2 = \underline{\hspace{3cm}}

Select INTERSECT to find the solution(s).

$(\underline{\hspace{0.8cm}}, \underline{\hspace{0.8cm}})$ and $(\underline{\hspace{0.8cm}}, \underline{\hspace{0.8cm}})$

---

12. $_nP_r = \dfrac{n!}{(n-r)!} = \underline{\hspace{1cm}}$ Student \underline{\hspace{1cm}} is correct. Student \underline{\hspace{1cm}} did not use the correct

\underline{\hspace{4cm}} for permutations.

---

13. *Use the Fundamental Counting Principle.*

$\underline{\hspace{1cm}} \cdot \underline{\hspace{1cm}} \cdot \underline{\hspace{1cm}} = \underline{\hspace{1.5cm}}$ choices

14. *Order is important.*

$_nP_r = \dfrac{\boxed{}!}{(\boxed{} - \boxed{})!} = \underline{\hspace{1cm}}$

$P = \dfrac{\text{single outcome}}{\text{number of permutations}} = \underline{\hspace{1cm}}$

---

15. *Isolate the square root.*

$\sqrt{x} = \underline{\hspace{1.5cm}}$

$x = \underline{\hspace{1cm}}$

Check. $\sqrt{(\underline{\hspace{0.8cm}})} + 2 = 8$

$\underline{\hspace{1cm}} = 8$

16. *Set the expressions equal to each other. Square both sides to solve.*

$\underline{\hspace{2.5cm}} = \underline{\hspace{2.5cm}}$

$x = \underline{\hspace{0.8cm}}$

---

17. $f(x) = |x + 4|$

x	-2	-1	0	1	2
y					

Sketch the graph.

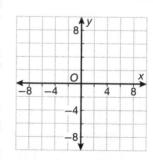

18. a. $x(x + 2) =$ _____

$x^2 +$ __$x -$ __$= 0$

Substitute.

$$x = \frac{-\square \pm \sqrt{\square^2 - 4\square\square}}{2\square}$$

$$= \frac{\square \pm \sqrt{\square}}{\square} = \underline{\quad} \pm \underline{\quad} \text{ or}$$

$x =$ ____ and $x + 2 =$ ____

dimensions: ____ by _____

b. perimeter $= 2(l + w) = 2(\underline{\quad} + \underline{\quad})$

$= \underline{\qquad}$

19. a. maximum height occurs at $t = -\dfrac{b}{2a}$,

so $t = -\dfrac{\square}{2\square} = \underline{\qquad}$

b. The ball hits the ground when $h = 0$.

Divide by -2.

$8t^2 - \underline{\quad}\, t - \underline{\quad} = 0$

Use the quadratic formula.

$$t = \frac{-\square \pm \sqrt{\square^2 - 4\square\square}}{2\square}$$

$$= \underline{\quad} \pm \underline{\qquad}; \, t = \underline{\qquad}$$

c. Substitute t from part **a.**

$h = -16(\underline{\quad})^2 + 14(\underline{\quad}) + 50 = \underline{\qquad}$

20. Substitute.

$$d = \sqrt{\frac{3\square}{2}} = \sqrt{\frac{\square}{2}}$$

$$d = \underline{\quad} \sqrt{\underline{\qquad}}$$

21. Make a table for each function.

$y \geq -\dfrac{3}{5}x + 3$

x	5	0	-5
y			

$y \geq \dfrac{3}{4}x + 3$

x	4	0	-4
y			

 Graph the equations.

22. The first equation has a variable, _____, for the initial height. The second equation

assumes that the initial height, _____, will have a value of _____.

23. y-intercept: _____

slope = _____

equation of boundary line:

$y =$ ___x ◯ ___

Shading shows that

y ◯ ___x ◯ ___

24. *Substitute 200 for h.*

_____ $= -16t^2 + 84t$

Set the equation equal to zero.

$0 = -16t^2 + 84t -$ _____

Find the discriminant.

$($___$)^2 - 4($___$)($___$) =$ _____

The discriminant is _____ than zero,

so the projectile _____ reach 200 feet.

25. *Set the equation equal to zero.*

$0 =$ ___x^2 ◯ ___$x +$ ___

Factor out the GCF. Solve for x.

___$(x^2 +$ ___$x +$ ___$) = 0,$

$x =$ ___

26.　100 ◯ 0

1.065 ◯ 1

Answer: _____

27. **a.** *Divide each term by −4.9.*

___$t^2 +$ ___$t =$ ___

b. 📰 Complete the square to find the

real-number solutions.

$t =$ ___ or $t =$ ___

c. $t =$ ___, since time cannot be a

_____ number.

28. $A(n) = ar^{n-1}$

_____. If $r = \frac{1}{3}$, the 5th term is

$($___$)($___$)^{\square}$ or _____.

If $r = -\frac{1}{3}$, the 5th terms is

$($___$)($___$)^{\square}$ or _____.

29. "Vertically compressed" means to "push

up or down" on the parabola, so the

parabola is _____.

30. They are _____ images of

each other, _____ across

the _____-axis.

New Concepts

Example **Graphing a Square-Root Function**

Make a table of $y = 2\sqrt{x} + 1$. Then graph the function.

$y = 2\sqrt{0} + 1 = 2(0) + 1 = 1$

$y = 2\sqrt{1} + 1 = 2(1) + 1 = 3$

$y = 2\sqrt{4} + 1 = 2(2) + 1 = 5$

$y = 2\sqrt{9} + 1 = 2(3) + 1 = 7$

x	y
0	1
1	3
4	5
9	7

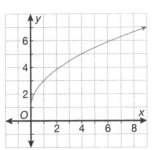

Example **Determining the Domain of a Square-Root Function**

Determine the domain.

$y = \sqrt{x - 4}$

The radicand must be ≥ 0.

Solve $x - 4 \geq 0$.

$x \geq 4$

The domain is all values of x greater than or equal to 4.

$y = 3\sqrt{\frac{x}{2} + 4} - 7$

Solve $\frac{x}{2} + 4 \geq 0$.

$\frac{x}{2} + 4 \geq 0$

$\frac{x}{2} \geq -4$

$x \geq -8$

The domain: $x \geq -8$

- The parent function of the square-root function is $y = \sqrt{x}$. This parent function can be transformed like other parent functions.

Transformations of the Graph of $f(x) = \sqrt{x}$
Vertical translation: The graph of $f(x) = \sqrt{x} + c$ is c units up from the parent graph if $c > 0$ and the graph is c units down from the parent graph if $c < 0$.
Horizontal translation: The graph of $f(x) = \sqrt{x - c}$ is c units to the right of the parent graph if $c > 0$ and the graph is c units to the left of the parent graph if $c < 0$.

Example **Translating the Square-Root Functions**

Describe the translation applied to the
parent function to form
$y = \sqrt{x} - 3$.

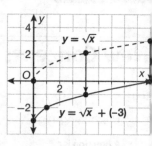

$\sqrt{x} - 3$ is of the form $f(x) = \sqrt{x} + c$.

$c = -3$. The -3 translates the
graph 3 units down.

Reflections of the Graph of $f(x) = \sqrt{x}$

If $f(x) = \sqrt{x}$, then $g(x) = -\sqrt{x}$ is a reflection of the graph of f
across the x-axis.

If $f(x) = \sqrt{x}$, then $g(x) = \sqrt{-x}$ is a reflection of the graph of f
across the y-axis.

Lesson Practice 📖 page 779

a. Graph $y = 3\sqrt{x + 1}$ using a table.

x	-1	0	3	8	15
y					

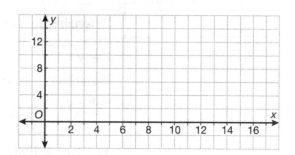

Determine the domain.

b. The radicand must be ≥ 0.

$\frac{x}{3} \geq 0$, so $x \geq$ _____

c. $x - 2 \geq 0$, so $x \geq$ _____

Describe the transformations applied to the parent function.

d. a shift of _____ unit(s) _____

e. a shift of _____ unit(s) to the _____

f. a _____ over the ____-axis, then
a shift of _____ unit(s) _____

g. a reflection over the _____-axis, then a shift
of _____ unit(s) _____

h. $t = 0.45\sqrt{8} = 0.45 \cdot \sqrt{} = \sqrt{} \approx$ _____ seconds

1. *Isolate the absolute value symbol.*

$|z + 5| = $ _____

Since $|z + 5|$ ◯ 0, the solution set

is _____.

2. *Set the equation equal to 0.*

$10x^2 = 70x$

_____$(x - $_____$) = 0$

$x = $ _____ and _____

3. $24x = 32x^2$

$x = $ _____ and _____

4. *Find the LCD.*

$5(\_\_)(\_\_) - 2(\_\_\_)(\_\_) = 5(\_\_\_)(\_\_)$

Eliminate extraneous solutions.

$x = $ _____

5. *Substitute.*

$y = \sqrt{(__)} - 1 = $ _____

Circle the answer.

A $\sqrt{2}$ **B** $\sqrt{7}$

C $2\sqrt{2} - 1$ **D** no solution

6. $y = \sqrt{10d}$

Substitute.

$y = \sqrt{10 \cdot \_\_\_}$

$y = \_\_\sqrt{\_\_}$

$y \approx $ _____

7. $\sqrt{\frac{4x}{3} - 1}$ ◯ 5

Square both sides. Solve for x.

x ◯ _____

8. _____ the parent function

$f(x) = \sqrt{x}$ _____ units to the _____.

Then, _____ the resulting

function _____ units up.

9. *See page 6 in the* Student Reference Guide.

$(\underline{})^2 - 4(\underline{})(\underline{}) = \underline{}$

10. Student _____ is correct. Student _____

did not set the equation equal to _____

before finding the values of _____, _____,

and _____.

11. Multiply $(x + 12)(x + 8)$.

$x^2 + \underline{}x + \underline{}x + \underline{} = \underline{}$

Simplify and rearrange.

$x^2 + \underline{}x + \underline{} = 0$

Calculate $b^2 - 4ac$: _____

_____ value(s) of x give(s) an area of 50.

12. a. $\underline{}x^2 + \underline{}x + \underline{} = 0$

b. $a = \underline{}$, $b = \underline{}$, and $c = \underline{}$

c. $b^2 - 4ac = \underline{}$

d. _____, because the discriminant

is $\bigcirc$ 0.

13.

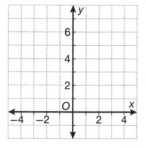

$(\underline{}, \underline{})$ and $(\underline{}, \underline{})$

14. Student _____ is correct. Student _____

did not _____ to both sides

when setting the equation equal to _____.

15. *Use substitution, then set equal to zero.*

$x^2 + (\underline{})x = 0$.

Factor.

$\underline{} (x \bigcirc \underline{}) = 0$

$x = \underline{}$ or $x = \underline{}$

Substitute to find the altitude.

$y = \underline{}$

16. $x^2 \bigcirc (\underline{})x \bigcirc (\underline{}) = 0$

Factor.

$x = \underline{}$ and $\underline{}$

Distance between x_1 and x_2:

$\underline{} - \underline{} = \underline{}$ units

If 8 cm = _____ units, the scale is _____

per _____ unit.

17.

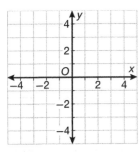

18. Let x = today's temperature

$x - 65 =$ ____ or $x - 65 =$ ____

The temperatures could have been ____

or ____.

19. *Arrange the ordered pairs so the x-values are increasing.*

The x-values increase by ____ for all four ordered pairs and the y-values _____

have a common ratio, the ordered pairs _____ satisfy an exponential function.

20. *Let m = number of motorcycles*
Let c = number of cars
Write a system of inequalities.

$c \bigcirc$ ____ $m \bigcirc$ ____

____ + ____ $\bigcirc$ 5

____ $c +$ ____ $m \bigcirc$ 8000

   Graph the system.

Choose 2 points in the region where the four solution sets overlap.

$c =$ ____ and $m =$ ____ or $c =$ ____ and $m =$ ____

21. *Write in standard form.*

$x^2 -$ ____ $x +$ ____ $= 0$

$x = \dfrac{-\square \pm \sqrt{\square^2 - 4\square\square}}{2\square}$

$=$ ____ $\pm$ ____ $=$ ____ or ____

22. ____! or ____ arrangements

Circle the answer.

A 3   **B** 6

C 12   **D** 24

23. When you are trying to find the number of _____ to pick items and when the _____ is important.

24. a. 60 ft = 60 · ____ = ____

b. $|d -$ ____ $| \bigcirc$ ____

____ $\bigcirc$ $d \bigcirc$ ____

c. shortest distance to pin 1:

____ $-$ ____ $=$ ____

25. Substitute: $y = \sqrt{2 \cdot \underline{\hspace{0.5cm}}} + 3 = \underline{\hspace{0.5cm}} + \underline{\hspace{0.5cm}} = \underline{\hspace{0.5cm}}$

---

26. *Substitute.*

Let x = height

$\underline{\hspace{1cm}} = \left(\frac{1}{2}\right)(x)(x + \underline{\hspace{0.5cm}})$

$0 = x^2 + \underline{\hspace{0.5cm}}x + \underline{\hspace{0.5cm}}$

$x = \underline{\hspace{0.5cm}}$ or $\underline{\hspace{0.5cm}}$

base $= x + \underline{\hspace{0.5cm}} = \underline{\hspace{0.5cm}}$

27. a. *Use $A(n) = ar^{n-1}$*

To find the total salary s including raises after n years, use 1.04 for r.

$s = \underline{\hspace{1.5cm}} \cdot (\underline{\hspace{1cm}})^n$

 b. *Find the x-coordinate of the intersection of $y = 40{,}000$ and $y = 32{,}000(1.04)^n$.*

$n = \underline{\hspace{0.5cm}}$

c. $s = 32{,}000(\underline{\hspace{0.5cm}})^{\square}$

$\approx \underline{\hspace{2cm}}$

---

28. *Square both sides.*

$\left(\sqrt{x+3}\right)^2 = (\underline{\hspace{0.5cm}})^2$

$\underline{\hspace{0.5cm}}x^2 - \underline{\hspace{0.5cm}}x - \underline{\hspace{0.5cm}} = 0$

---

29. Because the coefficient of x^2, (i.e. \underline{\hspace{0.5cm}})

is \underline{\hspace{2cm}} than 1, the graph

has been vertically \underline{\hspace{2cm}}

(which means the graph is

\underline{\hspace{2cm}} than the parent).

30. Both are \underline{\hspace{2.5cm}}

functions with the \underline{\hspace{1.5cm}} shape,

but $g(x)$ has been

\underline{\hspace{2cm}} stretched by

a factor of \underline{\hspace{1cm}}.

New Concepts

Math Language

A **cubic function** is a polynomial function in which the greatest power of any variable is 3.

• The parent function of the cubic function is $y = x^3$. The parent function can be transformed by translations and reflections like other parent functions.

Example **Graphing Cubic Functions**

Evaluate the cubic parent function $y = x^3$ and $y = -x^3$ for $x = -2$, $-1, 0, 1, 2$. Then graph the functions.

Make a table, then plot the points.

$y = x^3$

x	-2	-1	0	1	2
y	-8	-1	0	1	8

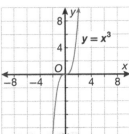

$y = -x^3$

x	-2	-1	0	1	2
y	8	1	0	-1	-8

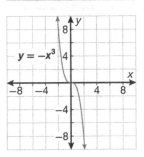

Example **Solving Cubic Equations by Graphing**

Solve $0 = x^3 - 1$
Graph $y = x^3 - 1$.

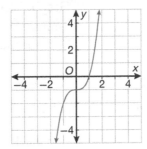

Find the x-intercept(s) since these are the x-values where $y = 0$. By inspection, the only x-intercept is at $x \approx 1$.

Solve $2 = -2x^3 - 7$

Move the terms to the right side, and write y on the left.
Graph $y = -2x^3 - 9$.

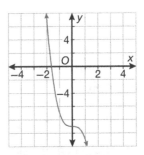

Find the x-intercepts. By inspection, the only x-intercept is at $x \approx -1.7$.

Example **Solving Cubic Equations Using a Graphing Calculator**

Solve with your graphing calculator. $-2x^2 = \frac{1}{2}x^3 - 1$

Move terms to the right side of the equation.

$0 = \frac{1}{2}x^3 + 2x^2 - 1$

Enter $Y1 = \frac{1}{2}x^3 + 2x^2 - 1$.

Use TRACE to estimate the value of the x-intercepts.

Use the ZERO function for better estimates of the x-intercepts.

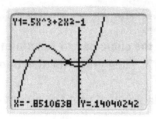

$x_1 \approx -3.9$, $x_2 \approx -0.8$, $x_3 \approx 0.7$

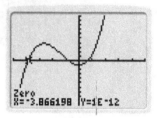

$x_1 \approx -3.87$, $x_2 \approx -0.79$, $x_3 \approx 0.66$

Lesson Practice 📖 page 785

a. Make a table and graph.

x	−2	−1	0	1	2
y					

b. $4x^3 =$ _____

Graph. Identify the x-intercept(s) by inspection.

$x =$ _____

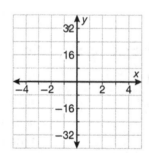

c. Rearrange.

$0 = -x^3 +$ _____

$y =$ _____

Graph. Identify x-intercept(s) by inspection.

$x \approx$ _____

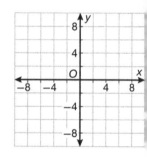

d. *Multiply each term by the LCD 4. Then write in standard form.*

_____ $x^3 +$ _____ $x^2 +$ _____ $= 0$

Graph. *Use the TRACE and ZERO functions to solve.*

$x_1 \approx$ _____ ; $x_2 \approx$ _____ ; $x_3 \approx$ _____

e. Set $Y1 =$ _____ . Graph.

Use the TRACE function to find V when $x \approx 25.5$.

$V \approx$ _____

1. *Factor the second denominator.*

   ____ $(x +$ ____ $)$

   LCD: ____ $(x +$ ____ $)$

   Multiply each term by the LCD.

   $x =$ ____

2. *Factor the second denominator.*

   ____ $(x +$ ____ $)$

   $x =$ ____

3. 📓 Make a table. Let $x = -3, 0,$ and 3.

   Graph.

   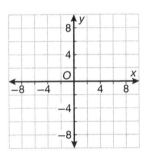

   $x =$ ____

4. *Cubic is degree 3.*

   Circle the answer.

   A $y = 3x - 4y$

   B $y = 6x^2 + 2$

   C $y = x^3 - 4x + 1$

   D $y = 10x^4 + 3x^2 - 5$

5. Complete the table.

x			
V	4	23	60

   When $V = 23, x =$ ____.

6. *Use your graphing calculator.*

   Set Y1 = _____.

   Use the TRACE function to find V when r is 2 in.

   $V \approx$ _____

7. The ends of the graph go in _____

   directions. The graph is a _____ curve.

   The curve crosses the x-axis at least

   _____ time(s) and at most _____ times.

8. *The parent function is $y = x^3$.*

   Example: _____

9. *Substitute.* $y = \sqrt{4(\underline{}) - 5}$

Simplify. $\sqrt{\underline{} - 5} \approx \underline{}$ $y \approx \underline{}$

10. Student _____ is correct. Student _____

incorrectly subtracted _____ from _____.

11. a. Make a table.

x	0	4	9	16
y				

 Graph the function.

b. If $x = 12, t \approx$ _____

12. *Discriminant* $= b^2 - 4ac$

$(\underline{})^2 - 4(\underline{})(\underline{}) = \underline{}$

$\underline{} \bigcirc 0$

_____ real solution(s)

13. Student _____ is correct. Student _____

is incorrect because the value of _____

is _____, not _____.

14. $A = (\underline{})(\underline{})$

If $A = 50$, $(\underline{})(\underline{}) = 50$.

Rearrange. $x^2 \bigcirc \underline{} x \bigcirc \underline{} = 0$

discriminant: $(\underline{})^2 - 4(\underline{})(\underline{}) = \underline{}$

Discriminant $\bigcirc$ 0, so _____, there

are dimensions for which $A = 50m^2$.

15. _____, because $200 = (\underline{})(\underline{})$

represents the area of the rectangle.

Write in standard form.

$\underline{} x^2 + \underline{} x + \underline{} = 0$

discriminant $= (\underline{})^2 - 4(\underline{})(\underline{})$

The discriminant is $\bigcirc$ 0, which

means there is _____ value of x that

makes the equation true.

16. *Arrange the ordered pairs so the x-values are increasing.*

The x-values increase by _____ for all

four ordered pairs and the y-values

_____ have a common ratio, so the

ordered pairs _____ satisfy

an exponential function.

17. *Isolate y in each inequality.*

$y \geq$ ____ x ◯ ____

$y \leq$ ____ x ◯ ____

Graph each inequality.

18. $48 = \frac{1}{2}($ _____ $)($ _____ $)$

Write in standard form.

x^2 ◯ ____ x ◯ ____ $= 0$

Factor to solve.

$x =$ _____ or $x =$ _____

$h =$ _____

$b =$ _____

19.

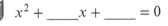

Find the x-intercept(s) to solve.

$x =$ _____

20. *Use the fundamental counting principle.*

_____ · _____ · _____

$=$ ____ area codes

21. *Substitute.*

Circle the answer.

A $y = x^2$
$y = x + 6$

B $y = x^2$
$y = 6$

C $y = x^2$
$y = -2x - 1$

D $y = x^2$
$y = -x + 6$

22. *Draw a sketch.*

The second _____ line could

intersect the parabola at least _____.

Since it _____ intersects the second

line, there is ____ solution to the system.

23. Let x = number of big bows
Let y = number of small bows

____ $x +$ ____ y ◯ 20

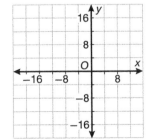

24. *Write in standard form.*

$x^2 +$ ____ $x +$ ____ $= 0$

$Y1 =$ _____

Use the ZERO function to find the solution(s).

Round to the nearest tenth.

$x =$ _____ and $x =$ _____

25. *Isolate x^2 and then take the square root of both sides of the equation.*

Circle the answer.

A 7   **B** ±7

C no solution   **D** ±7√1̄

26. Complete the pattern:

In the first set of calls, 3 people are notified.

1, 3, _____, _____. _____, _____, _____

_____, _____ ...

_____ sets of calls

27. a. $P = $ _____

    b. _____ $= 8$

    Isolate the radical. Then square both sides.

    $x = $ _____

28. The _____ sign indicates

that the "V" will open _____.

29. *Write the equations in the form $y = a|x - h| + k$. Compare the a-value in each equation to determine if the graph is compressed or stretched.*

$d = |60t - 90| = |60(t - \underline{\quad})|$

$= \underline{\quad}|t - \underline{\quad}|$

$d = |80t - 90| = |\underline{\quad}(t - \underline{\quad})|$

$= \underline{\quad}|t - \underline{\quad}|$

The graph would be _____.

30. slowest: _____

between fastest and slowest: _____

fastest: _____

Solving Simple and Compound Interest Problems page 788

New Concepts

See "Simple Interest Formula" on 📖 page 788.

Math Language

Principal is money that is invested or borrowed.

Interest is the amount of money paid for the use of that money.

Simple interest is paid on the principal only.

Compound interest is the interest paid on both the principal and on previously-earned interest.

Example **Finding Simple Interest**

An account is opened with $4000 and the bank pays 5% simple interest annually. **How much interest will it earn in 3 years?**

principal: $P = 4000$; rate: $r = 5\% = 0.05$; time: $t = 3$ years

$I = Prt$ — Write the formula for simple interest.
$\quad = 4000(0.05)(3)$ — Substitute the values of the variables.
$\quad = 600$ — Simplify.

The account will earn $600 interest in 3 years.

See "Compound Interest Formula" on 📖 page 790.

Example **Finding Compound Interest**

$5000 is invested. **Find the value of the investment after 10 years at 6% compounded quarterly.**

time: $t = 10$ years; $n = 4$; rate: $r = 6\%$

$A = P\left(1 + \frac{r}{n}\right)^{nt}$ — Write the formula.

$\quad = 5000\left(1 + \frac{0.06}{4}\right)^{4(10)}$ — Substitute the values of the variables.

$\quad = 5000(1.015)^{40}$ — Use the order of operations.

$\quad = 5000 \cdot 1.814018409$ — Simplify the power; do not round.

$\quad = 9070.09$ — Multiply; round to the nearest penny.

The value of the investment will be $9070.09.

Lesson Practice 📖 page 792

a. account opening balance: _____

annual simple interest: _____

number of years: _____

$I = Prt$

$I =$ _____ · _____ · _____

$\quad = \$$ _____

b. invested amount: _____

simple interest: _____

number of years: _____

$I =$ _____ · _____ · _____ $= \$$ _____

Add interest to principal to find account total.

_____ + _____ $= \$$ _____

c. $I = Prt$

$$562.5 = \underline{\hspace{1.5cm}} \cdot \underline{\hspace{1.5cm}} \cdot t$$

$$\underline{\hspace{1.5cm}} = \underline{\hspace{1.5cm}} \cdot t$$

$$\underline{\hspace{1.5cm}} \text{ years} = t$$

d. 15 months is the same as 1.25 years

$$\underline{\hspace{1cm}} = \underline{\hspace{2cm}} \cdot r \cdot \underline{\hspace{1cm}}$$

$$\underline{\hspace{1.5cm}} = r \cdot \underline{\hspace{1cm}}$$

$$\underline{\hspace{1.5cm}} = r \text{ or } \underline{\hspace{1cm}} \%$$

e. For interest compounded annually, $n = 1$, so $A = P(1 + r)^t$.

$$A = \underline{\hspace{2cm}}(1 + \underline{\hspace{1cm}})^{\square}$$

$$A = \underline{\hspace{1cm}}(\underline{\hspace{1cm}})^{\square}$$

$$A = \$\underline{\hspace{2cm}}$$

f. Use the formula for interest compounded other than annually: $A = P(1 + \frac{r}{n})^{nt}$.

$$A = \underline{\hspace{1.5cm}}\left(1 + \frac{\square}{4}\right)^{4t}$$

$$A = \underline{\hspace{1.5cm}}(\underline{\hspace{1cm}})^{4 \cdot \square}$$

$$A = \$\underline{\hspace{2cm}}$$

g. account balance: _____

simple interest: _____

Use the formula for simple interest. Add to find each total amount in the account.

Complete the table to find the amount in the account after 1, 2, 5, and 10 years.

Years	$Prt = I$	Account Total
1		
2		
5		
10		

h. account amount: _____

annual compounded interest: _____

Use the compound interest formula.

Complete the table to find the amount in the account after 1, 2, 5, and 10 years.

Principal	Rate	Years	Account Total
$2500	12%	1	
$2500	12%	2	
$2500	12%	5	
$2500	12%	10	

Use the tables in problems *g* and *h*.

i. Use the table in *g* to graph the account earning simple interest and the table in *h* to graph the account earning compound interest on one coordinate plane. Compare the growth over time.

The _____ interest account increases

_____ rapidly.

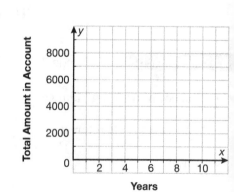

j. Find each investment, then compare.

The ___-year old man's investment will be worth more by $_____.

1. *Use the formula for simple interest.*

$I =$ _____ · _____ · _____

$I =$ _____

2. Simple interest is paid on the _____.

Compound interest is paid on the

_____ and the _____

earned.

3. *The y-intercept is the original value.*

$ _____ was originally invested.

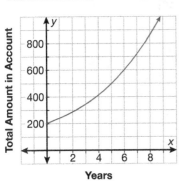

4. *Enter the function rule into the Y = editor. Look at the TABLE function to find the y-value of 4 million.*

The population will reach 4 million in

_____.

5. $I =$ _____ · _____ · _____ = _____

Add the interest and principal.

_____ + _____ = _____

Circle the answer.

A $924   **B** $1524

C $2586.26   **D** $92,400

6. *For interest compounded annually, n = 1, so*
$A = P(1 + r)^t$.

$A = ($_____$)(1 + $_____$)^{\square}$

$A = ($_____$)($_____$)^{\square}$

$A = $$ _____

7. $y = -3x^3$

$x =$ _____

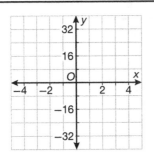

8. Student _____ is correct.

Student _____ used the

_____ power; "cubed"

means the _____ power.

9. *Evaluate the function for x = −2, −1, 0, 1, and 2.*

   $V =$ _____ ^{3}

   $V =$ _____

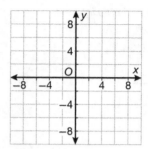

---

10. $y = x^3 + 5$

    a.

x	y
−2	
−1	
0	
1	
2	

    b.

    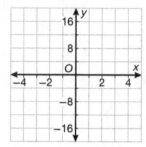

    c. $y = x^3 + 5$ $y =$ _____

---

11. $y = 3\sqrt{(7x + 2)} - 7$

    $y = 3\sqrt{(7(\underline{\quad}) + 2)} - 7$

    $y =$ _____

12. $y = 8\sqrt{x}$

    $y = 8\sqrt{\underline{\quad}}$

    $y \approx$ _____

---

13. Student _____ is correct. Student _____ just removed the

    _____ sign and set the entire right side _____

    than or _____ to zero.

14. $s = \sqrt{A}$

    $s =$ _____

---

15. $y \geq \dfrac{2}{5}x - 4$

    $y \leq 0$

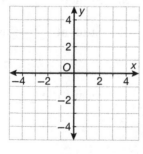

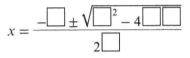

16. *Write the equation in standard form.*

$46 + 16x = -x^2 \longrightarrow$ _____

Use the quadratic formula: $x = \dfrac{-b \pm \sqrt{b^2 - 4ac}}{2a}$

$a =$ _____ $b =$ _____ $c =$ _____

$x = \dfrac{-\square \pm \sqrt{\square^2 - 4\square\square}}{2\square}$

17. *Multiply the number of possible choices for each finishing place.*

____ • ____ • ____ • ____ • ____ = _____

18. $y = 2x^2 - 6x + 1$

$y = -x - 4$

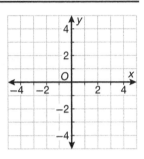

Solution: _____

$x =$ _____ + _____ = _____

$x =$ _____ − _____ = _____

19. *Discriminant* $= b^2 - 4ac$

_____^{2} − 4(_____)(_____)

Circle the answer.

A 0   **B** 1

C 2   **D** 3

20. The discriminant tells how many times

the graph of a _____

equation _____ or

_____ the x-_____.

21. *Write the equation in standard form.*

22.   Isolate the absolute value. Then write as a compound inequality.

$|4x - 3| + 1 > 10$

$x \bigcirc$ _____ OR $x \bigcirc$ _____

Solution: _____

23.
$$p = 4905\sqrt{x}$$

$$\underline{\hspace{2cm}} = 4905\sqrt{x}$$

$$\underline{\hspace{2cm}} = \sqrt{x}$$

$$\underline{\hspace{2cm}} = x$$

24.

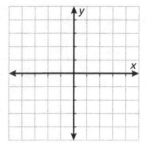

Vertex: (____, ____)

25. $I = Prt$

$$\underline{\hspace{1.5cm}} = \underline{\hspace{1cm}} \cdot \underline{\hspace{1cm}} \cdot t$$

$$\underline{\hspace{1.5cm}} = t$$

The money was borrowed for

$$\underline{\hspace{3cm}}.$$

26. *Use the formula for interest compounded other than annually:* $A = P\left(1 + \frac{r}{n}\right)^{nt}$, $n = 12$.

$$A = \underline{\hspace{3cm}}$$

27. $f(x) = 4(-2)^x$ is not an exponential

function because b is _____.

The range values are not all positive or all

negative, for example:

$f(2) = \underline{\hspace{1cm}}$ and $f(3) = \underline{\hspace{1cm}}$.

28. a. The pattern is to _____

each term by _____.

b. The next term in the sequence is

$$\frac{1}{\square} \bigcirc \underline{\hspace{1.5cm}} = \underline{\hspace{2cm}}.$$

29. *Use the formula for the axis of symmetry.*

$$x = -\frac{b}{2a} = \underline{\hspace{1cm}}$$

Substitute to find the y-coordinate.

$$y = 3x^2 - 12x + 2$$

$$y = 3(\underline{\hspace{1cm}})^2 - 12(\underline{\hspace{1cm}}) + 2$$

$$y = \underline{\hspace{1cm}}$$

The vertex is at (____, ____).

30. $f(x)$ is _____

$h(x)$ is _____

$g(x)$ is _____

$j(x)$ is _____

New Concepts

Math Language

Trigonometry is a branch of mathematics that deals with the relationships of the sides and angles of right triangles.

There are six **trigonometric ratios** that can be written using two sides of the triangle in relation to the angles of the triangle.

The six trigonometric ratios are defined as follows.

Sine, Cosine, and Tangent
$\text{sine of } \angle A = \dfrac{\text{length of leg opposite } \angle A}{\text{length of hypotenuse}} = \dfrac{a}{c}$
$\text{cosine of } \angle A = \dfrac{\text{length of leg adjacent to } \angle A}{\text{length of hypotenuse}} = \dfrac{b}{c}$
$\text{tangent of } \angle A = \dfrac{\text{length of leg opposite } \angle A}{\text{length of leg adjacent to } \angle A} = \dfrac{a}{b}$

Cosecant, Secant, and Cotangent
$\text{cosecant of } \angle A = \dfrac{\text{length of hypotenuse}}{\text{length of leg opposite } \angle A} = \dfrac{c}{a}$
$\text{secant of } \angle A = \dfrac{\text{length of hypotenuse}}{\text{length of leg adjacent to } \angle A} = \dfrac{c}{b}$
$\text{cotangent of } \angle A = \dfrac{\text{length of leg adjacent to } \angle A}{\text{length of leg opposite } \angle A} = \dfrac{b}{a}$

Example **Finding Trigonometry Ratios**

Use the right triangle to find sin B, cos B, and tan B.

$\sin B = \dfrac{\text{opposite}}{\text{hypotenuse}} = \dfrac{5}{13}$

$\cos B = \dfrac{\text{adjacent}}{\text{hypotenuse}} = \dfrac{12}{13}$

$\tan A = \dfrac{\text{opposite}}{\text{adjacent}} = \dfrac{5}{12}$

Find all six trigonometric ratios for $\angle A$ in the right triangle.

$a^2 + 4^2 = 5^2$ *First use the Pythagorean*
$a^2 + 16 = 25$ *Theorem to find the*
$\quad a^2 = 9$ *length of side a.*
$\quad a = 3$

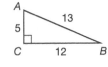

$\sin A = \dfrac{a}{c} = \dfrac{3}{5}$ $\qquad \csc A = \dfrac{c}{a} = \dfrac{5}{3}$

$\tan A = \dfrac{a}{b} = \dfrac{3}{4}$ $\qquad \cot A = \dfrac{b}{a} = \dfrac{4}{3}$

$\cos A = \dfrac{b}{c} = \dfrac{4}{5}$ $\qquad \sec A = \dfrac{c}{b} = \dfrac{5}{4}$

Find the missing measures.

a. $\sin A = \dfrac{\text{opposite}}{\text{hypotenuse}} = \dfrac{\square}{\square} = $ _____

$\cos A = \dfrac{\text{adjacent}}{\text{hypotenuse}} = \dfrac{\square}{\square} = $ _____

$\tan A = \dfrac{\text{opposite}}{\text{adjacent}} = \dfrac{\square}{\square} = $ _____

b. $b^2 + 3^2 = 5^2$ $b = $ _____

$\sin B = \dfrac{\square}{\square}$ $\cos B = \dfrac{\square}{\square}$ $\tan B = \dfrac{\square}{\square}$

$\csc B = \dfrac{\square}{\square}$ $\sec B = \dfrac{\square}{\square}$ $\cot B = \dfrac{\square}{\square}$

Use a graphing calculator for c–g.

c. $\sin 49° \approx$ _____

$\tan 49° \approx$ _____

$\cos 49° \approx$ _____

d. $\csc 67° \approx$ _____

$\cot 67° \approx$ _____

$\sec 67° \approx$ _____

e. *Use tan 36°.*

$\tan 36° = \dfrac{x}{40}$

_____ $\approx \dfrac{x}{40}$

_____ $\approx x$

f. $\sin 48° = \dfrac{x}{17}$ $\cos 48° = \dfrac{y}{17}$

_____ $\approx \dfrac{x}{17}$ _____ $\approx \dfrac{y}{17}$

_____ $\approx x$ _____ $\approx y$

g. $\tan A = \dfrac{\square}{\square}$

$A = \tan^{-1}(\tan A) = \tan^{-1}\left(\dfrac{\square}{\square}\right) \approx$ _____

$\tan B = \dfrac{\square}{\square}$ $B = \tan^{-1}(\tan B) = \tan^{-1}\left(\dfrac{\square}{\square}\right) \approx$ _____

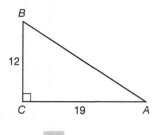

h. $\cos x = \dfrac{\square}{\square}$ $x = \cos^{-1}(\cos x) = \cos^{-1}\left(\dfrac{\square}{\square}\right) \approx$ _____

1. $\sin A = \dfrac{\text{opposite}}{\text{hypotenuse}} = \dfrac{\square}{\square}$

   $\cos A = \dfrac{\text{adjacent}}{\text{hypotenuse}} = \dfrac{\square}{\square}$

   $\tan A = \dfrac{\text{opposite}}{\text{adjacent}} = \dfrac{\square}{\square}$

2. $\sin A = \dfrac{\square}{\square}$

   $\cos A = \dfrac{\square}{\square}$

   $\tan A = \dfrac{\square}{\square}$

3. *An equation for direct variation is in the form* $y = kx$. *Use the coordinates to find k.*

   $\underline{\qquad} = k(\underline{\qquad})$

   $k = \underline{\qquad}$ $y = \underline{\qquad}x$

4. *Use a calculator.*

   $\sin 77° \approx \underline{\qquad}$ $\cos 77° \approx \underline{\qquad}$

   $\tan 77° \approx \underline{\qquad}$

5. Student $\underline{\quad}$ is correct. The tangent ratio is the $\underline{\qquad\qquad}$ leg over the $\underline{\qquad\qquad}$ leg.

   Student $\underline{\quad}$ used the $\underline{\qquad\qquad}$ leg over the $\underline{\qquad\qquad}$ leg.

6. *Let A = the measure of each acute angle. Let x = the length of each leg.*

   $180° = 90° + A + A$ $\sin A = \dfrac{x}{\square}$ $\sin \square = \dfrac{x}{\square}$

   $A = \underline{\qquad}$ $\underline{\qquad} \approx x$

7. **a.** *Find the length of the hypotenuse.*

   $\underline{\qquad}^2 + \underline{\qquad}^2 = c^2$

   $\underline{\qquad} + \underline{\qquad} = c^2$

   $\underline{\qquad} = c^2$

   $\underline{\qquad} = c$

   b. *Use tan A.*

   $\tan A = \dfrac{\square}{\square}$

   $\tan^{-1}(\tan A) = \tan^{-1}\left(\dfrac{\square}{\square}\right)$

   $\tan A \approx \underline{\qquad}$

8. *If the acute angles of a right triangle are equal, the legs are equal.*

   The tree is $\underline{\qquad}$ tall.

9. $I = prt$

   $I = \underline{\qquad} \cdot \underline{\qquad} \cdot \underline{\qquad}$

   $= \$\underline{\qquad}$

10. *Find the angle that is complementary to the angle of the dive.*

$$\cos \underline{\qquad}° = \frac{x}{3.4}$$

$$\underline{\qquad} \approx \frac{x}{3.4}$$

$$\underline{\qquad} \text{ miles} \approx x$$

11. The opposite leg is the leg of a right triangle that is _____ the acute angle. The adjacent leg is the leg that is next to the _____ angle, but is not the _____.

12. Student _____ is correct.

Student _____ found the _____ earned, but not the _____ value.

13. *Use the formula for annual compound interest: $A = P(1 + r)^r$.*

10-year account:

$$A = \underline{\qquad}(1 + \underline{\qquad})^{\square}$$

$$A = \underline{\qquad}$$

5-year account:

$$A = \underline{\qquad}(1 + \underline{\qquad})^{\square}$$

$$A = \underline{\qquad}$$

The account that pays _____% for _____ years will pay $_____._____ more.

14. *Find the y-value when x = 0.*

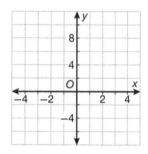

When $x = 0$, $y = \underline{\qquad}$.

15. Student _____ is correct.

Student _____ graphed $y = x^3$, or the _____ function.

16.

x	$V = x^3 + 3$
1	
2	
3	
4	
5	

$x = $ _____ for 30 cubic units

17. *First, write the equation in standard form.*

$$2x^2 - \underline{\qquad} + 9 = 0$$

Use the quadratic formula.

$$x = \underline{\qquad} \quad \text{or} \quad x = \underline{\qquad}$$

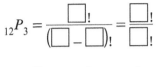

18. *There are 12 numbers taken 3 at a time.*

$$_{12}P_3 = \frac{\boxed{}!}{(\boxed{} - \boxed{})!} = \frac{\boxed{}!}{\boxed{}!}$$

$$= \underline{} \cdot \underline{} \cdot \underline{} = \underline{}$$

19. $x^2 + 5 = 9$

$$x^2 = \underline{}$$

$$x = \pm \underline{}$$

20. Graph the functions.

$$y = \frac{x^2}{8} + \frac{7}{4}$$

$$y = -\frac{9x}{8}$$

Intersection points:

$(\underline{}, \underline{})$,

$(\underline{}, \underline{})$

 Check.

21. *Discriminant* $= b^2 - 4ac$

$$\underline{}^2 - 4(\underline{})(\underline{})$$

$$= \underline{}$$

$b^2 - 4ac \bigcirc 0$, so there $\underline{}$

real solution(s).

22. *The domain is the values for x that make the radicand greater than or equal to 0.*

$$\underline{} \geq 0 \qquad x \geq \underline{}$$

Circle the domain of the function

$$f(x) = 2\sqrt{x + 6} - 1.$$

A $x \geq -5$ **B** $x \geq -6$

C $x \geq 6$ **D** $x \geq 0$

23. The graph of $f(x) = \sqrt{(x + 4)}$ can be

rewritten in the form $f(x) = \sqrt{(x - (\underline{}))}$.

This is a translation of the parent function

$\underline{}$ units to the $\underline{}$.

24. $3|8x + 2| < 12$

$|8x + 2| < \underline{}$ *Isolate the absolute-value.*

$8x + 2 \bigcirc \underline{}$ $8x + 2 \bigcirc \underline{}$

$8x \bigcirc \underline{}$ $8x \bigcirc \underline{}$

$x \bigcirc \underline{}$ $x \bigcirc \underline{}$

25. a. x and $\underline{}$

b. $x^2 + (\underline{})^2 = 74$

c. *Factor to solve.*

$$\underline{} = 74$$

$$\underline{} = 0$$

$$\underline{}(\underline{})(\underline{}) = 0$$

$\underline{}$ and $\underline{}$ or $\underline{}$ and $\underline{}$

26. $\csc 81° = \dfrac{1}{\sin 81°} \approx \underline{\hspace{1cm}}$ $\sec 81° = \dfrac{1}{\cos 81°} \approx \underline{\hspace{1cm}}$ $\cot 81° = \dfrac{1}{\tan 81°} \approx \underline{\hspace{1cm}}$

27. $f(0) = 15\left(\dfrac{4}{5}\right)^0 = \$\underline{\hspace{1.5cm}}$

$f(1) = 15\left(\dfrac{4}{5}\right)^{\square} = \$\underline{\hspace{1.5cm}}$

$f(2) = 15\left(\dfrac{4}{5}\right)^{\square} = \$\underline{\hspace{1.5cm}}$

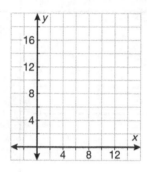

28. In the first system, the boundary lines are _____ because the points on those lines

_____ solutions. Whereas, the boundary lines in the second solution are

_____ and _____ in the solution set.

29. A half-life is the amount of time it takes

for _____ the substance to

remain.

There are _____ half-lives in 150

years.

30. a. horizontal asymptote: $y = \underline{\hspace{1.5cm}}$

b. vertical asymptote: $x = \underline{\hspace{1.5cm}}$

c. $y = \dfrac{2000}{x} + 2$

$= \dfrac{2000}{\square} + 2$

$= \underline{\hspace{1cm}} + 2$

$= \underline{\hspace{1.5cm}}$ rackets

Solving Problems Involving Combinations

page 804

New Concepts

Example Comparing Combinations to Permutations

A teacher puts 4 essay questions on a test. They are labeled A, B, C, and D. Students are required to answer 3 questions.

How many permutations of the 3 questions are possible?

$$_4P_3 = \frac{4!}{(4-3)!}$$

$$= \frac{4!}{1!} = \frac{4 \cdot 3 \cdot 2 \cdot 1}{1} = 24$$

There are **24 permutations of the 3 test questions.**

How many *combinations* of the 3 questions are possible?

The order of the questions does not matter. If a student hands in the test with questions A, B, and C answered, the teacher does not care whether the student answered A first, or B first, or C first. A test with ABC answered is the same as one with ACB, CAB, CBA, BCA, or BAC.

To find the number of different *combinations* of answered questions the teacher sees, list the 24 permutations. Then cross out the duplicate sets.

ABC	ABD	~~ACB~~	ACD	~~ADB~~	~~ADC~~
~~BAC~~	~~BAD~~	~~BCA~~	BCD	~~BDA~~	~~BDC~~
~~CAB~~	~~CAD~~	~~CBA~~	~~CBD~~	~~CDA~~	~~CDB~~
~~DAB~~	~~DAC~~	~~DBA~~	~~DBC~~	~~DCA~~	~~DCB~~

That leaves **4 combinations of the 3 test questions.**

- In the first Example, there are 6 times as many permutations as combinations. This makes sense because:
  for each set of 3 letters, there are $3 \cdot 2 \cdot 1 = 6$ possible orders.

    ABC   ABC, ACB, CAB, CBA, BCA, BAC

- To find the number of combinations of a group of items, the number of permutations is divided by the number of ways to order r items, $r!$.

- See "Combination Formula" on 📖 page 805.

Example Finding the Number of Combinations

At a restaurant 2 side dishes may be chosen from a total of 6 side dishes. **How many possible combinations are there?**

$$_6C_2 = \frac{6!}{2!(6-2)!}$$ *Substitute n = 6 and r = 2.*

$$= \frac{6!}{2!(4!)}$$ *Simplify inside parentheses.*

$$= \frac{6 \cdot 5 \cdot \cancel{4} \cdot \cancel{3} \cdot \cancel{2} \cdot \cancel{1}}{(2 \cdot 1)(\cancel{4} \cdot \cancel{3} \cdot \cancel{2} \cdot \cancel{1})}$$ *Expand the factorials. Cancel out common factors.*

$$= \frac{30}{2} = 15$$ *Multiply. Simplify.*

There are 15 ways to choose 2 side dishes.

Lesson Practice 📖 page 806

A teacher selects 2 students from a group of 5 students. Use this information for a and b.

a. How many permutations are possible?

$$_nP_r = \frac{n!}{(n-r)!} \qquad _5P_2 = \frac{\boxed{}!}{(5-\boxed{})!} = \frac{5 \cdot \boxed{} \cdot \boxed{} \cdot \boxed{} \cdot \boxed{}}{3 \cdot \boxed{} \cdot \boxed{}} = \frac{\boxed{}}{\boxed{}} = \underline{} \text{ permutations}$$

b. How many combinations are possible?

$$_nC_r = \frac{n!}{r!(n-r)!} \qquad _5C_2 = \frac{\boxed{}!}{2!(5-\boxed{})!} = \frac{5 \cdot \boxed{} \cdot \boxed{} \cdot \boxed{}}{(2 \cdot \boxed{})(3 \cdot \boxed{} \cdot \boxed{})} = \frac{\boxed{}}{\boxed{}} = \underline{} \text{ combinations}$$

c. 4 markers are chosen from a box of 8. How many combinations are there?

$$_\boxed{}C_\boxed{} = \frac{\boxed{}!}{4!(8-\boxed{})!} = \frac{8 \cdot \boxed{} \cdot \boxed{} \cdot \boxed{} \cdot \boxed{} \cdot \boxed{} \cdot \boxed{}}{(4 \cdot \boxed{} \cdot \boxed{} \cdot \boxed{})(4 \cdot \boxed{} \cdot \boxed{} \cdot \boxed{})} = \frac{\boxed{}}{\boxed{}} = \underline{}$$

d. 9 parents are chosen from a group of 22. How many combinations are there?

$$_\boxed{}C_\boxed{} = \frac{22!}{\boxed{}!(22-\boxed{})!}$$ 📓 Complete the calculation.   _____ combinations

e. There are 18 possible ingredients. A cook uses 4 to make soup. What is the probability he will pick beans, corn, rice and carrots?

$$_\boxed{}C_\boxed{} = \frac{\boxed{}!}{\boxed{}!(18-\boxed{})!}$$ 📓 Complete the calculation.

There are _____ possible combinations.

$P(\text{beans, corn, rice, carrots}) = $ _____

1. $_{15}C_4 = \dfrac{\square!}{4!(15-\square)!} = \dfrac{15 \cdot 14 \cdot 13 \cdot 12 \cdot 11 \cdot 10 \cdot 9 \cdot 8 \cdot \square \cdot \square \cdot \square \cdot \square \cdot \square \cdot \square \cdot \square}{(4 \cdot \square \cdot \square \cdot \square)(11 \cdot 10 \cdot \square \cdot \square \cdot \square \cdot \square \cdot \square \cdot \square \cdot \square \cdot \square \cdot \square)}$

$= \underline{\qquad}$

2. $_{11}C_4 = \dfrac{\square!}{4!(11-\square)!} = \dfrac{11 \cdot 10 \cdot 9 \cdot 8 \cdot \square \cdot \square \cdot \square \cdot \square \cdot \square \cdot \square \cdot \square}{(4 \cdot \square \cdot \square \cdot \square)(7 \cdot \square \cdot \square \cdot \square \cdot \square \cdot \square \cdot \square)} = \underline{\qquad}$

3. $_{9}C_7 = \dfrac{\square!}{7!(9-\square)!} = \dfrac{9 \cdot 8 \cdot \square \cdot \square \cdot \square \cdot \square \cdot \square \cdot \square \cdot \square}{(7 \cdot \square \cdot \square \cdot \square \cdot \square \cdot \square \cdot \square)(2 \cdot \square)} = \underline{\qquad}$

4. $_{12}C_5 = \dfrac{\square!}{5!(12-\square)!} = \dfrac{12 \cdot 11 \cdot 10 \cdot 9 \cdot 8 \cdot \square \cdot \square \cdot \square \cdot \square \cdot \square \cdot \square \cdot \square}{(5 \cdot \square \cdot \square \cdot \square \cdot \square)(7 \cdot \square \cdot \square \cdot \square \cdot \square \cdot \square \cdot \square)} = \underline{\qquad}$

5. In a \underline{\qquad\qquad}, the \underline{\qquad\qquad} of the items matters, but in a

\underline{\qquad\qquad} the \underline{\qquad\qquad} does not matter.

6. $_{8}C_3 = \dfrac{8!}{\square!(8-\square)!} = \dfrac{8!}{(8-\square)!} \cdot \dfrac{1}{\square!} = \dfrac{\dfrac{8!}{(8-\square)!}}{\square!} = \dfrac{_{8}P_3}{\text{number of ways to order } \square \text{ items}}$

7. $_{5}C_3 = \dfrac{\square!}{3!(5-\square)!}$

$= \dfrac{\square \cdot \square \cdot \square \cdot \square \cdot \square}{(\square \cdot \square \cdot \square)(2 \cdot \square)} = \underline{\qquad}$

Circle the answer.

A 10	**B** 12
C 20	**D** 60

8. $n = \underline{\qquad}$ $r = \underline{\qquad}$

$_\square C_\square = \dfrac{10!}{3!(10-\square)!}$

$= \dfrac{\square \cdot \square \cdot \square \cdot 7 \cdot 6 \cdot 5 \cdot 4 \cdot 3 \cdot 2 \cdot 1}{(\square \cdot \square \cdot \square)(7 \cdot 6 \cdot 5 \cdot 4 \cdot 3 \cdot 2 \cdot 1)}$

There are \underline{\qquad} combinations that can be

made from 10 different products.

9. *First factor the expressions.*

$(15x - 10) =$ ____($\qquad$) $(3x - 2) =$ _____   LCM = _____

---

10. $_8C_2 = \dfrac{\square!}{\square!(\square - \square)!} = \dfrac{\square \cdot \square \cdot \square \cdot \square \cdot \square \cdot \square \cdot \square \cdot \square}{(2 \cdot \square)(\square \cdot \square \cdot \square \cdot \square \cdot \square \cdot \square)} = \dfrac{\square}{\square} =$ ____

---

11. a. 📓 Complete the calculation.

$_{25}C_9 = \dfrac{\square!}{\square!(\square - \square)!}$

b. 📓 Complete the calculation.

$_{24}C_8 = \dfrac{\square!}{\square!(\square - \square)!}$

$P(\text{choosing 8 out of 24}) =$ _____

12. *Trigonometric ratios: SOH-CAH-TOA*

$\sin A = \dfrac{\square}{25}$ $\cot A = \dfrac{7}{\square}$

$\cos A = \dfrac{\square}{25}$ $\sec A = \dfrac{25}{\square}$

$\tan A = \dfrac{24}{\square}$ $\csc A = \dfrac{\square}{24}$

---

13. a. $a^2 + b^2 = c^2$

$12^2 + b^2 =$ _____ ^{2}

_____ $+ b^2 =$ _____

$b^2 =$ _____

$b =$ _____ feet

b. $\sin A = \dfrac{\square}{20}$

$\sin^{-1}(\sin A) = \sin^{-1}\left(\dfrac{\square}{20}\right)$

$A \approx$ _____ $^\circ$

14. Graph $\triangle ABC$.

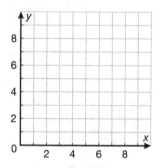

$AC =$ _____ $BC =$ _____

Use a trigonometric ratio to find the measure of $\angle A$.

$\tan A = \dfrac{\square}{\square}$ $A = \sin^{-1}\dfrac{\square}{\square} \approx$ _____ $^\circ$

---

15. $I = Prt$

$I = 9200($_____$)($_____$) = \$$_____

16. $A = P(1 + r)^t$

$A = 20,000(1 + \underline{\hspace{1cm}})^{\square}$

$= 20,000(\underline{\hspace{1cm}})^{\square}$

$= \$\underline{\hspace{1cm}}$

Subtract original amount from the ending amount.

$\$\underline{\hspace{1cm}} - 20,000 = \$\underline{\hspace{1cm}}$

17. $A = P\left(1 + \frac{r}{n}\right)^{nt}$

$r = \underline{\hspace{1cm}}$ $\quad n = \underline{\hspace{1cm}}$ $\quad t = \underline{\hspace{1cm}}$

Student $\underline{\hspace{1cm}}$ is correct.

Student $\underline{\hspace{1cm}}$ found the interest

compounded $\underline{\hspace{2cm}}$,

not $\underline{\hspace{2cm}}$.

18. $\dfrac{10!}{5!} = \dfrac{10 \cdot 9 \cdot \square \cdot \square \cdot \square \cdot \square \cdot \square \cdot \square \cdot \square \cdot \square}{\square \cdot \square \cdot \square \cdot \square \cdot \square}$

$= \underline{\hspace{2cm}}$

19. $\dfrac{4}{\sqrt{3} - 2} \cdot \dfrac{\sqrt{\square} + \square}{\sqrt{\square} + \square} = \dfrac{4\sqrt{\square} + \square}{\square - \square}$

$= \underline{\hspace{2cm}}$

20. *Use substitution.*

$x^2 - 5 = \underline{\hspace{1.5cm}}$

$x^2 - \underline{\hspace{1.5cm}} - 5 = 0$

$(x + \underline{\hspace{0.8cm}})(x - \underline{\hspace{0.8cm}}) = 0$

$x = \underline{\hspace{1cm}}$ $\qquad x = \underline{\hspace{1cm}}$

 Use y = 4x to determine the y-coordinates.

$y = 4(\underline{\hspace{0.8cm}}) = \underline{\hspace{1cm}}$

$y = 4(\underline{\hspace{0.8cm}}) = \underline{\hspace{1cm}}$

Solutions: $(\underline{\hspace{0.8cm}}, \underline{\hspace{0.8cm}})$ and $(\underline{\hspace{0.8cm}}, \underline{\hspace{0.8cm}})$

21. $y = -16t^2 + 75t + 2$

$-16t^2 + 75t + 2 = \underline{\hspace{1.5cm}}$

$-16t^2 + 75t - \underline{\hspace{1.5cm}} = 0$

Discriminant = b² – 4ac

$a = \underline{\hspace{1cm}}$ $\quad b = \underline{\hspace{1cm}}$ $\quad c = \underline{\hspace{1cm}}$

$\underline{\hspace{1cm}}^2 - 4(\underline{\hspace{0.8cm}})(\underline{\hspace{0.8cm}}) = \underline{\hspace{1.5cm}}$

The ball $\underline{\hspace{2cm}}$ reach a height of 45 ft.

22. $y = \sqrt{\dfrac{3}{\square}} + 2$

$= \sqrt{\dfrac{\square}{\square}} + 2 \approx \underline{\hspace{1cm}}$

23. Graph $x^3 - 27 = 0$ and find the x-intercept.

Answer: $\underline{\hspace{1.5cm}}$

24. parent cubic function:

$y = \underline{\hspace{1.5cm}}$

25. $x^2 = 45$

$$x = \pm\sqrt{\underline{}} = \pm\sqrt{(\underline{})(\underline{})} = \pm\underline{}\sqrt{\underline{}} \approx \pm\underline{}$$

26. a. Day 1: $A(1) = 500$

Day 2: $A(2) = 500 \cdot 5 = \underline{}$

Day 3: $A(3) = 25{,}000 \cdot 5 = \underline{}$

Use the geometric sequence formula
$A(n) = ar^{n-1}$.

$n = 5$ $\quad r = \underline{}$ $\quad a = 500$

$A(5) = 500(\underline{})^{\square - 1} = \underline{}$

b. Since $\frac{1}{4}$ of the cells die off each day, multiply r by $\frac{3}{4}$.

Use the geometric sequence formula $A(n) = ar^{n-1}$.

$$A(n) = \underline{}\left(\underline{} \cdot \frac{3}{4}\right)^{\square - 1}$$

c. $A(5) = 500(\underline{})^{\square - 1} = \underline{}$

27.
a.
$$\begin{cases} \underline{}t + \underline{}s \bigcirc 200 \\ t + s \bigcirc 250 \end{cases}$$

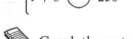 Graph the system. Use s as the vertical axis.

b. If 15 teachers buy tickets, it $\underline{}$ possible for the class to meet its goal because there $\underline{}$ an ordered pair with $\underline{}$ teachers in the solution set.

28. *Approximate the square when using the Quadratic Formula.*

$a = \underline{}$ $\qquad b = \underline{}$ $\qquad c = \underline{}$

$$v = \frac{-\square \pm \sqrt{\square^2 - 4\square\square}}{2\square} = \frac{-\square \pm \square}{\square}$$

$v \approx \underline{}$ and $v \approx \underline{}$

29. GCF: $-\square_z\square$

$-88z^3 - 2r^2z^3 - 30rz^3$

$= \underline{}(44 + \underline{} + \underline{})$

$= \underline{}(r^2 + \underline{} + \underline{})$

$= (\underline{})(r + \underline{})(r + \underline{})$

30. *How many 100-minute periods are in 10 hours?*

10 hours $= \underline{}$ minutes $\longrightarrow$ $\underline{}$ minutes $\div 100 = \underline{}$ half-lives

Use the exponential decay function $f(x) = k(b)^x$.

$x = \underline{}$ $\qquad b = \frac{1}{2}$ $\qquad k = \underline{}$

$f(\underline{}) = 320(\underline{})^{\square} = \underline{}$mg

Graphing and Comparing Linear, Quadratic, and Exponential Functions page 809

New Concepts

Math Language

A **function family** is a set of functions whose graphs have similar characteristics.

Example **Matching Function Families and Tables**

Identify the table of values to identify the function family.

x	-3	-2	-1	0	1	2	3
$f(x)$	$\frac{1}{27}$	$\frac{1}{9}$	$\frac{1}{3}$	1	3	9	27

Plot the points. Connect them using a smooth curve. As x increases, values for $f(x)$ increase at an increasing rate of change. This is exponential growth. **The function belongs to the exponential family.**

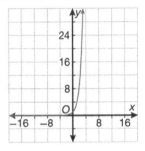

- Each type of function models a different type of real-world situation.

Function	Linear	Quadratic	Exponential
Parent	$f(x) = x$	$f(x) = x^2$	$f(x) = b^x$
Graph	line	parabola	exponential
Situation	constant rate of change	minimum or maximum value	values **always increasing at an increasing rate of change or always decreasing at a decreasing rate of change**

Example **Identifying an Appropriate Model**

Identify the appropriate model for each situation.

the height of a ball thrown upward from an initial height of 5 feet

The ball goes up, hits a maximum height, and comes back down. The path is a parabolic curve with a maximum value. **A quadratic function models the situation.**

the cost of a tank of gas when gas costs $3.25 per gallon

The price of gas is a constant. For each gallon put in the tank, the total cost increases by $3.25. **A linear function models the situation.**

Identify the function family represented by each graph.

a. A non-vertical straight line is a _____ function.

b. The point (0, 2) is a _____, so it is a _____ function.

c. A curve with _____ steepness is a _____ function.

Use the table of values to identify the function family.

d. x-values increasing by: ____ y-values increasing by: ____

constant rate of change? _____   _____ function

e. x-values increasing by: ____ y-values values _____ and then _____

constant rate of change? _____   📖 Graph.

The graph is a _____-shaped curved, so it is a _____ function.

Tell whether the function family is linear, quadratic, or exponential.

f. The graph is always increasing with a *constant rate.*

_____ function

g. The graph changes direction at a *maximum* of 3.

_____ function

h. The graph is *always increasing* and it *gets steeper* as x increases.

_____ function

Identify the appropriate model for each situation.

i. 📖 Sketch the arrow's path.

The arrow's path is a ____-shaped _____, so a(n) _____ function is the model.

j.

Hour	0	1	2	3	4	5
# of Particles	1000	500	___	___	___	___

The rate of change is _____, so a(n) _____ function is the model.

k. constant rate? _____   a(n) _____ function

1. Student _____ is correct.

   Student _____ wrote an equation that

   does not include an _____ term.

2. As x decreases, y always increases at an

   increasing rate of change, thus the graph is

   _____.

   function family: _____

3. At $(-2,$ _____ $)$, the graph has a

   _____.

   function family: _____

4. You can graph the _____

   function and then graph a series of

   _____ of it.

5. function: $f(x) =$ _____ $+$ _____

   function family: _____

   parent function: $f(x) =$ _____

6. Student _____ is correct.

   Student _____ used the formula for

   _____.

7. **a.** constant rate of change? _____

   function type: _____

   b. $f(x) =$ _____ $+$ _____

8. function: $f(x) =$ _____ $+$ _____

   function family: _____

9. Circle the answer.

   A quadratic   **B** linear

   C exponential   **D** none of these

10. $A = \frac{1}{2}($ _____ $)($ _____ $)$

    $= \frac{1}{2}($ _____ $)$

    function family: _____

11. function family: _____

12. In the function, x is the _____.

function type: _____

13. a. The order of the helpers _____ matter, so this is a _____.

$$22 \text{——} 4 = \frac{n!}{r!(n-r)!}$$

$$= \text{_____}$$

b. The choice of Shawn, Tonia, Torie, and Reid is _____ out of a possible _____

different groups, so the probability is _____.

14. Find the value of the trigonometric ratios.

$\sin 14° \approx$ ____._____

$\cos 14° \approx$ ____._____

$\tan 14° \approx$ ____._____

15. Student _____ is correct.

Student _____ used the wrong ratio.

x represents the _____ leg.

The ratio of the _____ leg over

the _____ is _____.

16. x represents the length of the triangle's

_____. 8000 is the length of

the leg _____ the given angle.

$$\text{_____} 11° = \frac{\square}{x}$$

$$\text{_____} \approx \frac{\square}{x}$$

$$x \approx \text{_____}$$

17. 📎 Graph.

Do the graphs intersect each other?

If so, at what point(s)?

Solution(s): _____

18. $b^2 - 4ac$

_____^{2} − 4(_____)(_____)

= _____ − _____

= _____

The discriminant is _____,

so the equation has _____ real solution(s).

19. The square root of a _____

number is not a real number, so the domain

is n ◯ _____.

There cannot be a _____ number

of cards, so we write the domain as

n ◯ _____.

20. _Make a table of values._ 📝 Graph.

At $x = 0$, $y =$ _____.

21. $A = P(1 + r)^t$

$A =$ _____$(1 + \_\_.\_\_)^\square$

$A = $ _____

interest earned: _____

_____ > _____

$I = Prt$

$I = ($_____$)($_._____$)($_____$)$

$I = $ _____

22. $A = P\left(1 + \frac{r}{n}\right)^{nt}$

$A = $ _____$\left(1 + \dfrac{\square}{\square}\right)^{(\square)(\square)}$

Circle the answer.

A $1282.04   **B** $2000

C $2653.30   **D** $2701.48

23. $_nC_r = \dfrac{n!}{r!(n-r)!}$

$_8C_3 = \dfrac{\square!}{\square!(\square - \square)!}$

$= \dfrac{\square}{(\square)(\square)}$

= _____

24. conjugate of $\sqrt{7} - 3\sqrt{5}$: _____ + _____

$$\frac{6}{\sqrt{7} - 3\sqrt{5}} \cdot \frac{\square + \square}{\square + \square}$$

$$= \frac{\square\sqrt{\square} + \square\sqrt{\square}}{\square + \square\sqrt{\square} - \square\sqrt{\square} - (\square \cdot \square)}$$

$$= \frac{\square\sqrt{\square} + \square\sqrt{\square}}{\square - \square} = \frac{-\square\sqrt{\square} - \square\sqrt{\square}}{\square}$$

25. *First divide so the coefficient of x^2 is 1. Then add $\left(\frac{b}{2}\right)^2$ to each side and factor.*

$$m^2 + \underline{\quad}m = \underline{\quad}$$

$$m^2 + \underline{\quad}m + \underline{\quad} = \underline{\quad} + \underline{\quad}$$

$$(m + \underline{\quad})^2 = \sqrt{\underline{\quad}}$$

$$m = \underline{\quad} \quad \text{or} \quad m = \underline{\quad}$$

26. a. $-\sqrt{x - 4} = $ _____

$\sqrt{x - 4} = $ _____

$x - 4 = $ _____

$x = $ _____

b. To isolate the radical, both sides of the equation must be _____ by _____.

c. 📓 Make a table of values and graph.

27. function family: _____

28. If an expression can be easily _____, the extra steps in the quadratic equation are not necessary.

29. $${}_nP_r = \frac{n!}{(n - r)!} = {}_6P_2 = \frac{\square!}{(\square - \square)!} = \underline{\quad} \cdot \underline{\quad} = \underline{\quad}$$

30. *If a and/or b is equal to 0, substitute and rewrite the equation.*

	Function Type	Graph Shape
a. $f(x) = ax^2 + bx + c$	_____	_____
b. $f(x) = \underline{\quad} + c$	_____	_____
c. $f(x) = \underline{\quad} + c$	_____	_____
d. $f(x) = \underline{\quad}$	_____	_____

Using Geometric Formulas to Find the Probability of an Event page 817

New Concepts

- Probability is the ratio of the number of favorable outcomes to the number of total possible outcomes. In geometrical probability, the areas of geometric figures represent the desired outcome and total outcomes of an event. The ratio of the areas is probability.

> **Example** Finding Geometric Probability with Rectangles
>
> **What is the probability that the bird lands in the tomato area?**
>
> $$\text{Probability} = \frac{\text{favorable outcomes}}{\text{total outcomes}} = \frac{\text{area with tomatoes}}{\text{area of whole garden}}$$
>
> 15 feet
>
> 10 feet
>
> 12 feet
>
> Tomatoes
>
> 3 feet
>
> $$= \frac{3 \cdot 12}{10 \cdot 15} \quad \textit{Use } A = l \cdot w \textit{ to find the area of each figure.}$$
>
> $$= \frac{36}{150} \quad \textit{Multiply.}$$
>
> $$P(\text{bird lands in tomatoes}) = \frac{6}{25} \quad \textit{Simplify.}$$

- When finding probability with circles, express area of the circles in terms of π. π's may cancel making simplification much easier.

> **Example** Finding the Probability of a Complement
>
> **What is the probability that the raindrop lands in the town, but not in the park?**
>
> Find the complement of the probability of the raindrop landing in the park.
>
> $$P(\text{not landing in park}) = 1 - P(\text{landing in the park})$$
>
> 5 miles
>
> Park
>
> 50 miles
>
> $$= 1 - \frac{\text{area of park}}{\text{area of town}}$$
>
> $$= 1 - \frac{5^2}{\pi(25)^2} \quad \textit{Use area formulas.}$$
>
> $$= 1 - \frac{25}{625\pi} \quad \textit{Simplify the powers.}$$
>
> $$\approx 0.99 \quad \textit{Subtract.}$$
>
> The probability of the raindrop landing in the town, but not in the park, is **99%**.

Math Language

The **complement** of an event is all the outcomes in the sample space that are NOT included in the event. The sum of the probability of an event and its complement is 1.

a. $P(\text{ball hits raft}) = \dfrac{\text{area of raft}}{\text{area of pool}}$

$$= \dfrac{2 \cdot \Box}{\Box \cdot \Box}$$

$$= \dfrac{\Box}{\Box}$$

b. $P(\text{glitter misses crown}) = P(\text{glitter hits center})$

$$P(\text{glitter hits center}) = \dfrac{\text{area of } \Box}{\text{area of plate}} = \dfrac{\pi\Box^2}{\pi\Box^2} = \dfrac{\Box}{\Box}$$

c. $P(\text{not in hole}) = 1 - \dfrac{\text{area of hole}}{\text{area of mask}}$

$$= 1 - \dfrac{\Box^2}{\pi\Box^2}$$

$$= 1 - \dfrac{\Box}{\pi\Box}$$

$$\approx \underline{\hspace{2cm}}$$

d. $P(\text{not in garden}) = 1 - \dfrac{\text{area of garden}}{\text{area of } \Box}$

$$= 1 - \dfrac{\frac{1}{2}\Box \cdot \Box}{\Box \cdot \Box}$$

$$= 1 - \dfrac{\Box}{\Box}$$

$$\approx \underline{\hspace{2cm}}$$

e. *It is not necessary to find all the areas.*

$$P(\text{not square}) = \dfrac{\text{area that does not include the square}}{\text{area of } \Box}$$

$$= \dfrac{\Box - \Box}{\Box}$$

$$= \dfrac{\Box}{\Box} = \dfrac{\Box}{\Box}$$

1. $P(\text{triangle}) =$

$$\frac{\text{area of } \square}{\text{area of } \square}$$

$$\frac{\frac{1}{2}\square \cdot \square}{\square^2} = \frac{\square}{\square}$$

2. Geometric probability is using

_____

_____ to calculate

the _____ and

_____ outcomes.

---

3. The system has _____ solution.

4. $P(\text{not triangle}) = \underline{\quad} - \dfrac{2 \cdot \frac{1}{2}\left(\square \cdot \square\right)}{\square \cdot \square}$

$$= \underline{\quad} - \frac{\square}{\square} = \frac{\square}{\square}$$

---

5. ${}_7C_2 = \dfrac{n!}{r!(n-r)!}$

$$= \frac{\square!}{\square!\left(\square - \square\right)!}$$

$$= \underline{\qquad}$$

6. $V = s^3$

$V = \underline{\qquad}^3$

$V = \underline{\qquad}$

---

7. $P(\text{circle}) =$

$$\frac{\text{area of } \square}{\text{area of } \square} = \frac{\pi\square^2}{\square \cdot \square} = \frac{\square}{\square} = \underline{\quad}$$

Circle the answer.

A ≈ 0.09 **B** ≈ 0.28

C ≈ 0.72 **D** ≈ 0.92

8. ${}_{20}C_8 = \dfrac{n!}{r!(n-r)!}$

$$= \frac{\square!}{\square!\left(\square - \square\right)!}$$

$$= \underline{\qquad}$$

---

9. shaded region =

area of _____ − area of _____

$$P(\text{shaded}) = \frac{\square^2 - \left(\frac{1}{2}(\square)(\square)\right)}{\pi\square^2}$$

$$= \frac{\square - \square}{\square} \approx \underline{\qquad}$$

10. Label the triangle.

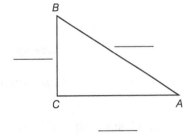

---

11. The domain is the values for x that make the radicand ≥ 0.

$x \bigcirc$ _____

12. Use the formula $A(n) = ar^{n-1}$

$A(4) =$ ___ $\cdot (-1.1)^{\square - \square}$

$=$ ___ $\cdot$ ___ $=$ _____

---

13. $P(\text{not biscuit}) = 1 - \dfrac{\text{area of } \square}{\text{area of } \square}$

$$\dfrac{12 \cdot \left(\pi \square^2\right)}{\square \cdot \square}$$

$$1 - \dfrac{\square}{\square} \approx 1 - \underline{\quad} \approx \underline{\quad}$$

14. Student _____ is correct.

Student _____ found the probability of

_____.

---

15. Using $A = s^2$, the area of the square is _____ square centimeters. The radius of the circle

is half the diameter, or ____ centimeters. Using $A = \pi r^2$, the area of the circle is _____.

Find the _____ of not landing in the circle by finding the _____

of the probability of landing in the circle. The formula is ____ $- \dfrac{\square}{\square}$ which is approximately

_____.

---

16. Draw a sketch.

red sectors: ____

not red sectors: ____

$P(\text{not red}) = \dfrac{\square}{\square}$

17. $P(\text{square}) = \dfrac{\square^2}{\frac{1}{2}(\square)(\square)} = \dfrac{\square}{\square} = \dfrac{\square}{\square}$

---

18. a. First find the number of smaller squares.

$P(\text{not landing on the same square}) = 1 - \dfrac{\square}{\square} = \dfrac{\square}{\square}$

b. $4 \cdot (\text{area of small square}) = 4 \cdot$ _____ $=$ _____

---

19. Student _____ is correct. A linear function must have a _____ rate of

change.

Student _____'s graph does not have a constant _____ of _____;

it gets _____ as x increases.

---

20. a. This is a _____

function because the graph is a

_____.

b. *Find the y-value at the vertex of the graph.*

$y =$ _____

21. This equation is in the

_____ function family.

---

22. Student _____ is correct.

Student _____ made _____ count.

23. *Discriminant* $= b^2 - 4ac$

$d =$ _____$^2 - 4($_____$)($____$)$

$d =$ _____

$d \bigcirc 0$, so there _____

_____ solution(s).

---

24. $P(\text{shaded}) = \dfrac{\pi\square^2}{\square} = \dfrac{\pi\square}{\square} \approx$ _____

25. $I = prt$

$I = ($_____$)($____$)($____$)$

$I =$ _____

_____ $+$ _____ $=$ _____

---

26. Graph the function and its translation.

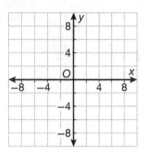

translation: $f(x) =$ _____

27. $\cos A = \frac{5}{7}$

$\cos^{-1}(\cos A) = (\cos^{-1})\left(\frac{5}{7}\right)$

Circle the answer.

A 44.4°   **B** 45.6°

C 0.71°   **D** 1.00°

28. *Divide both sides by 3 to make a=1, then add $\frac{b}{2}$ to both sides to make it a trinomial square.*

$3x^2 + 9x = 5.25$

$(\underline{\hspace{1cm}})(3x^2 + \underline{\hspace{1cm}} = \underline{\hspace{1cm}})$

$x^2 + \underline{\hspace{1cm}} = \underline{\hspace{1cm}}$

$x^2 + \underline{\hspace{1cm}} + \underline{\hspace{1cm}} = \underline{\hspace{1cm}} + \underline{\hspace{1cm}}$

$(\underline{\hspace{2cm}})^2 = (\underline{\hspace{2cm}})^2$

$x + \underline{\hspace{1cm}} = \underline{\hspace{1cm}}$ $x + \underline{\hspace{1cm}} = -\underline{\hspace{1cm}}$

$x = \underline{\hspace{1cm}}$ or $x = -\underline{\hspace{1cm}}$

29. *Subtract the probability of the bean bag landing in the shaded area from 1.*

$P = 1 - \dfrac{\pi\boxed{}^2}{\boxed{}} = 1 - \dfrac{\pi\boxed{}}{\boxed{}} \approx \underline{\hspace{1cm}}$

30. *Order matters.*

a. $6! =$ _____

b. $P = \dfrac{\boxed{}}{\boxed{}}$

Investigating Matrices page 826

Math Language

A **matrix** is a rectangular array of numbers in horizontal rows and vertical columns.

An **element** is an individual member of a matrix.

• A matrix organizes data from tables for display or for addition or subtraction with other matrices. The data are displayed within brackets [ ]. The dimensions of a matrix with m rows and n columns is $m \times n$. The elements are in the same m and n positions in the matrix as they were in the original table.

column ─────────────

row ──►

Type	Matinee	Regular
Child	$5	$7
Student	$6	$8
Adult	$9	$11

$$\begin{bmatrix} 5 & 7 \\ 6 & 8 \\ 9 & 11 \end{bmatrix}$$

same position

1. *Keep the elements in the same order.*

$$\begin{bmatrix} 10 & \underline{} \\ \underline{} & 2 \end{bmatrix}$$

2. _____ the numbers in the _____ row.

_____ + _____ = _____ sweatshirts

3. The matrix has _____ rows and _____ columns.

4. The dimensions of the matrix are _____ × _____.

5. The element in the third row, second column is _____.

6. The matrix would have _____ rows and _____ columns.

7. _____ the number of large hats sold on the first day, _____, and the second day, _____.

8. Put the data from each table into a _____ and then find the _____ of the values in the _____ row and _____ column of each _____.

9. *Add the elements that are in the same position within both matrices.*

$$\begin{bmatrix} \underline{} & 2 \\ 4 & \underline{} \end{bmatrix} + \begin{bmatrix} 8 & \underline{} \\ \underline{} & 7 \end{bmatrix} = \begin{bmatrix} \underline{} & \underline{} \\ \underline{} & \underline{} \end{bmatrix}$$

10. $\begin{bmatrix} 10 & \underline{} \\ 3 & \underline{} \\ \underline{} & \underline{} \end{bmatrix} - \begin{bmatrix} \underline{} & \underline{} \\ \underline{} & 5 \\ 4 & \underline{} \end{bmatrix} = \begin{bmatrix} \underline{} & \underline{} \\ \underline{} & \underline{} \\ \underline{} & \underline{} \end{bmatrix}$

Exploration 📖 **pages 827, 828**

Use your textbook to complete the Explorations.

Investigation Practice 📖 page 829

Use the tables in the textbook.

a. Put the data from each table into a _____. Label the first table _____ *A*

and the second table _____ *B*. Subtract the data in matrix _____ from matrix _____.

b.

$$\begin{bmatrix} \underline{} & \underline{} & \underline{} \\ \underline{} & \underline{} & \underline{} \\ \underline{} & \underline{} & \underline{} \end{bmatrix} - \begin{bmatrix} \underline{} & \underline{} & \underline{} \\ \underline{} & \underline{} & \underline{} \\ \underline{} & \underline{} & \underline{} \end{bmatrix} = \begin{bmatrix} \underline{} & \underline{} & \underline{} \\ \underline{} & \underline{} & \underline{} \\ \underline{} & \underline{} & \underline{} \end{bmatrix}$$

Paul made _____ more during the second summer.

c. In *A*, *B*, *C*, *D* order, put the *x*-coordinates in the first row of a matrix and the *y*-coordinates in the second row.

$$\begin{bmatrix} -2 & \underline{} & \underline{} & \underline{} \\ 3 & \underline{} & \underline{} & \underline{} \end{bmatrix}$$

Multiply the matrix by _____.

$$\underline{}A = \begin{bmatrix} -1 & \underline{} & \underline{} & \underline{} \\ \underline{} & -0.5 & \underline{} & \underline{} \end{bmatrix}$$